A HISTORY OF
WESTERN MUSIC
REVISED EDITION

Donald Jay Grout

PROFESSOR EMERITUS OF MUSICOLOGY, CORNELL UNIVERSITY

A HISTORY OF
WESTERN MUSIC

REVISED EDITION

W · W · NORTON & COMPANY · INC ·

NEW YORK

Copyright © 1973, 1960 by W. W. Norton & Company, Inc.

Library of Congress Cataloging in Publication Data

Grout, Donald Jay.
  A history of Western music.

  Bibliography: p.
  1. Music—History and criticism. I. Title.
ML160.G87 1973   780'.9   72–10089
  ISBN 0–393–09416–2

Printed in the United States of America

  2 3 4 5 6 7 8 9 0

Contents

Contents

Preface

A generation ago this book would have been called simply a "History of Music." Today's view is different, and the word *Western* in our title reflects the realization that the musical system of western Europe and the Americas is but one of several among the civilizations of the world. Two further limitations should be stated here: this book is concerned only with art music; and it emphasizes certain composers, works, and historical relationships. Fashions in history change with the generations, like fashions in musical taste. Of course a historian tries to be objective; but any general history of music is bound to reflect its writer's judgment as to which of the music of the past that he happens to know, and which aspects of the historical development of that music, are most worth attending to in the present.

The history of music is primarily the history of musical style, and cannot be grasped except by first-hand knowledge of the music itself. It is therefore essential to become acquainted with the *sound* of the musical examples cited in this book and to hear them *in their context;* for this reason, most of the examples have been selected from works which are conveniently accessible in standard editions or in anthologies of music, and these are listed in the Bibliography for each chapter.

An elementary knowledge of musical terms and of harmony—equivalent perhaps to a first-year course in theory—has been assumed. The Glossary contains brief definitions of terms not elsewhere defined in this book; but many of these are terms which a student who is ready to begin the study of the history of music should not need to look up, unless by way of reminder.

The Appendixes also contain suggestions for further reading. These lists are not intended as bibliographies. Most of the titles are in English, since many university undergraduates are not able to read a foreign language.

Particular thanks are due to Professor Otto Kinkeldey and Professor Paul Henry Lang. Both read all the chapters in manuscript and gave me much excellent advice, most of which I have followed. Other colleagues as well have given me the benefit of their specialized knowledge from time to time. I want to thank Dr. Emanuel Winternitz and Professor Carl Parrish for help with the illustrations; Mrs. Brian McGuinness for special assistance; and Mr. Harold Samuel, Music Librarian of Cornell University, for his quiet efficiency and never-failing patience.

Preface to the Revised Edition

The purpose of the Revised Edition is to improve this book, not to recast it entirely. Numerous changes, corrections, and some additions have been made, with a view to bringing the whole into line with the results of most recent research in all fields of the history of Western music. A new section on the period since 1950 has been added and the bibliographies and chronology updated.

I am especially grateful to the following scholars who have kindly provided extensive and expert advice on portions of the book that lay in areas of their special competence: to Professor Albert Seay, The Colorado College (medieval period); Professor Leeman Perkins, Yale University (Renaissance); Professor Joseph Kerman, Oxford University (English music of the sixteenth and early seventeenth centuries); Professor Christoph Wolff, Columbia University (Baroque); Jens Peter Larsen, Professor Emeritus, University of Copenhagen, and Professor Dénes Bartha, University of Pittsburgh (Classical period); Professor Gerald Abraham of Sussex, England (nineteenth century); and Professor William W. Austin, Cornell University (twentieth century). I have carefully considered all their very valuable counsels and have heeded most of them; any errors and shortcomings that remain in the following pages are mine alone.

Other friends and colleagues have responded to my occasional appeals for help or enlightenment. Particular thanks are due to Professor Paul Henry Lang, Professor R. M. Longyear, and Professor John D. Bergsagel for many helpful suggestions; to Professor Zofia Lissa and Dr. Wajciech Pazdro of Warsaw for information on the history of Polish music; and to Professors John Hsu and Don Randel of Cornell, Professor Lewis Lockwood of Princeton, Professor Edward Lowinsky of Chicago, Professor Eugene J. Leahy of Notre Dame, and Professor William G. Waite of Yale for information on special points.

I wish also to express appreciation to Mrs. Judith Bossert and Mrs. Martha Hsu of the Cornell University Libraries and to Mr. Richard Hunter and his amiable assistants in the Cornell Music Library. Finally, my thanks go to Mr. David Hamilton and Mrs. Claire Brook, of W. W. Norton and Company, Inc., for their painstaking care in the production of this revised edition.

Donald J. Grout
"Cloudbank," Spafford, New York
August, 1972

1

‖‖

The State of Music at the End of the Ancient World

Anyone living in a province of the Roman Empire in the fifth century of the Christian era might have seen roads where people used to travel and now travelled no more, temples and arenas built for throngs and now falling into disuse and ruin, and life everywhere becoming with each generation poorer, more insecure, and more brutish. Rome in the time of her greatness had imposed peace on most of western Europe as well as on considerable parts of Africa and Asia; but Rome had grown weak and unable to defend herself. The barbarians were pouring in from the north and east, and the common civilization of Europe was splintering into fragments which only after many centuries began to coalesce gradually into the modern nations.

The grand events of Rome's decline and fall stand out so luridly in history that it is hard for us even now to realize that, along with the process of destruction, there was quietly going on an opposite process of creation. This came to be centered in the Christian Church, which until the tenth century was the principal—and oftentimes the only—bond of union and channel of culture in Europe. The earliest Christian communities, in spite of three hundred years of sporadic persecution, grew steadily and spread to all parts of the Empire. After his conversion in 312, the Emperor Constantine adopted a policy of toleration and, what is more, made Christianity the religion of the imperial family. In 395 the political unity of the ancient world was formally broken up by the division into Eastern and Western Empires, with capitals at Byzantium and Rome. When after a terrible century of wars and invasions the last Western Emperor finally stepped down from his throne in 476, the foundations of the Papal power were already so firmly laid that the Church was ready to assume the civilizing and unifying mission of Rome.

The Greek Heritage

The history of Western art music properly begins with the music of the Christian Church. But all through the Middle Ages and even to the present time men have continually turned back to Greece and Rome for instruction, for correction, and for inspiration in their several fields of work; this has been true in music —though with some important differences. Roman literature, for example, never ceased to exert influence in the Middle Ages, and this influence became much greater in the fourteenth and fifteenth centuries when more Roman works became known; at the same time, too, the surviving literature of Greece was gradually recovered. But in literature, as well as in some other fields (notably sculpture), medieval or Renaissance artists had the advantage of being able to study and, if they so desired, imitate the models of antiquity. The actual poems or statues were before them. In music this was not so. The Middle Ages did not possess a single example of Greek or Roman music—nor, it may be added, are we today much better off. About a dozen examples—half of them mere fragments—of Greek music have been discovered, nearly all from comparatively late periods, but there is no general agreement as to just how they were meant to sound; there are no authentic remains of ancient Roman music. So we, as well as the men of medieval times, derive nearly all our knowledge of this art in the ancient civilizations at second hand from a few rather vague accounts of performances, but mostly from theoretical treatises and literary descriptions.

There was a special reason for the disappearance of the traditions of Roman musical practice at the beginning of the Middle Ages: most of this music was connected with social occasions on which the early Church looked with horror, or with pagan religious exercises which the Church believed had to be exterminated. Consequently every effort was made not only to keep out of the Church music which would recall such abominations to the minds of the faithful, but, if possible, to blot out the very memory of it. How much may have slipped in and been preserved, and how much may have survived outside the Church over the centuries, on one knows.

Yet there were some features of ancient musical practice that lived on in the Middle Ages if only for the reason that they could hardly have been abolished without abolishing music itself; further-

2

more, ancient musical theory was the foundation of medieval theory and was part of most philosophical systems. So in order to understand medieval music, we must know something about the music of ancient peoples, and in particular about the musical practice and theory of the Greeks.

Greek mythology ascribed to music a divine origin and named as its inventors and earliest practitioners gods and demigods, such as Apollo, Amphion, and Orpheus. In this dim prehistoric world, music had magic powers: people thought it could heal sickness, purify the body and mind, and work miracles in the realm of nature. Similar powers are attributed to music in the Old Testament: we need only recall the stories of David curing Saul's madness by playing the harp (I Samuel xvi: 14–23), or of the trumpet-blasts and shouting that toppled the walls of Jericho (Joshua vi: 12–20). In the Homeric Age, bards sang heroic poems at banquets (*Odyssey* VIII, 72–82).

Music in ancient Greek life and thought

From earliest times music was an inseparable part of religious ceremonies. In the cult of Apollo the lyre was the characteristic instrument, while in that of Dionysus it was the aulos. Both these instruments probably came into Greece from Asia Minor. The lyre and its larger counterpart, the kithara, were instruments with five to seven strings (later as many as eleven); both were used for solo playing and to accompany the singing or reciting of epic poems. The aulos, a double-pipe reed instrument (not a flute) with a shrill piercing tone, was used in connection with the singing of a certain kind of poetry (the dithyramb) in the worship of Dionysus, out of which it is believed the Greek drama developed. As a consequence, in the great dramas of the classical age—works by Aeschylus, Sophocles, Euripides—choruses and other musical portions were accompanied by, or alternated with, the sounds of the aulos.

Vase painting of Apollo playing a lyre and Artemis holding an aulos before an altar. The lyre was a loosely constructed instrument with a body made from a tortoise shell or wooden bowl over which was stretched a skin. Two horns or wooden arms projected upward from the bowl and supported a horizontal crosspiece to which strings were attached; the other ends of these arms were fastened to the underside of the sounding bowl after passing over a bridge. The lyre was played by plucking the strings either with the fingers or a plectrum. (Courtesy Metropolitan Museum of Art, Rogers Fund, 1907)

I. The State of Music at the End of the Ancient World

From at least as early as the sixth century B. C. both the lyre and the aulos were played as independent solo instruments. There is an account of a musical festival or competition held at the Pythian games in 586 B. C. at which one Sakadas played a composition for the aulos illustrating the combat between Apollo and the dragon —the earliest known piece of program music, and one which remained famous for centuries. Contests of kithara and aulos players, as well as festivals of instrumental and vocal music, became increasingly popular after the fifth century B. C. As instrumental music grew more independent the number of virtuosos multiplied; at the same time the music itself became more complex in every way. In the fourth century Aristotle warned against too much professional training in general music education:

> The right measure will be attained if students of music stop short of the arts which are practised in professional contests, and do not seek to acquire those fantastic marvels of execution which are now the fashion in such contests, and from these have passed into education. Let the young practise even such music as we have prescribed, only until they are able to feel delight in noble melodies and rhythms, and not merely in that common part of music in which every slave or child and even some animals find pleasure.[1]

Sometime after the classical age (about 450 to 325 B. C.) a reaction set in against technical complexities, and by the beginning of the Christian era Greek musical theory, and probably also its practice, had become simplified. Most of our surviving examples of Greek music come from relatively late periods. The chief are: two Delphic hymns to Apollo from about 150 B. C., a *skolion* or drinking song from about the same time or perhaps a little later, and three hymns of Mesomedes of Crete from the second century A. D. (see HAM, No. 7 for examples).

Although we do not know much about Greek music or its history, we can say that in three fundamental respects it was the same kind of music as that of the early Church. In the first place, it was primarily monophonic, that is, melody without harmony or counterpoint. There is some slight evidence of two-part music in Greece, but certainly the practice could not have been systematic or important. In the period when large vocal and instrumental ensembles were employed, it frequently happened that certain instruments would embellish the melody simultaneously with its plain performance by others in the ensemble, thus creating *heterophony*. But neither heterophony nor the inevitable necessity of singing in octaves when both men and boys took part constitutes true polyphony. In the second place, as far as we know, musical performances in the most flourishing period of Greek civilization were improvised.

[1] Aristotle, *Politics*, Book VIII, 6, 1341a 10, tr. B. Jowett in R. McKeon, ed., *The Basic Works of Aristotle*, New York, 1941, 1313. Cf. also Plato, *Laws*, II, 669E, 770A.

The performer was, to a certain extent, also the composer. This does not mean that what he did was completely spontaneous and unprepared; he had to keep within the universally accepted rules governing the forms and styles of music suitable for particular occasions, and he probably incorporated in his performance certain traditional musical formulas; but outside these restrictions he had considerable freedom. He was not playing or singing something he had memorized or learned from a score, and consequently no two performances of the "same" piece were exactly alike. Improvisation, in this or some similar sense, was characteristic of all ancient peoples. It prevailed also in our Western music up to perhaps the eighth century A. D., and the practice continued to affect musical styles for a long time even after precise musical notations were invented, as we shall see. ③Thirdly, Greek music was almost always associated with words or dancing or both; its melody and rhythm were most intimately bound up with the melody and rhythm of poetry, and the music of the religious cults, of the drama, and of the great public contests was performed by singers who accompanied their melody with the movements of prescribed dance patterns.

To say, however, that the music of the early Church resembled Greek music in being monophonic, improvised, and inseparable from a text, is not to assert a historical continuity. No direct historical connection from the one to the other can be demonstrated. *Greek musical theory* It was the theory rather than the practice of the Greeks that affected the music of western Europe in the Middle Ages; and it happens that we have much more information about Greek musical theories than about the music itself. Those theories were of two classes: (1) doctrines of the nature of music, its place in the cosmos, its effects, and its proper uses in human society; and (2) systematic descriptions of the materials and patterns of musical composition. In both the philosophy and the science of music the Greeks achieved insights and formulated principles, many of which have not been superseded to this day. Of course Greek thought about music did not remain static from the time of Pythagoras (*ca.* 500 B. C.), its reputed founder, to Claudius Ptolemy (2nd century A. D.), its last important expositor; the account which follows, though necessarily simplified, emphasizes those features that were most characteristic and most important for the later history of Western music.

The word *music* had a much wider meaning to the Greeks than it has to us. It was an adjectival form of *Muse*—in classical mythology any one of the nine sister goddesses who presided over certain arts and sciences. The verbal relation suggests that among the Greeks music was thought of as something common or basic to activities that were concerned with the pursuit of truth or beauty. In the teachings of Pythagoras and his followers, music and arithmetic were not separate; as the understanding of numbers was thought to be the key to the understanding of the whole spiritual and physical

I. The State of Music at the End of the Ancient World

Apollo holding a kithara. The kithara had a heavy body solidly joined together with a wooden sounding board and strong arms supporting a crossbar around which the strings were wound. This painting is on a Greek oil-vase from the middle of the fifth century B.C. *(Courtesy Metropolitan Museum of Art, gift of Mr. & Mrs. Leon Pomerance, 1953)*

universe, so the system of musical sounds and rhythms, being ordered by numbers, was conceived as exemplifying the harmony of the cosmos and corresponding to it. This doctrine was most thoroughly and systematically expounded by Plato, particularly in the *Timaeus* (in the Middle Ages the most widely known of his dialogues) and the *Republic.* Plato's views on the nature and uses of music, as interpreted later by medieval writers, exercised profound influence on the speculations about music and its place in education throughout that period.

Compare Wagner & Greeks

For some Greek thinkers music had also a close connection with astronomy, not only through the identity of mathematical laws that were thought to underlie both the system of musical intervals and the system of the heavenly bodies, but also through a particular correspondence of certain modes and even certain notes with the various planets. Such magical connotations and extensions of music were common among all Eastern peoples. The idea was given poetic form by Plato[2] in the beautiful myth of the "music of the spheres"; it is echoed by writers on music throughout the Middle Ages, and appears also in Shakespeare and Milton. Ptolemy, one of the most important of the ancient writers on music, was also the leading astronomer of antiquity—as, in our own day, many of the best amateurs of music are physical scientists.

The close union of melody and poetry is another dimension in which we may view the amplitude of the Greek's conception of music. Actually it is incorrect to speak of a "union," for to the Greeks the two were practically synonymous. When we now speak of "the music of poetry," we are conscious of using a figure of speech; but to the Greeks such music was actual melody whose intervals and rhythms could be precisely described. "Lyric" poetry meant

2 Plato, *Republic,* X, 617.

poetry sung to the lyre; "tragedy" incorporates the verb *aeidein*, "to sing." In fact, many of the Greek words that designate the different kinds of poetry, such as *ode* and *hymn,* are musical terms. Forms that lacked music were not designated at all. In the beginning of his *Poetics* Aristotle, after setting forth melody, rhythm, and language as the elements of poetry, goes on to say: "There is further an art which imitates by language alone . . . in prose or in verse. . . . This form of imitation is to this day without a name."[3] The Greek idea of music as essentially one with the spoken word has reappeared in diverse forms throughout the history of music; it is present, for example, in Wagner's theories about music drama in the nineteenth century. The search for a perfect union of words and music may, for some modern composers, mean no more than striving for correct rhythmic declamation of the text. For others it may have a more comprehensive meaning; it may be motivated by the belief that there is a power in music akin to the power of words for influencing human thought and action, and that therefore an artist, whether in music or words, is under obligation to exercise this power with due regard for its effect on others. Such a belief formed one of the most conspicuous and most important aspects of Greek thought about music.

The doctrine of *ethos,* or the moral qualities and effects of music, seems to be rooted in the Pythagorean view of music as a microcosm, a system of sound and rhythm ruled by the same mathematical laws that operate in the whole of the visible and invisible creation. Music, in this view, as not a passive image of the orderly system of the universe; it was also a force that could affect the universe—hence the attribution of miracles to the legendary musicians of mythology. A later, more scientific age emphasized the effects of music on the will and thus on the character and conduct of human beings. How music worked on the will was explained by Aristotle[4] through the doctrine of imitation. Music, he says, directly imitates (that is, represents) the passions or states of the soul—gentleness, anger courage, temperance, and their opposites and other qualities; hence, when one listens to music that imitates a certain passion, he becomes imbued with the same passion; and if over a long time he habitually listens to the kind of music that rouses ignoble passions his whole character will be shaped to an ignoble form. In short, if one listens to the wrong kind of music he will become the wrong kind of person; but, conversely, if he listens to the right kind of music he will tend to become the right kind of person.[5]

Both Plato and Aristotle were quite clear as to what they meant by the "right" kind of person; and they were agreed that the way

The doctrine of ethos

---

3 Aristotle, *Poetics,* 1, 1447a 28, tr. I. Bywater, in McKeon, *op. cit.*
4 Aristotle, *Politics,* 8, 1340a, b; cf. Plato, *Laws,* II, 665, 668–70, 812C.
5 Also see Plato, *Republic,* III, 401E.

I. The State of Music at the End of the Ancient World

An aulos player from a painting on a Greek drinking-cup of about 480 B.C. The player is shown holding the double pipes in his left hand; a leather band fastened over his face is pierced with two holes just large enough so that he can put the ends of the pipes in his mouth. (Courtesy Metropolitan Museum of Art, purchased by subscription, 1896)

to produce him was through a system of public education in which two principal elements were gymnastics and music, the one for the discipline of the body and the other for that of the mind. In the *Republic,* written about 380 B. C., Plato insists on the need for a balance of these two elements in education: too much music will make a man effeminate or neurotic; too much gymnastics will make him uncivilized, violent, and ignorant. "He who mingles music with gymnastic in the fairest proportions, and best attempers them to the soul, may be rightly called the true musician."[6] But only certain kinds of music are suitable. Melodies of expressive softness and indolence are to be avoided in the education of those who are being trained to become governors of the ideal state; for them, only the Dorian and Phrygian "tunes" are to be retained as promoting the virtues of courage and temperance respectively. Multiplicity of notes, complex scales, the blending of incongruous forms and rhythms, ensembles of unlike instruments, "many-stringed curiously-tuned instruments," even aulos-makers and aulos-players, are to be excluded from the state.[7] Furthermore, the foundations of music once established must not be changed, for lawlessness in art and education inevitably leads to licence in manners and anarchy in society.[8] For Plato the saying "Let me make the songs of a nation and I care not who makes its laws" would have expressed a political maxim; more than that, it would have been a pun, as the word *nomos,* with the

[6] Plato, *Republic,* III, 411.
[7] *Republic,* III, 398 ff.; also, *Laws,* VII, 812E.
[8] *Republic,* IV, 424; also, *Laws,* III, 700C.

general meaning of "custom" or "law," was used also to designate the melodic patterns of a certain type of lyric song.[9] Aristotle, in the *Politics* (about 350 B. C.) is less explicit than Plato about the particular rhythms and modes, and also less severe. He allows the use of music for amusement and intellectual enjoyment as well as for education;[10] but he agrees with Plato that all music used for educating the young should be regulated by law.

It may be that in thus limiting the kinds of music allowable in the ideal state both Plato and Aristotle were consciously opposing certain tendencies in the actual musical life of their time, particularly the use of enharmonic intervals, the use of certain rhythms connected with orgiastic rites, the independence of instrumental music, and the rise of professional virtuosos. But lest we be tempted to regard these philosophers as men so out of touch with the real world of art that their opinions on music cannot be of importance, these facts must be remembered: first, in ancient Greece a great deal more was included in music than we now understand by the word; second, we do not know how this music sounded, and it is not impossible that it really did have certain powers over the mind of which we can form no idea; third, there have been many instances in history of the state or some other authority prohibiting certain kinds of music, acting on the principle that this matter was important to the public welfare. Music was regulated in the early constitutions of both Athens and Sparta. The writings of the Church Fathers contain many warnings against specific kinds of music. Nor is the issue dead in the twentieth century. Dictatorships, both fascist and communist, have attempted to control the musical activity of their people; churches usually establish norms for the music that may be used in their services; all enlightened educators are concerned with the kinds of music, as well as the kinds of pictures and writings, to which young people are habitually exposed.

The Greek doctrine of *ethos,* then, was founded on the conviction that music affects character and that different kinds of music affect it in different ways. In the distinctions made among the many different kinds of music we can discern a general division into two classes: music whose effect was toward calmness and uplift, and music which tended to produce excitement and enthusiasm. The first class was associated with the worship of Apollo; its instrument was the lyre and its related poetic forms the ode and the epic. The second class was associated with the worship of Dionysus; its instrument was the aulos and its related poetic forms the dithyramb and the drama. This division makes apparent the two opposite yet

9 Cf. *Laws*, VII, 800.
10 *Politics*, 5–7.

parallel tendencies, usually distinguished as *classic* and *romantic,* or Apollonian and Dionysian, which have interacted throughout the history of music. (For a detailed treatment of Greek musical theory, see the Appendix to this chapter, pp. 27–34.

Music in ancient Rome

We do not know whether any significant contributions to either the theory or the practice of music were made by the Romans. They took their art music from Greece, especially after that country became a Roman province in 146 B. C., and it is possible that this imported culture replaced an indigenous Etruscan or Italian music of which we have no knowledge. The Romans invented or developed, chiefly for military purposes, some brass instruments of the trumpet and horn types. Many passages in the writings of Cicero, Quintilian, and others show that familiarity with music, or at least with musical terms, was considered a part of the education of a cultivated person, just as such a person was expected to be able to speak and write Greek.

A Roman matron playing a kithara is depicted in this Roman fresco of the first century A.D. *(Courtesy Metropolitan Museum of Art, Rogers Fund, 1903)*

During the great days of the Roman Empire (the first two centuries of the Christian era), art, architecture, music, philosophy, new religious rites, and many other cultural goods were brought in from the Hellenistic world. There are numerous reports of the popularity of famous virtuosos, of the prevalence of large choruses and orchestras, and of grandiose musical festivals and competitions. Many of the emperors were patrons of music; Nero even aspired to personal fame as a musician. With the economic decline of the Empire in the third and fourth centuries, the production of music on the large and expensive scale of earlier days ceased. Music-making there undoubtedly was, even in those troubled times, but little record of it has been preserved; after the fifth century, practically all traces of secular musical practice disappear. This, of course, does not mean that there was no secular music in the early Middle Ages. As for the ancient Romans, it is difficult to believe that the countrymen of Cicero, Virgil, and Horace could have been completely unoriginal in the field of music; yet we can only say that, if they did make any significant original contributions to the art, no evidence of the fact has so far come to light.

To summarize: although there is much uncertainty about details, we do know that the ancient world bequeathed to the Middle Ages certain fundamental ideas about music: (1) a conception of music as consisting essentially of pure, unencumbered melodic line; (2) the idea of melody intimately linked with words, especially in matters of rhythm and meter; (3) a tradition of musical performance based essentially on improvisation, without fixed notation, where the performer as it were created the music anew each time, though within communally accepted conventions and making use of certain traditional musical formulas; (4) a philosophy of music which regarded the art not as a play of beautiful sounds in a spiritual and social vacuum of art for art's sake, but rather as an orderly system interlocked with the system of nature, and as a force capable of affecting human thought and conduct; (5) a scientifically founded acoustical theory; (6) a system of scale-formation based on tetrachords (see pp. 27 ff. below); and (7) a musical terminology.

Part of this heritage (Nos. 5, 6, and 7) was specifically Greek; the rest was common to most if not all of the ancient world. Knowledge of it and ideas about it were transmitted, albeit incompletely and imperfectly, to the West through various channels: the Christian Church—whose rites and music were taken over in the beginning largely from Jewish sources, though without the Temple accessories of instruments and dancing—the writings of the Church Fathers, and early medieval scholarly treatises which dealt with music along with a multitude of other subjects.

The Early Christian Church

It is impossible for us to know exactly how much, and what, music from Greece or the mixed Oriental-Hellenistic societies around the eastern Mediterranean was taken into the Christian Church during the first two or three centuries of its existence. Certain features of ancient musical life were definitely rejected—for example, the idea of cultivating music purely for enjoyment as an art. Above all, the forms and types of music connected with the great public spectacles such as festivals, competitions, and dramatic performances, as also the music of more intimate convivial occasions, were regarded by many as unsuitable for the Church, not so much from any dislike of music itself as from the need to wean the increasing numbers of converts away from everything associated with their pagan past. This attitude involved at first even a distrust of all instrumental music. Yet the break may not have been complete. Just as early Christian theology was influenced by the philosophy of antiquity, so early Christian music may have taken over something—how much, or what, we cannot tell—from pagan sources.

More important, however, than any such possible external influences was the fact that the worship services of the earliest Christians were closely modelled on the Jewish synagogue services. Like them, they included readings from the holy books, psalms, hymns, prayers, and almsgiving—all elements that remain to this day in the liturgy of the Mass (where they are followed, of course, by the Eucharist, the celebration of the Last Supper). It is a safe assumption that, in music as well as liturgy, the early Church adopted the usual Synagogue practices, probably adding certain features taken over from the Temple worship. In both the Jewish and the Christian services, the characteristic styles and forms of the musical portions were adapted to, in fact conditioned by, their liturgical function. We may therefore note here briefly some of the general features of Hebrew music which found a place in early Christian worship and which eventually entered into the various types of Christian chant that developed in later centuries.

The Judean heritage

Among the Hebrews, psalms were sung in alternation between a soloist and the congregation; in one form of alternation, which later became important in Christian liturgy under the name of *responsorial psalmody*, the leader sang the first line of each psalm verse and the congregation responded by singing the second line. Such a method is particularly appropriate to the psalms, in which many of the verses have two parallel phrases, the second restating or continuing or amplifying the thought expressed in the first:

> Bless the Lord, O my soul, / and forget not all his benefits:
> Who forgiveth all thine iniquities; / who healeth all thy diseases.

A related form of singing was *antiphonal psalmody*, in which the two parts of the verse, or alternate verses, were sung in turn by two choruses. Still another usage inherited by the early Church from the Jewish service was the reciting of prescribed passages of Scripture by a soloist, using certain melodic formulas the essential outlines of which could be retained while details were varied to suit the requirements of a particular text.

As the early Church spread through Asia Minor and westward into Africa and Europe, it accumulated musical elements from diverse areas. The monasteries and churches of Syria were important in the development of antiphonal psalmody and for the use of hymns. Both these types of church song seem to have spread from Syria by way of Byzantium to Milan and other western centers. Hymn singing is the earliest recorded musical activity of the Christian Church (Matt. xxvi:30; Mark xiv:26). Pliny the Younger, about the year 112, reported the Christian custom of singing "a song to Christ as a god" in the province of Bithynia in Asia Minor.[11] It is likely that some of the hymns of the early Church were sung to what would now be called folk melodies, and it is possible that some of these melodies eventually found their way into the official chant repertoire.

The oldest surviving example of Christian church music is a hymn of praise to the Trinity, with Greek words and in Greek vocal notation, found on a papyrus at the site of the ancient Egyptian town of Oxyrhynchos and published in 1922. The date of the papyrus is toward the end of the third century. It contains only the last few lines of the hymn and is so mutilated that even these cannot be completely reconstructed. It was formerly thought that the Oxyrhynchos fragment proved a definite influence of Greek music in the early Church; but later research has indicated that, in spite of the Greek notation, the melody probably has a more Eastern provenance.

The Eastern Churches, in the absence of a strong central authority, developed different liturgies in the different regions. Although there are no surviving manuscripts of the music used in these Eastern rites *Byzantium* during the first few centuries of the Christian era, in recent years comprehensive studies of Jewish and Byzantine music have allowed us to infer a great deal about early Eastern church music.

The city of Byzantium (or Constantinople, now Istanbul) was rebuilt by Constantine and designated in 330 as the capital of his reunited Roman Empire. After the permanent division in 395 it remained the capital of the Eastern Empire for over a thousand years, until its capture by the Turks in 1453. During much of this time Byzantium was the seat of the most powerful government in Europe and the center of a flourishing culture which blended Hellenistic and Oriental elements. The music of the Byzantine Church continued to have some influence in the west until the final schism of the Eastern and Western Churches in 1054. Byzantine chant is also the ancestor of the music of the modern Greek Orthodox, the Russian, and other Eastern Churches.

The finest and most characteristic examples of medieval Byzantine music were the hymns. These originated from the short responses (*troparia*) between verses of the psalms, being furnished with music on the basis of melodies or melody-types perhaps taken over from Syria. These insertions gradually increased in importance and eventually developed into independent hymns, of which there are two principal kinds: the *kontakia,* which flourished in the sixth century, and the *kanones,* of the eighth to tenth centuries; *kanones* probably

---

[11] Pliny's phrase "carmen dicere" may mean reciting a poem or incantation, rather than singing.

adopted some of the melodies that had been used in the *kontakia*. These Byzantine hymns had an elaborate structure which was in contrast to the hymns of the Western Church. A *kanon* consisted usually of eight divisions (called *odes*), each of several strophes. Each of the eight odes of a *kanon* was sung to its own melody, which remained the same for every stanza of the ode. Each ode corresponded to a specific Biblical *canticle; canticles* are certain lyrical portions of the Bible, similar to hymns or psalms, which are sung in Church services at specified times. The canticles of the Byzantine Church, with one exception, still remain today in the liturgy of the Roman Catholic Church. The most important of these for the history of music is the Canticle of the Blessed Virgin Mary, the *Magnificat* (Luke i:46–55).

The texts of the Byzantine *kanones* were not wholly original creations, but rather commentaries or variations on the Scriptural models. Likewise, their melodies were not wholly original; they were constructed according to a principle common in all Eastern music, one quite different from Western ideas. The units of the structure were not a series of notes organized in a scale, but rather a group of given short motives; from these the singer was expected to choose certain motives and combine them to form his melody. Some of the motives were to be used for the beginning, some for the middle, and some for the end of a melody, while others were connecting links; there were also standard ornamental formulas (*melismas*). The singer's originality consisted in the way he combined the motives and varied them with ornamentation.

The motives in such a collection have different names in different musical systems—*rāga* in Hindu music, *maqām* in Arabian, *echos* in Byzantine, and by various terms translatable as *"mode"* in Hebrew. A *rāga, maqām, echos* or *mode* is, so to speak, a repertoire of melodic motives; all the motives of one group are unified in that they express more or less the same quality of feeling, are congruous in melody and rhythm, and are derivable from the same musical scale. The choice of a particular *rāga* or *mode* may depend on the nature of the text to be sung, or the particular occasion, or the season of the year, sometimes (as in Hindu music) on the hour of the day. The melodies of the Hebrew Synagogue chants have been classified on the basis of their *modes*. Byzantine music had a system of eight *echoi*, and the melodies in the collections for the *kanones* are classified according to this system.

The melodies of the Hebrew Synagogues and the Byzantine Church (as also those of the Western churches) had been passed along by oral tradition for centuries before being written down. Comparison of the oldest available records and consideration of other evidence have convinced modern scholars that both the ancient Jewish melodies and those of the earliest Christian churches were built on the principle of *modes;* in some cases it has been possible to ascertain with a high degree of probability the ancient melodic formulas. The importance of these discoveries for the history of early Western Church music is twofold:

(1) Many of the oldest Western chants are constructed according to the method used in Jewish melodies—that is, on the basis of melody-types and including a number of established melodic motives. In a few instances the resemblances between Jewish and Western chants are so close as to suggest either that the latter were taken over from the former or else that both were variants of one common form. Isolated melodic resemblances, however, are less important than the basic similarity of the method and principles of melodic construction used in both Hebrew and Christian chant. From this similarity we can conclude that the earliest Western Church music incorporated a great many Jewish elements, either directly from the Hebrew chants or indirectly as the original melodies had been modified in the various early Christian centers in Greece, Syria, Egypt, and other regions of the East. Just how the borrowing occurred, and what the respective contributions from the different centers were, are matters about which we have as yet little accurate knowledge.

(2) The Byzantine system of eight *echoi* had an important influence on the Western medieval theory of the eight church modes. Like the Western Church modes, the *echoi* were grouped in four pairs, and the four pairs had as their final tones respectively the four notes d, e, f, and g. How much the Byzantine system was influenced by Greek theory is uncertain, but the later Western medieval system was clearly a compound of the Byzantine *echoi* and the Greek *tonoi*. The *echoi* may be considered an earlier stage of a system of which the Western theory represents a logical culmination. The *echoi* were not scales, but rather collections of melodic motives. Western theorists started at this point, then deduced the scales out of which the respective groups of motives were formed, and finally attempted to relate these scales to the Greek system of *tonoi*. The results of this process appear in completed form as the Western modal system (Chapter II).

In the west, as in the east, local churches at first were relatively independent. Although they shared, of course, a large area of common practice, yet it is likely that each region of the west received the eastern heritage in a slightly different form; these original differences combined with particular local conditions to produce several distinct liturgies and bodies of chant between the fifth and the eighth centuries. Eventually all these local versions except one (the Ambrosian) either disappeared or were absorbed into the single uniform practice for which the central authority was Rome. From the ninth to the sixteenth centuries, in theory and increasingly in

Western liturgies

15

practice, the liturgy of the Western Church was regulated by the Church of Rome.

The principal early non-Roman liturgies were the *Gallican* in France, the *Mozarabic* in Spain, and the *Ambrosian* in Milan. In most of England the *Sarum* liturgy and chant were used from the late Middle Ages to the Reformation. The Gallican liturgy, which included both Celtic and Byzantine elements, was in use among the Franks until near the end of the eighth century. From the Gallican, the Roman liturgy took over certain portions of the present Good Friday service, including the *Improperia* (texts mainly from the Prophets, sung as representing the reproaches of Christ from the Cross), and two hymns: *Crux fidelis* (*O Faithful Cross*) and *Pange lingua . . . certaminis* (*Sing, my tongue, the glorious battle*).

In Spain the liturgy was influenced by the invasion of the Visigoths in the fifth century, who brought with them Eastern practices from Syria and Byzantium. The Spanish uses were given definite form by the Council of Toledo in 633, and after the Mohammedan conquest in the eighth century this liturgy was given its name, Mozarabic, though there is no reason to suppose any Arabian influence on the music. The Spanish was not officially replaced by the Roman rite until 1071, and even today some traces of it are retained in a few churches at Toledo, Salamanca, and Valladolid.

The most important Western Church center outside Rome, however, was Milan, a flourishing city with close cultural ties to Byzantium and the East; it was the chief residence of the western emperors in the fourth century, and later was made the capital of the Lombard Kingdom in northern Italy, which flourished from

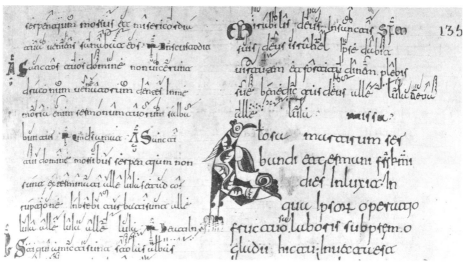

Mozarabic Chant, from a Missal of the Mozarabic rite containing Masses for saints' feasts. This page has parts of the Office for the Feast of St. Servandus and St. Germanus. (Courtesy British Museum)

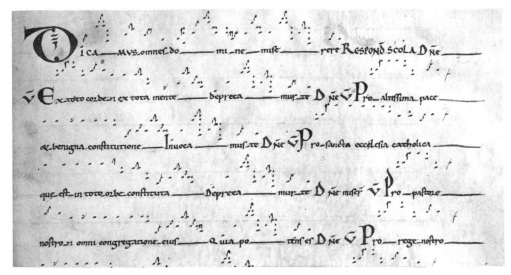

Gallican Chant. A folio from the eleventh-century Gradual of St. Yrieux, containing prayers of the Gallican liturgy. The music on this page is a litany for the Feast of St. Mark the Evangelist.

568 to 744. The Bishop of Milan from 374 to 397 was St. Ambrose, who first introduced antiphonal psalmody to the west. Owing to the importance of Milan and to the energy and high personal reputation of St. Ambrose, the Milanese liturgy and music exerted a strong influence not only in France and Spain but also at Rome, where antiphonal psalmody was adopted early in the fifth century. The songs of the Milanese rite later came to be known as Ambrosian Chant, though it is doubtful whether any of the music that has come down to us dates from the time of St. Ambrose himself. The Ambrosian liturgy with its complete body of chants has been maintained to some extent at Milan to the present day, in spite of various attempts to suppress it. Many of the chants in their present form are similar to those of the Roman Church, indicating either an interchange or a derivation from a common source. Where there are two versions of the same melody, if it is of an ornate type (such as an Alleluia) the Ambrosian is usually more elaborate than the Roman (see, for example, HAM, No. 10); and if a plain type (such as a Psalm Tone) the Ambrosian is simpler than the Roman.

An important addition to Western church music was the *hymn*. The singing of "hymns, psalms, and spiritual songs" is mentioned by St. Paul (Col. iii: 16; Eph. v: 18–20) and other writers of the first three centuries, but we do not know just what this consisted of. All the surviving hymn texts from these three centuries are Greek; one of them, *O gladsome light,* by an unknown author probably of the third century, is still sung at Vespers in the Greek church. Hymns were introduced in the West in the fourth century by St. Ambrose,

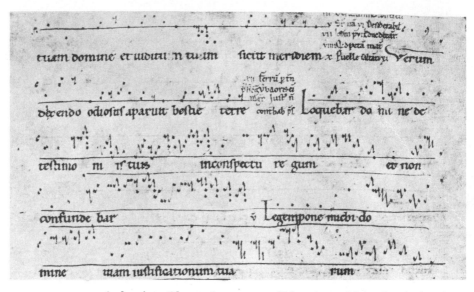

Ambrosian Chant, from a twelfth-century Manuale Ambrosiano. *This folio contains portions of the Office and Mass of the Feast of the Beheading of St. John the Baptist.*

according to an old tradition, though recent scholarship is inclined to credit this innovation to Hilary, Bishop of Poitiers (*ca.* 315–366). They were used in the Benedictine monastic liturgy in the sixth century, but did not become firmly fixed in the Roman rite until the eleventh century. Gradually, the meaning of *hymn* had been narrowed to denote a poem in strophic form, all the stanzas of which were intended to be sung to the same melody; the setting was mostly *syllabic* (one note to a syllable), and comparatively simple and tuneful—music originally for the congregation or the individual worshiper rather than for a trained choir or soloist. Many of the earliest hymn melodies were probably taken over from popular secular tunes. As to subject matter, the hymn is limited only by its general purpose of "celebrating Christian truths or events";[12] thus it need not be Scriptural—though there was a considerable struggle before the Church finally admitted non-Biblical hymns. In general, it may be said that hymns, in both form and content, are apt to express personal, individual sentiments, whereas other parts of the liturgy are by comparison more objective, public, and formal.

As the liturgy developed, and especially after the singing of hymns in the service was entrusted to the choir instead of the congregation, many of the earlier tunes were enriched by the addition of ornamental notes; also, new melodies of a sometimes quite ornate

[12] P. Wagner, *Einführing in die gregorianischen Melodien*, Leipzig, 1911, I, 42.

character arose. Beside the versified hymns there are a few with prose texts, among which the best known is the *Te Deum laudamus* ("We praise Thee, O God"), written probably in the latter part of the fourth century and sung now to a melody very similar to one which may have been used in the ancient Synagogue services and which has been preserved in Jewish tradition.[13] According to legend, at the moment when St. Ambrose baptized St. Augustine the two spontaneously improvised the *Te Deum* in alternate verses. This legend is thought to refer to what was undoubtedly a practice in the early Church, namely the creation of hymns under the inspiration of strong religious feeling, somewhat the way today new phrases of text and new melodic variations spontaneously arise during the enthusiasm of a revival meeting or a folk sing.

In addition to the main outlines of the liturgy, the body of responsorial and antiphonal psalmody, the reciting formulas, and the hymns, one other Jewish element became important in Western church music: the class of songs originally used in the Hebrew Synagogue as refrains, for example on the word "amen" or "alleluia." Such refrains were chanted responsively by the congregation after each verse or after the last verse of a psalm, and some of them later developed into independent song types, losing their primitive simple character and becoming more or less elaborate solo melodies. The alleluias were especially noteworthy because of their florid (melismatic) style, in which the last syllable was drawn out in ecstatic melody, soaring phrase after phrase "in gladness of heart outflowing, joy too full to be expressed in words."[14] The alleluia was introduced into the liturgy at Rome before the fourth century and was eventually incorporated in the Mass for every Sunday except during the fasting or penitential seasons.

Another species of Western chant that grew out of the synagogue songs with refrains was the *antiphon*. At first the antiphon, a verse or sentence with its own melody, probably was repeated after every verse of a psalm or canticle, like the phrase "for His mercy endureth forever" in Psalm 135/6. An example of a refrain occurs in the canticle *Benedictus es* (*Graduale*, pp. 16–17), which is sung on the four Saturdays in Advent. The melody of this refrain (*Et laudabilis et gloriosus in saecula*) is probably an ornate version of an originally simple congregational response. In later practice, the refrain was usually sung only at the beginning and end of the psalm; at the present day only the "intonation" or opening phrase of the antiphon is sung first, and the entire antiphon is heard after the psalm (examples, HAM, No. 11, MM, No. 1). Most an-

---

13 Eric Werner, *The Sacred Bridge*, London and New York, 1959, p. 342.
14 St. Augustine, "In Psalmum xcix enarratio, sermo ad plebem"; pr. Migne, *Patrologiae cursus completus, Series Latina*, XXXVII, 1272.

tiphons are in a fairly simple style, reflecting their origin as congregational or choral responsive songs. Some rather more elaborate pieces, originally antiphons, developed into separate chants—for example, the Introit, Offertory, and Communion in the Mass. The four *Marian antiphons* (so called, although they are really independent compositions rather than antiphons in the strict liturgical sense) are of comparatively late date, and are especially beautiful melodies (see Example II–1, page 39).

A form akin to the antiphon is the *responsory* or *respond,* a short verse which is sung by a soloist and repeated by the choir before a prayer or short sentence of Scripture, and repeated again by the choir at the end of the reading. The responsory, like the antiphon, was originally repeated by the choir, either wholly or in part, after each single verse of the reading; this early practice survives in a few present-day *responsoria prolixa* or Long Responsories (see HAM, No. 14).

The dominance of Rome

Although the manner in which the various elements of Eastern chant were adopted by the West during the first three Christian centuries is not altogether clear, one thing is certain: as far as the music is concerned there was no evolution from a simple to a more complex musical style. Many of the chants that were brought from the East were undoubtedly ornate, full of melismatic passages with opportunities for improvisation; and at least some of them may have been based on Oriental scale patterns with chromatic and enharmonic intervals. The course in the West must have been, at first, toward order and relative simplicity, a course made the more imperative by events of the early fourth century.

In 313 Constantine recognized the Christians as entitled to equal rights and protection along with other religions in the Empire; the Church at once emerged from its underground life, and during the fourth century Latin replaced Greek as the official language of the liturgy at Rome. As the prestige of the Roman Emperor declined, that of the Roman Bishop increased, and gradually the predominant authority of Rome in matters of faith and discipline began to be acknowledged.

With ever greater numbers of converts and ever growing riches, the Church began to build large basilicas, and services could no longer be conducted in the comparatively informal manner of early days. From the fifth to the seventh centuries many popes were concerned with revising the liturgy and music, a work in which they were greatly aided by the monks of the Order of St. Benedict (founded in 529). The post of Cantor, or chief solo singer (an institution inherited from the synagogue) was officially established; boy choirs, common at Jerusalem by the beginning of the fifth century, were introduced in the West; by the eighth century there existed at Rome a *Schola Cantorum,* a definite group of singers and teachers entrusted with the training of boys and men as church musicians. In all these steps the original basic distinction between solo and choral singing was retained, and as a consequence, to this day Roman chant preserves a division between the music of responsorial and solo psalmody on the one hand and that of antiphonal psalmody and hymnody on the other—the former being rhythmically flexible and melodically elaborate, the latter by comparison strict and simple.

The culminating reform of the liturgy and chant seems to have been in large part the work of Gregory I (The Great), Pope from 590 to 604. St. Gregory's achievement was so highly regarded that by the middle of the ninth century a legend began to take shape to the effect that he himself had composed all the melodies in use by the Church, under divine inspiration; he was depicted in manuscripts of this time as receiving the chants from the Holy Spirit, as a dove, and dictating them to a scribe (see illustration on p. 22). His actual contribution was probably much less than what later medieval tradition ascribed to him; so great a work could not have been accomplished in fourteen years. He recodified the liturgy and reorganized the Schola Cantorum; he assigned particular items of the liturgy to the various services throughout the year in an order that remained essentially untouched until the sixteenth century; he gave impulse to the movement which eventually led to the establishment of a uniform repertoire of chant for use throughout the Church in all countries. Whether St. Gregory actually composed any melodies is a different question.

There is a body of so-called Old Roman Chant, preserved in a few manuscripts dating from the eleventh to the thirteenth centuries. Many of these melodies are more or less similar to those we find in the present-day official chant books, though as a rule of less highly organized structure. It is possible that the Old Roman may represent earlier versions of the now accepted forms; on the other hand, the differences may be due not to chronology but simply to different regional practices. The whole matter is still unsettled. We may be certain, however, that neither the Old Roman nor the present official versions have come down to us literally and unchanged from the time of St. Gregory. Exactly how the chants were sung in his time no one knows, since the oldest manuscripts with musical notation do not appear until three hundred years later.

Nevertheless, the medieval tradition as a whole had a real historical basis. It is therefore appropriate that this whole body of music should be called, as it has been for over a thousand years, Gregorian Chant. It was given also, in the twelfth and thirteenth centuries, the designation *cantus planus* (*plainsong*) to distinguish it from the *cantus figuralis* or *mensuratus* (figural or measured song), the measured polyphonic music of the Middle Ages.

St. Gregory and scribe. At the moment depicted, the Saint is listening to what the dove (symbolizing the Holy Spirit) is whispering in his ear. The scribe, curious about the intermittent pauses in his master's dictation, has come out from behind the screen to peer at them, still holding his stylus in his hand. Presently, St. Gregory will resume his dictation and the scribe, returning behind the screen, will take it down.

The Gregorian chants are one of the great treasures of Western civilization. Like Romanesque architecture, they stand as a monument to medieval man's religious faith; they were the source and inspiration of a large proportion of all Western music up to the sixteenth century. They constitute one of the most ancient bodies of song still in use anywhere, and include some of the noblest artistic works ever created in pure melody.

The principal events and tendencies in the history of Western music to the time of Gregory the Great (making allowance for incomplete knowledge due to the lack of evidence on many points) may be summed up as follows: During the first three centuries of the Christian era the earliest forms of worship and their musical concomitants, taken over from the Hebrew Synagogue, were variously modified and expanded in different regions of the East. There was no uniform practice, and individual improvisation seems to have played a certain role. There were three main types of chant: the reciting formulas, the melismatic songs, and the refrains sung by the choir or congregation. The melodies of all these were built up according to the Jewish fashion of combining traditional standard melodic formulas within a given mode. There were three ways of performing: direct (without alternation), responsorial (alternation of soloist and chorus), and antiphonal (alternation of two choruses).

From the fourth to the sixth centuries all this system was as- similated by the Western churches; but the Western trend was toward a uniform practice, which eventually emanated from Rome. Probably the extremes of the inherited chant were modified, the melismatic tunes made somewhat plainer and the simple tunes some- what more ornate. More and more of the performance was handed over to an officially constituted body of trained singers. The reforms under Gregory I and his successors aimed to organize the whole body of chant in a uniform manner for the entire Western Church, embracing diverse types and practices in one orderly system; con- currently with this change the performance of chants in the service came to be entrusted to a separately constituted body of trained singers. So the first stage of Western music seems to have been one in which an early emphasis on ecstasy and individual liberty was succeeded by emphasis on order and discipline. Thus the Gregorian age may be called the first "classical period" in the history of West- ern music.

This was the main stream of history—main stream, that is, insofar as recorded history goes. Undoubtedly in those six centuries, as in all times, people sang and played their own music outside the church. But what it was that they sang and played we do not know, for no record of it survives. What little we hear about it comes mainly from incidental references, usually hostile, in contemporary clerical writings that are mainly concerned with church matters. We do know, of course, that in later periods the Church continually took over secular music and musical practices, and it is likely that some- thing of this kind occurred during the first Christian centuries— likely, moreover, that the exchange worked in both directions; but as to extent and manner of it we can do little more than speculate.

During these early centuries, also, the musical theory and philos- ophy of the ancient world—or as much of it as was accessible after the "time of troubles" and the barbarian invasions—was being *The Church* gathered up, summarized, modified, and transmitted to the West. *Fathers* Most notable in this work was Martianus Capella in his encyclopedic *and music* treatise entitled *The Marriage of Mercury and Philology* (early fifth century) and Anicius Manlius Severinus Boethius (ca. 480–524) with his *De institutione musica* ("The Principles of Music"; early sixth century). Boethius was the most influential authority on music in the early Middle Ages and his ideas are quite typical of the period. Like the Pythagoreans and Plato, he regards music as a corollary of arithmetic, thus as exemplifying in sounds the fundamental prin- ciples of order and harmony that prevail throughout the universe. His division of the subject is threefold: *musica mundana* ("cosmic" music), referring to the "music of the spheres" and the orderly mathematical relations observable in the behavior of the stars, the planets, and the earth—that is, in the macrocosm; *musica humana*, referring to the ways in which such harmonious relations are imprinted on and exemplified in the soul and body of man—the microcosm; and *musica instrumentalis,* or audible music produced by instruments (including, by implication, the human voice), which exemplifies the same principles of order, particularly in the acoustical ratios of musical intervals. The picture of the cosmos which Boethius and the other ancient writers drew in their discussions of *musica mundana* and *musica humana* is reflected in the art and literature of the later Middle Ages, notably in the structure of Paradise in the last canto of Dante's *Divine Comedy*. Remnants of the doctrine of *musica humana* survived through the Renaissance and indeed linger on to this day, in the form of astrology.

Like the Greeks, Boethius emphasizes the influence of music on character and morals. Music thus becomes important as an element in the education of the young and, in its mathematical-theoretical aspects, as an introduction to more advanced philosophical studies; hence music finds a place, along with arithmetic, geometry, and astronomy, in the *quadrivium,* the four higher subjects comprised in the medieval educational system of the seven liberal arts. *De musica* was in use as a textbook at Oxford as late as the eighteenth century.

In placing *musica instrumentalis*—which is practically the entire art of music as we understand it now—in the third and presumably lowest category, Boethius is motivated by his conception of music on the whole as an object of knowledge rather than an expression of feeling. Music, he says, is "the skill of examining carefully the diversity of high and low sounds by means of reason and the senses."

The illumination from the eleventh-century Uta Evangeliary represents a symbolic diagram of the music of the spheres as described by Boethius in the perfect consonances corresponding to the Trinity which are woven into the design. (Courtesy Kathi Meyer-Baer)

Therefore, the true musician is not the singer or player—as we might say today, the "mere performer"—nor the one who only makes up songs by instinct without knowing the meaning of what he does, but the philosopher, the critic, he "who possesses the faculty of judging, according to the speculation or reason, appropriate and suitable to music, of modes and rhythms and of the classes of melodies and their mixtures of all those things" that pertain to the subject.[15]

With this basic orientation, especially coupled as it was with a firm belief in the power of music to influence for good or ill the characters of those who listened to it, we can well understand that the philosophers and churchmen of the early Middle Ages did not strongly dwell on the idea—which we take for granted in our day— that music might be heard solely for the sake of esthetic enjoyment, for sheer pleasure in the play of beautiful sounds. They did not deny, of course, that the sound of music is pleasurable; but they maintained that all pleasures must be judged in accordance with the Platonic principle that beautiful things exist to remind us of divine and perfect beauty and therefore those seeming beauties of the world which inspire only self-centered enjoyment, or desire of possession, are to be rejected. Music, consequently, was to be judged by its power to uplift the soul to contemplation of divine things. This view is at the root of many of the pronouncements about music which we find in the writings of the Church Fathers (and later, by some theologians following the Protestant Reformation).

Specifically, their philosophy was that music is the servant of religion. Only that music is worthy to be heard in church which by means of its charms opens the mind to Christian teachings and disposes it to holy thoughts. Since they believed that music without words cannot do this, they at first excluded instrumental music from public worship, though the faithful were allowed to use a lyre to accompany the singing of hymns and psalms in their homes and on informal occasions. On this point the Fathers ran into difficulty, for the Old Testament and especially the psalms are full of references to the psaltery, harp, organ, and other musical instruments. How were these to be explained? The usual recourse was to allegory: "the tongue is the 'psaltery' of the Lord . . . by the 'harp' we must understand the mouth, which is put in vibration by the Holy Spirit as by a plectrum . . . the 'organ' is our body. . . ." These and many similar explanations were typical of an age which delighted in allegorizing Scripture.

The exclusion of certain kinds of music from the worship services of the early Church also had practical motives. Elaborate singing, large choruses, instruments, and dancing were, through long habit, associated in the minds of the first converts with pagan spectacles.

---

[15] From the translation in SR, 86 (=SRA, 86).

I. The State of Music at the End of the Ancient World

Until the feeling of pleasure attached to these kinds of music could be somehow transferred from the theatre and the marketplace to the church, they were distrusted; better be "deaf to the sound of instruments" than give oneself up to those "diabolical choruses," those "lascivious and pernicious songs." "Is it not absurd that they who have listened to that mystical voice of the Cherubim from Heaven should deliver their ears over to the dissolute songs and ornate melodies of the theatre?" But God, taking pity on the weakness of man, has "mingled with the precepts of religion the sweetness of melody . . . the harmonious melodies of the psalms have been added so that those who are still children should in reality be building up their souls even while they think they are only singing the music."[16]

"Some claim that I have ensnared the people by the melodies of my hymns" says St. Ambrose, adding proudly, "I do not deny it."[17] There were doubtless some in the Church who despised music and indeed tended to regard all art and culture as inimical to religion; but there were others who not only defended pagan art and literature but were themselves so deeply sensitive to beauty that they actually feared the pleasure they experienced in listening to music, even in church. The well-known words of St. Augustine express this dilemma:

> When I call to mind the tears I shed at the songs of Thy Church, at the outset of my recovered faith, and how even now I am moved not by the singing but by what is sung, when they are sung with a clear and skilfully modulated voice, I then acknowledge the great utility of this custom. Thus vacillate I between dangerous pleasure and tried soundness; being inclined rather (though I pronounce no irrevocable opinion upon the subject) to approve of the use of singing in the church, that so by the delights of the ear the weaker minds may be stimulated to a devotional frame. Yet when it happens to me to be more moved by the singing than by what is sung, I confess myself to have sinned criminally, and then I would rather not have heard the singing. See now the condition I am in! Weep with me, and weep for me, you who so control your inward feelings that good results ensue. As for you who do not thus act, these things concern you not. But Thou, O Lord my God, give ear, behold and see, and have mercy upon me, and heal me—Thou, in whose sight I am become a puzzle to myself; and this is my infirmity.[18]

16 Sts. Jerome, Basil, John Chrysostom; in Gérold, *Les Pères de l'église*, pp. 86, 92, 94–96; for a list of additional citations on this subject, see Abert, *Die Musikanschauung des Mittelalters*, p. 77, note 1.

17 Migne, *op. cit.*, XVI, 1017.

18 Saint Augustine, *Confessions*, X, Ch. 33, tr. J. G. Pilkington in Whitney J. Oates, ed., *Basic Writings of Saint Augustine*, New York, 1948. Quoted by permission of Random House. In 387 A.D., St. Augustine began a treatise *On Music*, of which he completed six books. The first five, after a brief introductory definition of music, deal with the principles of meter and rhythm. The sixth, written somewhat later, goes into psychology, ethics, esthetics, and theology, but has very little to say about music.

The conflict between sacred and secular in art is not peculiar to the Middle Ages. People have always generally agreed that some kinds of music, for one reason or another, are simply not appropriate for use in church. Different churches, different communities, and different ages have fixed the boundary at different points, though the line is not always perfectly clear. The reason that it was sometimes drawn so close to the ascetic extreme in the early period lies in the historical situation. The Church in the beginning was a minority group charged with the task of converting the entire population of Europe to Christianity. To do this it had to establish a Christian community clearly set off from the surrounding pagan society and so organized as to proclaim by every possible means the urgency of subordinating all the things of this world—even the good things and especially the best things, such as the arts—to the eternal welfare of the soul. Thus in the opinion of many, the Church, like an army going into battle, could not afford to carry excess baggage in the shape of music not strictly necessary to its task. In Toynbee's great metaphor, the Church was "the chrysalis out of which our Western society emerged." Its "germ of creative power"[19] in the realm of music was embodied in the Gregorian Chant. The Christian missionaries travelling the ancient Roman roads in the early Middle Ages carried these melodies to every part of western Europe. They were one of the seeds from which, in the fullness of time, our Western music developed.

APPENDIX: The Greek Musical System

With regard to the more technical aspects of Greek musical theory, three factors are mentioned as affecting the *ethos* of a melody: the rhythm, the genus, and the mode. Our information about the first two of these is fairly clear. The rhythm of a Greek song was the rhythm of the poetic text, and in all likelihood the rhythmic system of instrumental music was the same as that of vocal. The basis of the system was quantitative: division into long and short syllables, forming various poetic feet (as the iambus, trochee, etc.), which in turn were combined into verse patterns. Stress accent does not seem to have played an important part, at least in classical times. (The later Middle Ages revived the method of measuring musical rhythm by long and short units grouped in a manner analogous to the poetic feet—the *rhythmic modes*.)

To understand the term *genus* in the context of Greek music we must know that their basic group of intervals was the *tetrachord*, that is, a group of four notes the highest and lowest of which were a perfect fourth apart. This interval is a critical one in all musical systems, and it is practically certain that the Greeks received the tetrachord organization from some Eastern source. In any event, this and the other intervals of the musical scale were mathematically

Tetrachords and genera

19 Arnold J. Toynbee, *A Study of History*, 10 vols., London, 1935–39, I, 57–58.

determined through the measurement of vibrating strings by Pythagoras or his disciples about the end of the sixth century B. C., and expressed in terms of proportions (2:1, octave; 3:2, fifth; 4:3, fourth, etc.) which are still basic to modern acoustical theory. The two outer notes of the tetrachord, being formed of an interval which could always be sung in correct tune, were regarded as fixed, while the inner notes were movable. It seems probable that in the prehistoric stage of Greek music there was only one note in this inner musical space, lying at some indefinite point quite close to the lower fixed note and making a pattern which we might notate approximately as an Example I–1a.

The oldest extant Greek musical treatise, the *Harmonics* of Aristoxenus (*ca.* 330 B.C.) presents a highly developed melodic system organized by means of tetrachords of three principal types or genera: *enharmonic, chromatic,* and *diatonic.* Examples I–1b and I–1c show the (conjectured) evolution of each of these three types from the (supposed) primitive type. Here again the notation of the two inner notes is only approximate. Aristoxenus describes three varieties or "shades" of the chromatic and two of the diatonic tetrachord, formed by locating the two inner notes at various points within the bounding interval of the perfect fourth; but he admits that the possible number of shades is theoretically infinite. In contrast to Pythagoras, Aristoxenus maintains that the true method of

EXAMPLE I–1   Tetrachords

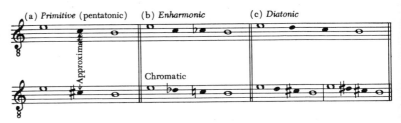

determining intervals is by the ear, not by mathematical calculation; and his method of measurement is not by proportions but by a fractional system in which the whole tone is divided into twelve equal parts. We can infer from Aristoxenus's descriptions and from accounts in later theorists that the ancient Greeks, like most Eastern peoples to the present day, were able to sing (or play) and hear a great variety of micro-intervals that have no place in our Western scales and that they commonly made use of such intervals in their music. Obviously such distinctions would make possible certain qualities in a melody of which we can hardly form a clear idea, and which must have had an effect in determining the *ethos* of a particular composition.

Two tetrachords could be combined in either of two ways. If the last note of one was also the first note of the other, the tetrachords were said to be *conjunct;* if there was a whole tone between, the tetrachords were *disjunct* (see Example I–2 where T = whole tone and s = semitone). Eventually the *Greater Perfect (complete) System* evolved—a two-octave scale made up of conjunct and disjunct tetrachords in the manner shown in Example I–3. The lowest *A* in this system was regarded as an added tone (*proslambanomenos*).

EXAMPLE I–2   Conjunct and Disjunct Tetrachords

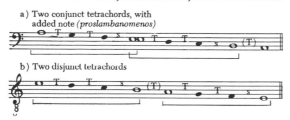

Middle *a* was called *mese* (middle), and the *b* above it *paramese* ("next to middle"). Each of the other notes had a double name, in which the first word gave the position of the note in its tetrachord and the second word was the name of the tetrachord itself (thus *a'*,[20] for example, was called *"nete hyperbolaion"*):

Note	Position	Tetrachord	Translation of Names
a'	Nete	⎫	Nete: "lowest"
g'	Paranete	⎬ Hyperbolaion	Paranete: "next to lowest"
f'	Trite	⎭	Trite: "third"
e'	Nete	⎫	Hyperbolaion: "of the extra"
d'	Paranete	⎬ Diezeugmenon	(tetrachord)
c'	Trite	⎭	Diezeugmenon: "of (the tetrachord of) disjunction"
b	Paramese		
a	Mese		
g	Lichanos	⎫	Lichanos: "index finger"
f	Parhypate	⎬ Meson	Parhypate: "next to highest"
e	Hypate	⎭	Hypate: "highest"
			Meson: "of the middle" (tetrachord)
d	Lichanos	⎫	
c	Parhypate	⎬ Hypaton	Hypaton: "of the highest"
B	Hypate	⎭	(tetrachord)
A	Proslambanomenos		

EXAMPLE I–3   The Greater Perfect System

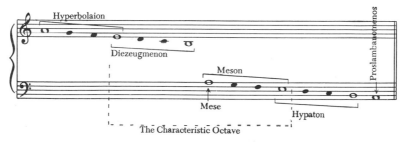

It will be noticed that in the Greek terminology the words "low" and "high" are used with meanings opposite to ours. This is because the names were taken from the relative position of the strings of the lyre; the instrument was held by the player so that the low-

[20] See Glossary, *Note designation*.

29

pitched strings were farther from the ground than the high-pitched ones. *Lichanos* is obviously derived from the fingering of the lyre. The name of the tetrachord *diezeugmenon* comes from the fact that the interval *b-a* is the whole tone between two disjunct tetrachords, the "point of disjunction"—in Greek, *diazeuxis*.

In Example I–3 the outer or fixed tones of the tetrachords have been rendered in modern notation with open (white) notes. The two inner tones of each tetrachord (shown in black notes) could, as was explained above, be altered in pitch to produce the various shades and the enharmonic and chromatic genera; but regardless of pitch modification these notes retained the same names (*paranete, trite; lichanos, parhypate*) as in the diatonic genus.

There was also a *Lesser Perfect System* which consisted of the octave from *a* to *A* as in the Greater Perfect System, with an added conjunct tetrachord (called *synemmenon*: "hooked") made of the notes d'-c'-b♭-a.

The Greater Perfect System was, at least in origin, a theoretical structure arrived at by adding a conjunct tetrachord at either end of the central octave *e'-e*. This octave was the one within which, as far as we can tell, most Greek melodies were sung and played. It was early named the Dorian "key" (*tonos*), in the same way that we give a letter name to a key to indicate its relative position in a pitch series. Various theorists distinguished as many as fifteen keys, some above and some below the Dorian. Ptolemy in his *Harmonics* (*ca.* A. D. 150) reduced the number to seven.

The modes

With this much by way of preface, we are ready to consider what Plato and Aristotle meant by a *mode*. "The musical modes" says Aristotle, "differ essentially from one another, and those who hear them are differently affected by each. Some of them make men sad and grave, like the so-called Mixolydian; others enfeeble the mind, like the relaxed modes; another, again, produces a moderate and settled temper, which appears to be the peculiar effect of the Dorian; the Phrygian inspires enthusiasm."[21] Whether we regard the essential quality of the central octave of the Greater Perfect System—the Dorian octave *e'-e*—as consisting in the pitch at which it lies or in the pattern of tones and semitones formed by its notes (descending T–T–s–T–T–T–s), we can perceive nothing about it capable of producing a moderate and settled temper or indeed any other state of mind. It is apparent, then, that Aristotle does not mean by "mode" any abstraction, such as an octave of the Greater Perfect System; or if he does, he considers it part of the entire musical substance from which the abstraction was made, the general expressive quality of the melodies and melodic turns characteristic of a certain mode; and he clearly connects with these also the particular rhythms and poetic forms associated with that mode. In saying that the Phrygian inspires enthusiasm, therefore, he means something similar to but very much more definite than the kind of thing we mean when we say that the key of D major has an energetic and cheerful sound, or that C minor has a character of heroic tragic tension.

What was there about a mode in Greek music that could affect listeners so markedly? And what was the principle of difference among the modes that caused such strikingly different effects to be

[21] *Politics,* 1340a, p. 40 ff. Cf. Plato, *Republic,* III, p. 398 ff.

imputed to them? No one today knows with certainty the answers to these questions. No writer contemporary with Plato and Aristotle gives a clear technical description of a mode, and not enough of the music is preserved to enable us to verify and amplify the statements of the theorists. Lacking direct evidence, we resort to hypothesis. There are two principal theories, one old and one more recent:

The older theory held that a mode in Greek music was essentially similar to a mode in medieval music, namely, *a certain octave scale pattern of tones and semitones* with a definite tonal center. In this theory, the modes were differentiated by the different interval patterns of their octave scales, that is, by the different distribution of tones and semitones. Thus the (diatonic) Dorian mode was the pattern exemplified in the octave *e′–e* of the Greater Perfect System; the Phrygian was the pattern of the octave *d′–d,* the Lydian that of *c′–c,* and so on.

This theory was opposed by the claims that different scale patterns were not in use in Plato's and Aristotle's time; that the only octave species known or in practical use was the one exemplified (in its diatonic form) in the central octave *e′–e* of the Greater Perfect System; that other octave species were differentiated only later by theorists, and remained for many centuries apparently of only theoretical importance; that the word Plato and Aristotle use for mode (*harmonia*) was not a technical musical term but a general word of various meanings; and that when *harmonia* is used by a writer presumably expert in musical terminology it either clearly has a meaning that has nothing to do with modality, or else is treated as if it were synonymous with key (*tonos*).

Consequently, according to the newer and more generally accepted theory, *a mode is a key,* and the different modes were different keys—that is, transpositions of one basic octave pattern to different pitch levels. Thus the Phrygian and Lydian modes were not (as we would say) the white-key octave scales from d and c respectively, but simply the octave pattern (descending) T–T–s–T–T–T–s starting respectively on f♯ and g♯. The *ethos* of a mode, according to this theory, was a matter not of the order of tones and semitones in the scale pattern, but of higher and lower pitch.

Stated thus baldly, this view is not without its difficulties. For example, how could a mere transposition by one tone up or down account for the difference in *ethos* which Plato postulates between the Dorian and the Phrygian modes? One would have to assume that there was something like a standard pitch and that listeners were able instantly to recognize and respond to different pitch levels in relation to this standard—assumptions both extremely improbable and completely unsupported by evidence. The transposition theory is therefore usually modified in the following ways:

Most Greek instruments and melodies had a range of not more than one octave. The different keys (*tonoi*) therefore would have to be capable of being realized within this compass, which is the musical space of the *characteristic octave e′–e* in the Greater Perfect System. If the basic diatonic interval pattern of (descending) T–T–s–T–T–T–s is thought of as in the Phrygian key, that is, as starting from f♯′, those of its notes that fall within the space of the characteristic octave would occur as e′–d′–c♯′–b–a–g–f♯; and likewise if the pattern were in the Lydian key starting from g♯′, its notes within the characteristic octave would be e′–d♯′–c♯′–b–a–g♯, while

I. The State of Music at the End of the Ancient World

EXAMPLE I-4   Species of the Characteristic Octave

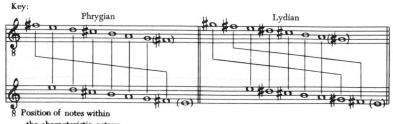

Position of notes within
the characteristic octave:

the two top notes g♯'–f♯' would appear as g♯–f♯, that is, one octave
below their (theoretically) original pitch (see Example I–4); and similarly with the other keys. The list of keys according to Ptolemy
is shown in Example I–5.

As a consequence of an actual or assumed transposition of the
basic interval pattern to seven different pitch levels, seven correspondingly different patterns of intervals result within the characteristic octave *e'–e*. These seven different appearances or *species*

EXAMPLE I-5   The Keys According to Ptolemy

of the octave eventually came to be named after the keys from which they were derived; the names originally applied to the keys in column A of Example I–5 were transferred, by a natural association of ideas, to the octave patterns of column B. But this probably did not happen before the time of Ptolemy, in the second century A. D. Moreover, there is no suggestion that the species ever had the character of a mode, that is, an ordered disposition of the notes according to their function in relation to one or more focal points, such as we find in the medieval church modes with their dominants and finals. The errors of the older theory, it is claimed, consisted in regarding the octave species as primary and the keys as derivative, and in ascribing a modal character to the octave species.

This modification of the transposition theory does not seem to make clear in what sense one key can sound higher or lower than another, since apparently the only transposition it allows is a theoretical one whose only audible effect would be a redistribution of the tones and semitones within one and the same octave range; nor does it bring us any closer to an understanding of the differences among the several modes or keys. A second supporting hypothesis seeks to meet the latter objection.

There is some reason to suspect that in all the different keys one note—the *mese* of the Greater Perfect System—had special importance as a central tone of frequent recurrence in melodies, a tone functioning perhaps somewhat like the dominant (or possibly the tonic) in our system. If this were the case, the differing relations of the other notes to this immutable "dominant" *a* would probably produce a characteristic set of melodic motives in each mode, peculiar to that mode and giving to it a special quality which could never be deduced solely from its pitch or its scale species. This suggests the possibility that the modes may have been complex structures similar to the Indian *rāgas* and Arabian *maqamât*—that is, patterns or general melodic types, with each of which certain specific rhythms and certain tetrachord genera were associated. This thought goes a long way toward explaining the definite ethical quality which ancient writers ascribe to each mode. There may have been other associations not technical or musical, such as traditions, customs, and more or less unconscious acquired attitudes toward different types of melody; it is also possible that originally the names "Dorian," "Phrygian," etc. may have referred to particular types of music or manners of performance characteristic of the various races from whom the Greek people of historic times were descended; about all these things we can do little more than guess. We may be practically certain, at any rate, that whatever music was actually being played and sung by the common people of Greece in ancient times took little or no account of the various artificial systems of "learned" music propounded by the philosophers and theorists.

To repeat—we do not know, and in all probability we shall never know, exactly what were the modes about which Plato and Aristotle wrote, or how these may have been different from the modes as understood by later writers. "It is impossible for us to give a detailed description of Greek . . . music . . . There is not sufficient evidence."[22] Each of the various hypotheses about the modes has claims to credi-

---

[22] Werner Jaeger, *Paidea: The Ideals of Greek Culture*, tr. G. Highet, New York, 1943, II. 225.

bility, and each is warmly defended by its champions. No field of musicology has produced a richer crop of disputation from a thinner soil of fact. Altogether, the sources consist of some twenty treatises, most of them fragmentary, the earliest written about 350 B. C. and the latest about 350 A. D.; and six melodies, with about an equal number of musical fragments, spanning the same seven centuries. How much could a historian from some future civilization deduce about tonality in our Western music in the period from 1250 to 1950 if he had no more than this to work from?

II

Gregorian Chant and Secular Song in the Middle Ages

Gregorian Chant and the Roman Liturgy

In studying the history of music it is of course necessary to learn certain facts about musical forms and styles in the different historical periods; but it is even more necessary to get to know the music itself. The facts are but dry bones; the music alone gives them life and meaning. It is especially important to bear this in mind in studying Gregorian Chant, which is unfamiliar music to many people. The chants should be listened to and sung until the student becomes accustomed to their sound; and at every stage of this growing acquaintance, he should not only consider their beauty, but also be aware of the relation of the chants to the relevant historical and analytical information which it is the purpose of this chapter to present.

This admonition is the more urgent because, with the change from Latin to the vernacular in the liturgy since the Second Vatican Council of 1962–65 Gregorian Chant has virtually disappeared from the regular services of the Catholic Church. In Europe, it is still in use in some monasteries and for certain services in some of the larger parochial churches; in America, it is cultivated much less. Even though in theory Latin remains the official language and Gregorian Chant the official music of the Church, in practice the traditional chants have been mostly replaced by music thought suitable for the entire congregation to sing: simplified versions of the more familiar Gregorian melodies; new melodies, often of a cheap commercial sort, of little or no musical value; or occasional experiments in more sophisticated popular styles. Even when sung to the authentic melodies, the vernacular speech rhythm alters the musical character of the Chant, while the direct intelligibility of the English words detracts from the objective quality which it possessed with its Latin text.

There seems no likely prospect for eventual restoration of Gregorian Chant on any considerable scale. Nevertheless, and regardless of its current practical status, a knowledge of the Chant is both valuable for its own sake and essential for understanding the history of music (not only church music) in the Middle Ages, the Renaissance, and even in later times.

The nature of Gregorian Chant

When we hear Gregorian Chant for the first time, we are apt to have a negative impression of it. We are struck not so much by what is there as by what is not there. We feel the lack of supporting harmony or accompaniment; we miss clearly defined time values and regular accents; we notice that the melodic line sometimes turns strangely and often does not cadence on the expected note; and we are perhaps resentfully conscious that the music makes no attempt to thrill our senses or entangle our emotions. We may incorporate these impressions in a definition: Gregorian Chant consists of single-line melody sung to Latin words by unaccompanied men's voices, in a flexible rhythm articulated by means other than regular accentuation, in a scale system different from our major or minor; and it has an impersonal, objective, other-worldly quality in which sensuous beauty and emotional appeal are largely subordinate to expression of the religious content of the text.

A sharp cleavage between sacred and secular is so ingrained in our thinking that it requires an effort to realize that in the Middle Ages people did not regard sacred music as completely separate from everyday experience. Many of the Gregorian melodies were as familiar as any common folk tune today. Children learned them in school. Some of them were sung by the congregation, which in those days included practically every inhabitant of a community. Many medieval folk songs and other secular compositions were adapted from church melodies, and the church in turn adapted secular melodies to its own use. Dante frequently mentions in the *Divine Comedy* particular chants, assuming them to be familiar to his readers. All in all, Gregorian Chant in the Middle Ages was music of the people as well as music of the Church.

Gregorian Chant, while beautiful as sheer music, is not meant to be listened to for its own sake; as an adjunct to worship, it is strictly functional music. Consequently, in order to understand the music it is essential to know something of the liturgy within which it has its place. We shall therefore first consider the main outlines of the Catholic Latin liturgy as prescribed since the late sixteenth century, without dwelling on the modifications of detail that are currently in process of adoption, along with the change from Latin to the vernacular, since the Second Vatican Council. What follows, then, is a generalized description (using the present tense for convenience) of what we may call the historically settled form of post-medieval Roman liturgy—which, though not identical in all respects with earlier medieval forms, is close enough to them in essentials to serve our purpose.

The two principal classes of services are the *Office* and the *Mass*. There are eight *Offices,* or *Canonical Hours,* which are celebrated every day at stated times in a regular order, though their public recitation is generally observed only in monasteries and certain cathedral churches: *Matins* (before daybreak), *Lauds* (at sunrise), *Prime, Terce, Sext, Nones* (respectively at about 6 a.m., 9 a.m., noon, and 3 p.m.), *Vespers* (at sunset) and *Compline* (usually immediately after Vespers). The Gregorian music for the Offices is collected in a liturgical book called the *Antiphonale* or *Antiphonar*. The principal features of the Offices are the chanting of psalms with their antiphons, the singing of hymns and canticles, and the chanting of lessons (passages of Scripture) with their responsories. From the musical point of view the most important Offices are Matins, Lauds, and Vespers. Matins includes some of the most ancient chants of the Church. Vespers has the canticle *Magnificat anima mea Dominum* ("My soul doth magnify the Lord," St Luke 1:46–55); and inasmuch as this Office is the only one that admitted polyphonic singing from early times, it is especially important to the history of sacred music. A feature of Compline is the singing of the four votive antiphons of the Blessed Virgin Mary, the so-called "Marian" antiphons, one for each of the main divisions of the Church year:[1] *Alma Redemptoris Mater* ("Sweet Mother of the Redeemer") from Advent to February 1; *Ave Regina caelorum* ("Hail, Queen of the Heavens") from February 2 to Wednesday of Holy Week; *Regina caeli laetare* ("Rejoice Queen of Heaven") from Easter to Trinity Sunday; and *Salve Regina* ("Hail, O Queen") from Trinity until Advent. (See illustration on p. 38, and Example II–1.)

The Roman liturgy

The Mass, although its liturgy was developed later than that of the Offices, is the principal service of the Catholic Church. The

[1] The principal seasons of the liturgical year are:
Advent, starting with the fourth Sunday before Christmas;
Christmas, including the twelve days to
Epiphany (January 6th) and following weeks; the
Pre-Lenten season, beginning nine weeks before Easter;
Lent, from Ash Wednesday to Easter;
Eastertide, including Ascension (forty days after Easter) and continuing to
Pentecost or *Whitsunday,* ten days after Ascension or seven weeks after Easter; and
Trinity, from the first Sunday after Pentecost to the beginning of Advent.
Advent and Lent are sometimes called the "penitential" seasons.

Salve Regina *as it appears in modern Gregorian notation in the* Liber Usualis.

word "Mass" comes from the service's closing phrase: *Ite missa est* ("Go, [the congregation] is dismissed"); the service is also known in other Christian churches under the names of the Eucharist, the Liturgy, Holy Communion, and the Lord's Supper. The culminating act of the Mass is the commemoration of re-enactment of the Last Supper (Luke xxii:19–20; I Cor. ii:23–26), the essential parts of the ceremony being the offering and consecration of the bread and wine and the partaking of these by the faithful. All that part of the Mass which precedes this was derived originally from the ancient Jewish ritual, to which the specifically Christian Eucharist was added. In the Catholic Church there are two ways of celebrating Mass. In a *Low Mass,* the words are said by the priest in a low voice, and the congregation follows the service silently; in a *High Mass* the service is recited and sung audibly (in a "high" voice) either completely in Gregorian Chant or in Chant and polyphonic music.

EXAMPLE II–1   Antiphon: *Salve Regina*

MODE 1

Sal - ve*† Re- gi - na, ma-ter mi - se - ri - cor-di - ae:

Vi - ta, dul - ce - do, et spes nos - tra, sal - ve.

Ad te cla - ma - mus, ex - su - les, fi - li - i He - vae.

Ad te sus - pi - ra - mus, ge-men - tes et flen - tes in hac

la - cri - ma - rum val - le. E - ia er - go, Ad-vo - ca - ta

no - stra, il - los tu - os mi - se - ri - cor - des o - cu - los

ad nos con - ver - te. Et Je - sum, be- ne - di - ctum fructum ven -

tris tu - i, no - bis post hoc ex - si - li - um os - ten-de.

O cle - mens: O pi - a:

O dul - cis *Vir- go Ma - ri - a.

Hail, O Queen, Mother of mercy, our life, our sweetness and our hope! To thee we cry, banished children of Eve; to thee we send up our sighs, mourning and weeping in this vale of tears. Turn then, our Advocate, thine eyes of mercy toward us; and after this our exile, show unto us the blessed fruit of thy womb, Jesus. O clement, O loving, O sweet Virgin Mary.

† This modern transcription reproduces certain signs that accompany the neumes in the manuscript. The asterisk indicates where the chant alternates between soloist and choir, or between the two halves of the choir. The straight lines under some pairs of notes are extensions of the sign for a slight lengthening of the notes. The small notes correspond to a sign probably indicating a light vocalization of the first ("voiced") consonant in such combinations as *ergo, ventris*. The wavy line represents a sign which probably called for a slight ornamenting of the note, perhaps something like a short trill or mordent.

In its historically settled form the liturgy of the Mass begins with the *Introit;* originally this was an entire psalm with its antiphon, chanted during the entrance of the priest (the *antiphona ad introitum,* or "antiphon for the entrance"), but later was shortened to only a single verse of the psalm with an antiphon. Immediately after the Introit the choir sings the *Kyrie,* to the Greek words *Kyrie eleison* ("Lord have mercy upon us"), *Christe eleison* ("Christ have mercy upon us"), *Kyrie eleison,* each invocation being sung three times. Next follows (except in the seasons of Advent and Lent) the *Gloria,* begun by the priest with the words *Gloria in excelsis Deo* ("Glory be to God on high") and continued by the choir from *Et in terra pax* ("And on each peace"). Then come the prayers (*Collects*) and the reading of the *Epistle* for the day, followed by the *Gradual* and Alleluia, both sung by a soloist or soloists with responses by the choir. In penitential seasons the Alleluia is replaced by the more solemn *Tract.* After the reading of the *Gospel* comes the *Credo,* begun by the priest *Credo in unum Deum* ("I believe in one God") and continued by the choir from *Patrem omnipotentem* ("the Father Almighty"). This, together with the sermon if any, marks the end of the first main division of the Mass; now follows the Eucharist proper. During the preparation of the bread and wine the *Offertory* is sung. This is followed by various prayers and the *Preface* which leads into the *Sanctus* ("Holy, holy, holy") and *Benedictus* ("Blessed is He that cometh"), both sung by the choir. Then comes the *Canon* or prayer of consecration, followed by the Lord's Prayer and the *Agnus Dei* ("Lamb of God"). After the bread and wine have been consumed, the choir sings the *Communion,* which is followed by the singing of the priest's *Post-Communion* prayers. The service then concludes with the dismissal formula *Ite missa est* or *Benedicamus Domino* ("Let us bless the Lord"), sung responsively by the priest and choir.

The texts of certain parts of the Mass are invariable; others change according to the season of the year or the dates of particular feasts or commemorations. The variable portions are called the *Proper of the Mass (Proprium missae).* The Collects, Epistle, Gospel, Preface, and the Post-Communion and other prayers are all part of the Proper; the principal musical portions of the Proper are the Introit, Gradual, Alleluia, Tract, Offertory, and Communion. The invariable parts of the service are called the *Ordinary of the Mass (Ordinarium missae),* and include the Kyrie, Gloria, Credo, Sanctus, Benedictus, and Agnus Dei. These parts are sung by the choir, though in early Christian times they were also sung by the congregation. Since the fourteenth century, they are the texts most often set to polyphonic music, so that the term "Mass" is frequently used by musicians to refer only to these items, as in Bach's *Mass in B Minor* or Beethoven's *Missa solemnis.* Incidentally, neither Bach's nor Beethoven's Mass is appropriate for liturgical use; and there are many other settings of the Ordinary which are inappropriate for use in church because of their undue length, textual repetitions, or generally ornate character.

A special Mass, also often (though only since the middle of the fifteenth century) set polyphonically, is the Mass for the Dead, or Requiem Mass, so called from the first word of its Introit, which begins *Requiem aeternam dona eis Domine* ("Grant them eternal rest, O Lord"). The Requiem Mass has its own Proper which does not vary with the calendar. The Gloria and Credo are omitted, and the sequence *Dies irae, dies illa* ("Day of wrath, O dreadful day") is inserted after the Tract. Modern settings of the Requiem (for example, those by Mozart, Berlioz, Verdi, and Fauré) include certain texts of the Proper, such as the Introit, the Offertory *Domine Jesu Christe*, the Communion *Lux aeterna*("Light eternal"), and sometimes the Responsory *Libera me, Domine* ("Deliver me, O Lord").

The Gregorian music for the Mass, both Proper and Ordinary, is published in a liturgical book, the *Graduale*. The *Liber Usualis,* another book of Gregorian music, contains a selection of the most frequently used chants from both the *Antiphonale* and the *Graduale*. Texts of the Mass and Offices respectively are published in the Missal (*Missale*) and the Breviary (*Breviarium*).

When the chants are to be read or sung from an edition in modern plainsong notation, the following information will be necessary: the staff is of four lines, one of which is designated by a clef as either c′ (**c**) or f (**f**). These clefs do not indicate absolute pitches; they are only relative. The usual method of performance today is to interpret all the notes (which are called *neumes*) as having essentially the same duration regardless of shape; a dot after a neume doubles its value. Two or more neumes in succession on the same line or space, if on the same syllable, are sung as though tied. A horizontal dash above a neume means it should be slightly lengthened. *Composite* neumes (single signs representing two or more notes) are to be read from left to right in the normal manner, except for the *podatus* or *pes* (**c**), in which the lower note is sung first. A neume, whether simple or composite, never carries more than one syllable. Flat signs, except in a signature at the beginning of a line, are valid only until the next vertical division line or until the beginning of the next word. The little sign at the end of a line is a guide to show the position of the first note in the following line. An asterisk in the text shows where the chorus takes over from the soloist, and the signs *ij* and *iij* indicate that the preceding phrase is to be sung twice or three times. For an example of a chant in modern Gregorian notation and its transcription in ordinary modern notation, see pages 38 and 39.

Modern Gregorian notation

The melodies of Gregorian Chant are preserved in hundreds of manuscripts dating from the ninth century and later. These manuscripts were written at different times and in widely separated areas. Very often the same melody is found in many different manuscripts: and it is remarkable that these manuscripts record the melody in almost identical form—very close, indeed, to the form in which it appears in the present-day liturgical books. How are we to interpret this fact? One possibility, of course, is to say that the melodies must have come from one source and must have been transmitted with great accuracy and fidelity, either by purely oral means or with the help of some early notation of which no specimens have survived. Something of this sort was substantially the interpretation advanced by writers of the eighth and ninth centuries, coupled with statements to the effect that the "one source" was St. Gregory himself. Modern scholarship has shown this interpretation to be untenable without serious modification. How, then, can we account not only for the agreement among the earliest manuscripts but also for the fact that all these manuscripts were written not at Rome nor even in Italy, but at various centers in what are now France, Switzerland, and the western part of Germany—in other words, in the territory of the Frankish kingdom of Charlemagne (742–814)?

It may be remarked that both the systematic writing down of the chant melodies and their ascription to divine inspiration (through St. Gregory) coincide with a determined campaign by the Frankish monarchs to unify their polyglot kingdom. One necessary means to this end was a uniform liturgy and music of the churches, binding on the entire population. Rome, so venerable in the imagination of the Middle Ages, was the natural model, particularly after Charlemagne was crowned there in 800 as head of the Holy Roman Empire. He and his successors undertook to replace the Gallican liturgies in Frankish lands by Roman usages. Great numbers of liturgical-musical "missionaries" travelled between Rome and the north in the late eighth and ninth centuries, and a potent weapon in their propaganda was the legend of St. Gregory and the divinely inspired Chant. Naturally, their efforts met with resistance and a great deal of confusion ensued before unification was finally achieved. Writing down the melodies would then have been one way of assuring that henceforth the chants would be sung everywhere the same.

There is another, or rather a supplementary, hypothesis[2] to account for the reduction of the chants to musical notation in the ninth century. Everything that we know about their history before that time goes to show that they were indeed transmitted orally, but not

---

[2] Set forth persuasively, with supporting evidence, by Leo Treitler in " 'Improvised' and 'Composed' Music in the Medieval West," in *Improvisation in Music, East and West,* ed. Ella Zoris and Leonard B. Meyer, University of Chicago Press, in prep.

in fixed, unalterable versions learned by heart from a written document or from a teacher. In the first Christian churches and up to about the eighth century the singing of the chants was *improvisatory*: not, of course, "free" spontaneous improvisation, but performance in which traditional melodic structures or "melody-types" associated with particular parts of the liturgy or particular seasons of the church year furnished a basis on which the singer embroidered, making use also of certain standard melodic formulas in the course of his improvisation. This is the same principle we have already met in connection with ancient music and which is still operative among many peoples (see above, pp. 14–15). That such a system demands prodigious powers of memory need not be surprising; comparable feats were required of the bards who recited the Homeric poems and the medieval epics before these were eventually written down, and one can hear similar performances today in connection with long "epic chants" in parts of Central Asia and Eastern Europe.[3] By the late eighth century, however, the number of texts in the liturgy had increased to a point where singers were beginning to have difficulty in adapting so many different sets of words to the traditional basic melodic schemes. As a result, it became necessary to fix the melodies in writing. The earliest musical notation did not give an exact picture of the melody; the signs were rather in the nature of a reminder to the singer of something he already knew pretty well. Meanwhile, the pressure for uniformity was on. Musical notation—first of the "reminder" sort and later of precise intervals—appeared only after a large measure of uniformity had already been achieved within the frame of improvisatory performance. Notation, in short, was a consequence of that uniformity as well as a means of perpetuating it.

Just what were the melodies that were brought from Rome to the Frankish lands? No one can answer this question with certainty. The recitation tones, the psalm tones, and some others of the simplest types were very ancient and may have been preserved practically intact from the earliest years; some thirty or forty antiphon melodies may have originated in St. Gregory's time; a great many of the more complex melodies—Tracts, Graduals, Offertories, Alleluias—must have been in use (perhaps in simpler versions) at Rome before being spread to the north; and it may be that some of the early melodies are preserved in the manuscripts of the Old Roman Chant. Whatever the case, we may suspect that in its new home much, if not all of this imported music underwent changes before finally being written down in the form in which we find it in the oldest manuscripts. Furthermore, a great many new melodies and new forms of chant

[3] See descriptions in "Traditional Recitation Forms of Epic Chants" in International Musicological Society, *Report of the Tenth Congress, Ljubljana 1967* Kassel and Ljubljana, 1970, 359–99.

grew up in the north after the ninth century. In sum: practically the whole body of the chant as we now know it comes to us from Frankish sources that either incorporate Roman materials to an unknown extent or else represent new music of northern origin. In a strict historical sense, therefore, it is incorrect to call the Chant as a whole "Gregorian." But since the name after all does have some historical justification, and since "Gregorian Chant" is a term well established and consecrated by centuries of use, we may continue to accept it—making a distinction, where necessary, between the Roman or Gregorian heritage and the later Frankish changes and additions.

Classes, Forms, and Types of Gregorian Chant

All chants may be divided into those with *Biblical* and those with *non-Biblical* texts; each of these divisions may be subdivided into chants with *prose* texts and those with *poetical* texts. Examples of Biblical prose texts are the lessons of the Office, and the Epistle and Gospel of the Mass; of Biblical poetical texts, the psalms and canticles. Non-Biblical prose texts include the *Te Deum,* many antiphons, and three of the four Marian antiphons; chants with non-Biblical poetical texts are the hymns and sequences.

Chants may also be classified according to the manner in which they are (or were, in earlier times) sung as *antiphonal* (alternating choirs), *responsorial* (alternating soloist and choir), or *direct* (without alternation).

Still another classification is based on the relation of notes to syllables. Chants in which most or all of the syllables have a single note each are called *syllabic;* those characterized by long melodic passages on a single syllable are called *melismatic.* This distinction is not always clear-cut, since chants that are prevailingly melismatic usually include some syllabic sections or phrases, and many chants otherwise syllabic have occasional short melismas of four or five notes on some syllables. This type of chant is sometimes called *neumatic.*

In general, the melodic outline of a chant reflects the normal modern accentuation of the Latin words by setting the prominent syllables on higher notes or by giving such syllables more notes. But this rule has many exceptions even in a moderately florid chant; and of course it cannot be fully applied in recitative-like chants, where many successive syllables are sung to the same note, or in hymns, where every strophe has to be sung to the same melody. Moreover, in florid chants the melodic accent often has greater importance than the word accent; consequently we may find long melismas on weak syllables, particularly final syllables, as on the final "a" of "alleluia" or the last syllable of words like "Dominus," "exsultemus," or "Kyrie." In such chants the important words and syllables of a phrase are emphasized and made clear by setting them more simply, so that they stand out in contrast to the rich ornamentation of the unstressed syllables. In Gregorian Chant there is hardly ever any repetition of the text; word-painting or similar pointed reflection of single words or images is exceptional. The melody is adapted to the rhythm of the text, to its general mood, and to the liturgical function which a chant fulfills; no attempt is made to adapt the melody to special emotional or pictorial effects. This is not to say that Gregorian Chant is inexpressive, but only that it does not have that quality musicians call *espressivo*.

Every Gregorian melody is divided into phrases or periods[4] corresponding to the periods of the text. These sections are marked off in the modern chant books by a vertical line in the staff, shorter or longer according to the importance of the subdivision. In the great majority of Gregorian phrases, the melodic curve has the form of an arch ⌒; it begins low, rises to a higher pitch where it remains for some time, then descends at the end of the phrase. This simple and natural design is worked out with great subtlety and in many varied combinations; for instance, the melodic arch may extend over two or more phrases, or include lesser arches. A less common melodic design, characteristic of phrases beginning with an especially important word, starts on a high note and descends gradually to the end.

As far as general aspects of form are concerned, three main types of chants may be distinguished: the forms exemplified in the psalm tones, of two balanced phrases corresponding to the two balanced parts of a typical psalm verse; strophic form, exemplified in hymns, in which the same melody is sung to several stanzas of text; and free forms, which include all other types, and do not lend themselves to concise description. Free chants may combine a number of traditional melodic formulas, or may incorporate such formulas in an otherwise original composition; they may arise from the expansion or development of a given melody-type; or they may be entirely original.

We shall now examine some of the more important categories of chants used in the Mass and Office, beginning with syllabic and proceeding to melismatic kinds.

The chants for the recitation of prayers and readings from the Bible are on the border between speech and song. They consist of

---

4 *Phrase* and *period* are used here as roughly synonymous and in a general sense, not with the special technical meaning given to them in treatises on plainsong.

Reciting and psalm tones

a single *reciting note* (usually a or c'), to which each verse or period of the text is rapidly chanted. This reciting note is also called the *tenor,* or (in later times) the *dominant;* occasionally the upper or lower neighboring note will be introduced to bring out an important accent. The reciting note may be preceded by a two- or three-note introductory formula called the *initium;* at the end of each verse or period there is a short melodic cadence. Similar to these recitation tones, but slightly more complex, are standard formulas called *psalm tones;* there is one tone for each of the eight church Modes and an extra one called the *Tonus peregrinus* or "foreign tone." The psalm tones and those for the readings of the Epistle and Gospel, are among the oldest chants of the liturgy; they may have been taken over directly from chants of the Hebrew synagogue. Likewise very ancient are the slightly more ornate tones for the Preface and Lord's Prayer. All the psalms are sung antiphonally in the Offices to one or another of the tones, and this same general type of melodic formula also occurs in many other chants. A psalm tone consists of the *initium* (used only in the first verse of the psalm), *tenor, mediatio* (semicadence in the middle of the verse), and *terminatio,* or final cadence. Usually the last verse of a psalm is followed by the *Doxology* or *Gloria Patri* ("Glory be to the Father"); in the chant books the closing words of the Doxology are indicated by vowels below the last notes of the music, thus: *euouae.* These vowels are an abbreviation for the last six syllables of the phrase *et in secula sEcUlOrUm, AmEn* ("world without end, Amen").

Antiphons

Antiphons are more numerous than any other type of Chant; about 1250 are found in the modern *Antiphonale.* However, many antiphons employ the same melody-type, making only slight variations to accommodate the text, a practice which goes back to the Jewish origins of early Church music. Since antiphons were originally intended for a group of singers rather than for a soloist, the older ones are usually syllabic or only slightly florid, with stepwise melodic movement, limited range, and comparatively simple rhythm. The antiphons of the canticles are somewhat more elaborate than those of the psalms. Many antiphons were composed for additional feasts that were introduced from the ninth to the thirteenth centuries; to this same period belong a number of antiphons not attached to particular psalms, which are independent pieces for use in processions and for other special occasions. The difference between the early and the late types may be realized by comparing the end of the antiphon *Laus Deo Patri* ("Praise to God the Father"; Example II–2) with the eloquent closing period of an eleventh-century antiphon to St. Afra, *Gloriosa et beatissima Christi martyr* ("Glorious and most blessed martyr of Christ"; Example II–3),

EXAMPLE II–2   Antiphon: *Laus Deo Patri* (*Liber Usualis*, p. 914)

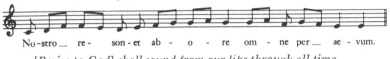

No-stro_ re - son-et ab - o - re om - ne per_ ae - vum.

[Praise to God] shall sound from our lips through all time.

composed by Hermann of Reichenau, commonly known as Hermannus Contractus ("the cripple"; 1013–54).

EXAMPLE II–3   Antiphon: *Gloriosa et beatissima,* Hermann of Reichenau

Pro   no - stris re - - a - ti -

bus   in - - - ter - - - ce - de.

Intercede for us guilty ones.

Moderately ornate forms of antiphonal psalmody are found in the Introit and Communion of the Mass. The Introit, as noted above, was originally a complete psalm with its antiphon. In the course of time this part of the service was very much shortened, so that today the Introit consists only of the original antiphon, a single psalm verse with the customary *Gloria Patri,* and the repetition of the antiphon. The tones for the psalm verses in the Mass are slightly more elaborate than the psalm tones of the Office. The Communion, coming at the end of the Mass as a counterpart to the Introit at the beginning, is a short Chant, often consisting of only one verse of Scripture. In contrast to the Introit, which is apt to be comparatively animated, the Communion usually has the character of a quiet close to the sacred ceremony.

Introit and Communion

The most highly developed chants, musically, of the Mass are the graduals, alleluias, tracts, and offertories. The tract was originally a solo song. The gradual and alleluia are responsorial; the offertory was probably at first an antiphonal chant, but today no trace of the original psalm remains, and what must have been the original antiphon is performed now as a responsorial chant by soloist and choir.

The tracts are the longest chants in the liturgy, partly because they have long texts and partly because their melodies are extended by the use of melismatic figures. All tract melodies are in either the second or the eighth mode; most tracts in each mode have a similar melodic structure. The tracts in the second mode have for their texts chiefly words of penitence and sadness; they are longer and more serious than the tracts in the eighth mode, which most often

Tracts

are set with texts of hope and assurance. This difference may be in part related to the fact that mode II has a minor third and mode VIII has a major third. A good example of a tract in mode II is *Eripe me, Domine* ("Deliver me, O Lord"), sung in the Good Friday service. One of the most beautiful tracts of mode VIII is *Sicut cervus* ("Like as the hart"), from the service of Holy Saturday. The musical form of the tracts in both modes is a complex variation of a simple formula very like a psalm tone; each verse of the tract is divided by a mediatio as in a psalm tone, and the characteristic reciting notes or tenors of psalmody are present. There are certain recurring melodic formulas which are found in many different tracts, and regularly in the same place—at the mediatio, at the beginning of the second half of the verse, and so on. These features—the construction of so many melodies on only two basic patterns, the form (a psalm recitation ornamented with melismas), and the presence of standard melodic formulas—all suggest that in the tracts we have a survival, probably in elaborated form, of some of the music from Gregorian or even pre-Gregorian times. If this is true, it would suggest that originally there were only two modes, instead of eight as in the Byzantine and later Western systems, and that these two original modes were what we should now call "minor" and "major" in character.

Graduals

The graduals were also among the types of Chant that came from Rome to the Frankish churches, probably already in a late, highly developed form. Their melodies are more florid than those of the tracts and their structure is essentially different. A gradual in the modern chant books is a shortened responsory; it has an introductory refrain or *respond*, followed by a single verse of the psalm. The refrain is begun by a soloist and continued by the choir; the verse is sung by a soloist with the choir joining in on the last phrase. Graduals occur in seven of the eight modes. A large number written in mode II are variants of a single melodic type which is exemplified in the Easter Gradual *Haec dies quem fecit Dominus* ("This is the day which the Lord hath made"; Example II–4).

Another important group of graduals are those in mode V, whose melodies often give the impression of being in F major owing to the frequent outlining of the f-a-c' triad[5] and the frequent use of the B-flat. Certain melismatic formulas recur in different graduals; some of the melodies are made up almost entirely of such formulas joined together, in a manner similar to the tracts and the Hebrew synagogue chants.

Alleluias

Alleluias consist of a refrain, on the single word "alleluia," and a verse, followed by repetition of the refrain. The customary manner of singing is as follows: the soloist (or soloists) sings the word "alleluia"; the chorus repeats this and continues with the *jubilus*,

[5] For an explanation of pitch designations, see Glossary under *Note designation*.

a long melisma on the final "ia" of "alleluia"; the soloist then sings the verse, with the chorus joining on the last phrase, after which the entire alleluia with jubilus is sung by the chorus. The "alleluia" is moderately florid; the jubilus is, of course, melismatic. The verse usually combines shorter and longer melismas; very often the last part of the verse repeats part or all of the refrain melody. The

EXAMPLE II–4   Gradual: *Haec dies*

MODE 2

Haec di - es,* quam fe - cit Do - mi - nus: ex - sul - te - mus, et lae - te - mur in e - a.

℣ Con-fi-te - mi - ni Do - mi - no, quo - ni - am bo - nus: quo - ni - am in sae cu - lum mi - se - ri-cor - - di - a* e - jus.

This is the day which the Lord hath made; we will rejoice and be glad in it. O give thanks unto the Lord; for he is good; for his mercy endureth forever.

The first part is called the "Response"; it is sung by chorus, except for the opening phrase (up to the asterisk), which is for a soloist. The second part, called the "Verse" (beginning at the sign ℣, the usual abbreviation for *versus* or "verse") is for a soloist, with the chorus joining at the end on the "ejus."

alleluias thus have a design different from that of any other pre-Frankish type of chant: their musical form is outlined by systematic repetition of distinct sections. The repetition of the alleluia and jubilus after the verse results in a three-part (*ABA*) pattern; this is subtly modified when melodic phrases from the refrain are incorporated in the verse. Moreover, both refrain and verse are often related in some kind of *AAB* form; and within the general schemes, the melody may be organized by the repetition or echoing of motives, musical rhyme, systematic combination and contrast of melodic curves, and similar devices, all signs of a well developed sense of musical construction.

It may be significant that compositions of this character begin to appear among the alleluias—relatively late chants in which there is a great deal of melody without words and which stem from a time when the need for purely musical principles of order, of the sort above listed, would have begun to be felt. From this point of view it is interesting to compare the alleluias with the graduals and tracts. The last two are outgrowths of an archaic style of Eastern provenance in which the melody is evidently a product of the kind of improvisation described earlier (see p. 14), based on large generalized melody-types and incorporating standard small melodic formulas. Many of the alleluias, by contrast, approach a style based on more modern and Western principles of order; they begin to suggest means of control over the musical material more typical of composed than of improvised music. Alleluias continued to be written until the end of the Middle Ages, and important new forms developed out of them after the ninth century.

Offertories

The offertories are similar in melodic style to the graduals. Originally, offertories were very long chants sung by both congregation and clergy during the ceremony of presentation of bread and wine; when this ceremony was curtailed, the offertory also was shortened, but curious traces of its original use are evident in the occasional text repetitions. At one time, perhaps, these may have been optional, so that the singers could lengthen or shorten the chant according to the time required for the presentation of offerings. The offertories embrace many varieties of form and mood, and show the same techniques of motivic repetition and musical rhyme as do the alleluias. The melismas of the offertories are closely related to the text, and often serve an expressive as well as a decorative purpose.

Chants of the Ordinary

The chants for the Ordinary of the Mass probably were originally quite simple syllabic melodies sung by the congregation; these were replaced, after the ninth century, by other settings. The syllabic style is still maintained in the Gloria and Credo, but the other chants of the Ordinary are now somewhat more ornate. The Kyrie, Sanctus, and Agnus Dei, by the nature of their texts, have three-part sectional arrangements. The Kyrie, for example, suggests the following setting:

> A   *Kyrie   eleison*
> B   *Christe   eleison*
> A   *Kyrie   eleison*

Since each exclamation is uttered three times, there may be an *aba* form within each of the three principal sections. More sophisticated versions of the Kyrie may have the pattern *ABC,* with motivic interconnections: parts *A* and *B* may be similar in outline and have identical final phrases (musical rhyme); the last repetition of part *C* may be expanded by repeating the initial phrase, the last section of which will be similar to the first phrase of part *A.* In an analogous fashion, the Agnus Dei may have the form *ABA,* though sometimes the same music is used for all sections:

> A   *Agnus Dei . . . miserere nobis* ("Lamb of God . . . have mercy
> upon us")
> B   *Agnus Dei . . . miserere nobis*
> A   *Agnus Dei . . . dona nobis pacem* ("Lamb of God . . . grant us
> peace")

The Sanctus is likewise divided into three sections; a typical distribution of musical material is as follows:

> A   *Sanctus, sanctus, sanctus* ("Holy, holy, holy")
> B   *Pleni sunt caeli et terra* ("Heaven and earth are full")
> B'   *Benedictus qui venit* ("Blessed is He that cometh")

Later Developments of the Chant

Between the fifth and the ninth centuries the people of western and northern Europe were converted to Christianity and the doctrines and rites of the Roman Church. Gregorian Chant was established in the Frankish Empire before the middle of the ninth century; and from then until near the close of the Middle Ages all important developments in European music took place north of the Alps. This shift of musical center occurred partly because of political conditions. The Mohammedan conquests of Syria, North Africa, and Spain, completed by 719, left the southern Christian regions either in the hands of the infidels or under constant threat of attack. Meanwhile, various cultural centers were arising in the north. During the sixth, seventh, and eighth centuries, missionaries from the Irish and Scottish monasteries established schools in their own lands and on the Continent, especially in Germany and Switzerland. A resurgence of Latin culture in England early in the eighth century produced scholars whose reputation extended to continental Europe; and an English monk, Alcuin (who, incidentally, also wrote a treatise on music), helped Charlemagne in his project to revive education throughout the Frankish empire. One of the results of this eighth- and ninth-century Carolingian renaissance was the development of a number of important musical centers, of which the most famous was the monastery of St. Gall in Switzerland.

The influence of the northern musical spirit had important consequences for Gregorian Chant. First of all, the range of expression was enlarged, as had been mentioned in connection with the history of the antiphon. The earlier Gregorian Chant was essentially an objective, impersonal art. Its esthetic may be compared to that of Byzantine mosaics, in which people are depicted not as personal, private beings, but rather as types, as representatives of certain public concepts, unaffected by moods or passions. The figure of the Virgin in Byzantine art is never an individual, human, and suffering mother; instead, she is depicted as the Mother of the Redeemer and the Queen of Heaven. She is also represented in this hieratical aspect in classical Gregorian Chant; the *Mater dolorosa* ("Mother of Sorrows") does not appear until the late Middle Ages.

A second result of northern influence on Gregorian Chant was that the melodic line became modified through the introduction of more skips, especially by the interval of a third. An illustration of the northern use of skips is the melody of the sequence *Christus hunc diem* ("Christ [grants] this day"), written in the early tenth century. The tendency of all northern melody is toward organization by thirds; the ultimate consequence of this was the gravitation of all music, including the Chant, toward harmonic organization in major or minor. And finally, northern composers created not only new melodies but also new forms of Chant. All these developments were concurrent with the rise of secular monodic song and the earliest experiments in polyphony; but it will be convenient to continue the history of the Chant here and take up these other matters later.

Tropes

A *trope* was originally a newly composed addition, usually in neumatic style and with a poetic text, to one of the antiphonal Chants of the Proper of the Mass (most often to the Introit, less often to the Offertory and Communion); later, such additions were made also to Chants of the Ordinary (especially the Gloria). The earliest tropes served as prefaces to the regular chant; at a later stage, tropes are found also in the form of interpolations between the lines of a chant. The custom of troping seems to have originated in northeastern France or the Rhineland in the ninth century—possibly even earlier. An important center of troping was the Monastery of St. Gall, where the monk Tuotilo (d. 915) was distinguished for compositions in this form. Tropes flourished, especially in monastic churches, in the tenth and eleventh centuries; in the twelfth century they gradually disappeared.

The terms trope and troping have often been used in an extended

sense to designate *all* additions and interpolations to a chant, thus
including the *sequence,* for example, as a subclass under "tropes."
Even interpolations in the text of the Gloria, found in some polyphonic Masses of later periods, have been called "tropes." Such
extended usages may be justified in some contexts, but when discussing the various types of additions to medieval Chant it is better
to restrict the word to its original meaning as described above.[6]

In the early manuscripts of chants are to be found from time to
time certain rather long melodic passages which recur, practically
unchanged, in many different contexts: sometimes as a passage in a
regular liturgical chant, sometimes included in a separate collection,
and in either situation sometimes with words and sometimes without. These are not short melodic formulas such as might be introduced into an improvisational performance, but long, definitely
shaped melodies which were evidently widely known and used,
either in melismatic form or underlaid with different texts. Such
melodies, and similar ones not in the "recurring" category, were
typically Frankish creations, though doubtless some of the oldest of
them were adapted from Roman models. Long melismas of this sort
came to be attached to the Alleluia in the liturgy—at first simply as
extensions of the chant but later, in still larger and more elaborate
forms, as new additions. Such extensions and additions were given
the name *sequentia* or "sequence" (from the Latin *sequor,* to follow),
perhaps originally because of their position "following" the alleluia.
When equipped with a text, the proper name for them is *prosa*
(diminutive, *prosula*), alluding to the prose form of their texts—
though the same word "sequence" is often used loosely for both the
texted and untexted versions. Where and how they first arose is hard
to say. There is a story that a monk of St. Gall, Notker Balbulus
("the stammerer"; ca. 840–912), "invented" the sequence when he
began to write words syllabically under certain long melismas as an
aid to memorizing the tune. Even if the story is true—and there is
no particular reason to doubt it—it does not follow that the music
always existed first and the words came later. At first, no doubt, this
was the case; later, probably tune and text were created simultaneously. Syllabic prose texts were added to melismatic passages in
other chants as well as those of the Alleluia; the so-called "Kyrie
tropes," the names of which survive in the modern liturgical books
as the titles of certain Masses (for example, *Kyrie fons bonitatis,*
No. II in the *Liber Usualis*), were at one time *prosulae* consisting of
words added syllabically to the melismas of the original chant.

The sequence or *prosa* early became detached from particular
liturgical chants and began to blossom forth as an independent form

Sequences

---

[6] See Richard Crocker, *The Early Trope Repertory of Saint Martial de Limoges,*
Princeton, 1970, chs. I and II.

of composition. Hundreds of them appeared all over western Europe from the tenth to the thirteenth centuries and even later. In church, they may have been sung to the accompaniment of organ and bells. Popular sequences were imitated and adapted to secular uses; there was considerable mutual influence between sequences and contemporary types of semisacred and secular music, both vocal and instrumental, in the late Middle Ages.

In its fully developed independent form the sequence is based on the principle of repetition: each strophe of the text is immediately followed by another with exactly the same number of syllables and the same pattern of accents; these two strophes are sung to the same melodic segment, which is repeated for the second strophe. The only exceptions are the first and last verses, which usually do not have parallels. Although any two paired strophes are identical in length, the length of the next pair may be quite different. The typical sequence pattern may be represented thus: *a bb cc dd . . . n; bb, cc, dd . . .* represent an indefinite number of strophic pairs and *a* and *n* the unpaired verses.

One of the most celebrated sequences is *Victimae paschali laudes* ("Praises to the Paschal Victim"), ascribed to Wipo, chaplain to the Emperor Henry III in the first half of the eleventh century; in it the classical sequence form of paired strophes is plainly evident, as is also the common device of unifying the different melodic segments by similar cadential phrases. The twelfth-century *prosae* of Adam of St. Victor illustrate a later development in which the text was regularly versified and rhymed. Some later rhymed sequences approach the form of the hymn—for example, the well-known *Dies irae,* attributed to Thomas of Celano (early thirteenth century), in which a melody with the pattern *AA BB CC* is repeated twice (though with a modified ending the second time), just as a hymn melody is repeated for successive stanzas.

Most sequences were abolished from the Catholic service by the liturgical reforms of the Council of Trent (1545–63), and four only were retained in use: *Victimae paschali laudes,* at Easter; *Veni Sancte Spiritus* ("Come Holy Ghost"), on Whitsunday; *Lauda Sion* ("Zion, praise") by St. Thomas Aquinas, for the festival of Corpus Christi; and the *Dies irae.* A fifth sequence, the *Stabat Mater* ("By the Cross the Mother Standing," ascribed to Jacopo da Todi, a Franciscan monk of the thirteenth century) was added to the liturgy in 1727.

No one can listen to the *Dies irae* without realizing that the new spirit which came into music after the eleventh century involved, among other things, a feeling for dramatic expression. Just as in ancient Greece the drama had grown out of religious rites, so in the west the earliest musical dramas grew out of the liturgy—or, to be exact, out of tropes. One of the earliest of these liturgical dramas was based on a tenth-century trope preceding the Introit of the Mass

Liturgical dramas

for Easter. The original trope, in dialogue form, represents the three Marys coming to the tomb of Jesus. The angel asks them, "Whom seek ye in the sepulchre?" They reply, "Jesus of Nazareth," to which the angel answers, "He is not here, He is risen as He said; go and proclaim that He has risen from the grave" (Mark xvi:5–7). Contemporary accounts indicate not only that this dialogue was sung responsively, but also that the singing was accompanied by appropriate dramatic action.

Similar little scenes were performed in connection with the Christmas liturgy, and on other occasions, and in time the action was expanded to include incidents preceding and following the original scene. As the scope and subject matter of the plays was enlarged and acting grew more realistic, spoken dialogue was introduced. Eventually the plays were detached from the regular church service; hymns and songs of a popular nature were introduced in addition to the Chants, and the texts became a mixture of Latin and the vernacular. Songs for the congregation to sing were introduced, and probably also trumpet fanfares and other instrumental effects. Different stories from the Bible were dramatized in this way, for example the story of Daniel in the lions' den, of Herod's slaughter of the Innocents, and many others. Many of the Easter plays used the familiar sequence *Victimae paschali laudes,* and the performances often concluded with the singing of the *Te Deum.* The liturgical drama at its height in the twelfth and thirteenth centuries was extremely popular all over Western and Central Europe, and recent modern revivals of some of these works have had considerable success. The naive mixture, in the originals, of sacred and secular elements well illustrates the interpenetration of these two areas in late medieval times.

Medieval Musical Theory and Practice

There were two types of musical treatises in the Middle Ages: speculative and practical. The former kind dealt with such matters as the ethos of music and its importance as a mental discipline in preparation for higher philosophic studies. The mathematical aspects of music received much attention, especially as applied to the exact determination of intervals. We need not linger over the authors of speculative works, of whom the chief was Boethius; his treatise, though not designed as a textbook, actually established the pattern of medieval education in music insofar as the subject was taught in the quadrivium with arithmetic, geometry, and astronomy. A few similar works, modeled on, and to a large extent copied from, Boethius, were produced by later authors. The subject matter of much medieval musical theory is now subsumed under acoustics, aesthetics, and the psychology of music.

A great many students in the Middle Ages intended, or at least aspired, to enter clerical orders, and their training was directed to this end. Educational institutions were the monasteries and the schools attached to cathedral churches. In the monasteries the musical instruction was primarily practical, with a scattering of non-musical subjects at an elementary level. The cathedral schools tended to give more attention to speculative studies and it was chiefly these schools which, from the beginning of the thirteenth century, prepared students for the Universities. But most formal education in medieval times was oriented toward practical matters, and most of the musical treatises reflect this attitude. Their authors pay their respects to Boethius in an introductory chapter or two and then turn, with evident relief, to more pressing topics. Some of the instruction books are in verse; others are written as dialogues between a preternaturally eager student and an omniscient master—a reflection of the customary oral method of teaching with great emphasis on memorizing.[7] There were visual aids in the shape of diagrams and tables; there was also the *monochord,* a contrivance consisting of one vibrating string stretched over a long wooden resonator, with a movable bridge to vary the resonating lengths of the string and so demonstrate the different intervals, for either theoretical or practical purposes. Students were taught to sing the intervals, to memorize chants, and, later, to read notes at sight. The treatises deal with these matters and then usually go on to something that would now be called "theory"—that is, the study of intervals in combination and the correct use of consonance and dissonance in composition. In connection with all this, the treatises will also discuss musical notation and the system of the eight modes (or, as medieval writers called them, the *tones*) of music.

The Church modes

The development of the medieval modal system was a gradual process, not all the stages of which can be clearly traced. In its complete form, achieved by the eleventh century, the system recognized eight modes, differentiated according to the position of the tones and semitones in a diatonic octave built on the *finalis* or *final;* in practice this note was usually—not invariably—the last note in the melody. The modes were identified by numbers, and grouped in pairs; the odd-numbered modes were called *authentic* ("original"), and the even-numbered modes *plagal* ("derived"). A plagal mode always had the same final as its corresponding authentic mode. The authentic modal scales were notated as white-key octave scales rising from the notes *d* (mode I), *e* (mode III), *f* (mode V), and *g* (mode VII), with their corresponding plagals a fourth lower (Example

---

[7] The dialogue form was still used in Renaissance treatises such as Morley's *Plain and Easy Introduction* of 1597, and even as late as Fux's *Steps to Parnassus* of 1725.

*Guido of Arezzo and Bishop Theo-
bald of Arezzo with the monochord.
From a twelfth-century German
manuscript.*

II–5). It must be remembered, however, that these notes do not stand
for a specific "absolute" pitch —a conception foreign to Gregorian
Chant and to the Middle Ages in general—but were chosen simply
so that the distinguishing interval patterns could be notated with
minimum use of accidentals.

The finals of each mode are shown in Example II–5 as ▯ . In
addition to the final, there is in each mode a second note, called the
tenor (as in the psalm tones; see above, p. 46) or *confinalis* ("co-final")
or *dominant* (shown in Example II–5 as ○), which sometimes functions as a secondary tonal center. The finals of the corresponding
plagal and authentic modes are the same; but the dominants are
different. A handy way to identify the dominants is to remember
these facts: 1) in the authentic modes the dominant is a fifth above
the final; 2) in the plagal modes the dominant is a third below the
dominant of the corresponding authentic mode; 3) whenever a
dominant would fall on the note B, it is moved up to C.

A mode is identified by its final, its dominant, and its range. A
plagal mode differs from its corresponding authentic mode by having
a different dominant and a different range: in the authentic modes
the entire range lies above the final, whereas in the plagal modes the
final is the fourth note from the bottom of the octave. Thus modes I
and VIII have the same range, but different finals and dominants.

The only accidental properly used in notating Gregorian Chants
is B♭. Under certain conditions the B was flatted in modes I and II,
and also occasionally in modes V and VI; if this was consistently
done, these modes became exact facsimiles of the modern "natural"
minor and major scales respectively. Accidentals were necessary, of
course, when a modal melody was transposed; if a chant in mode I,
for example, were written on G, a flat would be required in the
signature.

EXAMPLE II–5   The Medieval Church Modes

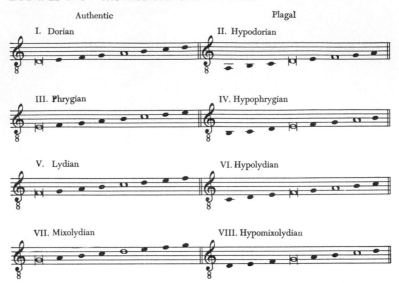

The particular quality of a mode is not merely a result of its range or its scale pattern of tones and semitones. These are matters of theory—and medieval modal theory undoubtedly arose, like musical theory in all ages, as an attempt to explain and systematize already existing practice. The concrete reality, therefore, is to be found in the melodies themselves, the particular turns of phrase characteristic of each mode and each type of chant. A "modal scale" is only a catalogue of the tones which were or could have been used in the melody of a chant or of any other composition. Some chants remain entirely within the range of a fifth above the final and one note below; others use the entire octave range with perhaps one note beyond in either direction; still others, like the sequence *Victimae paschali laudes,* cover the entire combined range of the authentic mode and its corresponding plagal. Some chants even combine the characteristics of two modes that have different finals; such chants cannot be definitely assigned to either one mode or the other. In short, the correspondence of theory and practice is no more exact for medieval modal melodies than for any other type of actual music in any period.

In the tenth century, theorists tried to identify the system of church modes with the ancient Greek keys; because of an understandable vagueness about their meaning, the Greek names were applied to the wrong modes, as may be seen by comparing Example I–5 with Example II–5. Although the modern liturgical books do not use the Greek names (preferring a classification by numerals), they are still in general use elsewhere, especially in textbooks on counterpoint. Thus modes I and II are now often called Dorian and Hypodorian, modes III and IV Phrygian and Hypophrygian, modes

V and VI Lydian and Hypolydian, and modes VII and VIII Mixolydian and Hypomixolydian.

Why were there no modes on *a, b,* and *c'* in medieval theory?
The original reason was that if the modes on *d, e,* and *f* were sung
with the flatted *b* (which was legally available), they became equivalent to the modes on *a, b,* and *c',* and consequently, these three
modes were superfluous. The modes on *a* and *c,* which correspond
to our minor and major, have been recognized theoretically only
since the middle of the sixteenth century: the Swiss theorist Glarean
in 1547 set up a system of twelve modes by adding to the original
eight, two modes on *a* and two on *c,* respectively named Aeolian and
Hypoaeolian, Ionian and Hypoionian. Some later theorists recognize
also a "Locrian" mode on *b,* but this is not often used.

For the teaching of sight singing an eleventh-century monk, Guido
of Arezzo, perfected a method which had as its basis the memorizing
of six tones in the pattern *c–d–e–f–g–a;* in this pattern a semitone   *The hexachord*
falls between the third and fourth steps and all other steps are   *system*
whole tones. Guido pointed out, as an aid to memorizing the pattern, that in a familiar hymn, *Ut queant laxis,* six phrases each began
with one of the notes of the pattern in regular ascending order—
the first phrase on *c,* the second on *d,* and so on. (See Example II–6.)
The initial syllables of the words of these six phrases became the
names of the notes: *ut, re, mi, fa, sol, la.* We still learn them this
way today, except that we say *do* for *ut* and add a *ti* above *la.* The
semitone, it will be noticed, is always the interval *mi–fa.*

This hexachord, or pattern of six notes, could be found at different places in the scale: beginning on C, on G, or (by flatting
the B) on F. The hexachord on G used the B-natural, for which
the sign was ♮ , "square b" (*b quadrum*); the F hexachord used
the B–flat, which had the sign ♭ , "round b" (*b rotundum*). Although these signs are obviously the models for our ♮, ♯, and ♭, their
original purpose was not the same as that of the modern accidentals;
originally they served to indicate the syllables *mi* and *fa.* Because the

EXAMPLE II–6   Hymn: *Ut queant laxis*

Ut que-ant la - xis *re* - so - na - re fi - bris *Mi* - ra ge - sto -

rum *fa* - mu - li tu - o - rum, *Sol* - ve pol - lu - ti

La - bi - i re - a - tum, San - cte Jo - an - nes.

*That thy servants may freely sing forth the wonders of thy deeds,
remove all stain of guilt from their unclean lips, O Saint John.*

square form of the B was called "hard" and the rounded form "soft," the G and F hexachords were called respectively the "hard" (*durum*) and "soft" (*molle*) hexachords; the one on C was called the "natural" hexachord. The whole of the musical space within which medieval composers worked and with which medieval theorists were concerned extended from G (which was written as the Greek letter Γ, and called *gamma*) to e″; within this range every note was named not only by its letter, but also according to the position is occupied within the hexachord or hexachords to which it belonged. Thus gamma, which was the first note of its hexachord, was called *gamma ut* (whence our word *gamut*); e″, as the top note of its hexachord, was *e la*. Middle c′, which belonged to three different hexachords, was *c sol fa ut* (see Example II–7). The similarity to the Greek system of nomenclature is obvious. Both the Greek and the medieval note names were retained by theorists until well into the sixteenth century, but only the medieval names were in practical use.

EXAMPLE II–7   The System of Hexachords

In order to learn any melody that exceeded a six-note range, it was necessary to change from one hexachord to another. This was done by a process called *mutation*, whereby a certain note was taken as if it were in one hexachord and quitted as if it were in another, the way a pivot chord is used in modern harmony. For instance, in the Kyrie *Cunctipotens Genitor Deus*, Example II–8, the fifth note *a* is taken as *la* in the C hexachord and quitted as *re* in the G hexachord; the reverse mutation occurs on the third note *a* of the following phrase:

EXAMPLE II–8   Kyrie: *Cunctipotens Genitor Deus*

A special pedagogical aid was the so-called "Guidonian hand." Pupils were taught to sing intervals as the teacher pointed with the index finger of his right hand to the different joints of his open left hand; each one of the joints stood for one of the twenty notes of the system, but any other note, such as F♯ or E♭, was considered as "outside the hand." No late medieval or renaissance music textbook was complete without a drawing of this hand.

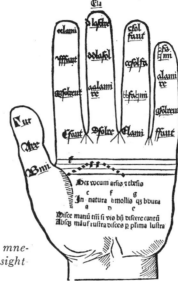

The "Guidonian Hand," a mnemonic device used as an aid to sight-singing.

One task that occupied the theorists of the Middle Ages was developing an adequate musical notation. As long as the chants were transmitted orally, and a certain latitude was tolerated in the application of the texts to the traditional melodies, all that was needed was an occasional reminder of the general outline of the tune. Beginning sometime before the middle of the ninth century, signs (neumes) were placed above the words to indicate an ascending melodic line (╱), a descending one (╲), or a combination of the two (∧). These neumes probably were derived from grammatical accent marks like those still used in modern French and Italian. Eventually, a more precise way to notate a melody was required, and by the tenth century scribes were placing neumes at varying heights above the text to indicate more exactly the course of the melody; these are called "heighted neumes." Sometimes dots were added to the solid lines to indicate the relationship of the individual notes within the neume, and thus make clearer what intervals the neume represented. A decisive advance was made when a scribe drew a horizontal red line to represent the pitch f, and grouped the neumes about this line; in time a second line, usually yellow, was drawn for c′. By the eleventh century Guido of Arezzo was describing a four-line staff then in use, on which letters indicated the lines for f, c′ and sometimes g′—letters which eventually evolved into

Notation

our modern clef signs.

This invention of the staff made it possible to notate precisely the relative pitch of the notes of a melody, and freed music from its hitherto exclusive dependence on oral transmission. It was an event as crucial for the history of Western music as the invention of writing was for the history of language. The staff notation with neumes was still imperfect, however; it conveyed the pitch of the notes, but did not indicate their relative durations. Signs showing rhythm do exist in many medieval manuscripts, but modern scholars have not been able to agree about what they meant. There is evidence that different note shapes once indicated different durations, and that from the ninth to the twelfth centuries definite long and

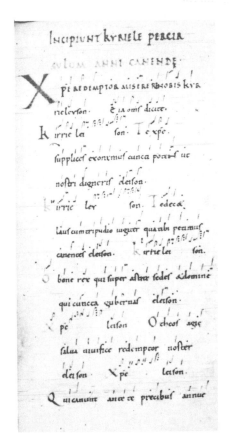
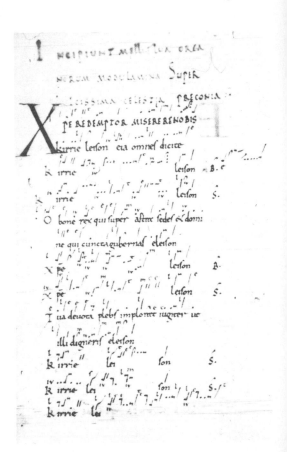

Two pages from the Winchester Troper Manuscript, Cambridge, Corpus Christi 473. On the left (f55) is the chant, a "troped Kyrie," that is, a Kyrie with insertions; on the right (f135) is the added organal part intended to be sung with the chant. The melody of the chant is that of the "ad libitum" Kyrie No. vi (Te Christe Rex supplices) in the modern liturgical books (see Liber Usualis, *p. 78)*

short time values were used in singing the chants; but this manner of singing seems to have gone out of use after the twelfth century. The modern practice is to treat the notes of a chant as if they all had the same basic value; notes are grouped rhythmically in twos or threes, these groups being in turn flexibly combined into larger rhythmic units. This method of interpretation has been worked out in great detail by the Benedictine monks of the Abbey of Solesmes under the leadership of Dom André Mocquereau, and has been approved by the Catholic Church as being in conformity with the spirit of her liturgy. The Solesmes editions of the modern liturgical books, being intended for practical use rather than historical study, include a number of interpretive signs which are not in the original manuscripts. Whether or not the Solesmes method of singing Gregorian Chant is the final word on the subject only time will tell; at any rate, it is infinitely preferable to the corrupt editions and performances that were current from the sixteenth to the nineteenth centuries.

Very little information is available on the way Gregorian Chant was performed in the Middle Ages; there is certainly no reason to suppose that it was always sung in the same way. In general, the *Performance* cultivated vocal tone was probably more pinched and nasal than that used today, and a falsetto was sometimes employed. Tempo was slower at the more solemn festivals, and morning services were supposed to be sung at a higher pitch than evening services. Occasionally admonitions appear in the manuscripts to singers against carelessness and self-display; these suggest that the problems of a medieval choirmaster were not so different from those of a modern one.

To what extent, if at all, the organ was used to accompany the singing of the Chant remains an open question. In ancient times and in the early Middle Ages, the organ was a raucous and somewhat unwieldy instrument, favored for large public ceremonies both secular and sacred. We hear of organs in some churches as early as the sixth century, but the descriptions suggest that they were used only for processions and perhaps also to accompany the singing of hymns by the congregation. The organ does not seem to have been used regularly with the choir in the Mass much before the thirteenth century, by which time a keyboard had replaced the old awkward mechanism, and the tone of the pipes had been softened.

Nonliturgical and Secular Monody

If we were to judge solely from the surviving music and the treatises, we should have to conclude that all through the Middle Ages up to the eleventh century practically no music was heard or performed except in Church. Such a conclusion, improbable and actually incorrect, would be no more accurate than the opposite claim that a flourishing secular music was deliberately ignored and left unrecorded by the monks. As usual, the truth probably lies somewhere between these two extremes.

So far as we can find out, the main medieval musical development was Gregorian Chant; in comparison, the earliest extant examples of contemporary secular musical forms can almost be described as primitive. To be sure, the Chant was notated and hence preserved fairly completely; whether if we had equally complete knowledge about the secular music of the sixth to the eleventh century we should find it equally interesting is simply an unanswerable question.

Early secular forms

As might be expected, the oldest preserved specimens of secular music are songs with Latin texts. The earliest of these form the repertoire of *Goliard songs* from the eleventh and twelfth centuries. The Goliards—named after a probably mythical patron, Bishop Golias—were students or footloose clerics who migrated from one school to another in the days before the founding of the great resident universities. Their vagabond way of life, deprecated by respectable people, was celebrated in their songs, of which numerous manuscript collections were made. The subjects of the texts are drawn largely from the eternal trinity of youthful masculine interest: wine, women, and satire. The treatment is sometimes delicate and sometimes not; the spirit is decidedly keen and informal, as one may readily sense when listening to some of the modern musical settings in Carl Orff's *Carmina Burana*. Only a little of the original Goliard music is notated in the manuscripts, and that little is in staffless neumes; therefore, modern transcriptions are conjectural unless a melody happens to have been preserved in some other source in a more exact notation.

Another kind of monophonic song written in the period from the eleventh to the thirteenth century is the *conductus*. Conducti are outstanding illustrations of how vague the dividing line was between sacred and secular music in the Middle Ages. They originally may have been sung at moments when an actor in a liturgical drama or a celebrant in the Mass or some other service was formally "conducted" in procession from one place to another. Their texts were metrical verses, like the texts of sequences of the same period; but their connection with the liturgy was so tenuous that by the end of the twelfth century the term *conductus* was applied to any nonliturgical Latin song, generally of a serious character, with a metrical text, on either a sacred or a secular subject. One important feature of the conductus was that, as a rule, its melody was newly composed, instead of being borrowed or adapted from Gregorian Chant or some other source.

The characteristic aspects of the secular spirit of the Middle Ages are, of course, most clearly reflected in the songs with vernacular texts. One of the earliest known types of vernacular song was the *chanson de geste*—an epic narrative poem recounting the deeds of national heroes, sung to simple melodic formulas, a single one of which might serve unchanged for each line throughout long sections of the poem. The poems were transmitted orally and not reduced to writing until a comparatively late date; virtually none of the music has been preserved. The most famous of the *chansons de geste* is the *Song of Roland,* the national epic of France, which dates from about the second half of the eleventh century, though the events it relates belong to the age of Charlemagne.

The people who sang the *chansons de geste* and other secular songs in the Middle Ages were the *jongleurs* or *ménestrels* ("minstrels"), a class of professional musicians who first appear about the tenth century: men and women wandering singly or in small groups from village to village, from castle to castle, gaining a precarious livelihood by singing, playing, performing tricks, and exhibiting trained animals—social outcasts often denied the protection of the laws and the sacraments of the Church. With the economic recovery of Europe in the eleventh and twelfth centuries, as society became more stably organized on a feudal basis and towns began to grow up, their condition was ameliorated, though it was a long time before people ceased to regard them with mingled feelings of fascination and revulsion. "People of no great wit, but with amazing memory, very industrious, and impudent beyond measure," Petrarch wrote of them. In the eleventh century, they organized themselves into brotherhoods, which later developed into guilds of musicians offering professional training like a modern conservatory.

Jongleurs

The minstrels, as a class, were neither poets nor composers in exactly the sense we give to those terms. They sang, played, and danced to songs composed by others or taken from the common domain of popular music, no doubt altering them or making up their own versions as they went along. Their professional traditions and skill played a part in an important development of secular music in western Europe—that body of song commonly known today as the music of the troubadours and the trouvères.

These two words mean the same thing: finders or inventors; *troubadour* was the term used in the south of France, *trouvère* the term used in the north. In the Middle Ages the words apparently were applied to anyone who wrote or composed anything; modern usage which restricts them to two particular groups of musicians is therefore historically inaccurate. "Troubadours" were poet-composers who flourished in Provence, the region now comprising southern France; they wrote in Provençal, the *langue d'oc.* Their art, taking its original inspiration from the neighboring Hispano-Mauresque culture of the Iberian peninsula, spread quickly northward, especially to the provinces of Champagne and Artois. Here the "trouvères," active throughout the thirteenth century, wrote in

Troubadours and trouvères

the *langue d'oïl,* the dialect of medieval French that became modern French.

Neither troubadours nor trouvères constituted a well-defined group. Both they and their art flourished in generally aristocratic circles (there were even kings among their number), but an artist of lower birth might be accepted into a higher social class on the ground of his talent. Many of the poet-composers not only created their songs but sang them as well. Alternatively, they could entrust the performance to a minstrel. Where the extant versions differ from one manuscript to another, they may represent versions of different scribes—or, perhaps, various renditions of the "same" song by different minstrels who had learned it by rote and afterward dealt with it in their own way, as happens whenever music is transmitted orally for some time before being written down. The songs are preserved in collections (*chansonniers*), some of which have been published in modern edition with facsimiles. Altogether, about 2600 troubadour poems and over 260 melodies have been preserved, and about 4000 trouvère poems and 1400 melodies.

The poetic and musical substance of the troubadour and trouvère songs is often not profound, but the formal structures employed show great variety and ingenuity. There are simple ballads and ballads in dramatic style, some of which require or suggest two or more characters. Some of the dramatic ballads evidently were intended to be mimed; many obviously call for dancing. Often there is a refrain which, at least in the older examples, must have been sung by a chorus. In addition, and especially in the south, they wrote love songs—the subject par excellence for troubadour song. There are songs on political and moral topics, and songs whose texts are debates or arguments, frequently on an abstruse point of courtly love. Religious songs are characteristically northern and appear only late in the thirteenth century. Each of these general types of song included many subtypes each of which followed quite strict conventions about subject matter, form, and treatment.

A favorite genre was the *pastourelle,* one of the class of dramatic ballads. The text of a pastourelle always tells the following story: a knight makes love to a shepherdess who usually, after due resistance, succumbs; alternatively, the shepherdess screams for help, whereupon her brother or lover rushes in and drives the knight away, not without blows given and received. In the earliest pastourelles, all the narration was monologue; it was a natural step, however, to make the text a dialogue between the knight and the shepherdess. Later, the dialogue came to be acted as well as sung; if one or two episodes were added, and if the rescuing shepherd appeared with a group of rustic companions, and the performance were decked out with incidental songs and dances, the result was a little musical play. One such play, in fact, is the famous *Jeu de Robin et de Marion,* written

Adam de la Hale, also called the Hunchback of Arras, was born in Arras about 1230 and died at Naples about 1288. Gifted as both poet and composer, he is depicted here in a miniature from the Chansonnier d'Arras.

by Adam de la Hale, the last and the greatest of the trouvères, about 1284. It is uncertain whether all the songs in this work were written by Adam himself or whether they were popular chansons incorporated in the play. A few of them have polyphonic settings.

The pastourelles and other ballad songs were aristocratic adaptations of folk material. The Provençal love songs, on the other hand, were aristocratic from their inception. Many were openly sensual; others concealed sensuality under the veil of chivalric or "courtly" love, represented as a passion more mystical than fleshly. Its object, to be sure, was a real woman, and usually another man's wife; but she was conventionally adored from a distance, with such discretion, respect, and humility that the lover is made to seem more like a worshipper, content to suffer in the service of his ideal Love, the source of all his aspiration. The lady herself is depicted as so remote, calm, lofty, and unattainable that she would be stepping out of character did she condescend to reward her faithful lover. The whole affair is rather abstract, and the chief interest lies in the intellectual subtleties of the situation. It is significant that trouvère songs praising the Virgin Mary have the same style, the same vocabulary, and sometimes the same melodies that were also used to celebrate earthly love.

Some idea of the style of medieval knightly love poetry may be gained from the following two stanzas of a song by Jaufré Rudel, a twelfth-century troubadour:

> When the days lengthen in the month of May,
> Well pleased am I to hear the birds
> Sing far away.

> And when from that place I am gone,
> I hang my head and make dull moan,
> Since she my heart is set upon
>   Is far away.
>
> Yet shall I know no other love but hers
> And if not hers, no other love at all.
>   She hath surpassed all.
> So fair is she, no noble, I would be
> A captive in the hosts of paynimrie
> In a far land, if so be upon me
>   Her eyes might fall.[8]

Techniques of troubadour and trouvère melodies

The melodic settings of both troubadour and trouvère songs were generally syllabic with occasional short melismatic figures; it is probable that in performance melodic ornaments were added and that the melody was varied from stanza to stanza. The range is narrow, frequently no more than a sixth and hardly ever more than an octave. The modes seem to be chiefly the first and seventh, with their plagals; certain notes in these modes were probably altered chromatically by the singers in such a way as to make them almost equivalent to the modern minor and major. There is some uncertainty about the rhythm of the songs, especially with regard to the oldest extant melodies, which are notated in a way that does not indicate the relative time values of the notes. Some scholars maintain that these songs were sung in a free, unmeasured rhythm such as that notation seems to imply; others, however, believe that they were given some fairly regular rhythm and that the melody was measured by long and short notes corresponding in a general way to the accented and unaccented syllables of the words. Divergence of opinion on this point is shown by five different modern transcriptions of the same phrase in Example II–9.

In trouvère songs the phrases are almost always clear cut, fairly short (three, four, or five measures in a modern transcription in ¾ time), and with a definite, easily retained melodic profile. The troubadour melodies are less sectional and often suggest a freer rhythmic treatment. It may be said in general that the trouvère songs show an affinity to French folk song with its piquant irregularity of phrasing, whereas troubadour songs are a little more sophisticated and a little more complex in their rhythmic patterns.

The repetition, variation, and contrast of short, distinctive musical phrases naturally produce a more or less distinct formal pattern. Many of the troubadour and trouvère melodies repeat the opening phrase or section before proceeding in a free style. But on the whole the melodies in the original manuscript sources do not fall so neatly

---

[8] Translation by Helen J. Waddell, *The Wandering Scholars*, London, 1927. Used by permission of Constable, the publishers.

EXAMPLE II–9   Troubadour melody: *Reis glorios,* Guiraut de Bornelh
(1173–1220)

Reis glo- ri- os, ve- ray lums   e   clar -   tatz

Glorious King, true light and clarity.

into categories as the designations in some modern collections suggest. These formal designations, in fact, properly apply only to the poetic, not to the musical, form of the songs. In the fourteenth century, when some of these monophonic tunes are incorporated into polyphonic compositions, they begin to be molded into the characteristic patterns of ballade, virelai, and rondeau (these forms are described in Chapter IV), of which most melodies of the troubadours and trouvères show only indistinct outlines. Phrases are modified on repetition and shadowy resemblances, elusive echoes of earlier phrases, are heard; but the main impression is one of freedom, spontaneity, and apparent artlessness.

Many of the trouvère songs have *refrains,* a recurring line or pair of lines in the text which usually also involve the recurrence of the corresponding musical phrase. The refrain was an important structural element. Songs with refrains perhaps evolved out of dance songs, the refrains being originally those portions that were sung by all the dancers in chorus. After the songs were no longer used to accompany dancing, the original refrain may have been incorporated into a solo song.

The art of the troubadours was the model for a German school of knightly poet-musicians, the *Minnesinger.* The love (*Minne*) of which they sang in their *Minnelieder* was even more abstract than troubadour love, and sometimes had a distinctly religious tinge. The music is correspondingly more sober; some of the melodies are in the ecclesiastical modes, while others veer toward major tonality. As

Minnesinger

69

nearly as can be inferred from the rhythm of the texts, the majority of the tunes were sung in triple meter. A common Minnesinger form is what is called in German a *Bar*—*AAB*—in which the same melodic phrase, *A,* is repeated for the first two units, called *Stollen,* of a stanza, and the remainder, *B,* called the *Abgesang,* has new melodic material. This pattern is the same as that often used for the Provençal *canzo;* like the canzo, the *Bar* form sometimes involves recurrence of all or part of the *Stollen* phrase in the course of the *Abgesang.* Texts of the Minnesingers included loving depictions of the glow and freshness of the spring season, and dawn songs or watcher's songs (*Wächterlieder*) sung by the faithful friend who keeps guard and warns the lovers of the approach of dawn. Both French and Germans wrote songs of religious devotion, many of them inspired by the Crusades; one of the most beautiful of the German is Walther von der Vogelweide's *Crusader's Song.*

Meistersinger

In France toward the end of the thirteenth century the art of the trouvères came to be carried on more and more by cultured middle-class citizens instead of predominantly by nobles as in earlier times. A similar movement took place in Germany in the course of the fourteenth, fifteenth, and sixteenth centuries; the eventual successors of the Minnesinger were the *Meistersinger,* stolid tradesmen and artisans of German cities, whose lives and organization have been well portrayed by Wagner in his opera *The Mastersingers of Nuremberg.* Hans Sachs, the hero of this opera, was an historical figure, a Meistersinger who lived in the sixteenth century. The art of the Meistersinger was so hedged about by rigid rules that their music seems stiff and inexpressive in comparison with that of the Minnesinger. The Meistersingers' guild had a long history, and was finally dissolved only in the eighteenth century.

*Other kinds
of song*

In addition to monophonic secular songs, there were also in the Middle Ages many monophonic religious songs not intended for use in church. These songs were expressions of individual piety; they had vernacular texts and were written in a melodic idiom that seems to be derived about equally from church plainchant and popular folk song. The few surviving English songs of the thirteenth century show a variety of moods and suggest a much more extensive musical life than is now possible to reconstruct. Spanish monophonic songs include a large number of *cantigas,* hymns to the Virgin; these have been preserved in a large late thirteenth-century collection, and resemble in many ways the music of the troubadours. Contemporary Italian monophonic songs were the *laude;* they were sung by processions of penitents, and have music of a vigorous, popular character. Related to the *laude* are the flagellants' songs (*Geisslerlieder*) of fourteenth-century Germany. The lauda was still cultivated in Italy after the penitential craze of the thirteenth and fourteenth centuries had passed, and eventually the texts were given polyphonic settings.

Medieval Instrumental Music and Instruments

Dances in the Middle Ages were accompanied not only by songs but by instrumental music as well. The *estampie,* of which several English and Continental examples exist from the thirteenth and fourteenth centuries, was a dance piece, sometimes monophonic and sometimes polyphonic, in several sections (*puncta*), each of which was repeated (compare the sequence); the first statement ended with an "open" (*ouvert*), or incomplete, cadence; the repetition ended with a "closed" (*clos*), or full, cadence. In some *estampies* the cadences of all the *puncta* are identical or similar.

Estampies happen to be the earliest known examples of an instrumental repertoire that doubtless goes back far beyond the thirteenth century. It is unlikely that the early Middle Ages had any instrumental music other than that associated with singing or dancing, but it would be completely incorrect to think that the music of this period was exclusively vocal. We cannot be certain that even Gregorian Chant was always and everywhere sung unaccompanied. Although we do not know what music was played on instruments prior to the thirteenth century, we do know that instruments existed and were played. This knowledge comes not from the musical manuscripts, which never name an instrument or even indicate whether one is to be used; nor from the older musical theorists, for it was not until about 1300 that any writer dealt extensively with instrumental music. For the earliest period, whatever information we have comes from scattered literary references, from representations in reliefs and sculptures, and especially from miniatures and similar pictorial decorations in Psalters and other books. There are, in addition, many references to instruments in twelfth- and thirteenth-century French poetry.

The Roman lyre survived into the Middle Ages, but the oldest characteristically medieval instrument was the *harp,* which was imported to the Continent from Ireland and Britain some time before the ninth century. The principal bowed instrument of medieval times was the *vielle* or *Fiedel,* which had many different names and a great variety of shapes and sizes; it is the prototype of the viol of the Renaissance and the modern violin. The thirteenth-century vielle had five strings, one of them usually a drone. This is the instrument with which jongleurs are most often depicted, and with which they probably accompanied their singing and recitations. Another stringed instrument was the *organistrum;* described in a tenth-century treatise, it was a three-stringed vielle played by a revolving wheel turned by a crank, the strings being stopped by a set of rods instead of by

King David holds his harp while musicians below play the bell chimes, recorder, vielle, and positive organ. A miniature from a late eleventh-century Bible.

the fingers. In the early Middle Ages, the organistrum was apparently a large instrument requiring two players, and was used in churches; after the thirteenth century it degenerated into a smaller form, from which the modern hurdy-gurdy is descended.

An instrument that appears frequently in the Middle Ages is the *psaltery,* a type of zither played either by plucking, or more often by striking, the strings—the remote ancestor of the harpsichord and clavichord. The *lute* was known as early as the ninth century, having been brought into Spain by the Arab conquerors; but it did not come into common use in other countries much before the Renaissance. There were *flutes,* both the recorder and the transverse types, and *shawms,* reed instruments of the oboe variety. *Trumpets* and *horns* were used only by the nobility; the universal folk instrument was the *bagpipe. Drums* came into use by the twelfth century, chiefly to beat time for singing and dancing.

In the Middle Ages there were, in addition to the great organs in churches, two smaller types, the *portative* and the *positive.* The portative organ was small enough to be carried (*portatum*), perhaps suspended by a strap around the neck of the player; it had a single rank of pipes, and the keys were played by the right hand while the left worked the bellows. The positive organ also could be carried but had to be placed (*positum*) on a table to be played and required an assistant for the bellows.

Most of these instruments came into Europe from Asia, either by way of Byzantium or through the Arabs in North Africa and Spain. Their early history is obscure and their nomenclature often inconsistent and confusing. Furthermore, in the absence of precise expert description one cannot be sure whether an artist has drawn an actual instrument or an impressionistic one, or to what extent a poet is indulging in mere fancy when, as often happens, he tells of extraordinary instrumental ensembles. We can be sure, however, that music in the Middle Ages was much brighter and had a more variegated instrumental color than the music manuscripts alone suggest.

Angel musicians play the zither, timbrels or drums, and bagpipe. Early fourteenth-century marbles by Giovanni Balduccio da Pisa. (Courtesy Duveen Brothers, Inc.)

From the twelfth century onward the attention of composers was increasingly absorbed by polyphony. The monophonic songs of the troubadours and trouvères were a special artistic expression of the feudal upper classes; they were essentially the product of gifted amateur musicians rather than of professional composers. This was also true of the Minnelieder and the semipopular religious *cantigas* and *laude*—they were written by amateurs, and as in most amateur composing, the tendency was toward a conservative style and idiom.

II. Gregorian Chant and Secular Song in the Middle Ages

Monophonic music—songs and dances—continued to be performed in Europe until well into the sixteenth century; but, with the exception of Guillaume de Machaut, few professional composers of the first rank are known to have written in this style after the thirteenth century. We therefore turn our attention now to the rise of polyphony and its first flowering in the Middle Ages.

The Beginnings of Polyphony and the Music of the Thirteenth Century

Historical Background of Early Polyphony

The eleventh century is of crucial importance in Western history. The years 1000–1100 A.D. witnessed a revival of economic life throughout western Europe, an increase in population, reclamation of wastelands, and the beginning of modern cities; the Norman conquest of England, important strides toward the recovery of Spain from the Muslims, the First Crusade; a revival of culture, with the first translations from Greek and Arabic, the beginnings of the universities and scholastic philosophy, and the rise of Romanesque architecture. The cultural independence of the West was marked by the growth of vernacular literature and symbolized by the final schism between the Western and Eastern Churches in 1054.

The eleventh century was equally crucial in the history of music. During this time certain changes were beginning—changes which, when eventually worked out, would result in giving to Western music many of its basic characteristics, those features which distinguish it from other musics of the world. Those changes may be summarized as follows:

(1) *Composition* slowly replaced improvisation as a way of creating musical works. Improvisation, in one form or another, is the normal way in most musical cultures and was probably the exclusive

way in the West up to about the ninth century. Gradually the idea arose of composing a melody once for all instead of improvising it anew each time on traditional melodic pattern-structures; and thenceforward a piece of music could be said to "exist," in the way in which we ordinarily think of it now, apart from any particular performance.

(2) A composed piece could be taught and transmitted orally, and might be subject to alterations in the course of transmission. But the *invention of musical notation* made it possible to write music down in a definitive form, which could be learned from the score. The score, in other words, was a set of directions which could be executed whether or not the composer was present. Thus composition and performance became separate acts instead of being combined in one person as before, and the performer's function became that of a mediator between composer and audience.

(3) Music began to be more consciously structured and made subject to certain *principles of order*—for example, the theory of the eight modes, or the rules governing rhythm and consonance; such principles were eventually formulated into systems and set forth in treatises.

(4) *Polyphony* began to replace monophony. Of course, polyphony as such is not exclusively Western; but it is our music which, more than any other, has specialized in this technique. We have developed polyphonic composition to a unique degree and, it must be admitted, at the expense of rhythmic and melodic subtleties that are characteristic of the music of other highly civilized peoples, India and China for example.

It must be emphasized that the changes we have been describing all took place very gradually; there was no sudden, sharp break with the past. Monophony continued: some of the finest specimens of monophonic chant, including antiphons, hymns, and sequences, were produced in the twelfth and thirteenth centuries. Improvisation continued after the eleventh century and many stylistic details of the new composed music were taken over—as has always been the case—from improvisational practice. Nevertheless, in looking back over the whole historical development, we can now see that it was in the eleventh century that the first stages of a new and different musical system began to be manifest. During the first thousand years of the Christian era the Western Church had absorbed and converted to its own use all that it could take from the music of antiquity and the East. By about 600 A.D. the absorption and conversion were practically complete, and during the next four hundred years the material was systematized, codified, and disseminated throughout western Europe. This heritage was not abandoned. Polyphonic sacred compositions up to the end of the sixteenth century incorporated plainchant along with other borrowed musical materials. Meanwhile polyphony had begun to develop independently of such borrowings and independently of the Church. By the sixteenth century composers were discovering new realms of expression and inventing new techniques to master them; and this is the period of music history in which we are still living—though, it is true, we may now be near the end of it.

Early Organum

There are good reasons to believe that polyphony existed in Europe long before it was first unmistakably described. It was probably used chiefly in nonliturgical sacred music; it may have been employed also in folk music, and probably consisted of melodic doubling at the third, fourth, or fifth, along with a more or less systematic practice of heterophony—that is, by performing the same melody simultaneously in ornamented and unornamented form. Needless to say, there are no surviving documents of this supposed early European polyphony; but the first clear description of music in more than one voice, dated about the end of the ninth century, manifestly refers to something already being practiced, and is not a proposal of something new. In this treatise, *Musica enchiriadis* ("Handbook of Music") and in a contemporary commentary on it, the *Scholia enchiriadis,* two distinct kinds of "singing together" are described, both being designated by the name *organum* (pronounced or'-gan-um). In one species of this early organum, a plainsong melody in one voice, the *vox principalis,* is duplicated at a fifth or a fourth below by a second voice, the *vox organalis;* either voice or both may be further duplicated at the octave and at other intervals, as shown in Example III–1.

In another kind of early organum the two voices start at the unison; the *vox principalis* moves upward until it forms the interval

EXAMPLE III–1   Parallel Organum

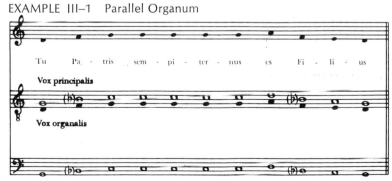

Thou art the everlasting Son of the Father.

(Facsimile of original in Apel, *Notation of Polyphonic Music,* p. 205.)

of a fourth with the *vox organalis*, whereupon both proceed in parallel fourths until they come together again on a unison at the cadence (Example III–2). Duplication of the voices is possible in this as in the first type.

EXAMPLE III–2   Organum with Parallel Fourths

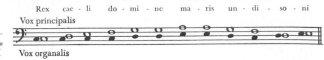

King of Heaven, Lord of the wave-sounding sea.

(Facsimile of original in Parrish, *Notation of Medieval Music*, plate XXa.)

Despite the fact that no theorist in the tenth century and only one in the eleventh so much as mentions organum, during this time it was undoubtedly being sung—improvised—and the idea of two simultaneous distinct voices seems to have gradually caught on. Organum in its first stage—where the added voice simply duplicates the original at a fixed interval—was hardly susceptible of development, and its mention in the theory books may have been no more than an attempt to account theoretically for certain examples of its use in contemporary musical practice. Extant musical examples of the eleventh century show important progress toward melodic independence and equal importance of the two voices: contrary and oblique motion become regular features. These are illustrated in Example III–3; a complete transcription appears in HAM, No. 26a. As a rule the *vox organalis* sings above the *vox principalis*, though the parts frequently cross; and rudimentary rhythmic diversity is shown by the *vox organalis* occasionally singing two notes against one of the *vox principalis*. In all eleventh-century organa the consonant intervals are the unison, octave, fourth, and fifth; all others occur only incidentally and are treated as dissonances requiring resolution. The rhythm is that of plainsong, on which the pieces are always based.

The oldest large collection of pieces in organum style is contained in two eleventh-century manuscripts known collectively as the Winchester Troper and consisting of a repertory of troped chants used at Winchester Cathedral. The music, in two voices, is notated in heighted neumes without staff lines (see illustration, p. 62), so ·that the precise intervals can be determined only with great difficulty and uncertainty—though in some cases a melody may be identical with one that has been preserved in a later, more exact notation, and can be reconstructed.

Polyphonic setting in the eleventh century was not applied to all parts of the liturgy, but was chiefly used in the troped sections (such as the Kyrie, Gloria, or Benedicamus Domino) of the Ordinary, in certain parts of the Proper (especially graduals, alleluias, tracts, and sequences), and in responsories of the Office. Even then, only those portions were set polyphonically which in the original chant were sung by soloists. In performance, therefore, polyphonic sections alternated with sections of monophonic chant; polyphony was sung by solo voices and the monophonic chant by the full choir in unison.

EXAMPLE III–3   Eleventh-century Organum

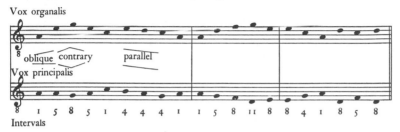

By the end of the eleventh century, polyphony had developed to a point where composers were able to combine two *melodically* independent lines by using oblique and contrary motion. Harmonic intervals had been stabilized by the invention of precise pitch notation on a staff. Two other essentials had still to be achieved: the ability to combine two or more *rhythmically* independent melodies; and a precise method of notating rhythm.

The development of notation was hastened by the growth of polyphony. As long as there was only one melody, a certain leeway in pitch and rhythm could be allowed; but when two or more melodies were to be played or sung together from a score, not only the pitches had to be made clear but also some means had to be devised to show the rhythmic relationships.

Florid Organum

A new type of organum appears early in the twelfth century. Examples are preserved in one manuscript at the monastery of Santiago de Compostela in the northwest corner of Spain and in three manuscripts from the Abbey of St. Martial at Limoges in south-central France. In this kind (called variously "florid," "melismatic," or "St. Martial" organum), the original plainchant melody (played or sung) lies always in the lower voice; but each note is prolonged so as to allow the upper (solo) voice to sing phrases of varying length against it. It is not always clear from the notation whether the upper voice was sung in a free non-rhythmic manner or was subject to definite rhythmic patterns. In either case, it is obvious that this new kind of organum not only greatly increased the length of pieces but also deprived the lower voice of its original character as a definite tune, making it in effect rather a series of

A page from a St. Martial manuscript showing the organum Lux descendit. *(Courtesy of the British Museum)*

single notes, like "drones," with melodic elaborations above—a device common in some eastern European folk singing as well as in many non-Western musical systems. Clearly it was a style that could have originated, and probably did, in improvisation; the versions in the manuscripts may have actually been taken down in the first place from improvised performances.

The term *organum* properly refers only to the style in which the lower voice holds long notes; when both parts came to move in similar measured rhythm, as happened later in the twelfth and early thirteenth centuries, the usual medieval term was *discant*. Since florid organum was at first applied in a two-voice texture, one designation for it was *organum duplum vel purum* ("double or pure organum"). By extension, *organum* has also come to have other meanings: it is sometimes used as a general term to denote all polyphonic music based on Gregorian Chant up to about the middle of the thirteenth century; it is used (like the modern word *sonata*) as the name of a *type* of composition, so that we can speak of "an organum" or "the organa" of a composer; and finally *organum* is the Latin word for any musical instrument, and also refers particularly to the organ. It is necessary not to confuse these different meanings; for example, when contemporaries called a certain composer *"optimus organista,"* they were not calling him an "excellent organist," but an "excellent composer of organa," that is, of compositions like the ones now being discussed.

The phrases in medieval organum usually begin and always end with one of the consonant intervals (unison, octave, fifth, and rarely, fourth), and throughout each phrase these intervals are the most prominent. Thirds and sixths, seconds and sevenths, are used as supplementary tones, seconds and sevenths especially being often treated as sharply dissonant "appoggiaturas." Example III–4 (given completely in HAM, No. 27b) shows this use of intervals. Since the rhythmic interpretation of the original notation is not certain, the points at which the voices came together may not have been exactly those shown in modern transcriptions.

EXAMPLE III–4   Florid Organum, twelfth-century

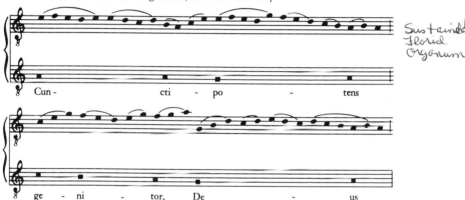

The texts of the St. Martial organa are like the texts of the eleventh-century organa; tropes of the *Benedicamus Domino* are especially frequent. As a rule the two voices have the same words; occasionally the lower voice carries the original plainsong text, while the upper voice sings the melody to the words of a trope. As in the earlier organum, sections of unison chant alternate with sections of polyphony; further variety is obtained by contrasting sections in the older note-against-note style with sections in the new or florid organal style. Since the lengthening of the single tones of the lower voice in these organa made the original plainsong melody unrecognizable, this is probably one reason why the new manner was at first applied so extensively to tropes and other non-liturgical texts, which were not held in as much reverence as words and melodies of the regular liturgy. The lower voice, because it sustained or held the principal melody, came to be called the *tenor,* from the Latin *tenere,* to hold; and this word was used to designate the lowest part of a polyphonic composition until after the middle of the fifteenth century.

Organum in the florid style could have been sung from a notation that did not specify the relative time values of the notes in the two voices. The two parts were written one above the other—*score notation*—fairly well-aligned vertically, and with vertical lines on the staff to mark off the phrases; two singers, or one soloist and a small group, could not easily go astray. But in pieces whose rhythmic structure was more complicated—for example, if one or both melodies were laid out in regular rhythmic patterns formed by longer and shorter tones of definite relative time values—some way had to be found of distinguishing between long and short notes and indicating their relative durations.

The late medieval (and the modern) notations of Gregorian Chant do not indicate this; indeed, there was no felt need to specify it, for by the twelfth century the Chant was evidently being sung either in free rhythm or in a rhythm tied to that of the text. The troubadour and trouvère melodies also could be written down in this notation, for if in performance any systematic difference was made between long and short values it depended not on the shape of the notational signs but on the meter of the poetry; here also, as in the chant, there was only one melodic line to be considered.

Uncertainties of note duration and rhythm which were not of serious practical importance in solo or monophonic singing could, however, cause chaos when two or more simultaneously sounding melodies were involved. This was true even in florid organum, since at least one of the voices might be melismatic and therefore textless; and when a syllabic text was used, it was often a prose text which had no regular rhythmic pattern.

The Rhythmic Modes

The system which eleventh- and twelfth-century composers devised for the notation of rhythm proved adequate for all polyphonic music until well into the thirteenth century. It was based on a fundamentally different principle from that of our notation: instead of showing fixed relative durations by means of different note signs, it indicated different *rhythmic patterns* by means of certain combinations of single notes and especially of note-groups. By about 1250, these patterns were codified as the six rhythmic modes, identified as a rule simply by number:

I. ♩ ♪   IV. ♪ ♩ ♩.
II. ♪ ♩   V. ♩. ♩.
III. ♩. ♪ ♩   VI. ♪ ♪ ♪

As can be seen, the patterns correspond to the metrical feet of French and Latin verse. Mode I, for example, corresponds to the trochee, a long syllable followed by a short one in the ratio of 2 to 1.

The whole system may have been suggested by St. Augustine's *De musica* ("On Music," begun in 387 A.D.) which is in effect a treatise on rhythm and which was well known to theorists of the later Middle Ages. Modes I and V were the first to be used in practice; II and III were introduced later; Mode VI can be understood as a variant of I or II; Mode IV was less often used.

Theoretically, according to the system, a melody in Mode I should consist of an indefinite number of repetitions of the pattern ♩ ♪, each phrase ending with a rest which replaced the second note of the pattern, thus:

$$\text{♩ ♪♩ ♪|♩ ♪♩ ⅞ |♩ ♪♩ ♪|}_{\text{etc.}}$$

In practice, however, the rhythm of such a melody would be more flexible than such a scheme shows. Either of the notes ♩ ♪ could be broken into shorter units, or the two notes of the pattern could be combined into one, and various other means for variety were available; also, a melody in Mode I might be sung over a tenor which held long notes not strictly measured, or which might be organized in the pattern of Mode V:

$$\text{♩. ♩. |♩. ⅞ |♩. ♩. |}_{\text{etc.}}$$

An actual melody which can be interpreted in Mode I may be seen in the upper voice of Example III–6.

The basis of the system of rhythmic modes was a threefold unit of measure called by theorists a *perfectio*—a "perfection." In order to adapt to this, the original classical poetic pattern of Modes III and IV had to be modified. Ostensibly, these two modes corresponded to the dactyl (♩ ♫) and the anapest (♫ ♩); in the system of rhythmic modes, they become ♩. ♪♩ and ♪♩ ♩.. Undoubtedly the reason for this change was to make it possible to combine Mode III (and later, IV) with Mode I, which was the original mode, in what we should now call a six-beat measure; and this practical motive was strongly reinforced by the medieval feeling for the mystical perfection of the number 3, a symbol of the Trinity, as against the "imperfect" number 2. At any rate, all medieval polyphony until the fourteenth century, insofar as it was in measured rhythm at all, was dominated by ternary division of the "beat," producing an effect like that of the modern 6/8 or 9/8 meter.

The required rhythmic mode was indicated to the singer by the choice and order of the notes. *Ligatures*, compound signs derived from the compound Gregorian neumes, denoting a group of two, three, or more tones, were one important means of conveying this information. For example, if a melody were notated as in Example III–5a—a single three-note ligature followed by a series of two-note ligatures—a singer would sing it in a rhythm that can be expressed in the modern notation of Example III–5b; in other words, the

EXAMPLE III–5   Use of Ligatures to Indicate a Rhythmic Mode

particular series of ligatures in Example III–5a signaled to the singer that he was to use the first rhythmic mode. The other rhythmic modes could be shown in equivalent ways. Departures from the prevailing rhythmic pattern, change of mode, or repeated tones (which could not be indicated in a ligature) necessitated modifications of the notation which are too complex and lengthy to be described in detail here. (The entire system is explained in William G. Waite's *The Rhythm of Twelfth-Century Polyphony;* the student may make a beginning by comparing the transcription in Example III–6 with the original shown in the illustration on page 88).

Notre Dame Organum

It must not be supposed that the system of rhythmic modes was invented at one stroke, or that the system was invented first and the music written to conform to it. The opposite is true: the system and its notation were developed gradually during the twelfth and early thirteenth centuries to fill the needs of a school of polyphonic composers who were active at Paris, Beauvais, Sens, and other centers in the north-central part of France. Two composers of this school— the first composers of polyphony whose names are known to us— were Leonin, who lived in the third quarter of the twelfth century, and Perotin, who lived perhaps in the last part of the twelfth century and the first part of the thirteenth (1183?–1238?). Both men apparently were choirmasters at the Church of Notre Dame (predecessor to the cathedral now known by that name). Their compositions, together with those of their anonymous French contemporaries, are known collectively as the music of the Notre Dame school.

The entire art of polyphonic composition from the twelfth to the middle of the fourteenth centuries developed primarily in northern France and radiated to other parts of Europe. The highest achievements in organum especially were the work of the Notre Dame school; organum was sung in other regions of France, in England, Spain, and Italy, but less extensively and in less highly developed form than at Paris, probably often being improvised by the singers on festal occasions. The great bulk of the music in both the Mass and the Office was still monophonic Gregorian Chant, and newly composed monophonic songs are still found in the same manuscripts that contain organa and other polyphonic pieces.

Three principal styles or types of composition are represented in the music of the Notre Dame school and the later thirteenth century: organum, conductus, and motet. Leonin wrote a cycle of two-part graduals, alleluias, and responsories for the entire church year, called the *Magnus liber organi* ("The Great Book of Organum"). The *Magnus liber* no longer exists in its original form, but its contents have survived in various manuscripts at Florence, Wolfenbüttel, Madrid, and elsewhere; some of them are available in modern editions or facsimiles. (See list on pages 743–44. A reconstruction and transcription of the two-part organa from *Magnus Liber* forms the second part of Waite's *Rhythm of Twelfth-Century Polyphony*.)

The Leonin style

As an example of Leonin's style, let us take the setting of the Easter gradual *Haec dies quam fecit Dominus* ("This is the day which the Lord hath made"; a reproduction of the first part of this piece in the original notation is illustrated below, on page 88). A comparison of the plainsong gradual (see Example II–4) with the polyphonic setting shows that the original chant, approximately two and one-half minutes long, has been expanded to about six minutes of music. Only the solo portions of the chant, however, have been expanded; the chorus sections have been left in simple plainsong. This contrast of solo voices in polyphony alternating with chorus voices in unison is the principal formal characteristic of the piece. But within the polyphonic sections themselves there is further contrast.

The first section, through the words "haec dies," is given in Example III–6; the entire piece is transcribed in Waite, *op. cit.* pp. 120–26. The style looks at first like that of the older melismatic or florid organum; the plainsong melody, stretched out into indefinite unmeasured long notes, forms the tenor. Could this actually have been sung by one soloist? It would seem more likely that it was played on a stringed instrument or on the organ, or at least carried by several singers, who could take breaths at different times. Above the long notes of the tenor, a solo voice sings textless melismatic phrases, broken at irregular intervals by cadences and rests.

The exact note values of this upper voice (called the *duplum*) in a modern transcription are not to be taken too literally. The interpretation of some details of modal notation is not absolutely certain; besides, the desired effect seems to be one of expressive improvisation over a series of slowly changing "drone" notes. It was formerly thought that the notation of the upper voice in organum duplum signified a completely free, unmeasured rhythm. This view no longer prevails; still, within the framework of the modal rhythm in such a piece as this some flexibility of delivery certainly seems called for. Some passages in contemporary theoretical writings suggest that in this style the singer used considerable freedom, making the long notes longer and the short ones shorter than the written values.

III. The Beginnings of Polyphony and the Music of the Thirteenth Century

Did the upper solo voice sing any words, or were the notes to be vocalized on the corresponding vowel of the tenor part? The latter is usually assumed, but we do not know for certain. It has even been suggested that the textless upper line was played on an instrument above a sung tenor part; but the character of the melody

EXAMPLE III–6   First section of Organum Duplum, *Haec dies*

William G. Waite, *The Rhythm of Twelfth-Century Polyphony*, New Haven, 1954, Part 2, pp. 102–22. The original notation is shown in the illustration on page 88. The only two single note signs are the *longa* or *long* ▌ and the *brevis* or *breve* ■ ; ligatures of various shapes are combinations of longs and breves. In this kind of notation, neither the long nor the breve has a fixed duration; their time value depends on the context, on their position in the pattern. Brackets in the transcription indicate either ligatures in the original (as in measures 2–4 and generally elsewhere) or a stepwise descending group of small diamond-shaped notes called *conjunctura* or *currentes* attached to a single long (measures 5, 31, 32–33, 34–35, 37). Currentes attached to a ligature are shown by slurs (measures 20, 45. Phrases or periods in the original are marked off by small vertical strokes; these are shown in the tenor of the transcription by apostrophes and in the upper voice as a rule by rests. The apostrophe in measure 11 of the upper voice is a breathing mark; those in measures 4 and 33 represent a vertical dash that may have, in conjunction with the preceding note, indicated a short trill or similar ornament. The sign ♪ stands for a *plica*, a short upward or downward dash affixed to a single note (as in measures 4 and 33) or to the final note of a ligature (measures 11, 13, 26, 27). Originally a sign for an ornamental or passing tone, the plica is used in modal notation to divide a longer note into two shorter ones; it takes its time value from the note to which it is attached.

so strongly implies vocal rendition that the theory of instrumental performance seems implausible. The melody as a whole strongly suggests a style derived from improvisatory practice. Typical is the non-periodic, rather loosely structured flow; there is a clearly climactic passage at measures 36–40 and there are a couple of little sequential repetitions (measures 26–28, 30–33). The held high a at the beginning is an example of the usual introductory gesture in most examples of organum; it is balanced by the high a at the end. There are some melodic formulas that recur often in other two-voice organa. Two cadential formulas are incorporated: descent by step after an upward leap, in measures 4–5 (identical in 56–57), 9–10, 19–20, 34–35; and descent by a "triadic" figure, in measures 25 and 29. (This figure relates to the conspicuous descending fifths of measures 2 and 6). All the phrases except one begin and end, as is the normal rule, on one of the perfect consonances (fifth, unison, or octave); and fifths, fourths, and octaves are the most prominent harmonic intervals throughout.

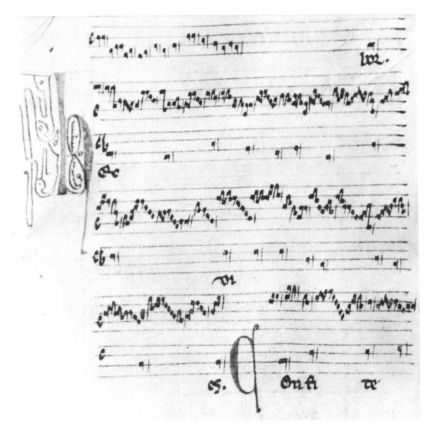

Organum [Leonin], Haec dies quam fecit Dominus, *from the Wolfenbüttel manuscript 628.*

After a choral unison interlude, consisting of the original plain-song chant from the words "quam fecit" through "laetamur in ea" ("let us rejoice in it"), the two-voice texture is resumed. But beginning with the word "Domino" a quite different style is heard (Example III–7). The tenor now sings short notes in strictly measured rhythm; the upper voice, which moves in still faster notes, likewise takes on a more distinctly rhythmic character. Both parts sing in notes of definitely measured duration, in contrast to the more flexible rhythm of the previous section. As has already been mentioned, the style in which all the parts are in measured rhythm came to be called discant; it did not exclude occasional short melismas, particularly at cadential points, but for the most part the two voices moved according to the rhythmic modes.

EXAMPLE III–7   Beginning of Clausula from *Haec dies*

The choice of whether to use organal or discant style was not a matter of caprice. It was based on the general principle that in those portions of the original chant which were syllabic or only slightly florid—in other words, in the portions where there were comparatively few notes to a syllable—the organal style with long sustained tones in the tenor was appropriate; but in those portions where the original chant was itself highly melismatic, it was necessary for the tenor to move along more quickly in order not to lengthen the whole piece unduly. Such sections, built over the more melismatic portions of the chant and written in discant style, were called *clausulae.* Each clausula was kept distinct, with a definite final cadence. Leonin's *Haec dies* organum of Examples III–6 and 7 has in all three clausulae, with a contrasting section in organal style between the second and third. After the last discant section the chorus finishes the piece with the concluding few phrases of the plainsong gradual on which the organum is based.

One of the distinctive features of the Leonin style was the juxtaposition of old and new elements, passages of organum of the florid

EXAMPLE III–8   Tenors on "Domino" from *Haec dies*

1. Gregorian (Graduale, *p. 241*)

2. Two-voice clausula (Leonin, W1, fol. 27'; see Example III–7)

3. Two-voice clausula (Perotin? W1, fol. 46'; HAM 30)

4. Three-voice clausula (Perotin? W1, fol. 81; HAM 31)

1)

5. Motet (W2, fols. 126–127; HAM 32c; cf. Las Huelgas Ms., No. 131)

6. Motet (Montpellier Ms., No. 190)

7. Motet (Montpellier Ms., No. 193)

8. Motet (Montpellier Ms., No. 221)

1) e´ in original

type alternating and contrasting with the livelier rhythmic discant clausulae. As the thirteenth century went on, *organum purum* was gradually abandoned in favor of discant; in the course of this development, clausulae first became quasi-independent pieces, and eventually evolved into a new form, the *motet*.

The work of Perotin and his contemporaries may be regarded as a continuation of that done by Leonin's generation. The basic formal structure of the organum—an alternation of unison chant with polyphonic sections—remained unchanged by Perotin, but within the polyphonic sections there was a continuing tendency toward greater rhythmic precision. Not only were the older rhapsodic portions of the florid organa often replaced with discant clausulae; many of the older clausulae were replaced with faster

Perotin organum

2) c′ in original

movements in definite and stylized patterns. The tenor of Perotin's organum was characteristically laid out in a series of reiterated identical rhythmic motives, corresponding usually to the fifth or third rhythmic mode; these tenors, in, modern transcription, give the effect of distinct binary grouping in two, or multiples of two, measures—see Example III–8. Moreover, the tenor melody, which in Perotin's style was typically in shorter notes than the tenors of Leonin, often had to be repeated wholly or in part in order to bring a section out to the length the composer desired. Both these kinds of repetition—of rhythmic motive and of melody—were also part of the formal structure of the later thirteenth-century motet. Nos. 7 and 8 of Example III–8, and also Example III–11, where the tenor is laid out in identical repeated rhythmic patterns, actually foreshadow the technique of the fourteenth-century "isorhythmic" motet which we shall study in the next chapter (see pages 116–45).

An important innovation made by Perotin and his contemporaries was the expansion of organum from two voices to three or four voices. Since the second voice was called the duplum, by analogy the third and fourth were called respectively the *triplum* and *quadruplum*. These same terms also designated the composition as a whole; a three-voice organum was called an *organum triplum,* or simply *triplum,* and a four-voice organum a *quadruplum.*

The three-voice organum, or triplum, became standard in the Perotin period and remained in favor for a long time; examples have been found in manuscripts dating from the second half of the thirteenth century. Two fairly distinct styles are usually present in a long organum triplum, either intermingled or alternated. Most tripla begin with long-held notes of the chant in the tenor, and two voices moving above in measured phrases. This style corresponds to the sustained-note portions of Leonin organum, differing only in the more regular rhythmic quality of the upper voices. In a typical Perotin organum, an opening section of this sort will be followed by one or more discant sections in which the tenor is also measured, though it moves less rapidly than the upper voices. As the composition proceeds, sections in sustained-tone style blend and alternate with sections in discant style; the latter as a rule correspond to the melismatic parts of the original chant, and the sections in sustained-tone style to the more syllabic parts of the chant.

Despite the three or four voices of Perotin's larger organa, the music really moves in only two tonal strata: a static or slower-moving tenor contrasting with a faster-moving shorter-phrased duo or trio above. It is thus, in a sense, an elaboration of the older *organum duplum.* The total compass seems surprisingly narrow, extending altogether only from the lowest to the highest notes of the tenor voice range; the two or three upper parts all move within the same musical space, continually crossing and intertwining, and occasionally passing below the line of the tenor part, which is normally the lowest. Occasionally a phrase will be repeated with some of the voices interchanged—see for example the duplum and triplum at measures 26–33 of Example III–9. Such voice interchange (sometimes called by the German term *Stimmtausch*) occurs also in both motets and conducti of the thirteenth century. Because of the constant intertwining of voices, the piano is of all instruments the least well adapted to suggest the correct sound of this music; only voices—preferably solo for the upper parts—or melody instruments will do so. At the beginnings of phrases usually, at cadences always, and on strong beats generally, the only intervals sounded are those accepted as consonances in the Middle Ages (octave, fifth, fourth); but within the phrase the parts move in a strongly independent, linear fashion, not excluding frequent consecutive parallel fifths, unisons, or octaves, and continually producing sharp clashes both among themselves and against the tenor.

The melodies often have a dance-like lilt. Individual voice lines may be shaped by means of repeated melodic motives or short melodic sequences, as in measures 10–15 of the duplum of Example III–9. Although a triad as such is seldom actually sounded, thirds are so prominent in the texture that the total harmonic effect—the harmonic structure—of a Perotin organum is that of a succession of triads, one on each of the notes of the original chant as set forth in the tenor. An organum may thus be regarded as the lengthened shadow of a chant. The sustained-note sections, which sometimes involve as many as a hundred or more measures of a modern transcription in 6/8 time over one unchanging tenor tone, form great blocks of fundamentally static harmony, markedly different from the quick-moving harmonic rhythm of the discant sections. Yet even the latter do not have the quality of harmonic movement to which we are accustomed in music of the eighteenth and nineteenth centuries, organized around clearly related tonal centers and working with dominant-tonic relationships; one cannot properly speak of chord *progressions* in Perotin, but only of chord *successions.*

The musical shape of a Perotin organum is defined by the design of the Gregorian chant on which the piece is built, much as the plan of a Gothic cathedral is defined by the form of the Cross; in both arts the basic sacred symbol has almost unlimited possibilities for expansion and enrichment, depending on the creative fantasy of the artist. A melody used in this way as the basis of a polyphonic composition was called a *cantus firmus* or "fixed song"; if the melody was taken from some already existing source, that fact might be indicated by calling it a *cantus prius factus,* or "song previously made."

With respect to color, in the modern meaning of the quality of the sound of a composition, there are two particularly impressive

EXAMPLE III–9   Organum Quadruplum: *Sederunt principes*, Perotin

features in the triple and quadruple organa of the Perotin period:
the kaleidoscopic hues and shades of sound, punctuated by flashes
of dissonance within the basic sonority of a single triad, produced
as the upper voices interweave their mazy patterns around an unchanging tenor note; and the broad contrasts between one section
and another obtained by varying the vowel qualities of the text.
Few composers since Perotin have so largely exploited this particular resource, and none with finer artistry; it is especially prominent
in the great four-part organa, where the relentless triple rhythms
and shifting powerful sound masses combine to produce an effect
of often overwhelming grandeur.

The foregoing observations are based on the assumption that the
performance of these organa in the early thirteenth century was
by voices which sang only the words found in the written scores.
This is in fact the most likely hypothesis; but in view of the mystery
that shrouds all details of musical practice in this period we cannot
exclude the possibility that instruments may have taken part as well,
doubling the voice parts in unison. Since both boys and men sang
at the Cathedral of Notre Dame, it has been surmised that the upper
voices of Perotin's organa were doubled at the octave; but there
seems to be better historical evidence for a different manner of performance, one that seems rather strange to us, in which boy's voices
sang the tenor notes while the melismatic upper parts were taken
by soloists in falsetto. In any event, melodic embellishments and
vocal ornaments were undoubtedly inserted by the solo singers.

Part of Perotin's Organum Quadruplum Sederunt Principes *as it appears in the Medicean Library manuscript Pluteus 29, 1, fol. 6ʳ (see Example III–9).*

Polyphonic Conductus

The tripla and quadrupla of Perotin and his generation are the summit of purely ecclesiastical polyphony in the early thirteenth century. The conductus, of which there are numerous examples up to about 1250, developed from quasi-liturgical sources such as the hymn and the sequence, but was extended to include secular words. Its texts were like those of the eleventh- and twelfth-century monophonic conductus: they were metrical Latin poems, hardly ever liturgical, though often on sacred themes; if they were secular, they dealt seriously with moral questions or historical events.

The polyphonic conductus written by Perotin and by other composers of the Notre Dame era had a less complex musical style than organum. The music of the polyphonic conductus was written in two, three, or four voices which, as in organum, were held within a comparatively narrow range, crossing and recrossing, and were organized harmonically around the consonances of the octave, fourth, and fifth. Thirds sound prominently in some conducti, though the interval was not yet accepted as a perfect consonance. Voice interchange is fairly frequent.

As usual with music of this period, the basis of the rhythm was a triple division of the beat; but typically in conducti the voices moved in nearly the same rhythm, so that the effect was—to use a modern term—chordal, in contrast to the greater rhythmic variety of the voices in organum. This thirteenth-century chordal manner of writing is often referred to as "conductus style," and sometimes was used in compositions other than conducti: for instance, two-part or three-part settings of hymns, sequences, ballads, and rondeaux were written in this style throughout the twelfth and thirteenth centuries, as were also some early thirteenth-century motets. Example III–10 (transcribed completely in HAM, No. 39) illustrates the conductus style.

Characteristics of the conductus

The polyphonic conductus of the early thirteenth century was distinguished not only by its pseudo-chordal texture; it had two

EXAMPLE III–10   Early Thirteenth-century Conductus

At this opening of the year, in this January, let us turn to our labors, supported by our virtues.

For a transcription based on a different source, and adopting a different rhythmic mode, see Janet Knapp, ed., *Thirty-five Conductus for Two and Three Voices,* Collegium Musicum No. 6, New Haven, 1965, p. 38.

further identifying characteristics. First, the words, for the most part, were set syllabically. An exception to this rule occurs in some conducti which introduce fairly long textless passages, called *caudae*, at the beginning, at the end, and sometimes also before important cadences and elsewhere. These caudae (literally, "tails"; compare the word "coda"), which sometimes incorporated pre-existing clausulae, often introduced variety of rhythm among the voices similar to the rhythmical contrasts in organum, so that a mixture of conductus and organum styles resulted.

A second distinguishing characteristic of thirteenth-century polyphonic conducti was that the tenor, instead of being taken from an ecclesiastical chant or some other pre-existing source, was often a newly composed melody which served as a *cantus firmus* for one particular composition. The conductus, therefore, was the first expression in the history of Western music of the concept of a completely original polyphonic work, independent of borrowed melodic material, although the new melody was used in the same way as any other *cantus firmus*.

In the manuscripts the conducti are notated in the same manner as organa, that is, in score arrangement: the corresponding notes of each voice part are in vertical alignment, and the text is written only under the lowest (tenor) part. Probably they were performed in the way this suggests, by voices singing all parts and with the melismas vocalized in the same way as the melismatic sections of organum; as in organum, also, instruments may have doubled some or all of the voices. Some scholars maintain that only the tenor was sung, and that the upper voices were played on instruments; if this is true, then any melismas at the beginning and end probably were purely instrumental.

Both organum and conductus gradually dropped out of favor after 1250, and during the second half of the thirteenth century the most important type of polyphonic composition was the motet.

The Motet

Leonin, as we have seen, had introduced into his organa distinct sections (*clausulae*) in discant style. The idea evidently fascinated composers of the next generation—so much so that Perotin and others produced hundreds of discant clausulae, many of them designed as alternates or substitutes for those of Leonin and other earlier composers. These "substitute clausulae" were interchangeable; as many as five or ten might be written over the same tenor, and from these a choirmaster could select any one for a particular occasion. Presumably, the added upper voice or voices originally had no words; but sometime before the middle of the century words began to be fitted to them—usually tropes or paraphrases, in rhymed Latin verse, of the tenor text. Eventually, the clausulae cut

Origins and general features

loose from the larger organa in which they had been imbedded and began life on their own as separate compositions—in much the same way that the sequence, after starting out as an appendage to the alleluia, later became independent. Probably because of the addition of words, the newly autonomous substitute clausulae were called _motets_. The term comes from the French _mot,_ meaning "word," and was first applied to French texts that were added to the duplum of a clausula. By extension, "motet" came to signify the composition as a whole. The Latin form _motetus_ is customarily used to designate the second voice (the original duplum) of a motet; when there are more than two voices, the third and fourth have the same names (triplum, quadruplum) as in organum.

Thousands of motets were written in the thirteenth century; the style spread from Paris throughout France and to all parts of western Europe. Three of the most important surviving manuscripts have been published in modern editions with commentaries and facsimilies; the Montpellier Codex, a miscellaneous collection of 345 pieces, chiefly motets, the majority of which date from about the middle of the century; the Bamberg Codex, a collection of 108 three-voice motets of slightly later date; and the Las Huelgas Codex, preserved at a monastery near Burgos in Spain, which, although written in the fourteenth century, contains organa, conducti, and 58 motets of the thirteenth century.

Since most motets have a different text in each voice, the usual way of identifying a motet is by a compound title made up of the _incipit_ (the first word or words) of each of the voice parts in turn, beginning with the highest—as in Examples III–11, 12, 13, and 14.

Most motets are anonymous; many are found in more or less varying forms in different manuscripts, and often it is impossible to say which of several versions is the earliest. New words were set to old music, and new music to old words. The same melody served for both sacred and secular texts. The same tenor might be found in different manuscripts, each time with a different duplum above it (possibly recording different improvised performances.) A motet originally in three parts might lose one of its upper voices and survive as a two-part composition; more often, a third or fourth voice would be added to an earlier two- or three-voice motet; or a new upper voice might be substituted for an older one, the other parts remaining unchanged. Sometimes a motet would lose its tenor, leaving only the two upper voices. (Some instances of this found in the manuscripts were at first thought to be examples of conductus.) In short, the stock of motet melodies, both tenors and upper parts, lay in the public domain; composers and performers freely helped themselves to the music of their predecessors without acknowledgment and altered it without notice.

The earliest type of motet, based on the substitute clausula with Latin texts supplied for the upper voices, was soon modified in

EXAMPLE III–11   Motet: *O Mitissima (Quant voi)—Virgo—Hec dies*

lo *nun - ci - an - te,* *Vir - go es post et an - te.*

Triplum, upper line *(from the Bamberg Codex): O sweetest Virgin Mary, beg Thy Son to give us aid and relief against the deceiving wiles of the demons and their wickedness.*

Triplum, lower line *(from the Montpellier Codex): When I see the summer season returning and all the little birds make the woods resound, then I weep and sigh for the great desire which I have for fair Marion, who holds my heart imprisoned.*

Motetus: *Virgin of virgins, Light of lights, restorer of men, who didst* various ways. (1) It was a natural step to discard the original upper voices, and instead of putting words to one or more pre-existing melodies, to keep only the tenor and write one or more new melodies to go with it. This practice gave the composers much more freedom in the selection of texts, since they were able to set to music the words of any poem instead of having to choose or write one that would fit a given musical line; and as a further consequence, they had much greater possibilities for variety of rhythm and phrasing in the melodies. (2) Motets were written to be sung outside the church services, in secular surroundings; the upper voices of these motets were given a secular text, usually in the vernacular. Motets with French words in the upper voices still used a plainsong melody as *cantus firmus;* but as the *cantus firmus* served no liturgical function, there was no point in singing the original Latin text, so probably these tenors were played on instruments. (3) It had become customary before 1250 to use texts that were different in words, though related in meaning, for the two upper voices in a three-voice motet. Both texts might be in Latin, or both in French, or (rarely) one in Latin and the other in French. This kind of three-part motet with different texts (not necessarily in different languages) in the upper voices became standard in the second half of the thirteenth century, and the principle of polytextuality was even carried over sometimes into the ballade and virelai of the fourteenth century.

In the first half of the thirteenth century practically all the motet tenors had Latin texts taken from the repertoire of clausula tenors in the *Magnus Liber*. Since these clausulae had originally been written over melismatic portions of the chant, their texts at most consisted of only a few words, sometimes only a single word or even part of a word. Consequently, the motet tenors had very short texts—phrases such as *Haec dies, Domino, Quoniam, In seculum* (from the Easter gradual *Haec dies*), or perhaps a single syllable, such as *Go,* from the word *Virgo* in the Verse of the gradual *Benedicta et venerabilis es*. Even if the actual text were longer than a phrase, the motet manuscripts give only the incipit under the tenor line, probably on the assumption that if the piece was to be used in church the singers would know the rest of the words, and if elsewhere, the words were not needed. Tenors tended to be laid out in regular repetitive rhythmic patterns, such as those shown in Example III–8 (Nos. 5, 7, 8), the tenors of Example III–11, and the motet illustrated on pages 112–13.

After the middle of the thirteenth century, particularly after 1275, motet tenors were taken from sources other than the Notre Dame books; Kyries, hymns, and antiphons were used. After 1250, composers also began to use tenors taken from contemporary secular

---

bear the Lord: through *Thee, O Mary, let grace be given as the angel announced: Thou art Virgin before and after.*
Tenor: *This is the day [which the Lord hath made]*.

chansons and from instrumental estampies. Paralleling this broadening of the repertoire was a progressive relaxation in the way the rhythmic modal formulas were used, and hence an increasing rhythmic flexibility. Also, as the century went on composers acquired a more sophisticated feeling for continuity of line in the motet as a whole; instead of making the phrase endings of the motetus and triplum always coincide with the rests in the tenor pattern, they learned to begin and end phrases at different points in the different voices (as in Example III–12) and so avoid the "start-and-stop" effect which is noticeable in motets like Example III–11.

As a rule, the poems used as texts for motets were not of particularly high literary quality; they abound in alliteration, stereotyped images and expressions, extravagant rhyme schemes, and capricious stanza forms. Frequently, certain vowels or syllables are emphasized in all the voices either simultaneously or in echo fashion, so that a similarity of ideas in the texts is reinforced by a similarity of vowel sounds: notice, for example, in the motet *O mitissima —Virgo—Haec dies* (Example III–11) the persistent recurrence of the "i" of "dies" in the Latin texts of the two upper voices.

Motet texts

No attempt was made to express musically any emotional or pictorial connotations of the text, beyond such commonplace practices as suggesting upward or downward movement by ascending or descending passages, or breaking the melodic line with a rest to suggest sighing. However, just this absence of any close expressive correspondence made it possible to use the same melody for different sets of words, both sacred and secular. Thus Example III–11 occurs in one manuscript with sacred Latin words in the triplum, and in another manuscript with secular French words. There are many other cases of such transference in the thirteenth century. Despite their apparent differences, the combination of texts in a motet was not haphazard. In the early motets, the upper voice or voices were paraphrases of the tenor text; and in the later Latin motets, a similar connection of thought was usually maintained, a kind of counterpoint of ideas among the three texts paralleling the counterpoint of tones among the three melodies.

In the French motets—that is, motets with French words in both motetus and triplum—there was, naturally, seldom any connection between the texts of the upper voices and the Gregorian tenor, which functioned simply as a convenient, traditional, instrumentally performed *cantus firmus*. The two French texts were almost always love songs. The triplum was usually gay, and the motetus complaining, and both poems were usually in the style of the contemporary trouvère works, as in Example III–12.

The admixture of sacred and secular elements in a motet, however incongruous or even irreverent it may appear to us, must be understood from the medieval point of view, which recognized no such gulf between those two realms as exists in modern thought.

A motet was not one piece, but many, like a garment that serves different purposes according to the weather or the occasion. Any of the upper voices might be sung by itself as a solo melody. A motet like *Quant voi—Virgo—Haec dies* (Example III–11) could, by omitting the triplum, be performed as a sacred duet; by playing the tenor and motetus on vielles, it could be transformed into a secular solo with accompaniment.

The union of the voices was not a homogeneous ensemble like that of a modern trio or quartet; even when all were sounded together, each kept a certain detachment, not so much blended as juxtaposed, like figures in a medieval painting that exist on the same physical surface but not in the same visual space. The unity of the voice parts was conveyed by harmonic consonances, by the echoing of vowel sounds among the voices, and often also by more subtle means not immediately apparent to the senses—that is, by symbolical relations of ideas, relations that would have been grasped by a medieval listener more easily than by us. Such symbolical unity was felt to be strong enough to override even a difference of language between the motetus and the triplum. This is the case with *Quant voi—Virgo—Haec dies:* the tenor theme is from the gradual for Easter Sunday; Easter suggests spring; and spring, by universal agreement among poets, if not by an immutable law of nature, suggests love. From imagined love for an idealized shepherdess to spiritual love for the Mother of God was but a step—for medieval man a short step indeed: as earthly spring prefigured the eternal spring-time of the Resurrection, so earthly love was the analogue of divine love, and Marion the shepherdess an earthly image of Mary, Queen of Heaven. Once we understand such a habit of thought, we can understand how secular and sacred texts could be combined without either incongruity or irreverence.

A considerable number of French motets incorporate in one or more of their upper voices, usually at the end of the stanza, a *refrain,* a line or two of poetry which exists in identical form in other songs of the thirteenth century, and which therefore has the character of a quotation. The citation of refrains from other pieces became less frequent in motets of the second half of the century, and was typically restricted to motets with French tenors.

In early motets, the motetus and triplum were essentially alike in character: they intertwined in a moderately lively movement with similar slight modifications of a basic rhythmic mode, but remained practically indistinguishable as far as melodic style was concerned. In the later period, composers often sought to introduce distinctions in style not only between the upper voices and the tenor, but also between the two upper voices themselves. This kind of later motet is sometimes called *Franconian,* after Franco of Cologne, a composer and theorist who was active from about 1250 to 1280. The triplum had a longer text than the motetus, and was given a

The Franconian motet

EXAMPLE III–12   Motet: *Pucelete—Je languis—Domino*

M'a-mi-e - te la bru-ne - te, jo-li- e - te - ment Bele a - mi - e,

giés moi, douce a - mi - e Ces- te

qui ma vie en vo bail - lie A - vés te-nu - e tant,

ma - la - di - e Qu'a - mours

Je voz cri mer - ci en sous - pi - rant.

ne m'o - ci - e.

Triplum: *The fair maid, pretty, polite, and pleasing, the delightful one whom I desire so much, makes me joyful, gay, and loving. No nightingale in May sings so gaily. I shall love with all my heart my sweetheart, the fair brunette. Fair friend, who hast held my life in thy command so long, I cry you mercy, sighing.*
Motetus: *I languish with the sickness of love; I had rather that this kill me than any other illness; such death is very pleasant. Relieve me, sweet friend, of this sickness lest love kill me.*

rather fast-moving melody with many short notes in short phrases of narrow range; against this triplum, the motetus sang a comparatively broad, long-breathed, lyrical melody. A charming example of a Franconian style motet is *Pucelete—Je languis—Domina* (Example III–12). Each voice in this motet is in a different rhythmic mode. The tenor is in the fifth mode; the motetus moves for the most part in the ♩ ♩ pattern of the second mode; the triplum moves in a version of the sixth mode, with the first note broken into two shorter ones (♩ ♩ ♩ = ♫ ♩ ♩).

The musical contrast between the two upper voices in this piece is supported by the texts. The triplum is a chatty description of a lady's attractions, and the motetus a conventional plaint by her despairing lover. The tenor text, *Domino,* simply refers to the source of this melody (the setting of the word "Domino" in the chant *Benedicamus Domino*—see *Liber Usualis,* p. 124 or HAM, No. 28a) and has nothing to do with either motetus or triplum, since this part would have been played rather than sung.

Another development in the rhythm used in motets involved the tenor. In the middle thirteenth century, one of the most conspicuous traits of the motet was the tenor's rigid rhythmic scheme; indeed, much of the effect of freedom and freshness in the unsymmetrically-phrased triplum depended on its contrast with the more regularly laid out motetus and especially with the persistence of a strongly marked and unvarying tenor motive. Toward the end of the thirteenth century, however, even the tenor was sometimes written in a more flexible style approaching that of the other two parts. *Pucelete —Je languis—Domino* is an early example of the use of a freer tenor; the (instrumental) lowest voice, with its diversified phrasing and quiet movement, is assimilated into the texture, instead of standing out in aggressive isolation after the fashion of the earlier motet tenor.

The two tendencies just described—the one toward greater diversity and the other toward greater homogeneity of texture— were to a certain extent contradictory. By the late thirteenth century, they were not ordinarily found together in the same composition. Rather, the trend at this time was toward the emergence of two distinct types of motets: one with a fast, speech-like triplum, a slower motetus, and a Gregorian (though instrumentally performed) tenor in a strict rhythmic pattern; and the other, usually on a French secular tenor, in which all voices proceeded in more nearly equal rhythm, although the triplum was frequently most important melodically.

The first type of motet is often called after Petrus de Cruce (Pierre de la Croix), one of the few identifiable thirteenth-century composers, who was active from about 1270 to 1300. He wrote motets in which the triplum attained an unprecedented speed in comparison with the lower voices, the long notes being broken up into shorter and shorter values (see Example III–13; the entire piece is in HAM, No. 34). This necessitated slowing down the tempo. The breve (transcribed as ♩ in Example III–13), originally a "short" note as the name implies and normally in mid-thirteenth century taken at about M.M. 132, thus came by the end of the century to signify a duration closer to M.M. 60; and this in turn led eventually, as the process of metrical "inflation" continued in the fourteenth century, to the semibreve becoming the new unit of the beat.

It is probable that in a motet like Example III–13 both tenor and

EXAMPLE III–13   Motet: *Aucun—Lonc—Annun[tiantes]*,
Petrus de Cruce

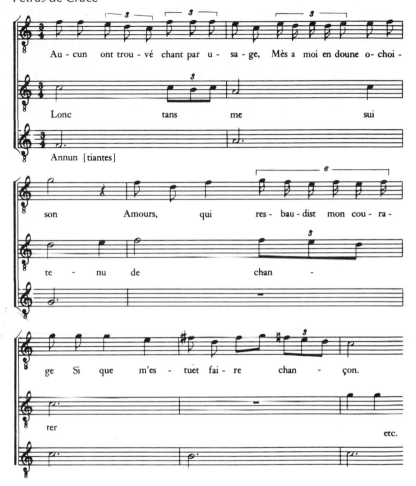

Triplum: *Some invent their song from habit, but it is love that gives me incentive, rejoicing my heart so that I must make a song.*
Motetus: *Long time have I refrained from singing.*

motetus were played on instruments, thus making the piece in effect a solo song with sustained accompaniment.

The motet with similar rhythm in all voices is illustrated in Example III–14, *On parole—A Paris—Frèse nouvele* (a complete transcription is in HAM, No. 33b). As is usual with French tenors, the lowest voice of this motet is to be sung, not played. The piece is a vocal trio celebrating the joys of life in the city of Paris; the tenor theme, repeated three times, may be a couple of Parisian street cries.

Changes in the rhythmic structure of the motet in the course of the thirteenth century were more extensive than changes in its harmonic vocabulary. In 1300, as in 1200, the fifth and octave were the accepted correct consonances for strong beats. The fourth had come more and more to be treated as a dissonance. Thirds were beginning to achieve theoretical status as consonances, though they were not actually being used much more often at the end of the century than they had been at the beginning. The harmonic rhythm of a motet was, at least after the middle of the century, that of the tenor part; that is to say, each note of the tenor carried its own chord, so that in works in the style of Petrus de Cruce, where the tenor notes were extremely long in comparison with those of the triplum, a characteristic contrast existed between a rapid melodic

EXAMPLE III–14   Motet: *On parole—A Paris—Frèse nouvele*

Triplum: *They speak of beating and winnowing and of digging and plowing, but these pastimes do not please me; for there is no life so good as to be at ease.*
Motetus: *At Paris, night and morning, one finds good bread and good clear wine, good meat and good fish, and all sorts of company.*
Tenor: *Fresh strawberries! Wild blackberries!*

movement and long-drawn-out harmonic changes. After 1250, cadences began to be written more often in forms that were to remain
standard for the next two centuries; these are given in Example
III–15.

EXAMPLE III–15   Cadence Forms

   Musicians and audiences of the thirteenth century gave much less
attention than we do to the harmonic or vertical dimension of music.
Provided the ear was satisfied by the recurrence of consonance at
the proper points, any degree of dissonance was tolerated between.
Passages like that in Example III–16 were not uncommon in motets
of four voices around the middle of the century; the strong-beat
dissonances (marked by asterisks) were justified by Franco's rule that
"he who shall wish to construct a quadruplum . . . ought to have
in mind the melodies already written, so that if it be discordant with
one it will be in concord with the others." Even in three-part writing
it was thought sufficient to make the triplum consonant with *either*
the motetus or the tenor on strong beats. Moreover, the dissonant
clashes practically always occurred casually as a result of the uninhibited progression of the various melodic lines.

EXAMPLE III–16   Passage from a Montpellier Motet

   The modern listener must also realize that the musical sounds produced by medieval performers were not the same as those produced
by modern instruments and voices. Singers and players probably

cultivated a comparatively light, clear, thin tone, free of the continuous vibrato which characterizes nearly all present-day musical sounds and which in itself precludes perfect accuracy of pitch; consequently, the texture of medieval music in performance would have been more transparent than anything we ordinarily experience.

Notation in the thirteenth century

Progress in rhythm in the thirteenth century was accompanied by changes in notation. As has been explained, the rhythmic organization of music in the first half of the century was based on the rhythmic modes, in which no note sign had a fixed value and the chief means of indicating a mode as well as variants within the modal pattern were the meter of the words or the use of ligatures. But now the rise of the motet created difficulties. Modal notation could still be used for the tenors, where either there were no words or else each single syllable was stretched out under a long melisma. But the texts of the upper voices of motets were often not in any regular meters; moreover, these texts were set syllabically, that is, with one syllable to one note. Ligatures were useless here because of the unbreakable rule that a ligature could never carry more than one syllable. It was necessary somehow to stabilize the relative durational values of the written notes so that a performer could easily tell what rhythm was demanded.

Franconian notation

Various ways to approach this ideal were proposed, but the codification of a practicable system was the work of Franco of Cologne, who in his *Ars cantus mensurabilis* (*The Art of Mensurable Music*), written sometime between 1250 and 1280, established rules for the time values of single notes, ligatures, and rests. Franco's system of notation remained in use through the first quarter of the fourteenth century and many of its features survived until the middle of the sixteenth century.

Franconian notation, like that of the rhythmic modes, was based on the principle of ternary grouping. There were four single-note signs: the double long: ■┐ ; the long: ■ ; the breve: ■ ; and the semibreve: ◆ . The basic time unit, the *tempus* (plural, *tempora*), was the breve. A double long always had the value of two longs; a long might be perfect (three *tempora*) or imperfect (two *tempora*); a breve normally had one *tempus,* but might under certain conditions have two, in which case it was called an *altered* breve; similarly the semibreve might be either *lesser* (1/3 of a *tempus*) or *greater* (2/3 of a *tempus*). Three *tempora* constituted a *perfection,* equivalent to a modern measure of three beats.

The main principles governing the relationships of the long and the breve are indicated in the following table, where the perfect long is transcribed as a dotted half-note:

¶ ¶ = 𝅗𝅥· | 𝅗𝅥·

¶ ∎ ¶ = 𝅗𝅥 𝅘𝅥 | 𝅗𝅥·   (First long imperfect)

¶ ∎ ∎ ¶ = 𝅗𝅥· | 𝅘𝅥 𝅘𝅥 | 𝅗𝅥·   (Second breve altered)

¶ ∎ ∎ ∎ ¶ = 𝅗𝅥· | 𝅘𝅥 𝅘𝅥 𝅘𝅥 | 𝅗𝅥·

¶ ∎ ∎ ∎ ∎ ¶ = 𝅗𝅥 𝅘𝅥 | 𝅘𝅥 𝅘𝅥 𝅘𝅥 | 𝅗𝅥·   (First long imperfect)

¶ ∎ ∎ ∎ ∎ ∎ ¶ = 𝅗𝅥 𝅘𝅥 | 𝅘𝅥 𝅘𝅥 𝅘𝅥 | 𝅘𝅥 𝅘𝅥   (Both longs imperfect)

¶ ∎ ∎ ∎ ∎ ∎ ∎ ¶ = 𝅗𝅥 𝅘𝅥 | 𝅘𝅥 𝅘𝅥 𝅘𝅥 | 𝅘𝅥 𝅘𝅥 | 𝅗𝅥·   (First long imperfect, last breve altered)

Any of these relationships could be changed by introducing a dot, which indicated a division between two perfections; for example:

¶· ∎ ¶ = 𝅗𝅥· | 𝅘𝅥 𝅘𝅥   (Second long imperfect)

¶ ∎· ∎ ¶ = 𝅗𝅥 𝅘𝅥 | 𝅘𝅥 𝅘𝅥   (Both longs imperfect)

¶ ∎· ∎ ∎ ¶ = 𝅗𝅥 𝅘𝅥 | 𝅘𝅥 𝅘𝅥 | 𝅗𝅥·   (First long imperfect, third breve altered)

¶ ∎ ∎· ∎ ¶ = 𝅗𝅥· | 𝅘𝅥 𝅘𝅥 | 𝅘𝅥 𝅘𝅥   (Second breve altered, second long imperfect)

Similar principles regulated the relations of the semibreve to the breve. In addition, Franco established signs for rests, and set down rules on how to recognize notes in ligatures as longs, breves, or semibreves.

The Franconian system allowed the breve to be divided into not more than three semibreves. When Petrus de Cruce began writing music in which four or more notes were to be sung within the time value of one breve, he simply used as many semibreves as he needed for the syllables of the text, sometimes indicating their grouping by dots. Thus, although values shorter than a lesser semibreve were actually in use by the end of the thirteenth century, there were at first no specific notational signs to represent them. Eventually, of course, a scheme of organization, with appropriate notation, was set up to apply to these groups of four or more semibreves.

One further notational change came about as a result of the evolution of thirteenth-century motet style. The earliest motets were written in score, like the clausulae from which they were derived. As the upper voices acquired longer texts, and as each syllable had to have a separate note-sign, composers and scribes soon found that

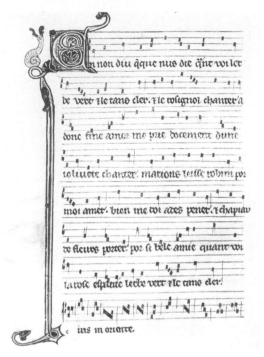

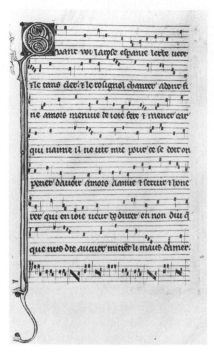

these voices took a great deal more room on the page than did the tenor, which had fewer notes and which, being melismatic, could be written in the compressed modal notation of ligatures. To write all the parts in score would mean that there would be long vacant stretches on the tenor staff, a waste of space and costly parchment (see Example III–13). Since the upper voices sang different texts, it was natural to separate them; and so in a three-voice motet, the triplum and the motetus came to be written either on facing pages or in separate columns on the same page, with the tenor on a single staff extending across the bottom. This arrangement may be seen in the illustrations above, which show the motet *En non Diu— Quant voi—Eius in oriente* in the original notation of the Mont-pellier and Bamberg Codices. (This piece is transcribed in MM, No. 10.) The writing of the voices in different places on the same or facing pages is called *choirbook* format, and was the usual way of notating polyphonic compositions after 1230 until the sixteenth century.

Other Late Thirteenth-Century Forms

The word *cantilena* was used in a loose sense by some late medieval writers to designate a whole class of secular songs, both monophonic and polyphonic. As a rule, polyphonic songs of this nature have a

(Left) Two facing pages of the motet En non Diu—Quant voi—Eius in oriente *as it appears in the Montpellier manuscript.*
(Right) The same motet as it appears in the Bamberg Codex.

single text, with the voice parts moving in uniform phrases and the chief melodic interest in the upper line or lines. Cantilena is defined in a more restricted sense in a treatise written at Paris about 1300 by Johannes de Grocheo, in which he describes the various forms and types of music currently in use. Under polyphonic music Johannes mentions, along with motet, organum, and conductus, a kind of "cut-up song" called *hocket*. (The word is thought to be derived from the Latin *ochetus,* literally "hiccup"). In hocket, the flow of melody is interrupted by the insertion of rests, generally in such a way that the missing notes are supplied by another voice so that the melody is divided between the voices (compare Webern's orchestration of the Ricercare from Bach's *Musical Offering;* the device also occurs in the music of some non-Western peoples). Passages in hocket occur occasionally in secular conducti and motets of the late thirteenth century and more frequently in the early fourteenth century. Pieces in which hocketing was used extensively were themselves called hockets. Such compositions might be either vocal or instrumental. A fast tempo is implied in an instrumental hocket; indeed, theorists distinguished three tempos: slow for motets in which the breve in the triplum was subdivided into many shorter notes (the Petrus de Cruce style motets); moderate for those in which there were not more than three semibreves in a breve (the Franconian motets); and fast, for hockets.

Two other forms of composition being written around 1300 were the *rota* and *rondellus*. The rota was simply a round or canon: the most famous example is *Sumer is icumen in,* which probably dates from about 1240. This piece, of English origin, shows many traits characteristic of English medieval music, especially its full chordal texture, its free use of thirds as consonances, and its distinct major tonality. Below the canon two tenors sing a *pes* ("foot," i.e. a repeated bass motive) with continuous interchange of the voices.

The *rondellus* was a song in which all parts were systematically interchanged by each voice singing every phrase in turn; in effect, therefore, each section was like a round, except that all the voices began together instead of entering one after another:

a	b	c		d	e	f
b	c	a		e	f	d
c	a	b		f	d	e

Summary

The period from the middle of the twelfth to the end of the thirteenth century may be regarded as a distinct epoch in the history of music. It is commonly known under the name of *ars antiqua* —the "old art" or manner of composing, so called by modern scholars in contrast to the *ars nova* or "new art" of the fourteenth century—and is chiefly remarkable for the rapid growth of polyphony and the rise of three types of polyphonic composition: organum and conductus in the Notre Dame period, to about 1250, and the motet in the second half of the thirteenth century. All this activity centered around Paris, so that for one hundred and fifty years all western European polyphonic music was dominated by French composers. The principal technical achievements of these years were the codification of the rhythmic modal system and the invention of a new kind of notation for measured rhythm—both examples of the growing tendency to make explicit the rational principles underlying the art of musical composition and to give the composer more control over the way in which his works were to be performed.

The spirit of the music was objective. Composers strove for a cool balance of musical elements within a strong formal framework, an ideal evident in all the essential characteristics of the music: adherence to the system of rhythmic modes with triple grouping of the beats; dependence on the Chant as the basis for composition; deliberately limited range of sound; strongly linear texture; an elemental harmonic vocabulary of fifths and octaves; and avoidance of chromaticism and other devices of merely sensuous appeal.

At the beginning of the thirteenth century practically all polyphonic music was sacred; by the end of the century, although there was yet no clear distinction between sacred and secular musical styles, polyphonic settings were being written for both sacred and secular texts. One polyphonic form, the late thirteenth-century motet, became, as it were, a microcosm of the cultural life of its time. The structure of the motet, with its motley concourse of love songs, dance tunes, popular refrains, and sacred hymns, all held together in a rigid formal mold based on Gregorian plainsong, is analogous to the structure of Dante's *Divine Comedy,* which likewise encompasses and organizes a universe of secular and sacred ideas within a rigid theological framework.

By the end of the thirteenth century, however, this neatly closed medieval universe was beginning to dissolve, to lose both its inner coherence and its power to dominate events. Signs of the dissolution appeared in the motet as in a mirror: gradual weakening of the authority of the rhythmic modes, relegation of the Gregorian tenor to a purely formal function, exaltation of the triplum to the status of a solo voice against the accompanying lower parts. The road was open to a new musical style, a new way of composing, in an age that was to look back on the music of the latter half of the thirteenth century as the old, the old-fashioned, the outdated way.

IV

French and Italian Music
of the Fourteenth Century

General Background

Comparatively speaking, the thirteenth century was an era of stability and unity, the fourteenth one of change and diversity. The chief symbol of the contrast was the state of the Papacy: in the thirteenth century the authority of the Church, centered in the Popes at Rome, was generally respected and acknowledged as supreme, not only in matters of faith and morals but also to a great extent in intellectual and political affairs; in the fourteenth century this authority, and especially the supremacy of the Popes, began to be widely questioned. For the greater part of the century—from 1305 to 1378—the Popes, in exile from the prevailing anarchy and tumults of Rome, resided at Avignon in southeastern France (the "Babylonian Captivity"); for a further thirty-nine years—until 1417—there were two and sometimes three rival claimants to the Papacy (the "Great Schism"). Criticism of this state of affairs, as well as of the often scandalous and corrupt life of the higher clergy, became increasingly sharp, and was expressed not merely in writings but also in various divisive and heretical movements that were the forerunners of the Protestant Reformation.

The thirteenth century witnessed the perfecting of a universal philosophy that reconciled revelation and reason, the divine and the human, the claims of the kingdom of God and those of the political states of this world, in one unbroken and harmonious order of thought. The philosophy of the fourteenth century, on the other hand, tended to regard human reason and divine revelation as disjunct, each restricted to and authoritative in its own sphere: the Church having the care of men's souls and the state looking out for their earthly concerns, but neither subject to the other. Thus were laid the ideological foundations for the separation of religion from science and of the Church from the State, doctrines which for good and ill have prevailed in our society since the close of the Middle Ages. *[margin note: Separation of church and state.]*

The centrifugal movement of fourteenth-century thought was paralleled by social trends: slackening of economic progress, and the economic dislocations caused by the terrible ravages of the Black Death (1348–50) and the Hundred Years' War (1338–1453) led to urban discontent and peasant insurrections; the growth of cities in the previous two hundred years had brought increased political power to the middle classes and caused a corresponding decline of the old feudal aristocracy. By the fourteenth century chivalry was becoming a mere form, a code of manners and ceremonies rather than a vital force. The medieval ideal of the political unity of Europe gave way before the actuality of separate, independent powers: France developed in the direction of a centralized absolute monarchy, and the Italian peninsula was divided into many little rival states—whose rulers, however, often emulated one another in their patronage of art and letters. *[margin note: France—more centralized authority]*

The increasing independence and importance of secular interests were shown in the continued growth of vernacular literature: Dante's *Divine Comedy* (1307),[1] Boccaccio's *Decameron* (1353) and Chaucer's *Canterbury Tales* (1386) are some of the great literary landmarks of the fourteenth century. The same period saw the beginnings of *humanism,* involving a renewal of the study of classical Latin and Greek literature, which was to be one of the most important influences in the later Renaissance. In painting, Giotto (ca. 1266–1337) made the first definitive break away from the formalized Byzantine style toward naturalistic representation of objects. Literature, education, and the arts alike participated in a movement away from the relatively stable, unified, religiously centered viewpoint of the thirteenth century toward absorption in the varied and changing phenomena of human life in this world. *[margin note: Secular Works]* *[margin note: Turn to Greek thought.]*

The change, of course, was slow; it was a gradual shift in emphasis, not a sudden reversal of values. Many tendencies and traits characteristic of the fourteenth century had appeared before 1300, and many features of the thirteenth century persisted for a long time after that date. Nor was the change necessarily or in all respects for the better. Every age preserves and develops some elements from the past,

---

[1] On the references to music in Dante, see Kathi Meyer-Baer, *The Music of the Spheres,* Appendix III, and the same author's "Music in Dante's *Divina Commedia*" in *Aspects of Medieval and Renaissance Music,* J. LaRue, ed., New York, 1966.

Giotto's art marks the beginning of the realistic movement in Italy. This fresco (dated 1350) in the Arena Chapel, Padua, shows Joachim and Anna at the Golden Gate.

but it also inevitably rejects others; whether the result in any given instance is an improvement or the reverse is a question that cannot always be decided with complete objectivity.

Musical background

Ars nova—the "new art" or "new technique"—was the title of a treatise written about 1316–18 by the French composer and poet Philippe de Vitry (1291–1361). The term was so apt that it has come to be used to denote the musical style which prevailed in France through the first half of the fourteenth century. Musicians of the time were quite conscious of striking out a new path, as is shown not only by the title of de Vitry's treatise but also by that of another French work, Jean de Muris's *Ars novae musicae (The Art of the New Music,* 1319). On the opposite side was a Flemish theorist, Jacob of Liège, who in his encyclopedic *Speculum musicae (The Mirror of Music,* ca. 1330) vigorously defended the "old art" of the late thirteenth century as against the innovations of the "moderns."

The chief technical points at issue were (1) acceptance in principle of the modern duple or imperfect division of the long, breve (and, eventually, semibreve) into two equal parts, as well as the traditional triple or perfect division into three equal (or two unequal) parts; and (2) the use of four or more semibreves as equivalent to a breve—already begun in the motets of Petrus de Cruce—and, eventually, of still smaller values.

The *Ars Nova* in France

It is typical for the fourteenth century that composers produced far more secular than sacred music. The motet, which had begun as a sacred form, had been to a great extent secularized before the end of the thirteenth century, and this trend continued. The earliest fourteenth-century musical document from France is a beautifully decorated manuscript, dating from 1316, of a satirical poem, the *Roman de Fauvel*. In one of the manuscripts of this work are interpolated about 130 pieces of music, constituting in effect an anthology of the music of the thirteenth and early fourteenth centuries. Most of the *Fauvel* pieces are monophonic, but the collection includes also 33 polyphonic motets. Among these, along with other examples of late thirteenth-century style, are several that introduce the new duple division of the breve. Many of the texts are denunciations of the clergy, and there are many allusions to contemporary political events. Such allusions were characteristic of the motet in the fourteenth century, as they had been of the conductus in an earlier period; and the motet in the fourteenth century came to be used as the typical form of composition for the musical celebration of important ceremonial occasions both ecclesiastical and secular, a function it retained through the first half of the fifteenth century.

Five of the three-part motets in the *Roman de Fauvel* are by Philippe de Vitry; at least five other motets of his are found in the Ivrea Codex, which was written about 1350. De Vitry appears to have been one of the outstanding composers of his time. His motet tenors are often laid out in segments of identical rhythm, on the same principle we have already encountered in some motets of the late thirteenth century (see Examples III–8 and 11); as in some earlier motets also, the rhythmic formula may be varied after a certain number of repetitions. But now, all this takes place on a much larger scale than before: the tenor is longer, the rhythms are more complex, and the whole line moves so slowly, so ponderously, under the faster notes of the upper voices that it is no longer recognizable as a melody, but functions rather as a foundation on which the piece is constructed.

As the fourteenth century went on, theorists and composers evidently began to think of such a motet tenor as being constituted by two distinct elements: the set of intervals, which they called the *color;* and the pattern of rhythm, called the *talea* (a "cutting" or segment). Color and *talea* might be joined in various ways: for example, if the two were of the same length, the *color* might be repeated with the *talea* in halved (or otherwise diminished) note values; or the *color* might consist of three *taleae,* and might then be repeated with the *taleae* in diminished values; or again, *color* and *talea* might be of such differing lengths that their endings did not coincide, so that some repetitions of the color would begin in the midst of a *talea.* Motets having a tenor constructed in some such way as these just described are called *isorhythmic* ("equal rhythm") motets. In some instances the upper voices as well as the tenor may be written isorhythmically (or "isometrically"), and the technique was also occasionally applied to compositions in other forms.

The isorhythmic motet

2 Color =
3 Talea

Example IV–1 shows the tenor of an isorhythmic motet. Since there are eighteen notes in the *color* and twelve in the *talea,* it takes three statements of the latter to make two of the former; consequently, the second and fourth statements of the *color* begin with the seventh note (disregarding rests) of the *talea.* After three *taleae* the entire pattern is repeated in halved note values. Furthermore, in the particular motet (given complete in Vol. II, pp. 119–22 of *Polyphonic Music of the Fourteenth Century*) both motetus and triplum are also isorhythmic.[2]

EXAMPLE IV–1 Tenor of Motet: *De bon espoir—Puisque la douce—Speravi,* Guillaume de Machaut

The basic idea of isorhythm, as we have seen, was not new in the fourteenth century; but during this period and on into the fifteenth century it came to be applied in ever more extended and complex ways. Isorhythm was a way of giving unity to long compositions which had no other effective means of formal organization. True, the interlocked repetitions of *color* or *talea,* extending over long stretches of the music, might be anything but obvious to the ear. Yet the isorhythmic structure, even if not immediately perceived, does

---

[2] An early example of a quasi-isorhythmic tenor may be seen in MM, No. 10 (transcribed from the illustration on page 112 above). The first half (nineteen notes) of the tenor chant melody (*Graduale,* p. 58) begins in the rhythm ♩ ♪♩ 𝄽. Starting with the second note of measure 7, this phrase of melody is repeated, this time however beginning on the second note of the tenor pattern, thus: ♪♪ 𝄾♩ ; in other words, *talea* and *color* are "out of phase" from measure 7 to the first note of measure 13. At measure 14 begins the eighteen-note second half of the tenor melody, repeated beginning at measure 20, both times in the rhythm ♩ ♪♩ 𝄾.

A miniature depicting a charivari; from the Roman de Fauvel, *an early fourteenth-century musical manuscript. Fauvel was a symbolic horse or ass whose name was made up from the first letters of Flaterie, Avarice, Vilanie, Variété, Envie, and Lascheté. (After Gérold)*

have the effect of imposing a coherent form on the entire piece; and the very fact of the structure's being concealed—of its existing, as it were, at least partially in the realm of abstraction and contemplation rather than as something capable of being fully grasped by the sense of hearing—would have pleased a medieval musician.

We have already seen how important such mystic, supra-sensory factors were in the organum of the thirteenth century, as evidenced by the retention of liturgical Gregorian themes in the tenor even when the original melody was so lengthened or rhythmically distorted as to be unrecognizable (see Examples III–6 and 9). The same delight in concealed meanings, sometimes extending to deliberate, capricious, almost perverse obscuring of the composer's thought, runs like a thread through late medieval and early Renaissance music.

We may think of this as a typically medieval propensity, but it is present also in other historical periods: one finds it in Bach, and in such a work as Alban Berg's *Wozzeck* (1925), concerning which the composer, after alluding to his incorporation of traditional musical forms, adds: "No one . . . no matter how aware he may be of the musical forms contained in the framework of the opera, of the precision and logic with which it has been worked out . . . pays any attention to the various fugues, inventions, suites, sonata movements, variations, and passacaglias about which so much has been written."[3] Berg's attitude is essentially the same as that of fourteenth-and fifteenth-century composers toward the use of the isorhythmic construction in their motets.

Guillaume de Machaut

The leading composer of the *ars nova* in France was Guillaume de Machaut (1304?–77), whose works were preserved in excellent manuscripts and have been published in modern editions. Machaut was born in the province of Champagne in northern France. He was educated as a cleric and took holy orders; at about the age of twenty he became secretary to King John of Bohemia, whom he accompanied on military campaigns over many parts of Europe. After King John's death at the battle of Crécy in 1346, Machaut entered the service of the French court and eventually ended his days in retirement as a Canon at Rheims. Machaut was famous not only as a musician but also as a poet. His musical works include examples of most of the forms that were current in his time, and show him as a composer of mingled conservative and progressive tendencies.

Most of Machaut's 23 motets were based on the traditional pattern: an instrumental liturgical tenor and different texts in the

[3] Postscript to W. Reich's "Guide to Wozzeck," *MQ*, 38 (1952), 21.

Guillaume de Machaut in his study. Amour is presenting to him his three children Doux Penser, Plaisance, and Espérance. A miniature by the Maître aux Bouqueteaux in a manuscript of Machaut's works.

two upper voices. They continue the contemporary trends toward greater secularity, greater length, and much greater rhythmic complexity. Isorhythmic structure sometimes involves the upper parts as well as the tenor. Considerable use is made of hocket in these motets, but the only work of Machaut's specifically called a "hocket" is an apparently instrumental three-part motet-like piece with an isorhythmic tenor whose melody came from the Gregorian intonation of the word "David" in an Alleluia verse.

Machaut's monophonic songs may be regarded as continuing the trouvère tradition in France. They comprise eighteen *lais,* a twelfth-century form similar to that of the sequence, and about twenty-five songs which he called *chansons balladées,* though the more common name for them is *virelai.* Characteristic of the virelai is the form *Abba . . . ,* in which *A* stands for the refrain, *b* the first part of the stanza (which is repeated) and *a* the last part of the stanza (which uses the same melody as the refrain). If there are several stanzas the refrain *A* is usually repeated only after the last stanza.

Machaut also wrote a few polyphonic virelais, with an accompanying instrumental tenor part below the vocal solo; in these he occasionally introduced the device of a musical rhyme between the endings of the two melodic sections.

It was in his polyphonic virelais, *rondeaux,* and ballades—the so-called "formes fixes"—that Machaut showed most clearly the progressive tendencies of the *ars nova.* The rondeau, like the virelai, made use of only two musical phrases, combined typically in the pattern *ABaAabAB* (capital letters indicate the refrain of the text). The rondeau form had great attraction for poets and musicians of the late Middle Ages. Many of the songs in Adam de la Hale's *Jeu de Robin et de Marion* are rondeaux, some of them polyphonic; and there are motet tenors from the thirteenth century which are in rondeau form. Machaut's *rondeaux* have a highly sophisticated musical content, and one of them is an often cited example of ingenuity. Its enigmatic tenor text—"Ma fin est mon commencement et mon commencement ma fin" ("My end is my beginning and my beginning my end")—means that the melody of the tenor is that of the topmost voice sung backward; the melody of the contratenor also illustrates the text, because its second half is the reverse of its first half.

One of Machaut's most important achievements was the development of the "ballade" or "cantilena" style. This style is exemplified in his polyphonic virelais and *rondeaux,* as well as in the forty-one *ballades notées,* so called to distinguish them from his poetic ballades without music. Machaut's ballades, whose form was in part a heritage from the trouvères, normally consisted of three or four stanzas, each sung to the same music and each ending with a refrain. Within each stanza the first two lines (or first two pairs of lines) had the same music, although often with different endings; the remaining lines within each stanza, together with the refrain, had a different melody, the ending of which might correspond to the ending of the first section. The formula for the ballade is thus similar to that of the *Bar* of the Minnesinger; it may be diagrammed *aabC*, in which *C* stands for the refrain.

Machaut wrote ballades with two, three, and four parts and for various combinations of voices with instruments; but the typical setting was for high tenor solo voice with two lower, more slowly moving instrumental parts. These instrumental parts, the tenor and the contratenor, were similar in melodic style and moved within the same range, constantly crossing; in effect they constitute a kind of accompaniment and support for the solo (see Example IV–2; the entire composition is transcribed in HAM, No. 45).

EXAMPLE IV–2   First section of Ballade: *Je puis trop bien,* Guillaume de Machaut

All too well can I compare my lady to the image Pygmalion made: it was of ivory, so beautiful, so peerless, that he loved it more than Jason did Medea.

The music is organized in distinct phrases, each ending with a definitive cadence. Most of the principal cadences take the form illustrated in Example III–15, but with the difference that now the cadences on **G** and **C** are chromatically altered so as to make them like the one on **F**: in other words, *both* the upper two notes of the penultimate three-note chord are brought within a half-step of their note of resolution, making in effect what could be called a double leading tone (to use modern terminology). In addition, various melodic and rhythmic ornamentations are sometimes introduced; one such ornamental cadence formula, in which the upper leading tone moves down to the sixth before rising to the tonic, became almost a mannerism in the music of the late fourteenth and early fifteenth centuries (see Example IV–3). This figure is sometimes called the *Landini cadence* after its supposed inventor, the fourteenth-century Italian composer Francesco Landini.

EXAMPLE IV–3   The "Landini Cadence"

Machaut: *Ballade*   Landini: *Ballata*

Filippo da Caserta: *Ballade*   Ciconia: *Mass*   Dufay: *Chanson*

Although we still hear many parallel fifths and many pungent dissonances in Machaut, the total effect is less strange to our ears than that of thirteenth-century music, owing to the pervading milder sonorities of the third and sixth and to the general sense of harmonic order. Most admirable is the finely-wrought, flexible melodic line in the solo voice, in which the new lyricism of the fourteenth century speaks with an accent of sincerity that often imparts warmth even to the stylized language of chivalric verse. Machaut himself declared that true song and poetry could come only from the heart (*Qui de sentiment non fait/son dit et son chant contrefait*), and once he sent a new composition to a friend with the message "I have *listened* to it several times and it pleases me right well."

The most famous musical composition of the fourteenth century is Machaut's *Messe de Notre Dame* (*Mass of Our Lady*), a four-part

IV. French and Italian Music of the Fourteenth Century

setting of the Ordinary of the Mass together with the dismissal formula *"Ite, missa est."* This was not the first polyphonic setting of the Ordinary; there had been a half-dozen more or less complete earlier cycles. But Machaut's is important because of its spacious dimensions and four-part texture (unusual at the time), because it is clearly planned as a musical whole, and because it is by any standard a first-rate work. In the twelfth and thirteenth centuries composers of polyphonic music had been chiefly interested in texts from the Proper of the Mass, for example the Graduals and Alleluias in Leonin's and Perotin's organa; they sometimes set parts of the Ordinary too, but when these pieces were performed together in one service, their selection and combination were fortuitous. No one seemed to care whether the Kyrie, Gloria, Credo, Sanctus, and Agnus Dei were in the same mode or based on the same thematic material or musically unified in any particular way. This attitude prevailed until about the second quarter of the fifteenth century; although fourteenth- and early fifteenth-century composers did write music for the Ordinary, they did not as a rule attempt to relate the different movements musically. In the manuscripts the different parts of the Mass were usually separated, all the Glorias being placed together, followed by all the Credos, and so on; the choirmaster could choose from these collections what he considered appropriate individual items for the complete Ordinary to be performed. Machaut's *Messe de Notre Dame,* therefore, insofar as he seemed to regard the five divisions of the Ordinary as one musical composition rather than separate pieces, was exceptional not only for its time but for the next seventy-five years as well. The means by which musical unity is achieved in this work are not easy to define; the relationship between movements is based on similarity of mood and general style rather than obvious thematic interconnections, although some commentators have called attention to the recurrence of a certain musical motive throughout the work:

EXAMPLE IV–4 Motive of Machaut Mass

The Kyrie, Sanctus, and Agnus Dei are based on Gregorian tenors and are wholly or partly isorhythmic. Both the Gloria and the Credo, probably because of the length of their texts, are given a straight conductus-like setting in syllabic style; their extraordinarily austere music, full of parallel progressions, strange dissonances, chromatic chords, and abrupt pauses, is organized in a free strophic form, a series of musical "stanzas" articulated by conspicuous similar cadences. For the most part the music of the Mass remains on a lofty, impersonal plane, without attempting to reflect any of the emotional suggestions implicit in the text. There is, however, one striking exception in the Credo: at the words "ex Maria Virgine" ("of the Virgin Mary") the movement suddenly slows to long-held chords, thus bringing this phrase into strong relief. In the Masses of later composers it became customary to set off this entire portion of the Credo, from the words "Et incarnatus est" ("And He was incarnate") through "et homo factus est" ("and He was made man"), by the same means, using a slower rhythm and more impressive style to emphasize these central statements of the Creed.

It is impossible to tell with certainty just how Machaut's Mass was meant to be performed. All the voice parts may have been doubled by instruments. It seems likely that the contratenor part, in view of its general melodic style and the fact that in some of the manuscript sources it has no text, was played rather than sung; in the isorhythmic movements, at least, the tenor part also may have been played on or doubled by an instrument. In the Gloria and Credo there are numerous short interludes, always for tenor and contratenor, that are almost certainly instrumental. But what instruments were used, and to what extent, we cannot say. Nor do we know for what occasion the work was written, despite a persistent but unfounded legend that it was for the coronation of the French King Charles V in 1364; whatever the occasion, it must have been one of unusual solemnity and magnificence.

Machaut was a typical fourteenth-century composer in that his sacred compositions formed only a small proportion of his total output. The relative decline in the production of sacred music in this period was due partially to the weakened prestige of the Church and to the ever increasing secularization of the arts. In addition, the Church itself had become critical of the use of elaborate musical settings in the service. From the twelfth century on, there had been numerous ecclesiastical pronouncements against complicated music and against displays of virtuosity by the singers. The burden of these complaints was twofold: it was objected, first, that such practices distracted the minds of the congregation and tended to turn the Mass into a mere concert; and second, that the words of the liturgy were obscured and the liturgical melodies made unrecognizable. One effect of this official attitude apparently was to discourage the composition of polyphonic church music in Italy. However, polyphony appeared there in connection with the practice of *alternatim* performance of the Ordinary of the Mass, where the choir would sing one phrase in plainsong and the organist would play the next phrase, adding a line of florid counterpoint above the notes of the chant. Furthermore, on occasion choirs improvised simple polyphony in discant style over the written notes of a chant. In this way they conformed literally to a degree of Pope John XXII, issued from Avignon in 1324, which permitted "on festal days or in solemn Masses and in the Divine Office, some concords (such as the octave, fifth, and fourth) that enrich the melody and which may be sung above the simple ecclesiastical chant, in such manner however that the integrity of the chant itself shall remain undisturbed."

Composition of motets and Mass sections meanwhile continued to develop mainly in France. Sometimes a particular section in a Mass would be written in the style of a motet with an instrumental tenor, sometimes as a choral conductus-like movement with text in all the voices. In addition to these two styles, both of which had been used by Machaut, composers of the later fourteenth and early fifteenth centuries wrote Masses and hymns in cantilena style—that is, for solo voice, usually with two accompanying instrumental parts. A few Masses and hymns made use of a liturgical *cantus firmus;* for example, a Gregorian Kyrie might be adapted as the tenor of a polyphonic Kyrie in motet style, or a Gregorian hymn, more or less ornamented, might appear as the upper voice in a ballade-like setting of the same text.

Italian Trecento Music

Italian music in the fourteenth century (the "trecento") has a history different from that of French music in the same period, due mostly to differences in the social and political climate. Conditions of virtual anarchy in much of the Italian peninsula and especially in the city of Rome contrasted with the increasing power and stability of the French monarchy. There was no tradition of polyphony in Italy, nothing comparable to the thirteenth-century organum and motet in France. So far as can be ascertained, all music in Italy up to the fourteenth century, and the bulk of it even then, was monophonic. At the courts, Italian *trovatori* of the thirteenth century had followed in the footsteps of the troubadours. Folk singing of course there had been in Italy as elsewhere, all through the Middle Ages, often associated with instruments and dancing; but none of this music has been preserved. Only the monophonic *laude,* the processional songs already mentioned (p. 70), have come down to us in manuscripts. Polyphony in Italian church music of the fourteenth century, as we have said, was largely a matter of improvisation. The Italians at this time seemed allergic to erudite styles of composition. They had no use for the *cantus firmus* technique and were but little interested in the structural complexities of the motet. The Italian spirit expressed itself rather in spontaneous, flowing melodies and comparatively simple textures.

The principal centers of Italian fourteenth-century music were in the central and northern part of the peninsula, notably at Bologna,

Padua, Modena, Perugia, and above all at Florence, a particularly important cultural center from the fourteenth through the sixteenth centuries. Florence is the scene of two celebrated works of literature, the *Decameron* of Boccaccio and the *Paradiso degli Alberti* of Giovanni da Prato. From these writings and others of the time we learn how music, both vocal and instrumental, accompanied nearly every activity of Italian social life. In the *Decameron,* for example, each of the company varies the day's round of stories with singing and dancing:

> The tables being cleared away, the queen bade bring instruments of music, for that all the ladies knew how to dance, and also the young men, and some of them could both play and sing excellent well. Accordingly, by her commandment, Dioneo took a lute and Fiammetta a viol and began softly to sound a dance; whereupon the queen and the other ladies . . . struck up a round and began with a slow pace to dance a brawl; which ended, they fell to singing quaint and merry ditties.
> . . . Emilia, by the queen's commandment, leading the round, the ditty following was sung by Pampinea, whilst the other ladies responded. . . . After this they sung sundry other songs and danced sundry dances and played upon divers instruments of music.[4]

It is possible that some of the music to which Boccaccio refers was polyphonic; but if so, the polyphony was probably either improvised or performed from memory. Very few actual examples of Italian polyphony have been preserved which can be dated earlier than about 1330. After that date, however, the stream flows more abundantly, as evidenced by several fourteenth-century manuscripts written either in Italy or southern France. The most copious source —though unfortunately late and not altogether reliable—is the magnificent Squarcialupi Codex, so called from its former owner, the Florentine organist Antonio Squarcialupi (1416–80). This codex, which was copied probably about 1420, is now in the Medicean Library at Florence. Written on vellum and richly ornamented in bright colors, it contains 352 pieces, mostly for two and three voices, by twelve composers of the fourteenth and early fifteenth centuries. A miniature portrait of each composer appears at the beginning of the section containing his works.

Three types of secular Italian composition are represented in the Squarcialupi Codex and the earlier manuscripts: *madrigal, caccia,* and *ballata.* The fourteenth-century madrigal, one of the first polyphonic genres to be cultivated in Italy, has many traits that suggest some historical connection with the French thirteenth-century polyphonic conductus. Madrigals were usually written for two voices; their texts were idyllic, pastoral, amatory, or satirical poems of two or three three-line stanzas. The stanzas were all set to the same

The madrigal

---

4 *Decameron,* Day I, Prologue; tr. John Payne, 1931.

music; at the end of the stanzas an additional pair of lines, called the *ritornello,* was set to different music with a different meter. Both voices had the same text and both apparently were meant to be sung, perhaps with instrumental doubling. Although the two melodic lines flowed in similar smooth vocal style, the upper was embellished with melismatic passages; the longest of these were placed—as in the conductus—at the beginning and just before the principal cadences, though similar shorter passages might occur elsewhere too.

The caccia

The caccia is another form which may have owed something to foreign examples. In fourteenth-century France there was a type of piece called a *chace,* with lively pictorial-descriptive words and a melody of popular cast designed to be sung in strict canon. Similar pieces are found in a Spanish manuscript, the *Llibre Vermell,* written about 1400. The Italian caccia, which seems to have flourished chiefly from 1345 to 1370, was likewise canonic, for two equal voices at the unison; but it usually had also, unlike the French and Spanish examples, a free supporting instrumental part in slower movement below. Its poetic form was irregular, though many *cacce,* like madrigals, had a ritornello, which was not always in canonic style. Both the French and Italian words have the same meaning: "hunt" or "chase." As the name of a type of composition, they have also a punning sense, alluding to the canon (Latin *fuga,* "flight") and also, in the case of the caccia, to the subject matter of the text, which typically described a hunt or some other scene of animation, such as a fishing party, a bustling market-place, a party of girls gathering flowers, a fire, or a battle. Vivid realistic details—shouts, bird songs, horn calls, exclamations, dialogue—all are brought out with spirit and humor in the music, often with the aid of hocket and echo effects. Similar realistic devices were sometimes taken over into the Italian madrigal and ballata, as they had been also into the French virelai.

Composers in the fourteenth century had what seems to us a strange attitude toward the use of imitation as a technique. They either wrote strict canons or eschewed systematic imitation almost entirely. Canons, especially in the form of "rounds," have always been a favorite musical form for convivial social entertainment (compare the English seventeenth-century *catch*—a word probably derived from "caccia"); composers' use of canon in the fourteenth-century chace and caccia was undoubtedly a reflection of contemporary popular practice, comparable in its way to the light-hearted convivial canons of Purcell, Mozart, and other later composers. Canons are found sporadically in Italian madrigals and *ballate;* but continuous systematic free imitation, pervading all the voices of a composition, does not come into general use before the last part of the fifteenth century.

The polyphonic ballata, the third type of Italian secular fourteenth-century music, flourished later than the madrigal and caccia, and showed some influence of the French ballade style. Originally the word ballata signified a song to accompany dancing (Italian *ballare*, to dance); the thirteenth-century *ballate* (of which no musical examples have survived) were monophonic dance songs with choral refrains. The ballata form was used for the lauda, and in this connection lost some of its dance characteristics, though in Boccaccio's *Decameron* the ballata or "ballatetta" is still associated with dancing. A few early fourteenth-century monophonic *ballate* have been preserved, but most of the examples in the manuscripts are for two or three voices, and date after 1365. These purely lyrical, stylized, polyphonic *ballate* resemble in form the French virelai. They have a two-line refrain (*ripresa*) which was sung at both the beginning and the end of a six-line stanza. The first two pairs of lines in the stanza (which were called the *piedi*) had their own musical phrase, while the last pair (the *volta*) used the same music as the refrain.

The ballata

The leading composer of *ballate* was Francesco Landini (1325–97), the foremost Italian musician of the fourteenth century. Blind from boyhood as a result of smallpox, Landini nevertheless became a well-educated man, an esteemed poet (like Machaut and de Vitry), and a master of the theory and practice of music; a virtuoso on many instruments, he was especially known for his skill at the organetto, a small portative organ, which he played "as readily as though he had the use of his eyes, with a touch of such rapidity (yet always observing the measure), with such skill and sweetness that beyond all doubt he excelled beyond comparison all organists who can possibly be remembered."[5]

Francesco Landini.

How was it performed

Landini is one of the principal characters in Giovanni da Prato's *Paradiso degli Alberti*. This book, though not written before 1425, purports to record scenes and conversations from the year 1389; among the short stories (*novelle*) contained in it—stories set in a framework similar to that of Boccaccio's *Decameron* and Chaucer's *Canterbury Tales*—is one supposed to have been related by Landini himself. At another place in the *Paradiso* the following agreeable incident is recorded:

> Now the sun rose higher and the heat of the day increased, and the whole company remained in the pleasant shade; and as a thousand birds were singing among the verdant branches, someone asked Francesco [Landini] to play the organ a little, to see whether the sound would make the birds increase or diminish their song. He did so at once, and a great wonder followed: for when the sound began many of the birds were seen to fall silent, and gather around as if in

[5] From an account by a fourteenth-century Florentine chronicler, Filippo Villani.

amazement, listening for a long time; and then they resumed their song and redoubled it, showing inconceivable delight, and especially one nightingale, who came and perched above the organ on a branch over Francesco's head.[6]

Landini wrote no music to sacred texts. His extant works comprise about 90 two-part and 50 three-part *ballate,* besides a couple of cacce and a dozen madrigals. The two-part *ballate* are evidently early works; their style in general resembles that of the madrigals, save that the melodic line is more ornate. Many of the three-part *ballate* are, like the French ballades, for solo voice with two accompanying parts. The ripresa of a Landini ballata is given in Example IV–5; the entire piece appears in HAM, No. 53.

Performance

It should be stressed that there was no uniform, fixed way of performing this or indeed any other music of the fourteenth century. The fact that one part lacks a text is not conclusive evidence for regarding it as instrumental, since another manuscript may show the same part furnished with words; and conversely, the presence of a text does not always imply exclusively vocal performance. We may suppose, however, that the tenor parts of Landini's *ballate* and Machaut's ballades, with their long notes, frequent wide skips, and customary notation with many ligatures (which precludes syllabic rendition of a text, since it was a rule that only one syllable might be sung to a ligature), were conceived as primarily instrumental. The contratenor parts were evidently composed after the superius (the highest part) and tenor, with the purpose of completing the harmonic sonority. For the contratenor, again, we may often suppose an instrumental rendition; but many contratenors are equally suitable for singing, and many are furnished with texts. The superius is always vocal in character, and often quite florid. But this part also could have been played; the description quoted above of Landini's rapid manner of playing the organetto suggests a style of playing to which the superius parts of his madrigals and some of his *ballate* would be quite adaptable. Furthermore, we must keep in mind the likelihood of instrumental doubling (perhaps with added embellishments) of a sung melody and also the possibility of alternation of instrument and voice; for example, the florid melismas at the beginning and end of a madrigal may have been played and the rest of the part sung, and both conceivably by the same performer. Finally, evidence exists that vocal pieces were sometimes played entirely instrumentally, with added embellishments in the melodic line. This instrumental art of embellishment was largely one of improvisation, but sometimes such pieces were written down; thus the Robertsbridge Codex of about 1325 has organ arrangements of three motets, and the Faenza Codex from the first quarter of the fifteenth century contains, in addition to keyboard pieces based on

---

[6] *Il Paradiso degli Alberti,* A. Wesselofsky, ed., Bologna, 1867, III, 112–13.

EXAMPLE IV–5   Ripresa of Ballata: *Amor c'al tuo suggetto,*
Francesco Landini

A - mor, c'al   tuo   sug- get- to o- mai da' le - - - - na, Sot - to tu - o gio - go vi - vo san - ça pe - - - na.

Love, who to thy slave now givest life, under thy yoke I live with-out suffering.

plainchant for parts of the Mass, ornate keyboard versions of Machaut's ballades and of madrigals and *ballate* by Italian fourteenth-century composers, including Landini.

One of the charms of Landini's music, in addition to the graceful vocal melody, is the suavity of the harmonies. There are no parallel seconds and sevenths, such as abounded in the thirteenth century, and few parallel fifths and octaves. Full triad sonorities are plentiful, though they are never used as either first or final chords. Landini's three-part madrigal *Sy dolce non sonò* is exceptional in being constructed on an isorhythmic tenor, and one senses that the composer was not entirely at ease with this difficult technique. On the other hand, in *De dimmi tu* a canon at the fifth between tenor and contratenor does not constrain him in the least; this madrigal, in fact, is one of Landini's most beautiful compositions.

Toward the end of the fourteenth century the music of Italian composers began to lose its specific national characteristics and to be absorbed into the contemporary French style. The trend was noticeable especially after the return of the Papal Court from Avignon to Rome in 1377. Italians wrote songs to French texts and in French forms, and their works often appear in late fourteenth-century manuscripts in French notation. Still another factor entered the situation at this time, one whose eventual importance could not have been foreseen. About the year 1390 the composer and theorist Johannes Ciconia (ca. 1340–1411) came from Liège and settled at Padua; there and in the neighboring city of Venice he had a very successful musical career. As it turned out, Ciconia was the first of a long line of Netherlandish, French, English, and (later) Spanish musicians who flocked to Italy in the course of the fifteenth century. They were welcomed—some of them so warmly, indeed, that for many years practically every important musical post in that country was held by a foreigner. Unquestionably, the music these men wrote was strongly influenced by what they heard and learned in Italy; but the Italian contribution, though very important, was chiefly indirect. No native Italian composer of first rank arose in the fifteenth century. As far as the record tells, Italian music—in the sense of a distinctive national style such as existed in the *trecento*—might be said to have gone underground for a hundred years, to emerge once more into the light of history only at the beginning of the sixteenth century.

French Music of the Late Fourteenth Century

It is a paradox typical of the time that the Papal Court at Avignon was a more important center for secular than for sacred music. Here and at other courts in southern France a brilliant chivalric society flourished, providing a congenial environment for the work of many late fourteenth-century French and Italian composers. Their music consisted chiefly of ballades, virelais, and *rondeaux* for solo voice with supporting instrumental tenor and contratenor parts. Most of the texts were probably written by the composers themselves. Some of the ballades include reference to contemporary events and personages, but the majority of all the pieces are love songs. Many of them are works of refined beauty, with sensitive melodies and delicately colored harmonies, examples of aristocratic art in the best sense of the word. Their musical style is matched by the visual appearance of some pages in the manuscripts, with their fanciful decorations, intermingled red and black notes, ingenious complications of notation, and occasional caprices such as the writing of a love song in the shape of a heart (see illustration below) or a canon in the shape of a circle.[7]

Comp. of French compared to Italian Music.

7 See facsimiles of both in MGG II, plate 55; color facsimiles of other pages from the famous Chantilly manuscript of the late fourteenth century are in MGG I, plate 28; II, plate 34; Apel, *Notation*, facsimile 83, p. 413.

Belle bonne, *the splendid "Musical Heart" by Baude Cordier from the Chantilly Codex, ca. 1400.*

IV. French and Italian Music of the Fourteenth Century

Rhythm

One feature of French secular music of this period is a remarkable rhythmic flexibility. The solo melody in particular exhibits the most subtle nuances: the beat is subdivided in many different ways, and the line of the phrase is broken by pauses in hocket, or held in suspense through long-continued syncopation—as though the composers had tried to capture and fix in notation the free, rubato-like delivery of a singer. This flexibility is illustrated in Example IV–6; the leisurely melodic line reflects the opening words of the ballade text: "En attendant"—"While waiting." (The entire piece appears in HAM, No. 47 and in Apel, *French Secular Music,* No. 49)

EXAMPLE IV–6   Beginning of Ballade: *En attendant,* Jacob de Senleches

For the original notation, see Apel, *The Notation of Polyphonic Music,* 1953, facsimile 87, p. 423. This page is from the manuscript at Modena, Bib. Estense, L. 568, fol. 39v; the piece is also found in the Chantilly manuscript No. 68 on fol. 44v.

Rhythmic complexity penetrates the very texture of all this late fourteenth-century French music: voices move in contrasting meters and in contrasted groupings within the beat; harmonies are refracted and purposely blurred through suspensions and syncopations. No doubt sometimes the fascination of the technique caused it to be carried to extremes that degenerated into mannerism; but, properly used, it was an indispensable element of the style. Example IV–7 (the two lowest staves are merely a reduction of the parts, not an accompaniment) shows a typical phrase from a rondeau by Anthonello da Caserta, a late fourteenth-century Italian composer who may be said to have excelled the French at their own game. Here the syncopation gives the effect of a delayed entrance by the soloist; the rhythmic subtlety of the passage is of an order not to be matched in any other music before the twentieth century, yet everything falls logically into place. Noteworthy is the delightful effect of the sixth at measure 2, the coquettish hesitation between Bb and B♮ after the first rest in the solo part, and the way in which the contratenor sounds now above, now below the tenor, so that the real bass of the harmony is in first one then the other of these voices, and is sometimes revealed in one by the cessation of the other (marked in the example by an asterisk). We may imagine the sheer variety of sonorities resulting from these two lower parts being played on instruments of contrasting timbres—say a trombone for the tenor and an English horn or a viola for the contratenor, with a recorder doubling the voice in the superius.

Since most of the phrase quoted in Example IV–7 is a melisma, the text has been omitted. The entire composition may be found in Apel's *French Secular Music of the Late Fourteenth Century*, No. 29. Accidentals below or above the notes are not in the original. The so-called "partial signatures"—different signatures in different voices—were common in the fourteenth and fifteenth centuries.

The sophisticated music of the southern French courts was designed for auditors of exceptional cultivation and performers of professional skill. Its formidable rhythmic and notational complexities began to go out of fashion by the end of the fourteenth century. Meanwhile, contemporary with developments in the south, in the latter part of the century a simpler type of secular polyphony existed in northern France, cultivated by guilds of musicians who were in a sense heirs of the trouvère tradition. Their poems had a popular character: instead of the polished sentiments of courtly love, they offered realistic scenes of the hunt and the marketplace, sometimes introducing imitations of bird songs. The music had a corresponding liveliness and freshness, with vigorous straightforward rhythms like those of folksong. It is probable that this simpler art flourished more widely than the few examples preserved in fourteenth-century manuscripts would suggest. Whether it had any influence on composers in the south of France is doubtful.

Chromaticism and *Musica Ficta*

A special flavor is imparted to much fourteenth-century music, both French and Italian, by the use of chromatically altered notes. Chromatic alteration was common at cadences in which otherwise there would have been a whole step between the seventh note of the modal scale and its upward resolution to the final, as for instance at a cadence on D, illustrated in Example IV–8a and b. This species of chromatic alteration was enjoined by a rule that the interval of a third contracting to a unison must be made minor, and a sixth expanding to an octave must be made major. As a rule in cadences of the type shown in Example IV–8b, *both* the upper two notes of a penultimate three-note chord would be raised, thus making what we have called a double leading tone—Example IV–8c. Cadences on G and C were altered similarly to those on D (see Example IV–3, and compare Example IV–2, measures 8 and 15). Cadences on E,

IV. French and Italian Music of the Fourteenth Century

EXAMPLE IV–7   Rondeau: *Dame zentil*, Anthonello da Caserta

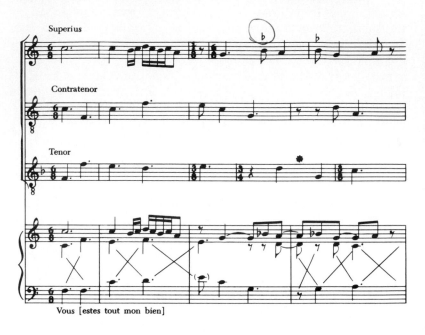

Vous [estes tout mon bien]

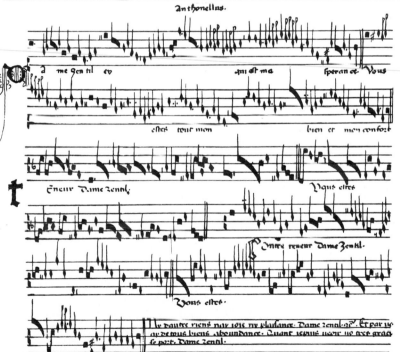

The sharp near the end of line one in the original above belongs with the B, not the C; it signifies that the note is *mi,* that is, B-natural. (Ms. Modena, Bib. Estense, L. 568, fol. 38v., *ca.* 1410)

however, usually remained in their unaltered modal form—Example IV–8d.

EXAMPLE IV–8   Chromatic Alteration at Cadences

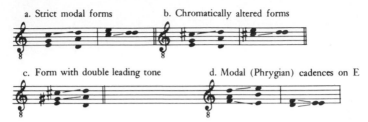

a. Strict modal forms

b. Chromatically altered forms

c. Form with double leading tone

d. Modal (Phrygian) cadences on E

Elsewhere than at cadences, chromatic alteration was used in order to avoid sounding a diminished fifth or an augmented fourth above the lowest note of a chord, and especially to avoid in a melody the tritone interval F–B♮, which later came to be called *"diabolus in musica,"* the devil in music. Chromatics might also be introduced to make a smoother melodic line, or for no other reason than *"causa pulchritudinis,"* simply because they sounded well—literally, "for the sake of beauty"; but for this, of course, no rules could be given.

Chromatic alterations in fourteenth-century music would make no difficulty for modern performers if only the composers or scribes had been considerate enough to write them down in the manuscripts. Unfortunately for us, they did not always do so, and even when they did they were not always consistent: the same passage may be found in different manuscripts with different written accidentals. Furthermore, accidentals might be omitted in the score and singers and players left to make the necessary alterations according to the rules—or, as it might happen, according to their own fancy. Since in this way notes might be introduced that were not provided for in the Guidonian system (see page 60), the result was called *musica ficta* or *musica falsa*—"fictitious" or "false music." Manuscripts of the fourteenth and early fifteenth centuries, especially the Italian ones, are relatively well supplied with accidentals, but after 1450 they largely disappear; and it is still not certain whether this reflected a real change in the sound—a reversion to the purity of the diatonic modes —or whether (as is more likely) it was simply a matter of notation, and the performers continued to apply chromatic alterations as before. In view of these uncertain factors a careful modern editor will not insert any accidentals in this music that are not found in the original sources, but will indicate, usually above or below the staff, those that he believes were applied by the performers.

Notation

Obviously, anything like a detailed description of fourteenth-century notation is beyond the scope of this book. We shall try to indicate only some of the main principles that guided Italian and French musicians in working out a notation for the new alternative duple or triple subdivision of longer notes, the introduction of many new short note values, and the great rhythmic flexibility which marked music of the latter part of the century.

The basis of the Italian system was described by Marchetto da Padua in his *Pomerium* of 1318. (This section is translated in SR, 160–71 [SRA, 160–71].) Briefly, the method consisted in dividing semibreves into groups set off by dots, supplemented by certain letter signs to indicate the various combinations possible in duple and triple subdivisions and by newly invented note forms to mark exceptions to the general rules of grouping and to express shorter note values. This kind of notation, particularly convenient as it was for florid melodic lines, served well for Italian music until the latter part of the century; by then it began to be supplemented and was eventually replaced by the French system, which had proved itself better adapted to the musical style of that time.

The French system was an extension of Franconian principles. The long, the breve, and the semibreve could each be divided into either two or three notes of the next smaller value. The division of the long was called *mood*, that of the breve *time*, and that of the semibreve *prolation*; division was *perfect* if it was triple, *imperfect* if duple. Two new note forms were introduced to indicate values shorter than the semibreve: the *minim* ♩, one-half or one-third of a semibreve; and the *semiminim* ♪, one-half of a minim. The framework of the system thus was as follows:

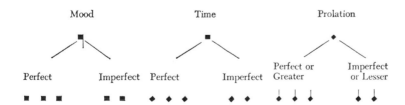

Eventually the original signs for perfect and imperfect mood were dropped and simplified signs for time and prolation were combined: a circle indicated perfect time and a half-circle imperfect time; a dot inside the circle or half-circle indicated greater prolation, and the absence of a dot lesser prolation thus:

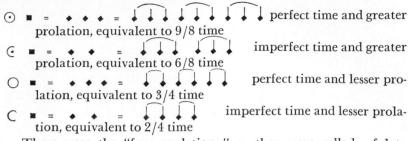

These were the "four prolations," as they were called, of late medieval music theory.

The half-circle ⊂, has come down to us as the modern sign for 4/4 time. Our ₵ with its corresponding designation "alla breve," is a relic of the late medieval and renaissance system of "proportions" whereby the unit of movement (the "beat") could be transferred from the normal note values to other note values in an indicated ratio—in this case, in the ratio 1 : 2, thus transferring the beat from the usual semibreve to the breve.

About 1425 all the forms pictured above began to be written as "white" notes, that is with black outlines unfilled (⌐ ▢ ◇ ♩); the semiminim became ♩, and shorter notes were devised *ad libitum* by adding flags to the semiminim (♪ ♫ ♫ etc.). These are essentially the forms of present-day notes; the change from diamond-shaped to rounded heads took place toward the end of the sixteenth century.

In addition to the signs shown above, the French notation employed other devices. They used dots, though not always with the same meanings as in Italian scores. Red notes served to show perfection or imperfection where the normal reading would indicate the opposite interpretation, to show that the notes were to be sung at half (or some other fraction) of their normal value, and for a multitude of other purposes. "White" note forms were used with similar special meanings. The different voices might be notated with different prolational signatures, and signatures might be frequently changed in one and the same voice line. Occasionally, the different prolations were also used for a shorthand notation of canons where the imitating voice or voices proceeded at a different rate from that of the leading voice: the melody would be written only once, but provided with two or more different time signatures. Such "mensuration canons" became more common in the fifteenth and sixteenth centuries, as we shall see. Fourteenth-century composers also worked out ingenious ways to indicate syncopation, which was a prominent feature in some melodic lines in the latter part of the century (see Example IV–7).

Instruments

A full and accurate account of instrumental music in the fourteenth and fifteenth centuries is impossible, for the simple reason that the music manuscripts practically never tell even whether a given part is instrumental or vocal, let alone specify the instruments. If composers had had in mind some particular combination of voices and instruments, there was no reason why they should not have marked it clearly on the page. The fact that they did not do so probably means that they were content to rely on custom or tradition for the manner of performing their music, and did not feel that specific directions were needed.

We know from pictorial and literary sources that the most usual way of performing polyphonic music in the fourteenth and early fifteenth centuries was with a small vocal and instrumental ensemble, normally with only one voice or one instrument to a part. There is also some evidence to suggest that, in pieces in cantilena style, the solo voice part was simultaneously played on an instrument which added embellishments, thus making heterophony. We can be fairly sure that certain parts, such as the Latin tenors in isorhythmic motets and the textless tenors in Landini's three-part *ballate,* were instrumental rather than vocal. But beyond a few general principles like these we can discern no uniform rules; apparently performances varied according to circumstances, depending on what singers or players happened to be at hand, or on the taste or caprice of the performers.

For out-of-doors music, for dancing, and for especially festive or solemn ceremonies, larger ensembles and louder instruments were employed; the fourteenth-century distinction betwen "high" (*haut*) and "low" (*bas*) instruments referred not to pitch, but to loudness. The low instruments most used in this century were harps, vielles, lutes, psalteries, portative organs, flutes, and shawms; among the high instruments were horns and trumpets. Percussion instruments, including small bells and cymbals, were common in ensembles of all kinds. The prevailing quality of tone was clear, bright, or shrill; instruments, if one may judge from the art of the time, were grouped not in families of homogeneous timbre (like a string quartet, for example), but in contrasting colors, such as viol, lute, harp, and trombone; or viol, lute, psaltery, flute, and drum. Crescendo and diminuendo were probably unknown. Although polyphonic vocal music was probably never sung unaccompanied in this period, motets and other vocal pieces were sometimes performed with instruments alone. There was also, of course, a large repertoire of instrumental dance music, but as these pieces were generally either improvised or played from memory, not many written examples have been preserved.

The earliest keyboard instruments of the clavichord and harpsichord type were invented in the fourteenth century, but do not seem to have come into common use until the fifteenth century. In addition to the portative organ or organetto, there were positive organs; and large organs were being installed in an increasing number of churches. A pedal keyboard was added to organs in Germany toward the end of the fourteenth century. A mechanism of stops enabling the player to select different ranks of pipes at will, and the addition of a second keyboard, were achievements of the early fifteenth century.

Summary

One of the most striking characteristics of the fourteenth century was the massive transfer of emphasis from sacred to secular composition. Corresponding to this shift of interest, and partly as a consequence of it, we see innovations in general musical style. Most obvious among these is the greater diversity and freedom of rhythm, carried by some late composers to almost fantastic extremes. Throughout the fourteenth century there is also a growing sense of harmonic organization, a definite planning of progressions to center about certain tonal areas. The "imperfect" consonances—thirds and, to a lesser degree, sixths—begin to occur more often on strong beats, though the final sonority is still always a unison, octave, or empty fifth. Passages of parallel thirds and sixths appear, while parallel fifths and octaves become rarer. Chromatic alteration by means of *musica ficta* helps to stabilize cadential points and give more flexibility to the melodic line. The range of voices is slowly extended upward. The abstract linear style of the thirteenth-century motet loses its dominance, though it continues to exist alongside the more melodic-harmonic idiom of cantilena texture; and in connection with the latter there is a growing search for sensuous attractiveness. In France, the motet continues as a special form of composition, no longer mainly liturgical but becoming more political and ceremonial in function as well as more intricate in structure. New forms of composition are developed. Some, like the caccia and (possibly) the madrigal, seem to derive rather closely from popular musical practice; some, like the ballata and other songs with refrains, go back to the thirteenth century and, more remotely, to popular models. The sophisticated types, the "formes fixes," which likewise continue an earlier tradition, are literary as well as musical in conception: the virelai; the ballade; and the rondeau, which was increasing in favor toward the end of the century and beginning to branch out into more complex types.

By the year 1400 the two formerly distinct musical styles of France and Italy had begun to merge. As we shall see in the next chapter, this incipient international style was to be augmented in the fifteenth century by streams from other sources, chiefly England, France, and the Netherland area.

The thirteenth century was the last great unitary medieval musical era: organum, conductus, and motet were different manifestation of one fundamental style. The fourteenth century, though still medieval, was a time of relatively rapid change. Some of its music sounds experimental, tentative; some of it seems affected and a bit over-refined, like the manners and costumes of its knightly patrons. Of course there was actually much more music than meets the eye of even the most diligent searcher among the manuscripts; folk songs, dances, improvised music of all kinds, went for the most part unrecorded as lying outside the interest of those who wrote and preserved the musical documents. Most of what has come down to us was composed for the pleasure of aristocratic, cultivated listeners or amateurs; but contemporary pictures and writings show that the practice of music, both vocal and instrumental, was widespread among all social classes.

V

Medieval to Renaissance: English Music and the Burgundian School in the Fifteenth Century

English Music to the End of the Fifteenth Century

The first few decades of the fifteenth century in France and Italy do not seem to have produced any outstanding composers or any great innovations in musical style. Venice was the principal center in northern Italy; Rome, with the Papal chapel, rose to importance after 1420. Composition was still mainly in the secular forms; cantilena texture was increasingly favored and was even carried over to some extent into the motet (itself quasi-secular and ceremonial) and settings of the Mass. The long-range trend was toward an international style, already foreshadowed by the presence of Ciconia and other northerners in Italy in the early 1400s; to this new style, decisive contributions were made toward the middle of the century by English composers.

English music, like that of northern Europe generally, had been characterized from earliest times by a rather close connection with folk style and, by contrast with Continental developments, a certain disinclination to carry abstract theories to extremes in practice.

General features

Thus there had always been a tendency in English music toward major tonality (as opposed to the modal system), toward greater harmonic unity (as opposed to the independent lines, divergent texts, and harmonic dissonances of the French motet), toward greater fullness of sound, and toward a freer use of thirds and sixths than in the music of the Continent. It was in the writings of English theorists around 1300 that the third was first recognized as a consonant interval, and a twelfth-century example of parallel thirds occurs in a *Hymn to St. Magnus,* patron saint of the Orkney Islands. The practice of writing in parallel thirds or parallel sixths was common in English polyphonic compositions of the thirteenth century.

The works of the Notre Dame school were known in the British Isles, as we gather from the fact that one of the principal source manuscripts of this repertoire, Wolfenbüttel 628 (called W$_1$) was copied in Scotland. This manuscript contains, in addition to Notre Dame compositions, many works thought to be of British origin. These pieces consist for the most part of two-voice tropes and sequences; they are similar to syllabic conducti, but with the upper voice slightly more melismatic than the tenor, which is usually a liturgical or quasi-liturgical melody, often freely paraphrased.

Three-part conducti and motets were composed in England in the thirteenth century and were also known on the Continent; for instance, the English motet *Alle psallite—Alleluia* is found in the Montpellier Codex. (The tenor is given in Example V–1; the entire piece in HAM, No. 33a.) This motet illustrates the freedom with which English composers adapted the form of the French motet. The tenor, instead of being cramped into an unvarying rhythmic formula, is organized in such a way as to present three phrases, each repeated, which seem to grow organically one out of another while the duplum and triplum interchange their melodies at each repetition of the tenor phrase—a favorite device in English music of this period. As shown in Example V–1, the tenor is related to a plainsong Alleluia and was perhaps inspired by it; similar melodies occur in other contemporary motets of this type. The fresh, folklike quality of all the melodic lines and the harmonious blending of the voices are other English traits, such as may be heard also in the famous *Sumer* canon.

It must be remembered in connection with English medieval church music that the basic repertoire of chant was that of the Sarum rite, the melodies of which differ to some extent from those of the Roman rite which we find in the *Liber Usualis* and other modern chant books. Not only English, but also many Continental composers in the fifteenth century, used the Sarum rather than the Roman versions of plainchant as *cantus firmi* in their compositions.

EXAMPLE V–1   Tenor of *Alle psallite—Alleluia*

The chief sources of our knowledge of English fourteenth-century music are a number of manuscript fragments containing works that point to the existence of a school of composition centering at Worcester Cathedral. These works comprise chiefly tropes of various sections of the Ordinary of the Mass, selections from the Proper of the Mass, motets, and conducti. Most of the motets are oldfashioned, but a few closely resemble in spirit and technique *Alle psallite—Alleluia.*

Fourteenth Century

The conducti and some of the conductus-like tropes of the Ordinary exhibit a new stylistic feature, one that had begun to appear as early as the thirteenth century and was to be of great importance in the music of the early fifteenth century: the melodic line is accompanied by two other voices in generally parallel motion, in such a way as to produce, from time to time, successions of chords that would be described in modern terms as first-inversion triads or sixth chords (marked with brackets in Example V–2; the complete piece is given in HAM, No. 57b). This kind of writing reflects the English national predilection for thirds and sixths and for full, harmonious sounds. It may have originated in the same frequent practice of voice-exchange in thirteenth-century English music that led to such forms as the rondellus. It was recognized in theory and practice by the establishment of rules for "discanting," that is, for singing an unnotated part against a *cantus firmus,* the added part moving note-against-note in equal rhythm with the given melody and always forming consonances with it. By the late thirteenth century, the rules for discanting forbade consecutive perfect fifths and octaves, but allowed a limited number of consecutive parallel thirds or sixth. One consequence was the rise of a peculiarly English sonority, marked by a generally homophonic texture (in contrast to the can-

EXAMPLE V–2   Gloria from Fourteenth-century English Mass

Lau - da - mus te. Be - ne - di - ci - mus te. A - do- ra - mus te.

Glo - ri - fi - ca - mus te.

We praise Thee. We bless Thee. We adore Thee. We glorify Thee.

tilena and motet textures of Continental music) and permeated to an extraordinary degree with the sound of the "softer" harmonic intervals of the third and sixth—including the sound of that particular combination which we call the $\frac{6}{3}$ chord.

English music was becoming known on the Continent in the early part of the fifteenth century. Perhaps due to the English example, the sound of sixth-chord progressions so fascinated Continental composers that from about 1420 to 1450 this manner of writing affected every form of composition. The usual name for it is *fauxbourdon*—a term whose exact significance and etymology are still in dispute.[1] In the strict sense, a *fauxbourdon* was a composition written in two voices which progressed in parallel sixths with octaves interspersed and always with an octave at the end of the phrase; to these written parts an unnotated third part was added in performance, moving constantly at a fourth below the treble. The actual sound of fauxbourdon, then, was like that of the passages of $\frac{6}{3}$ chords in English works; the difference in principle was that in fauxbourdon the principal melody was in the treble, whereas in English compositions that used a *cantus prius factus* this usually was heard in the middle or the lowest voice.

The fauxbourdon technique was used chiefly for settings of the simpler Office chants (hymns and antiphons) and of psalms and

Fauxbourdon

[1] The various proposed etymologies of *fauxbourdon* and the related words *falsobordone, fabordón, faburden* are discussed in an article by Robert A. Hall, Jr., "L'etimologia di 'falsobordone,'" in *Archivio Glottologico Italiano* LIII (1968) 141–47. The author suggests ultimate derivation from a French construction *fors-bordon*, that is, a line of music outside of, different from, added to, the *bordon* or "bass" (i.e., the contratenor)—on the analogy of the medieval French *forsborc* (modern *faubourg*), meaning "outside the city."

psalm-like texts like the Magnificat and the Te Deum. However, the important practical consequence of this device was not the production of such pieces of these, but the emergence, around the middle of the century, of a new style of three-part writing. In this style the principal melodic line is in the upper voice, so that in this respect it resembles the cantilena of the fourteenth century; but there are important differences. In the older cantilena style the two lower voices stood as it were apart, holding to a slower rhythm and serving as a more or less neutral background for the melody. Now, by contrast, the top voice and the tenor are coupled as if in a duet; these two voices—and eventually the contratenor as well—become more nearly equal in importance, in melodic quality, and in rhythm (though the treble may be enlivened by ornamental tones); and all three are assimilated in what is, by comparison with the previous century, a more consonant sound and a more harmonious progression of sonorities within the phrase. This new style exercised a strong influence on all types of composition—an influence in the direction of homophonic texture, consonant harmonies, full triad sonority, and acceptance of the $\frac{6}{3}$ sonority as a conspicuous element in the harmonic vocabulary.

The Old Hall Manuscript

The chief collection of English music of the early part of the fifteenth century is the Old Hall Manuscript. It contains 147 compositions dating from about 1350 to 1420, of which approximately four-fifths are settings of various sections of the Ordinary of the Mass and the remainder are motets, hymns, and sequences. Most of the Mass settings are in the chordal "discant" style, modified in some instances by greater melodic activity in the top voice; they often incorporate plainchant melodies in one of the inner voices. Thus, one *Sanctus* by Leonel Power has a four-part setting with a liturgical *cantus firmus* in the tenor voice, which more often than not lies above the contratenor. This type of setting, with the plainsong melody in the next-to-lowest voice of a four-part texture, is historically important as a forerunner of the manner of using a plainsong tenor in the Masses of the late fifteenth and early sixteenth centuries. Other Mass sections in the Old Hall manuscript are in cantilena style, with the principal melody in the treble; in still others, a plainsong melody appears now in one voice, now in another, as a "migrant" *cantus firmus*. About one-seventh of the compositions in this collection, including both Masses and settings of other texts, are in the style of the isorhythmic motet. Among the composers named in the Old Hall manuscript is one "Roy Henry," probably King Henry IV of England, who reigned from 1399 to 1413.

John Dunstable

There was in the first half of the fifteenth century a considerable number of English composers whose works are found in Continental manuscripts of the period, and through whom the characteristic features of English musical style became known. Their influence is attested by a French poem of about 1440 which speaks of the *"contenance angloise"* (English countenance, or qualities) which contributed to making contemporary Continental music so "joyous and bright" with "marvelous pleasantness." Allusion is made particularly to the leading English composer of the time, John Dunstable (*ca.* 1385–1453). Part of Dunstable's life was probably spent in the service of the English Duke of Bedford, Regent of France from 1422 to 1435 and commander of the English armies that fought against Joan of Arc; the extensive English possessions and claims in France in this period partly explain the presence of Dunstable and many other English composers on the Continent as well as the spread of their music.

Dunstable's compositions, of which about sixty are known, include examples of all the principal types and styles of polyphony that existed in his lifetime: isorhythmic motets, sections of the Ordinary of the Mass, secular songs, and three-part settings of miscellaneous liturgical texts. His twelve isorhythmic motets testify to the continued vitality of this ancient and venerable form of composition in the early fifteenth century. His most celebrated motet, a four-part setting that combines the hymn *Veni creator spiritus* and the sequence *Veni sancte spiritus,* is not only a splendid example of isorhythmic structure, but also a thoroughly impressive piece of music, embodying the English preference for full-bodied sonority with complete triads. Some of the sections of the Ordinary of the Mass, which comprise about one-third of Dunstable's known works, are also constructed on a liturgical melody set forth isorhythmically in the tenor. Only a few secular songs are attributed to Dunstable; of these, *O rosa bella* and *Puisque m'amour* are excellent examples of the expressive lyrical melodies and clear harmonic outlines of the English music of their time.

[handwritten margin notes: Listened to. Had no thot of climax tension & release. It seems to go on & on very Monotonous. Use of isorythmics to keep the sound going.]

Most numerous and most important historically among Dunstable's works are the three-part sacred pieces—settings of antiphons, hymns, and other liturgical or Biblical texts. These are composed in various ways: some have a *cantus firmus* in the tenor part; others have a florid treble line and a borrowed melody in the middle voice, which moves for the most part in thirds and sixths above the tenor; others have an ornamented liturgical melody in the treble (see Example V–3); and still others are freely composed, without borrowed thematic material. A piece of this last type is the antiphon *Quam pulcra es* (Example V–4; pp. 154–56), a work that we shall analyze in some detail, since it not only exemplifies Dunstable's style but also illustrates some important historical developments.

Dunstable's three-part sacred works

In *Quam pulcra es* the three voices are similar in character and of nearly equal importance; much of the time they move in the

EXAMPLE V–3   Treble of Motet: *Regina caeli laetare,* John Dunstable

same rhythm and usually pronounce the same syllables together: the musical texture is that of conductus, and the short melisma at the end of the word "alleluia" is in accordance with the ornamented conductus style. A composition like this one was not limited by a *cantus firmus,* nor by any prescribed scheme of structure, as in an isorhythmic motet, nor by any prescribed pattern of repetitions or sections, as in the *formes fixes* like the virelai or rondeau. The form of the music, therefore, was a matter for the composer's free choice, limited only insofar as he might wish to follow any suggestions of a formal outline that were implicit in the text. In this instance Dunstable has divided the piece into two sections. Section one (measures 1–38) comprises, in shortened form, verses 6, 7, 5, and 11 of Chapter vii of *The Song of Solomon;* section two, beginning with "et videamus," is on verse 12, with an added "alleluia." The longer first section is punctuated near the end by the held notes on the word "veni" ("come"); its pattern of subdivision is 9 + 9 + 11 + 8 measures, with cadences on C, C, D, and G. The second section subdivides, though less neatly, into (4 + 3) + (6 + 3) + 4 measures, with cadences on F, D, C, D, and C. The musical subdivisions of the first section correspond to the modern division of the text into verses; those of section two are less distinct, just as the subdivisions of the text are less clearly marked than in section one, but the "alleluia" is definitely set off by its melisma and the livelier melodic and harmonic rhythm as the final cadence is approached.

Not only is the musical form in its main outlines determined by the text; the outline of many phrases also is molded to the rhythm of the words, as may be noted in the declamation by repeated notes of "statúra túa assimiláta est," "mála Púnica," and "íbi dábo tíbi." Other details to be noted are: the conspicuous melodic intervals of a third in the topmost voice, and the occasional outlining of a triad in the melody (for example, measures 1–5, 43, 55); and the use of fauxbourdon style, particularly at the approach to a cadence (as in measures 12–15).

Among English musicians on the Continent after Dunstable may be mentioned Walter Frye (fl. 1450), composer of Masses, motets, and chansons; and John Hothby (d. 1487), who worked at Lucca and elsewhere in Italy for a great part of his life. Meanwhile, development of English music at home continued. One form that was especially cultivated was the *votive antiphon,* a sacred composition in honor of some particular saint or, most often, of the Virgin Mary. A large collection of such pieces, in elaborate polyphonic settings for five to nine voices, is preserved in a choirbook from the late fifteenth century at Eton College. The full sonority of these works, the alternation of larger and smaller voice-groups, and the large-scale division into sections of perfect, then imperfect time, are characteristic of votive antiphon and Mass composition in England through the first half of the sixteenth century.

Votive antiphons

Another form of English composition that flourished in the fifteenth century was the *carol.* Originally the carol, like the rondeau and ballata, was a monophonic dance song with alternating solo and chorus portions. By the fifteenth century it had become stylized as a setting, in two or three (sometimes four) parts, of a religious poem in popular style, often on a subject of the Incarnation, and frequently written in a mixture of English and Latin rhyming verses. In form the carol consisted of a number of stanzas all sung to the same music, and a *burden* or refrain with its own musical phrase, which was sung at the beginning and then repeated after every stanza. The carols were not folk songs, but their fresh, angular melodies and lively triple rhythms give them a distinctly popular character and an unmistakably English quality. The Incarnation carols were probably used to accompany religious processions or other religious ceremonies at the Christmas season.

The carol

EXAMPLE V–4   *Quam pulcra es,* John Dunstable

How fair and how pleasant art thou, O love, for delights! Thy stature is like to a palm tree, and thy breasts to clusters of grapes. Thine head upon thee is like Carmel; thy neck is a tower of ivory. Come, my beloved, let us go forth into the field . . . and see whether the tender grapes appear and the pomegranates but forth: there will I give thee my loves.[2]

[2] *Song of Solomon* (King James version) vii:6–7, 5, 4, 11–12. The text in the order used by Dunstable is found in the *Antiphonale Sarisburiense*, facsimile ed., London, 1901–25, 528–29.

The Evolution of Musical Style in the Late Middle Ages

Dunstable's *Quam pulcra es* represents a trend in musical composition which had become continuously stronger throughout the fourteenth century. The history of musical style can be regarded from one point of view as a continual contest between the *contrapuntal* and the *harmonic* principles, that is, between independence of melodic lines on the one hand and unity of harmonic effect on the other. The general line of evolution in the late Middle Ages was away from the contrapuntal and toward the harmonic principle. The thirteenth-century motet had been primarily contrapuntal in style; emphasis was on the independent melodic lines, with comparatively little attention being given to the harmonies. During the fourteenth century the trend was in the direction of a growing feeling for the importance of harmonic organization and for the sensuous effect of harmonic combinations. Sharp dissonant clashes between melodic lines began to be avoided; the cantilena style, with one principal melody supported by subordinate lower parts, was a step in the direction of harmonic, as opposed to contrapuntal, organization of music; the rise of fauxbourdon, and the gradual penetration into all types of composition of the sonority of sixth chords, was still another step toward the dominance of the harmonic principle.

Another indication of the change in emphasis from contrapuntal toward harmonic texture in the fourteenth century was the change in attitude toward the words in vocal music. The polytextual thirteenth-century motet was replaced by the new fourteenth-century forms which typically had a single text—treated either as a solo, as in the French ballade; or distributed between the voices in such a way as to keep the words always clearly understandable, as in the Italian madrigal; or pronounced simultaneously, as in fauxbourdon.

Another aspect of the change in musical style between the thirteenth and the fifteenth centuries was a gradual turning away from interest in abstract, nonsensuous principles of construction toward pleasure in sounds for their own sake and toward a clarity of structure immediately apparent from the music itself, without reference to esoteric meanings.

From another point of view, we may summarize the course of musical evolution from 1225 to 1425 as a movement from the *motet* principle to the *conductus* principle: from the French Gothic motet with its stylized liturgical *cantus firmus,* highly independent melodic

𝒮𝓌𝑒𝓈

lines, multiple texts, rigidly logical abstract structure, and relative indifference to harmonic progression or suavity of effect, to the secularized style of the mid-fifteenth century with its fusion of French, Italian, and English qualities. In this new international style, a liturgical *cantus firmus* is either altogether absent or, if present, is incorporated into the musical ensemble without dominating it; dissonance is at a minimum; the form is determined either by the musical device of repeated and contrasted sections or by the literary form of the single text; and the harmonies, enriched by the employment of thirds and sixths as consonant intervals, begin to assume significance in the shaping of the phrase and of the work as a whole. Dunstable's *Quam pulcra es* is an example of this new style, which had favorable soil for growth in fourteenth-century England because English composers had continued to cultivate the conductus and conductus-like style of composition after these had largely fallen out of use on the Continent.

The fifteenth-century motet

Quam pulcra es is classified in the standard edition of Dunstable's works as a "motet." This word, which we have hitherto used to denote the French form of the thirteenth century and the isorhythmic form of the fourteenth and early fifteenth centuries, had begun in the fourteenth century to take on a broader meaning. Originally, a motet was a composition on a liturgical text for use in church; as we have seen, by the later thirteenth century the term was applied to works with secular texts as well, including even those which used a secular melody as a tenor *cantus firmus*. In the isorhythmic motets of the fourteenth and early fifteenth centuries the tenors were usually Gregorian melodies, and these motets retained the traditional characteristics of a liturgical *cantus firmus*, multiple texts, and strongly contrapuntal texture. The isorhythmic motet was a conservative form, participating only to a slight degree in the general evolution of musical style during the late fourteenth and early fifteenth centuries; by 1450 it had become an anachronism, and disappeared. A few motets were written after that date with plainsong *cantus firmus* tenors, but without otherwise much resembling the older medieval types.

Meanwhile, in the first half of the fifteenth century the term "motet" began to be applied also to settings of liturgical or even secular texts in the newer musical style of the time. This broader meaning of the term has prevailed up to the present day: a motet, in this usage, means almost any polyphonic composition on a Latin text other than the Ordinary of the Mass, and thus includes such diverse forms as antiphons, responsories, and other texts from the Proper and the Office. From the sixteenth century onward, the word was also applied to sacred compositions in languages other than Latin. This usage, though regrettable in some respects, is so widely accepted that we shall have to retain it, remembering however that within the general class "motet" there are many different subclasses which must sometimes be distinguished. In particular, special categories are usually made of the *Magnificat* canticle and the *Lamentations.*

The Burgundian School[3]

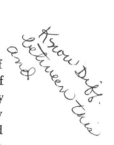

The Dukes of Burgundy, although feudal vassals of the Kings of France, were virtually their equals in power. During the second half of the fourteenth century and the early years of the fifteenth, by means of a series of political marriages and a course of diplomacy that took full advantage of their Kings' distress in the Hundred Years' Wars, they acquired possession of territories comprising most of what are today Holland, Belgium, northeastern France, Luxembourg, and Lorraine; these they added to their original fiefs, the medieval Duchy and County of Burgundy in east central France, and ruled over the whole as virtually independent sovereigns until 1477. Though their nominal capital was Dijon, they had no fixed principal city of residence but sojourned from time to time at various places in their dominions. The main orbit of the peripatetic Burgundian court after the middle of the century was around Lille, Bruges, Ghent, and especially Brussels, an area comprising modern Belgium and the northeastern corner of France. Most of the leading northern composers of the late fifteenth century came from this general region and many of them were connected in one way or another with the Burgundian court.

All the Dukes of Burgundy were active patrons of art and music. Hubert and Jan van Eyck were among the painters who had enjoyed their protection. Like most great nobles, they maintained a *chapel,* with an accessory corps of composers, singers, and instrumentalists who furnished music for church services, probably also contributed to the secular entertainment of the court, and accompanied their master on his journeys. Chapels with elaborate musical resources were being established all over Europe in the late four-

---

[3] It has been remarked that the Holy Roman Empire of the Middle Ages was in fact neither holy nor Roman nor an empire. In like manner it has been objected (Henry L. Clarke, "Musicians of the Northern Renaissance," in Jan LaRue, ed., *Aspects of Medieval and Renaissance Music,* 67–81) that the Burgundian School was, strictly speaking, neither Burgundian nor a school: that "Burgundian" did not connote nationality nor even a single geographical area, nor "school" a center of musical instruction for the training of composers. Historical labels are matters of convenience, and most of them are necessarily somewhat inaccurate. "Burgundian School" is established in usage since P. H. Lang's *Music in Western Civilization* (1941); it is convenient, specific, and sufficiently accurate as designating the principal northern musicians of the generation of Dufay and Binchois to be retained in preference to the broader term "Franco-Flemish" for this group.

A fête champêtre *at the court of Duke Philip the Good (1396–1467) of Burgundy. The musicians, ever present on these occasions, serenade the Duke's party, which is at the center. Hunters are chasing game in the background. This painting, dated 1430–31, is ascribed to Jan Van Eyck.*

teenth and early fifteenth centuries; Popes, emperors, kings, and princes competed for the services of eminent composers and singers. Tinctoris, a Flemish theorist writing about 1475, tells how the proffered rewards in honor and riches so stimulated the growth of talent that in his day music seemed like "a new art, the course of which was among the English with Dunstable at their head, and contemporary with him in France Dufay and Binchois."

The court and chapel of Philip the Good, ruler of Burgundy from 1419 to 1467, were the most resplendent in Europe, and his influence as a patron of music was so extensive that the name "Burgundian" has been given both to the style of music and the composers who flourished during his reign. The term, of course, does not connote nationality. The Burgundian chapel, numbering fifteen to twenty-seven musicians, in the early part of the century was recruited chiefly from Paris; later, it was made up of musicians from England and various parts of the Continent, but most numerous were those from the Franco-Belgian region. In addition to his chapel, Philip the Good maintained a band of minstrels—trumpeters, viellists, lutenists, harpists, organists—which included Frenchmen, Italians, Germans, and Portuguese. The cosmopolitan atmosphere of such a fifteenth-century court was accentuated by numerous visits from foreign musicians and by the fact that the members of the chapel themselves were continually on the move, migrating from one service to another in response to "better offers." Under such circumstances a musical style could not be other than international; the prestige of the Burgundian court was such that the kind of music cultivated there influenced other European musical centers, such as the chapels of the Pope at Rome, the Emperor in Germany, the kings of France and England, and the various Italian courts, as well as cathedral choirs—the more so because many of the musicians in these other places either had been at one time, or hoped some day to be, in the service of the Duke of Burgundy himself.

Guillaume Dufay is commonly named as one of the chief figures of the Burgundian School, although he was perhaps never a regular member of the ducal chapel. Dufay was born about 1400 in the Burgundian province of Hainaut (the present Franco-Belgian border region). He seems to have journeyed to Paris and Italy soon after completing his early education as a choir boy at Cambrai, and

Guillaume Dufay

Guillaume Dufay (ca. 1400–1474) and Gilles Binchois (ca. 1400–1460), the leading Burgundian composers, are shown together in this miniature from Le Champion des Dames. *(Bettmann Archive)*

from 1428 to 1433 was a member of the Papal chapel at Rome. After a two-year interlude in the service of the Duke of Savoy (whose territories at that time included parts of the present northwestern Italy and western Switzerland as well as the French province of Savoy), Dufay rejoined the Pope's chapel at Florence and Bologna from 1435 until 1437. The events of the next fifteen or twenty years of his life are not clearly known; he travelled much, and was a welcome guest at many European courts. Dufay was ordained a priest sometime around 1420 and studied canon law in France. He was thus an exceptionally well-educated man, and he was appointed to influential offices in the Church not because of his music—although he was greatly admired as a composer—but because of his learning. We hear of him from time to time at the court of Burgundy, but whether as a regular member of the chapel or only an honorary one is uncertain. The closing years of his life were passed in honorable retirement at Cambrai, where he had held appointment as a Canon of the Cathedral since 1436. Already before his death in 1474, and for a generation after, he was celebrated as one of the greatest composers of his time and the teacher of many famous musicians.

The works of Dufay and his contemporaries have been preserved in a large number of manuscripts, mostly of Italian origin. The

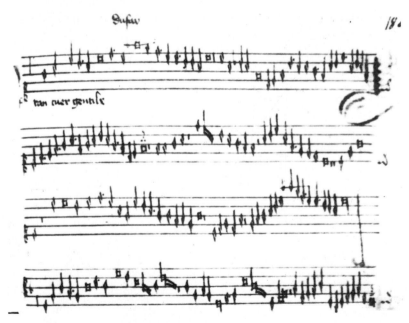

The superius of Dufay's chanson Franc cuer gentilx, *in the manuscript Trent 92. A transcription is given in Example V–5.*

EXAMPLE V–5   Chanson: *Franc cuer gentilx,* Guillaume Dufay

Gentle noble heart, gracious above all other ladies,
Rich in honor and adorned with every good . . .

most important of these are a manuscript now in the Bodleian Library at Oxford (Canonici misc. 213), copied in northern Italy about 1460 and containing over 300 works dating from about 1400 to 1440; and the Trent Codices, six volumes now in the library of the National Museum in the Castello del Buonconsiglio at Trent, containing altogether 1585 compositions written between 1420 and 1480. Transcriptions from these and other manuscripts of the period are plentifully available in modern editions.

The principal types of composition of the Burgundian School were Masses, Magnificats, motets, and secular chansons with French texts. The prevailing combination of voices was the same as in the French ballade and the Italian ballata: tenor and contratenor both moving within the range c to g', and a treble or *discantus* normally not exceeding the compass of a tenth (a to c″ or c′ to e″). As in the fourteenth century, the intention was for each line in performance to have a distinct timbre and the whole a transparent texture, with predominance of the discantus as the principal melody. The style in general may be regarded as a combination of the homophonic suavity of fauxbourdon with a certain amount of melodic freedom and contrapuntal independence, including occasional points of imitation. The typical discantus line flows in warmly expressive lyrical phrases, breaking into graceful melismas at the approach to important cadences—see Example V–5.

The Burgundian cadence formula was still for the most part that of the fourteenth century (Example III–15), and the "Landini" embellishment figure was very common (Example IV–3); but along with this older type of cadence, another began to appear which was in effect a dominant–tonic progression and which, in three-part writing, nearly always involved crossing of the two lower voices; see Example V–6a and b.

The feeling for chord progressions of this character became more marked throughout the fifteenth century; and after about 1460 the normal cadence formula was one that would be described in modern terminology as V–I. It must be understood, however, that the composers did not think of such progressions with the implications attached to the modern terms we are using to describe them. Music theorists until after the middle of the sixteenth century did not even recognize the triad as an entity, still less any tonal-functional chord progressions. Their unit was not the chord, but the interval between a pair of voices. Thus in Example V–6a and b the bass, and in V–6c and d the bass and alto, are to be thought of as "added" parts which fill out the vertical sonorities and accommodate themselves to the intervallic progressions of the essential soprano-tenor framework— which here (as in the cadential formulas of Examples III–15 and IV–8) is moving by rule to a perfect interval (the octave) from the next preceding imperfect interval (the sixth).

EXAMPLE V–6   Cadential Formulas

(a) Dufay: *Motet*

(b) Binchois: *Rondeau*

(c) Dufay: *Mass*

(d) Dufay: *Mass*

The great majority of the compositions of the Burgundian School were in some form of triple meter, with frequent cross rhythms resulting from the combination of the patterns ♩ ♩ ♩ and ♫♫ ♫♫; see Example V–6b and d. Duple meter was used principally in subdivisions of longer works as a means of contrast.

In the fifteenth century, *chanson* was a general term for any polyphonic setting of a secular poem in French. The Burgundian chansons were, in effect, accompanied solo songs. Their texts—nearly always love poems—were most often in the pattern of the rondeau, sometimes the traditional form with a two-line refrain, sometimes an expanded form such as the *rondeau quatrain,* which had a four-line stanza and refrain. The chansons were the most characteristic productions of the Burgundian School. The chief center of their cultivation was the Burgundian court itself, and the outstanding master of the genre was Gilles Binchois.

The Burgundian chanson

Binchois was born at Mons about 1400. In early life he seems to have combined the pursuit of music with a military career; later he took clerical orders, and from 1430 until his death in 1460 was in service as a musician at the court of Duke Philip the Good. Binchois' chansons excel in the expression of a tender melancholy, just touched with sensuous longing. The moving charm of the melodies, the clear, bright-colored sound of the ensemble, and the miniature proportions of the whole contrive to suggest to our minds the picture of a visionary world, remote yet strangely familiar, standing at the threshold between the Middle Ages and the modern era. So strong was the spell of this Burgundian musical style that the tradition of it lingered in Europe long after the downfall of the Duchy of Burgundy as an independent political power.

Gilles Binchois

In their church music the Burgundian composers at first developed no distinctive sacred style, but wrote both motets and Masses in

Burgundian motets

the manner of the chanson, with a freely melodic solo treble coupled with a tenor and supported by a contratenor part in the usual three-voice texture. The treble might be newly composed, but in many cases it was an embellished version of a chant (for example, Dufay's *Alma Redemptoris Mater*). This use of a liturgical *cantus firmus* was fundamentally different from the way such a theme was used in the tenor of the old thirteenth- and fourteenth-century motet. There the liturgical melody was no more than a mystical base for the structure; as long as it was present, no matter how distorted in rhythm and regardless of whether any hearer could recognize it, its purpose was fulfilled. In Burgundian motets, on the contrary, the Gregorian melodies were meant to be recognized; they were not only a symbolic link with tradition, but also a concrete, musically expressive part of the composition. The influence of fauxbourdon style on the Burgundian motet may be recognized in the prevailing homophonic texture and relatively frequent sixth chords of Dufay's *Alma Redemptoris Mater,* his *Veni Creator Spiritus* and, in a simpler form quite close to strict fauxbourdon, some of his other hymn settings.

In addition to motets in the modern chanson style, Dufay and his contemporaries still occasionally continued the custom—exemplified by Ciconia at Venice and many later fourteenth-century composers—of writing isorhythmic motets for solemn public ceremonies—an archaic musical style, like an archaic literary style, being appropriate for such circumstances. Dufay's four-part isorhythmic motet, *Nuper rosarum flores—Terribilis est locus iste,* written for the consecration of the church of Santa Maria del Fiore (the "Duomo") at Florence in 1436, was long famous. It is of interest to know that the overall rhythmic proportions as well as many details of Dufay's motet correspond exactly with the proportions of the cupola of the Duomo, which had been designed by the famous Renaissance architect Filippo Brunelleschi in terms of the "musical proportions" of ancient treatises.[4] An eyewitness of the service of dedication, at which Pope Eugene IV officiated in person, wrote of the bright-robed company of trumpeters, viellists, and players of other instruments, and of the singing choirs that struck the listeners with awe, so that with sound of music and perfume of incense and sight of the beautiful decorations:

> the senses of all began to be uplifted. . . . But at the elevation of the Most Sacred Host the whole space of the temple was filled with such choruses of harmony, and such a concent of divers instruments, that it seemed (not without reason) as though the symphonies and songs of the angels and of divine paradise had been sent forth from Heaven to whisper in our ears an unbelievable celestial sweetness. Wherefore in that moment I was so possessed by ecstasy that I seemed

[4] See Charles W. Warren, "Brunelleschi's Dome and Dufay's Motet," *MQ* 59 (1973), 92–105.

to enjoy the life of the blessed here on earth; whether it happened so to others present I know not, but concerning myself I can bear witness.[5]

It was in settings of the Mass that composers of the Burgundian period first developed a specifically sacred musical style, and moreover began an evolution which by the end of the century made this form the principal vehicle for the thought and effort of composers. We have already noted the increased number of polyphonic settings of the Mass in the late fourteenth and early fifteenth centuries. Previous to about 1420 the various sections of the Ordinary were composed as separate pieces (Machaut's Mass and a few others excepted), though occasionally such separate items might be brought together by a compiler into a unified cycle. A central achievement of the fifteenth century was to establish as regular practice the polyphonic setting of the Ordinary as a musically unified whole. At first only a pair of sections (for example, Gloria and Credo) would be brought into perceptible musical relationship; gradually the practice was extended to all five divisions of the Ordinary. The motive for this development was the desire of musicians to give coherence to a large and complex musical form; moreover, similar cyclical groupings of the plainsong chants of the Ordinary had existed as early as the beginning of the fourteenth century.

Burgundian Masses

Of course a certain feeling of musical unity resulted simply when all five parts of the Ordinary were composed in the same general style, which on the Continent in the early fifteenth century was usually that of the ballade or chanson. If in addition each movement took an appropriate chant from the *Graduale* for a *cantus firmus* (which would usually appear in ornamented form in the treble), the impression of unity was strengthened—but by liturgical association rather than by musical resemblance, since the plainsong melodies were not necessarily thematically related. (A Mass using Gregorian themes in this way is called a *missa choralis* or Plainsong Mass.) The most practical way of achieving a definite, perceptible musical interconnection of the various sections of a Mass was to use the same thematic material in each. At first the connection consisted only in beginning each movement with the same melodic motive, usually in the treble (a Mass that uses this device is sometimes called a "motto Mass"); but this technique—which the Englishman John Hothby at Lucca had used also in his settings of the Magnificat— was soon superseded by or combined with another, namely the use of the same *cantus firmus* in every movement. The resulting cyclical musical form is known as a *cantus firmus Mass* or *Tenor Mass*. The earliest cyclical Masses of this kind were written by English com-

[5] From an account by Giannozzo Manetti, quoted in Dufay, *Opera omnia*, de Van and Besseler, eds., II, xxvii.

posers, but the form was quickly adopted on the Continent and by the second half of the fifteenth century had become the customary one.

The tradition of the medieval motet suggested the placing of the borrowed melody in the tenor; but the new conception of music in the fifteenth century required that the lowest voice be free to function as a foundation for the desired harmonic progressions, particularly at cadences. To use as the lowest voice a given melodic line which could not be essentially modified would have limited the composer's freedom and possibly have led to harmonic monotony. This difficulty was resolved by making the tenor the next-to-lowest voice, placing below it a part at first called *contratenor bassus* ("low contratenor"), later simply *bassus;* placing above the tenor a second contratenor called *contratenor altus* ("high contratenor"), later *altus;* and retaining in the highest position the treble part, called variously the *cantus* ("melody"), *discantus* ("discant"), or *superius* ("highest" part). These four voice parts came into being about the middle of the fifteenth century, and this distribution has remained, with few interruptions, the standard one to our own day.

Another heritage from the medieval motet was the custom of writing the tenor of a *cantus firmus* Mass in longer notes than the other parts and in isorhythmic fashion—either imposing a certain rhythmic pattern on a given plainsong melody and repeating it with the same pattern, or keeping the original rhythm of a given secular tune and altering the successive appearances of the melody by making them now faster, now slower, in relation to the other voices. Thus, as in the isorhythmic motet, the identity of the borrowed tune might be quite thoroughly disguised, the more so that it lay now in an inner voice and not in the lowest one as in the fourteenth century; nonetheless its regulative power in unifying the five divisions of the Mass was undeniable. The melodies used as *cantus firmi* were taken from the chants of the Proper or the Office, or else from a secular source, most often the tenor part of a chanson; in neither case did they have any liturgical connection with the Ordinary of the Mass. The name of the borrowed melody was given to the Mass for which it served as a *cantus firmus;* in Dufay's Mass *Se la face ay pale (If my face is pale)*, the tenor is taken from one of the composer's own chansons. A favorite tenor was the song *L'homme armé (The Armed Man)*, on which nearly every composer of the late fifteenth and sixteenth centuries wrote at least one Mass.

L'homme armé, Example V–7, was perhaps a folk song. Example V–8 shows how Dufay used it as the tenor of the first Agnus Dei in a Mass. (Other parts of this Mass using the same tune are in HAM, No. 66.) In Example V–8, the text is given as it appears in the original manuscript. Evidently the exact adjustment of the syllables to the notes was left to the singer; the tenor may have been

EXAMPLE V–7   *L'homme armé*

L'hom-me, l'hom-me, l'homme ar - mé, l'homme ar - mé, L'homme ar - mé doibt
on   doub - ter, doibt on doub - ter.   On   a   fait par - tout cri - er
Que chas - cun se viengue ar - mer D'un hau - bre - gon de   fer.

*The armed man is to be feared; everywhere it has been proclaimed
that everyone should arm himself with an iron coat of mail.*

played rather than sung. The rhythmic complication of measures
22–23 is notable.

A *cantus firmus* was not necessarily used continuously throughout
a Mass. For example, in Dufay's Mass the *L'homme armé* tune is
absent from a long section of the Osanna and does not appear at
all in the Benedictus. Also, the prevailing four-part texture in a Mass
was frequently replaced by duet or trio sections, which usually
were composed freely, without a *cantus firmus*. The *cantus firmus*
itself might be subjected to various rhythmic modifications, or
elaborated melodically, or be inverted, or sung backwards ("*cancrizans*," literally "crabwise"; this device is used by Dufay in the
third Agnus Dei of his *L'homme armé* Mass). In fact, it may be remarked that fifteenth- and sixteenth-century Masses on *L'homme
armé* are especially notable for complications of this sort. Composers seemed to think that the *Armed Man* had issued a challenge
to their ingenuity which they were obliged to accept on pain of professional disgrace.

Another *cantus firmus* used by Dufay and other fifteenth-century
composers is of special interest as being one evidence of the pervasive
English influence on the Continent. Scholars for a long time were
unable to trace the original of this *cantus firmus,* which is designated
in Dufay's Mass by the single word *caput* ("head"). No such melody
to this word could be found anywhere in the whole body of Roman
plainchant. Eventually it turned up in an English source, as the
final long melisma of an antiphon that was used only in the Sarum
(not in the Roman) rite. Dufay may have taken it over from an
earlier (lost) Mass by an English composer.[6]

Dufay's four-part *cantus firmus* Masses are late works, dating for
the most part after 1450. It is clear that in such compositions as

[6] The whole story may be read in M. F. Bukofzer's *Studies in Medieval and
Renaissance Music,* 226–310. The three fifteenth-century *Caput* Masses are published in *Collegium Musicum,* Number Five (Yale University, 1964).

EXAMPLE V–8 Agnus Dei from the Mass *L'homme armé,*
Guillaume Dufay

Lamb of God that takest away the sins of the world, have mercy [on us].

these we are no longer dealing with typically Burgundian music in the style of the chansons and chanson-like motets and Masses of the earlier part of the century. Some of the new features in the *cantus firmus* Masses of Dufay are indicative of a new musical style which rose to a dominating position after 1450, and which in some respects seemed to signalize a revival of medieval ideals of church music. On the whole, however, the course of development after about 1430 tended to emphasize those features which were to differentiate the musical style of the Renaissance from that of the late Middle Ages: control of dissonance, predominantly consonant sonorities including sixth chords, equal importance of voices, melodic and rhythmic congruity of lines, four-part texture, and occasional use of imitation. From this point of view it would not be unreasonable to classify Dufay and Binchois, and in some respects Dunstable also, as early Renaissance composers.

VI

The Age of the Renaissance: Ockeghem to Josquin

General Features

Humanistic Principles

The period from about 1450 to 1600[1] in the history of music is now generally known as "the Renaissance," a term which, like "Gothic" for the late Middle Ages or "Baroque" for the seventeenth and early eighteenth centuries, has been borrowed from art history. *Renaissance* was used by art historians to designate fifteenth- and sixteenth-century styles of painting, sculpture, and architecture; its use was gradually extended to all cultural manifestations of these two hundred years, including music (which the earliest writers on Renaissance civilization, Burkhardt and Symonds, had largely ignored). As the word gained in content it lost in precision. Its literal meaning is "rebirth," and many writers and artists of the fifteenth and sixteenth centuries view the achievements of their own time as a revival of the glories of Greece and Rome, a revival stimulated in part by discoveries of many ancient works of art and literature. No comparable discoveries of ancient music were made, so there could be no literal "rebirth" in the same sense as in the other fields. The

[1] As with all historical periods, the exact boundary dates are necessarily arbitrary. Some music historians would see the Renaissance as beginning around 1420, or still earlier; English music historians tend to place the beginning nearer to 1550, at least for their own country. Some place the end at about 1570 (see Blume, *Renaissance and Baroque Music*, New York, 1967), while others would extend it well into the seventeenth century. Changing boundaries and conceptions of the Renaissance are surveyed in Wallace K. Ferguson, *The Renaissance in Historical Thought*, Cambridge, Mass., 1948.

essentials of Greek musical theory had been handed down through the Middle Ages; Renaissance theorists diligently studied such of the ancient treatises as were available and sought to apply their teachings to the contemporary musical scene. Descriptions of the marvelous effects of ancient music led to some attempts in the sixteenth century to discover the lost secret of its power in the hope of reviving its glories. Projected revival of the chromatic and enharmonic genera of Greek music by the theorist Vicentino (1555), as well as later experiments that led eventually to opera, were among the consequences of the eager Renaissance interest in the music of antiquity.

Also to be considered is the more general meaning of Renaissance as a rebirth of the human spirit, a revival of standards of culture. During the fifteenth and sixteenth centuries areas of learning were *Social* broadened to include secular studies that had been neglected in the *conditions* earlier Christian centuries, and there was a decided inclination to use the results of such studies for the benefit of man in this world as well as for his salvation in the next. This specifically human and secular orientation was the essence of the movement known as *humanism,* an important aspect of the Renaissance. Artists and writers began to use secular as well as religious subject matter, and to want to make their works understandable and delightful to men as well as acceptable to God.

Furthermore, Renaissance men were convinced that theirs was an age both different from and better than immediately preceding times: "The world is coming to its senses as if awaking out of a *The* deep sleep," Erasmus said. The medieval sense of unbroken historical *Renaissance* continuity with the ancient world vanished, and instead men's minds *spirit* vaulted back to a kind of Golden Age of antiquity, half real and half mythical, which (as many felt) had been lost for a thousand years but which now was to be recovered, first by the imagination and then in actual life and art. Consequently there was exultation in the present, and each generation felt that it had excelled its predecessors: Tinctoris in 1475 thought that no music worth hearing had been written before 1440; the Swiss theorist Glarean in 1547 was persuaded that no one could ever surpass the music of Josquin des Prez (d. 1521); for Zarlino, an Italian composer and theorist writing in 1558, the acme of musical art was reached in the works of his contemporary, Willaert; the Florentine composers active about 1590 believed that their new kind of solo singing was the true reincarnation of ancient Greek music and therefore the best music that had been achieved in modern times, and that it was destined to supersede all the polyphonic developments of the fifteenth and sixteenth centuries. The whole temper of the age was optimistic and buoyant.

Of course it is impossible to date precisely any such momentous and far-reaching change in human attitudes, habits, and institutions as is implied in the idea of the Renaissance. The beginnings of the change have been traced to the fourteenth century, to Giotto, Petrarch, Boccaccio, and Landini. The movement developed earliest and most fully in Italy, whence it later radiated to other parts of Europe in variously modified forms. The so-called High Renaissance of the fifteenth and early sixteenth centuries witnessed the careers of such important artists and writers as Botticelli, Leonardo da Vinci, Michelangelo, Raphael, Cellini, Ariosto, and Machiavelli. New ideas naturally did not entirely supplant the old, nor did they flourish without opposition. Just as many Renaissance traits had appeared before the fifteenth century, so many medieval characteristics persisted after that time, and of course many counter currents developed. Many of the humanistic and pagan tendencies of the Renaissance, for example, were vigorously opposed by the Catholic Church in Italy after the middle of the sixteenth century.

Historical events

From our own vantage point in time, we can see that certain historical and cultural events of the late fifteenth and early sixteenth centuries appear to signal the end of the Middle Ages and the beginning of the modern era. In 1453, the year of Dunstable's death, the Turks captured Constantinople, the capital and last stronghold of the eastern Roman Empire, thereby severing the last visible link with the world of antiquity; many Byzantine scholars fled to Italy, where their presence stimulated the study of the Greek language and of ancient Greek literature and philosophy. The invention of printing from movable type was made at about the same time. The rediscovery of America by Columbus in 1492 was followed by other voyages of discovery and the eventual colonization of the western hemisphere. Finally, the two great universal medieval institutions— the Catholic Church and the Holy Roman Empire—were both splintered. The Reformation begun by Martin Luther in 1517 divided the Church into Catholic and Protestant branches. As for the Empire, its authority had long since become a mere shadow, and its territory, embracing approximately the extent of modern Germany, Austria, and a portion of the Netherlands, comprised merely one state of the European community.

And now, what of music in the years 1450 to 1600? Here the picture is anything but simple. Generally speaking, the Renaissance witnessed a spectacular increase of musical culture. More music was composed and performed than in any previous age. Moreover, music in the Renaissance tended to become more autonomous—not in the romantic sense of "art for art's sake" but in the sense that composers now felt able and free to create works that should be aesthetically satisfying as well as serviceable for particular social requirements. For the first time, all available musical resources came to be used: the entire chromatic scale, the full practicable range of voices and instruments. No longer bound by fixed poetic forms, vocal music achieved a new and intimate union with the text; texts themselves were taken from a wider range of literature and were generally of better literary quality than before. Independent instrumental forms of music developed.

Musicians in the Renaissance continued to live as they had done in the late Middle Ages: they depended on patronage. As before, the largest patron was the Church, but steadily growing support came from secular sources as well. Strict professional standards were becoming more widely accepted; musicians on the whole enjoyed more prestige than ever before, and the idea of the "great composer" made its first tentative appearance. As the number of professional performers and interested amateurs increased throughout the sixteenth century, a new kind of writing about music began to appear: "how to do it" books, manuals of instruction for players and singers, including instructions for improvisation; at the same time, the more general aspects of music theory received attention from many competent thinkers.

One of the most important factors in the growth of music during the Renaissance was the rise of music printing. The art of printing books from movable type, perfected by Johann Gutenberg by 1450, was applied to liturgical books with plainchant notation about 1473. *Music printing* Examples of music printed from wood blocks appear in a few books of theory or instruction in the late fifteenth century; this method continued, either alone or in combination with printing from type, into the early sixteenth century but eventually died out except for a few sporadic instances. The first collection of polyphonic music printed from movable type was brought out in 1501 by Ottaviano de'Petrucci at Venice. By 1523 Petrucci had published fifty-nine volumes (including reprints) of vocal and instrumental music. His publications, especially the earliest ones, are models of clarity and accuracy. Petrucci used the method of triple impression, that is, one impression for the staff lines, another for the words, and a third for the notes. This was a long, difficult, and expensive process; some printers in the sixteenth century reduced it to two impressions, one for the words and one for the music. Printing from a single impression—that is, from pieces of type which printed staffs, notes, and text in one operation—was apparently first practiced by John Rastell in London about 1520 and first applied systematically on a large scale by Pierre Attaingnant at Paris beginning in 1528. Music printing began in Germany about 1534 and in the Netherlands in 1538; Venice, Rome, Nuremberg, Paris, Lyons, Louvain, and Antwerp became the principal centers.

Most published ensemble music in the sixteenth century was printed in the form of partbooks—one small volume, usually of oblong format, for each voice or part, so that a complete set was requisite for performances. Partbooks were intended primarily for

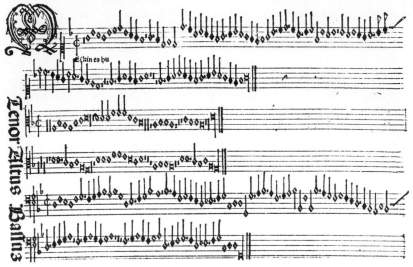

A page from Harmonice Musices Odhecaton, *a collection of 96 part-songs by Franco-Netherlandish composers, the first such book to be printed from movable type. Ottaviano de'Petrucci (1466–1539) published it at Venice in 1501. Petrucci's editions are highly prized for their neat presswork.*

use at home or in social gatherings. Most church choirs continued to use the large handwritten choirbooks; new ones were still being copied in the sixteenth century, although a few publishers also printed large choirbooks.

Meanwhile, in the early part of the sixteenth century a change had been taking place in the method of writing music. Composers formerly had written the various voice-parts successively, beginning probably with the tenor and adding the superius and then the other voices in turn. Now they began to conceive and to write the parts simultaneously, as a whole. In conformity with this changed approach they used a score for composing. The theorist Lampadius (1537) gives a short example of a score with barlines and dates its invention from the time of Josquin and Isaac. Manuscript scores appear in large numbers from 1560 on; the earliest printed ensemble score appears in 1577.

The application of the art of printing to music was obviously an event of far-reaching consequence. Instead of a few precious manuscripts laboriously copied by hand and liable to all kinds of errors and variants, a plentiful supply of new music was now made possible—not exactly at a low price, but still less costly than equivalent manuscripts, and of uniform accuracy. Furthermore, the existence of printed copies meant that now many more works of music would be preserved for performance and study by later generations.

Insofar as it is possible to define a Renaissance musical style, the following general features may be noted.

The characteristic "ideal" sound was that of four or more voice lines of similar character in a homogeneous tone color, instead of three more or less dissimilar lines in contrasting timbres as in the Middle Ages. The lines were of equal importance in that all shared equally in presenting the musical motives in a texture of imitative counterpoint; however, the two outer voices had special functions in defining tonal centers, and the makeup of some church choirs suggests that the soprano line was given some prominence in performance.

Renaissance musical style

The ideal performing medium was an unaccompanied vocal ensemble (*a cappella*)—"ideal" both in that one feels this to have been the kind of sound most composers had in mind, and also in that it was not always heard in actual performances. The fact that instrumentalists (except the organist) are seldom listed among the personnel of church choirs in the first half of the sixteenth century suggests that *a cappella* singing was customary, at least in the larger churches of Italy, at this time; after about 1560, however, instruments seem to have been generally used in combination with the voices.

Saviour of Church music in Renaissance is Palestrina

Bass - given foundation of harmonic structure

Units of vertical sonority were the combinations we call the triad and the $\frac{6}{3}$ chord—conceived, however, not as such but rather in terms of intervallic relationships and progressing according to the requirements of melodic movement and harmonic consonance within a modal framework.[2] The bass was gradually given the function of a harmonic foundation, even when it was imitating the other voices.

By the end of the fifteenth century some "rules" for *musica ficta*—that is, for the performers' application of accidentals not specified in the score—had achieved fairly general currency. These rules, which were given further currency by printed treatises at the end of the 15th and beginning of the 16th centuries, included the following:

Musica ficta

(1) In direct melodic leaps of a fourth or a fifth, or melodically outlined fourths and (except in certain contexts) fifths, the intervals should be perfect.

(2) Except in certain contexts, "Una nota supra la semper est canendum fa" (one note beyond la should be sung as fa)—that is, when the melody proceeds upward only a single step from la, that step should be a semitone.

(3) Except in certain contexts, harmonic intervals of the fourth, fifth, and octave should be perfect.

(4) (a) When the two voices of a third proceed stepwise outward to a fifth, or the two voices of a sixth stepwise outward to an octave, the imperfect interval (that is, the third or sixth) should be major. Similarly, when the two voices of a third proceed inward to a unison, the third should be minor.

[2] A brief compendium of sixteenth-century theory relating to these matters may be read in the selections from Glarean's *Dodecachordon* (1547) and Zarlino's *Istituzioni* (1558) printed in SR 219–55 (SRRe, 29–65).

(b) Especially in suspension-cadences, the sixth immediately preceding the octave should be major.

(5) If the final harmony of a piece contains a third, it should be major.

(6) Some theorists also say that in certain circumstances the middle note of each of the following melodic groups should be raised a semitone: a–g–a, d–c–d, g–f–g.

There is no general agreement on the order of priority in the application of these rules in cases where two or more of them would conflict. Conventions governing their application doubtless varied from place to place and from time to time.

The presence of explicit accidentals in manuscripts and prints of the period can be used to support the idea that the rules they seem to illustrate were current, or, on the other side of the argument, that they were not self-evident. Undoubtedly, there was a growing tendency in the first half of the sixteenth century for composers to make intended accidentals explicit.[3]

Rhythm

With regard to rhythm, two distinct tendencies were apparent in the Renaissance: (1) the music might move with fluid rhythm either in a contrapuntal texture with systematic free imitation involving all the voices, or in a freely improvisatory style, as in certain types of lute and keyboard pieces; or, (2) the movement might be by strongly marked rhythmic patterns in a predominantly chordal texture, as in instrumental dance pieces and certain kinds of secular vocal compositions. These two tendencies represent two different traditions; they interact to some extent in the sixteenth century, but on the whole they remain differentiated.

Music and words

Renaissance music became both more closely united with words and more independent of words. On the one hand there was a constant and successful effort throughout the sixteenth century to make the texts in vocal music more easily understandable and to make the music immediately and strikingly express the images and especially the feelings suggested by the text; at the same time the rise of instrumental music bears witness to the urge to create musical forms which should be complete and satisfying as purely musical entities, not needing the support of words. The esoteric devices of medieval music, such as isorhythm or the use of unrecognizable fragments of Gregorian Chant, died hard, especially in the innately conservative realm of sacred composition; but on the whole, the trend of the Renaissance was away from concealed meaning (except for occasional playful manifestations) and toward making the content of music such as could be grasped by any listener with the requisite sensibility.

Finally, although the older cantilena texture of a solo voice with instrumental accompaniment was not entirely dropped during the

---

[3] This summary is quoted by permission from a statement prepared by Professor Arthur Mendel for the Josquin Festival-Conference at New York in June, 1971.

Title page of Silvestro di Ganassi's Fontegara, *1535. A recorder consort and two singers are shown performing from printed part-books.*

Texture

Renaissance, for a long time it was neglected. The fundamental nature of most Renaissance music suggests general equality of the voices, yet many pieces in contrapuntal style were actually performed by a vocal soloist with instruments playing the other parts. Also, a certain number of pieces were frankly written as solos with accompaniment; but it was not until near the end of the sixteenth century that this particular type of composition rose to special prominence.

The foregoing generalizations will acquire more meaning as we study specific examples of the music of the Renaissance. Meanwhile, we should remember that none of these features was absolutely new; all had been foreshadowed in the fourteenth and early fifteenth centuries. The difference is that what was then exceptional now became typical. Of course, many medieval traits survived in the music of the late fifteenth and early sixteenth centuries; for example, there was a notable revival of the medieval spirit, and to some extent also of medieval technical procedures, in church music toward the end of the fifteenth century. Renaissance ideals were not everywhere dominant; some of the Protestant churches in the sixteenth century were distrustful not only of these ideals but of any elaborate music whatever.

For convenience we may distinguish two main overlapping periods in the history of Renaissance music. Until well into the sixteenth century the prevailing style was international, relatively uniform, and largely dictated by composers from northern France and the Lowlands. As the sixteenth century progressed, diverse national styles arose; and after about 1550, the progress of music was marked by the growing dominance of these styles and by new departures that foreshadowed the Baroque era.

In this and the next two chapters we shall divide the complex history of Renaissance music in the following way: the present chapter will deal with the principal composers and musical forms from the late fifteenth century to about 1520. Chapter VII will be concerned with the Catholic church music of the period from 1520 to 1550, with the beginnings of national styles and of instrumental music, and the flowering of the madrigal and related forms in the middle and late sixteenth century. In Chapter VIII we shall follow the growth of sacred music in the Lutheran and other Protestant churches in the sixteenth century, the Catholic church music of the latter half of the sixteenth century, the instrumental music of the same period, and the rise of the Venetian school, the immediate predecessor of the Baroque.

The Netherlands Composers

The period between 1450 and 1550 in the history of music has been called "the age of the Netherlanders." During this time most of the important musical posts on the continent of Europe were held by composers who came from the region comprising the present territory of central and southern Holland, Belgium, and the northeastern part of France near the Belgian border. The word "Netherlands" in the fifteenth and sixteenth centuries did not connote nationality; in modern terms we should have to call some of the Netherlandish composers French, some Belgian, and some Dutch. Older histories of music speak of three "Netherlands Schools," the first of these being the group which we have designated as "Burgundian." Other terms used or advocated include "Flemish," "Franco–Flemish," "Franco–Belgian," "Franco–Netherlandish," or simply "Northern." The choice is of little consequence, and we shall use any or all of the above names as may be most convenient. The essential thing to remember is that they all designate not race or nationality, but either (a) a certain geographical area or (b) a certain musical style which, however modified from composer to composer or from generation to generation, retains permanent common features that appear in most of the music written in Europe up to about 1570.

The dominance of the Northerners, which had begun early in the fifteenth century, is vividly illustrated in the careers of their chief composers and performers between 1450 and 1550: most of these men passed a large part of their lives in the service of the Emperor (service which might take them to Spain, Germany, Bohemia, or Austria), the King of France, the Pope, or one of the Italian courts. In Italy, the courts or cities of Naples, Florence, Ferrara, Modena, Mantua, Milan, and Venice were the chief centers for the diffusion of the art of the Netherlanders. Their music was regarded as the proper style for cultivated composers, and musicians of all countries willingly learned from them.

The period after the middle of the fifteenth century is represented by the later works of Dufay and the compositions of Johannes Ockeghem. As is true of many other Netherlands composers, the exact date (1430?) and place of Ockeghem's birth are unknown. We first hear of him as a singer in the choir of the Cathedral at Antwerp in 1443. In 1452 he entered the chapel of the King of France, and in 1465 was made its leader (*maître de chapelle*), which post he held until his death in 1495. He was celebrated not only as a composer but also as the teacher of many of the leading Netherlanders of the next generation. It was customary in the fifteenth century to compose laments or *déplorations* on the death of famous musicians; in one such *Déploration sur le trépas de Jean Ockeghem* which was set to music by Josquin des Prez in 1497, the tenor intones the Gregorian theme of the Introit from the Requiem Mass ("Requiem aeternam"—"grant them eternal rest") while the other four voices lament in the mannered poetic language of the time with its mythological allusions and repeated puns—all of which, however, does not prevent the composer from expressing in his music a profound and touching sorrow:

Johannes Ockeghem

Nymphes des bois, déesses des fontaines,	Nymphs of the woods, goddesses of the fountains,
Chantres experts de toutes nations,	Skilled singers of all nations,
Changez vos voix tant clères et haultaines	Change your voices so clear and proud
En cris tranchants et lamentations.	To sharp cries and lamentations.
Car Atropos, très terrible satrappe,	For Death, terrible satrap,
A vostre Ockeghem attrappé en sa trappe,	Has caught your Ockeghem in his trap,
Vray trésorier de musique et chief d'oeuvre,	True treasurer of music and chef d'oeuvre,
Doct, élégant de corps et non point trappé;	Learned, handsome in appearance, and not stout.
Grant dommaige est que la terre le coeuvre.	Great pity that the earth should cover him.
Acoutrez vous d'habits de deuil:	Clothe yourselves in mourning,
Josquin, Piersson, Brumel, Compère,	Josquin, Piersson, Brumel, Compère,
Et plourez grosses larmes d'oeil:	And weep great tears from your eyes,

Perdu avez vostre bon père.   For you have lost your good
                                father.
Requiescant in pace. Amen.   May they rest in peace. Amen.[4]

This lament, which was reprinted at Antwerp as late as 1545, is one of several that were written on the death of Ockeghem. A miniature in a French manuscript of about 1530 shows Ockeghem and eight other singers of his chapel singing a Gloria from a large manuscript choirbook on a lectern (see p. 184), in the usual fashion of the time.

Ockeghem's style   Ockeghem does not seem to have been an exceptionally prolific composer. His known works comprise about twelve Masses, ten motets, and some twenty chansons. The relatively large number of Masses reflects the fact that in the second half of the fifteenth century this was the principal form of composition, in which the composer was expected to demonstrate most fully his skill and imagination. Most of Ockeghem's Masses are similar in general sonority to Dufay's *Se la face ay pale,* with four voices of essentially like character in a contrapuntal texture of independent melodic lines. However, the bass, which before 1450 rarely sang below c, is now extended downward to G or F, and sometimes as much as a fourth lower in special combinations of low voices; otherwise the ranges normally are the same as in the early part of the century. Example VI–1 shows the ranges used; the compass of the superius corresponds to that of the modern alto; the tenor and contratenor (the "tenor altus") are in nearly the same range, and frequently cross each other in the part-writing. The result, as compared with

EXAMPLE VI–1   Normal Ranges of Voice Parts in the Late Fifteenth Century

Burgundian style, is a fuller, thicker texture, a darker and at the same time a more homogeneous sound. This effect is reinforced by the character of Ockeghem's melodic lines, which are spun out in long-breathed phrases, in an extremely flexible rhythmic flow much like that of melismatic plainchant, with infrequent cadences and few rests (see Example VI–2).

To vary the sonority Ockeghem, following the example of earlier fifteenth-century composers, wrote whole sections as trios or duets, omitting one or two of the normal four voices; or he set one pair of

---

4 For transcription, facsimile, and commentary, see Edward Lowinsky, ed. *The Medici Codex of 1518* (MRM III–V). Line 7 of the poem alludes to Ockeghem's position as treasurer of the Abbey of St. Martin in Tours. The four names in line 11 are those of famous composers of the time ("Piersson" is Pierre de La Rue).

EXAMPLE VI–2   Agnus Dei II from the Mass *Mi-mi,* Johannes Ockeghem

[etc.]

voices against another pair, a device in natural accord with contemporary musical theory (which derived all vertical sonorities from
a primary intervallic relation between two voices) and one which
occurs often in early sixteenth-century music both sacred and secular.
Another way by which Ockeghem achieved contrast was to write
occasional passages in which all parts sing in identical rhythms,
producing a chordal or homophonic texture. This manner of writing in the vocal music of the fifteenth and sixteenth centuries is now
sometimes called "familiar style"; among the earlier Franco–Netherlandish composers it was rare, and was apparently reserved for
passages where they desired to place special emphasis on the words.
In the latter half of the sixteenth century it became much more
common.

Ockeghem's harmonic vocabulary is by no means oriented toward
the modern tonal system. In fact, the sound of his church music is
more austerely modal, and thus closer to the spirit of Gregorian
Chant, than that of the Burgundians. This is one sign of a general
tendency on the part of composers in the second half of the fifteenth
century to create a style of church music different from that of
secular music, instead of, as in the earlier period, writing Masses and
motets in a style practically indistinguishable from that of the
chanson. The uncertainties with respect to *musica ficta* become
especially troublesome in the work of Ockeghem and his followers;
it is very difficult to tell with assurance how far the apparently
rather strict modality of Ockeghem may have been modified in
practice by the use of accidentals, particularly for raising the leading
tone at cadences.

In general, Ockeghem did not rely heavily on imitation in his
Masses; there are many imitative passages, but these seldom involve
all the voices, and the technique is used only incidentally, not continually and systematically as it later was in the sixteenth century.

*The
Netherlands
canon*

Johannes Ockeghem and the singers of his chapel

One class of compositions, however, the *canons,* are a conspicuous exception to this general rule. Ockeghem, in common with his contemporaries, took delight in writing music in which the audible structure was supported by another, concealed structure of a theoretically rigid nature; it was the same propensity as that which led medieval composers to write isorhythmic motets, partly for sheer pleasure in the exercise of technical virtuosity, and partly as a public demonstration of professional skill. With the Netherlanders these displays of technique took the form of canons.

The method of writing canon is to derive one or more additional voices from a single given voice. The additional voices may be written out by the composer, or they may be sung from the notes of the given voice, modified according to certain directions. The additional voice may be derived in various ways. For example, the second voice may start at a certain number of beats or measures after the original one; the second voice may be an inversion of the first—that is, move always by the same intervals but in the opposite direction; or the derived voice may be the original voice backward —called a *retrograde* canon, or *cancrizans* ("crab") canon.

Another possibility is to make the two voices move at different rates of speed; canons of this sort are sometimes called *mensuration* canons, and they may be notated by prefixing two or more different mensuration signs (see pp. 141–42) to a single written melody. In a mensuration canon the ratio between the two voices may be simple augmentation (second voice moving in note values twice as long as the first), simple diminution (second voice in values half as long), or some more complex ratio. Of course, any of the devices just described may be used in combination. Furthermore, in any instance the derived voice need not be at the same pitch as the original one, but may reproduce its melody at some chosen interval above or below. A composition may also involve *double canon,* that is, two canons (or even more) being sung or played simultaneously. Two or more voices may proceed in canon while other voices move in independent lines. All in all, it is evident that considerable complication is possible.

An example of canonic writing is Ockeghem's *Missa prolationum,* every movement of which is constructed as a double mensuration canon making use of various intervals and various combinations of time signatures. Example VI–3 shows the beginning of the second Kyrie from this Mass. Each of the two parts in the original notation has two mensuration signatures— ○ and ◖ in the superius, ⊙ and ◔ in the contra—and two C clefs, one with each signature. In the transcription (Example VI–3b) the two top voices represent the superius and the lower voices the contra, with appropriate reduction of the original note values.

A composition somewhat similar to the *Missa prolationum* is Ockeghem's *Missa cuiusvis toni,* a Mass which can be sung "in any mode" by reading the music according to one or another of four

EXAMPLE VI–3 Kyrie II from the *Missa prolationum,* Johannes Ockeghem

b. Transcription

different clef combinations and making the necessary adjustments to avoid the occurrence of the interval F–B♮ either melodically or harmonically with the bass; see Example VI–4.

The importance of these and similar flights of virtuosity can easily be exaggerated. They hold a fascination for everyone who enjoys puzzles, musical or otherwise; and the nature of language is such that things of this kind lend themselves more readily to verbal explanation and may be more easily remembered than many more essential matters about these composers. It is less important to know that Ockeghem wrote canons than to realize, by listening to his music, that in the comparatively few compositions where he does use such artifices, they are most artfully hidden; they do not in the least inhibit his ability to communicate through the music, even to listeners untutored in the "science" of musical composition. It is very unlikely that anyone listening to the *Missa prolationum,* unless he were exceptionally attentive or had been alerted beforehand, would

EXAMPLE VI–4   Qui tollis from *Missa cuiusvis toni,* Johannes Ockeghem

186

Thou that takest away the sins of the world, receive our prayer.

realize that he was hearing a series of mensuration canons; but when the underlying scheme of the work is known, one must admire all the more the smooth melodic lines, the harmonious proportions, and the apparent ease with which the music moves despite the formidable technical problem which the composer has set himself.

Ockeghem and the other Netherlanders seem to have believed that as far as the ordinary listener was concerned the perfect canon, like the perfect crime, must not even be suspected, much less detected. They took a sly pleasure in concealed ingenuity, which may be regarded as a survival of medieval habits. In the late fifteenth century, this love of mystification occasionally manifests itself as a kind of guessing-game between composer and performer. The directions for deriving the second voice (or for singing the written one) are sometimes hinted in an intentionally obscure or jocular fashion instead of being plainly stated: thus "Clama ne cesses"— "Cry without ceasing," that is, ignore the rests; and others more enigmatic. It is significant that when music began to appear in printed form in the sixteenth century the publishers took care always to furnish a solution to such riddles. The word "canon," incidentally, did not have the same meaning in the fifteenth century that it has today, namely a composition or passage in strict imitation. Such a piece in the fifteenth century was called a *fuga* ("flight"). *Canon* originally meant the "rule" or direction according to which the second voice was derived.

Some of Ockeghem's Masses, like Dufay's *Se la face ay pale,* are based on a *cantus firmus,* using a given melody more or less systematically as the framework for every movement. For example, the Mass *De plus en plus* uses for its *cantus firmus* the tenor part of a Binchois chanson; the Mass *Ecce ancilla* is based on a plainsong antiphon. In most of Ockeghem's *cantus firmus* Masses the treatment of the given melody is quite free (his Mass *L'homme armé* is exceptional in this respect); in his *Missa caput* (modelled after Dufay's Mass of the same title) the borrowed plainsong melody is written in the alto clef, as in Dufay's Mass, but with a verbal canon (i.e., a "rule") directing that it be sung an octave lower, thus becoming in effect the lowest voice of the ensemble. Another means of unity in some of Ockeghem's Masses is the practice of beginning every section with the same opening motive.

In the fifteenth and sixteenth centuries, Masses without a *cantus firmus* took their titles from the mode in which they were written (for example, *Missa quinti toni,* "Mass in Mode V") or from some peculiarity of structure (for example, Ockeghem's *Missa cuiusvis toni*). Ockeghem's Mass *Mi-mi* probably derives its name from the first two notes of the bass voice, e–A, both of which in the Guidonian solmization (see Example II–7) were sung to the syllable "mi." A Mass having neither a *cantus firmus* nor any other identifying peculiarity, or one whose source the composer did not wish to indicate, was often called a *Missa sine nomine,* "without a name."

The essential quality of Ockeghem's church music is difficult to describe. The low range, the nonpulsatile rhythms, the prevailing texture of nonimitative counterpoint, the seemingly random harmonic progressions, and especially the long-breathed, winding melodies, unarticulated either by regular cadences or melodic sequences —all combine to produce an effect of vastness and mystery, a suggestion of inward rapture rising from the contemplation of thoughts embodied in the sacred text. Certainly there is no other polyphonic sacred music that so perfectly reflects the ideal of mysticism, of otherworldliness, in religious worship. And that spirit becomes all the more evident when the singing is by a chorus rather than by solo voices.

Ockeghem's church music

This important change in the manner of performing church music had come about gradually during the first half of the fifteenth century. All through the Middle Ages polyphony had been sung by solo voices, the chorus being used only for unison plainchant. But in the Old Hall manuscript, and in some English and Italian manuscripts of the 1420s and 30s, we begin to find unequivocal directions for certain passages to be rendered by several singers on a part, that is, by a chorus (not necessarily a large group) instead of by an ensemble of soloists. By the middle of the century, choral performance of church music—alternating with duets or trios for solo voices—seems to have been the rule. (For most secular vocal music throughout the Renaissance, however, solo voices remained the normal medium.) Choruses were not large by modern standards. An ensemble of thirty singers was exceptional; eight or twelve was a more usual size. The customary manner of performance was from a single large choirbook placed on a lectern, with the music written large enough so that all the singers could read from the same open pages (see illustration, p. 184). Apparently in the few churches where the choir was sufficiently skilled, performances were *a cappella;* but instrumental doubling or replacement of human voices was probably common, and on especially festive occasions instruments might always be brought in.

Ockeghem's Masses show an extreme reaction against the Burgundian chanson-style Mass and motet of the early fifteenth century; a more even balance between mystic withdrawal on the one hand and articulate expressiveness on the other was restored in the next generation of Franco–Flemish church composers, many of whom directly or indirectly were pupils of Ockeghem. The three most eminent figures of this generation were Jacob Obrecht, Henricus Isaac, and Josquin des Prez, all born around the middle of the century—Obrecht near Antwerp, Isaac perhaps at Bruges, and Josquin somewhere in the territory of Hainaut. All received their earliest musical training and experience in the Netherlands. All traveled widely, working in various courts and churches in different countries of Europe. The careers of these three composers, like those of most of their contemporaries, well illustrate the lively continual interchange in musical matters that went on in the fifteenth and sixteenth centuries between northern and southern Europe, between the Franco–Belgian centers and those of Italy and (somewhat later) Spain. It is natural, therefore, that we should find in their music a diversity, a mixture, and to some extent a fusion, of northern and southern elements: the serious tone, the leaning toward rigid structure, the intricate polyphony, the smoothly flowing rhythms of the Netherlands; the more spontaneous mood, simpler homophonic texture, more distinct rhythms, and more clearly articulated phrases of the Italian style.

Jacob Obrecht

Few details are known of the life of Jacob Obrecht (*ca.* 1452–1505). He held important positions at Cambrai, Bruges, and Antwerp; he probably made several visits to Italy. He was at the court of Ferrara in 1487–88; he returned there to join the ducal Chapel in 1504, but died of the plague within a year.

Obrecht's works include some two dozen Masses, about an equal number of motets, and a number of chansons and instrumental pieces. Most of his Masses are built on *cantus firmi*, either secular songs or liturgical Gregorian melodies; but there is much variety in the treatment of these borrowed themes. In some Masses the entire melody is used in every movement; in others, the first phrase of the melody is used in the Kyrie, the second in the Gloria, and so on. Some Masses may have two or more liturgical *cantus firmi* in combination; the *Missa carminum* introduces about twenty different secular tunes. Throughout the Masses occur frequent canonic passages.

Obrecht's style

Obrecht thus employed the typical Netherlandish techniques, but with considerable freedom and originality. His Masses and motets differ from those of Ockeghem first of all by reason of the more spontaneous, impulsive quality of his musical imagination. One feels that Obrecht is constantly trying new things; his fancy occasionally leads him into bizarre experiments, but it manifests itself chiefly in the freshness and expressive warmth of his melodic lines. Related to this expressive quality is a complex of stylistic traits which together make for distinctness of outline, an immediately perceptible articulation of the musical flow. Obrecht's melody is typically Netherlandish in its smoothly vocal curves and its richly melismatic character; but unlike the long, winding, rapt, unbroken line of Ockeghem, Obrecht's melody is organized into relatively short though perfectly proportioned phrases with periodical cadences, supported always by clear and appropriate harmonies.

An excellent example of Obrecht's style is the three-voice motet

Parce Domine. (Example VI–5; the entire motet appears in MM, No. 18.) The two upper voices are pervaded by the motive of a stepwise-descending fourth, a motive like a gesture of supplication, which

EXAMPLE VI–5 Basic motive from Motet: *Parce Domine,* Jacob Obrecht

unifies these two parts without much obvious imitation and likewise binds them thematically to the lowest voice, which has the same descending interval as its underlying structural feature. This lowest voice, with its longer note-values, frequent pauses, and plain syllabic text setting, contrasts with the other two parts, serving in the manner of a *cantus firmus* melody (its only "harmonic" interval is the fifth e–A at the end). The theorist Glarean, writing over a generation afterwards (1547), cites this piece as an example of the "Aeolian" mode on A, one of the modes which he added to the traditional list of eight.[5] The divisions of the music correspond to those of the text:

Text	*Measures*	*Cadence on*
Parce, Domine	1–10	E
populo tuo	11–18	A
quia pius es	18–27	A
et misericors.	27–34	G
Exaudi nos in aeter-		
num, Domine.	34–45	A

Notice the overlapping of cadences; the careful treatment of dissonance in passing tones and suspensions; the frequent pairing of the two upper voices in successions of imperfect consonances (thirds and sixths), typically at the approach to a cadence; and the climactic effect obtained by combining this device with the long-held notes of the bass in the final five measures.

Not all of Obrecht's music shows these characteristics of his style so clearly as this motet, which is evidently a late work; but the contrast with Ockeghem is nearly always perceptible.

In addition to these general stylistic characteristics, Obrecht also uses from time to time certain supplementary devices—repetition of motives, ostinato figures, and melodic sequences—to give shape and coherence to his music. With respect to free imitation, Obrecht stands about midway between fifteenth- and sixteenth-century practice: he uses the technique fairly constantly, although in his church music it is more evident in the motets than in the Masses. In those motets based on a liturgical Chant, the Chant melody, or fragments of it, often appears in all the voices, so that the melodic substance of

[5] *Dodecachordon,* Bk. III, ch. 13; English tr., Miller, ed., II, 252, 327.

the *cantus firmus* permeates the entire musical tissue instead of being confined to a single voice, as had been the general rule with earlier composers. This practice was later carried much further.

An example of the way Obrecht blended older and newer style traits in his motet *O beate Basili* (HAM, No. 76a). The framework of this piece consists of a liturgical melody in canon at the fifth between the inner voices; the other two voices, though participating to a slight extent in the thematic material, for the most part go their independent nonimitative ways. A favorite sonority of this period is illustrated by the many passages in which the two outer voices are coupled in parallel tenths.

The chanson

Although polyphonic church music, especially settings of the Ordinary of the Mass, had achieved greater prestige in the second half of the fifteenth century than at any time in the previous two hundred years, there was no lack of secular composition in this period. The miniature proportions typical of the early Burgundian school were being expanded into larger musical forms; late Burgundian chansons of 1460–80 show a gradually increasing use of imitative counterpoint, involving at first only the superius and tenor voices, later all three. Binchois's *Filles à marier* has a sustained tenor and contratenor (possibly instrumental) supporting two soprano voices written in free imitation and a vivacious syllabic style. A concise, syllabic, strongly rhythmic type of melody is also found in the middle section of Ockeghem's *Ma maîtresse* (HAM, No. 74); here it makes a contrast to the first section, which is in the most elegant Burgundian courtly manner. Most of Ockeghem's chansons, as well as those of his hardly less famous contemporary Antoine Busnois (d. 1492), made use of the traditional *formes fixes* of courtly poetry. These were to be replaced in the next generation by verses in freer form—often strophic poems with refrain—and embracing a wider range of subject matter.

The chansons of Ockeghem, Busnois, and their successors were immensely popular. Certain favorites, such as Ockeghem's *Ma bouche rit* and Josquin's *Adieu mes amours,* appear over and over again in manuscripts and prints from many different countries. Chansons were freely altered, rearranged, and transcribed for instruments. Above all, they provided an inexhaustible supply of *cantus firmi* for Masses; sometimes the superius, sometimes the tenor voice of a chanson would be selected for this purpose. Thus Ockeghem used the superius of his *Ma maîtresse* complete and unchanged for the Gloria of a Mass, the first section in the contratenor and the second section later in the tenor, so that the same melody which served once for "My mistress and my own dear love" is sung to the words "And on earth peace, good-will to men"—an example of the religious conversion of a secular melody extremely common in this period. Obrecht's Mass *Je ne demande* takes over not only the tenor but also material from the other voices of a four-part chanson by Busnois.

The chanson in the generation of Obrecht, Isaac, and Josquin may be studied in one of the most famous of all music anthologies, the *Harmonice Musices Odhecaton A,* which was published by Petrucci at Venice in 1501. The title means "One hundred songs [actually there are only ninety-six] of harmonic [that is, polyphonic] music"; the letter "A" indicates that this is the first of a series of such collections, of which the other volumes, the *Canti B* and *Canti C,* were in fact issued in 1502 and 1504. The *Odhecaton* is a selection of chansons written between about 1470 and 1500; it includes pieces ranging from late Burgundian composers to the "modern" generation. Somewhat more than half of the chansons are for three voices, and these in general are written in the older styles. Among the composers represented in the collection are Isaac, Josquin, and two of their contemporaries, Alexander Agricola (*ca.* 1446–1506) and Loyset Compère (*ca.* 1455–1518). Petrucci and later Italian music printers issued a great number of chansons by French or Franco–Netherlandish composers in collections during the first half of the sixteenth century.

The Odhecaton

In all three of the Petrucci publications mentioned above, most of the chansons have either no words or only a text-incipit; this circumstance has led to the belief that these pieces were intended for instruments. Yet many of the same chansons are found in contemporary manuscripts wholly or partially furnished with words. As with the music of the Italian *trecento,* the presence of a text did not necessarily imply vocal performance nor did its absence necessarily imply instrumental performance. In the great majority of cases either was admissible, as was also a mixture of the two. For example, Obrecht's *Tsaat een meskin (Odhecaton,* No. 92), although it has been edited as an "instrumental canzona," may just as well have been sung.

The four-voice chansons of the *Odhecaton* show the way in which the form was developing at the beginning of the sixteenth century toward a fuller texture, a more completely imitative counterpoint, clearer harmonic structure, greater equality of voices, and closer union of the older and newer elements in the chanson style. Duple meter was replacing the more common triple meter of the Burgundian period. Many of these chansons, like contemporary Masses, used either a popular tune or a single voice from some earlier chanson as a *cantus prius factus.*

During the first two decades of the sixteenth century various types of chanson were cultivated by Franco-Flemish composers who were associated more or less closely with the French royal court at Paris. Some of these chansons were entirely original compositions; others incorporated already existing melodies. One of the latter kind is illustrated in Josquin's *Faulte d'argent* (HAM, No. 91): here the composer has taken a tune and text of popular origin and set it in

EXAMPLE VI–6   Canon from Chanson: *Faulte d'argent*, Josquin des Prez

strict canon at the lower fifth between the contratenor and the *quinta pars* ("fifth part"; see Example VI–6); around this the other three voices weave a network of close imitation, but without ever sacrificing clarity of texture. Another favorite procedure of Josquin, as also of his younger contemporary Antoine de Fevin (*ca.* 1470–1511), was to place a similarly borrowed melody in the tenor and enclose it with two outer voices which echo motives from the tune in a light-hearted play of imitative counterpoint—an adaptation of the *cantus firmus* technique. Still another method was to use separate motives from a given melody in a free four-part polyphonic texture. Again, the tune, or a paraphrased version of it, might be heard in the highest voice. In all these and other ways composers in the period 1500–1520 aimed to blend popular elements with the courtly and contrapuntal tradition of the chanson.

Josquin des Prez

Throughout the history of Western music, periods of exceptionally intense creative activity have occurred, during which the curve of musical production rises to a notable peak. The early sixteenth century was such a period. Out of the extraordinarily large number of

Josquin's career

first-rank composers living around 1500, one, Josquin des Prez, must be counted among the greatest of all time. Few musicians have enjoyed higher renown while they lived, or exercised more profound and lasting influence on those who came after them. Josquin was hailed by contemporaries as "the best of the composers of our time," the "Father of Musicians." "He is the master of the notes," said Martin Luther. "They must do as he wills; as for the other composers, they have to do as the notes will." Cosimo Bartoli, a Florentine man of letters, wrote in 1567 that Josquin was without peer in music, even as Michelangelo in architecture, painting, and sculpture: "Both opened the eyes of all those who now take pleasure in these arts and shall find delight in the future."

Josquin was born about 1440 in the province of Hainaut, the present Franco-Belgian border region. From 1473 to at least 1479, and probably longer, he was a member of the ducal chapel of the Sforza family in Milan, and perhaps remained under the patronage of Cardinal Ascanio Sforza until the latter's death in 1505. From 1486 to 1494 we hear of him from time to time at the Papal Chapel in Rome; from 1501 to 1503 he apparently was in France, perhaps at the court of Louis XII. In 1503 he was appointed *maestro di capella* at the court of Ferrara, but in the next year he left Italy for France. Toward the end of his life he returned to his natal region and died at Condé-sur-l'Escaut in 1521. His compositions were published in large numbers of sixteenth-century printed collections, and also occur in many of the manuscripts of the time. They include altogether about eighteen Masses, one hundred motets, and seventy chansons and other secular vocal works.

The high proportion of motets in Josquin's output is noteworthy. In his day the Mass was still the traditional vehicle by which a composer was expected to demonstrate mastery of his craft; but because of its liturgical formality, unvarying text, and established musical conventions, the Mass offered little opportunity for experimentation. The motets were freer; they could be written for a wide range of texts, all relatively unfamiliar and hence suggesting interesting new possibilities for word-music relationships. In the sixteenth century, therefore, the motet, rather than the Mass, came to be the most progressive form of sacred composition.

Very few of Josquin's works can be dated definitely, but it is apparent that his music includes both traditional and modern elements. He is the composer who more than any other may be said to stand at the border between the Middle Ages and the modern world. The conservative features of his work, as might be expected, are most conspicuous in the Masses. Most of these use a secular tune as a *cantus firmus,* and they abound in exhibitions of technical ingenuity. In the Mass *L'homme armé super voces musicales,* Josquin

*Josquin's
Masses*

195

transposes the familiar fifteenth-century tune to successive degrees of the hexachord (the *"voces musicales"*), beginning it on C for the Kyrie, on D for the Gloria, and so on.

Josquin's Masses illustrate many of the techniques and devices that were commonly used in the sixteenth century. The theme of the Mass *Hercules dux Ferrariae* offers an example of what the sixteenth century called a *soggetto cavato,*[6] a "subject [or theme] carved out" of a word or sentence by letting each vowel indicate a corresponding syllable of the hexachord, thus:

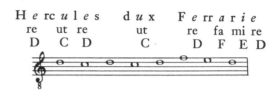

Hercules, or Ercole I, Duke of Ferrara from 1471 to 1505, from whose name this theme was derived, was a patron for whom Josquin wrote at least two other works in addition to this Mass.

Parody Masses   Josquin's Mass *Malheur me bat* is an instance of a procedure that became more common later in the sixteenth century. This Mass is based on a chanson by Ockeghem; but instead of only a single voice, all the voices of the chanson are employed at one time or another and subjected to free fantasy and expansion. A Mass which thus takes over not merely a single voice, but several—including (to varying degrees) the characteristic motives, progressions, or even the general structure and the musical substance—of some pre-existing chanson, Mass, or motet, is called a *parody Mass.* (This somewhat unfortunate term, of 19th-century German coinage, refers only to a method of composition and has no pejorative meaning; an alternative term is "derived Mass.") Obviously, in such cases the extent of borrowing can vary tremendously; more important, so can the degree of originality in treatment of the borrowed material. One extreme would consist merely in putting new words under old music, a procedure sometimes called "parody" but better denoted by the word *contrafactum.* A *cantus firmus* Mass with a borrowed tune in the tenor part exemplifies the typical fifteenth-century method; in an extension of this practice, motives from the given melody may be heard in other voices besides the tenor. The decisive step toward the parody Mass

---

[6] The *soggetto cavato* is not peculiar to the sixteenth century. One need only recall the many pieces written on the theme B–A–C–H (*b-flat, a, c, b-natural*)—for instance, Liszt's organ fantasia. The supplement to a special number of the Paris *Revue Musicale* for October, 1922, is entitled: *"Hommage à Gabriel Fauré; Sept pièces de piano sur le nom de Fauré: F fa, A la, U sol, R ré, E mi, par Louis Aubert, Georges Enesco, Charles Koechlin, Paul Ladmirault, Maurice Ravel, Roger-Ducasse, Florent Schmitt."*

is taken when the chosen model is no longer a single melodic line but a whole texture of contrapuntal voices. Foreshadowings, isolated instances of the new technique appear sporadically in Mass music from the fourteenth century on; the trend accelerates greatly in the early sixteenth century. The full-fledged parody Mass—which not only borrows musical material to a significant extent but also makes something new out of it, especially by means of combining borrowed motives in an original contrapuntal structure with systematic imitation among all the voices—finally replaces the *cantus firmus* Mass as the dominant form by about 1540.

In Josquin's Mass *Faysans regres* there is a fascinating mixture of motives from secular and sacred sources. This Mass takes its theme from the second part of a rondeau by Walter Frye, an English composer of the mid-fifteenth century who was perhaps associated with the Burgundian court. (The same theme was used in a chanson by Alexander Agricola, published in Petrucci's *Canti C* of 1504.) Josquin, taking over only a single phrase of the melody, constructs the tenor of his Mass from beginning to end on nothing but this four-note motive, transposed to different scale degrees and subjected to a myriad of rhythmic variations; in the Agnus Dei it is combined with another motive (in the altus) from the first part of the original chanson. In addition, in the Kyrie, Gloria, and Credo, Josquin introduces appropriate Gregorian melodies. The superius uses only these liturgical motives and figures derived from them; the melodic material of the altus comes chiefly from the superius, and that of the bassus from either the superius or the tenor. Example VI–7 shows how expertly Josquin worked.

EXAMPLE VI–7   Kyrie from the Mass, *Faysans regres*, Josquin des Prez

In thus using a *cantus firmus* or *cantus prius factus* (a "melody previously made") in his Mass, Josquin was following the universal custom of his time. By the sixteenth century, of course, this custom had already been long established, going back some five hundred years to the earliest days of polyphonic church composition. We can understand how, in the sixteenth century as well as in the twelfth, composers might wish to show their veneration for the sacred liturgical melodies by adorning them with all the resources of their art. But why use secular tunes? If they needed a single theme to give musical unity to a long work, why not take a plainsong chant, or invent a theme of their own? Why interlard the solemn words of the Mass with reminiscences of *My Mistress* or *The Armed Man* or some other worldly—or even obscene—chanson? Partly, of course, for the sheer fun of getting away with it: those who were not in the know (surely the vast majority of the congregation and probably also of the clergy) would not be likely to recognize the tune at all, particularly if it were well hidden in the tenor. For those who might recognize it there would be the pleasure of hearing from time to time something familiar in an otherwise incomprehensible stream of complicated sound—a pleasure to which church congregations in all ages have been addicted.

From the composer's point of view the secular tunes offered certain advantages as frameworks for organizing a long polyphonic movement: their musical shape was more pronounced than that of plainsong and their harmonic implications more definite. *L'homme armé*, for instance, was popular at least partly because of its distinct three-part form and its strong balance of harmonies. Moreover, Renaissance composers were not obsessed by the need for absolute originality, an idea which has become important in music only since the nineteenth century. Composers felt it was no more irreverent to use a familiar tune in a Mass than to depict a familiar object in a religious painting; the important thing was not the tune or the object, but what the composer or painter did with it. In borrowing *Faysans regres* for a Mass, Josquin was no more indebted to Frye than Beethoven later was to Diabelli for the theme of a set of variations.

Although Josquin's individuality is apparent in his Masses despite their adherence to traditional forms and practices, it was in the motets that he made his most original contributions; a good example is the beautiful four-voice *Ave Maria* based in part on a Gregorian melody (see MM, No. 19). This work illustrates the style which came to be characteristic of the entire sixteenth century. Each phrase of the text has its own musical motive, which is first presented in imitation by each voice in turn; the musical sentence thus initiated comes eventually to a cadence, and a similar sentence, on the next phrase of the text and with its own musical motive, begins. But the cadences are concealed by overlapping, so that while some of the voices are still finishing one sentence, others are begining the next, and the music continues without obvious division into sections. This was the basic plan of a sixteenth-century motet. However, the plan was subject to various modifications in order to avoid the danger of monotony arising from the same kind of texture too long continued and in order to achieve clear formal outlines and proportioned structure in the work as a whole.

Josquin's motets

Some of the means that Josquin used to attain this balance and formal articulation were: (1) the repetition of phrases, either literally or with added voices; or—frequent with Josquin and not uncommon with other composers of the time—with contrasting pairs of voices; (2) division of the work into large sections, set off by simultaneous cadencing of all voices and by the introduction of changes in meter and tempo; (3) a rounded three-part form, resulting from the similarity of sections one and three and their contrast with section two; (4) a purposive approach to cadences: the cadence of one part may be signalized by a long preparation on the dominant with threefold repetition of the bass motive and the coming together of all voices

Motet structure

in a chordal ensemble at the end; or by a similar piling-up of voices and a marked quickening of the harmonic pulse as well as of the movement of the individual voice-parts and increasing use of dissonances. This "drive to the cadence" was characteristic of all Netherlands polyphony between 1480 and 1530.

Another example of Josquin's three-part structure is found in *Tu pauperum refugium* (Example VI–8; also HAM, No. 90) which is itself the second half of a complete motet.[7] The peculiar character of the third mode (Phrygian) and the effective use of chordal style in phrases fitted closely to the accent of the words contribute toward the somber, deeply moving quality of this music. The hymnlike middle section with its slightly lilting triple rhythm (Example VI–8b) is typical of many passages in Josquin's work, and offers a suitable foil, appropriate also to the text, to the first and third sections. The voice pairing at the beginning of section three on the

[7] It has occasionally been suspected that this motet (I. Pars *Magnus es tu Domine*) may not be an authentic work of Josquin. While evidence from the sources is not unambiguous, the preponderance is in favor of authenticity. Certainly from the viewpoint of style there is no room for doubt as far as *Tu pauperum refugium* is concerned. Exactly similar procedures of text treatment and voice pairing may be found in many other works of Josquin—see for example the five-voice motet *Miserere mei Deus* (Smijers ed., No. 37; *Motetten*, Bundel VIII, 58 ff.), especially measures 284–90, 338–53.

EXAMPLE VI–8   Motet: *Tu pauperum refugium,* Josquin des Prez

a. *Thou refuge of the poor*

b. *And now, Redeemer, Lord*

c. *In Thee I hope, in Thee I trust*

words "in Thee I hope—in Thee I trust" (Example VI–8c) is an exceptionally fine use of this common device, suggested here naturally by the parallelism of the words.

The closing measures of this motet of Josquin illustrate another common early sixteenth-century usage, the prolongation of the cadence by a pedal point in one or more voices while the others oscillate gently back and forth before coming finally to rest. The last chord, as is usual in this period, consists of only the octave and fifth which, being perfect consonances, were regarded as more appropriate for the final sonority than a combination that included the imperfect consonance of the third.

The harmonic progressions in Josquin's music, though of course conceived within modal theory, show in practice the increasing pull of the dominant-tonic relationship. One sign of this is the conduct of the bass line with its frequent movement by fourths and fifths (see Example VI–8).

Josquin was particularly praised by his contemporaries for the care he took to suit his music to the text. One of the most puzzling matters involved in preparing modern editions or performances of early sixteenth century music is that of text underlaying—fitting the syllables of the text to the notes of the music—since most manuscripts and printed partbooks of the time are noncommittal in this respect. Printers and scribes were not always careful about placing a syllable directly under the note (or the first of a group of notes) to which it was to be sung, and there was no sign, like the modern slur, for indicating the duration of a syllable. Instead, a word of, say, three syllables is placed below or in the general vicinity of a passage of perhaps seven or eight notes to which the word obviously should be sung, with no hint of how the notes are to be distributed over the syllables. Moreover, the placing of the words is seldom identical in different contemporary manuscripts or editions of the same piece. Modern editors and conductors, in underlaying the text of choral works from this period, must often go by a combination of guesswork and musical common sense—and our musical common sense is not necessarily the same as that of the early sixteenth century.

Text and music

All the vocal music of Josquin's time shows the influence of humanism, and doubtless also that of the chanson and contemporary Italian popular forms like the frottola and lauda, in the effort for a more understandable text and better adherence to correct accentuation of the words; in effect, this was a reaction against the highly florid, melismatic style of Ockeghem and the other early Netherlands composers, who evidently were so preoccupied with the music that they were willing to leave the details of text underlaying entirely to the trained judgment of the singers.

Josquin's care for correct declamation is most apparent in the syllabic passages (especially those in familiar style) of his motets. *Tu pauperum refugium* is particularly instructive because it has a mixture of syllabic and melismatic styles. In the syllabic passages the setting of the Latin words is faithful both to the grammatical accent and to the emotional sense as well. But Josquin sometimes abandons the strictly syllabic setting for the sake of depicting the words even more graphically: at "laborantium" (the "heavy-laden"), by poignant suspensions; and at "errantium" (the "erring," or wandering ones; those who have lost the track) by a deliberately halting, directionless line in the altus. Among the wonderful tonal pictures in this motet is one at the words "ne unquam obdormiat in morte" ("lest ever [my soul] sleep the sleep of death"), where the drooping, descending lines of the voices going down one after another to the low dark tones of their register seem to bring the image of Death itself before us (Example VI–9).

EXAMPLE VI–9   Motet: *Tu pauperum refugium,* Josquin des Prez

Lest ever my soul sleep the sleep of death.

"Suiting the music to the meaning of the words, expressing the power of each different emotion, making the things of the text so vivid that they seem to stand actually before our eyes . . ."—these words are from a famous description of the music of a later Franco-Netherlandish composer,[8] but they apply equally well to Josquin. The author adds: "This kind of music is called *musica reservata*." This strange term (literally, "reserved music") seems to have come into use shortly after the middle of the sixteenth century to denote the advanced or "new" style of those composers who, motivated by a desire to give strong and detailed reflection of the words, introduced chromaticism, harmonic freedom, ornaments, and contrasts of rhythm and texture in their music to a degree hitherto unknown. There is also, perhaps, the implication that such music was "re-

Musica reservata

---

[8] Wolfgang Boetticher, *Orlando Di Lasso*, I, 240. The passage refers to the *Penitential Psalms* of Orlando Di Lasso, which were written about 1560 and published in 1584. The author was Samuel Quickelberg, a Dutch scholar and physician residing at the court of Munich; the date of his description is 1565.

EXAMPLE VI–10   Motet: *Absalon fili mi,* Josquin des Prez

served" for hearers who were capable of appreciating it. The expression *musica reservata* occurs occasionally in other writings of the late sixteenth and early seventeenth centuries with various meanings that are not clearly explained. Insofar as it refers to vivid musical expression of moods and images suggested by the text, one may justly call Josquin its originator, or at least its precursor.

Compositions in syllabic chordal style, like *Tu pauperum refugium,* are a minority of his total production; but expressive rendition of the text is common in his more conventional contrapuntal style as well. The ending of the motet *Absalon fili mi* (*O my son Absalom*: David's lament, II Samuel xviii:33) has an extraordinary passage of tone-painting on the words "but go down weeping to the grave" (Example VI–10). Here the voices descend not only melodically but also harmonically, taking the music through the circle of fifths from Bb to Gb. This shows Josquin as a bold experimenter, for the early sixteenth century as a rule never went beyond Eb, and even this note occurred only rarely.

Josquin excelled as a tone-painter not only of death and gloom, however. Many of his chansons overflow with cheerful spirits or a robust humor reminiscent of Beethoven's scherzos. In the sacred works there are passages like the tender lyric interlude in triple rhythm from the second part of the Christmas motet *Mittit ad Virginem,* that "combination of cradle song, pastorale, and angelic hymn"; or the playful musical punning on the last two words of the motet *Virgo prudentissima,* which ends *electa ut sol* ("clear as the sun"; Song of Solomon, vi:10), giving occasion for a procession of *ut-sols* to stalk through the four voices in turn:

or the incomparable prayer for peace to the Lamb of God at the end of the Mass *Pange lingua.*

Josquin was a composer of the period of transition between medieval and modern times, as Monteverdi was between the Renaissance and Baroque, Handel between the Baroque and Classical periods, and Beethoven between the Classical and Romantic. Josquin and Beethoven resemble each other in many ways. In both, the strong impulse of personal utterance struggled against the limits of the musical language of their time. Both were tormented by the creative process, and worked slowly and with numerous revisions. Both had a sense of humor; both, because of their independent attitude, had trouble with their patrons. Both, in their best works, achieved that combination of intensity and order, individuality and universality, which is the mark of genius. It may be added that both annoyed fastidious critics for the same reasons: "He lacked moderation, and the judgment that comes from sound learning, so that he did not always properly curb the violent impulses of his imagination." This was said by the Swiss theorist Glarean[9] about Josquin, whom he nevertheless admired above all other composers.

Some Contemporaries of Obrecht and Josquin

A general history of music must, for lack of space, renounce all hope of doing justice to the many excellent composers of the early sixteenth century who were contemporary with Obrecht and Josquin. Henricus Isaac (*ca.* 1450–1517), a Netherlander by birth, was in the service of Lorenzo the Magnificent at Florence from about 1484 to 1492; he later spent several years in Rome, and in 1497 became court composer to the Emperor Maximilian I at Vienna and Innsbruck. Toward the end of his life he returned to Italy, eventually settling at Florence, where he died in 1517.

Henricus Isaac

Isaac was a prolific composer in all the forms current in his time; he absorbed into his own style musical influences from Italy, France, Germany, and the Netherlands, so that his output is more fully international in character than that of any other composer of his generation. He wrote a large number of songs with French, German, and Italian texts, and many other short chanson-like pieces which, since they occur without words in the sources, are usually regarded as having been composed for instrumental ensembles. During his first sojourn at Florence, Isaac undoubtedly composed music for some of the *canti carnascialeschi,* "carnival songs" which were sung in gay processions and pageants that marked the Florentine holiday seasons.[10] The melody of one of his German polyphonic songs, *Isbruck, ich muss dich lassen (Innsbruck, I now must leave thee),* was later adapted to sacred words and became widely known under the title *O Welt, ich muss dich lassen (O world, I now must leave thee).*

Isaac's sacred compositions include some thirty settings of the Ordinary of the Mass and a cycle of motets based on the liturgical texts and melodies of the Proper of the Mass (including many sequences) for a large portion of the church year. This monumental cycle of motets, comparable to the *Magnus liber* of Leonin and Perotin, was commissioned by the church at Constance, and is known

9 Dodecachordon, 1547, III, xxiv.
10 See Walter Rubsamen, "The Music for 'Quant'è bella giovinezza' and Other Carnival Songs by Lorenzo de' Medici" in Charles S. Singleton, ed., *Art, Science, and History in the Renaissance,* Baltimore, 1968, 163–84.

as the *Choralis Constantinus*. Its musical style is representative of the Netherlands practice of Isaac's time: a prevalent texture of imitative counterpoint is clarified by repetitions and melodic sequences, and it is often evident that Isaac took particular care to emphasize important or dramatic words. Many of the melodic lines, especially in the altus and bassus voices, have a rather unvocal character which is not uncommon in the works of this period, and which may or may not indicate that the composer had instrumental performance in mind.

One of the foremost Franco-Netherlandish composers of the early sixteenth century was Pierre de La Rue (*ca.* 1460–1518), whose numerous Masses and motets still await a comprehensive modern edition. The supreme example of his technical skill is the Mass *Ave Sanctissima*. This is a parody Mass based on a motet which is perhaps by La Rue himself although it is also attributed to another Franco-Flemish composer, Philippe Verdelot (d. *ca.* 1545). La Rue's *Ave Sanctissima* is for six voices, and is written entirely in canon: from three notated voices three others are derived by canonic imitation at the fourth above, at various distances in each movement. The miracle, however, is not the technique but the music itself, for within this rigid and extremely difficult technical framework La Rue created one of the most beautiful settings ever made of the Mass.

Another important contemporary of Obrecht and Josquin was the Franco-Netherlander Jean Mouton (*ca.* 1459–1522). Mouton held several positions in France before beginning his long period of service in the royal chapel under two kings, Louis XII and Francis I. Described by the theorist Glarean as one of the "emulators" of Josquin, Mouton wrote Masses and motets that are remarkable for their smooth-flowing melodic lines and skillful use of various unifying devices. He was highly esteemed in Italy as well as in France, and is of particular historical interest also as a teacher of Adrian Willaert (*ca.* 1490–1562), a Netherlander who was to become the leading early figure in the rise of the Venetian school (see below, pp. 288 ff.).

VII

New Currents in the
Sixteenth Century

The Franco-Flemish Generation
of 1520-1550

The thirty years between 1520 and 1550 witnessed a constantly growing diversity of musical expression. In every country new types and forms of vocal music began gradually to modify the dominant cosmopolitan style of the Netherlands; the amount and importance of instrumental music also increased. The generation of Netherlanders after Josquin was not unaffected by these changes. Those who lived abroad, especially those in Italy and southern Germany, were naturally influenced by acquaintance with the musical idioms of their adopted homes.

For a time, church music (which is always conservative) resisted the changes; indeed, some composers tended to return to the continuous contrapuntal style of Ockeghem, as though in reaction against the too highly personal and adventurous experiments of Obrecht and Josquin. Even these conservative composers, however, almost wholly abandoned the canons and similar devices of the older school. In the Mass the parody method of composition gradually replaced the older technique of a single *cantus firmus*. Liturgical chants were still commonly used as the melodic substance of both Masses and motets, but in general they were treated quite freely. In both motets and Masses, composers were beginning to write for five or six voices in preference to the earlier standard four.

VII. New Currents in the Sixteenth Century

Nicolas Gombert

The Netherlands motet style of the period 1520–50 is found in the works of Nicolas Gombert (*ca.* 1500–*ca.* 1556), supposedly a pupil of Josquin, who as an official of the chapel of the Emperor Charles V accompanied the court on numerous voyages and worked at Vienna, Madrid, and Brussels. His motet *Super flumina Babilonis* (HAM, No. 114) exemplifies this motet style: a continuous series of imitative sentences with interlocking cadences, save for a single short contrasting section in triple meter and fauxbourdon harmonies; a generally smooth and uniform texture, without many rests, with all dissonances carefully prepared and resolved—quite undramatic in effect as compared with many of the works of Josquin, though not without a sensitive feeling for the rhythm and general mood of the text. The majority of Gombert's 169 motets are divided into two approximately equal parts or sections; in some instances these are thematically connected by making the closing portions identical in both text and music.

Jacobus Clemens

Another important Netherlands composer of this period was Jacob Clement or, in Latinized form, Jacobus Clemens (*ca.* 1510–*ca.* 1556); he was called "Clemens non Papa," probably to distinguish him from a poet named Jacobus Papa who lived in the same city of Ypres. Clemens worked in Paris for some time in the 1530s, returning to the Netherlands in 1540. His compositions include chansons, 15 Masses, over 200 motets, and 4 books of Psalms (*Souterliedeken*) with Dutch texts, written in simple three-part polyphony and using tunes of popular origin.

All but one of Clemens's Masses are of the "parody" type. His motets are similar in style to Gombert's, though the phrases are somewhat more clearly distinguished, and the melodic motives more carefully shaped to the sense of the words. His *Vox in Rama,* on a text of unusually intense and pathetic character, illustrates a theory about "secret chromatic passages" in works by Netherlands composers of the mid-sixteenth century. According to this theory, these passages require in performance the alteration of certain notes by flatting—alterations not marked by accidentals in the music but plainly hinted by certain notational procedures; when these alterations are carried out, they lead to temporary modulations into remote flat keys.

Example VII–1 (the entire piece is given in HAM, No. 125) shows how unnotated chromatics may have been applied. The flat sign before the b′ in the second measure of the superius, which plainly occurs in the manuscript, is unnecessary, since this b′ would have been flatted in any case by the singer in accordance with the ordinary rule of *musica ficta* to avoid the melodic tritone f′-b′♮. This superfluous flat sign in measure 2 is the hint to flat the b in the following measure of the tenor part, and this alteration also serves to keep the imitation of the phrase (indicated by brackets in the ex-

EXAMPLE VII–1   Motet: *Vox in Rama,* Clemens non Papa

ample) exact. But the flatting of this tenor b requires in turn that
the next note, e′, of the tenor also be flatted (to avoid the tritone
bb-e′♮), and this in turn involves the flatting of the b and e′ of
the altus in measure 4. The altus e′b in turn requires the bass in
this measure to conform by flatting its e, which in turn compels
the Ab in the superius and tenor on the last beat of this measure.
(Compare a similar process in Example VI–10.) The spiral is halted
and a return made to the normal modality by the a♮ on the first beat
of the altus in measure 6.

We cannot enter here into a discussion of the complicated arguments for and against this secret chromatic interpretation; but if
the theory is essentially correct—and it seems extremely probable
that it is—this music is another interesting manifestation of the age-
old delight in mystification and concealed meanings in music, as
well as a demonstration of the lengths to which composers of this
period would go to achieve a striking effect suggested by the emotional content of the text. It should be added that such unusual
secret modulations are found in the music of only a few composers,
and always in connection with words of exceptional significance.
Moreover, they are not essential, since the plain diatonic reading
of the notes is always possible—in Example VII–1, for instance, by
disregarding the added flats above the notes; the chromatic reading
was, as it were, "reserved" for those who understood the composer's
secret intentions.

The Masses and motets of Isaac's Swiss pupil, Ludwig Senfl (*ca.*
1490–1543), who worked chiefly at the Bavarian court of Munich,
are rather conservative in style, as is generally the case with composers in Germany at this period. Senfl's principal achievements,
however, were in other fields; he wrote many German secular songs
and also some sacred works on German texts for the Lutheran
church.

*Adrian
Willaert*

Not only the motets of Senfl, but also and more typically those of Gombert and Clemens, who worked chiefly in the north, exemplify what may be called a conservative direction in the Netherlands motet style of the first half of the sixteenth century. A somewhat different line of development stems from Adrian Willaert, the most notable Netherlander in Italy during this period. Born around 1490 in Flanders, Willaert studied composition with Mouton at Paris. After holding various positions in Rome, Ferrara, and Milan, Willaert was appointed director of music in St. Mark's cathedral at Venice in 1527. Here he remained until his death in 1562, conducting, composing, and training many eminent pupils, through whom his fame and influence spread all over Italy. Willaert, representing the tradition of Josquin, Mouton, and other composers associated with the French Court, must be regarded as one of the principal founders of the Venetian school and a pioneer of new tendencies that were to become increasingly important in the second half of the century. His *Victimae paschali laudes* (HAM, No. 113), published in 1559 in a collection called *Musica nova* (*New Music*) but written probably many years earlier, shows both old and new features. There is a plainsong *cantus firmus* (first in the *sextus* then in the *quinta pars*), but instead of standing out as a rigid scaffolding, it is blended into the full rich harmonies of the other five voices. Instead of flowing melismatic lines and continuous systematic imitation, we have short phrases moving within a narrow compass, with mostly syllabic texting and many repeated notes. Care is taken to make the words understood and to reflect in the music their natural accentuation. The bass is not primarily melodic, but serves rather as the foundation of a musical texture that approaches homophony. All these are precursory signs of a coming new style in which Italy was to take the lead after the middle of the sixteenth century.

The Rise of National Styles

ITALY

Although Franco-Netherlandish composers were scattered all over Western Europe in the early sixteenth century, and their idiom was a common international musical language, each country also had its own distinctive music which was certainly better known and probably better enjoyed by most people than the learned art of the northerners. Gradually in the course of the sixteenth century these various national idioms rose to prominence and eventually caused the Netherlands style to be modified in varying degrees. The process was most clearly marked in Italy. The change from foreign to native musical leadership in that country is vividly illustrated by the following sequence of events: about 1520 the Belgian Adrian Willaert came to Italy and in 1527 was made director of the music at St.

Mark's Cathedral in Venice, the most prestigious musical position in Italy. Among Willaert's many Italian pupils was Andrea Gabrieli (*ca.* 1520–86), who later held positions at St. Mark's and whose pupil and nephew, Giovanni Gabrieli, became the most celebrated Venetian composer of his generation. In 1609 a promising young German composer, Heinrich Schütz, came to Venice to study with Giovanni Gabrieli. Thus, in the space of less than a century Italy had supplanted the Netherlands as the center of European musical life, and her primacy then established endured for two hundred years. In all European countries, musical dependence on the Netherlands at the beginning of the sixteenth century was replaced by dependence on Italy at the beginning of the seventeenth; but in the meantime each country had also developed a national school of its own.

When Petrucci started to print music at Venice in 1501, he began with chansons, Masses, and motets; but then, from 1504 to 1514, he published no fewer than eleven collections of strophic Italian songs, set syllabically to music in four parts, having marked rhythmic patterns, simple diatonic harmonies, and a definitely homophonic style with the melody in the upper voice. These songs were called *frottole* (singular, *frottola*), a generic term which embraces many sub-types.

The frottola

The frottola flourished in the late fifteenth and early sixteenth centuries. Probably the usual method of performance was to sing the upper voice and play the other parts as accompaniment. The singer might deal quite freely with the written notes, and especially might introduce an improvised melismatic flourish—a little "cadenza"—at one or more of the principal cadences. In spite of the simplicity of their music and the uninhibited freedom of many of their amorous and satirical texts, the *frottole* were not popular or "folk" music; their milieu was the Italian courts, especially those of Mantua, Ferrara, and Urbino. The *frottole* were perhaps a national reaction against the artificial sentiments and the contrapuntal style of the Netherlands chanson. The principal composers were Italians, though Netherlanders living in Italy also wrote a few. The frottola is historically important as a forerunner of the Italian madrigal; the extent of its influence on the style of the French chansons that began to appear in the 1520s is uncertain.

The religious counterpart of the frottola was the polyphonic *lauda* (pl. *laude*), a popular nonliturgical devotional song. (See discussion of monophonic *laude* on p. 70). The texts were sometimes in Italian, sometimes in Latin; these were set to four-part music, the melodies being often taken from secular songs. Two books of *laude* were published by Petrucci in 1507 and 1508. *Laude* were commonly sung in semi-public devotional gatherings, either a cappella or possibly with instruments playing the three lower voices. Like the *frottole,* the *laude* were for the most part syllabic, homophonic, and

The lauda

regularly rhythmic, with the melody practically always placed in the highest voice. In their simple harmonic settings they were often remarkably expressive. Related in mood and purpose to liturgical music, the *laude* nevertheless seldom incorporated Gregorian themes, nor did they show many traces of the Franco–Flemish church style. On the contrary, it was the Netherlanders in Italy who undoubtedly learned from the lauda and the frottola (as well as from the old Burgundian fauxbourdon) some of the potentialities of harmonic writing and simple syllabic text setting; passages in familiar style in the music of many late sixteenth-century composers (Palestrina and Victoria, for example) are probably indebted to the tradition of the lauda.

FRANCE

In the fifteenth and early sixteenth centuries it is difficult to speak of a French musical idiom distinct from that of Burgundy or the Netherlands. The culture of Burgundy, as well as that of most of the Netherlands provinces, was French. Pierre de La Rue and Josquin des Prez, though of Flemish descent, were culturally French, and their very names are probably French translations of Flemish names.

The new
French chanson

French was always the language of the chanson as Latin was of the Mass. But although French composers of Masses and motets in the early sixteenth century continued to write in a slightly modified version of the international style of the Netherlands, chanson composers in this period and during the long reign of Francis I (1515–47) developed a type of chanson that was more distinctively national in both poetry and music.

Such works appeared in the publications of the first French music printer, Pierre Attaingnant, who between 1528 and 1552 brought out in Paris more than fifty collections of chansons, about 1,500 pieces altogether. Other publishers soon followed Attaingnant's lead. The popularity of the chanson is attested by hundreds of transcriptions for the lute and arrangements for solo voice with lute accompaniment which were published during the sixteenth century in both France and Italy.

The typical chansons of the earliest Attaingnant collections resembled in many respects the Italian frottola and the *canti carnascialeschi*. They were light, fast, strongly rhythmic songs for four voices, syllabic, with many repeated notes, predominantly in duple meter with occasional passages in triple meter, and predominantly homophonic with the principal melody in the highest voice, but not excluding short points of imitation; one is illustrated in Example VII–2. They had distinct short sections which as a rule were repeated so as to form an easily grasped pattern, such as *aabc* or *abca*. The texts covered a considerable range of verse forms and subjects, a favorite topic being some amatory situation that might allow the poet occasion for all sorts of pleasant comments and equivocal allusions. Not all the texts, however, were frivolous.

EXAMPLE VII–2 Chanson: *Fy, fy d'amours,* Claudin de Sermisy

(1.) Fy, fy d'a-mours et de leur al-li-an — — n'est qu'a-bus, tour-ment et dur mar-ty — — re

(2.) Coust, dueil, en-nuy, tra-vail et def-fi-an — — ce Ce n'est qu'a-bus tour-ment et dur mar-ty — re
n'est qu'a-bus, tour-ment et dur mar-ty — — re
ce Et si ne font qu'a· l'ame et au corps nuy — re.

(3.) Plu-sieurs ont veu de fol-les gens des-truy —
de fol-les

Et Dieu
re Et Dieu lais-ser pour leurs a-mours ser-vir
(etc.)
Et Dieu
Et dieu lais — — ser

Bah! Their love and their alliance are nothing but abuse, torment, and hardship, blows, mourning, boredom, labor and mistrust; in fact, all they do is harm the soul and the body. Several have seen foolish people destroy and abandon God in order to devote themselves to love.

The two principal composers of chansons in the first Attaingnant collections were Claudin de Sermisy (*ca.* 1490–1562) and Clément Janequin (*ca.* 1485–*ca.* 1560). Janequin was particularly celebrated for his descriptive chansons in free form, songs not unlike the Italian fourteenth-century caccia, introducing imitations of bird calls, street cries, and the like. The most famous of Janequin's descriptive chansons was one entitled *La Guerre,* traditionally supposed to have been written about the Battle of Marignan (1515); it is the ancestor of innumerable "battle" pieces in the sixteenth century and afterward. The leading composer of chansons at Paris after Sermisy and Janequin was Pierre Certon (*ca.* 1510–72) whose works ably continue the style founded by Sermisy.

The later Netherlands chanson

Besides Attaingnant and others at Paris, the principal publishers of chansons in the first half of the sixteenth century were Jacques Moderne at Lyons (publications 1532–60) and Tilman Susato at Antwerp (fourteen collections, 1543–55). The chansons published at Antwerp were mostly by Franco–Flemish composers, chiefly Gombert, Clemens non Papa, Pierre de Manchicourt (d. 1564) and Thomas Crécquillon (d. 1557). As a rule their chansons were somewhat more contrapuntal than those written by the Paris composers,

Title page for the second of seven volumes of Masses published by Attaingnant in 1532; it contains works by Mouton, Claudin (de Sermisy) and Pierre de Manchicourt. The scene shows a mass at the court of the King of France, Francis I.

with fuller texture, more melismatic lines, and a less marked rhythmic beat. These men, in fact, continue the older Netherlands chanson tradition, influenced, however, by the French example toward a style more homophonic than that of the early sixteenth-century Netherlanders.

Susato and other Netherlands publishers also issued a few polyphonic songs with texts in their own language. Practically all the chanson writers, French and Netherlandish, also produced Masses and motets; Manchicourt in particular was a distinguished composer for the church. Like the earlier chansons, those of the sixteenth century were used as material for Mass themes, and many of them also served as models for parody Masses.

Polyphony developed later in Germany than in the other countries of Western Europe. The monophonic art of the Minnesinger flourished at the German courts through the fourteenth century, and that of the Meistersinger in the cities and towns from about 1450 and more especially throughout the sixteenth century. Franco-Flemish musicians begin to be heard of in Germany from about 1530.

GERMANY

With the rise of a prosperous mercantile civilization, a distinctive type of German polyphonic *Lied* (song) came into existence. The *Lochamer Liederbuch* (*Lochamer Songbook*) of 1452, one of the earliest collections of German polyphonic songs, contains both monophonic melodies and three-part settings with the leading melody in the tenor part. Similar three-part settings are found in the *Glogauer Liederbuch* of about the same date.

The German
Lied

Lieder composers skillfully combined German melodic material with a conservative method of setting and a contrapuntal technique derived from the Netherlands. The first real masters of the polyphonic Lied were Isaac and his contemporary Heinrich Finck (1445–1527). In Isaac's *Zwischen Berg und tiefem Tal* (*Between Mountain and Deep Valley*) a characteristically German melody—perhaps original, perhaps borrowed, perhaps even a folk song—is presented, phrase by phrase, in canon by the bass and tenor; the other two voices anticipate each phrase with brief imitations in quicker rhythm. Part of this Lied is given in Example VII–3; the entire piece appears in HAM, No. 87. In performance possibly only the tenor was sung, the other parts being taken by instruments.

Another excellent composer of *Lieder* was Paul Hofhaimer (1459–1537), court organist of the Emperor Maximilian. With Ludwig Senfl, the Lied reached artistic perfection; some of his *Lieder* are, in all respects except the language of the text, full-fledged motets of the Netherlands type, and most beautiful examples of that style. Senfl also wrote many shorter songs on folklike tenor tunes, filled with picturesque or humorous touches, yet always exhibiting a certain earthy, serious quality that seems inseparable from the German musical feeling.

VII. New Currents in the Sixteenth Century

EXAMPLE VII–3   Lied: *Zwischen Berg und tiefem Tal*, Henricus Isaac

Between mountain and deep valley lies an open road.

Collections of German *Lieder* continued to be published during the first half of the sixteenth century, chiefly at Nuremberg, which was a leading center of German culture at this time. After 1550, German taste veered to Italian madrigals and villanellas, and consequently the Lied declined in importance or took on Italianate characteristics. Meanwhile, however, it had provided the musical model and a great deal of the musical material for the chorales or hymns of the Lutheran church.

One kind of song, written in other countries as well but mostly in Germany, was the *quodlibet* (literally, "whatever you like"), a piece made up of different songs or fragments of songs thrown together often with the apparent aim of making an incongruous and absurd mixture of texts; the musical sense of many quodlibets, however, was sound and even quite artistic. Another minor genre of this period in Germany, an outgrowth of humanistic studies, was musical settings of classical Latin verses, for example, the *Odes* of Horace. These pieces were in strict chordal style, with a rhythm determined by combining long and short note values which corresponded exactly with the long and short syllables of the poetry; they were sometimes designed to be used as aids to instruction in school courses in classical literature.

The quodlibet

Comparatively little of the earliest polyphonic music of Spain has been published. By the late fifteenth century the works of Burgundian and Netherlands composers were known and sung in Spain; at the same time a national school of polyphonic composition was arising, a school which, like the one in Germany, incorporated some popular elements and held out for a long time against foreign influences. The principal genre in Spanish secular polyphony toward the end of the fifteen century was the *villancico,* which may be regarded as the Spanish analogue of the Italian frottola. A short strophic song with a refrain, typically with the pattern *aBccaB,* villancicos had the principal melody in the top voice, and were probably intended to be performed by a soloist with accompaniment of two or three instruments. They were collected in songbooks (*cancioneros*) and many were also published as vocal solos with lute accompaniment. The principal poet and composer of the early sixteenth century was Juan del Encina (1469–1529), whose pastoral plays usually ended with a villancico.

SPAIN

Spanish sacred polyphony, like that of all continental Europe in the late fifteenth and early sixteenth centuries, was strongly under the influence of the Netherlands style. Gombert, Manchicourt, Crécquillon, and other Netherlanders worked from time to time in Spain, and Spanish manuscripts of the period include many works by Franco–Flemish masters. Within its basic framework of Netherlands technique, however, Spanish sacred music was marked by a particular sobriety of melody and moderation in the use of contrapuntal artifices, together with a passionate intensity in the expression of religious emotion. These qualities may be heard in the motet *Emendemus in melius (Let us Amend)* by Cristóbal de Morales *(ca.* 1500–53), the most eminent Spanish composer of the early sixteenth century and one who had acquired fame in Italy during his residence at Rome from 1535 to 1545 as a member of the Papal chapel. *Emendemus in melius* is a penitential motet (the words occur as a Responsory in the service of Ash Wednesday); Morales has chosen to reinforce the mood by using a fifth voice, musically and textually independent of the other four, which proclaims insistently like a warning trumpet the grim reminder "Remember, O man, that dust thou art and to dust thou shalt return." This technique was not uncommon in the period: essentially, the device is a *cantus firmus* in the form of an ostinato phrase which centers alternately on the final (E) and dominant (A) of the mode (see Example VII–4; the entire motet is in HAM, No. 128). The other voices are notably plain, almost austere; they bring into relief, by means of repeated notes or wide leaps, occasional salient phrases of the text, for example, the tenor and bass at the words *Attende Domine* ("Hearken to us, O Lord"). Interesting also with respect to text treatment is the way in which Morales tends to cluster the suspensions around words that are most strongly colored with emotion: *peccavimus* ("we have sinned"), *mortis* ("of death"), *invenire non possimus* ("we cannot find"), *miserere* ("have mercy"); as these words are repeated, the expression each time is intensified by increased use of suspensions.

EXAMPLE VII–4 *Cantus firmus of Motet: Emendemus in melius,* Cristóbal de Morales

Remember, man, that dust thou art and to dust thou shalt return.

Morales was one of a large number of Spanish composers in the sixteenth century; some of these men worked entirely in their own country, while others, like Morales and Victoria, were closely associated with the music of the church at Rome. As in Germany and Italy, so also in Spain: after the middle of the sixteenth century the traditional Netherlands technique was gradually absorbed into a new style of both sacred and secular music, a style determined in large part by national characteristics.

To varying degrees and at varying intervals of time, the eastern countries of Europe participated in the general musical developments of the late medieval and Renaissance periods. As far as Catholic church music was concerned, there was a common basis in Gregorian Chant, examples of which are found in eastern manuscripts from as early as the eleventh and twelfth centuries. Everywhere, elements of foreign origin intermingled with native popular traditions; melodies of sequences, tropes, and liturgical dramas were adapted to vernacular texts. Influences came from western composers who served from time to time at eastern royal courts, and from musicians of eastern Europe who were trained in Germany, France, or Italy. Contemporary Franco-Flemish music was known in Bohemia during the reign of Emperor Charles IV (1347–78). Works by Flemish theorists were studied at the Universities of Prague and Cracow from the end of the fourteenth century. The earliest examples of Polish polyphony date from the thirteenth century. By the sixteenth century Polish and Bohemian composers were writing chansons, Masses, and motets as well as music for lute, organ, and instrumental ensembles. Polish organ tablatures are particularly important in this period. The leading composers of Catholic church music were Wacław of Szamotuł (ca. 1520–ca. 67) in Poland, and in Bohemia, Jacobus Gallus (1550–91) and Jan Trajan Turnovský, sometimes called the "Bohemian Palestrina".

EASTERN EUROPE

Production of music in England had declined during the disturbances of the Wars of the Roses (1455–85); when a revival began in the reign of Henry VII (1485–1509), English composers seem to have worked in comparative isolation. Contemporary developments in Continental music were known, but no Netherlands musicians came to England until after 1510, and the new style of continuously imitative counterpoint was adopted but slowly. Isolated earlier examples apart, it was first applied systematically in Psalm settings and motets from about 1540. Meanwhile, native production of secular music continued. Manuscripts from the reigns of Henry VII and Henry VIII (*reg.* 1509–47) reveal a variety of songs and instrumental pieces in three- and four-part settings, reflecting various facets of court life—which at this period in England did not by any means exclude popular elements.

ENGLAND

However, most of the surviving English polyphonic music of the late fifteenth and early sixteenth centuries is sacred, consisting chiefly of Masses, Magnificats, and votive antiphons. Many of these works illustrate the English predilection for a fuller sonority of five or six voices as against the more common imitative four-part texture of contemporary Continental music. Correspondingly, there is evident a strong feeling for the harmonic dimension of music and for the possibilities of obtaining sonorous variety through the use of contrasting voice groups. An English peculiarity, which persisted throughout the century, was the writing of long melismatic passages

219

over a single syllable of the text, a kind of free vocalization which often, in the coda sections of motets, led to passages of extraordinary beauty and expressiveness.

Two leading English composers at the beginning of the sixteenth century were William Cornyshe (*ca.* 1468–1523) and Robert Fayrfax (*ca.* 1464–1521), the former distinguished chiefly for his secular songs and the latter for Masses and other sacred works. An important younger contemporary of theirs was Nicholas Ludford (*ca.* 1485–*ca.* 1557), composer of some of the best Mass settings of the early sixteenth century. Undoubtedly the greatest English musician of this period, however, was John Taverner (*ca.* 1495–1545), a man whose career included four years as choirmaster in an Oxford college, a short term of imprisonment for heresy, and an active part in the suppression of the monasteries as an agent of Thomas Cromwell in 1538–39. Taverner's festal Masses and Magnificats are mostly in the full, florid English style of the early part of the century, with occasional sequential passages and some use of imitation. An example is the Mass *Gloria tibi Trinitas,* said to have been performed at the Field of the Cloth of Gold, the famous meeting between King Henry VIII and Francis I of France near Calais in 1520. Taverner's *Western Wynde* Mass is one of three on this tune by English composers of the sixteenth century; all three are peculiar in that they treat the *cantus firmus* not in any of the conventional ways, but rather as a series of variations, in a manner similar to English keyboard variations of the later part of the century. In some of his shorter sacred works, Taverner makes use of a simple chordal style, with antiphonal choral effects.

Toward the middle of the century the leading English composers were Christopher Tye (*ca.* 1500–73), Thomas Tallis (*ca.* 1505–85), and Robert Whyte (*ca.* 1530–74). Most important was Tallis, whose musical production bridges early and late sixteenth-century English styles and whose career reflects the religious upheavals and bewildering political changes that affected English church music in this period. Under Henry VIII, Tallis wrote Masses (including one parody Mass) and votive antiphons; under Edward VI (*reg.* 1547–53), music for the English service and anthems to English texts; from the reign of Queen Mary (1553–58), when Catholicism was temporarily restored, come a number of Latin hymns and (probably) a large seven-voice Mass *Puer nobis;* under Queen Elizabeth, Tallis set music to both Latin and English words. His late works include two sets of *Lamentations* which are among the most eloquent of all settings of these verses from the prophet Jeremiah, texts which first attracted the attention of composers shortly after the middle of the fifteenth century and which in the sixteenth century formed a distinct type of church composition. Among Tallis's earlier works the motet *Audivi vocem de caelo* (*I heard a voice from Heaven*) is an excellent specimen of mid-sixteenth-century English style; by that time the principle of imitation had been fully admitted by English composers. One remarkable feature of the work (and it is a feature of much English music of the sixteenth century) is the essential vocality of the melodies; one senses on hearing or singing them that they have been conceived not as an interplay of abstract melodic lines, but as an interplay of *voices*—so closely is the melodic curve wedded to the natural cadence of the words, so imaginatively does it project their content, and so naturally does it lie for the singer. For instance, note the effect of Tallis's apparently simple closing measures on the word "venit," given in Example VII–5; the entire motet is in HAM, No. 127.

EXAMPLE VII–5   Closing measures of Motet: *Audivi vocem de caelo,* Thomas Tallis

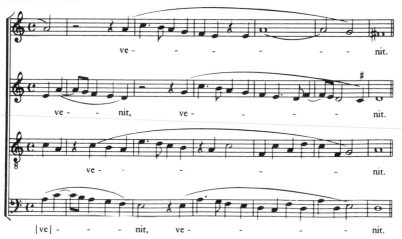

The Rise of Instrumental Music

Although the period from 1450 to 1550 was primarily an era of vocal polyphony, the same hundred years witnessed a growth of interest in instrumental music on the part of serious composers and the beginnings of independent styles and forms of writing for instruments. This statement does not imply that there was no instrumental music before 1450. As we have already seen, instruments took part with voices in the performance of every type of polyphonic music in the Middle Ages, although we cannot be certain of the extent or the exact manner of their participation. Moreover, a great deal of music was performed purely instrumentally, including on occasion many of the compositions we customarily regard as at least partly vocal; medieval manuscripts, such as the Robertsbridge and Faenza codices, which include keyboard arrangements and elaborations of cantilenas and motets, undoubtedly represent only a fraction of the music that was transcribed in this way; and in addition independent instrumental music, in the form of dances, fanfares, and the like, has not come down to us apparently for the reason that it was always either played from memory or improvised.

So the seeming increase in instrumental music after 1450 is to a considerable degree an illusion; it means only that now more of this music began to be written down and that consequently we are in a position to know something definite about it. The fact that it was written down at all reflects an improvement in the status of instrumental musicians, who, in the Middle Ages, had been regarded for the most part with contempt or condescension. Even so, the written and printed documents do not by any means preserve all the instrumental music of the Renaissance, since there was still a great deal of improvisation; and much of the notated instrumental (as well as some of the vocal) music of this period was elaborated in performance by improvised embellishments.

One sign of the sixteenth century's growing regard for instrumental music was the publication of books which describe instruments or give instructions for playing them. The first such publication was in 1511; others followed in increasing numbers throughout the century. It is significant that from the outset most of these books were written not in Latin but in the vernacular; they were addressed not to theorists, but to practical musicians. From them we can learn some of the problems of pitch, temperament, and tuning in this period, and can observe the importance that was attached to improvising ornaments on a given melodic line.

Instruments

In Sebastian Virdung's *Musica getutscht und ausgezogen* (*A Summary of [the science of] Music in German*) of 1511, and much more fully in the second volume of Michael Praetorius's *Syntagma musicum* (*Treatise of Music*) of 1618, there are descriptions and woodcuts of the various instruments in use during the sixteenth century. Two things are of particular interest: the extraordinary number and variety of wind instruments, and the fact that all instruments were built in sets or families, so that one uniform timbre was available throughout the entire range from bass to soprano. This is in keeping with the Renaissance ideal of a homogeneous sound mass; the "chest" or "consort"—the complete set—of three to eight recorders or viols, for example, corresponded to the complete "family" of voices ranging from bass to soprano.

Besides recorders, the principal wind instruments were the shawms (double-reed instruments), cromornes (or krummhorns, also with a double reed, but softer than the shawms), and cornetts (made of wood or ivory, with cup-shaped mouthpieces); the trumpets and trombones were softer in tone than their modern counterparts. The viols differed in many details of construction from the present-day

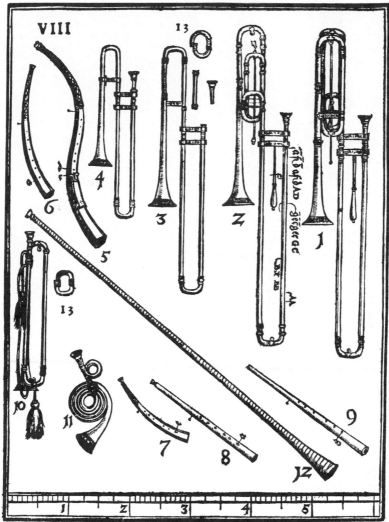

1. 2. Quart-Poſaunen. 3. Rechte gemeine Poſaun. 4. Alt-Poſaun. 5. Cornol Groß Tenor-Cornet. 6. Recht ChorZinck. 7. Klein DiſcantZinck / ſo ein Quint höher. 8. GeraderZinck mit eim Mundſtück. 9. StillZinck. 10. Trommet. 11. JägerTrommet. 12. Hölgern Trommet. 13. Krumbbügel auff ein gantz Thon.

A plate from Michael Praetorius's Syntagma musicum, *showing sets of Renaissance horns: trombones (Nos. 1, 2, 3, and 4); cornetts (Nos. 5, 6, and 7, curved; Nos. 8 and 9, straight); trumpets (Nos. 10, 11, and 12); and (No. 13) a crook by the use of which a horn player could achieve extra tones.*

violin family of bowed instruments: the neck was fretted, there were six strings tuned a fourth apart with a major third in the middle (as *A-d-g-b-e'-a'*), and the tone was more delicate, finer, less *espressivo*—because without vibrato—than that of modern instruments of the violin type.

Hans Burgkmair: Maximilian with his Musicians. *This well-known woodcut depicts the Emperor in the midst of his musicians. Among the instruments shown are the organ, harp, a harpsichord-type instrument, drums, kettledrum, lute, trumpet, viol, flute, cromorne, recorders, and trumscheit. (Courtesy Metropolitan Museum of Art)*

An appreciation of the difference between the sound of those characteristic Renaissance instruments, the recorder and viol, and that of the modern instruments which have supplanted them, the transverse flute and the violin, is important for understanding the music of the entire period. The medieval distinction of *haut* and *bas,* or "loud" and "soft" instruments still prevailed, but as compared with our modern sonorities the volume of sound in the Renaissance was less and its range smaller; the colors within that range, although multitudinous and diversified, were less penetrating, less charged with intensity than those to which we are accustomed. It is likely that in the relative quietness of the musical world of the Renaissance details of line were more easily audible, as well as nuances of color and feeling which our more resistant sensibilities can apprehend only with difficulty today.

Another indication of the Renaissance ideal was the rise to prominence of solo instruments which could by themselves cover the entire compass of tones with a uniform sonority. The tone of the organ began to be varied by the addition of solo stops and stops of softer sound, which could be combined with the unvariable principals and mixtures of the medieval instrument. By about 1500 the large church organ was similar in essentials to the instrument as we know it today, although the pedal keyboard was employed in Germany and the Netherlands long before it was adopted in other countries. The medieval portative organ did not survive beyond the fifteenth century, but the sixteenth century had small positive organs, including the regal, which had reed pipes of a delicately strident tone.

There were two types of clavier instruments, the clavichord and the harpsichord. In the clavichord, the tone was produced by a metal tangent which struck the string and remained in contact with it; the tone was delicate, but within narrow limits its volume could be controlled by the performer and a slight vibrato could be imparted. Instruments of the harpsichord type were built in different shapes and sizes, and were known under various names (virginal, spinet, clavecin, clavicembalo, among others); in all these the sound was produced by a quill plucking the string. The tone was more robust than that of the clavichord, but could scarcely be shaded by varying the pressure on the key; different timbres and degrees of loudness were possible only by a special mechanism of stops. The clavichord was essentially a solo instrument for use in small rooms; the harpsichord was used for both solo and ensemble playing.

By far the most popular household solo instrument of the Renaissance was the lute. Lutes had been known in Europe for over five hundred years; before the end of the sixteenth century they were being built in various sizes, often of costly materials and with exquisite workmanship. A Spanish type of lute, the *vihuela de mano,* had a guitar-like body; but the standard lute was pear shaped. It had one single and five double strings, tuned *G-c-f-a-d'-g'*; the neck was fretted and the pegbox turned back at a right angle. The usual method of playing was to pluck the strings with the fingers. Chords, melodies, runs and ornaments of all kinds, even contrapuntal pieces, could be performed on the lute; it was used as a solo instrument, to accompany singing, and in ensembles, and a skilled player could produce a great variety of effects. A special kind of notation was invented for lutenists, called *tablature,* the principle of which was to show, not the pitch of each sound, but the point at which the finger had to stop the strings in order to produce the required pitch. (See illustrations pages 250, 338.) Tablatures were devised also for viols and keyboard instruments.

The lute

[handwritten margin note:] aristocratic instrument most popular at the time.

VII. New Currents in the Sixteenth Century

Relation of instrumental to vocal music

At the opening of the sixteenth century instrumental music was still closely associated, both in style and performance, with vocal music. Instruments could be used to double or replace voices in polyphonic compositions, both secular and sacred. In the Office, the Magnificat was frequently performed in alternation between the choir and organ, the even-numbered verses being sung and the odd-numbered ones played; short organ pieces designed thus to be used as substitutes for portions of the service normally sung were called *verses* or *versets,* and might incorporate some or all of the melody of that part of the chant which they replaced. A similar procedure was sometimes applied to sections of the Mass, especially the Kyrie and Gloria. Organ pieces on liturgical or other *cantus firmi* were also written as independent works. These instrumental compositions were analogous to vocal *cantus firmus* motets.

Instruments also served to accompany singing. In the frottola and perhaps also in the villancico, the lower voices were frequently played; *Lieder,* chansons, and madrigals were also sometimes performed as vocal solos with instrumental accompaniment. In such performances, the written parts might be simply taken as they were, either by an instrumental ensemble or by a solo instrument like a lute or harpsichord; or for convenience a lutenist or harpsichordist might make for himself a tablature or score of the voice-parts he was to play, and in so doing might simplify the texture, reducing contrapuntal passages to a more nearly chordal form. The practice of making simplified instrumental versions of complex polyphonic pieces continued throughout the sixteenth century, and was the origin of the basso continuo of the Baroque period. Many *frottole* and other vocal pieces of the early sixteenth century were republished as solo songs with the accompanying voice-parts arranged in tablature for the lute. There was also in the sixteenth century a considerable literature of solo songs with accompaniments. These pieces were probably written originally for the lute—or rather, the *vihuela da mano,* since Spanish composers were among the first in this field. An important early collection containing lute songs by Luis Milán (*ca.* 1500–*ca.* 61) was published in 1536 at Valencia. Milán often gave two different versions of the accompaniment, one the plain quasi-contrapuntal two or three parts as they might have been written for voices, and the other a free, elaborate lute version filled with rapid scale passages in virtuoso style.

The intimate connection between instrumental and vocal style in the sixteenth century is illustrated by the fact the majority of publications of vocal music stated that the pieces could be either sung or played. Such phrases as "convenables tant á la voix comme aux instrumens," "per cantar e sonar,"—"apt for the voices or viols," "to be sung and played"—continually recur, especially after about 1540, on the title pages of both motet and chanson collections.

Moreover, a great deal of the music specifically designated as instrumental in the early part of the century was essentially nothing other than transcribed vocal music. But usually in the performance of such pieces, and frequently in the published versions as well, certain adaptations were made. Chief among these were the freer use of chromatic alteration—or at least the specification of such alterations according to the principles of *musica ficta*—and the ornamentation or *coloration* of the melodic lines, the addition of passing tones, runs, cadenzas, and other embellishments of all kinds.

The adaptation of vocal pieces to instrumental performance led naturally to certain species of instrumental compositions which, while not necessarily derived from any particular vocal piece, were obviously patterned on vocal prototypes. Such were the imitative *ricercar* and the *canzona,* instrumental counterparts respectively of the motet and chanson. The word *ricercar* comes from an Italian verb meaning both "to seek" or "search out," and "to attempt" or "try." Both of these meanings are reflected in the different types of instrumental pieces which in the first half of the sixteenth century are called *ricercari*. The earliest ones are improvisatory in character with sporadic bits of imitation; later ones achieve clearer form by means of some repetition of phrases and balanced passages of paired imitation. By 1540, *ricercari* appear which consist of a succession of themes without marked individuality or contrast, each developed in imitation and interlocked with the next by overlapping the cadence—in effect, a textless imitative motet. *Ricercari* of this kind were usually intended for ensemble playing, but they were written also for keyboard instruments and for the lute; they differ from strict vocal style simply by freer voice leading and by the addition on the printed pages of typically instrumental embellishments. However, the same name ricercare continued to be applied both to motet-like pieces of this kind and also the improvisatory type, as well as to pieces in a mixture of those two styles.

Instrumental forms: the ricercar

Canzona is the Italian word for "chanson." An instrumental canzona in Italy was called a *canzon da sonar* ("chanson to be played") or *canzona alla francese* ("chanson in the French style"). Canzonas were written for both ensembles and solo instruments. The development of the canzona as an independent instrumental form in the second half of the sixteenth century had important historical consequences.

Canzona

Social dancing was more widespread and more highly regarded in the Renaissance than it had ever been in western history. A considerable part of the instrumental music of the sixteenth century, therefore, consists of dance pieces for lute, keyboard, or ensembles; these are no longer improvised, as they were in the late Middle Ages, but are written out in tablatures or partbooks, and appear in printed collections issued by Petrucci, Attaingnant, and other pub-

Dance music

An early sixteenth-century court scene. In the foreground, four couples dance "the great ball," a ceremonious pavane, while musicians accompany them on flute, trumpets, and drums.

lishers. As befits their purpose, these pieces usually have clearly marked and quite regular rhythmic patterns, and are divided into distinct sections. There is little or no contrapuntal interplay of lines, though the principal melody may be highly ornamented or colored. Commonly the dances were grouped in pairs or threes, and these groups are the historical precursors of the instrumental dance suite of later times. A favorite combination was a slow dance in duple meter followed by a fast one in triple meter on the same tune, the second dance thus constituting a variation of the first. One instance of this kind of pairing of dances is the combination, frequently found in French publications of the sixteenth century, of *pavane* and *gaillarde*. Similarly paired dances are found in Polish tablatures of the same period (See Example VII–6).

The dance pieces of the early sixteenth century owed little to vocal models, and in them, therefore, the characteristics of instrumental style could be freely developed. Much dance music, of course, in the sixteenth century as in later ages, became detached from its original purpose and developed into stylized pieces which retained the characteristic rhythms and general outlines of dances but which were obviously not intended for actual dancing—any more than the waltzes of Chopin were intended for ballroom waltzing.

The growth of instrumental style was related to the widespread practice of improvisation in the Renaissance. The peculiarly instru-

EXAMPLE VII–6   *Czayner Thancz* from the Tablature of John of Lublin
(ca. 1540)

mental traits in the earliest written or printed instrumental music of
the sixteenth century undoubtedly were for the most part only the
spelling out in notation of procedures that were already common
in practice. The sixteenth-century performer had two main ways
to improvise: ornamentation of a given melodic line; or the addition
of one or more contrapuntal parts to a given *cantus firmus.* The
latter method was called *discantus supra librum* ([extemporized]
discant on [a melody written in] a book), *contrappunto alla mente*
(literally, mental counterpoint) or *sortisatio* (extemporization, as
opposed to *compositio* or written composition), and was regarded
by teachers in the early sixteenth century as a very important
discipline in a composer's training. The favorite courtly dance of
the late fifteenth and early sixteenth centuries, the *basse-danse,* was
an example of this method of improvisation: it was traditionally

*Improvisatory
pieces*

performed as an improvised counterpoint over a borrowed tenor or *cantus firmus. Discantus supra librum* was often combined with the other method of improvisation in the sixteenth century, namely the addition of improvised embellishments to a given melody.

Compositions in improvisatory style, not based on any given *cantus firmus* but unfolding freely, often in a somewhat rambling fashion, with varying textures and without continued adherence to a definite meter or form, are found among the earliest specimens of music for solo players (this style being obviously unsuited to ensembles). Such pieces appeared under various names: prelude or *preambulum, fantasia,* or *ricercare.*

Variations

One other new form of composition, the *theme and variations,* probably began with the Spanish lute and keyboard composers in the first half of the sixteenth century. Here, as in other instrumental forms, the works of the great Spanish organist and composer Antonio de Cabezón (1510–66) were outstanding. His keyboard variations on the *Song of the Cavalier* (HAM, No. 134) present the complete theme successively in the uppermost voice (twice), the tenor, the alto, and the bass, accompanied each time by a different contrapuntal network in the other parts—a basically simple scheme which is worked out with admirable taste and a satisfying sense of continuity from beginning to end. A form related to the theme with variations was the composition on a short ostinato pattern, the prototype of the later chaconne and passacaglia.

✳ The Madrigal and Related Forms

The Italian madrigal of the sixteenth century had practically nothing in common with the madrigal of the fourteenth century but the name. The *trecento* madrigal was a strophic song with a refrain (ritornello); the early sixteenth-century madrigal as a rule made no use of a refrain or any other feature of the old *formes fixes* with their patterned repetitions of musical and textual phrases. It was a through-composed setting of a short poem, constructed as a series of (usually) overlapping sections, some contrapuntal and some homophonic, each based on a single phrase of the text. To this extent its form resembled that of the motet. The artistry of the composers was shown in their ability to infuse this quasi-sectional form with a sense of continuity and proportioned climax, always reflecting and enhancing the spontaneous flow of the poetry. There are no more perfect examples in music of art concealing art. One important means of continuity was the harmonic organization, which in most madrigals is a fascinating blend of modern major tonality and ancient modality.

Most of the works composed in the first period of madrigal production, from about 1520 to 1550, were set for four voices; after the middle of the century five voices became the rule, although six-part settings were not infrequent. The word "voices" is to be taken literally: the madrigal was a piece of vocal chamber music intended for performance with one singer to a part; as always in the sixteenth century, however, instrumental doubling or substitution was possible and doubtless common.

Although essentially similar in form to the motet, the madrigal was usually more varied and vivid. Of course it was not subject to the restrictions of style that prevailed in church music; and the free atmosphere of the secular surroundings in which madrigals were sung encouraged experimentation. Consequently, madrigal composers developed pictorial and expressive writing to an extraordinary degree, and particularly experimented with harmonic boldness. Moreover, some madrigals of the second half of the century show the Renaissance a cappella ideal of equal voices being transformed into the Baroque ideal of dominating solo parts against a firm harmonic bass and chordal background. In these respects, the madrigal was the most progressive form of composition in the late sixteenth century, as the motet had been in the earlier part of the century and the Mass before that.

Most madrigal texts were sentimental or erotic in subject matter, with scenes and allusions borrowed from pastoral poetry. Usually the text ended with an epigrammatic climax in the last line or two. Some madrigal poetry, especially in the early part of the century, was stereotyped and of little literary merit; some Italian composers, however, used verses by Petrarch, Sannazaro, Ariosto, or (toward the end of the century) Tasso. Madrigals were sung in all sorts of courtly social gatherings; in Italy they were sung especially at meetings of the academies, societies organized in the fifteenth century in many cities for the study and discussion of literary, scientific, or artistic matters. The output of madrigals and similar polyphonic songs in Italy was enormous: some two thousand collections (counting reprints and new editions) were printed between 1530 and 1600, and the flood of production continued well into the seventeenth century.

Madrigal texts

The leading early composers of Italian madrigals were Phillipe Verdelot (*ca.* 1480–1545), a Franco-Fleming who worked at Florence and Rome; Costanzo Festa (*ca.* 1490–1545) of Rome, one of the few Italians in the Papal chapel in the early sixteenth century and one of the first Italian composers to offer serious competition to the Netherlanders; Adrian Willaert at Venice; and Jacob Arcadelt (*ca.* 1505–*ca.* 60), a northerner who for a time was head of the Pope's chapel and later became a member of the Royal chapel at Paris. All the composers wrote chansons as well as madrigals, and there was probably a good deal of mutual influence between the two forms. Festa's madrigal *Quando ritrova* (Example VII–7; the entire piece is in HAM, No. 129) is a case in point: the homophonic setting, the

Early madrigal composers

231

EXAMPLE VII–7   Madrigal: *Quando ritrova*, Costanzo Festa

*When I find my shepherdess in the meadow, with the sheep in the
pasture, I approach her and greet her.*

In the left margin (handwritten notes):

1. Early Madrigal
   Modal but
   tends toward
   Major tonality
2. Text and music
   are together
   in that accents
   of music suit
   accent words.
   Definite Dance
   Rhythms.
3. Cadence weakened
   by flow
4. Alternation
   back & forth
   between
   polyphony &
   homophony
5. Tone Painting

symmetrical phrasing, and the occasional repetitions in the music
following the structure of the poetry, are all symptomatic of a stage
at which the madrigal still somewhat closely resembles the French

EXAMPLE VII–8   Madrigal: *Voi ve n'andat'al cielo*, Jacob Arcadelt

a. Thou risest to heaven.

b. *I would gladly rise in flight but, struggling, I fall back in pain and tears.*

c. *Behold my [heart] which thou holdest enclosed within thee.*

chanson and the Italian frottola.

In the madrigals of Arcadelt (first publication *ca.* 1538), the style becomes more contrapuntal and the texture and spirit more refined;

the voice parts are more nearly equal in melodic interest, and the music does not follow quite so rigidly the scheme of the verses. The pictorial effects in *Voi ve n'andat' al cielo* (Example VII–8; the entire piece appears in HAM, No. 130) are noteworthy: for example, the rising line at *cielo* (heaven, Example VII–8a), echoed at *levarmi a volo* (rise in flight, Example VII–8b); the suggestion of helpless struggle by the repeated *struggendo mi torno* (but, striving, I fall back, Example VII–8b); and the allargando-like repeated closing cadence with the E♭, reserved until this point in the piece to underline the important *in voi chiuso* (enclosed within thee, Example VII–8c). The text as a whole is a good example of the sort of *double-entendre* often met with in Renaissance poetry: the art of pretending to conceal erotic allusions under a veil of ordinary language.

Cipriano de Rore

Important innovations in the madrigal were made with the publication in 1542 of the first book of five-part madrigals by Cipriano de Rore (1516–65). Rore was a Netherlander who worked in Italy chiefly at Ferrara and Parma, although he also for a short time held the post of music director at St. Mark's in Venice as successor to his master Willaert. Rore's publications included five books of madrigals for five voices and three books for four voices; these and other works were issued repeatedly in new printings and editions throughout the second half of the sixteenth century.

Rore's preference for serious poetry of high literary quality set a standard for all subsequent madrigal composers. His favorite author was Petrarch; and whatever bad effects the vogue of Petrarch may have had for the development of Italian literature in this period, his verses were perfect for madrigal composers. He was "the ideal poet for an art that was striving for a perfect, secular, and sensuous expression, but whose means were still restricted."[1] Among the texts set by Rore was a cycle of eleven madrigals on Petrarch's *Vergini*, stanzas of invocation to the Virgin Mary which form the conclusion of his cycle of poems *On the Death of Madonna Laura*. (Madrigals of this sort, on texts of pious devotion, are fairly numerous in the sixteenth century and form a special class commonly called *madrigali spirituali*.) Other composers also found inspiration in the work of Italy's great fourteenth-century poet; for example, Willaert's *Musica nova* of 1559 contains twenty-five madrigals of which all but one are settings of sonnets by Petrarch.

Beginning with Rore, the normal setting of the Italian madrigal is for five voices, the fifth voice (*quinta pars*) being usually paired with one of the other four as a second tenor or second soprano. But the expansion of the form in this period was not alone a matter of sonority. All the dimensions were enlarged; in contrast to the

[1] Alfred Einstein, *The Italian Madrigal*, I, 190.

regularity of the frottola and early madrigal in which each line of text was set to its own line of music, the text of the later sixteenth-century madrigal was handled freely, almost capriciously, the music now moving ahead, now lingering over a particular phrase or word to give it a special intensity: this point is illustrated in Rore's *Da le belle contrade,* Example VII–9, with the realism of the exclamations beginning at *t'en vai* (thou goest); the obvious but effective device of using a single voice for the words *sola mi lasci* (thou leavest me solitary); the dramatic pause before the climax at *ahi, crud'amor* (ah, cruel love); and the long, mournful descent of this phrase to *finisc'in pianto* (end in tears). Yet with all this detail the larger proportions of the piece are not neglected. The agitated rhythms and wayward harmonies of the middle portion (the entire piece appears in HAM, No. 131) are enclosed by two sections of clear F-major tonality in phrases of regular length, with a symmetrical repetition of the closing phrase.

One result of the composers' desire to depict vividly the emotions of the text was their use of venturesome harmonic progressions, of which Example VII–9 furnishes instances. The rise of chromatic writing in the sixteenth century was to some extent due to experiments that sought to revive the chromatic and enharmonic genera of Greek music; but composers like Rore also deliberately used chromatics for artistic reasons. Chromatic passages were always written in a homophonic style, so that emphasis was given to the striking character of the chord successions; effects like the juxtaposition of the A-major and C-minor triads (Example VII–9, measures 11 and 12) became common expressive devices.

Chromaticism of this kind has nothing to do with a notation, called "chromatic," which came into fashion around the middle of the sixteenth century, and which was nothing but the writing of music in four-four time (signature $\mathbf{C}$) instead of the older $\mathbf{\cent}$, resulting in the use of shorter notes (for example, $\downarrow$ to signify about the same duration that had been formerly signified by $\flat$). The preponderance of black notes on the page gave the notation its name "chromatic," that is, "colored" as opposed to the "white" signs of the older notation. The possibility of using black (filled-in) forms of normally white (unfilled) note heads allowed composers to set words like "dark," "night," and "blind" in blackened note forms, and often composers would do this even though it made no difference in the actual sound, but was merely a bit of eye music capable of being appreciated only by the singers who were looking at the page. This point illustrates the fact that madrigals were written and sung mostly for the delectation of the performers rather than for an audience—that they were, in a word, social music, and not concert pieces.

Among the many northern composers who shared in the development of the Italian madrigal after the middle of the century, three

EXAMPLE VII–9   Madrigal: *Da le belle contrade*, Cipriano de Rore

*Thou goest, alas! Farewell! Thou leavest me solitary. Farewell! What
will become of me here, forgotten and sorrowing? Ah, cruel Love!
Uncertain and brief are thy pleasures, and it pleases thee that the
highest joy should end in tears.*

in particular must be mentioned: Orlando di Lasso, Philippe de
Monte, and Giaches de Wert. Orlando di Lasso (1532–94) is most important as a church composer, but his was a universal genius equally
at home with the madrigal, the chanson, and Lied. Philippe de
Monte (1521–1603), like Lasso, was prodigiously productive in
both the sacred and secular fields; he began writing madrigals in his
youth in Italy and continued uninterruptedly through the many
years of his service under the Habsburg Emperors in Vienna and
Prague. He published thirty-two collections of secular madrigals, in
addition to three or four books of *madrigali spirituali*. Giaches de
Wert (1535–96), though Netherlandish by birth, spent nearly his
entire life in Italy; he further developed the style of madrigal composition begun by Rore and exercised an important influence on
Monteverdi.

The leading madrigalists toward the end of the century were
Italians. Luca Marenzio (1553–99) was a composer of remarkable
artistry and technique, in whose works contrasting feelings and
visual details were depicted with utmost virtuosity. As was typical
of madrigal composers of the late sixteenth century. Marenzio

*Netherlands
madrigalists*

Luca Marenzio

237

mainly used pastoral poetry as his texts. One of the most celebrated of his madrigals is a setting of a Petrarchan sonnet in which the mood of the opening lines:

Solo e pensoso i più deserti campi	Alone, thought-sick, I pace where none has been,
Vo misurando a passi tardi e lenti	Roaming the desert with dull steps and slow[2]

is suggested by means of a slow chromatic scale in the topmost voice, rising without a break from g′ to a″ and returning to d″,

2 *The Sonnets of Petrarch,* Joseph Auslander, tr., 1931. Quoted by permission of the publishers, Longman, Green and Co.

EXAMPLE VII–10   Madrigal: *Io pur respiro,* Gesualdo

. . . give an end [at once] to life and to [my] great pain.

while the other voices form a background of expressively drooping figures for the first line and all but come to a dragging halt for the second—a masterpiece of sensitive musical imagery, harmonic refinement, and skilful contrapuntal writing.

The height of chromaticism in the Italian madrigal was reached not in the works of Marenzio but in those of Carlo Gesualdo, Prince of Venosa (*ca.* 1560–1613), a picturesque character who was both "musician and murderer," as his biographer puts it. In some of his later madrigals Gesualdo carries chromatic harmony to a point that almost suggests Wagner. Sometimes with Gesualdo the chromaticism is mere mannerism, style for style's sake; but at its best it is a sincerely felt and deeply moving response to the text (see Example VII–10; the entire madrigal appears in HAM, No. 161). *Carlo Gesualdo*

The musician who served as a transition figure from the sixteenth century to the seventeenth—that is, from the Renaissance to Baroque—was Claudio Monteverdi (1567–1643), one of the major composers in the history of western music. Monteverdi was born at Cremona and received his earliest training from Marc' Antonio Ingegneri, head of the music in the cathedral of that city. In 1590 Monteverdi entered the service of Vincenzo Gonzaga, Duke of Mantua, and in 1602 became master of the ducal chapel. From 1613 until his death in 1643 he was choirmaster at St. Mark's in Venice. *Claudio Monteverdi*

The works of Monteverdi with which we are concerned at present are the first four books of madrigals, published respectively in 1587, 1590, 1592, and 1603. In these madrigals Monteverdi, without going to such extremes as Gesualdo, demonstrated his mastery of the madrigal technique of the late sixteenth century, with its smooth combination of homophonic and contrapuntal part-writing, its faithful reflection of the text, and its freedom in the use of expressive harmonies and dissonances. But there were certain features—not altogether absent in the music of his contemporaries—which showed that Monteverdi was moving swiftly and with remarkable assurance toward the new style of the seventeenth century. For example, many of the musical motives are not melodic but declamatory, in the manner of recitative; the texture often departs from the Renaissance ideal of equal voices and becomes a duet over a harmonically supporting bass; and certain formal practices characteristic of the Baroque are foreshadowed. As an example of the flexible, animated, vivid, and variegated style of Monteverdi's sixteenth-century madrigals, rich in musical invention, humorous and sensitive, audacious yet perfectly logical in harmonies, the five-voice madrigal *Ohimè, se tanto amate,* first published in Book IV in 1603, will repay study. (Example VII–11; the entire piece is in HAM, No. 188.) A work like this represents the limits of the a cappella madrigal style, the culmination of a century of development.

The madrigal was not the only type of Italian secular polyphony in the sixteenth century. Among the lighter varieties of song was

EXAMPLE VII–11 Madrigal: *Ohimè, se tanto amate,* Monteverdi

a.

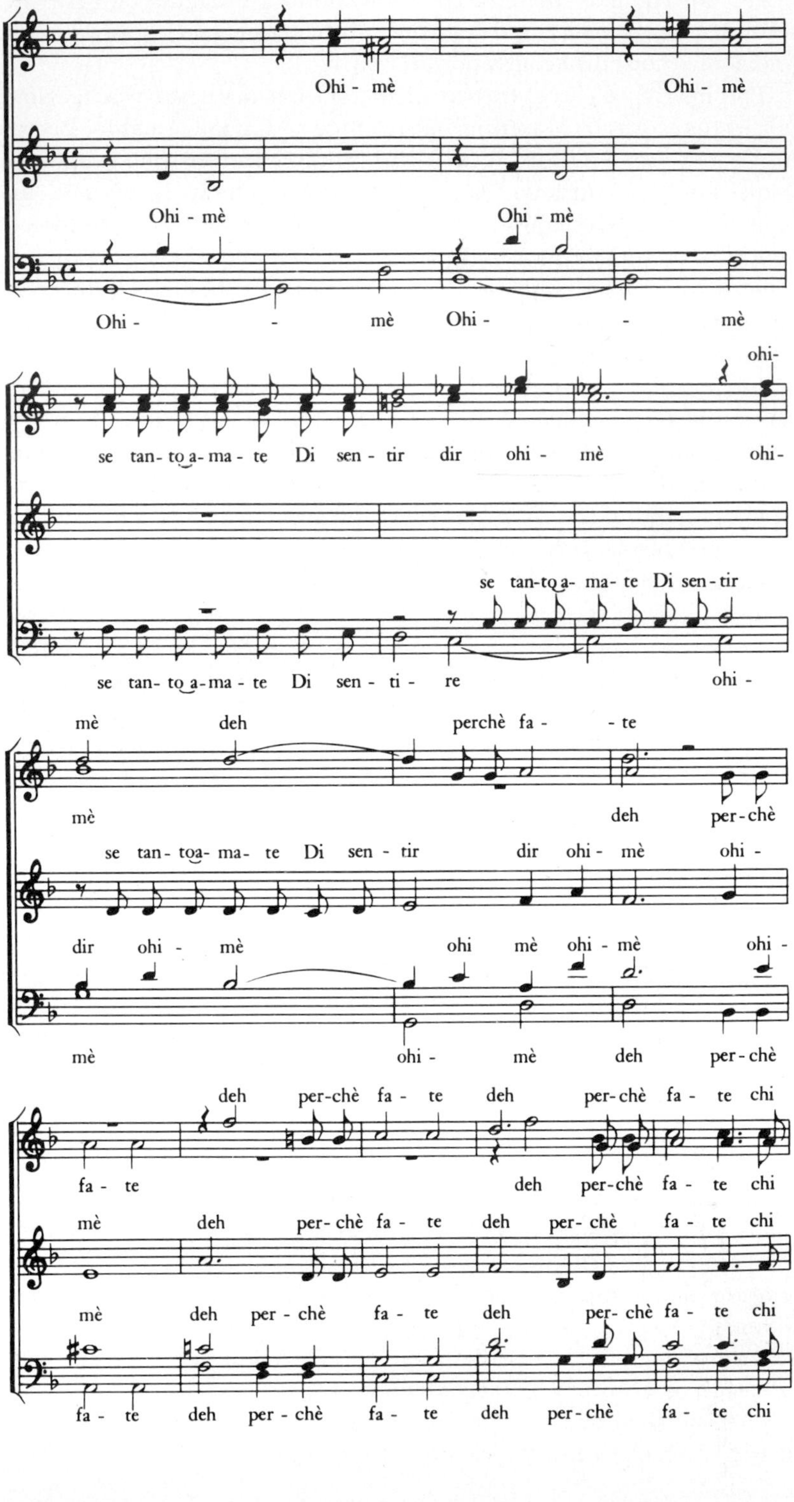

a. *Alas! If you love so much to hear me say "Alas!" why do you cause to die him who says "Alas!"*

b. *. . . then you will have from me thousands and thousands of sweet "alas's".*

VII. New Currents in the Sixteenth Century

Other Italian secular vocal forms

the *canzon villanesca* (peasant song) or *villanella,* which first appeared around Naples in the 1540's and flourished chiefly in the Neapolitan area. The villanella was a three-voice, strophic, lively little piece in homophonic style, in which composers often deliberately used parallel fifths—originally to suggest its supposedly rustic character, later perhaps to caricature the suave correctness of the madrigals, which were often parodied in both the words and music of the villanella. Neither the villanella nor any of the other lighter types of Italian song are to be regarded as distinctively popular or nationalistic; they were written by the same Italians and Netherlanders who composed serious madrigals, and were meant for the same sophisticated audiences. In the course of time the villanella became like the madrigal and gradually lost its own identity.

By the end of the sixteenth century the most important lighter forms of Italian vocal polyphony were the *canzonetta* ("little song") and the *balletto.* These two forms are similar; they are written in a neat, vivacious homophonic style, with clear major-minor harmonies and distinct, evenly phrased sections which are often repeated. *Balletti,* as the name suggests, were intended for dancing as well as singing or playing; a "fa-la-la" refrain is one of their characteristics. The leading composer of *canzonette* and *balletti* was Giacomo Gastoldi (d. 1622). Both forms were extremely popular in Italy, and were imitated by German and English composers.

While native composers and national forms of music were coming to the fore in Italy during the second half of the sixteenth century,

GERMANY

an opposite development was occurring in Germany. The various courts and municipalities, following the example set by the Emperor in his chapel, began from about 1550 to hire first Netherlanders and then Italians for the most influential musical positions in the country. These composers did not attempt to impose their foreign tastes; on the contrary, they were for the most part quickly assimilated into German musical life and made important contributions to the secular Lied and to both Lutheran and Catholic church music. Consequently, the kind of German music exemplified in the works of Senfl was gradually transmuted into a more international, cosmopolitan style which intermingled German, Franco-Flemish, and Italian characteristics.

Chief among the international composers in Germany in the sixteenth century was Orlando di Lasso, who entered the service of

Orlando di Lasso

Duke Albrecht V of Bavaria in 1556 or 1557, became head of the ducal chapel in 1560, and remained in that post at Munich until his death in 1594. Among the vast number of Lasso's compositions were seven collections of German *Lieder.* The Lied *Ich armer Mann* has somewhat uncouth verses which Lasso matched with appropriate music (see Example VII–12; the entire piece is given in GMB, No.

EXAMPLE VII–12   Lied: *Ich armer Mann,* Orlando di Lasso

I, poor man, what have I done? I have taken a wife. [It would be better if I had never done it; how often I have rued it you may well imagine:] all day long I am being scolded and nagged, [at bedtime and at table].

125). Lasso's setting no longer surrounds a familiar tune in the tenor by a web of counterpoint, as was done in earlier German *Lieder;* instead, he sets the text in the manner of a madrigal, with all the parts having equal importance in the variegated interplay of motives, bits of imitation, echoes, and mock-pathetic melismas at the phrase *muss ich im hader stahn* (I must always be bickering).

In the same year in which this piece was published (1576), Jacob Regnart (*ca.* 1540–99), another Flemish composer and a member of the Imperial Chapel, published the first volume of his *Kurzweilige teutsche Lieder zu dreyen stimmen nach art der Neapolitanen oder Welschen Villanellen (Entertaining German songs for Three Voices in the Manner of the Neapolitan or Italian Villanelle*). This publication of Regnart's was one of many similar collections in the late sixteenth century attesting to the popularity of the Italian style in Germany.

A fruitful union of Italian sweetness with German seriousness was achieved in the music of the greatest German composer of the late sixteenth century, Hans Leo Hassler. Born at Nuremberg in 1564, Hassler was studying in 1584 with Andrea Gabrieli at Venice; from 1585 until his death in 1612 he held various positions at Augsburg, Nuremberg, Ulm, and Dresden. His works comprise instrumental ensemble and keyboard pieces, canzonets and madrigals with Italian texts, German *Lieder,* Latin motets and Masses, and settings of Lutheran chorales. The two *Lieder, Ach Schatz* (HAM, No. 165) and *Ach, süsse Seel'* (GMB, No. 152) are good examples of Hassler's music, and show his suave melodic lines, sure harmonic structure, and clearly articulated form with its varied repetitions and balanced echoing of motives. Hassler's work stands nearly at the end of the age of German Renaissance polyphony for equal voices. The only notable German composers in this style after Hassler were Johann Hermann Schein (1586–1630) and Heinrich Schütz (1585–

1672); but their *Lieder* and madrigals in Italian style were youthful works, and both men were more important for the Baroque than for the Renaissance.

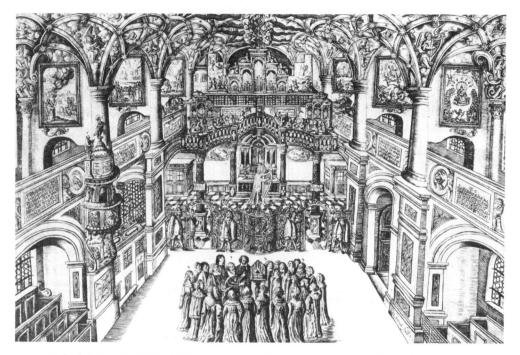

Heinrich Schütz (1585–1672) surrounded by his singers in the Chapel of the Elector of Saxony in Dresden; he was master of the Chapel from 1617 to his death.

In France and the Netherlands the chanson continued to flourish in the second half of the sixteenth century. The old polyphonic tradition remained alive longest in the north, as may be seen from two books of chansons published by the Dutch composer Jan Sweelinck (1562–1621) in 1594 and 1612. In France, however, the tradition was modified by a lively interest in the Italian madrigal, the effects of which on French music were particularly evident in the period from 1560 to 1575. One of the principal mediators of the Netherlandish-Italian influence in France was Orlando di Lasso, whose powerful musical personality impressed itself on the chanson as on every other type of vocal composition in the later sixteenth century. Many of Lasso's chansons with French texts are written in a tight polyphonic texture with close imitations and sudden changes of pace in tense, delightfully humorous settings; others are in the homophonic style of the Parisian chanson, with varied rhythms which seem to spring spontaneously from each nuance and accent of the text. An example of a homophonic chanson, which also

FRANCE

245

illustrates Lasso's gift for penetrating to the essential qualities of a style, is *Bon jour, mon coeur* (HAM, No. 145a).

Other chanson composers in France in the latter part of the sixteenth century were Claude Le Jeune (1528–1600), Guillaume Costeley (1531–1606), and Jacques Mauduit (1557–1627). Many of Le Jeune's chansons are serious polyphonic works in several sections for five or more voices, and have other points of similarity to the Italian madrigals of the Rore period. The later Italian madrigal experiments (for example, those of Marenzio and Gesualdo) were not favorably received in France; on the other hand, the villanella and balletto had many French imitators.

Musique
mesurée

Along with the polyphonic chanson, a different type of chanson appeared in France about 1550. These new chansons were strictly homophonic, short, strophic, often with a refrain, and usually performed as a solo with lute accompaniment. They were at first called *vaudevilles,* a word whose etymology and precise meaning are obscure; later this type of song was known as an *air* or *air de cour* (court tune). The forms taken by these compositions in homophonic style with a musical meter bound to the meter of the text reflected the experiments of some poets and composers who in 1570 formed an *Académie de Poésie et de Musique* (Academy of Poetry and Music) under the patronage of King Charles IX. The poet Jean-Antoine de Baïf wrote strophic French verses in ancient classical meters (*vers mesurés à l'antique*), substituting for the modern accentual principle the ancient Latin usage of long and short syllables; and composers (Le Jeune, Mauduit, and others) set these verses to music for voices, strictly observing the rule of a long note for each long syllable and a note half as long for each short syllable. The variety of verse patterns thus produced a corresponding variety of musical rhythms in which duple and triple groupings freely alternated. This *measured music (musique mesurée)*, as it was called, was too artificial a creation to endure for long, but it did serve to introduce nonregular rhythms into the later *air de cour,* a feature which remained characteristic of this form as it was developed by a school of French composers in the first half of the seventeenth century; and after about 1580, the *air de cour* was the predominant type of French vocal music.

ENGLAND

The golden age of secular song in England came later than in the Continental countries. In 1588 (incidentally, the year of the Spanish Armada), Nicholas Yonge published at London, *Musica transalpina,* a collection of Italian madrigals in English translation; many of these madrigals had been circulating in manuscript for several years before Yonge's book came out. Four more anthologies of Italian madrigals appeared in the next decade; these publications gave impetus to the rise of the English madrigal school which flourished in the last decade of the sixteenth century and continued, with de-creasing momentum, in the early years of the seventeenth century. The leading composers were Thomas Morley (1557–1602), Thomas Weelkes (*ca.* 1575–1623), and John Wilbye (1574–1628). Morley, earliest and most prolific of the three, specialized in lighter types of madrigal and in the related forms of the *ballett* and *canzonet*. Balletts were derived from the like-named Italian form, especially the *balletti* of Gastoldi (see HAM, Nos. 158, 159). They are songs mainly homophonic in texture with the tune in the topmost voice, in dance-like meter (as the name suggests), with distinct sections set off by full cadences and with repetitions resulting in formal patterns such as AABB or the like, and with two or three strophes sung to the same music. There is a refrain, often sung to the syllables *fa-la,* whence the pieces were sometimes called *fa-la*'s. Canzonets, likewise imitated from Italian models, also have some repetition of sections, and are rather short and light in mood; otherwise, they resemble regular madrigals in both form and texture.

The English madrigal differs from its Italian prototype basically in the greater attention it gives to the overall musical structure, in its "preoccupation with purely musical devices, a reluctance to follow the Italians in splitting up compositions mercurially at the whim of the text. The English madrigalist is first of all a musician; his Italian colleague is often more of a dramatist."[3] Madrigals, balletts, and canzonets were all written primarily for unaccompanied solo voices, though many of the published collections of partbooks indicate on the title page that the music is "apt for voices and viols," presumably in any available combination. Ability to read a part, either vocally or instrumentally in such pieces, seems to have been expected of educated persons in Elizabethan England.

A comprehensive idea of the English madrigal may be obtained from *The Triumphes of Oriana,* a collection of twenty-five madrigals by different composers, edited and published by Thomas Morley in 1601 after the model of a similar Italian anthology called *Il trionfo di Dori* published in 1592. Each of the madrigals in Morley's collection presumably acclaims Queen Elizabeth I (reg. 1558–1603), and each madrigal ends with the words "Long live fair Oriana," a name from the conventional vocabulary of pastoral poetry often applied to Elizabeth.

The English madrigal

A large proportion of English madrigal texts are pastoral poems, for the most part anonymous. An example of a madrigal with a pastoral text is John Bennet's *Thyrsis, sleepest thou?* (MM, No. 28). The different pictorial suggestions in the text—as at the words "holla," "hold up," "cuckoo," "sighed," "drive him back"—are wittily taken up in Bennet's music. This kind of light, humorous spirit is typical of many English madrigals; even when the text professes to languish and lament for love, it is obvious that both poet

[3] Joseph Kerman, *The Elizabethan Madrigal,* 254

and composer are concerned more with elegance of expression than with sentiment, and that the emotional attitude of the piece is generally one of tongue in cheek. However, this does not preclude touches of serious or pathetic expression when these are motivated by the text. The mood of the madrigal is variegated, one of shifting light and shade. As Morley himself said "You must in your music be wavering like the wind, sometimes wanton, sometimes drooping, sometimes grave and staid, otherwhile effeminate . . . and the more variety you show the better shall you please."[4]

The expressive and pictorial traits in the music of the madrigals are combined with accurate, nimble declamation of the English texts. The accents of the words are maintained independently in each voice (to appreciate this feature fully, remember that the barlines of modern editions did not exist in the original), so that the ensembles produce sparkling counterpoints of endless rhythmic vitality. Moreover, with all the sharpness of detail, the long line of the music is never obscured. Bennet's *Thyrsis* reflects the madrigal's blend of major and medieval tonalities: despite its signature of two flats, for the most part it is written in F major; but it also is strongly attracted toward the subdominant key of B♭ because of the flatted seventh degree characteristic of the Mixolydian mode. On the other hand, Morley's *My bonny lass* (HAM, No. 159) comes out clearly in G major, with a nice balance of tonic and dominant harmonies.

There is little chromaticism of an extreme sort in English madrigals; composers occasionally resorted to chromatic harmonies for the special purpose of expressing distress or grief, as in the remarkable opening of the second part of Weelkes's *O Care, thou wilt despatch me* or the ending of his *Cease sorrows now;* but such passages are not frequent.

Pre-eminent for serious expressiveness within a sensitively molded musical whole are the madrigals of Wilbye. His mastery can only be adequately illustrated by a longer example than we have space for, but something of his particular quality may be heard in these measures from a six-part madrigal published in 1609 (Example VII–13).

Lute songs

Ayre – Strophic Songs

The solo song with accompaniment for lute and viol, popular on the continent since the early part of the sixteenth century, was taken up in England as early as 1589, but its most flourishing period came at and after the turn of the century—coinciding thus with the decline of the madrigal. The leading composers in this field were John Dowland (1562–1626) and Thomas Campion (1567–1620). Dowland's *First Book of Songs or Ayres,* first published in 1597 and the most widely reprinted of all Elizabethan prints, was but one of many such collections. The poetry of the English ayres is considerably better

---

[4] *Plaine and Easie Introduction* (1597) in SR, 275 (SRRe, 84).

EXAMPLE VII–13   Madrigal: *Long Have I Made These Hills,* John Wilbye

than that of the madrigals. The music as a rule lacks the madrigalesque pictorial touches and the mood is uniformly lyrical, but the ayres—especially those of Dowland—are remarkable for sensitive text-declamation and melodic subtlety. The lute accompaniments, while always carefully subordinated to the voice, have a certain amount of rhythmic and melodic independence. The voice and lute parts are usually printed on the same page in vertical alignment, evidently so the singer could accompany himself. In some collections the songs are printed both this way and in an alternative version with the lute part written out for three voices and the staffs so arranged on the page that singers or players sitting around a table could all read their parts from the same book (see illustration). These vocal and instrumental versions rarely differ except in slight details. The

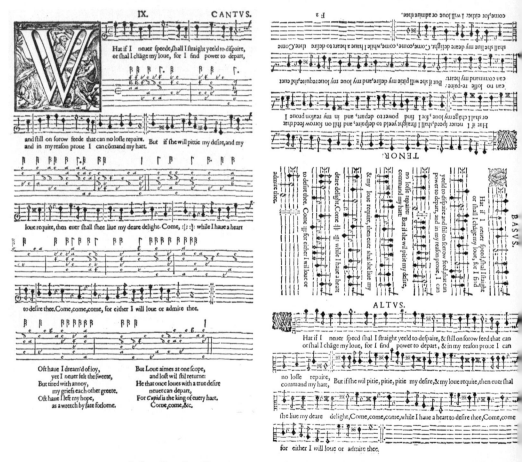

John Dowland's song, What if I never speed, *for solo voice with lute accompaniment in tablature (left), and in an optional arrangement for voices (right). This song appeared in Dowland's* The third and last booke of songs and aires. Newly composed to sing to the lute. *For transcription, see HAM, No. 163. (Courtesy Trustees of the British Museum, London)*

alternative four-part version might be performed with either voices or instruments or both; some of these versions are quite similar to madrigals.

Along with the madrigal and the ayre, both of which were more or less indebted to foreign examples, there continued a native English tradition which in the latter half of the sixteenth century manifested itself in the form of *consort songs,* that is, solo songs or duets with accompaniment of a consort of viols and, at a later stage, the addition of a chorus. Likewise in the native tradition were polyphonic songs for either vocal or mixed vocal-instrumental performance, on texts ranging over a great variety of subjects from secular to sacred (the latter, however, being designed for household use, not for church). These are frequently called "madrigals," but they are really a distinct species. They maintain a relatively conservative, somewhat abstract style, concentrating on musical qualities and avoiding the detailed text-painting characteristic of the madrigal. The outstanding composers here were William Byrd (1543–1623) and Orlando Gibbons (1583–1625).

VIII

Church Music and Instrumental Music in the Late Renaissance

The growth of a vivid and flexible secular musical language in the Italian and English madrigals, and the rise to prominence of the solo song with simple harmonic accompaniment, were the most important sixteenth-century developments toward the style of the seventeenth century. By the end of the sixteenth century the center of musical interest had shifted from sacred to secular composition. This shift is clearly defined by events which occurred in 1594 and 1597. In 1594, the year of Shakespeare's *Romeo and Juliet,* both Palestrina and Lasso, the two greatest late sixteenth-century Continental masters of Catholic Church music, died; in the same year, Gesualdo's first book of madrigals was published. In 1597 Morley published his *A Plaine and Easie Introduction to Practicall Musicke,* summing up the compositional practice of the late Renaissance; the first collection of English lute songs appeared, as did Gabrieli's *Symphoniae sacrae,* a landmark of early Baroque style; and (probably) the first performance of an opera, Peri's *Dafne,* was given in 1597.

Yet the latter half of the sixteenth century was by no means exclusively secular. At the same time that the madrigal was at its height in Italy and the solo song was entering upon its new career, while the first works of clearly Baroque character were being produced, and the earliest experiments toward opera were being made, a new and important body of church music was being written to meet the needs of the new Protestant churches. And as though in response to this challenge, the ancient forms of Roman Catholic Church music, the Mass and the motet, rose to new splendor at the hands of Lasso, Palestrina, Byrd, and a host of other late sixteenth-century composers.

The Music of the Reformation in Germany

When Martin Luther posted his ninety-five theses on the church door at Wittenberg in 1517, he had no intention of initiating a movement that would result in the formation of organized Protestant churches completely separate from Rome. Even after the break was irreparable, the Lutheran church still retained much of the traditional Catholic liturgy, along with a considerable use of Latin in the services; and similarly, much Catholic music, both plainsong and polyphony, was kept, sometimes with the original Latin text, sometimes with the original text translated into German, or sometimes with new German texts adapted to the old melodies (called *contrafacta* or parodies).

Martin Luther

The position of music in the Lutheran church, especially in the sixteenth century, reflected Luther's own convictions on this subject. He was a lover of music, a singer, a composer of some skill, and a great admirer of Netherlands polyphony and of the works of Josquin des Prez in particular; he believed strongly in the educational and ethical power of music and wanted all the congregation to take some part in the music of the services. And although he altered the words of the liturgy to conform to his own views on certain theological points, Luther also wished to retain Latin in the service, partly because he thought it had value for the education of the young. These views, personal and official, were in some respects inconsistent; and in applying them, different local congregations evolved a number of different usages. Large churches with trained choirs generally kept much of the Latin liturgy and Latin polyphonic music; for smaller congregations or for optional use, Luther published as early as 1526 a *German Mass* (*Deudsche Messe*), which followed the main outlines of the Roman Mass, but with many changes of detail: the Gloria was omitted; new recitation tones were used, adapted to the natural cadence of the German language; several parts of the Proper were omitted or condensed, and for the remainder, as well as for most of the Ordinary, German hymns were substituted. But Luther never intended either this formula or any other to prevail uniformly in the Lutheran churches, and almost every imaginable combination and compromise between the Roman usage and the new ideas could be found somewhere in Germany sometime in the sixteenth century. Latin Masses and motets continued to be sung, and Latin remained in the liturgy at some places even into the eighteenth century: at Leipzig in Bach's time, for example, considerable portions of the services were still sung in Latin.

The Lutheran chorale

The most distinctive and important musical contribution of the Lutheran church was the strophic congregational hymn called in German a *Choral* or *Kirchenlied* (church song) and in English a *chorale*. Since most people today are acquainted with these hymns chiefly in four-part harmonized settings, it must be pointed out that the chorale, like plainsong and folk song, consists essentially of only two elements, a text and a tune; but—also like plainsong and folk song—the chorale lends itself to enrichment through harmony and counterpoint and can be expanded into large musical forms. As most Catholic church music in the sixteenth century was an outgrowth of plainsong, so much Lutheran church music of the seventeenth and eighteenth centuries was an outgrowth of the chorale.

Four collections of chorales were published in 1524, and others followed at frequent intervals. From the outset, these songs were intended for congregational singing in unison, without harmonization or accompaniment. The notation in some of the books is like that of the contemporary Gregorian Chant, and thus does not indicate the relative duration of the notes; more commonly, however, the melodies are given in precise mensural notation, and oftentimes have quite complex rhythmic patterns. It does not seem likely that such complex patterns were followed literally in performance, especially when we remember that the congregation had to sing both words and notes from memory; more probably, the chorales were sung with notes of fairly uniform length, perhaps with modifications suggested by the natural flow of the words, and with a pause of indefinite length on the final note of each phrase.

For a long time the demand for suitable songs in the Lutheran church far exceeded the supply. Luther himself wrote many chorale verses, for example, the well-known *Ein' feste Burg* (*A mighty fortress*); it has never been definitely established that Luther wrote the melody of this chorale (first printed in 1529), though the music is generally ascribed to him. Many chorale tunes were newly composed, but even more were made up entirely or partly from songs already existing. Thus the Gregorian hymn *Veni Redemptor gentium* became *Nun komm' der Heiden Heiland* (*Come, Saviour of the nations*); familiar nonliturgical spiritual songs were taken over, for example, the mixed Latin-German Christmas hymn *In dulci jubilo* or the German Easter song *Christ lag in Todesbanden* (*Christ lay in death's dark prison*), later rearranged by Luther on the model of the Easter sequence *Victimae paschali laudes.*

A particularly important class of chorales were the *contrafacta* or "parodies" of secular songs, in which the given melody was retained but the text was either replaced by completely new words or else altered so as to give it a properly spiritual meaning. The adaptation of secular songs and secular polyphonic compositions for church purposes was common in the sixteenth century, as we have already seen in the history of the Mass. Perhaps the most famous and certainly one of the most beautiful of the contrafacta was *O Welt, ich muss dich lassen* (*O world, I now must leave thee*), adapted from Isaac's Lied, *Innsbruck, I now must leave thee*. A later and somewhat startling example was the tune from Hassler's Lied *Mein Gmüth ist mir verwirret* (*My peace of mind is shattered* [by a tender maiden's charms]), which about 1600 was set to the sacred words *Herzlich thut mich verlangen* (*My heart is filled with longing*) and later to *O Haupt voll Blut und Wunden* (*O sacred head now wounded*). The transfiguration of the opening phrase of this song from Hassler's original version into two of the settings in Bach's *Passion according to St. Matthew* is shown in Example VIII–1.

Contrafacta

EXAMPLE VIII–1

a. Hassler, *Mein Gmüth ist mir verwirret*

b. J. S. Bach, *Passion according to St. Matthew*

c. J. S. Bach, *Passion according to St. Matthew*

New chorale texts were written in great numbers throughout the sixteenth and seventeenth centuries, and some new tunes were adapted, although a large number of chorales from the early Reformation period were retained. Some chorale tunes from the sixteenth and seventeenth centuries are still to be found in most Protestant hymnals of the present day: Luther's *A mighty fortress,* Hassler's *O sacred head,* and Crüger's *Now thank we all our God* are examples. But it is regrettable that, on the whole, American Protestants do not make greater use of this spendid musical heritage.

Lutheran composers early began to write polyphonic settings for chorales. In 1524 Luther's principal musical collaborator, Johann Walter (1496–1570), published a volume of 38 German chorale settings together with five Latin motets; this collection was expanded, with a larger proportion of Latin motets, in subsequent editions, of which the fifth and last appeared in 1551. A more important collection of 123 polyphonic chorale arrangements and motets was issued at Wittenberg in 1544 by Georg Rhaw (1488–1548), the leading music publisher of Lutheran Germany. Unlike Walter's work, this was a compilation of pieces by all the leading German and Swiss-German composers of the first half of the sixteenth century, including Ludwig Senfl, Thomas Stoltzer (*ca.* 1475–1526), Benedictus Ducis (*ca.* 1490–1544), Sixtus Dietrich (*ca.* 1490–1548), Arnold von Bruck (*ca.* 1470–1554), and a Netherlander, Lupus Hellinck (*ca.* 1495–1541). The chorale settings in these and other sixteenth-century collections naturally varied considerably in style; some used the older technique of the German Lied, with the plain chorale tune in long notes in the tenor, surrounded by three or more parts in free-flowing polyphony, with independent motives and little use of imitation; others were like the Franco-Flemish motets, with each phrase of the chorale being developed imitatively through all the voices; still others were in a simple, almost chordal style. Through the first half of the century there was a general trend toward this last style of simplified writing, and also toward placing the tune in the soprano instead of in the tenor.

Polyphonic chorale settings were not intended for the congregation, but for the choir. Probably only the melody was sung, in unison and perhaps instrumentally doubled; the remaining parts may have been taken by the organ or with any other instruments that were available. A common method of performance was to alternate stanzas of the chorale sung in this way with stanzas sung by the congregation in unison without accompaniment. In the last third of the century a gradual change took place; more and more frequently chorales began to be published in *cantional* style, that is, in plainly chordal, hymn-like, rhythmically straightforward settings with the tune in the topmost voice. In the sixteenth century congregational singing was still probably unaccompanied; after 1600 it gradually became the custom

Polyphonic chorale settings

Bach's Heritage

for the organ to play all the parts while the congregation sang the tune. The first collection in cantional style was Lucas Osiander's (1534–1604) *Fünfzig Lieder und Psalmen* (*Fifty Chorales and Psalms*) in 1586. The chief composers of cantional settings in the early seventeenth century were H. L. Hassler (1608), Michael Praetorius (1571–1621) in his *Musae Sioniae,* 1607–10, and Johann Hermann Schein (1586–1630), in his *Leipziger Kantional* (1627).

By the end of the sixteenth century many Lutheran regions of Germany had returned to the Catholic faith, and the line between Protestant north and Catholic south was fixed substantially as it has remained to this day. With this definitive separation, a new and distinctive kind of Lutheran polyphonic church music emerged. Composers of chorale settings during the early Reformation had aimed at preserving the words and melody of the chorale intact; that is, they treated the chorale the way medieval composers of organa had treated Gregorian Chant, as something established and not to be altered, to be adorned but not to be interpreted in any personal expressive sense. By the end of the sixteenth century this attitude had changed. Led by the example of Lasso, Protestant German composers began to do what Catholic composers had done in the fifteenth century—to use the traditional melodies as the basic material for free artistic creation, to which they added individual interpretation and pictorial details. These new settings were called *chorale motets.*

The chorale motet

An example of the Lutheran chorale motet is the *bicinium* (two-part song) based on the chorale *Our Father,* by Michael Praetorius (Example VIII–2; see also HAM, No. 167a, and GMB, No. 160).

Composers of chorale motets could, and did, break away altogether from the traditional chorale tunes, though they still used melodic

EXAMPLE VIII–2   Bicinium: *Vater unser,* Michael Praetorius

du uns al - le heis-sest gleich, Brü - der

le heis - sest, der du uns al - le heis-sest gleich, Brü-der sein und

sein und dich ru - fen an, und willt das Be - ten

dich ru - fen an und willt das Be -

von uns han, und willt das Be - ten von uns han

ten von uns han, und willt das Be - ten von uns han,

Our Father in Heaven, who dost bid us all alike to be brothers and to call upon Thee, and desirest prayers from us.

material related to the chorale or Lied style. The appearance of these motets confirmed the division which has existed ever since in Protestant church music between simple congregational hymns and more elaborate music for a trained choir. The leading composers of German motets at the turn of the sixteenth century were Hassler, Johannes Eccard (1553–1611), Leonhard Lechner (*ca.* 1550–1606), and Michael Praetorius. Their work established the Lutheran church music style in Germany and opened the road to a development that culminated over a hundred years later in J. S. Bach.

Reformation Church Music
Outside Germany

The Psalter

The effect that the Reformation had on music in France, the Netherlands, and Switzerland was quite different from developments in Germany. Jean Calvin (1509–64) and other leaders of the reformed Protestant sects opposed much more strongly than did Luther the retention of elements of Catholic liturgy and ceremonial. To a general distrust of the allurements of art in services of worship was added a particular prohibition of the singing of texts not found in the Bible. As a consequence, the only notable musical productions of the Calvinist churches were the Psalters, rhymed metrical translations of the Book of Psalms, set to melodies either newly composed or, in many cases, of popular origin or adapted from plainchant. The principal French Psalter was published in 1562, with psalm texts translated by Clément Marot and Théodore de Bèze set to melodies selected or composed by Loys Bourgeois (*ca.* 1510–*ca.* 1561). The psalms were originally sung in unison and unaccompanied in the church services; for devotional use at home, settings were made in four and more parts, with the tune in either the tenor or the soprano, sometimes in simple chordal style and sometimes in fairly elaborate motet-like arrangements. Eventually some of the simpler four-part settings were also used in public worship.

The most important French composers of Psalm settings were Claude Goudimel (*ca.* 1505–72) and Claude Le Jeune; the most important Netherlands composer was J. P. Sweelinck. Translations of the French Psalter appeared in Germany, Holland, England, and Scotland, and many of the French tunes were taken over by the Reformed churches in those countries. In Germany many Psalter melodies were adapted as chorales (see Example VIII–3a). In Holland the translation of 1566 replaced an earlier Dutch Psalter, the *Souterliedekens* of 1540, the melodies of which had been taken from contemporary popular songs and were later given three-part settings by Clemens non Papa.

The French model also influenced the most important English Psalter of the sixteenth century, that of Sternhold and Hopkins (1562), and was even more influential for the Scottish Psalter of 1564. A combination of the English and the French-Dutch traditions, embodied in the Psalter brought out by Henry Ainsworth at Amsterdam in 1612 for the use of the English Separatists in Holland, was brought to New England by the Pilgrims in 1620, and remained in use many years after the appearance of the first American Psalter, the *Bay Psalm Book* of 1640. ✗ Most important early aid to education

The French Psalter melodies on the whole are suave, intimate, and somewhat austere in comparison with the forthright, vigorous quality of most of the German chorales. Since the Calvinist churches discouraged musical elaboration, the Psalter tunes were seldom expanded into larger forms of vocal and instrumental music, as were the Lutheran chorales; and consequently they are much less conspicuous in the general history of music. Yet as devotional music they are excellent; their melodic line, which prevailingly moves by step, has something of the quality of plainsong, and the phrases are organized in a rich variety of rhythmic patterns. It is surprising that so few of the melodies from the French Psalter of 1562 are found in modern hymnals: the best-known example is the tune sung originally

EXAMPLE VIII–3   Melodies from the French Psalter of 1562, with some Later Adaptations.

The transgression of the wicked saith within my heart that there is no fear of God [before his eyes].

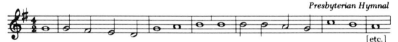

Arise ye servants of the Lord, which by night [stand] in the house of the Lord.

to Psalm 134, used in the English Psalters for Psalm 100 and hence known as "Old Hundredth" (Example VIII–3b).

A Pre-Reformation movement in Bohemia led by Jan Hus (1373–1415) resulted in the effectual banishment of polyphonic music and instruments from the church until the middle of the sixteenth century. The Hussites sang simple (usually monophonic) hymns of folklike character. As the earlier strictness was gradually relaxed, music in parts though still in note-against-note style came to be permitted. In 1561, a group known as the Czech Brethren published a hymnbook with texts in the Czech language and melodies borrowed from Gregorian Chant, secular songs, or French Calvinist Psalms in four-part settings. The Czech Brethren, later called the Moravian Brethren, emigrated to America in the early eighteenth century where their settlements—especially the one at Bethlehem, Pennsylvania—became important centers of music.

The Reformation made little lasting progress in Poland, but one of its products was the publication at Cracow in 1586 of a Psalter with Polish texts in four-part musical settings by Mikolaj Gomólka (*ca.* 1535–81).

The Church in England was formally separated from the Roman Catholic communion in 1534 under Henry VIII. Since the grounds of this action were political rather than doctrinal, no immediate changes in liturgy or music were involved. However, English was gradually substituted for Latin in the church service, and this change was confirmed under Edward VI in 1549 by the Act of Uniformity, which decreed that the liturgy as set forth in the English Book of Common Prayer would thenceforward be the sole permissible one for public use. There was a brief return of Roman Catholicism under Queen Mary (*reg.* 1553–58); but on the accession of Elizabeth I in 1558 the English rites were restored and the Church of England was established essentially in its present-day form.

Anglican church music

All this, of course, had repercussions on church music. In 1548, Edward VI admonished the Dean and Chapter of Lincoln Minster that henceforth they must sing only English, "settyng thereunto a playn and distincte note, for every sillable one"[1]—in other words, a plain, syllabic, homophonic style. Such a drastic change from the highly ornate, florid, massive medieval Catholic music of the early part of the century must have struck English composers as catastrophic. Fortunately, the more extreme demands were later modified so far as to allow for some counterpoint; some of the Latin motets of Tallis and Byrd remained favorites in English translation. Also, Queen Elizabeth specifically provided for the continued use of Latin in certain collegiate chapels and churches where that language was presumably familiar to the congregations. Still, the end result of the changes in language and liturgy was the rise of a new body of English church music. Tye and Tallis contributed to it, although their output in this field was neither so extensive nor so important as in that of Latin church composition. William Byrd, though a Roman Catholic, wrote five Services and about sixty anthems for Anglican use; some of this music is equal in quality to his Latin motets and Masses. Orlando Gibbons (1583–1625) is often called the father of Anglican church music; his works, despite the fact that they derive their technique from the Latin tradition, are thoroughly English in spirit. Thomas Weelkes and Thomas Tomkins (1572–1656) should also be mentioned among the early composers of English church music.

The principal forms of Anglican music are the *Service* and the *anthem*. A complete Service consists of the music for the unvarying portions of Morning and Evening Prayer (corresponding respectively

---

[1] Quoted in Reese, *Music in the Renaissance*, p. 796.

to the Roman Matins and Vespers) and of that for Holy Communion, which corresponds to the Roman Mass but which had a less important place in the Anglican musical scheme—often only the Kyrie and the Creed were composed. A Service is either a "Great Service" or a "Short Service"; these terms refer not to the number of items composed but to the style of the music used, the former being contrapuntal and melismatic, the latter chordal and syllabic. One of the finest examples of Anglican church music is the *Great Service* of Byrd.

The English anthem corresponds to the Latin motet. There are two types of anthems. One, which later came to be called a "full" anthem, was for chorus throughout, usually in contrapuntal style and (ideally, though not always in practice) unaccompanied; an example is Tomkins's *When David Heard* (HAM, No. 169), an extraordinarily moving and beautiful setting of this emotional text. The "verse" anthem was for one or more solo voices with organ or viol accompaniment, and with brief alternating passages for chorus. This type, which certainly originated from the consort song, was most popular in England during the seventeenth century.

The Counter Reformation

The years around 1560 were especially fateful for sixteenth-century Catholic church music. The capture and sack of Rome by Spanish and German mercenaries in 1527 had dealt the death blow to the secular phase of the Renaissance in Italy. Advocates of reform came to power in Church affairs. The Reformation in the north, and the loss or threatened loss of England, the Netherlands, Germany, Austria, Bohemia, Poland, and Hungary, all made more urgent the work of Counter Reformation. From 1545 to 1563, with numerous intermissions and interruptions, a Council was held at Trent in northern Italy to formulate and give official sanction to measures for purging the Church of abuses and laxities.

With respect to Church music (which constituted only a small part of the Council's work), the principal complaints heard at the Council of Trent were about its frequently secular spirit, as evidenced by Masses based on secular *cantus firmi* or parodied from chansons, and the complicated polyphony which made it impossible to understand the words. In addition, criticism was voiced about excessive use of noisy instruments in church, and the bad pronunciation, carelessness, and generally irreverent attitude of the church singers; in 1555 the Pope delivered a memorable reprimand to the choir of St. Peter's on this subject. The final pronouncement of the Council of Trent on these matters was extremely general, however; it merely stated that everything "impure or lascivious" must be avoided in order "that the

House of God may rightly be called a house of prayer." The imple-
mentation of this directive was left to the diocesan Bishops, and a
special commission of Cardinals was appointed to oversee its en-
forcement in Rome. The Council touched on no technical points
whatever: neither polyphony nor the parodying of secular models
was specifically forbidden.

There has long been a legend that when the Council of Trent was
being urged to abolish polyphony, Palestrina composed a six-voice
Mass to demonstrate that the polyphonic style was by no means
incompatible with a reverent spirit and did not necessarily interfere
with an understanding of the text; Palestrina thus became the "savior
of church music." We cannot be sure that the legend is wholly false.
The Mass in question was the one published in 1567 as the *Mass of
Pope Marcellus;* it may have been written during the brief pontifi-
cate of Marcellus II (1555) or, more likely, later and dedicated to the
memory of that Pope. Its precise connection with the Council of
Trent is not clear. The council was undoubtedly influenced in its
final decisions by the music of Jacobus de Kerle (*ca.* 1532–91), a
Flemish composer who in 1561 set to music a series of *preces speciales*
(special prayers) which were sung at sitting of the Council and which
by their transparent part-writing, frequent use of homophonic idiom,
and sober, devotional spirit amply convinced the Council of the
value of polyphonic music and silenced those few extremists who had
been inclined to oppose it.

The essential effect of the Council's decrees was to recognize and
sanction stylistic tendencies in church music which were already
established, particularly at Rome, by the middle of the century.
This new style aimed at a smoothly curved, prevailingly stepwise
melodic line, comparative regularity of rhythm, simplification of
counterpoint, frequent use of homophony, pure diatonic harmony,
and clarity of text; in general, composers strove to avoid secular
suggestion and to emphasize the ethical as against the merely
aesthetic function of music in church. Although parody Masses were
still being written, if a composer did use a secular model, he often
tactfully disguised that fact by calling the resulting work a *"Missa
sine nomine."* The consequence of such ideals, stimulated as they
were by the action of the Council of Trent and the atmosphere of
the Counter Reformation, was a style of composition whose greatest
representative was Giovanni Pierluigi da Palestrina.

Palestrina is the name of the small town near Rome where the
composer was born in 1525 or 1526. He served as a choirboy and
received his musical education at Rome; then, in 1544, he was appointed organist and choirmaster in his native town. In 1550 he
became choirmaster of the Cappella Giulia at St. Peter's in Rome;
in 1554 he published his first book of Masses, dedicated to his patron
Pope Julius III. After a brief engagement in 1555 as a singer in the

Palestrina

IOANNIS PETRI
Loysij Praeneſtini in baſilica
S. Petri de vrbe capellae
Magiſtri.
MISSARVM LIBER PRIMVS.

Title page of the first published work by Palestrina (Valerio & Luigi Dorico, Rome, 1554); the engraving shows the composer presenting the music to Pope Julius III.

Papal chapel, he took over the post of choirmaster at St. John Lateran (Rome), and six years later moved on to a similar but more important position at Santa Maria Maggiore. From 1565 to 1571 he taught at a newly founded Jesuit Seminary in Rome. In 1571 he was recalled to St. Peter's, where he remained as choirmaster until his death in 1594.

Palestrina twice refused offers which would have taken him away from Rome: one from the Emperor in 1568 (Philippe de Monte eventually took this position) and another from Duke Guglielmo Gonzaga at Mantua in 1583; although Palestrina did not accept the duke's invitation, he did write nine Masses for the ducal chapel which have only recently been rediscovered.

During the latter part of his life, Palestrina supervised the revision of the music in the official liturgical books to accord with the changes already made in the texts by order of the Council of Trent and to purge the chants of "barbarisms, obscurities, contrarieties, and super-fluities" which had come into them, according to Pope Gregory XIII, "as a result of the clumsiness or negligence or even wickedness of the composers, scribes, and printers."[2] This task was not completed during Palestrina's lifetime, but was continued by others until 1614, when the Medicean edition of the Gradual was published. This and other editions, more or less divergent, remained in use in various countries until the definitive reform of the Chant that was embodied in the Vatican Edition of 1908.

By far the greatest part of Palestrina's work was sacred: he wrote 102 Masses, about 450 motets and other liturgical compositions, and 56 spiritual madrigals with Italian texts. His 83 secular madrigals are not particularly outstanding examples of their kind, and in later life he "blushed and grieved" to have written music for profane love poems.

No other composer before Bach is so well known by name as Palestrina, and no other composer's technique has been subjected to more minute scrutiny. He has been called "the Prince of Music" and his works the "absolute perfection" of church style. It is generally recognized that, better than any other composer, he captured the essence of the sober, conservative aspect of the Counter Reformation in a polyphony of utter purity, detached from any secular suggestion. The Palestrina style is exemplified most clearly in his Masses; its objective, coolly impersonal quality is most appropriate to the formal and ritualistic texts of the Ordinary. The basis of his style is, of course, the Franco-Flemish imitative counterpoint; voice parts flow in continuous rhythm, with a new melodic motive for each phrase of the text. Palestrina's most important predecessors at Rome had been Festa, Arcadelt, and Morales, all of whom had adhered in their church music to the conservative, anti-secular, strictly liturgical principles which were typical of the Roman school and which are so fundamental in Palestrina's works.

The Palestrinian style

There can be no doubt that Palestrina had thoroughly studied the works of the Netherlands composers and made himself master of their technical accomplishments. Some of his early Masses were written in the old-fashioned *cantus firmus* style, including the first of the two Masses he wrote on the traditional *L'homme armé* melody. Also reminiscent of the older Flemish tradition are Palestrina's early *Missa ad fugam*, which is written throughout in double canon, and another Mass, *Repleatur os meum* of 1570, which introduces canons systematically through the various movements at every interval from

2 *Brief on the Reform of the Chant*, in SR, 358 (SRRe, 167).

the octave down to the unison, ending with a double canon in the last Agnus Dei. Canons are by no means lacking in Palestrina's later Masses, though seldom carried through so rigorously as in these two works. Another of Palestrina's conservative traits was that in a time when composers normally were writing for five or more voices, a considerable number of his compositions were for four voices only; about one-fourth of his motets, one-third of his Masses, and nearly one-half of his madrigals are so written.

A more significant reflection of Palestrina's churchly attitude is the fact that of his 102 Masses no fewer than 79 are built on themes from Gregorian Chant; this figure includes those parodied on motets or similar pieces which themselves were based on plainsong, such as the Mass *Veni sponsa Christi*. This matter is more than one of mere statistics. Gregorian Chant is the very earth out of which Palestrina's music grows, the only background against which his music can be properly heard and understood. Palestrina not only uses melodic substance from the Chant; its essential spirit and its technical procedures he takes up and transfigures in his polyphony.

Palestrina's harmony

For example, take the melodic line of any individual voice-part of a typical piece such as the first Agnus Dei from the famous *Mass of Pope Marcellus* (Example VIII–4; the entire piece appears in HAM, No. 140): long-breathed, flexibly articulated in rhythmic measures of varying length; prevailingly stepwise, with few repeated notes, moving for the most part within the range of a ninth, easily singable, the few skips greater than a third never dramatically exploited but smoothed over by returning to a note within the interval of the skip—in all, an even, natural, elegant curve of sound.

Purity of line is matched by purity of harmony. Characteristic of Palestrina is the complete—one might say, studied—avoidance of chromaticism, that new expressive resource which was being so thoroughly explored by the more progressive contemporary composers. Even in his secular madrigals Palestrina was conservative in this respect; the more so in his sacred works, and above all in the Masses, where the peculiarly intense, personal, carnal quality of chromatic harmonies would have been for him an unthinkable secular intrusion. Only the essential alterations required by the rules of *musica ficta* are tolerated.

The elements of Palestrina's harmony are the same as those of all sixteenth-century composers: the melodic lines combine to make what we now call triads and chords of the sixth. Typical also of the sixteenth century is the frequency of bass movement by a fourth or fifth, periodically producing cadences which more or less clearly define certain tonal centers. Thus in measure 7 of Example VIII–4 we have a cadence on G, but with the effect of finality avoided by the conspicuous third, the B, in the soprano and the uninterrupted eighth-note movement in the tenor and alto. The cadence on G at measure 13 is reached by way of the descending fifths A–D–G in the bass and is followed at once by a still further descending fifth to C at measure 15—this time, however, with a much more definitive cadence formula and consequently stronger cadential feeling. The kind of tonality defined by such means as these is characteristic of most sixteenth-century music, from Josquin on. We may think of it, if we like, as lying somewhere between the modally regulated polyphony of the fifteenth century and the tonal harmonic system of the

EXAMPLE VIII–4   Agnus Dei I from the *Pope Marcellus Mass,* Palestrina

eighteenth century with its hierarchy of tonics, dominants, and functional secondary chords. We must not, however, think of sixteenth-century harmony in "evolutionary" terms; it is not to be regarded either as an "improvement" over Dufay or as a mere stage of "progress" toward Bach. Tonality in the sixteenth century exists in its own right and operates consistently by its own methods.

The diatonic character of the harmony and especially the discreet handling of dissonance give Palestrina's music a consistent serenity and transparency not matched by any other composer's. Another beauty of sixteenth-century polyphony—as indeed of all good vocal polyphony—lies in the management of sonority, the grouping, spacing, and doubling of voices in vertical combination. By varying the voice grouping, a large number of subtly different shadings, of sonorities, can be obtained from the same chord, some of which will be better balanced or more effective than others, although each conceivably can be useful in a particular situation or for a particular coloristic or expressive effect. The vertical sonorities in Palestrina, arrived at always by logical and natural movement of the various voices, are among the most homogeneous and satisfying of those in any sixteenth-century music; and these sonorities account in part for the variety and sustained interest found in long works that are built entirely on what might seem an extremely limited harmonic vocabulary. Palestrina seldom uses particular registers or a particular spacing for dramatic reasons; his effects are purely in the realm of sonority, as though he wished to demonstrate how many different ways a plain triad or first inversion may be sounded by four or five or six unaccompanied voices. To take a simple example: in the first Agnus Dei from Palestrina's Mass *Veni sponsa Christi* (transposed version: see MM, No. 24) the combinations F–A–C or A–C–F occur twenty-one times. We may perhaps hear all these as harmonically identical—that is, as versions of the F-major triad—but in terms of actual sound there are eighteen different combinations and spacings of the chord (Example VIII–5).[3]

EXAMPLE VIII–5   Sonorities of the F-major triad in the Agnus Dei I from the Mass *Veni sponsa Christi,* Palestrina

The rhythm of Palestrina's music, like that of all sixteenth-century polyphony, is compounded of the rhythms of the various voices plus a collective rhythm resulting from the harmonic and contrapuntal combination of the lines. Example VIII–6 represents the first seven measures of Example VIII–4 but with each voice barred in accordance with its own natural rhythm; this example shows graphically how independent the individual lines are. However, the collective rhythm, heard when all the voices are sounding, gives the impression of a fairly regular succession of $\frac{2}{2}$ or $\frac{4}{4}$ "measures," set off not by stress accents but mostly by the changes of harmony and the placing of

---

[3] Given the four voices with the ranges of this piece, there are 229 possible sonorities of the F-major triad with its first inversion—excluding all merely unison-octave combinations, all combinations of A and C without F, and all combinations with C as the lowest note, but allowing all other combinations of 2, 3, or 4 voices, and allowing doubling and crossing of voices.

EXAMPLE VIII–6   Rhythms in Agnus Dei I from the *Pope Marcellus Mass*, Palestrina

suspensions on strong beats. This gently marked regularity of rhythm is characteristic of the Palestrina style.

This same Agnus Dei also illustrates how Palestrina unifies a composition by purely musical means. Externally, the movement resembles a typical motet by Gombert: each phrase of the text has its own musical motive, and the contrapuntal development of each motive is merged with that of the next by means of overlapping cadences. But in Palestrina's work the connection between motives is more than one of mere succession; an organic unity is achieved in part through the harmonic organization and in part through systematic repetition. At the strongly defined cadence on C at measure 15, a new motive is introduced. From this point to the end we hear a series of phrases each of which is repeated almost exactly as far as the harmonic structure is concerned, though with changes in the relative position of the voice parts and in some melodic details, thus:

measures 16_4–20_3 = 20_4–24_3
measures 24_4–29_1 = 29_4–34_1
measures 34–38 = 38–42 (a minor third lower)
measures 42–45 = 46–50
measures 50–54: Coda (plagal cadence)

Most of Palestrina's church compositions, and in particular his Masses, were in contrapuntal style, with a texture consisting of several rhythmically independent and equally important voice parts. However, Palestrina also used the more modern homophonic or chordal conception of texture in his litanies and lamentations, and in one of his most celebrated works, the *Improperia*. This composition is written entirely in chordal style, and was designed to be chanted in the manner of the harmonized Psalm tones that were widely used in Italian and Spanish churches during the sixteenth century. There are also a number of short motets by Palestrina written entirely in familiar style. The *Stabat Mater*, for double chorus, is almost completely homophonic. More typically, however, Palestrina used a mixture of contrapuntal and homophonic textures in varying proportions within the same piece. In the Masses, the movements with longer texts (the Gloria and Credo) are more homophonic—partly to reduce the time required for their performance, partly because a homophonic setting allows the words to be more easily understood, and partly for contrast with the polyphonic movements (Kyrie, Sanctus, Angus Dei), in which there is inevitably more repetition of the text. Palestrina's motets, for the most part, are contrapuntal with occasional phrases in familiar style.

It should not be inferred that Palestrina's music is expressionless or that he does not try to reflect in it the sense of the words. On the contrary, he shows his sensitiveness to the text not only in his use of the stock pictorial touches (ascending passages on "ascendit" and the like) of the period, but also in the care he takes to give each word its correct accentuation. Moreover, the emotional connotation of the words does not go unmarked. It is only that in the Masses and, for the most part, in the motets as well, this matter is treated so delicately, with such reserve, is held so strictly within the bounds of liturgical propriety, that it may easily escape an ear attuned to the grosser language of the madrigalists or even of other church composers of Palestrina's time. Yet in such a passage as the "Crucifixus" of the *Missa brevis* (Example VIII–7) the emotional tone of the words "crucifixus" (He was crucified), "passus" (He suffered), and

EXAMPLE VIII–7   Crucifixus from the *Missa brevis,* Palestrina

"resurrexit" (He rose again) is conveyed perfectly, though by the simplest possible technical means. In some of his later motets, especially the cycle from the *Song of Songs* (1584), Palestrina permitted himself somewhat richer colors and more full-bodied sonorities—but these are always held in restraint, never used for mere dramatic or external effect.

Palestrina's style was the first in the history of Western music to be consciously preserved, isolated, and imitated as a model in later ages when composers quite naturally were writing altogether different kinds of music. His work has come to be regarded as embodying the musical ideal of certain aspects of Catholicism which were especially emphasized in the nineteenth and early twentieth centuries. Partly because of this fact, partly because of the legends that have clustered around his name, and partly because of ignorance of the works of other great Catholic church composers of the fifteenth and sixteenth centuries, Palestrina's reputation has long been higher than either his music or his historical position actually warrants. No one can doubt that his art fulfills two of St. Thomas's three requirements: it possesses, to a supreme degree, harmony and radiance; but as to wholeness, that is another matter. It is a body of music that is not merely Catholic (as was the work of Dunstable, Ockeghem, and Josquin); it is specifically Roman Catholic music of the Counter Reformation and not completely representative of even that limited period. The active, aggressive, colorful, confident spirit of the Counter Reformation is reflected in Baroque architecture and the music of the Venetian composers; the Counter Reformation's ideals of conservatism, inwardness, purification, and concentration—equally important, but not the whole—are embodied in the music of Palestrina. It is not true that his music sums up the achievement of Renaissance polyphony: on the contrary, he rejected—justifiably, in view of his purposes—some of the most important musical innovations of the sixteenth century. His great and venerable art is the expression of medieval mysticism in an intentionally restricted, and in some respects archaic, Renaissance musical vocabulary.

Some contemporaries of Palestrina whose musical style was related to his must be only briefly mentioned. Giovanni Maria Nanino *Contemporaries* (*ca.* 1545–1607), Palestrina's pupil and his successor at Santa Maria *of Palestrina* Maggiore and later director of the Papal Chapel, is to be counted among the foremost composers of the Roman school. Felice Anerio (1560–1614) was a pupil of Nanino who in 1594 succeeded Palestrina as official composer to the Papal Chapel. Giovanni Animuccia (*ca.* 1500–71) was Palestrina's predecessor at St. Peter's. He is noted chiefly for his *laude* written for the Congregation of the Oratory at Rome. This Congregation grew out of meetings organized by a priest (later canonized), Filippo Neri, for religious lectures and spiritual exercises, which were followed by the singing of *laude;* the name came from the original place of meeting, the "oratory" (prayer

chapel) of one of the Roman churches. The *laude* and similar devotional songs—Palestrina himself contributed a few pieces to this
repertory—later were occasionally given in the form of dialogues or
otherwise dramatized.

Next to Palestrina, however, the most important composer of the
Roman school was the Spaniard, Tomás Luis de Victoria (*ca.* 1549–
1611). As the career of Morales indicated, there was a close connection between Spanish and Roman composers throughout the sixteenth century. Victoria came to Rome in 1565, probably studied
with Palestrina, and followed him as teacher at the Seminary in
1571; returning to Spain about 1595, he became chaplain to the
Empress Maria, for whose funeral services he wrote a famous
Requiem Mass in 1603. His compositions are exclusively sacred.
Though his style is like that of Palestrina, Victoria often infuses
his music with a mystical intensity, a quality which makes it both
thoroughly personal and typically Spanish. A good example of his
work is the motet *O vos omnes:* instead of the gentle, even rhythm of
Palestrina, the lines are broken as if into sobbing ejaculations;
arresting vivid phrases with repeated notes (*attendite*– behold) give
way to cries of lamentation, underlined by poignant dissonances
(*sicut dolor meus*—like unto My sorrow). Palestrina's art may be
compared to that of Raphael; Victoria's, with its passionate religious
fervor, is like that of his contemporary, El Greco. Even in his more
conventional motets this fervent spirit is always immanent in Victoria's music.

Victoria

Other notable Spanish composers of church music were Francisco
Guerrero (1528–99), who worked in various Spanish cities and went
to Rome in 1574; and the Catalan, Juan Pujol (*ca.* 1573–1626), who
belongs chronologically to a later period, but whose style is still
essentially that of the Palestrina-Victoria school.

The last of the illustrious line of sixteenth-century Franco-Flemish
composers were Philippe de Monte and Orlando di Lasso. Unlike
Palestrina and Victoria, a large part of their work was secular.
Nevertheless, Monte produced 38 Masses and over 300 motets in
which he demonstrated his mastery of contrapuntal technique and
his faithfulness to the Netherlands musical tradition, although not
without some more modern touches.

*Orlando
di Lasso*

Orlando di Lasso ranks with Palestrina among the great composers
of sacred music in the late sixteenth century. But whereas Palestrina
was above all the master of the Mass, Lasso's chief glory is his motets.
His settings of the penitential psalms[4] (about 1560), though perhaps
the best known of his church works, are not fully representative. In
both his career and his compositions, Lasso was one of the most
cosmopolitan figures in the history of music. By the age of twenty-

---

4 Psalms 6, 32, 38, 51, 102, 130, 143 in the King James version of the Bible;
6, 31, 37, 50, 101, 129, 142 of the Vulgate.

four he had already published books of madrigals, chansons, and motets, and his total production eventually amounted to over 2000 works. The principal collection of his motets, the *Magnum opus musicum* (*Great Work of Music*) was published in 1604, ten years after his death. In contrast to Palestrina's considered, restrained, and classic nature, Lasso had an impulsive, emotional, and dynamic temperament. In his motets both the over-all form and the details are generated from a pictorial, dramatic approach to the text; an example of this may be heard in the motet *In hora ultima,* where a portentous announcement of the Day of Judgment is followed by abrupt musical depictions of those worldly vanities which in that hour "shall perish":

. . . tuba, tibia, et cythara,	. . . trumpet, flute, and harp,
jocus, risus, saltus,	joking, laughing, and dancing,
cantus et discantus.	song and descant.

Even in motets of a more conventional type, Lasso's attention to details of the text is evident. The distinctive technical features of his musical style seem to be an outgrowth of this attitude: the melodic movement is frequently by leap; phrases are uneven in length; texture is freely varied to suit the emotional or pictorial suggestions in the words; the harmonic rhythm is often rapid and irregular; and the expressive values of harmonic combinations are exploited.

In the latter years of his life, under the influence of the spirit of the Counter-Reformation, Lasso devoted himself wholly to setting sacred texts, particularly spiritual madrigals, renouncing the "gay" and "festive" songs of his youth for music of "more substance and energy." However, one cannot properly speak of a "Lasso style"; the man is too versatile for that. Netherlands counterpoint, Italian harmony, Venetian opulence, French vivacity, German gravity, all are to be found in his work, which more fully than that of any other sixteenth-century composer sums up the achievements of an epoch and in many ways looks forward to the age of the Baroque.

William Byrd

The last of the great Catholic Church composers of the sixteenth century was William Byrd of England. Byrd was born in 1543 and as a boy probably studied music under Thomas Tallis. He was appointed organist of Lincoln Cathedral in 1563; about ten years later he moved to London to take up his duties as a member of the Royal Chapel, which post he held until the end of his life despite the fact that he remained a Roman Catholic. From 1575 he possessed, at first jointly with Tallis and, after the latter's death in 1585, on his own account, a monopoly grant for the printing of music in England. He died in 1623.

Byrd's works include English polyphonic songs, keyboard pieces, and music for the Anglican Church; undoubtedly his best vocal compositions are his Latin Masses and motets. In view of the contemporary religious situation in England, it is not surprising that Byrd wrote only three Masses (respectively for three, four, and five voices); yet these are beyond doubt the finest settings of the Mass written by an English composer.

Byrd's earlier motets were probably intended for private devotional gatherings; but the two books of *Gradualia* (1605, 1607) were designed for liturgical use. In the dedication of the *Gradualia* of 1605 occurs a passage of significance for the understanding of Byrd's conception of the relation of words to music:

> I have found there is such a power hidden away and stored up in those words [of Scripture] that—I know not how—to one who meditates on divine things, pondering them with detailed concentration, all the most fitting melodies come as it were of themselves, and freely present themselves when the mind is alert and eager.

Byrd seems to have been the first English composer to absorb Continental imitative techniques to a point where they are used imaginatively and without any sense of constraint. The texture of his music is pervaded by the same essentially English quality of vocality that we have already noticed in the music of Tallis. Byrd's treatment of dissonance is sometimes unconventional, and often

EXAMPLE VIII–8   *Ave verum,* William Byrd

O sweet, gracious Jesus, son of Mary, have mercy on me.

extraordinarily beautiful in effect. A particular feature of his music, found also in that of other English composers of the period, is the use of the same note in both its diatonic and chromatically altered form in close juxtaposition, or even simultaneously (Example VIII–8). This usage, of course, must be understood in its proper context of unaccompanied vocal music, although similar clashes are common also in contemporary English string and keyboard writing.

Excellent examples of Byrd's style may be found in the motets *Ego sum panis vivus* (printed MM, No. 25) and *Non vos relinquam,* No. 37 of the second book of *Gradualia* (printed in HAM, No. 150). The latter is unequalled as a musical expression of Christian joy, rising steadily from the first note to a superb climax of exultation. Such a work well illustrates the difference between the liturgically centered, objective art of Palestrina and Byrd's more intimate, subjective language.

Instrumental Music of the Later Sixteenth Century

In the latter half of the sixteenth century, the Mass, the motet, and the madrigal were coming to the end of a long period of development. By the end of the century these had reached an apex of beauty that was not to be surpassed in any succeeding age, and their relative importance declined after 1600. Instrumental music, on the other hand, was steadily increasing both in quantity of output and in the skill with which composers were learning to write idiomatically and to manipulate and expand musical forms independently of a text; this growth continued without interruption into the following century.

During the late sixteenth century, instruments were still associated with the performance of most vocal music. Only at the Sistine Chapel in Rome, and in a few other chapels with a choir of competent singers, was polyphonic church music consistently sung unaccompanied. Elsewhere the organ, lute, viols, or other instruments accompanied, doubled, or substituted for voices, and organists developed a huge repertory of music for use in church services, including preludes, interludes, and arrangements of liturgical melodies. In secular music, the lute continued popular both for solos and in ensembles; clavier instruments were coming into wider use, and hundreds of pieces were written for chamber music ensembles.

Late sixteenth-century instrumental music can best be surveyed by dividing it into four classes: compositions derived from vocal models, dances, improvisatory pieces, and variations. This classification is of course imperfect, since the categories are not of the same order; they

Student Collegium musicum. *In this engraving by Crispyn de Passe the Elder (1564–1637), a group of students is shown singing and playing. Among the instruments are a violin, a lute, a harpsichord and a string bass. The presence of both ladies and wine indicate that music was not the only order of business!*

relate respectively to source, function, style, and form of compositions. Consequently, any given work may belong to more than one class, as, for example, a dance in the form of variations. It is therefore essential to regard these four classes not as so many pigeon-holes but rather as *basic principles of procedure* which are operative in the composition of instrumental music in the late sixteenth century, and one or another of which usually can be regarded as the *main* principle in any actual work of that period.

Of the compositions derived from vocal models a large number are nothing more than transcriptions of madrigals, chansons, or motets, decorated by turns, trills, runs, and other embellishments. The art of melodic ornamentation (coloration) had reached a high level by the end of the sixteenth century, and was applied in both vocal and instrumental performances. Originally ornamentation had been improvised, but as time went on composers began to write out their embellishments, and it is probable that many details of instrumental writing in the early Baroque era were the outgrowth of sixteenth-century improvisatory practice. German organ composers of the late sixteenth century are called "colorists" because their works consist so largely of embellished arrangements of vocal melodies.

Compositions derived from vocal models

A good example of an organ hymn based on a vocal *cantus firmus* is the beautiful setting of *Pange lingua* by the French organist Jean Titelouze (1563–1633). A similar type of piece, found only in English sources, is the *In nomine,* which has a curious history. The earliest keyboard pieces to be so called were transcriptions of the Benedictus of a Mass by Taverner; at the words "Benedictus qui venit *in nomine* Domini" (Blessed is he that cometh in the name of the Lord), Taverner used the melody of an antiphon, *Gloria tibi Trinitas* (*Glory to thee, O Trinity*: *Liber usualis,* 914). Keyboard composers who subsequently used the melody gave it the title *In nomine,* but the origin both of the title and of the melody itself remained for a long time a mystery to historians. English composers used the *In nomine* melody in a large number of contrapuntal fantasias for viols and, less often, for keyboard instruments.

Another favorite *cantus firmus* for keyboard and ensemble works consisted of the six notes of the hexachord (*ut, re, mi, fa, sol, la*), around which English composers wrote many ingenious counterpoints. One celebrated "hexachord fancy" by John Bull (*ca.* 1562–1618) takes the hexachord through all twelve keys in turn. This extraordinary composition was probably modeled after a Sinfonia of Alfonso della Viola (d. *ca.* 1570), one of several Italian composers in the sixteenth and seventeenth centuries who experimented with radical chromaticism.[5] Since Bull's "fancy" appears in the Fitzwilliam Virginal Book as a keyboard piece, it has been suggested that some approximation to equal temperament must have been known in England by the end of the sixteenth century; however, the keyboard version we have may be only a condensed score of a fantasy for four viols.

Keyboard and ensemble *ricercari* in the manner of vocal motets were composed throughout the sixteenth century, but more important historically was the development of the canzona. Originally, the canzona was an instrumental composition with the same general style as the French chanson—that is, light, fast-moving, strongly rhythmic, and with a fairly simple contrapuntal texture. The composers of instrumental canzonas took over these characteristics from the chanson, as well as the typical opening rhythmic figure ♩ ♩ ♩| ♩ or ♩ ♫ | ♩, which occurs in nearly all canzonas. More lively and entertaining than the sober and somewhat abstruse ricercar, the canzona became in the late sixteenth century the leading form of contrapuntal instrumental music. The earliest Italian examples (apart from mere transcriptions) were for organ; about 1580, Italian composers began to write ensemble canzonas as well. The organ canzonas were the forerunners of the fugue; these two terms were used synonymously in Germany as early as 1607. The ensemble canzonas, on the other hand, eventually developed into the *sonata da chiesa* (church sonata) of the seventeenth century.

The canzona

---

[5] For accounts of such experiments see Edward Lowinsky, "Echoes of Adrian Willaert's Chromatic 'Duo' in Sixteenth- and Seventeenth-Century Compositions" in Harold Powers, ed., *Studies in Music History: Essays for Oliver Strunk,* Princeton, 1968, 183–238, and footnote references.

The essential step in this development was the division of the canzona into a number of more or less distinct sections. Many of the earliest canzonas had a single theme, or perhaps several themes very similar in character, treated contrapuntally in one continuous and unchanging movement. Others, however, introduced themes of somewhat contrasting character, each theme in turn going through its contrapuntal working-out and then yielding to the next. Since the themes themselves were noticeably different from each other in melodic outline and rhythm, the piece as a whole began to take on the aspect of a series of contrasting sections—even though the divisions between sections were usually concealed by overlapping of the cadences. Example VIII–9 shows the four themes in a canzona of this type written by the Netherlander Jean de Macque (*ca.* 1550–1614; the entire piece is given in EE, No. 25).

A further stage in the direction of independent sections is illustrated in Example VIII–10, themes from an instrumental piece by the Venetian composer, Andrea Gabrieli (*ca.* 1520–86). (The entire piece is given in HAM, No. 136. Although it was called ricercare, it is of the canzona type, an indication of the looseness of terminology in this period.) The themes are more contrasting than those in de Macque's canzona, and moreover the second sec-

EXAMPLE VIII–9   Themes from a Canzona, Jean de Macque

tion of the piece is set off from the others by being written in a predominantly homophonic style. The opening section is repeated in its entirety after section four.

This composition of Gabrieli's thus illustrates also an important structural principle—repetition. Of course, the ideas of contrast and repetition were not new; both are basic in musical composition, and both appear in Western music from its earliest beginnings. But before the sixteenth century the use of repetition and contrast was dictated largely by liturgical requirements, or by the poetic form of the text, or by the nature of a dance pattern. In independent instrumental pieces, such as the canzonas, the decision to use these

EXAMPLE VIII–10   Themes from a Ricercare, Andrea Gabrieli

devices is made for purely musical reasons: to give coherence and variety to polyphony intended only to be listened to, without the distractions or support of ritual, dancing, or text. This new approach embodied in the late sixteenth-century canzona, and in similar contemporary forms with other names—capriccio, ricercare, fantasia, fancy, and the like—was important, for in it was implicit the later development of independent instrumental music.

In the latter half of the sixteenth century, dance music for lute, keyboard instruments, and ensembles was published in increasing amounts. Some dances were simple arrangements of tunes for popular use, but the majority seem to have been written for social occasions in the homes of the bourgeoisie or the courts of the aristocracy. The ballet, which had flourished earlier in the Burgundian and the Italian courts, was imported into France toward the end of the sixteenth century; the earliest French ballet music extant is that for the *Ballet comique de la reine* (*The Queen's Dramatic Ballet*), which was given at Paris in 1581.

Dance pieces

The tendency already present in the early sixteenth century to group dances in pairs or threes continued, as did the writing of stylized dance music. The English excelled in this type of piece; examples are Orlando Gibbons's *Pavane Lord Salisbury* and especially the pavanes of William Byrd, which are among his finest compositions. Often a stylized dance movement was used as the subject for a set of variations. The favorite pairs of dances in the late sixteenth century were the *pavane* (*padovano*, *paduana*) and *galliard;* or the *passamezzo* and *saltarello*. In either pair the first dance was slow and stately and in duple time, and the second dance was a more lively movement in triple time, usually on the same melody or a variation thereof. The second dance is sometimes called in German sources the *proportio* or *proportz*, a name surviving from the terminology of fifteenth-century notation.

The *allemande* or *alman,* a dance in moderate duple meter, came into favor about the middle of the sixteenth century, and was retained, in stylized form, as a regular item in the dance suites of later times. The *courante,* another regular constituent of the later suites, also appeared in the sixteenth century. A whole class of dances were called *branle;* 26 different kinds of branles are described in the *Orchésographie* of Thoinot-Arbeau (1588), the most important treatise on dancing in this period. The principal late sixteenth-century dances are listed, with interesting comments about their musical structure, by Morley in his *Plaine and Easie Introduction*.

The chief form of keyboard music in improvisatory style in the latter half of the century was the *toccata*. This word comes from the Italian verb *toccare* (to touch), and carries the suggestion of an organist improvising at the keyboard. As an example, we may take a toccata by the Venetian organist Claudio Merulo (1533–1604; Example VIII–11; the entire composition is in HAM, No. 153).

Improvisatory pieces

Merulo begins by taking advantage of the organ's power to sustain tones indefinitely; the first section is a succession of broadly con-

EXAMPLE VIII–11 Toccata Sections, Claudio Merulo

ceived harmonies in F major (Example VIII–11a) cadencing first on the tonic and then moving to a half cadence on the dominant. The numerous suspensions and other long-held dissonances are quite idiomatic to the organ. The harmonic structure is animated in all the voices by embellishments and scale passages in freely varied rhythms—ornaments probably played with a rather free rubato-like delivery. A contrasting middle section is, in effect, a short ricercare with three themes, each in turn developed by imitation (Example VIII–11b). The last ricercare theme soon dissolves into ornamental work followed by rapidly changing harmonies that lead to a cadence on the tonic. After this middle section comes a passage similar to the opening but with harmonies more broadly laid out and with even more fantastic play of brilliant running passages. The majestic slowing down of the harmonic rhythm in the coda, coupled with the increasing animation and ever wider sweep of the runs, makes a most impressive climax (Example VIII–11c).

The toccata was a specialty of the Venetian organ composers. Merulo, publishing at the very end of the century (1598 and 1604), was the first to introduce the ricercare-like middle section as described in the above example. Most sixteenth-century toccatas were simply in one movement, in straight improvisatory style. Various names were used for pieces of this sort: *fantasia, intonazione, prelude,* and others.

A rather different kind of improvisatory writing is found in some keyboard pieces toward the end of the sixteenth century, pieces in which the composer seems to wander dreamily through a maze of strange harmonies, as an organist might when quietly improvising. Example VIII–12 shows a passage from a work of this sort, appropriately entitled *Consonanze stravaganti* (*Roving Harmonies*), by Jean de Macque. (The entire composition is in HAM, No. 174). The peculiar chromaticism of this example is reminiscent of

EXAMPLE VIII–12   *Consonanze stravaganti,* Jean de Macque

    * *So in original; delete* a?
    ** *So in original; delete* d?

Gesualdo, with whom de Macque was associated for a time at Naples. The style is a forerunner of the beautiful chromatic toccatas of the seventeenth-century Roman organist, Frescobaldi.

The extraordinary flowering of the variation form in the late sixteenth century was due primarily to a school of English keyboard composers called the *virginalists* from the name of the principal keyboard instrument of the time. The leading composer in this group was William Byrd; important among his colleagues were Orlando Gibbons and Thomas Tomkins. Of the many manuscript collections of keyboard music which were made in England in this period, beginning with the *Mulliner Book* (*ca.* 1540–85), the most comprehensive is the *Fitzwilliam Virginal Book,* a manuscript compiled about 1620, which contains nearly 300 compositions written in the late sixteenth and early seventeenth centuries. Among these pieces are madrigal transcriptions, contrapuntal fantasias, dances, preludes, descriptive pieces, and many sets of variations.

English keyboard music

The title page of Parthenia, *(1611), one of the first English music books printed from engraved plates. This collection pre-dated the* Fitzwilliam Virginal Book *and presented the works of three outstanding English composers, William Byrd, John Bull, and Orlando Gibbons.*

Most of the variations in the *Fitzwilliam Virginal Book* are on slow dance tunes (as Bull's *Spanish Paven*) or familiar songs (as Munday's *Goe from my window*). Many folk tunes of the time also served as subjects for variation.

The tunes used as the basis for the variations as a rule were short, simple, and song-like, regular in phrasing, with a clear binary or ternary pattern set off by distinct cadences. The variations follow in uninterrupted sequence, sometimes a half-dozen of them, sometimes as many as twenty or even more. Each variation preserves the structure of the theme: the same articulations, the same cadences, the same harmonic plan. Sometimes the melody is presented intact throughout an entire set of variations, passing occasionally from one voice to another. More often, in some of the variations the melody is broken up by figuration, so that its original profile is only suggested. Sometimes this decorative figuration is derived from some phrase of the melody itself, but as a rule it is freely invented. Some of the passage work, particularly in the variations by Bull, has a high order of virtuosity, if not always important musical content; evidently fast scale-playing and similar feats of technical skill had the same fascination for composers and players then as in the nineteenth century.

In most English virginal music, however, mere technical display is not a prominent feature. Each variation commonly makes use of one main type of figuration; and sometimes the two halves of a variation, or two successive variations, will be paired by the use of the same figure in the right hand for one and in the left hand

A seventeenth-century double spinet or virginal, with an ornamental and painted case, made by Ludovicus Grovvelus of Flanders. The right-hand instrument can be removed from the case and used as a portable virginal. (Courtesy Metropolitan Museum of Art, the Crosby Brown Collection of Musical Instruments, 1889)

for the other, as in the third and fourth variations of Bull's *Spanish Paven*. Apart from such pairing, the only comprehensive plan in most sets of variations was to increase the animation as the work progressed—although with intermittent quieter interludes. Changes of meter were sometimes introduced, and once in a while a composer would show off his learning by writing a variation using two or three different meters simultaneously. Quite often the last variation was slower, a broadened restatement of the theme with fuller sonority and richer harmonization. The technique may be studied with pleasure in the charming little set of variations by Farnaby on *Loth to depart*.

The *Fitzwilliam Virginal Book* and other contemporary collections are eloquent witnesses to the quality of sixteenth-century English composers. It is not surprising that in the early seventeenth century English musicians were influential in the northern countries of Europe. John Dowland served from 1598 to 1607 as lutenist to the King of Denmark. Peter Philips (1561–1628) and Richard Deering (*ca.* 1580–1630) were among the English Catholics who emigrated to the Continent; their music was published chiefly in the Netherlands. William Brade (1560–1630) held various positions in Denmark and Germany, and published in the latter country a number of suites for viols. John Bull went to Brussels in 1613, and from 1617 until his death served as organist of the Cathedral at Antwerp. Whether or not he and Sweelinck were personally acquainted, it is certain that the latter knew the music of Bull and his English contemporaries and was influenced by it in writing his own works for clavier, which include several excellent sets of variations.

English composers on the Continent

Toward the Baroque: The Venetian School

In the sixteenth century, Venice was (next to Rome) the most important city of the Italian peninsula. An independent city state, geographically secure and isolated on her lagoons (though she held some colonies on the mainland), in political policy aloof from the quarrels of her neighbors, nominally a republic but actually a tightly-knit oligarchy, and the chief port for European trade with the East, Venice had reached the summit of her power, wealth, and splendor in the fifteenth century. Wars and other misfortunes reduced her position in the sixteenth century, but the flourishing civilization that was the outgrowth of her past prosperity continued without obvious abatement.

Social conditions in Venice

The heart and center of Venetian musical culture was the great eleventh-century cathedral of Saint Mark, with its Byzantine domes, its bright gold mosaics, and its spacious interior swimming in dim greenish-golden light. Like Venice itself, Saint Mark's was independent: its clergy, including the musicians, were more directly responsible to the Doge than to any outside ecclesiastical authority. Most of the exalted civic ceremonies of Venice took place in the Cathedral and in the vast *piazza* which it faced. Thus most Venetian music was conceived as a manifestation of the majesty of both State and Church, and was designed to be heard on solemn and festive occasions when that majesty was publicly displayed with every possible array of sound and pageantry. In addition to these circumstances it must be remembered that the life of Venice had little of the ascetic, devotionally centered quality that was characteristic of Rome. Venice took her religion more easily; her spirit was hedonistic, extrovert. Her wide commercial interests, and especially her centuries-old trade with the East, had given her a peculiarly cosmopolitan, flamboyant atmosphere.

Music in the Cathedral of Saint Mark was supervised by officials of the State, and no pains or expense were spared to keep it worthy of Venice's high traditions. The position of choirmaster at the Cathedral was the most coveted musical post in all Italy. There were two organs, and the organists, chosen after stringent examination, were always renowned artists. Choirmasters in the sixteenth century were Willaert, Rore, Zarlino, and Baldassare Donati; organists included Jacques Buus, Annibale Padovano, Claudio Merulo, Andrea Gabrieli, and his nephew, Giovanni Gabrieli (*ca.* 1557–1612). All these men were not merely conductors and players, but famous composers as well; and it will be seen that as the century went on the northerners (Willaert, Rore, Buus) were succeeded by native Italians.

Many Venetian composers of the sixteenth century contributed notably to the madrigal, and Venice produced the best organ music of all Italy. Venetian music was characteristically of full, rich texture, homophonic rather than contrapuntal, varied and colorful in sonority. In the motets, massive chordal harmonies were the rule, rather than the single intricate polyphonic lines of the Netherlanders.

From the time of Willaert, and even before that, the Venetian church composers had often written for double chorus, the two separate choirs which in Saint Mark's were placed with the organs on opposite sides of the church. The use of such *cori spezzati* (divided choirs) was not original with Venice or peculiar to it (Palestrina's *Stabat Mater,* for example, is written for double chorus); but the practice was congenial to, and further encouraged, the homophonic type of choral writing and the broad rhythmic organization which the Venetian composers preferred. Moreover, Venice was not committed, as was Rome, to the ideal of a cappella

Venetian polychoric motets

performance. Not only the organ, but many other instruments as well—trombones, cornetts, viols—sounded with the voices. In the hands of Giovanni Gabrieli, the greatest of the Venetian masters, the motet was expanded to unheard-of proportions: two, three, four, even five choruses were employed, each with a different combination of high and low voices, each intermingled with instruments of diverse timbres, answering one another antiphonally, alternating with solo voices, and joining for massive sonorous climaxes. An example is Gabrieli's motet *In ecclesiis*. In such works a new principle of composition was established, namely the contrast and opposition of sonorities; this principle became a basic factor in the *concertato* style of the Baroque period.

Instrumental music

The famous *Sonata pian' e forte* of Gabrieli is essentially nothing else than a double-chorus Venetian motet for instruments. This composition owes its prominent place in music history books less to its intrinsic musical worth than to the fact that it is one of the first instrumental ensemble pieces printed which designates particular instruments for each part: the first orchestra consists of a cornett and three trombones, the second of a viol (*"violino"*) and three trombones.

Another innovation in Gabrieli's sonata was the indication, both in the title and in the score itself, of *"pian[o]"* and *"forte"*; the former rubric is used when each orchestra is playing alone and the latter when both are playing together. This is one of the earliest instances of dynamic markings in music. As for the term *sonata*, it was used occasionally in the sixteenth century in a very general way for almost any kind of ensemble instrumental composition, and implied nothing about form. The only connection of the sixteenth-century "sonatas" with the sonata of the Baroque and Classical periods is nominal.

The same collection in which Gabrieli's sonata was published (*Sacrae symphoniae*, 1597) also contains a *canzon in echo* for eight cornetts and two trombones, with an optional arrangement using the organ, and a *canzon da sonar* for viol, cornett, and nine trombones. It must be remembered that in the sixteenth century trombones came in five sizes from bass to soprano and that their tone was considerably softer than that of the modern instrument. The cornett was a wooden instrument with cup-shaped mouthpiece; its mild tone blended well with that of other instruments in an ensemble.

Venetian influence

The Venetian school, everywhere admired as the most progressive in Italy, exercised wide influence in the late sixteenth and early seventeenth centuries. Pupils and followers of Gabrieli were numerous in northern Italy and were scattered all over Germany and Austria. The most famous of his direct pupils was the German Heinrich Schütz. A notable proponent of Venetian style in northern Germany was Hieronymus Praetorius (1560–1629) of Hamburg. Jacob Handl (1550–91), a Slovenian by birth—known also by the

Latin form of his name, Jacobus Gallus—worked at Olmütz and Prague; most of his works, particularly his motets for double chorus, show a close affinity with Venetian style. Handl's best-known composition is a four-part motet in familiar style, *Ecce quomodo moritur justus,* which breathes the pure devotional spirit of Palestrina. The motets of Hans Leo Hassler, a German pupil of Andrea Gabrieli, are prevailingly polychoric, with typical Venetian fullness of sound and richness of harmony. In Poland, the polychoric style was cultivated by Mikolaj Zielenski (d. 1615) and many others.

Summary

This discussion of music in the second half of the sixteenth century has many times overstepped the arbitrary boundary of the year 1600 which we set as the limit of the Renaissance period. The reason, of course, is that changes in musical style occur gradually, in complex ways, and at different times in different places. Development of the English madrigal school, for example, continued in the seventeenth century, but it has been dealt with in this section because the style of the English madrigal is more closely allied to Renaissance music than to Baroque. Certainly, late Renaissance traits persisted well into the seventeenth century; and many features of the early Baroque began to be manifest long before the end of the sixteenth.

To speak of "traits" or "features" of Renaissance or Baroque music, however, implies that there are certain characteristics by which we can identify a given piece as at least predominantly one or the other, regardless of the exact date of its composition. In discussing Renaissance music, we listed five general features; let us now see how each of these was affected by the changes that took place between 1450 and 1600.

The characteristic texture of similar contrapuntal voice parts was still the rule in the work of Palestrina, Lasso, Byrd, and Gabrieli, at the end of the sixteenth century, as it had been in the music of Ockeghem and Josquin. This texture, more than any other single feature, separates Renaissance music from Baroque. On the other hand, homophony, both in its pure form as familiar style and as a centripetal tendency curbing the independence of contrapuntal lines, had begun to invade all forms of polyphonic writing. Its dominance in the Venetian school is one sign of the approaching Baroque. The outlines of major-minor tonality were already taking shape in much of the music of Palestrina, Lasso, Byrd, and Gabrieli.

Texture

Rhythm, supported by systematic harmonic progressions within the sixteenth-century tonal system, had become comparatively steady and predictable by the end of the century, even in the contrapuntal style of Palestrina and in such apparently free compositions as the Venetian organ toccatas. The barline in the modern editions of

Rhythm

Palestrina, Gabrieli, and Byrd is no longer the intrusion it sometimes seems to be in modern editions of Ockeghem and Josquin. The Baroque begins with a conspicuous revolt against rhythmic regularity; but it ends by embracing this regularity completely, within the framework of the eighteenth-century tonal system.

Music and words

Musica reservata, the pictorial and expressive touches in the madrigal, Gesualdo's chromatic aberrations, and the splendorous sonorities of the Venetian massed choruses, are all signs of the sixteenth-century drive toward vivid outward expression in music. The Baroque carries this drive to still greater lengths, and embodies it in the new forms of cantata and opera. With the rise of pure instrumental forms (the ricercare, canzona, and toccata), Renaissance music had already begun to transcend words; this line of development also continues without a break through the Baroque and beyond. Finally: whereas the solo songs of the Renaissance were lyrical pieces, hardly different in style from madrigals, one of the chief innovations of the Baroque was the discovery that the solo song could be used as a vehicle for dramatic expression. The violent states of feeling expressed by Gesualdo and Gabrieli in an ensemble of voices are by the Baroque composers expressed in a solo with instrumental accompaniment.

Most important aspect of Baroque
Concertato - (Singing back & forth)
Three Aspects of Music
Venetian
Roman   our modern music - 1950 is
Lutheran   like this.
                These schools dictated this.
→ Luther → Bach → (Mozart, Haydn) Beethoven, Brahms
        → Wagner → Vaburn → Berg - Schwanburg →
        Stockhausen →
Roman - Palestrina → tried to protect & preserve Catholic Church
        heritage.

IX

Early Baroque Music

General Characteristics of the Baroque

The word *Baroque* has recently been brought into the vocabulary of music history to designate both a chronological period extending from about the end of the sixteenth century to the middle of the eighteenth, and the style of music typical of that period.[1] As with other epochs, the boundary dates are only approximations, since many characteristics of Baroque music were in evidence before 1600 and many were disappearing before 1750. But it is possible and convenient to take these dates as the approximate limits within which certain ways of organizing musical material, certain ideals of musical sound, and certain kinds of musical expression developed from diverse and scattered beginnings to an assured and workable system, exemplified at its highest in the works of Johann Sebastian Bach and of George Frideric Handel.

What are the characteristics of Baroque music? To answer this question, we must consider how that music is related to the surroundings which produced it. The use of the term *Baroque* to describe the music of 1600–1750 suggests that historians believe its qualities are in some ways similar to the qualities of contemporary architecture, painting, literature, and perhaps also science and phi-

[1] Earlier designations—"thoroughbass period," "period of the *concertato* style" —relate only to technical aspects of music and fail to support the important connections between music and other aspects of the culture of the time; moreover, neither thoroughbass nor the concertato style is present in all music of the period. On usage of the term "baroque," see Robert H. Hall, Jr., "Meditation on a Baroque Theme," *The Modern Language Journal* XLVI/1 (January, 1962), 3–8.

losophy. We must believe that a connection exists, not only in the seventeenth century, but in all eras, between music and the other creative activities of man: that the music produced in any age must reflect, in terms appropriate to its own nature, the same conceptions and tendencies that are expressed in other arts contemporary with it. For this reason general labels like *Baroque, Gothic,* and *Romantic* are often used in music history instead of designations that might more precisely describe purely musical characteristics. It is true that these general words are liable to be misunderstood. Thus *Baroque,* which perhaps comes from a Portuguese word meaning "of irregular shape," was long used in the pejorative sense of "abnormal, bizarre, exaggerated, in bad taste, grotesque"; the word is still defined thus in the dictionaries, and still carries at least some of that meaning for many people. However, the music written between 1600 and 1750 is not on the whole any more abnormal, fantastic, or grotesque than that of any other period, and the pejorative connotations of *Baroque* do not apply to it.

Geographical and cultural background

Baroque music was dominated by Italian ideas. From the mid-sixteenth to the mid-eighteenth centuries, Italy remained the most influential musical nation of Europe. One should say *region* rather than *nation,* for the Italian peninsula was split into areas ruled by Spain and Austria, the Papal States, and a half-dozen smaller independent states which allied themselves from time to time with larger European powers and in general heartily distrusted one another. Yet political sickness apparently does not preclude artistic health: Venice was a leading musical city all through the seventeenth century despite her political impotence, and the same was true of Naples during most of the eighteenth century. Rome exerted a steady influence on sacred music and for a time in the seventeenth century was an important center of opera and cantata; Florence had her brilliant period near the beginning of the seventeenth century.

FRANCE

As for the other European countries during the Baroque era, France in the 1630s began to develop a national style of music which resisted Italian influences for over a hundred years. In Germany the already weakened musical culture of the sixteenth century was overwhelmed by the calamity of the Thirty Years' War (1618–48), but despite political disunity there was a mighty resurgence in the following generations, climaxing in Johann Sebastian Bach. In England the glories of the Elizabethan and Jacobean ages faded with the period of the Civil War and the Commonwealth (1642–60); a brief brilliant revival toward the end of the century was followed by nearly complete capitulation to Italian style.

ITALY

The musical primacy of Italy during the Baroque was not absolute, but even in the countries that developed and maintained their own distinctive national idiom the Italian influence could not be escaped. It was prominent in France through the first half of the seventeenth century especially; the composer whose works did most to establish the national French style after 1660, Jean-Baptiste Lully, was an Italian by birth. In Germany in the latter part of the century, Italian style was the principal foundation on which German composers built; even the art of Bach owed much to Italy, and Handel's work was as much Italian as German. By the end of the Baroque period, in fact, the music of Europe had become an international language with Italian roots.

The years between 1600 and 1750, during which the Americas were colonized, were a period of absolute governments in Europe. Many of the European courts were important centers of musical culture. The most imposing of these, and the model for all lesser establishments in the late seventeenth and early eighteenth centuries, was the court of Louis XIV of France (*reg.* 1643–1715). Other patrons of music included Popes, emperors, kings of England and of Spain, and rulers of smaller Italian and German states. City states, such as Venice and many of the north German towns, also supported and regulated musical establishments, both ecclesiastical and secular. The Church itself, of course, continued to support music, but its role was relatively less important in the Baroque era than it had been in earlier times. Along with aristocratic or civic or ecclesiastical patronage, "academies" (that is, organizations of private persons) in many cities supported musical activities. Commercial concerts as we know them today, however, open to the public on payment of a fee, were not a feature of the Baroque. The first such undertaking was in England in 1672; Germany and France followed in 1722 and 1725 respectively, but the movement did not become widespread until after the middle of the eighteenth century.

Literature and other arts flourished along with music in the Baroque era. To realize the magnificence of this age in the history of western civilization it is only necessary to recall the names of a few of the great writers and artists who were working in the seventeenth century: in England, John Donne and Milton; in Spain, Cervantes; in France, Corneille, Racine, and Molière. The Netherlands, relatively quiescent musically, produced the paintings of Rubens, Rembrandt, and many other artists almost as famous; Spain, somewhat isolated and of secondary importance in music, could boast of the work of Velasquez and Murillo, Italy had the sculptor Bernini (*Ecstasy of St. Theresa,* 1647) and the architect Borromini (Church of St. Ivo in Rome, *ca.* 1645). Above all, the seventeenth century was one of the great ages in the history of philosophy and science: the work of Bacon, Descartes, and Leibniz, of Galileo, Kepler, Newton, and a host of others scarcely less important, established the foundations of modern thought. "A brief, and sufficiently accurate, description of the intellectual life of the European races during the succeeding two centuries and a quarter up to our own

Literature and art

The Cornaro Chapel in the church of Santa Maria della Vittoria in Rome. Bernini's illusionistic altarpiece showing the Ecstacy of St. Teresa of Avila is the focus of a dramatic setting of richly colored marbles, with the figures of the Cornaro family seated in balconies witnessing the visionary experience.

times is that they have been living upon the accumulated capital of ideas provided for them by the genius of the seventeenth century."[2]

In a world whose thought was being thus radically stirred, the language of music did not remain unchanged. Just as the seven-

New musical ideas

teenth-century philosophers were discarding outmoded ways of thinking about the world and establishing other more fruitful ra-

[2] Alfred North Whitehead, *Science and the Modern World*, New York, 1925, 57–58.

tionales, the contemporary musicians were seeking out other realms of the emotions and an expanded language in which to cope with the new needs of expression. And as the philosophers at first tried to develop new ideas within the frame of older methods, so the musicians at first tried to pour into musical forms inherited from the Renaissance the powerful impulses toward a wider range and greater intensity of emotional content—for example, as did Gesualdo in his madrigals and Giovanni Gabrieli in his motets. Consequently, a certain discrepancy between intention and form can be sensed in much (not in all) of the music of the first half of the seventeenth century, which accounts in part for its somewhat disappointing effect. Often a composer seems to be trying to say something for which the right vocabulary of sounds and rhythms has not yet been invented, and only the greatest geniuses of the period, like Monteverdi, ever overcome this handicap. By the middle of the seventeenth century, however, new resources of harmony, color, and form had been achieved—a common language with a firm vocabulary, grammar, and syntax, in which composers could move freely and could adequately express their ideas.

Despite continuous change, certain musical features remained constant throughout the Baroque era. One of these was a distinction drawn between various styles of composition. This distinction did not describe a diversity of individual idioms within one common style, nor even a diversity of manner between simpler and more complex types of writing, such as had existed in the sixteenth century, for example, between the frottola and the balletto on the one hand and the madrigal on the other. It was rather an acknowledged stylistic difference which writers of the time described in various ways. Monteverdi, for example, in 1605 distinguished between a *prima prattica* and a *seconda prattica*, or first and second "practices." By the first, he meant the style of vocal polyphony derived from the Netherlanders, represented in the works of Willaert, codified in the theoretical writings of Zarlino, and perfected in the music of Palestrina; by the second he meant the style of the modern Italians such as Rore, Marenzio, and himself. The basis of the distinction for Monteverdi was that in the first practice music dominated the text, whereas in the second practice the text dominated the music; hence it followed that in the new style the old rules might be modified and, in particular, dissonances might be used freely to make the music conform to the expression of feeling in the text. Others called the two practices *stile antico* and *stile moderno* (old and modern style), or *stylus gravis* and *stylus luxurians* (sober and ornamented style); this last designation implied the use of fast notes, unusual skips, and a well-marked melody, as well as dissonances.

The two practices

More complex and comprehensive systems of style classification appeared by the middle of the century. Most generally accepted was a broad threefold division into *ecclesiasticus* (church), *cubicularis* ("chamber" or concert), and *theatralis* or *scenicus* (theatre) styles; within these categories, or cutting across them, were many subdivisions. Theorists were following a strong tendency of the time when they aimed thus to describe and systematize all musical styles, regarding each one as distinct and each as having its particular social function and appropriate technical characteristics.

Idiomatic writing

Another feature of Baroque music was that composers began to be attracted by the idea of writing music specifically for a particular medium, such as the violin or the solo voice, rather than music that might be either sung or played or performed by almost any combination of voices and instruments, as could many pieces composed in the sixteenth century. The violin family began to replace the older viols, and composers developed an idiomatic violin style; wind instruments were technically improved and came to be used for their specific color and capabilities; an idiomatic style for keyboard music arose; indications for dynamics began to appear; and the art of singing, promoted by famous teachers and virtuosi, advanced very rapidly in the seventeenth century. Instrumental and vocal styles began to be differentiated, eventually becoming so distinct in the minds of later Baroque composers that they consciously used vocal idioms in instrumental writing, and vice versa.

The affections

One trait common to all Baroque composers was the effort they made to express, or rather represent, a wide range of ideas and feelings with the utmost vividness and vehemence by means of music. This effort was, in a way, an extension of the Renaissance idea of *musica reservata*. But whereas in the sixteenth century the emotions represented were relatively restricted and the presentation was held within the bounds of an aristocratic concept of moderation and detachment, in the Baroque these barriers were down. Composers struggled to find musical means for the expression of *affections* or states of the soul, such as rage, excitement, grandeur, heroism, lofty contemplation, wonder, or mystic exaltation, and to intensify these musical effects by means of violent contrasts. In Baroque architecture, sculpture, and painting the normal forms of objects were sometimes distorted, as though past the natural limits of the medium, to reflect the passionate intensity of the artist's thought; in Baroque music, also, the limits of the old order of consonance and dissonance, of regular and equable rhythmic flow, were being broken down. But music, since it is not conditioned, as are sculpture and painting, by the necessity of representing natural objects nor, as is architecture, by the unyielding physical properties of the medium and a functional character, is able to expand in whatever directions the imagination of a composer may suggest. In fact, such expansion is natural to music; and in the seventeenth century it was an important stimulus both to the development of music itself and also to its increasing relative importance.

[handwritten margin note: This is a coordination between texts & music but this was a reserved kind of Symbolism in Renaissance]

The music of the Baroque was thus not primarily written to express the feelings of an individual artist, but to represent the affections; these were not communicated haphazardly or left to individual intuition, but were conveyed by means of a systematic, regulated vocabulary, a common repertory of musical *figures* or devices. Such figures included the comparatively simple, obvious pictorial touches common in Renaissance vocal music, but went beyond these into much greater detail. The musical figures of the seventeenth century were systematized in contemporary theoretical treatises on the analogy of the figures or special devices of language used in rhetoric, and were given corresponding names. Thus the Baroque composers, from Monteverdi to Bach, consistently used particular devices of melody, rhythm, harmony, texture, and so on—even figures that might violate the ordinary rules of composition—to illustrate and enforce the literal or implied meaning of words or passages in a text. Their musical language, consequently, has a far more specific vocabulary than we ordinarily expect, and we need to be aware of this if we are to understand what they are saying. They used the same vocabulary in instrumental as well as vocal music, with similar implied meanings. In addition, the process of musical composition itself was conceived, by analogy with the rules of rhetoric, as consisting of three steps: *inventio*, the "finding" of a subject, or basic musical idea; *dispositio*, the planning or layout of the divisions or "subheads" of the work; and *elaboratio*, the working-out or elaboration of the material.

The doctrine of figures (*Figurenlehre*) was developed chiefly by German theorists of the seventeenth and early eighteenth centuries; in effect, it amounted to little more than a codification of what composers were already doing, plus the elaborate (and sometimes rather strained) analogies with the venerable and highly respected art of rhetoric. To conceive music as expressing "clear and distinct ideas" doubtless reflected the teachings of Descartes, whose philosophy dominated the thought of the seventeenth century.

Diversity of styles and idioms, together with the effort made to represent vividly and precisely objects, ideas, and feelings, brought into Baroque music factors that were somewhat incompatible. Baroque music shows conflict and tension between the centrifugal forces of freedom of expression and the centripetal forces of discipline and order in a musical composition. This tension, always latent in any work of art, was eventually made overt and consciously exploited by Baroque musicians; and this acknowledged dualism is the most important single principle which distinguishes between the music of this period and that of the Renaissance. The dualism is apparent in the existence of Monteverdi's two "practices." It is also evident in the two ways the Baroque treated rhythm: (1) regular metrical barline rhythm on the one hand; and (2) free unmetrical rhythm, used in recitative or improvisatory solo instrumental pieces, on the other.

Dualism:
Rhythm

Regular dance rhythms were, of course, known in the Renaissance; but not until the seventeenth century did most music begin to be written and heard in *measures*—definite patterns of strong and weak beats. At first these patterns were not regularly recurring; the use of a single time signature corresponding to a regular succession of harmonic and accentual patterns, set off by barlines at regular intervals, was common only after 1650. By the late Baroque, it had become customary for a composer to establish a distinctive rhythmic pattern at the beginning of a composition or movement, and to hold predominantly to this basic pattern throughout; the piece thus represented a single "basic affection," and made only sparing use of contrasting material.

Along with strictly measured rhythm, Baroque composers also used an irregular, inconstant, flexible rhythm in writing instrumental toccatas and vocal recitatives. Obviously the two rhythms could not be used simultaneously; but they were frequently used successively for deliberate contrast, as in the customary pairing of toccata and fugue or recitative and aria.

Sound ideal: the basso continuo

The basic sound ideal of the Renaissance was a polyphony of independent voices; the sound ideal of the Baroque was a firm bass and a florid treble, held together by unobtrusive harmony. The idea of a musical texture consisting of a single melody supported by accompanying harmonies was not in itself new; something like it had been used in the cantilena style of the fourteenth century, in

A portion of Sfogava con le stelle *by Giulio Caccini (ca. 1546–1618), as printed in* Le nuove musiche, *a collection published in Florence in 1602.*

the Burgundian chanson, in the early frottola, in the sixteenth-century lute songs, and in the Elizabethan ayre. The ideas that were new in the Baroque were the emphasis on the bass, the isolation of the bass and treble as the two essential lines of the texture, and the seeming indifference to the inner voice lines. This indifference was perfectly pictured in a system of notation used during the Baroque, called the *thoroughbass* or *basso continuo:* the composer wrote out the melody and the bass; the bass was played on one or more *fundament* or *continuo* instruments (clavier, organ, lute), usually reinforced by a sustaining instrument such as a bass gamba or violoncello or bassoon; and above the bass notes the keyboard or lute player filled in the required chords, which were not otherwise written out. If these chords were other than common triads in root position, or if non-harmonic tones (such as suspensions) or added accidentals were

The bass has own rhythms.

A modern edition of the same portion of Caccini's Sfogava con le stelle, *with the basso continuo realized by a modern scholar, Dr. Carol MacClintock, as published in her book* The Solo Song, 1580–1730 *(New York, 1972).*

to be played, the composer could so indicate by little figures or signs placed above or below the bass notes.

The *realization*—the actual playing—of such a *figured bass* varied according to the nature of the composition and the taste and skill of the player, who had a good deal of room for improvisation within the framework set by the composer: he might play simple chords, introduce passing tones, or incorporate melodic motives in imitation of the treble or bass parts. (A modern edition of compositions with a figured bass usually indicates in smaller notes the editor's conception of a proper realization: see the piece by Caccini and its realization on the preceding pages.) The realization of the basso continuo was not always essential: that is to say, many pieces were provided with a continuo even though all the notes necessary for the full harmony were already present in the notated melodic vocal or instrumental parts. In motets or madrigals for four or five voices, for example, the continuo instrument actually did no more than double or support the voices. But for solos and duets the continuo was usually necessary to complete the harmonies as well as to produce a fuller sonority.

The new counterpoint

It might seem that the Baroque basso continuo implied a total rejection of the kind of counterpoint written in the sixteenth century and earlier. As a matter of fact, this was true when the continuo was used alone as accompaniment to a solo, unless the composer chose to give the bass line itself some melodic significance, for the thoroughbass *was* a radical departure from all previous methods of writing music. But it must be remembered that a firm bass and florid treble was not the only kind of musical texture in the Baroque. For a long time, composers continued to write unaccompanied motets and madrigals; some instrumental ensemble pieces, as well as all solo keyboard and lute music, made no use of the basso continuo; most important, even in ensembles where the continuo was used, counterpoint did not disappear. But the new counterpoint of the seventeenth century was different from that of the Renaissance. It was still a blending of different melodic lines, but the lines all had to fit into the regulative framework of a series of harmonic chord progressions explicitly defined and sounded by the continuo: it was, in short, a harmonically governed counterpoint, whose melodies were subordinated to the harmonic scheme.

Dissonance and chromaticism

Within the harmonies thus defined, composers eventually were able to use dissonance quite freely, just because the underlying harmonies were so clear. Much dissonance in the early seventeenth century was experimental; toward the middle of the century dissonance almost disappeared; then, in the last part of the Baroque, it returned, incorporated in a complex system of tonal organization. Chromaticism followed a similar development from anarchy to order to freedom. Gesualdo's chromatic harmonies in the early seventeenth century were disorderly—or rather, their only order was that imposed by the intuitive fancy of an inventive mind searching for new and striking sounds to express the emotional content of the text. Throughout the seventeenth century the use of chromaticism was usually restricted to improvisatory pieces, like the toccatas of Frescobaldi and Froberger. But the late Baroque composers were able to employ it freely, as they did dissonance, within the framework of a thoroughly worked-out and perfected harmonic system.

That system was the major-minor tonality familiar to us in the music of the eighteenth and nineteenth centuries: all the harmonies of a composition organized in relation to a triad on the key note or tonic supported primarily by triads on its dominant and subdominant with other chords secondary to these, and with temporary modulations to other keys allowed without sacrificing the supremacy of the principal key. This particular tonal organization had long been foreshadowed in music of the Renaissance, especially that written in the latter half of the sixteenth century. Rameau's *Treatise on Harmony* (1722) completed the theoretical formulation of the system, but it had existed in practice for at least forty years before.

The major-minor system

Like the medieval modal system, the major-minor system evolved out of musical practice over a long period of time. The habitual, long-continued use of root movement by a fourth or fifth, of sequences of secondary chords issuing in a cadential progression, and of modulations to the most nearly related keys eventually required a consistent theory to summarize and account for their existence in practice. Just as the constant use in the early Middle Ages of certain characteristic melodic formulas eventually led to the theory of the modes, so the constant use in the seventeenth century of certain characteristic formulas led to the theory of major-minor tonality. The basso continuo was important in the later stages of this theoretical development because it emphasized the harmonic progressions by isolating them, as it were, in a special notation different from the notation of the melodic lines. The basso continuo was the road over which music travelled from counterpoint to homophony, from a linear-melodic to a chordal-harmonic structure. After the middle of the eighteenth century, when the system of harmonic relationships had become so firmly established that there was no further need to make it explicit by continually sounding the basic chord progressions, the basso continuo gradually disappeared.

Early Baroque Opera

Inasmuch as vocal music was still the paramount interest of most composers in the early seventeenth century, our study of the principal forms and types of composition will begin with the most conspicuous new form of Baroque vocal music, the opera.

An opera is a drama which combines soliloquy, dialogue, scenery, action, and continuous (or nearly continuous) music. Although the

Forerunners

earliest works which we now call operas date only from the very end of the sixteenth century, the association of music with drama goes back to ancient times. The choruses, at least, in the plays of Euripides and Sophocles were sung, and so perhaps was the dialogue. The medieval liturgical dramas were sung, and music was used, albeit incidentally, in the religious mystery and miracle plays of the late Middle Ages. It is also quite likely that some trouvère chansons and even some motets of the thirteenth century may occasionally have been given in dramatic form. In the theatre of the Renaissance, where so many tragedies and comedies were imitated from or inspired by Greek examples, choruses were sometimes sung, especially at the opening or the ending of an act; moreover, between acts of a comedy, an *intermezzo* or *intermedio*—an interlude of pastoral, allegorical, or mythological character—was usually given; these *intermedi* frequently were quite elaborate musical productions, with choruses, soloists, and instrumental ensembles.

Most of the leading Italian madrigal composers of the sixteenth century wrote music for *intermedi,* and by the late sixteenth century dramatic motifs were invading the madrigal itself. The representation of feeling was reinforced by devices in the music suggesting the appropriate acts, such as sighing, weeping, or laughing. In those madrigals which had dialogues for texts, action was musically suggested by using different combinations of voices to represent the different speakers. Still closer to the idea of opera were madrigals in which the composer took for his text a dramatic scene from a poem —Tasso's epic, *Jerusalem Delivered,* and Guarini's pastoral, *The Faithful Shepherd,* are examples. In many madrigals of the late sixteenth century the idiom of the music was also diverted toward drama, and words were set in a chordal syllabic declamatory style which contrasted with the normal polyphonic texture.

The most thoroughgoing attempts to adapt the madrigal to dramatic purposes, however, were madrigal cycles, in which a series

Madrigal cycles

Interest in nature begins

of scenes or moods was represented, or a simple comic plot was presented in dialogue; the characters were set off by contrasting groups of voices and short solos. These works are now usually called *madrigal comedies,* a rather unfortunate designation, since they were not intended for stage performance but only for concerts or private entertainment. Their music was, for the most part, light, lively, and humorous, with little contrapuntal interest but well adapted to the spirit of the words. The most famous madrigal comedy was *L'Amfiparnaso* (*The Slopes of Parnassus*), by the Modenese composer Orazio Vecchi (1550–1605), published in 1597. Adriano Banchieri of Bologna wrote a number of similar cycles around the end of the century, but the form was short-lived.

There are two points of special interest about the late sixteenth-century madrigals, *intermedi,* and madrigal comedies as predecessors of the opera. First, many of these works had pastoral scenes and subjects. The pastoral was a favorite literary genre in the Renaissance and by the end of the sixteenth century had come to be the predominant form of Italian poetical composition. As the name implies, pastorals were poems about shepherds or similar rural subjects. They were loosely dramatic, and recounted leisurely tales of idyllic and amatory character; but above all the form demanded from the poet skill in conveying the atmosphere of a remote, fairy-tale world of nature refined and civilized, peopled by simple rustic youths and maidens and the ancient—and for the most part harmless—deities of the fields, woods, and fountains. The uncomplicated subject matter, the ideality of the landscape, and the nostalgic mood of yearning for an unattainable earthly paradise made pastoral poetry attractive to composers; in the imaginary world of the pastoral, music seemed not only the natural mode of speech but moreover the one thing needful to give substance to the poets' visions and longings. Pastoral poetry was at once the last stage of the madrigal and the first stage of the opera.

The pastoral

The second point of interest is that in many of the *intermedi* and madrigal cycles the composer had to set two distinct kinds of text, each of which demanded a particular musical treatment. Almost any dramatic scene has two elements: the narrative or dialogue by which a situation is developed, and the reaction of the participants, the outpouring of feelings that arise out of the situation thus created. Poetry that conveyed reflection or feeling was well suited to the madrigal style, assuming, as the sixteenth century did, that the thoughts and emotions of an individual could be appropriately expressed by a group of singers; consequently, when a madrigal composer picked a text from a pastoral play, he almost always chose a monologue which expressed an inner mood, a state of feeling at a nodal point in the drama, rather than a passage of narrative or a dialogue by which the external action was advanced. Some attempts were made toward the end of the century to deal with expository texts in madrigal settings—for example, the dialogues in madrigal comedies and in a few other madrigals of the period. On the whole, however, these pieces, interesting as experiments and not without a certain charm, were unrealistic in effect and incapable of being developed further. Clearly, what was required was a style of solo singing that could be used for dramatic purposes.

Textual settings

Monody

The best way to express something

That style came into being as a by-product of the Renaissance veneration for classical antiquity; it was announced as a rediscovery of ancient Greek solo song and was given an appropriate Greek name: _monody_ (monodia: from _monos_, alone and _aidein_, to sing). Solo singing was certainly not new in the late sixteenth century. Aside from the common practice of improvising solo melodies over a given bass for the recitation of epic poems, and the many songs composed for solo voice and lute, it was not rare in the sixteenth century for polyphonic madrigals to be sung as solos with instrumental accompaniment; this type of solo was especially frequent in the _intermedi_. Moreover, many late sixteenth-century madrigals were written in a style that strongly suggests a soprano solo with chordal accompaniment. In the 1580's Luzzasco Luzzaschi (1545–1607) composed some "solo madrigals," songs for one, two, or three solo soprano voices with accompaniment for harpsichord. These pieces, however, were not genuine monodies; essentially they were madrigals of rather solidly harmonic texture, with the lower voices played and the upper solo part or parts decorated with coloratura passages.

Real monody aimed at a quite different kind of melody and, moreover, distinguished clearly between solo and accompaniment. Strict fidelity to the supposed Greek models would doubtless have required that the accompaniment be abolished altogether; although it was not abolished, it was minimized to the utmost, reduced in fact to a few simple chords. These provided an almost impalpable background for the solo voice, which declaimed in free rhythm, following the natural accent and flow of the words; the melodic line was thus halfway between speech and song. The idea of monodic singing in imitation of the Greeks seems to have been first suggested by a Roman scholar, Girolamo Mei, to a circle of musicians and literati at Florence who resolved to put the idea into practice. This group, the so-called Florentine Camerata, had as one of its earliest spokesmen Vincenzo Galilei (ca. 1520–91), father of the famous astronomer. Galilei, himself a madrigal composer of some competence, in 1581

The Florentine Camerata

published a _Dialogue about Ancient and Modern Music_. In this work, following the doctrines of Mei, Galilei attacked the theory and practice of vocal counterpoint as exemplified in the Italian madrigal. His argument was, in brief, that for every phrase of poetry there was but one, unique melody of tones and rhythms that perfectly expressed it. Therefore, when several voices simultaneously sang different melodies and words, in different rhythms and registers, music could never be consistent with text; when some voices were low and others high, some rising and others descending, some moving in slow notes and others in fast, the resulting chaos of contradictory impressions served only to show off the cleverness of the composer and the ability of the performers in a style of music which, if of any value at all, was suitable only for an ensemble of instruments. Word-painting, imitations of sighing, and the like, so common in the sixteenth-century madrigal, Galilei dismissed as childish. The correct way to set words, Galilei said, was to use a solo melody which would merely enhance the natural speech inflections of a good orator. Galilei tried his hand at monodies of this sort, setting some verses from Dante's *Inferno* for tenor solo with accompaniment of viols; this music has not been preserved.

In the last decade of the sixteenth century, the leaders in Italian monodic writing were Jacopo Peri (1561–1633) and Giulio Caccini (*ca.* 1546–1618). Both were singers by profession and consequently felt less bound than Galilei by the austerities of a theory that would, if consistently applied, not only have abolished counterpoint but also have severely limited the art of solo singing. As it was, Caccini soon developed a style of song which, while aiming first of all at clear and flexible declamation of words, nevertheless admitted certain embellishments of the melodic line at appropriate places; he thus introduced into monody an element of vocal virtuosity, which in the sixteenth century had been manifested by the improvisation of ornaments (scales, turns, runs, passing notes, and the like) on any note of a melody without regard to the character of the text. The earliest surviving compositions in the Florentine monodic style are some songs written by Caccini in the 1590s and published in 1602 under the title of *Le nuove musiche (New Music).*[3]

The monodic style quickly made its way into all kinds of music, both secular and sacred, in the early years of the seventeenth century. It was the one thing needed to make opera possible, for it provided a medium by which both dialogue and exposition could be conveyed in music clearly, quickly, and with all the necessary freedom and flexibility for truly dramatic expression. In 1600, Peri and Caccini jointly set to music a pastoral-mythological drama, *Euridice,* by Ottavio Rinuccini (1562–1621), which was publicly performed in that year at Florence in connection with the festivities in honor of the marriage of Henry IV of France and Marie de' Medici. In the following year each composer published a version of his own, and these two are the earliest surviving complete operas.

The first opera

Ottavio Rinuccini was a member of the Florentine Camerata; he wrote the librettos of several other early operas also. *Euridice* was the well-known myth of Orpheus and Eurydice, treated in the currently fashionable manner of the pastoral and modified so as to have a happy ending, in view of the joyful occasion for which it was

[3] To appreciate the subtleties of the relationship of music to text, the use or ornaments, and the manner of performance desired by the composer, examples from *Le nuove musiche* (MM, No. 30; HAM, No. 184; GMB, Nos. 172 and 173; WM, No. 49) should be studied in connection with Caccini's preface, which itself contains many musical illustrations (SR, 377–92; SRB, 17–32). The ornamental version in GMB, No. 173, is not Caccini's but the editor's.

written. The music of both Caccini and Peri consists for the most part of recitative over a generally slow-moving bass; such unvarying monodic declamation without vocal ornaments was called *stile rappresentativo* (representative or, perhaps, theatre style). This recitative, which is liable to seem to us thin and formless, is said to have made an extraordinary impression on listeners in 1600. Their interest was probably partly due to the novelty of the style and partly to the sensitive way in which the composers and singers were able to interpret the inner melody of the words in the vocal line while the shifting emotions of the poetry were mirrored in the changes of harmony. In addition, the monotony of the recitative was broken with occasional passages of a more melodic character or by short simple choral refrains. In these departures from the literal requirements of monodic theory, Peri and Caccini foreshadowed the distinction that was made in later operas between the recitative and the more fully musical portions such as arias and choruses.

Opera thus began as an experimental attempt to revive Greek music for the delectation of a little circle of learned amateurs. It

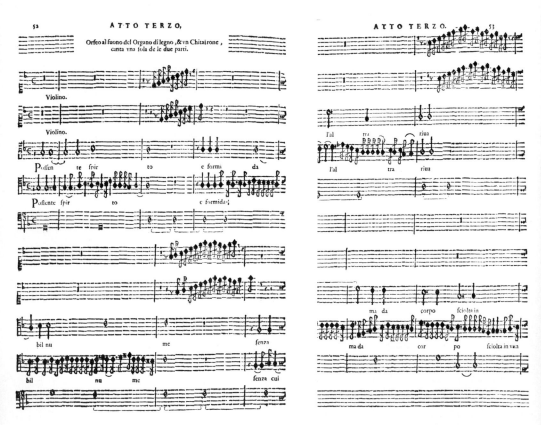

Beginning of Orfeo's aria Possente spirto, *from Act III of Monteverdi's* Orfeo. *For a transcription, see LSS, No. 63.*

might have died an early death had not the poets and composers realized that the form had to have a richer musical content. The composer who first wrote operas with this richness, and who therefore is perhaps best entitled to be called the creator of opera, was Claudio Monteverdi.

Orfeo, the first of Monteverdi's operas, was performed at Mantua in 1607. Its subject matter is the same as that of the Florentine *Euridice* operas, but expanded into full five-act length. The music likewise may be said to take the Florentine *stile rappresentativo* as its point of departure, but it soon leaves its model behind. The representation of emotions is stronger and more varied; the harmonies are more expressive; the recitatives no longer depend solely on the words for continuity but are organized into perceptible musical forms. Moreover, Monteverdi introduced many solo airs, duets, madrigal-like ensembles, and dances, which together make up quite a large proportion of the work and furnish a needed contrast to the recitative. One of the arias, Orfeo's *Possente spirto* in Act III, shows us how singers embellished a melody; in this aria Monteverdi wrote out the desired ornaments on an extra staff below the melodic line, furnishing a different set of ornaments for each strophe of the air. Consequently, we have a rare and probably quite authentic picture of how the early Baroque singers ornamented melody, although we are still uncertain how to translate some of Monteverdi's notes into actual performance.

Claudio Monteverdi

Greatest Contribution

Monteverdi's treatment of the orchestra in *Orfeo* is especially interesting. Florentine operas had used only a few lutes or similar instruments for accompaniment; in conformity with the monodic ideal, these were placed behind the scenery and kept as inconspicuous as possible. Monteverdi's orchestra in *Orfeo,* on the other hand, numbered about forty instruments, including flutes, cornetts, trumpets, trombones, a complete family of strings, and several different continuo instruments. In many places the composer, in order to make the dramatic situation more vivid, specified exactly which instruments were to play. Furthermore, the score contains twenty-six brief orchestral numbers; these include an introductory "toccata" (a short fanfare-like movement twice repeated) and several ritornellos, that is, short interludes which recur between stanzas of a song or at other places, and thus contribute to the musical unity of the work.

The large orchestra of *Orfeo* was not an innovation of Monteverdi's, but an attempt to organize the traditional large performing groups of the old mystery plays and *intermedi.* The attempt was not followed up in the later operas of Monteverdi or those of other seventeenth-century composers; for a long time after *Orfeo,* the opera orchestra consisted only of strings and harpsichord (or other continuo instruments).

5 act length

The music of Monteverdi's next opera, *Arianna* (1608), has been lost except for a few fragments and one number, a *Lament*. This famous song was universally admired in the seventeenth century as a perfect example of the monodic style, one which when well sung never failed to move the auditors to tears. Monteverdi later arranged the melody as a five-part madrigal and afterwards used it again to set a sacred text.

Roman composers of opera

Apparently little progress was made in opera during the twenty years after Monteverdi's *Orfeo,* for the next important school of composers is found at Rome in the 1630's. Here, as might be expected, operas were written on sacred subjects and ensembles held a prominent place. The most important early Roman opera was *Sant' Alessio* (1632), based on the life of the fifth-century Saint Alexis, with music by Stefano Landi (*ca.* 1590–*ca.* 1655). Roman composers also produced a number of pastoral operas and, strangely enough, it was at Rome that the comic opera began its independent career; the first writer of comic opera librettos was a nobleman of the church, Giulio Rospigliosi, who later became Pope Clement IX.

Roman - Stressed Recitativ

In the music of the Roman operas we can observe the separation of solo singing into two clearly defined types, recitative and aria. The monodic declamation of Monteverdi's *Orfeo* (and this remained true also of his later operas) was semimelodic; in Landi's work, and still more in the Roman comic operas, this original semimelodic recitative became a rather dry, quick movement with many repeated notes, lacking definite musical contour and supported by thin and musically insignificant harmonies in the continuo—became, in short, more like the recitative in the Italian operas of Mozart and Rossini, a mere vehicle for the rapid delivery of words. Melody and all other elements of musical interest gradually were concentrated in the songs or arias, which now began to assume rather definite shapes: strophic arias, arias over a ground bass, and (most often) arias in a loose two-part form with the sections framed by orchestral ritornellos. The many concerted vocal pieces in the Roman operas are derived from the madrigal tradition, modified of course by the presence of a continuo and by the more regular rhythm of the seventeenth century.

Landi's *Sant' Alessio* has an overture consisting of a slow chordal introduction followed by a livelier canzona movement. The prelude or *sinfonia* before Act II is another orchestral canzona, but without the slow introductory section. The two-movement form of the first overture (slow chordal—fast contrapuntal, sometimes with a closing reminiscence of the slow movement) later became the accepted pattern for the seventeenth-century opera overture. In France, it acquired certain special characteristics; the form became known as the *French overture* (see p. 349), and as such was one of the dominant instrumental forms of the middle and late Baroque.

The chief later Roman opera composer was Luigi Rossi (1597–1653). His *Orfeo* (Paris, 1647), on a libretto by Francesco Buti, is based on the same subject as the earlier operas of Caccini, Peri, and Monteverdi. This work illustrates the change that had come over the opera libretto during the first half of the seventeenth century. The antique simplicity of the myth is almost totally buried under a mass of irrelevant incidents and characters, spectacular scenic effects, and incongruous comic episodes. The intrusion of the comic, the grotesque, and the merely sensational into a supposedly serious drama was a common practice of Italian librettists during most of the seventeenth century. It was an indication that the integrity of the drama was no longer of first importance, as it had been with the early Florentines and Monteverdi, and that the ancient Greek and Roman myths had come to be regarded merely as conventional material to be elaborated upon in any way that promised to provide entertainment and offer good opportunities to the composer and singers. The decline of the libretto coincided with the development of an imposing style of theatre music. Rossi's *Orfeo* is, in effect, a succession of beautiful arias and ensembles well calculated to make the hearer forgive its faults as a drama.

In part, the deterioration of the opera libretto and the changes in the character of the music were the consequences of presenting opera in public performance rather than to private audiences. This step was taken when the first public opera house was opened at Venice in 1637. Before many years Venice had become the operatic capital of Italy, a position she retained until the end of the seventeenth century. Venetian composers, or composers trained in the Venetian school, were also responsible for the spread of Italian opera to the cities of southern Germany in this period.

Monteverdi wrote his two last operas for Venice: *Il ritorno d'Ulisse* (*Ulysses' Homecoming*) and *L'incoronazione di Poppea* (*The Coronation of Poppea*), performed respectively in 1641 and 1642. *Poppea* is in many respects Monteverdi's operatic masterpiece. It lacks the varied orchestral colors and the large instrumental and scenic apparatus of *Orfeo*, but excels in the depiction of human character and passions through music, being in this respect far in advance of any other seventeenth-century opera. The recitative is wonderfully concentrated and expressive, and is smoothly combined with more definitely outlined musical forms such as arias and duets. Modern revivals have proved that *L'incoronazione di Poppea*, far from being an opera of merely historical interest, is a masterpiece of living art, as able now as in the seventeenth century to stir the deepest emotions of those who listen to it.

One of the leading Venetian opera composers was Monteverdi's pupil, Pier Francesco Cavalli (1602–76). The steady demand for new works at Venice is reflected in the quantity of Cavalli's output. Of his forty-one operas, the most celebrated was *Giasone* (1649), a full-blown score with scenes in which arias and recitatives alternate, though the two styles are always kept carefully distinct. Two other Cavalli operas, *Ormindo* (1644) and *Calisto* (1651), have been recently revived, with alterations and additions that would probably have astonished the composer. Cavalli's music has neither the fine construction nor the penetrating psychological insight of Monteverdi's: it aims at broad striking effects and is best in scenes of violence and passion, as in the celebrated "Incantation" sung by the sorceress Medea in the first act of *Giasone*.

The operas of Marc' Antonio Cesti (1623–69) are more polished but less forceful in style than those of Cavalli; Cesti excels in lyrical arias and duets. His most famous opera is *Il pomo d'oro* (*The Golden Apple*), which was performed at Vienna in 1667 on the occasion of the wedding of Emperor Leopold I. As a festival opera, it was staged without regard to expense and therefore includes some features that were not common at Venice, such as an unusually large orchestra and many choruses. *Il pomo d'oro* was remarkable also for its lavish scenic effects. The use of elaborate machinery to make possible the representation of naval battles, sieges, storms, shipwrecks, descents of gods from the sky, and miraculous sudden transformations of all kinds had become a regular practice at Venice, but the

"The Palace of Paris," a sumptuous scene for the first act of Marc' Antonio Cesti's Il pomo d'oro. *This typically Baroque setting was designed by Ludovico Burnacini, an important seventeenth-century theatre architect.*

staging of *Il pomo d'oro* surpassed anything hitherto attempted in opera. Cesti's music is appropriately formal rather than deeply dramatic. The stately instrumental preludes (called "sonatas") that open each act are typical examples of the Venetian opera overture of this period.

By the middle of the seventeenth century Italian opera had assumed the main outlines of form it was to maintain without essential change for the next two hundred years. The principal features of this form were: (1) concentration upon solo singing with (for a long time) comparative neglect of ensembles and of instrumental music; (2) separation of recitative and aria; and (3) introduction of distinctive styles and patterns for the arias. This development was accompanied by a complete reversal in the relation of text and music: the Florentines had considered music accessory to poetry; the Venetians treated the libretto as hardly more than a conventional scaffolding for the musical structure.

Vocal Chamber Music

At the opening of the seventeenth century composers were confronted with two disturbing new problems. The first involved monody: could the rhythmic flexibility and the lifelike dramatic power of the solo recitative be absorbed into a system of vocal music based on counterpoint of several equally important parts? If so, what means of formal coherence could be devised? Then there was the basso continuo: within the bare texture of a supporting bass and one or two high voices could any resources be found to equal the ample sonority of the older contrapuntal music?

Of course there were two obvious, though unfruitful, ways to avoid these questions. A composer could ignore counterpoint and concentrate on monody, as the early Florentine composers had done; or he could ignore monody and stick to the old way of counterpoint, perhaps conceding to modernity the use of a basso continuo. However, the future of music lay neither with the ultraradical monodists nor with the ultraconservative contrapuntists. The issues had to be faced: reconciliation of the new with the traditional is a task that confronts every artist in his own generation, and one that can be evaded only at the price of artistic suicide. The way in which composers of the early seventeenth century effected their reconciliation can perhaps be more clearly understood by regarding it as a process of gradual enrichment and formal stabilization of the monodic style. Many different means were employed, of which two were of particular importance: (1) the use of the bass, as well as the entire harmonic structure, to give formal coherence to a composition; and (2) the use of the *concertato* principle to supply variety of texture and contrapuntal interest.

Imp. Page

The bass as a
unifying force

⌐ In the many collections of monodies that were published during the early part of the seventeenth century one of the most important means of obtaining unity was to keep the same bass for every stanza of the text while varying the melody of the solo part at each repetition of the bass pattern. Such an arrangement is called *strophic variation*. The bass might not be identical in every repetition, but its outline was maintained so that the same succession of harmonies occurred in every strophe. This is the scheme, for example, of the coloratura aria *Possente spirto* from the third act of Monteverdi's *Orfeo;* in simpler form, it also occurs in the strophic arias of Caccini's *Nuove musiche.*

For such songs the bass might be freely invented, in which case it was usually a mere series of notes without any particular melodic shape. There were, however, traditional bass patterns or *grounds,* many of them inherited from sixteenth-century dances or improvisatory practices, which composers might use instead of inventing a bass of their own. These traditional bass grounds were quite short and with easily recognizable outlines. If they were not long enough to accommodate an entire stanza of poetry, they were repeated over and over again, either unchanged *(ostinato bass),* transposed, or varied by rhythmic and melodic elaboration of the essential few notes. These repeated bass patterns of one kind or another served as unifying devices in hundreds of compositions, both instrumental and vocal, of the Baroque period. One favorite was the *romanesca* bass, the essential outline of which is given in Example IX–1.

EXAMPLE IX–1   Outline of *romanesca* bass.

Imp.

A particularly important class of *ostinato* patterns appears in pieces called *chaconne (ciacona)* or *passacaglia (passecaille).* The origin and early history of these types are obscure, but both evidently arose in Spain sometime late in the sixteenth century as frameworks for improvisation, probably in connection with dancing. Characteristic of both as we find them in the works of seventeenth-century composers is the continuous repetition of a four-bar formula in triple meter and slow tempo. The formula may be: (1) a series of harmonies, either simply I–IV–V–I or with additional or different harmonies between the first I and the final V–I; or (2) a melodic figure decending stepwise through the tetrachord from tonic to dominant (see Example IX–2). This figure will appear most often or most prominently in the bass, but it may also migrate to other voices and may be melodically varied. Around the middle of the seventeenth century, a keyboard piece built on a repeated series of harmonies—formula (1) above—would probably be called a chaconne, while one

EXAMPLE IX–2   Descending tetrachord figures (sometimes called "Passacaglia Bass")

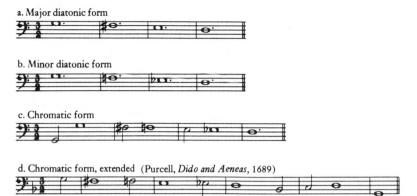

a. Major diatonic form

b. Minor diatonic form

c. Chromatic form

d. Chromatic form, extended (Purcell, *Dido and Aeneas*, 1689)

featuring the descending melodic tetrachord would be more likely to be called a passacaglia. Both obviously belong to the general category of *variation*. The nomenclature, however, was never fully consistent; by the end of the century, not only were the formulas themselves sometimes expanded, but also any distinction that might have existed between the terms "chaconne" and "passacaglia" had vanished—as may be seen from the titles of pieces from which Examples IX–3a–d are taken.

A widespread development of the early seventeenth century was the rise of the *concertato* style. This adjective comes from the same root as *concert* and *concerto*; it connotes not only "sounding together"—as in a "consort" of instruments—and the common meaning of the Italian verb *concertare* (to make sure, to reach agreement), *The concertato style*

EXAMPLE IX–3   Bass Patterns

a. Buxtehude (ca. 1637–1707): Ciacona

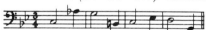

b. Bach: Passacaglia (ca. 1717)

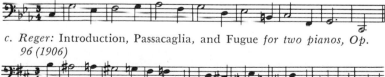

c. Reger: Introduction, Passacaglia, and Fugue *for two pianos, Op. 96 (1906)*

d. Hindemith: Cardillac *(1926)*

but also some idea of competition or emulation, as in the Latin *concertare* (to contend or dispute).[4] The *concertato* style, then, is one in which different musical elements are engaged not always in uniform array, as in counterpoint or monody, but in a manner which deliberately emphasizes the contrast of one voice or instrument against another, or of one group against another, or of a group against a solo. The origins of the *concertato* style of the Baroque lie in the polychoral works of the Venetian school and in the many polyphonic madrigals of the late sixteenth and early seventeenth centuries in which two or three voices, or a solo voice, are brought into prominence against the background of the ensemble.

The growth of the *concertato* style, along with other developments, can be followed in the fifth, sixth, seventh, and eighth books of Monteverdi's madrigals, published respectively in 1605, 1614, 1621, and 1638. It is fascinating to observe the greatest composer of his time succeed in fusing the heterogeneous musical elements of the early seventeenth century into an eloquent language, firm in structure, varied in color, alternately joyous and sad, robust and tender, warlike and peaceful, responsive to every suggestion of the text.

All these madrigals, beginning with the last six of Book V, have a basso continuo, and many call for other instruments as well. Solos, duets, and trios are set off against the vocal ensemble; there are instrumental introductions and recurring instrumental interludes (ritornellos). The seventh book is entitled *Concerto* and is described as consisting of "madrigals and other kinds of songs." Book VIII, *Madrigals of War and Love,* is especially noteworthy for the variety of forms and types, including madrigals for five voices; solos, duets, and trios with continuo; and large works for chorus, soloists, and orchestra. Among the finest compositions in this volume is the madrigal *Hor che'l ciel e la terra* (*Now that heaven and earth*) for six voices, two violins, and continuo, a masterpiece of moods and sonorities, of abundantly varied harmonies and vivid dramatic contrasts.

In the eighth book also are two *balli* (semidramatic ballets) and another work in the *genere rappresentativo* or theatre style, the *Combattimento di Tancredi e Clorinda* (*The Combat of Tancred and Clorinda*), which had been performed at Venice in 1624. This is a setting of a portion of the twelfth canto of Tasso's *Jerusalem Delivered* describing the combat between the crusader knight Tancred and the pagan heroine Clorinda, ending with the latter's death. The bulk of Tasso's text is straight narrative, which Monteverdi gives to a tenor soloist in recitative; the few short speeches of

---

4 There may also be in the word "concerto" some echo of the Latin *conserere,* meaning to unite for contest, as in the expression *conserere manum* = to join in close combat, hand-to-hand fighting. Insufficiently rehearsed performances of concertos may make this etymology seem quite plausible.

ALTO PRIMO

MADRIGALI

GVERRIERI, ET AMOROSI

Con alcuni opuſcoli in genere rappreſentatiuo, che ſaranno
per breui Epiſodij fra i canti ſenza geſto.

LIBRO OTTAVO

DI CLAVDIO MONTEVERDE

Maeſtro di Capella della Sereniſſima Republica di Venetia.

DEDICATI

Alla Sacra Ceſarea Maeſtà

DELL' IMPERATOR

FERDINANDO III

CON PRIVILEGIO.

IN   VENETIA   C

Appreſſo Aleſſandro Vincenti. MDCXXXVIII.

The title page of a part book for Claudio Monteverdi's eighth book of madrigals, the Madrigals of War and Love, *"with other small works in the* genere rappresentativo . . . ," *Venice, 1638. (New York Public Library)*

Tancred and Clorinda are sung by a tenor and soprano who are instructed during the singing of the narrative to mime the actions described. The instruments (string quartet with bass gamba and continuo), in addition to accompanying the voices, play interludes in which various parts of the action are imitated or suggested: the galloping of horses, the clash of swords, the excitement of combat. For such purposes Monteverdi invented a kind of music which he called the *stile concitato* or "excited style"; one device prominent in the *stile concitato* was the rapid reiteration of a single note, either with quickly spoken syllables in the voice or instrumentally as a string tremolo in rhythm. (An example of one of the *concitato* sections from the *Combattimento* appears in HAM, No. 189). The *stile concitato,* born of the urge for a more perfect musical representation of the text, was one of Monteverdi's many contributions to the ever-expanding language of music in the early seventeenth century.

The complex Baroque musical style thus was achieved by the interaction of diverse elements. Monody and madrigal were combined; formal articulation was approached through the organization of the bass and the harmonies and through systematic use of ritornellos; texture was varied by use of the *concertato* style. As a result, the representational and pictorial power of music was enlarged and intensified. All these developments coincided with a reaction, especially strong after 1630, against considering the text the only or chief unifying factor in serious vocal composition; the innate requirements of the music became more important to composers as they began to discard the original concept of music as merely a transparent veil for text. The gradual separation of recitative and aria left the composer free to write aria melody unhampered by the necessity of following every nuance of the text; and arias began to unfold in graceful, smoothly flowing phrases supported by simple harmonies, most often in slow triple meter with a persistent single rhythmic motif (Example IX–4). This *bel canto* style of vocal writing was a creation of Italian composers; it was imitated in all countries and was influential in both vocal and instrumental music throughout the Baroque and after.

Forms of vocal solo music

Italian vocal chamber music in the first half of the seventeenth century was published in collections of madrigals, arias, dialogues, duets, and the like. From the beginning of the century Italian composers had turned out thousands of monodies—solo madrigals, stro-

EXAMPLE IX–4   Aria from *Giasone,* Pier Francesco Cavalli

ma - - te sù que - sto mio co - re, deh!

più, deh! più non stil - la - - te le gio - ie d'a - mo - re

de - li - zie mie care, fer - ma - te - vi quì,

etc.

*Delightful pleasures that bless the soul, remain in my heart; delay
no more the joys of love. O my dear pleasures, remain.*

phic arias, canzonets, and other songs in light dance-like rhythms; these pieces were certainly more widely known than any of the contemporary opera music, which was performed only a few times to restricted audiences. Monodies, on the other hand, were sung everywhere and were published in huge quantities. Caccini's *Nuove musiche* was the first important collection of monodies; the principal other early composer was Sigismondo d'India (*ca.* 1562–*ca.* 1630), whose solo songs, as well as his polyphonic madrigals and motets, mark him as an outstanding musical personality in early seventeenth-century Italy.

The form that eventually came to engage the chief attention of Italian composers was the *cantata* (literally, a piece "to be sung"). This word, like its counterpart, *sonata*, has been used to designate many different types of composition. In a collection published before 1620 it was applied to arias in the form of strophic variations. Neither that form nor any other was consistently followed by cantata composers during the next two or three decades. Toward the middle of the century *cantata* came to mean a composition usually for solo voice with continuo accompaniment, in several sections which often intermingled recitatives and arias, on a lyrical or sometimes quasi-dramatic text. Yet the Roman, Luigi Rossi, the first eminent master of this particular type of cantata, also wrote others which had simpler forms—either plain strophic songs, strophic variations, arias with ostinato bass, or arias in an *ABA* (called *da capo*) pattern. Other leading Italian cantata composers of the mid-seventeenth century were Giacomo Carissimi (1605–74)—whose chief field, however, was the sacred oratorio—and the opera composer, Marc' Antonio Cesti.

Other countries, although often strongly influenced by Italian models, nevertheless produced songs of distinctively national character. Solo songs were written by many German composers after about 1630, notably Heinrich Albert (1604–51) and Andreas Hammerschmidt (1612–75). In France, the *air de cour* flourished in the form of charming solos and duets, some of them independent vocal chamber music and others written for court ballets. English composers of the early and middle seventeenth century—Nicholas Lanier (1588–1666), John Wilson (1595–1674), Henry Lawes (1596–1622), and others—likewise wrote many songs with continuo accompaniment in connection with court masques as well as independent solos, some in a declamatory, recitative style, others purely tuneful in dance-like rhythms. All in all, vocal chamber music in the early seventeenth century appeared in many forms and styles, and combined elements of the madrigal, the concerto, monody, dance songs, national idioms, dramatic recitative, and the *bel canto* aria. As with all other branches of music, composers of the second half of the century had the task of establishing some degree of order and uniformity amidst this profusion.

Church Music

Sacred music, although by nature conservative, was affected as soon and almost as strongly as secular music by the innovations of the late sixteenth and early seventeenth centuries. Monody, the basso continuo, and the *stile concertato* were all applied to sacred texts. There was, of course, some opposition to the new styles, and indeed, in the Roman Catholic Church, Renaissance polyphony of the Palestrina type was never completely abandoned. Thus throughout the seventeenth century two distinct styles, one conservative (*stile antico*) and one progressive (*stile moderno*), were opposed. Many times both tendencies were manifest in one and the same composer: Monteverdi, for example, wrote in either *stile antico* or *stile moderno* with equal mastery and occasionally alternated the two in the same composition. Before the middle of the seventeenth century, Palestrina had become the supreme model for the conservative style. All composers were trained to write counterpoint based on Palestrina's practice, though in the course of time the details were modified: a basso continuo was often added, rhythms became more regular, and the older modes gave way to the major-minor system. Fux's famous treatise, *Gradus ad Parnassum* (*Steps to Parnassus;* 1725) finally codified this quasi-Palestrinian counterpoint, and remained the most influential textbook in the subject for the next two hundred years.

The conservative Roman counterpoint, although invaluable for study and discipline, was less important in actual early seventeenth-century composition than the style, stemming from the polychoric works of Giovanni Gabrieli and the Venetian school, which is today called the "colossal Baroque." Many composers in this period wrote sacred music for huge aggregations of singers and players, but the master of this style, and one of the major figures in seventeenth-century Catholic Church music, was Orazio Benevoli (1605–72). His festival Mass written for the consecration of the cathedral at Salzburg in 1628 calls for two eight-part choruses with soloists; each chorus is associated with three different instrumental combinations and each has its own basso continuo; there is, in addition, a third basso continuo for the whole ensemble. This formidable score takes up fifty-three staves. Benevoli's later works, written mostly for St. Peter's in Rome during the 1640s, give a more adequate idea of his true stature than does the somewhat unwieldy Salzburg Mass; these later works include Psalms, motets, and Masses for three, four, or more choruses, which are provided with a figured bass for the organ but which may equally well be sung unaccompanied. The choruses were stationed at separate places on different levels within the ample basilica of St. Peter's, so that the listeners felt they were enveloped in music from all directions—a truly grandiose and typically Baroque conception. The sonorities are graduated and combined with the utmost dex-

The Baroque polychoric style

terity, antiphonal effects alternating with massive climaxes, and the writing is so skillful that, in spite of the vastness of the plan, the texture remains always clear.

The polychoric style was cultivated in Italy throughout the seventeenth century by many composers whose works still await publication. Notable examples were also written in Spain, for example by Juan Cererols (1618–76), who for thirty years was head of the *escolania* or choir school of the famous Monastery of Montserrat.

Other styles in church music

One of the first composers to adopt the *stile moderno* in church music was Lodovico Viadana (1564–1645), who in 1602 published a collection called *Cento concerti ecclesiastici (One Hundred Church Concertos)* for solo voice, or various combinations of solo voices, with basso continuo. This arrangement was of great practical significance: it allowed a work to be performed, if necessary, with a small number of singers, and so eliminated the necessity for doubling or replacing vocal parts by instruments as had often been done in the sixteenth century.

Settings of sacred texts in monodic or in *concertato* style became common during the first half of the seventeenth century. Pure monody was used mostly for motets or nonliturgical devotional songs, as in the collection of *Arie devote* (1608) by the Roman composer Ottavio Durante; sacred arias of this kind were often ornamented with elaborate coloratura passages. The *stile concertato* —in the form of solos, duets, dialogues, trios, choruses, and diverse small or large combinations of voices and instruments—was applied to both motets and Masses. In this field as in others Monteverdi was a notable pioneer. His *Vespers* of 1610 is a magnificent setting of a complete liturgical office incorporating traditional Gregorian Chants as *cantus firmi* but making use of all the new musical resources of the time—recitative, aria, and all varieties of solo, choral, and instrumental groupings—in a unified artistic whole. That the original print of 1610 also included a Mass *In illo tempore,* parodied on a motet of Gombert and written in strict Flemish contrapuntal style, is an illustration of the contrast between *stile antico* and *stile moderno* typical of the early seventeenth century.

The sacred compositions of Monteverdi's Venetian period are for the most part in the *concertato* style, but treated in a completely free and sometimes operatic manner. One stirring Gloria for seven voices *concertate* with two violins and four viols or trombones (?1631) is a brilliant example of a personal, nonliturgical musical treatment of a liturgical text.

Oratorios

Not only the monodic and *concertato* styles but also the specific dramatic methods of opera were turned to sacred uses. In 1600 Emilio de' Cavalieri (*ca.* 1550–1602), a Roman nobleman associated with the Florentine Camerata, produced on the stage at Rome a morality play with music—in effect, a sacred opera with allegorical characters—entitled *La rappresentazione di anima e di corpo* (*The Representation of the Soul and Body*). This work incorporated verses from earlier *laude* and like them was intended as part of an informal devotional religious service at the oratory of S. Filippo Neri. The music is of little interest in itself, but doubtless was more effective in its proper setting with the appropriate costumes, scenery, and action.

Apparently this first experiment with sacred opera was not considered successful enough to be imitated; but during the first three or four decades of the century a number of semidramatic dialogues on sacred themes were produced, as well as similar works involving solos and choruses with orchestra and continuo; these compositions combined elements of narrative, dramatic dialogue, and meditation or exhortation, and were not usually intended for stage performance. Toward the middle of the century, works of this kind were called *oratorios,* though the word did not at first have any very precise connotation as to musical genre. The libretto of an oratorio might be in Latin (*oratorio latino*) or Italian (*oratorio volgare*). The principal master of the oratorio in the mid-seventeenth century was Giacomo Carissimi at Rome. A synopsis of Carissimi's most famous oratorio, *Jephtha,* will indicate what an oratorio written about 1650 was like:

The Latin libretto is based on the Book of Judges xi: 29–40, with some paraphrasing and some added material. The narrator (called the *storicus* or *testo*) introduces the story. Jephtha (tenor solo) makes his fatal vow that if the Lord will give him victory in the impending battle he will sacrifice whatever being first comes to greet him on his return home. This much is in monodic recitative. Jephtha's victory over the Ammonites is then recounted, with appropriate imitative effects and much *stile concitato,* in chorus, solo aria, and duet. The next scene, narrated by the *storicus* in recitative, relates how Jephtha returns to his home in triumph; he is met by his daugter and her companions with songs of rejoicing (solo arias, duets, choruses). Then follows the dialogue, in recitative, between Jephtha and his daughter. The chorus next tells how Jephtha's daughter goes away to the mountains with her companions to bewail her approaching untimely death. Her song, the words of which are not in the Biblical account, is a long, semimelodic, very affecting recitative, with echoes by two sopranos of a recurring cadential phrase. The work closes with a magnificent six-voice chorus of lamentation.

The oratorio was thus distinguished from the contemporary opera by its sacred subject matter, by the presence of the *testo* or narrator, by the use of the chorus for dramatic, narrative, and meditative purposes, and by the fact that oratorios were seldom if ever meant to be staged. Action was narrated or suggested, not presented. Both oratorio and opera used monodic recitative, arias, duets, and instrumental preludes and ritornellos. In addition to the oratorios with chorus there were solo oratorios, works which might well be described as sacred cantatas. Carissimi's *Judgment of Solomon* is of this sort except for its closing chorus of exhortation.

In Austria and the Catholic southern cities of Germany, sacred music during the Baroque remained wholly under Italian influence.

The new styles in Lutheran music Italian composers were particularly active at Munich, Salzburg, Prague, and Vienna. Composers in the Lutheran central and northern regions began early in the seventeenth century to utilize the new monodic and *concertato* techniques, sometimes with chorale tunes as melodic material, but often also without reference to traditional melodies. Along with these compositions in *stile moderno,* the Lutheran composers continued to write Renaissance chorale motets for some time, as well as motets based on one or more Biblical verses but without use of chorale tunes. Many motets by Hassler, Praetorius, and other early seventeenth-century composers were written in the massive polychoric style, which testifies to the admiration with which the Venetian school was viewed by German musicians.

Elements of the *concertato*—the instrumental accompaniments and the florid vocal solo passages—occasionally invaded the chorale motets, but monody and the *concertato* style were best adapted to compositions for a smaller number of performers. An important collection of such pieces was published in 1618 and 1626 at Leipzig by Johann Hermann Schein (1586–1630), entitled *Opella nova* [literally, *New Little Works*] *Geistliche Konzerte . . . auff jetzo gebräuchliche Italiänische Invention* (*Sacred Concertos in the Nowadays Customary Italian Manner*). In many respects the pieces are like Lutheran counterparts of some of Monteverdi's *concertato* madrigals. The collection consists chiefly of duets and a few solos on chorale texts; however, Schein does not always use chorale melodies. When he does he treats them with freedom, inserting vocal embellishments, breaking up the phrases and dividing them between the voices. There is a continuo and sometimes one or two concertizing solo instruments, with an occasional orchestral sinfonia or an ensemble for chorus and instruments. The pieces are analogous to the early Baroque Italian cantatas, except for the Biblical (or at any rate sacred) words and the fairly consistent use of traditional chorale tunes as a basis for the melodic invention. These sacred concertos of Schein were followed by a long series of similar works by Lutheran composers of the seventeenth century.

The greatest German composer of the middle seventeenth century, and one of the most important musical figures of the Baroque, was *Heinrich* Heinrich Schütz (1585–1672). After beginning university studies, *Schütz* Schütz was sent to Venice, where he studied with Giovanni Gabrieli from 1609 to 1612 and brought out his first published work, a collection of five-part Italian madrigals. From 1617 to the end of his life, Schütz was Master of the Chapel of the Elector of Saxony at Dresden, although during the disturbed times of the Thirty Years' War he spent several years as Court Conductor in Copenhagen. Schütz renewed his acquaintance with Italian music when he went to Venice in 1628 especially to meet Monteverdi, whom he greatly admired.

As far as is known, Schütz wrote no independent instrumental music. He is reputed to have composed the first German opera, as well as several ballets and other stage works, but the music of all these has been lost; our knowledge of him consequently rests almost entirely on his church compositions, which we possess in considerable quantity and variety, dating from 1619 to the latest years of his life. The simplest of these works are plain four-part harmonic settings of a German translation of the Psalter (1628). Contrasting with the Calvinist plainness of the Psalm settings are the Latin motets of the *Cantiones sacrae* (1625); in these motets a basically conservative Catholic contrapuntal style is enlivened by harmonic novelties and by traits derived from the madrigal, such as the musical representation of sleep and waking at the beginning of *Ego dormio et cor meum vigilat (I sleep, and my heart waketh;* Example IX–5).

Venetian magnificence and color appear frequently in Schütz: for example, in the *Psalmen Davids* (1619) for multiple choruses, soloists, and *concertato* instruments, where the massive colorful sonority of the colossal Baroque is combined with sensitive treatment of the German texts. Indeed, the fusion of Italian and German styles, begun by Hassler and others toward the end of the sixteenth century, was carried to completion by Schütz, who thus established the fundamental characteristics of German music for the remainder of the Baroque age. Only one significant element of the fully developed Lutheran Baroque style was lacking in his works: he seldom made use of traditional chorale melodies, although he set many chorale texts.

In 1636 and 1639, during years when war had sadly reduced the Electoral Chapel, Schütz published his *Kleine geistliche Konzerte (Little Sacred Concertos)*, motets for one to five solo voices with organ accompaniment. The year 1636 also saw the publication of the *Musikalische Exequien* (funeral music for Schütz's friend and patron Prince Heinrich Posthumus von Reuss), for soloists and choruses in various combinations with accompaniment of basso continuo. Another collection of German motets, written in a severe

EXAMPLE IX–5 *Ego dormio,* Heinrich Schütz

contrapuntal style, was the *Geistliche Chormusik (Spiritual Choral Music)* of 1648. Most important of Schütz's *concertato* motets are the *Symphoniae sacrae (Sacred Symphonies),* which were published in three series in 1629, 1647, and 1650. The first two of these are for various small combinations of voices and instruments, up to a total of five or six parts with continuo. All the motets of the *Symphoniae sacrae* are remarkable for vigorous melodic invention and strong rhythms; they frequently alternate duple and triple meter, the latter often being used for ritornello ensemble sections whose recurrence provides one element of formal unity.

Schütz's works, like those of his contemporaries, about in musical "figures." Example IX–5, for instance, shows the figure called *antitheton* or contrast. Some other figures are illustrated in Example IX–6:

a) *Pathopoiia:* chromatic line for expression of grief and pain (*through thy bitter sorrows*).

EXAMPLE IX–6 Figures in Schütz's works

a. Kleine geistliche Konzerte *I, 14 (SWV 295)*

durch dein bit - ter Lei - den

b. Kleine geistliche Konzerte *II, 31 (SWV 337)*

co - ro - - - nam

c. Musikalische Exequien, *Pt. I (SWV 279)*

so ist es Müh und Ar - beit

d. Kleine geistliche Konzerte *I, 15 (SWV 296)*

Furch - te dich nicht, ich bin mit dir
(Fear not, I am with thee)

b) *Circulatio:* a figure circling around one note; here depicting the circular shape of a crown (*coronam*).

c) *Suspiratio:* realistic imitation of sighing (*so is it weariness and labor*).

d) *Antitheton:* contrast, here fourfold: first motive descending, in slow duple ("imperfect") time with a *saltus dirusculus* (an "ominous" or "dreadful leap"), the diminished fourth (an abnormal or "wrong" interval to emphasize the idea of fear); second motive ascending, in fast triple ("perfect") time with a perfect fourth, a normal or "correct" interval for the idea of confidence and hope.

The last part of the *Symphoniae sacrae,* published after the end of the Thirty Years' War when the full musical resources of the Dresden chapel were again available, calls for as many as six solo voices and two instrumental parts with continuo, supplemented by a full choral and instrumental ensemble. Many of these works are broadly laid out as dramatically conceived "scenes," sometimes with a closing chorus of pious reflection or exhortation; they thus approach the plan of the later church cantata. The setting of the conversion of St. Paul is a splendid example of Schütz's dramatic and pictorial imagination, particularly in his use of the very common Baroque device of the echo on the words "Why persecutest thou me?"

Schütz's compositions of the oratorio type include his most famous work, *The Seven Last Words* (?1645). Here the narrative portions are set as solo recitative (in two instances, for chorus) over a basso continuo, while the words of Jesus, in free and highly expressive monody, are always accompanied by continuo and strings. There is a short introductory chorus and sinfonia; after the seventh Word the sinfonia is repeated, followed by another short closing chorus. The quality of this music seems to sum up in itself a quiet yet deeply felt piety, a personal, ardent, yet infinitely respectful devotion before the figure of the Saviour.

The *Christmas Oratorio* (1664) is on a larger scale. The narrative portions are given in rather rapid recitative over a continuo, while the "scenes" are treated separately with arias, choruses, and instrumental accompaniment in *concertato* style. Schütz's three Passions, written toward the end of his life, are by comparison austere, hieratical works: narrative and dialogue are both in a style of unaccompanied recitative which, in spirit although not in technical details, is like Gregorian Chant. The *turba* (crowd), that is, the chorus that represents the disciples, the priests, and other groups, is given motet-like unaccompanied settings. Schütz's *Seven Last Words*, oratorios, and Passions are the most significant examples of Lutheran music in these quasi-dramatic forms before J. S. Bach.

Instrumental Music

In the early seventeenth century, vocal music had to assimilate the new technique of monody, which brought about profound changes from the style of the sixteenth century; but instrumental music for the most part had only to continue along the paths that had already been well marked out before the end of the Renaissance. The transference of the monodic principle to instrumental music, as for example in sonatas for solo violin with continuo, was not complicated by consideration of a text. The basso continuo was easily adapted to instrumental ensembles; moreover, there was a small but steady production throughout the Baroque of ensemble pieces in imitative counterpoint which dispensed with the continuo or admitted it only optionally; while for solo keyboard and lute music, of course, the question of continuo did not arise at all.

Instrumental music in the first half of the seventeenth century was gradually becoming the equal, in both quantity and content, of vocal music. Forms were still far from being standardized, however, and designations were still confused and inconsistent. Nevertheless, certain basic ways of proceeding, resulting in certain general types of composition, may be distinguished in instrumental music of this period:

1. The ricercare type: pieces in continuous (that is, nonsectional) imitative counterpoint. These were called *ricercare, fantasia, fancy, capriccio, fuga, verset,* and other names; for the most part, these eventually coalesce into the fugue.

2. The canzona type: pieces in discontinuous (that is, sectional) imitative counterpoint, sometimes with admixture of other styles. These pieces lead to the Baroque *sonata da chiesa,* the most important line of development in seventeenth-century instrumental music.

3. Pieces based on a given melody or bass: principally the *theme and variations* (or *partita*), the *passacaglia* or *chaconne,* the *chorale partita,* and the *chorale prelude.*

4. Dances and other pieces in more or less stylized dance rhythms, either strung loosely together or more closely integrated: the *suite.*

5. Pieces in improvisatory style for solo keyboard instrument or lute: called <u>toccata</u>, *fantasia,* or *prelude.*

These classifications are useful as an introduction to a somewhat complex field; but it must be remembered that the categories are neither exhaustive nor mutually exclusive. For example, the procedure of varying a given theme is found not only in compositions specifically called "variations" but often in *ricercari,* canzonas, and dance suites as well; toccatas may include short ricercare-like sections; canzonas may have interludes in improvisatory style; in short, the various types interact and interlock in many ways.

In its purest form the seventeenth-century ricercare is a fairly short, serious composition for organ or clavier in which one theme is continuously developed in imitation. One example is the *Ricercar dopo il Credo* (MM, No. 34) by Girolamo Frescobaldi (1583–1643), who was organist of St. Peter's in Rome from 1608 until his death. Frescobaldi published it in 1635 in a collection of organ pieces called *Fiori musicali* (*Musical Flowers*) intended for use in the church service. This ricercare was part of the music for the *Missa della Madonna* (*Mass of the Blessed Virgin;* No. IX in the *Liber Usualis,* p. 40); as the title says, it was to be played "after the Credo." The piece is remarkable for the skillful handling of the chromatic lines and the subtle use of shifting harmonies and dissonances, producing the typically Baroque effect of quiet intensity that characterizes much of Frescobaldi's organ music.

On a larger scale than the simple ricercare, and with a more complex formal organization, is a type of early seventeenth-century keyboard composition usually called a *fantasia.* The leading fantasia composers in this period were the Amsterdam organist Jan Pieterszoon Sweelinck (1562–1621) and his German pupils, Samuel Scheidt

Ricercare

Fantasia

[Handwritten marginal notes:]

Summary of Instrumental

1. Prelude - def (Intro to something else)

2. Toccata — a touch piece. a light piece that could be thrown out at will.

3. Music for groundbass which is an ostenato. forms 1. Chacone *2. Passacaglia

4. Bach's Inventions + called (Keyboard)

5. Baroque Sonatas
1. Solo
2. Trio - for a keyboard & two or 3 instruments
3. Chamber - small group of instrum.

6. Dances 1. Jig

7. Tower music — Imp. for Brass in Germany

8. Orchestra Music 1. Concerto grosso 2. overture 3. Suite

(1587–1654) of Halle and Heinrich Scheidemann (*ca.* 1596–1663) of Hamburg. An example of the fantasia is the magnificent *Chromatic Fantasia* of Sweelinck (GMB, No. 158), the form of which is a continuous development of the initial chromatic subject; this subject always remains melodically unchanged, although rhythmically it is both augmented and diminished and several times treated in stretto. As the piece proceeds, different countersubjects and scale passages are combined with the principal theme, and the whole works up to an imposing climax. The music does not flow in absolutely unbroken continuity; despite the unifying power of the unchanging theme, the piece is plainly divided into sections, set off from one another by contrasting rhythms and textures. Moreover, the general plan—one theme presented in successive diverse aspects —has an obvious relation to the variation principle.

Titles like ricercare, fantasia, fancy, capriccio, sonata, sinfonia, and canzona were applied to polyphonic instrumental compositions in the early seventeenth century rather indiscriminately. In general it may be said that the ricercare and fantasia were built on a theme or themes of sustained legato character. The tendency was to develop the themes in such pieces in continuous imitative counterpoint, as in the fugue; and, as has already been mentioned, *fuga* was the name used for pieces of this sort in Germany from the earliest years of the seventeenth century. The canzona, on the other hand, had livelier, more markedly rhythmic melodic material and composers tended to emphasize division of this material into sections.

Consort (ensemble) music for viols flourished in England from the early decades of the seventeenth century when the works of Alfonso Ferrabosco the Younger (d. 1628) and John Coperario (Cooper; d. 1626) were popular. The fancies of John Jenkins, the leading composer in this field in the mid-seventeenth century, illustrate both the ricercare and the canzona: his early five-part contrapuntal fancies for viols and organ have ricercare-like melodic subjects, though often more than one subject is presented and there is a suggestion of sectional division; and his later three-part fancies for two violins and bass are like Italian trio sonatas in their light texture, tuneful themes, and division into sections of contrasting styles. In still other works Jenkins uses the term *fancy* for an introductory movement in imitative counterpoint followed by one or more dances or "ayres."

The contrapuntal fantasia for strings without basso continuo, the leading form of early seventeenth-century English chamber music, was cultivated even after the Restoration. The principal later composers were Matthew Locke (*ca.* 1630–77) and Henry Purcell (*ca.* 1659–95), whose fantasias for viols, written about 1680, are the last important examples of the species.

EXAMPLE IX–7 Keyboard Canzona, G. M. Trabaci

The continuous, monothematic ricercare gradually evolved toward the fugue; the multisectional canzona evolved toward the Baroque sonata. As in the sixteenth century, canzonas were written both for keyboard instruments and ensembles. Some distinctive features of the seventeenth-century canzona may be described by citing a series of examples. The first, an anonymous keyboard canzona (MM, No. 26), has three sections in contrasting rhythms, each developing a different theme in fugal imitation, with a closing cadenza-like flourish to round off the whole. In another keyboard canzona, by G. M. Trabaci (*ca.* 1580–1647), the contrasts between the five sections are more marked, but on the other hand a single theme is used throughout (Example IX–7; also see HAM, No. 191), as in the Sweelinck *Chromatic Fantasia* discussed above. A piece of this type is sometimes called a *variation canzona*. A similar structure is used in many of the keyboard canzonas by Frescobaldi and in those of his most distinguished German pupil, the Viennese organist Johann Jakob Froberger (1616–67). Some keyboard canzonas, however, and the majority of ensemble canzonas, dispensed with the variation technique and were cast in thematically unrelated sections—sometimes with many short periods only a few measures long, put together like a patchwork; and sometimes with fewer but longer sections, one or more of which might be repeated either literally or varied after intervening material and thereby serve as an element of unity. Ensemble canzonas of this kind were written by Tarquinio Merula (b. *ca.* 1600).

Merula himself called these pieces *canzonas*. A later composer would probably have called them *sonatas*. This term, the vaguest of all designations for instrumental pieces at the beginning of the seventeenth century, gradually came to mean compositions whose form was like that of the canzona but with special features. Pieces called sonatas in the early seventeenth century were often for one or two melody instruments, usually violins, with a basso continuo; whereas the true ensemble canzona was traditionally written with four parts which could almost always be played just as well without a continuo. Moreover, sonatas were frequently written for a particular instrument and hence took advantage of the idiomatic possibilities of that instrument; they were likely to have a somewhat free and expressive character, whereas the typical canzona had more of the formal, abstract quality of instrumental polyphony in the Renaissance tradition.

The differences, as well as the similarities, will be most clearly evident if we compare two of the earliest sonatas for solo violin and continuo, by Biagio Marini (*ca.* 1595–1665) with contemporary canzonas. Marini's sonata *La Gardana* (1617) is an early example of what may be called instrumental monody. The solo instrument is still not definitely specified: the rubric says the piece may be played on either "violin or cornett"—a common option in the seventeenth century. A short free introduction is followed by a rather jerky little melody with nothing especially violinistic about it, over a slowly moving bass. A short interlude in chordal style leads to a canzona-like melody over a more animated bass part; this section is then repeated with a slight ornamental variation of the tune. A later sonata by Marini, published in 1629, has contrasting sections, the last one of which—a canzona-like Allegro—is repeated. There are no other literal repetitions, although the recurring cadences on A and the alternation of rhapsodic with regularly metrical sections give a certain coherence to the piece. Most notable is the idiomatic violin style, which makes use of sustained tones, runs, trills, double stops, and improvised embellishments called *affetti;* (see Example IX–8; the entire piece with realization of the figured bass appears in GMB, No. 183). Less idiomatic, but with the usual contrast of sections, is a violin sonata by G. B. Fontana (d. *ca.* 1630), which is unified by the periodic return of the sarabande-like rhythm ♩. ♪ ♩ | ♩.

By the middle of the seventeenth century the canzona and the

EXAMPLE IX–8   Sonata, Biagio Marini

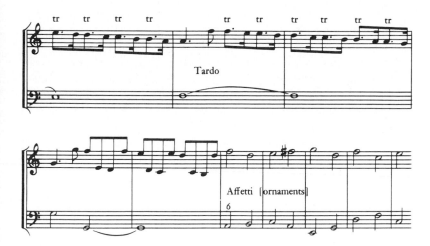

sonata had thoroughly merged, and the term *sonata* gradually replaced *canzona;* sometimes the name was expanded to *sonata da
chiesa,* since many of such pieces were intended for use "in church."
Sonatas were written for many different combinations of instruments; a common medium was two violins with continuo. The
texture of two treble melodic parts, vocal or instrumental, above a
basso continuo had a particular attraction for composers throughout the seventeenth century. Sonatas of this type are usually called
trio sonatas, and the two canzonas of Merula mentioned above may
be regarded as early examples.

The seventeenth century has been called "the age of the varia-
tion" because the variation principle permeates so many of the in-   *Variations*
strumental forms of the period. In a more specific sense, the *theme
and variations* is the continuation of a favorite type of keyboard
composition of the late Renaissance. Three techniques were used
in such pieces:

1) The melody could be repeated with little or no change, although it might be transferred from one voice to another and surrounded with different contrapuntal material in each variation.
This type is sometimes called the *cantus firmus variation.* The leading seventeenth-century composers were, in addition to the English
virginalists, Sweelinck and Scheidt.

2) The melody itself could be ornamented differently for each
variation; as a rule it remained in the topmost voice, with the underlying harmonies essentially unchanged. One of the leading composers
of this type of variation was the Hamburg organist Jan Adams
Reinken (1623–1722). Incidentally, it should be noted that the word
partite (divisions) was used in the early seventeenth century to

335

designate sets of variations; only later did it come to be applied to sets or suites of dances.

3) In a third type of variation, the bass or the harmonic structure, not the melody, is the constant factor. This is the most flexible of all Baroque variation forms, and was used for many important compositions of the late seventeenth and early eighteenth centuries. An early example is the set of *partite* by Frescobaldi on a variant of the romanesca bass, one of the favorite variations subjects of the seventeenth century. The outline of the romanesca bass is given in Example IX–1. In actual composition this outline was usually filled in and ornamented in various ways; the constant element in the variations was thus not alone the melodic line but also, or alternatively, a series of harmonies. The same method of composition was sometimes used in instrumental pieces called chaconnes or passacaglias, though on the other hand many such works do have a short clearly defined ostinato bass melody or continuously repeated ground.

An important class of Baroque organ compositions from middle and northern Germany were works based on chorale melodies. These pieces were produced in large numbers and in a great variety of forms after the middle of the seventeenth century, but there are examples already in the works of Sweelinck and Scheidt. In 1624, Scheidt published a large collection of compositions for the organ under the title *Tabulatura nova*—new, because instead of the old-fashioned German organ tablature, Scheidt adopted the modern Italian practice of writing out each voice on a separate staff. Among the chorale compositions of the *Tabulatura nova* are a notable fantasia on the melody *Ich ruf' zu dir* (*I Call to Thee*) and several sets of variations on other chorale tunes. There are also shorter organ settings of plainsong melodies, many variations on secular songs, and several monumental fantasias. The works of Scheidt, and his influence as a teacher, were the foundation of a remarkable development of North German organ music in the Baroque era.

Dance music in the seventeenth century continued to be produced in ever greater quantity and variety. Notable is the appearance in German collections at this time of numerous pieces called *Polnischer Tanz* (*Polish Dance*), *Polacca,* and the like—evidence of the extent to which the folk-based music of Poland was coming to be known in western Europe. Dance music was important not only in itself but also because dance rhythms began to permeate other music, both vocal and instrumental, sacred and secular. The characteristic rhythm of the sarabande, for example, and the lively movement of the gigue appear in many compositions that are not called dances at all. As in the sixteenth century, dances were written both for solo

Dance music

instruments and for ensembles.

The early seventeenth century is especially remarkable for the production in Germany of *suites* of dances for instrumental groups, commonly a set or consort of viols, although with the usual understanding that other instruments, such as violins or cornetts, might be substituted. The stimulus for the suites seems to have come largely from English composers living in Germany; probably it was the English influence also that led the Germans to extend the technique of thematic variation—already established in the pavane-galliard combination of the sixteenth century—to all the dances of a suite.

Suites

One of the most important collections of dances was J. H. Schein's *Banchetto musicale (Musical Banquet)*, published at Leipzig in 1617. The *Banchetto* contains twenty suites in five parts, each suite consisting of a *padouana,* a *gagliarda,* a *courente,* and an *allemande* with a *tripla* (a variation in triple meter of the allemande). The music is dignified, aristocratic, vigorously rhythmic, and melodically inventive, with that union of richness and decorum, of Italian charm and Teutonic gravity, so characteristic of the early Baroque in Germany. The typical Baroque device of the echoed phrase is common in Schein's dances. Some of the suites are obviously built on one melodic idea that recurs in varied form in every dance; in other suites the technique is more subtle, and melodic reminiscence is employed rather than outright variation of a theme. In all, however, a sound organic musical connection exists among all the dances of a given suite: they "finely correspond both in key and invention," as Schein claims in his foreword.

Among the dances sometimes included in a suite and sometimes published separately was the *intrada,* a piece usually of festive march-like character (though often written in triple meter) which, as the name suggests, might serve as the opening movement of a suite.

The conception of the suite as a musical entity, as one composition in several movements rather than a mere succession of short pieces each in a certain mood and rhythm, was a German contribution. In France, the great achievement of the early and middle seventeenth century was to establish a characteristic idiom and style for the individual dances. This achievement was a reflection of the fact that most French suites were not written for an ensemble but for a solo instrument—first the lute and later the clavecin (the French term for harpsichord). Lute music flourished in France during the early seventeenth century, culminating in the work of Denis Gaultier (*ca.* 1600–72). A manuscript collection of Gaultier's compositions entitled *La Rhétorique des dieux (The Rhetoric of the Gods)* contains twelve sets (one in each mode) of highly stylized

French lute and keyboard music

dances. Each set includes an allemande, courante, and sarabande, with other dances added apparently at random; each suite is thus actually a little anthology of short character pieces, many of which were given fanciful titles.

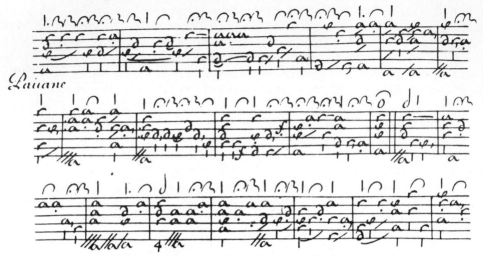

A page of Gaultier's La Rhétorique des dieux; *for a transcription, see HAM, No. 211.*

Since the lute was incapable of sustained tone, it was necessary to sketch in the melody, bass, and harmony by sounding the appropriate tones now in one register, now in another, leaving it to the imagination of the hearer to supply the implied continuity of the various lines (see HAM, No. 211). This was the *style brisé* or broken style which other French composers adapted to the harpsichord, together with certain features of the variation technique derived from the English virginalists; they also systematically developed the use of little ornaments (*agréments*), sometimes indicated by stenographic signs on the page and sometimes left to the discretion of the player. The French lute style was the source not only of important developments in keyboard music but also of the entire French style of composition in the late seventeenth and early eighteenth centuries.

The earliest important composer in the new keyboard idiom was Jacques Champion de Chambonnières (*ca.* 1602–72), the first of a long and brilliant line of French clavecinists among whom Louis Couperin (1626–61) and Jean Henri d'Anglebert (*ca.* 1628–91) should be especially mentioned. The new style was carried to Germany by Froberger, who established the allemande, courante, and sarabande as standard components of dance suites. In Froberger's manuscripts the suites end with a slow dance, the sarabande; in a later, posthumous publication of the suites in 1693, they were revised so as to end with a lively gigue. The fusion of genre pieces and dance rhythms in the mid-seventeenth century keyboard suite is well illustrated in one of Froberger's most famous compositions, a lament (*tombeau*) on the death of the Emperor Ferdinand IV; this piece, in the pattern and rhythm of an allemande, forms the first movement of a suite.

A different kind of improvisatory composition, already foreshadowed by some Italian keyboard works of the late sixteenth century, occurs in some of the toccatas of Frescobaldi. In contrast to the imposing objective grandeur and virtuosity of the Venetian school, these toccatas are in a reserved, subjective, mystical vein, with sustained harmonies and extraordinary original chord progressions. These works, exemplified by the well-known *Toccata for the Elevation* from the *Missa delli apostoli (Mass of the Apostles;* No. IV in the *Liber Usualis,* p. 25) in the *Fiori Musicali,* are the very essence of improvisatory style, although they utterly renounce technical display.

Improvisatory compositions

Other keyboard toccatas of Frescobaldi's, however, are related to the Venetian type: they allow scope for virtuosity and in form are a long series of loosely connected sections with great luxuriance of musical ideas. The various sections of these toccatas, the composer states, may be played separately, and the piece may be ended at any appropriate cadence if the player so desires; moreover, Frescobaldi indicates that the tempo is not to be subject to a regular beat but may be modified according to the sense of the music, especially by retarding at cadences.

A seventeenth-century Italian harpsichord in an elaborately sculptured Baroque case. (Courtesy Metropolitan Museum of Art, Crosby Brown Collection of Musical Instruments, 1889)

Baroque
Period in
Summary
① Secular music
increasing
importance
② Absolute music
increasing in
importance
because
3. Chordal style
in harmony
4. Donality
was firmly
established
Modal treatment
is out.
5. Tuning
Equal temperament
Equal distance
between the
half steps.
6. Figured Bass
7. Dynamics - Block or terrace dynamics.

More solidly formed though less exuberant toccatas were written by Froberger; in these, the free improvisatory passages provide a framework for systematically developed sections in the contrapuntal style of a fantasia. Froberger's pieces were the model for the later Baroque coupling of toccata and fugue, such as occurs in the works of Buxtehude or the familiar *Toccata in D minor* of Bach. Similar pairing of improvisatory and fugal styles was used by many German organ composers of the seventeenth century.

The confused and unsettled state of European politics during the first half of the seventeenth century is paralleled to some degree by the state of European music in that period. The Thirty Years' War in Germany, the Civil War in England, and the disturbances of the Fronde in France seem to have their counterpart in the conflict between the old and the new practices in music, the experimental character of early opera and cantata, and the untidiness of terminology in operatic and instrumental composition. The Treaty of Westphalia, the Restoration of Charles II, and the accession of Louis XIV introduced an era of comparative political stability and of unparalleled scientific and general intellectual progress in the second half of the century. The pervasive ideal of orderliness worked in the realm of music toward a synthesis of the discoveries of the earlier period and their establishment in relatively fixed styles and forms. This development we shall follow in the next chapter.

X

The Mature Baroque: Vocal Music

Opera, Cantata, Song

In the second half of the seventeenth century, opera spread through
Italy and outward to other countries. The principal Italian center
was Venice, whose opera houses were famous all over Europe.

Italian opera

The Venetian opera of this period, although by later standards
dramatically ridiculous, was scenically and musically splendid. The
plots were a jumble of improbable characters and situations, an
irrational mixture of serious and comic scenes, and served mainly
as pretexts for striking stage effects, pleasant melodies, and beautiful solo singing. Vocal virtuosity had not yet reached the dizzying
heights it attained in the eighteenth century, but the way was be
ing prepared. The chorus had practically disappeared, the orchestra
had little to do except accompany, and the recitatives were of only
slight musical interest: the aria reigned supreme, and its victory
in one sense marked the victory of popular taste over the aristocratic
refinement of the original operatic recitative of the Florentines
and Monteverdi, which was so intimately connected with the
rhythms and moods of the text.

Composers of the new aria did not entirely disregard the text,
but they considered it merely a starting point; they were chiefly
interested in the musical construction, the material for which they
drew from the rhythms and melodies of popular music—that is,
music familiar to the people in general. Some arias, indeed, were

*Agostini and
Sartorio*

GMB,
NO. 227

simply strophic songs in popular style—for example, the song *Se tu non m'ami o bella* (If thou wilt not love me, O fair one) from *Il ratto delle Sabine* (*The Rape of the Sabine Women*) by P. S. Agostini (*ca.* 1650–*ca.* 1690)—and even arias of a more pretentious character were dominated by march rhythms, or by the dance rhythms of the gigue, sarabande, or minuet. Ostinato bass was used in some arias, both as a means of musical organization and also in combination with dance rhythms, or skilfully adapted to the nuances of the text. Motives imitated from trumpet figures were used for martial or vehement arias, often being expanded into brilliant coloratura passages. An example is the aria *Vittrici schieri* (Victorious hosts) from the opera *Adelaide* (1672) by M. A. Sartorio (*ca.* 1620–*ca.* 1685). The coloratura had not yet become—as it had by the end of the century with some composers—an arbitrary vocal adornment for display of virtuosity; it was still serving a definite expressive function.

GMB,
NO. 223

Sartorio was one of the last of the Venetians who continued the heroic style of opera established by Monteverdi and Cavalli. In the works of Sartorio's follower Giovanni Legrenzi (1626–90) a milder, more genial temper prevails. The aria *Ti lascio l'alma impegno* (I leave my soul imprisoned with thee) from Legrenzi's *Giustino* (Venice, 1683) shows the combination of graceful nobility of melodic line and natural contrapuntal and constructive skill which is typical of Italian music in the late seventeenth century.

GMB,
NO. 231

In addition to Sartorio and Legrenzi, the most important Italian opera composers of the late seventeenth and early eighteenth centuries were Francesco Provenzale of Naples (1627–1704), Alessandro Stradella (1644–82), Carlo Pallavicino (1630–88), Agostino Steffani (1654–1728), and Alessandro Scarlatti (1660–1725). The qualities of Italian vocal style in arias that express strong feelings of sadness and pain are nowhere better exemplified than in the long melodic lines and expressive chromatic harmonies of *Lasciatemi morir* (Let me die) from Provenzale's opera *Il schiavo di sua moglie* (*His Wife's Slave*). The three-part *ABA* form of this aria, which was common in other contemporary Italian operas, foreshadows the fully developed da capo form of the eighteenth century.

HAM,
NO. 222

The aria *Tra cruci funesti* (Amidst fatal tortures) from Stradella's opera *Corispero* has a vigorous gigue-like rhythm, and consciously parodies for comic effect the stereotyped "fury-revenge" arias of the serious heroic operas. The accompaniment of this song is typical for the period: only harpsichord and bass are used to accompany the voice, but the arias are framed by orchestral ritornellos at the beginning and end. An aria accompanied only by harpsichord and bass, whether with or without orchestral ritornello, is known as a "continuo aria."

HAM,
NO. 241

Pallavicino and Steffani were two of the many Italian composers who in the late seventeenth and early eighteenth centuries carried Italian opera to the eagerly receptive German courts. Pallavicino worked chiefly in Dresden, Steffani at Munich and Hanover.

In his later works Steffani wrote amply proportioned arias and accompaniments of rich *concertato* texture; he nearly always managed to maintain an equal balance between form and emotional content in his music. One of the best Italian opera composers of his time, his works are important not only for themselves but also historically; they illustrate the transition from the style of the middle Baroque to that of the late Baroque, and they exerted influence on eighteenth-century composers, especially Keiser and Handel.

Steffani's aria *Un balen d'incerta speme* (A flash of uncertain hope) from the opera *Enrico detto il Leone* (*Henry the Lion;* Hanover, 1689) illustrates his early style. The aria has a da capo form of modest dimensions, with a contrasting middle section. The coloratura passages, though prominent, are neither excessive nor unrelated to the text: they occur on the pictorial words *balen* (flash) and *raggio* (ray), while the passage on *dolor* (pain) expresses the thought in typically Baroque fashion with chromatic melody and harmonic cross-relations. (Example X–1; the complete aria is given in HAM, No. 244.) Two other features of this aria occur fairly often in other arias of the late seventeenth and early eighteenth centuries:

EXAMPLE X–1   Aria, *Un balen* from *Enrico detto il Leone,* Steffani

è'l sol rag -   -   -   gio che m'a -

van - za frà le   nu - bi del do - lor

. . . is the only ray [of hope] that sustains me amidst the clouds of pain.

343

(1) it begins with a single phrase of the voice part which after a pause is repeated and then carried on in its natural development, a device sometimes called the *motto* beginning; the opening phrase is like a formal proclamation of the subject of the aria which is about to be heard; (2) the other feature is a *running bass*—a steadily flowing rhythm of eighth notes.

Lotti

It is instructive to compare this aria by Steffani, with its irregular phrase-lengths and occasionally awkward harmonies, with the aria, *Padre, addio* (Father, farewell; Example X–2; the complete aria appears in GMB, No. 270) from a Venetian opera of 1717, *Alessandro Severo* by Antonio Lotti (*ca.* 1667–1740). In Lotti's work the chord progressions are smooth and conventional, and the phrasing, while far from mechanical, is clear at first hearing; another characteristic typical of the later period is the gradual disappearance of the continuo aria; increasingly, the accompaniment to arias is played by the orchestra entirely. On the other hand, Lotti's accompaniment is devoid of contrapuntal interest, and the musical expression of the text is a little stylized, even artificial. For example, there is no compelling reason in the word itself for the long melismas on *ricordati* (remember); they are there only because the composer needs them to round out the phrase and make the pattern symmetrical.

EXAMPLE X–2 Aria, *Padre, addio* from *Alessandro Severo,* Antonio Lotti

ri - cor -   -   -   -   -

da - ti   di   me.

The Venetian style of Baroque opera on Italian texts, with its grandiose subject matter and generally serious musical treatment, continued in southern Germany well into the eighteenth century.

GMB, NO. 272

A late example was the festival opera *Costanza e fortezza* (*Constancy and Courage*) by the Viennese organist, theorist, and conductor Johann Joseph Fux, composed for the coronation of the Emperor Charles VI at Prague in 1723.

The Neapolitan style

In Italy even before the end of the seventeenth century there were distinct tendencies in opera toward stylization of musical language and forms, and toward a simple musical texture with concentration on the single melodic line of the solo voice, supported by ingratiating harmonies. The eventual result was a style of opera which was more concerned with elegance and external effectiveness than with dramatic strength and truth; but the dramatic weak-

344

nesses were often redeemed by the beauty of the music. This new style, which became dominant in the eighteenth century, was apparently developed in its early stages principally at Naples, and hence is often called the *Neapolitan* style.

One type of aria often found in Italian opera of this period is the *siciliana.* Derived from folksong, it consists of a rather melancholy, languid melody in 6/8 or 12/8 meter, usually in the minor mode; frequently at cadences the supertonic (the second degree of the scale) is flatted, thus producing the chord called the *Neapolitan sixth* (see Example X–3, measures 5 and 8).

Another notable feature of eighteenth-century Italian opera was the emergence of two distinct types of recitative. One type—which later was given the name *recitativo secco* (dry recitative) and was accompanied only with the harpsichord and a sustaining bass instrument—was used chiefly to get through long stretches of dialogue

EXAMPLE X–3   Aria, *Ricordati ch'io t'amo* from *L'Eraclea,*
Alessandro Scarlatti

Remember that I love you and serve you and am silent.

or monologue as quickly as possible with a minimum of musical interference. The second type—*recitativo accompagnato* or *stromentato* ([orchestrally] accompanied recitative)—was used for especially tense dramatic situations; the rapid changes of emotion in the dialogue were reinforced by the orchestra, which both accompanied the singer and punctuated his phrases by brief instrumental outbursts. There was also a type of melody which was neither so rhythmically free as the recitative nor so regular as the aria, but stood somewhere between the two; this kind of melody is called *arioso, that is,* "aria-like."

arioso

Between a recitative and an aria.

The struggle between the seventeenth-century Baroque opera and the newer style is evident in the works of Alessandro Scarlatti, who has generally been regarded as the principal founder of the Neapolitan school. Scarlatti's earliest operas were similar to those of Legrenzi and Stradella. In many of his later works, notably in *Mitridate* (Venice, 1707), *Tigrane* (Naples, 1715), and *Griselda* (Rome, 1721), the broad dramatic conception of the arias and the importance of the orchestra evidence Scarlatti's devotion to a serious musical ideal; but pressure from his patrons and the demands of his audiences sometimes induced him to write in a simpler, more immediately attractive idiom. An example of the lighter Italian style is the comic duet from *Gl'inganni felici* (*The Lucky Stratagems*), an opera performed at Naples in 1699.

By the beginning of the eighteenth century, Italian opera had been accepted by nearly every country in western Europe save France. Although a few Italian operas had been played at Paris toward the middle of the seventeenth century, the French for a long time would neither accept the Italian opera nor create one of their own. However, in the 1670s a national French opera was finally achieved under the august patronage of Louis XIV. With special features that distinguished it from the Italian form, it remained essentially unchanged until past the middle of the eighteenth century.

Opera in France

The characteristics peculiar to French opera were due to two powerful traditions in the national culture: the sumptuous and colorful ballet, which had flourished at the royal court ever since the *Ballet Comique de la Reine* of 1581; and the classical French tragedy, represented best by the works of Pierre Corneille (1606–84) and Jean Racine (1639–99). Tentative experiments in French opera were made by Robert Cambert (*ca.* 1628–77) beginning in 1659; but the first important composer was Jean-Baptiste Lully (1632–87), who succeeded in blending elements from the ballet and the drama in a form which he called a *tragédie lyrique* (tragedy in music).

Lully was an Italian who came to Paris at an early age, and who by astute business management and the favor of the king made him-

A contemporary engraving of a performance of Lully's Alceste *given in the candle-lit marble courtyard at Versailles. The orchestra can be seen seated in enclosures on both sides at the front of the stage; the royal personages directly face the singers.*

Jean-Baptiste Lully

self virtually the musical dictator of France. His librettist was Jean-Phillippe Quinault, an esteemed dramatist of the period; Quinault provided Lully with texts that satisfactorily combined serious (or, at least, not intentionally comic) plots on mythological themes with frequent long interludes of dancing and choral singing, the whole cleverly intermingled with adulation of the king, glorification of the French nation, long discussions of *l'amour,* and episodes of romantic and marvelous adventure. For these librettos Lully composed music that was appropriately pompous and that projected both the highly formal splendor of the French royal court and the somewhat intellectualized French preoccupation with the minutiae of courtly love and knightly conduct. Lully's music is most immediately attractive to modern ears in the massive spectacular choruses and in the rhythmical dances of the ballet scenes, for example the Chaconne

GMB, NO. 233

from *Roland.* Dances from Lully's ballets and operas eventually became widely popular in arrangements as independent instrumental suites, and many composers in the late seventeenth and early eighteenth centuries wrote dance suites in imitation of Lully's.

An original contribution of Lully was the treatment of recitative. Devising musical declamation for French words was by no means a simple task, since neither the rapid *recitativo secco* nor the quasi-melodic *arioso* of Italian opera was suitable to the rhythms and accents of the French tongue. Lully solved the problem by studying the style of declamation used in the French theatre and imitating it as closely as possible. Leaving nothing to the discretion of the singers, he notated his recitative in exact detail. The result, in the best instances, is an effect of genuine power, due not so much to the qualities of the melodic line or the harmony as to the way in which the music follows precisely the changing dramatic inflections and pauses of the text.

On the whole, the difference between recitatives and more melodic passages for solo voice is far less marked in French than in Italian opera. Fairly often Lully writes a recitative which is periodically interrupted by a recurring melodic phrase, as in the lament *O mort! venez finir mon destin déplorable* (O death, come and put an end to my unhappy fate) from *Persée*. GMB, NO. 232

Lully's operas contain many short songs in the graceful rhythm of the minuet or some other dance. In contrast to the Italian composers, Lully avoids coloratura writing, except for the purpose of briefly illustrating some pictorial detail (see Example X–4; the entire song is in HAM, No. 225).

EXAMPLE X–4   Air from *Alceste,* Lully

Et lais - sez   ré - gner sur les   on - - - - -

- - - - des.

And let [Zephyr] rule over the waves.

Other airs, less numerous but of greater musical interest, are poetical depictions of quiet scenes and of the contemplative feelings aroused by them. An example is *Bois épais* from the opera *Amadis* (1684; Example X–5). Musical mood-paintings of this kind—serious, restrained, elegantly proportioned, full of aristocratic yet sensuous charm—were much admired and frequently imitated by later composers.

Even before he began to write operas Lully had established the musical form of the *ouverture,* the "French overture." In the late seventeenth and early eighteenth centuries, instrumental pieces in this form not only introduced operas and other large composite works, but also appeared as independent compositions and sometimes constituted the opening movement of a suite, sonata, or concerto. The French overture has two parts. The first section is homophonic in style, slow in movement, majestic, with persistent dotted rhythm. The second section is more contrapuntal in texture (or at least usually starts out with some semblance of fugal imitation) and is comparatively fast-moving, though without ever sacrificing a certain grave and serious character; this section often ends The ouverture
Slow
Fast
Slow

EXAMPLE X–5   Air, *Bois épais* from *Amadis*, Lully

Bois é - pais   re - dou - ble ton   om - bre: Tu ne sau-

rais être   as - sez som-bre, Tu   ne peux trop ca - cher mon mal - heu- reux a - mour

Thick forest, redouble your shadows: you cannot be dark enough,
you cannot sufficiently conceal my unhappy love.

with an *allargando,* which sometimes includes a reference to the
characteristic rhythm and perhaps to the actual musical material of
the first section. Each section is marked to be repeated. Some later
opera overtures and other instrumental pieces begin in this way,
then continue with a number of additional movements. The original
aim of the *ouverture* was to create a festive atmosphere for the
opera that was to follow; Venetian overtures of the early seventeenth
century had served the same purpose. By the end of the century, the
Italian opera composers were beginning to write overtures, which
they called *sinfonie,* of quite a different type (see page 386ff.), but the
French remained faithful to their traditional form.

Lully's influence extended beyond the field of opera. The rich
five-part texture of his orchestration and his use of the woodwinds—
both for supporting the strings and in contrasting passages or movements for a trio of solo wind instruments (usually two oboes and
bassoon)—found many imitators in France and Germany. In the
latter country it was Georg Muffat (*ca.* 1645–1740) who first introduced Lully's style of composition and the French manner of
orchestral playing.

As far as the opera itself was concerned, the contemporaries and

1600's

followers of Lully in France did little more than continue the type which he had founded; the most important changes they made were to introduce occasional arias in the Italian style (which they called *ariettes*) and to expand still further the huge *divertissement* scenes which involved ballets and choruses. A development of this expansion was the appearance of a mixed form, the *opéra-ballet*, initiated in 1697 with *l'Europe galante* by André Campra (1660–1744).

Opera in England—or what was there known as "opera"—had a short career in the second half of the seventeenth century. During the reigns of James I (*reg.* 1603–25) and Charles I (*reg.* 1625–49), an aristocratic entertainment flourished which was somewhat similar to the French court ballet, namely the *masque*. Milton's *Comus*, produced in 1634 with music by Henry Lawes (1596–1662), is probably the best known masque. Masques continued to be given privately throughout the period of the Civil War (1642–49), the Commonwealth (1649–60), and the early years of the Restoration of Charles II (*reg.* 1660–85). The most elaborate of these private entertainments was *Cupid and Death* (1653), with music by Matthew Locke (*ca.* 1630–77) and Christopher Gibbons (1615–76); it includes many dances and other instrumental pieces, songs of various types, recitatives, and choruses.

English opera

Meanwhile, English opera had begun in a modest way under the Commonwealth, not because the English composers or public especially wanted operas, but because, although stage plays were prohibited, a play set to music could be called a "concert" and so avoid the ban. After the Restoration this pretext was no longer necessary, and thus nearly all of the English "semi-operas" of the seventeenth century are really plays with a large proportion of solos, ensembles, choruses, and instrumental music of all kinds. The only important exceptions were John Blow's *Venus and Adonis* (1684 or 1685) and Henry Purcell's *Dido and Aeneas* (1689), both of which are sung throughout.

John Blow (1649–1708) served two terms as organist of Westminster Abbey and also held the official positions of organist and composer in the Chapel Royal. *Venus and Adonis*, though entitled a "masque," is in reality an unpretentious pastoral opera, containing some charming and even moving music, in which the influences of the Italian cantata as well as of both the native English and the fashionable French styles of the period are discernible. The overture and prologue are obviously modeled on those of French opera; many of the airs and recitatives adapt the emotionally expressive curves of Italian *bel canto* to English words; other songs have more purely English rhythms and melodic outlines. The final threnodic chorus *Mourn for thy servant* is typically English in its simple, truthful interpretation of the text, its grave rhythms, flawless declamation, lucid part writing, and frequent harmonic audacities.

John Blow

Henry Purcell

Henry Purcell, the finest English musical genius after William Byrd and the last great English composer before the twentieth century, was a pupil of Blow; he served as organist of Westminster Abbey from 1679 and held other posts in the official musical establishments of London. In addition to many odes for chorus and orchestra, cantatas, songs, catches, anthems, Services, fancies, chamber sonatas, and keyboard works, he wrote incidental music for 49 plays, the largest and most important part of this theatre music being composed during the last five years of his life.

The opera *Dido and Aeneas* was written for a girls' boarding school at Chelsea, on a libretto by Nahum Tate, which, although crude in poetic details, dramatized the familiar story from Vergil's *Aeneid* in a fashion most satisfactory for musical setting. Purcell's score is a masterpiece of opera in miniature; the orchestra consists of strings and continuo, there are only four principal roles, and the three acts, including dances and choruses, take only about an hour to perform. The music shows that Purcell was able to incorporate in his own style both the achievements of the English school of the seventeenth century and the influences on that school from Continental sources. The overture is of the French type, and the homophonic choruses in dance rhythms suggest, although they surpass in tunefulness, the choruses of Lully. The minuet rhythm $\frac{3}{4}$ ♩ ♩ | ♩ ♫ | ♩ ♩ | ♩ of the chorus *Fear no danger to ensue,* beginning in alternate iambics and trochees ⏑ — | — ⏑ | ⏑ — | — , is especially reminiscent of French models.

Thoroughly English, however, is such an inimitable tune as *Pursue thy conquest, Love* or the melody of the chorus *Come away, fellow sailors* at the beginning of Act III, with its fascinating phraseology of 3 + 5, 4 + 4 + 4, 4 + 5 measures, and the sly mock-pathetic chromatics at the words "silence their mourning." The choruses, which throughout are freely intermingled with the solos, are an important part of the work. The closing chorus *With drooping wings* must certainly have been suggested to Purcell by the final chorus in Blow's *Venus and Adonis;* equally perfect in workmanship, it has a larger scale and a profounder depth of elegiac sorrow, the sentiment being supported by the musical suggestion of "drooping" and the impressive pauses after the word "never." The recitatives are neither the rapid chatter of the Italian *recitativo secco* nor the stylized rhythms of French operatic recitative, but free plastic melodies flexibly molded to the accents, pace, and emotions of the English text. Three of the arias are built entirely over a ground bass; the last of these—and one of the greatest arias in all opera—is Dido's lament *When I am laid in earth.* In its perfect adaptation of technique to expression this song is one of the landmarks of seventeenth-century music.

Apart from *Dido and Aeneas,* Purcell's output of dramatic music was all incidental music for plays. For most of the plays for which he wrote music he wrote only a few pieces and most of these few pieces were short ones. There are four or five plays, however, in which the musical portions are so extensive as to make them in effect operas within the seventeenth-century English meaning of the word —that is, dramas in spoken dialogue but with overtures, entr'actes, and long ballets or other musical scenes. Purcell's principal "operas" of this sort were *Dioclesian* (1690), *King Arthur* (1691), *The Fairy Queen* (1692; an adaptation of Shakespeare's *Midsummer Night's Dream*), *The Indian Queen* (1695), and *The Tempest* (1695). The solo and chorus *I call, I call, I call* from *King Arthur* give some idea of Purcell's style, but the variety, the wonderful virility, delicacy, and vividness of his theatre music can be fully appreciated only by studying and hearing the scores.

GMB, NO. 247

Unfortunately for English music, no composer appeared after Purcell who had sufficient stature to maintain the national tradition against the preference for Italian opera at the beginning of the eighteenth century. For two hundred years English opera remained a stepchild while English audiences lavished their enthusiasm on the productions of Italian, French, or German composers.

Despite the prevailing fashion for Italian opera at the German courts in the seventeenth century, a few cities supported German companies and gave operas in German by native composers. The most important center was the northern free city of Hamburg, where the first public opera house in Europe outside Venice was opened in 1678. The Hamburg opera existed until 1738, by which time the changed public taste would no longer support native opera on any considerable scale. During these sixty years, however, a number of German opera composers were active, and a national school of opera arose. Many librettos of German operas in this period were translated or imitated from the Venetian poets, and the music of the German composers was influenced by both Venetian and French models.

German opera

The principal native influences in the formation of German opera were the *school drama* and the German style of solo songs. School dramas were little plays of a pious, moral, or didactic character with inserted musical numbers, performed by students. They were fairly numerous in the sixteenth and early seventeenth centuries, but the practice of writing them died out during the Thirty Years' War. The serious religious tone of these works was preserved to some extent in the earliest Hamburg operas (many of which were on Biblical subjects) as well as in a curious earlier allegorical pastorale, *Seelewig* (1644), by the Nuremberg organist Sigmund Theophil Staden (1607–55).

The usual German word for "opera" around 1700 was *Singspiel,* that is, a play with music; many such works used spoken dialogue instead of recitative. When recitative was employed, it was usually in a style taken over practically without change from Italian opera; not until Mozart's *Magic Flute* (1791) did the German opera have a musical prosody as perfectly adapted to the German language as Lully's recitative was to French words. In their arias, however, the German composers of the seventeenth and early eighteenth centuries were both more eclectic and more independent. Occasionally they would write airs in French style and in the rhythms of French dances.

GMB, NO. 250

Other arias, such as *Schöne Wiesen* (Lovely Meadows) from Johann Sigismund Cousser's (1660–1727) *Erindo* (Hamburg, 1693), seem to combine German gravity with Italian elegance. More common in early German opera are short strophic songs with brisk forthright melodies and rhythms, songs that are essentially of native growth. These airs, so different in both form and spirit from the da capo arias of the contemporary Italian opera, give evidence of the vitality of the national popular musical style in seventeenth-century Germany, especially in the Lutheran northern regions where Italian influence was weakest.

Reinhard Keiser

The foremost, and most prolific, of the early German opera composers was Reinhard Keiser (1674–1739), who wrote over 100 works for the Hamburg stage between 1696 and 1734. Keiser's operas at their best represent a union of Italian and German qualities. In subject matter and general plan the librettos are like those of the Venetian operas, and the virtuoso arias even surpass their Italian counterparts in vigor and brilliance. The slower melodies, though lacking the suave perfection of the Italian *bel canto,* are serious and sometimes profoundly expressive; the harmonies are well organized in broad, clear structures. Keiser was no slave to the current Italian fashion of casting practically every aria in the da capo form; when he uses this pattern it is often with modifications, and in addition he introduces free arioso melodies not bound strictly to any rhythmic or formal scheme, as well as songs in purely German style. His accompaniments are of special interest, for Keiser shared the preference of most German Baroque composers for a comparatively full polyphonic texture in contrast to the Italian tendency to concentrate everything in the melody. Thus his arias abound in interesting basses and varied combinations of orchestral instruments which "concertize" or "compete" with the voice in independent melodic figures.

Another of Keiser's traits, which may be due to his German background, is his feeling for nature. In his most famous opera, *Croesus* (Hamburg, 1710), and in other works, there are pastoral scenes which the composer has handled with a freshness and naturalism rare in Italian opera of the time; the opening scene of the second act of *Croesus,* for example, combines the effect of rustic instruments with a melodic line realistically suggesting bird songs.

Keiser was apparently the first composer to write German comic operas. In the latter part of his life he set to music many farces of a trivial and even indecent character, works which contributed little to his musical reputation but are of some interest historically because they show how a first-rate composer of serious Baroque opera exhausted his powers in a vain effort to adapt himself to a narrowed public taste.

The national French opera survived in the early eighteenth century only because it was steadily supported by the state; the German opera, which like the English lacked such support, was helpless in the face of Italian competition. The only notable contemporary of Keiser who maintained to some degree the conservative standards of the serious Baroque opera in Germany during the first half of the eighteenth century was Georg Kaspar Schürmann of Wolfenbüttel (*ca.* 1672–1751); his most famous opera, *Ludovicus Pius* (*Louis the Pious*) was given at Brunswick in 1726.

GMB,
NO. 293

Along with opera, the other important Italian form of vocal composition in the second half of the seventeenth century was the cantata. After the early years of the century, the cantata had developed from monody with strophic variation to a form consisting of many short contrasting sections; in the second half of the century it finally settled into a more clearly defined pattern of alternating recitatives and arias—normally two or three of each—for solo voice with continuo accompaniment, on a text usually of amatory character in the form of a dramatic narrative or soliloquy, the whole taking perhaps ten to fifteen minutes to perform. Thus in both its literary and its musical aspects the cantata resembled a detached scene from an opera; it differed from opera chiefly in that both poetry and music were on a more intimate scale. Designed for performance in a room, without stage scenery or costumes, and for smaller and more discriminating audiences than those of the opera houses, the cantata kept always a certain elegance and refinement of workmanship that would have been out of place in opera. Because of its intimate character, also, it offered more opportunity than opera for experimental musical effects.

The cantata

Practically all the Italian opera composers of the seventeenth century were prolific composers of cantatas. In quantity as well as in quality the years from 1650 to about 1720 were astoundingly productive ones in Italy; but as is true of the operas, only a tiny fraction of these works is accessible in modern editions.

The most noted cantata composers after Carissimi, L. Rossi, and Cesti were Legrenzi and Stradella. A climax was reached toward the end of the century with the more than six hundred cantatas of Alessandro Scarlatti. His cantata *Lascia, deh lascia* (*Cease, O Cease*)

Alessandro Scarlatti

has many characteristics typical of the form. It begins with a short section of *arioso,* that is, a melody in slow tempo not so highly organized in form nor so regular in rhythmic pattern as an aria, with an expressive character midway between aria and recitative. (See Example X–6a; the entire cantata is given in GMB, No. 260.) The ensuing recitative is typical of the mature style of Scarlatti in its wide harmonic range: notice the modulation to the remote key of E♭ minor at the words *inganni mortali* (deceptions of mortal life; Example X–6b). Then follows a full da capo aria with long, supple melodic phrases over a bass in stately eighth-note rhythm, organized partly by the help of sequences and containing likewise some unusual harmonic progressions and chromatics expressive of the word "tormentar" (Example X–6c).

The pivot chord for a great many of Scarlatti's modulations is a diminished seventh, a rare chord in the works of his contemporaries and predecessors. Sometimes Scarlatti exploits the enharmonic ambiguity of this chord, but often he uses it rather for its marked pungency in leading to a cadence that might have been approached diatonically.

A second brief recitative, leading in rapid succession through various keys from F major to B minor, introduces a second da capo aria in E minor, the key of the opening movement. Although the

EXAMPLE X–6   Cantata: *Lascia, deh lascia,* Alessandro Scarlatti

La - scia,   deh la - scia al fi - ne   di tor - men -

tar - mi   più, di tor - men - tar - mi   più,

a. *Cease, O cease to torment me.*

b.

[fie - le] d'un i - dol trop-po in - gra - to tra gl'in - gan - ni mor -

ta - li; se sco - po all' i - re d'un av - ver - so fa - to:

b. . . . [bitterness] of an adored one too ungrateful, among the deceptions of mortal life; if it is the purpose of the wrath of adverse fate [only to make me die] . . .

c.

Ti bas - ti, A-mor cru - de - le, cru - de - le, più non mi tor - men -

tar, più non mi tor - men - tar ch'io vuò mo - ri - re,

c. Enough, cruel Love; torment me no more.

middle sections of both arias end in the dominant minor, the general tendency of the modulations throughout is toward the subdominant. The mood of tender melancholy, the elegant melodic lines, and the refinement of the harmonic workmanship are thoroughly characteristic of Scarlatti. A more extroverted style, like that of the opera, with more diatonic harmony and more elaboration in the melody, occurs in the cantata *Poichè ad Irene* (*Since to Irene*) by the Bolognese composer Domenico Gabrieli (*ca.* 1650–90). In this work the tonal organization is particularly clear: opening recitative in A minor; da capo aria in the same key with the middle section in the dominant; recitative in E minor; aria in C, the relative major, with sharply contrasting middle part in E minor; and closing recitative and arioso in A minor.

Although most cantatas of the seventeenth century were written for a solo soprano voice with continuo, there were many vocal chamber music works for more than one voice and also some with ensemble accompaniments and ritornellos. The vocal chamber duet, corresponding to the instrumental trio sonata with two equal high voices over a figured bass, was a favored medium, one in which Steffani was especially renowned; the style of Steffani's duets was imitated by many later composers, including Bach and Handel.

A form midway between cantata and opera was the *serenata,* a semidramatic piece usually written for some special occasion, which frequently had allegorical texts and typically was performed by a small orchestra and several singers. Stradella was one of the first composers of serenatas; his example was followed by Scarlatti, Handel, and most other composers of the late seventeenth and eighteenth centuries.

Song in other countries

The Italian chamber cantata was imitated or adapted in other countries, though to a lesser extent than Italian opera. In France Marc-Antoine Charpentier (1634–1704), a pupil of Carissimi, composed both secular cantatas and sacred oratorios in the Italian style. Italian influence remained strong on most of the French cantata composers of the early eighteenth century; thus Louis Nicolas Clérambault (1676–1749), who published five books of cantatas between 1710 and 1726, alternated recitatives in the manner of Lully with arias in Italian style, sometimes even with Italian words. In France there was also a modest but steady production throughout the seventeenth century of *airs* of various types, some attaching to the older tradition of courtly vocal music and others of a more popular cast.

The situation in Germany was similar; Keiser, Telemann, and others in the early eighteenth century wrote cantatas on Italian as well as on German texts. Among the many seventeenth-century German composers of solo songs the most notable was Adam Krieger (1634–66) of Dresden, a pupil of Scheidt; his *Neue Arien*

(*New Airs*), published in 1667 and 1676, were for the most part strophic melodies in a charmingly simple popular style with short five-part orchestral ritornellos, though occasionally he approached the form of the cantata with through-composed texts in contrasting movements. The use of orchestral accompaniments and ritornellos with solo songs was more common in Germany than in other countries, and many German composers also wrote songs and arias on sacred texts. Toward the end of the seventeenth century in Germany the song as a type of independent composition practically disappeared, being absorbed into composite forms—the opera or the cantata. Occasional songs in collections around the turn of the century are similar in style, if not in form, to opera arias.

England was of all western European nations the most remote from Italian influence in the seventeenth century. There were some attempts to imitate the new monodic recitative during the Commonwealth, and after the Restoration English musicians became acquainted with the works of Carissimi and Stradella; but the best song productions of English composers owed little to foreign models. In this genre as in all others the outstanding composer was Henry Purcell. In addition to the many songs written as theatre music, he wrote a large number of vocal solos, duets, and trios, many of which were published in 1698 in a collection called *Orpheus Britannicus*. A similar collection of songs by John Blow was issued in 1700 under the title *Amphion Anglicus*. A specialty of English composers in this period was the *catch*, a round or canon to be sung by a convivial group unaccompanied; the texts often were humorous, with ribald or obscene allusions.

The situation in England toward the end of the seventeenth century encouraged the composition of large works for chorus, soloists, and orchestra on festive subjects suited to ceremonial or state occasions. Examples are the Odes of Purcell, especially the magnificent *Ode for St. Cecilia's Day* composed in 1692. These works were the direct ancestors of Handel's English oratorios.

Church Music and Oratorio

The separation, so characteristic of the Baroque era, between conservative or "strict" style and progressive or "free" style is nowhere more vividly illustrated than in the music of the Roman Catholic Church during the later seventeenth and early eighteenth centuries. Hundreds of Masses and other liturgical compositions were written in the manner of the Roman school of Palestrina, many of them employing the Renaissance techniques of parody and *cantus firmus*. Frequently such works included canons and other learned contrapuntal artifices; they were sung by unaccompanied voices, or

GMB,
NO. 271

with instruments merely doubling the vocal parts. Their composers for the most part were men like Scarlatti, who were equally at home with the up-to-date musical language of the opera and cantata. A famous late example of this conservative church music was the *Missa di San Carlo,* known also as the *Missa canonica,* of Johann Josef Fux (1660–1741), composed at Vienna in 1716, every movement of which is built on elaborate but strictly canonic development of original themes. Fux mentions in his dedicatory letter that he composed this Mass particularly to revive the "taste and dignity of ancient music." But works of the old a cappella type, though considerable in quantity and interesting because they reflect the continued vitality of the Palestrina tradition, are less important for the history of church music than compositions in more progressive style.

The musical resources new at the opening of the seventeenth century—solo singing, the basso continuo, multiple choirs, the *concertato* treatment of voices and instruments—were eagerly taken up by church composers, and on the basis of the works of Monteverdi, Carissimi, Schütz, and other masters of the early and middle Baroque a further change of style occurred in the late seventeenth and early eighteenth centuries. During this time three other

This engraving by Martin Engelbrecht (1684–1756) depicts a singer being accompanied on a chamber or choir organ (Positiv).

new influences increasingly affected church music: the spread of opera with its pictorial and dramatic inventions; the establishment of definite formal types of instrumental composition; and the stabilizing of the major-minor tonal system. Important developments for concerted church music must have taken place in Italy in the seventeenth century, but so little of the Italian music of this period is accessible that it is impossible to trace them with any assurance, and for a clearer picture we must look to the Catholic centers in southern Germany—Munich, Salzburg, and especially Vienna, the seat of the Imperial Chapel. The four Emperors who reigned there from 1637 to 1740 not only supported music financially, but further encouraged it by their own interest and actual participation as composers.

South German church music in this period was the product of a union of Italian and German characteristics, and sums up many of the principal stylistic achievements of the Baroque. The Mass and other liturgical texts were set to music on a magnificent festive scale with choruses and solo ensemble sections freely intermingled, supported by full orchestral accompaniment as well as orchestral preludes and ritornellos. Especially elaborate choruses were written for the *Amen* of the Gloria and Credo in the Mass. Sequential repetitions became a common constructive device within a clearly outlined harmonic major-minor system.

[margin note: Distinctive about Church music at Vienna — German y England]

Church composers who worked at Vienna include Johann Heinrich Schmelzer (*ca.* 1623–80), Johann Kaspar Kerll (1627–93), Antonio Draghi (1635–1700), and Marco Antonio Ziani (*ca.* 1653–1715), as well as Fux, who in addition to works like the *Missa canonica* also composed Masses and motets with orchestral accompaniment.

In the Masses of Antonio Caldara (1670–1736), perhaps a pupil of Legrenzi, there are not only solo or ensemble sections within predominantly choral movements but also independent, self-contained solo arias and duets with concertizing instruments and orchestral ritornellos; these Masses thus have somewhat the aspect of a series of separate musical numbers, like an opera—although the operatic recitative was never used in liturgical compositions, and the full da capo aria form appeared but seldom.

The excerpt from Caldara's *Stabat Mater* (Example X–7; more of this is printed in GMB, No. 273) illustrates the contrapuntal texture and general layout of this Viennese church music and also the conventional repertoire of chromatic chords and cross relations that were employed to suggest a text of mournful mood.

The originators of this peculiarly plaintive early eighteenth-century chromaticism, which of course affects the melody as well as the harmony, were Italian—the north Italian composers Legrenzi and

EXAMPLE X–7 *Stabat Mater,* Antonio Caldara

The sorrowful Mother stood weeping [at the Cross] . . . who grieved and suffered.

Lotti, and especially the Neapolitans, Scarlatti and the younger Giovanni Battista Pergolesi (1710–36). Pergolesi's *Stabat Mater*, written only ten years later than Caldara's, exemplifies the fragile texture, the admirably balanced phrasing, and the lyrically senti- mental tone of much Italian religious music of the eighteenth cen- tury. Italian style predominates in the music of Johann Adolf Hasse (1699–1783), a German who studied and lived many years in Italy and who in addition to some 100 operas also wrote many oratorios, Masses, and other church compositions. *Pergolesi and Hasse*

The oratorio, although on sacred subjects, had a poetic rather than a biblical text; moreover, it was not bound by the conventional limitations of purely liturgical music, being intended rather for performance in what might be called sacred concerts, and thus often serving as a substitute for opera during Lent or at other seasons when the theatres were closed. After Carissimi's time, the Latin oratorio with choruses was largely abandoned in favor of the *oratorio volgare* (that is, oratorio with Italian words). Practically all composers of Italian opera in the Baroque also wrote oratorios, and as a rule there was little if any difference in musical style between the two. The chorus was retained to a slight extent in the oratorio, but most of the oratorio music was written as solos and duets, as in opera. The close connection between the two forms is suggested by the fact that most of the oratorios in the Catholic centers of South Germany in this period were, like the operas, on Italian texts. An example is *Gioaz* by Benedetto Marcello, performed at Vienna in 1726. Hasse's *La conversione di Sant Agostino* (*The Conversion of St. Augustine*), composed at Dresden in 1750, is an example of the oratorio in operatic style with an overture, recitatives, and da capo arias with coloratura and cadenzas; the choruses are short and unimportant. *Oratorio and motet*

HAM, NO. 281

Church music in France, like French opera, developed somewhat differently from Italian and southern German sacred music. Caris- simi's disciple, M.-A. Charpentier, introduced the Latin oratorio into France in a style that assimilated both Italian and French ele- ments. Charpentier's oratorios and other church music are works of substantial value; however, they seem not to have been widely known in France, and Charpentier exerted little influence on sub- sequent composers. At the Royal Chapel of Louis XIV the motet, using a biblical text, was the form principally cultivated by the official composers. There are a large number of later seventeenth- century motets for solo voices with continuo, much in the style of the currently fashionable secular cantata, as well as more elaborate motets and similar works for soloists, double choruses, and full orchestra by such composers as Lully, Charpentier, and Henri Dumont (1610–84)—pompous, occasionally splendid, but lengthy and frequently rather monotonous compositions.

The favorite church composer of the early eighteenth century at Paris was Michel-Richard Delalande or de Lalande (1657–1726), some of whose motets for chorus and orchestra are worthy examples of the grand style in ecclesiastical music of this period. Another eminent name in this field is that of François Couperin (1668–1733); his *Leçons de ténèbres* (1714), on texts from the Offices of Matins and Lauds for Holy Week for one or two solo voices with accompaniment in a spare *concertato* style, are uniquely impressive works.

Anglican church music

HAM,
NO. 242

The principal forms of Anglican Church music after the Restoration were the same as those of the early part of the century, namely anthems and Services. Among the many English church composers, John Blow and Henry Purcell were outstanding. Since Charles II favored solo singing and orchestral accompaniments, many anthems of the verse type were produced, such as Pelham Humfrey's (1647–74) *O Lord my God*. Anthems for coronation ceremonies were, of course, especially elaborate works; examples are Purcell's *My heart is inditing* or the splendid coronation anthems of Blow. Not a few of the composers of English Restoration verse anthems descended to triviality in their efforts to mimic the attractions of theatre music. A more even level of musical excellence was maintained in the less pretentious "cathedral" or "full" anthems for chorus without soloists, of which Purcell's earlier four-part *Thou knowest, Lord, the secrets of our hearts* is a beautiful example. Some of the best of Purcell's sacred music is found in his settings of nonliturgical texts, pieces for one or more solo voices usually in a rhapsodic arioso style with continuo accompaniment, evidently designed for private devotional use.

HAM,
NO. 268

One of the last of the native English church composers in the Baroque tradition was William Croft (1678–1727), whose verse anthem *Put me not to rebuke* is a sincerely expressive work, typical of the early eighteenth century in its tonal organization and frequent use of sequential patterns.

Lutheran church music

After the ravages of the Thirty Years' War church establishments in the Lutheran territories of Germany were quickly restored. The Baroque era, particularly the period from 1650 to 1750, was the Golden Age of Lutheran music. Its development was affected by two conflicting tendencies within the church. The Orthodox party, holding to established dogma and public institutional forms of worship, favored using all available resources of choral and instrumental music in the services. Opposed to Orthodoxy was the widespread movement known as Pietism, which emphasized the freedom of the individual believer; Pietists distrusted formality and high art in worship, and preferred the expression of personal feelings of devotion in music of more simple character.

The common musical heritage of all Lutheran composers was the chorale, the congregational hymn which went back to the earliest days of the Reformation. A few notable additions to the number of chorales were the hymns of Paul Gerhardt (1607–76) written toward the middle of the seventeenth century. Many of Gerhardt's texts were set to music by Johann Crüger of Berlin (1598–1662). Crüger edited and published in 1647 a collection entitled *Praxis pietatis melica* (*Practice of Piety in Song*), which became the most influential Lutheran songbook of the second half of the seventeenth century. The songs of the *Praxis pietatis melica* and its many successors, including the important Freylinghausen collection of 1704, were not originally designed for congregational singing but rather for use in the home; only gradually did these new melodies make their way into the official hymnbooks in the eighteenth century. Meanwhile the growing practice of congregational singing of the chorales with organ accompaniment encouraged settings in cantional style, in which the older metrical irregularities of the melody were gradually smoothed into uniform movement in equal notes, with the close of each phrase marked by a fermata—in short, the type of chorale setting familiar from the works of J. S. Bach.

The enormous increase in production of devotional songs in the latter part of the seventeenth century was accompanied by a general decline in both poetic and musical quality. Many of the Pietistic texts expressed self-centered and sentimental religious attitudes in extravagantly emotional language, while attempts to give the music a simple folklike quality too often resulted only in mediocrity. Not until after 1700 did the opposing currents of Pietism and Orthodoxy arrive at a mutually beneficial union. In the meantime developments of importance took place in Orthodox centers where the environment was favorable and the material resources adequate for the maintenance of high artistic standards.

Three distinct musical-textual elements were involved in these developments: the concerted style, with biblical text, as established in Germany by Schein, Scheidt, Schütz, and other composers of the early and middle seventeenth century; the solo aria, with strophic non-biblical text; and the chorale, with its own text and the tune which, as *cantus firmus*, might be treated in various ways. Combinations of these elements resulted in three basic types of composition: 1) the "concerto-aria" cantata, consisting of arias only (or arias and choruses), treated in *concertato* style; 2) the "concerto-chorale" cantata, consisting of chorales only, treated in *concertato* style; and 3) the "chorale-aria" cantata, consisting of both chorales and arias, the former either in simple harmonic settings or in *concertato* style. The following few examples must suffice to show something of the wide range and variety of production in the late seventeenth and early eighteenth centuries.

Schütz's tradition of concerted music for chorus, solo voices, and orchestra without reference to chorale melodies may be illustrated

EXAMPLE X–8   Chorus from Cantata: *Wenn der Herr die Gefangenen zu Zion*, Matthias Weckmann

by a chorus, *Die mit Tränen säen* (They that sow in tears) from a larger work by his pupil the Hamburg organist Matthias Weckmann (1619–74). Weckmann's treatment of the words "They that sow in tears shall reap in joy" is typically Baroque in the contrast between the two opposite moods suggested by the text. (Example X–8; the entire chorus is given in GMB, No. 212.)

Concerted church music

Another example of the concerted style, but for a smaller performing group, is a setting of the chorale *Wachet auf* (*Wake, awake*) for solo voice, strings, and continuo by Franz Tunder (1614–67) of Lübeck (Example X–9; the chorale appears in HAM, No. 214).

EXAMPLE X–9   Cantata: *Wachet auf,* Franz Tunder

Awake! the voice calls to us, the voice of the watchers high up on the tower; awake, thou city of Jerusalem! Midnight is this hour; it calls to us with a clear voice: Where are ye, wise maidens?

More subjective in mood, and showing some influence of Pietist sentiment, were the influential *Dialogues between God and a Believing Soul* by Andreas Hammerschmidt (1612–75), published in 1645 (Example X–10; the entire piece appears in HAM, No. 213). This work is remarkable for the skillful use of a trombone obbligato in the tenor register.

EXAMPLE X–10   Dialogue: *Wende dich, Herr,* Andreas Hammerschmidt

sei mir gnä - - dig,

da - ran.

Alto: *Turn thee, O Lord, and be merciful unto me.*
Bass: *Is not Ephraim my dear son and my beloved child? Because I*
remember well [*what I have said to him*] . . .

One of the principal Lutheran composers of the late seventeenth century was Dietrich Buxtehude (*ca.* 1637–1707), Tunder's son-in-law and his successor at Lübeck. Although the majority of Buxtehude's works were of the free *concertato* type he also wrote *chorale variations,* a form in which each stanza of a chorale in turn serves as a basis for elaboration by voices and instruments. His *Wachet auf* is written this way; its form consists of a short festive instrumental prelude or *sinfonia,* the outline of which seems to have been suggested by the first two phrases of the chorale melody; a first stanza of the chorale for soprano voice and orchestra (strings, bassoon, continuo), in 3/2 and 4/4 time, each phrase slightly ornamented in the voice and the vocal phrases separated by brief orchestral interludes, the whole being considerably extended by repetition of the last half of the chorale tune; a second stanza, bass voice with orchestra, treated similarly to the first stanza, but in brisk 3/4 rhythm; a third stanza, for two sopranos and bass, in 3/2, which is more compact, with short points of imitation on several of the chorale phrases, and which broadens out at the end to a sonorous climax. All movements are in the same key, D major, so that contrast is achieved mainly through change of texture and rhythm.

Buxtehude composed much of his church music for the *Abendmusiken,* public concerts following the afternoon church services at Lübeck during the Advent season. These appear to have been quite long, varied, quasi-dramatic affairs, musically somewhat like a loosely organized oratorio, incorporating dialogues, arias, chorales, and polyphonic choruses as well as organ and orchestral music. The *Abendmusiken* attracted musicians from all over Germany. J. S.

Bach journeyed over two hundred miles on foot to hear them in the autumn of 1705.

The variation form, so common in the Baroque period, is frequently found in chorale-based concerted compositions of the late seventeenth century. When a chorale melody was not used, composers felt free to employ a more flexible arrangement, alternating short solo arioso sections with ensemble and choral parts. Toward the end of the century a somewhat standardized pattern of concerted church music developed, consisting of a "motet-like opening chorus on a Bible verse, a solo movement or movements (aria or arioso) . . . and a final chorus setting a stanza of a chorale."[1] Free *concertato* without chorale prevails in the vocal works of Johann Pachelbel (1653–1706), most famous of a long line of composers working at or in the vicinity of Nuremberg. Like many of the composers in southern Germany, where Venetian influence remained powerful, Pachelbel frequently wrote for double chorus.

Not all Lutheran church music used German texts. Local usage varied, but at most places parts of the service were still sung in Latin. Hence we have from many composers of this period settings of the Magnificat, the Te Deum, and other standard Latin texts, including the Mass (usually in its Lutheran short form: Kyrie and Gloria only), as well as motets both Latin and German.

Until the end of the seventeenth century the texts of Lutheran compositions had consisted chiefly of passages from the Bible or the church liturgy, together with verses taken from or modelled on chorales. In 1700, Erdmann Neumeister (1671–1756) of Hamburg, an Orthodox theologian but a poet of decidedly Pietist leanings, introduced a new kind of sacred poetry for musical setting, in a form which he designated by the Italian term "cantata." Neumeister (and, after him, several other Lutheran poets of the early eighteenth century) wrote cycles of cantatas, intended to be used systematically throughout the church year. The characteristic feature of these church cantatas was the employment, in connection with the prescribed Biblical passages or hymns, of original poetic insertions which sought to expound the given scriptural text and to bring its meaning home to the individual worshipper through devout meditations of a subjective character. Each of the added poetic texts was designed to be composed either as an arioso or else as an aria, usually in da capo form and frequently with an introductory recitative. Neumeister and his imitators favored the free fancy of the composer by writing their poetry in the so-called "madrigal" style, that is in lines of unequal length with the rhymes irregularly placed; many of Bach's cantata texts and the arias in the *St. Matthew Passion* are in this madrigal style.

The widespread acceptance of this new cantata type was of car-

The Lutheran church cantata

J.S. Bach

— What is it

KNOW 6 kinds
of Passion
1. Plainsong –
2. Polyphonic
Prevalent (over)
around late
Ren. Fearly Baroque

[1] Henry Woodward, *A Study of the Tenbury Manuscripts of Johann Pachelbel.* Harvard doctoral dissertation (Typescript), 29.

371

3. Chorale
   Homophonic
   Style.
4. Motet
5. Oratorio
6. Bleeding
   Passion

dinal importance for Lutheran church music. Its poetic scheme reconciled Orthodox and Pietistic tendencies in a satisfactory blend of objective and subjective, formal and emotional elements; its musical scheme incorporated all the great traditions of the past—the chorale, the solo song, the concerted style—and added to these the dramatically powerful elements of operatic recitative and aria. Strictly speaking, the designation "cantata" is applicable only to compositions of the sort described above; concerted church compositions of the seventeenth and early eighteenth centuries in Lutheran Germany usually had no particular designations (though terms like "Kantate," "Konzert," and "Geistliches Konzert" were applied to them in various instances). However, as in the case of the word "motet," a somewhat loose practice now exists of applying "cantata" indiscriminately to nearly all types of concerted Lutheran Church music of the Baroque period, both before and after Neumeister's innovations.

J. S. Bach was the greatest master of the church cantata. His most important immediate forerunners were Johann Philipp Krieger of Weissenfels, who also composed operas; Johann Kuhnau (1660–1722), Bach's predecessor at Leipzig; and Friedrich Wilhelm Zachow (1663–1712) of Halle. Zachow's cantatas have a great variety of forms: recitatives and da capo arias are interminged with choruses, which sometimes make use of chorale melodies. The writing for both solo and chorus is brilliant in sonority and strong in rhythm; instruments are prominently used in *concertato* fashion. His works point directly and unmistakably to the cantatas of Bach, with which they have many characteristics in common.

Among the contemporaries of Bach notable for their church compositions should be mentioned Christoph Graupner (1683–1760) of Darmstadt; Johann Mattheson (1681–1764) of Hamburg, who wrote Passions and oratorios, and was also important as a scholar and essayist; and Georg Philipp Telemann (1681–1767), who worked at Leipzig, Eisenach, Frankfurt, and Hamburg. Telemann's immense production included 40 operas, 12 complete cycles of cantatas and motets (about 3000 pieces altogether), 44 Passions, and a large number of oratorios and other church compositions as well as hundreds of orchestral and chamber works.

Among the forms of church music in Lutheran Germany was the
. *historia,* a musical setting based on some biblical narrative, for example the story of Christmas or of Easter. The most important type of *historia,* however, was the *Passion.* Plainsong settings of the Gospel accounts of the suffering and death of Christ had existed since early medieval times. After about the twelfth century it was customary to have the story recited in semidramatic form, with one priest singing the narrative portions, another the words of Christ, and a third the words of the crowd (*turba*), all with appropriate contrasts of range and tempo. (The Passion was still sung in this

The Passion

way in some Catholic churches up to quite recent times.) After the late fifteenth century, composers made polyphonic settings of the *turba* portions in motet style, contrasting with the plainsong solo parts; this type of setting was known as the "dramatic" or "scenic" Passion. Johann Walter adapted the dramatic Passion to Lutheran use with German text in his *St. Matthew Passion* of 1550, and his example was followed by many subsequent Lutheran composers, including Heinrich Schütz. Often, however, the entire text would be set as a series of polyphonic motets—called the *motet Passion*. Motet Passion settings were made by various Catholic composers from about the middle of the fifteenth century; the most celebrated Lutheran motet Passions were those of Joachim a Burck (1568), Leonhard Lechner (1594), and Christoph Demantius (1631).

The rise of the concerted style in the late seventeenth century led to a new type of Passion which approximated the form of the oratorio and hence is called the *oratorio Passion;* this setting employs recitatives, arias, ensembles, choruses, and instrumental pieces, all of which lend themselves to a dramatic presentation, as in opera. Schütz's *Seven Last Words* was an early approach to this kind of musical treatment, although its text is a composite of all four Gospels instead of being taken, as was customary in the Passion, from one Gospel exclusively.

In the second half of the seventeenth century the Gospel text was expanded by the addition of, first, poetic meditations on the events of the story, which were inserted at appropriate points and set to music usually as a solo aria, sometimes with a preceding recitative; and second, by chorales traditionally associated with the story of the Passion, which were usually sung by the choir or congregation.

Among late seventeenth-century settings of the Passion the best known are those by Johann Sebastiani (1622–83) and Johann Theile (1646–1724), dating respectively from 1672 and 1673. The former presents the Gospel narrative from St. Matthew in recitatives and choruses, with a few orchestral interludes and interspersed chorales for solo voice. Theile's Passion, likewise based on St. Matthew's Gospel, is similar in form though somewhat more ornate in treatment; instead of chorales, however, a few strophic airs are inserted. Both works have the customary brief introductory and closing choruses.

In the early years of the eighteenth century, under the influence of Pietism, a new kind of Passion text appeared with Hunold-Menantes' *The Bleeding and Dying Jesus* (1704), in which the Biblical narrative was freely paraphrased with crude realistic details and tortured symbolic interpretations in the taste of the time. In similar vein was the popular Passion text of B. H. Brockes (1712), which was set to music by Keiser, Telemann, Handel, Mattheson, and some fifteen other composers in the eighteenth century. Even J. S. Bach drew upon it for some aria texts in his *St. John Passion.*

XI

The Mature Baroque: Instrumental Music

Up to now instrumental music has been discussed on the basis of musical forms derived from compositional procedures: the ricercare and other fugal forms; the canzona and sonata; variations and other pieces based on a *cantus firmus;* dances and the suite; the toccata and related improvisatory forms. However, instrumental composition in the later seventeenth and early eighteenth centuries will be discussed on a different basis, namely, the medium of performance: music for a keyboard instrument (organ, harpsichord, or clavichord); and music for an ensemble of instruments, whether a small (chamber) group or one of larger size.

The principal types of compositions associated with each of these media are:

Keyboard: toccata (prelude, fantasia) and fugue; arrangements of Lutheran chorales or other liturgical material (chorale prelude, verset, etc.); variations; passacaglia and chaconne; suite; sonata (after 1700).

Ensemble: sonata (*sonata da chiesa*), sinfonia, and related forms; suite (*sonata da camera*) and related forms; concerto.

Keyboard Music

The Baroque organ

The Baroque organ is familiar to all present-day musicians from the many modern instruments that have been built in imitation of the organs of the Baroque era, especially those of Gottfried Silbermann (1683–1753), the most famous organ builder of the early

The Baroque organ in the Abbey Church at Marmoutier (Alsace) was begun by Andreas Silbermann in 1710 and finished by his nephew Johann Andreas in 1746.

eighteenth century. The Baroque organ retained the clarity and brilliance of the older instruments with their numerous mixtures, but achieved a milder, more homogeneous ensemble, and in addition offered better facilities for bringing any desired single voice of the texture into prominence. Thus it was able to do justice both to counterpoint and to accompanied melody, as might be required.

The greatest development of organ music took place in Germany during the late seventeenth and early eighteenth centuries. In the north, continuing the tradition established in the early part of the century by Sweelinck and Scheidt, the chief figures were Georg Böhm (1661–1733) at Lüneburg and Buxtehude at Lübeck. A central group in Saxony and Thuringia (the Bach region) included Zachow and Kuhnau, as well as Johann Christoph Bach (1642–1703) of Eisenach. One of the most notable of the German organ composers was Johann Pachelbel of Nuremberg. There were many other organists in the south (at Munich, Vienna, and other cities), but their contributions to the literature of the instrument were less imposing than those of their northern colleagues, because in the Catholic service the organ functioned mostly as an instrument of accompaniment.

Three principal species of organ compositions were cultivated in the late Baroque in northern Germany: the *toccata*, the *fugue*, and the *organ chorale*. Each of these designations stands for a general class of compositions, and, as usual in this period, the nomenclature is unstable.

The toccata

Touch piece

The toccata was originally and always remained essentially a style of music which aimed to suggest the effect of an improvised performance. To this end it used many devices: irregular or free rhythm in contrast with a propulsive unceasing drive of sixteenth-notes; phrases deliberately kept indistinct or wilfully irregular; sudden sharp changes of texture. But mostly the effect of improvisation was maintained by means of a contrived uncertainty in the harmonic flow of the music: by quick erratic changes of direction or (at the opposite extreme) a slow-paced movement involving long, harmonically inert stretches marked usually by extended pedal points. The naturally capricious, exuberant character of toccatas was often intensified by making them vehicles for displaying a performer's skill at the keyboard and on the organ pedals; the demand made for virtuosity in playing the pedals was a feature that especially distinguished the German composers from all other organ composers of the time.

Toccatas best exhibit the outthrusting, fantastic, dramatic aspects of the Baroque spirit in music. It was equally characteristic of the Baroque, however, to discipline the freedom of the toccata, and in the most drastic manner, by yoking it with the ricercare in a union of musical opposites. Composers early began to incorporate in their toccatas well-defined sections of imitative counterpoint which contrasted with the otherwise prevailing rhapsodic style. These contrasting sections were especially necessary in long toccatas. Moreover, the desire for clearly articulated and symmetrical phrases became stronger as the seventeenth century wore on; and even in short toccatas without fugal interludes some measure of order was brought into the rhapsodic flow of sound by means of the two most common crystallizing devices of late Baroque music, the melodic sequence and sequential imitation. The Toccata in E minor by Pachelbel is a good example of this usage.

MM, NO. 37

Works which illustrate on a grand scale the Baroque conflict between impulse and order are the monumental organ compositions of the north German masters of the seventeenth century, above all those by Buxtehude. Buxtehude's toccatas are made up of sections in free style which alternate regularly with as long or longer sections of imitative counterpoint. They have a wonderful sense of movement and climax, with great variety in the figuration, and they take full advantage of the idiomatic qualities of the organ. Yet the soaring fantasy of the composer is held in balance by the architectural plan of the whole work. The opening is always in free improvisatory style, ending with a solid cadence; then follows a fugue, on a subject of salient melodic outline and with well-marked rhythm, fully developed in counterpoint; this merges at length gradually into a second toccata-like section, shorter than the first, and again leading to a cadence. At this point the composition may close; but as a rule Buxtehude goes on to a second and sometimes a third fugue, with brief interludes and a closing climactic section in toccata style. When there is more than one fugue, the subjects in the majority of cases are variants of a basic musical idea (see Example XI–1, the three fugue subjects from the toccata printed in HAM, No. 234). This use of the variation principle in a fugal type of composition is derived from the early seventeenth-century keyboard fantasies of Sweelinck and Scheidt, as well as from the variation canzona of Frescobaldi and the toccatas of Froberger.

Keyboard pieces like the one described above were called in the seventeenth century "toccata," "prelude," or some similar name, even though they included fugal sections. The simple coupling of two contrasted movements, a prelude in free or homophonic style and a fugue in contrapuntal style, is found only in the late Baroque; most seventeenth-century compositions called "Prelude and Fugue"

EXAMPLE XI–1   Varied Forms of a Fugal Subject, Dietrich Buxtehude by later editors show a relationship to the simpler Buxtehude type of toccata, that is, a toccata with one comparatively long fugal section in the middle.

The fugue

Fugues were also written as independent pieces. By the end of the seventeenth century the fugue had almost entirely replaced the old ricercare. The essential differences between the two are apparent in late seventeenth-century works (HAM, No. 249a–b) by Johann Krieger (1652–1735). The fugue subject has a more definite melodic character and a livelier rhythm than the ricercare subject; the ricercare develops in a placid, abstract manner without much variety or any marked climax, but the fugue drives ahead energetically to its close; the fugue has some short episodes (passages where the subject is not being heard in any voice) which are set off by a little lightening of the texture and sometimes also by the use of sequences; whereas the ricercare has fewer such passages and those few not sequential nor in any way different in texture from the rest of the piece. Moreover, the fugue has a tonal organization with a clear dominant-tonic relationship, while the conservative ricercare tends to stay closer to the old modal system.

Neither the fugues of Krieger, however, nor the ninety-four short fugues which Pachelbel wrote for use in the church service as preludes to the singing of the Magnificat give much more than a hint of the potentialities that were realized in the next generation. The final perfection of the fugue, as well as of all the other large musical forms characteristic of the late Baroque, was inseparable from the full development of the major-minor system of tonality with its hierarchy of keys, which made possible a systematic use of key relationships in the musical design of long movements.

Equal temperament

Corollary to this development was the gradual extension of the system of *equal temperament* to the tuning of keyboard instruments. In this tuning, the octave is divided into twelve exactly equal semitones, so that an instrument sounds equally in tune in any one of the twelve keys. Formulated by many theorists after the early sixteenth century, and apparently in actual use for lutes, viols, and other fretted instruments during the sixteenth and seventeenth centuries, the system or some practical approximation to it began to be generally applied to keyboard instruments on the Continent by the early years of the eighteenth century. J. K. F. Fischer's (*ca.* 1665–1746) *Ariadne musica* of 1715, a collection of keyboard preludes and fugues using nineteen different major and minor keys, was the principal forerunner of Bach's *Well-Tempered Clavier* (Book I, 1722), which uses all twenty-four keys.

Chorale compositions

The other principal class of organ composition of the late seventeenth and early eighteenth centuries comprises works based on a chorale melody. Organ composers in the seventeenth century used the chorale in three fundamental ways: as a theme for variations, as a subject for a fantasia, or as a melody to be presented with appropriate embellishment and accompaniment. These three ways of treating a chorale melody gave rise to three distinct types of composition: the *chorale partita,* the *chorale fantasia,* and the *chorale prelude.* The chorale partita, a set of variations on a chorale tune, was initiated early in the century by Sweelinck and Scheidt, and was continued, although with modifications in the technique, by later organ composers to the time of Bach and after. The chorale fantasia, also dating from the early part of the century, gradually moved away from the severe contrapuntal style of the fantasias of Scheidt. At the hands of Reinken, Buxtehude, and other north German composers, the form became extended. The treatment of the material became freer; each phrase of the chorale was worked out in turn and a great variety of figuration and texture was introduced, always with emphasis on brilliant virtuoso effects.

· Chorale prelude, a term often loosely applied to any organ composition based on a chorale melody, will be used here in a somewhat more restricted sense to denote relatively short pieces in which the entire melody is presented once in readily recognizable form. This form of the chorale prelude did not appear until after the middle of the seventeenth century. As the name implies, such pieces probably originated as functional liturgical music: the organist played through the tune, with accompaniment and ornaments *ad libitum,* as a prelude to the singing of the chorale by the congregation or choir; later on, when pieces in this same general style were written down, they were called "chorale preludes" whether or not they were intended to serve the original liturgical purpose. Naturally, many varieties of treatment are found: (1) Each phrase of the melody in turn may serve as the subject of a short fugal development, the whole piece thus taking on the form of a chain of fughettas. This form has an obvious resemblance to the chorale fantasia, but is more concise and more consistent in style. (2) In one particular type of chorale prelude, chiefly associated with the name of Pachelbel, the first phrase receives a fairly extended fugal treatment, after which this and all the following phrases in turn appear, usually in the top voice, in long notes with relatively little ornamentation; each such appearance is preceded by a short anticipatory imitative development of its characteristic melodic motive in short notes (that is, in diminution) in the other voices. Sometimes the opening fugal development is shortened and the first phrase introduced in the same manner as the ones following. (3) More numerous are chorale preludes in which the relation between melody and accompaniment is less exact. The accompaniment, while still borrowing many of its motives from the chorale tune, is treated much more freely and with greater variety from phrase to phrase; the melody, which usually begins at once without any introductory imitative material, is ornamented in an

The chorale prelude

379

imaginative, unstereotyped manner, and sometimes extended in a long melismatic phrase at the final cadence. The masters of this subjective and often highly poetic form of the chorale prelude were Buxtehude and Georg Böhm. (4) Finally, there are chorale preludes in which the melody, usually unornamented, is accompanied, in one or more of the lower voices, by a continuous rhythmic figure not related motivically to the melody itself. This type is not common in the seventeenth century, but is often found in Bach.

Organ music in the Catholic countries

The South German and Italian organists were not attracted by the austere mystic grandeur of the northern toccatas and fugues. Most organ music in the Catholic countries is in the forms of the ricercare, the variation canzona, *cantus firmus* pieces based on Catholic liturgical melodies (corresponding thus to the Protestant chorale preludes), and the early seventeenth-century type of toccata with only incidental episodes of counterpoint.

A notable Spanish organist of the Baroque was Juan Bautista José Cabanilles (1644–1712), composer of many *tientos* (that is, imitative *ricercari*), passacaglias, toccatas, and other works. Some of his tientos are in a chromatic idiom similar to Frescobaldi's *ricercari,* but there is a wide variety of forms and styles, from the severe ricercare to sectional pieces with the light texture and easy rhythmic grace of the eighteenth-century keyboard sonata. In general, the organ music of the southern countries, whether for the church service or for other purposes, was more graceful in manner and less weighty in content than that of the north.

A distinctive French Baroque school of organ music produced some attractive settings of popular airs and pieces resembling the overtures and expressive recitatives of French opera, as well as more learned, contrapuntal works and antiphonal "dialogues" for the three or four divisions of a large organ. This music has the typically French ornaments (*agréments*); many pieces were designed to exploit particular color possibilities on the organ, and the stops were often specified. Among the finest French organ music of this age are the "Masses" (versets and interludes to be played in the Mass) of François Couperin, which include specimens of all the distinctive types mentioned above. Couperin's noble organ music is one of the glories of the Baroque era in France, as was Buxtehude's in Germany.

Passacaglia and chaconne

The passacaglia or chaconne was another common form of composition in the late Baroque. In general it retained the same characteristics as in the early part of the seventeenth century: it basis was a simple four- or eight-measure harmonic pattern indefinitely repeated; on this rigid framework the composer exercised his ingenuity to provide continuity, variety, and a sense of progression to climax in the movement as a whole. Some passacaglias had a definite recurring bass melody; more often, however, the only recurring factor was the harmonic pattern, which itself might be somewhat varied in detail although it regularly preserved the original four- or eight-measure phrasing with periodic cadences.

The characteristic rhythm of the passacaglia and chaconne is a stately movement in triple meter. Both the chaconne and the related form of the ground or ground bass (in which there is a repeated bass melodic pattern as well as a repeated harmonic pattern) were applied not only to keyboard music but to instrumental and vocal ensemble works as well. All sorts of refinements of the basic scheme were possible. The *Passacaille ou Chaconne* from Couperin's first Suite for Viols (1728) maintains for 199 measures the regular 4 + 4-measure phrasing with only an occasional slight shortening or lengthening at cadences, but with numerous variations and alterations in the pattern (see Example XI–2). In one ground by Purcell the bass has a three-measure formula while the upper voices are so arranged that their phrase articulations always occur one measure later than those of the bass.

The term *clavier* (i.e. keyboard) is used to denote both the clavichord and the harpsichord. It is not always possible in the Baroque period, especially in Germany, to tell which of the two a composer intends in a given piece; sometimes it is even uncertain whether a clavier or an organ is the desired instrument. Though all the types of composition described in the preceding section were also used in clavier music, the two important forms of clavier music were the *theme and variations* and the *suite*.

Clavier music
Synonymous to all keyboard instruments

As has already been mentioned, variation of a given musical subject was one of the most widely used techniques in Baroque composition. This basic arrangement of a theme (air, dance, chorale, or the like) followed by a series of variations goes back to the early history of instrumental music. No essential change occurred in the late Baroque, although there was a tendency to abandon the earlier *cantus firmus* type of variation, except in chorale partitas. Many composers after 1650 preferred to write an original song-like melody (often called an *aria*) for the theme rather than borrow a familiar tune as earlier composers had commonly done.

Theme and variations

A large proportion of the clavier music of the late seventeenth and early eighteenth centuries is in the form of the *suite*. Two distinct varieties existed. In France, the *ordres* of François Couperin published between 1713 and 1730 consist each of a loose aggregation of many—sometimes as many as 20 or more—miniature pieces. Most of these are in dance rhythms, such as courante, sarabande, gigue, and so on, highly stylized and refined. Their transparent texture and delicate melodic lines decorated with many embellishments, as well as their conciseness and humor, are typical of French music of the time of the Regency. Most of them carry fanciful titles— *L'Engageante, Le Carillon de Cithère, Les Baricades Mistérieuses,*

The suite

EXAMPLE XI–2   *Passacaille ou Chaconne* from Suite No. 1 for Viols,
François Couperin

The lower line of music is for the second viol, together with the harpsichord realizing the basso continuo. In his two suites for "basse de viole," Couperin did not use the agrément signs that were typical of music for that instrument; instead he notated the agréments in the same manner as for his Pièces de clavecin. According to his Explication, they are to be interpreted as follows:

	pincé - simple	
	tremblement	
	port de voix pincé - simple	
	port de voix tremblement	
	aspiration	

Since each ornament begins on the beat and takes its time value from the note to which it is attached, the upper line of parts a and b of this example would be played approximately as follows:

The dotted sixteenths in part c should be slightly over-dotted, but not to the full extent of a double dot.

Les Gondoles de Délos, and the like—titles which seem to have only a tenuous connection with the music, but which in themselves are suggestive of the spirit of the age.

Couperin was the author of one of the most important practical musical treatises of the eighteenth century, *L'Art de toucher le clavecin* (*The Art of Playing the Clavecin*), published in 1716; among other matters Couperin gives precise instructions for fingering and for execution of the *agréments*. Both Couperin's music and his treatise had considerable influence on the keyboard style of J. S. Bach.

In Germany before the end of the seventeenth century the clavier suite (or *partita,* as it was also called) had assumed a definite order of four dances: allemande, courante, sarabande, and gigue. To these might be added an introductory movement or one or more optional dances placed either after the gigue or before or after the sarabande. The added dances as well as the general style of the writing reveal a continuing French influence on German clavier composers of this period, an influence equally evident in the clavier suites of contemporary Belgian composers. The dances of a partita, each distinguished by its characteristic rhythm and tempo, were all in the same key and cast in the same formal mould: a first section, modulating to the dominant (or relative major) and ending with a full cadence in the new key; a second section, usually somewhat longer than the first, beginning in the dominant (or relative major) and modulating through one or two closely related keys back to the tonic. Each section was to be repeated. Sometimes the closing measures of the second section would be a (transposed) recapitulation of those of the first section. This feature, but even more the standard modulation scheme of the dances, foreshadows the sonata-form of the Classical period.

The most important composers of the German keyboard suite, besides Froberger, were Pachelbel, Alessandro Poglietti (an Italian residing in Vienna; d. 1683), Johann Krieger, J. K. F. Fischer, Johann Kuhnau, and Georg Böhm. A contemporary of Bach and Handel was Gottlieb (= Theophil) Muffat (1690–1770), whose suites are examples of the pre-Classical style of the eighteenth century. In England, the charming harpsichord suites of Henry Purcell are the only notable representatives of this form.

Of the four standard dance movements, the allemande is usually in a moderately fast duple meter; it begins with a short upbeat, and presents a smooth continuous movement of eighth- or sixteenth-notes in which all the voices participate. The typical courante, which especially in older suites is thematically related to the allemande, is in moderate 6/4 time with the rhythmic figure ♩. ♪ ♩ ♩ ♩. ♪; often at cadences the last one or two measures of 6/4 are transformed in effect into measures of 3/2 by a shift of the accent. Sometimes the French courante is replaced by, or modified in the direction of, the Italian *corrente,* a faster dance in 3/4 time with more homophonic texture. The sarabande is a slow movement in 3/2 or 3/4 meter, often with the rhythmic pattern ♩ ♩. ♩ │ ♩ 𝅝 or ♩ ♩ ♩ │ ♩. ♪ ♩ , and generally in a more homophonic style than the allemande and courante. Sometimes the sarabande is followed by a *double,* that is, an ornamental variation of the original dance. The gigue, the finale of the suite, is sometimes in 4/4 time with dotted rhythm, but later more often in 12/8 (or 6/8, sometimes 3/8 or 3/4), with wide melodic skips and continuous lively movement of triplets. Quite often it is in fugal or quasi-fugal style; the second section may have the same subject as the first, but inverted. Italian suites, and suites influenced by Italian style, usually have a simpler and lighter texture and the dances depart in many ways from the German dances. The *ordres* of Couperin have many movements in rondeau form, in which one recurring theme alternates with different episodes or *couplets.*

Still another type of clavier suite, consisting of a number of French dances in no consistent order, was imitated from the orchestral ballet suites of the late seventeenth century. The international character of the late Baroque suite is strikingly demonstrated by the national origins of the dance movements: the allemande is probably German, the courante French, the sarabande Spanish (imported from Mexico), and the gigue Anglo-Irish.

The suite is represented in Germany by two composers who also produced notable compositions for the lute in the Baroque period: Esajas Reusner (1636–1679) and Silvius Leopold Weiss (1686–1750).

The sonata, which in the Baroque period was primarily a type of composition for instrumental ensemble, was first transferred to the clavier by Kuhnau in 1692. His *Frische Klavierfrüchte (Fresh Clavier-fruits),* published in 1696, consists entirely of sonatas. More interesting than these rather experimental pieces are the six sonatas Kuhnau published in 1700, which represent in music stories from the Old Testament, with titles such as "Saul's Madness Cured by Music," "The Combat between David and Goliath," or "Hezekiah's Illness and Recovery." These Biblical sonatas are attractive and well-constructed pieces, as well as amusing musical renditions of the stories. Instrumental program music was not unknown to the seventeenth and early eighteenth centuries; there are examples in the Fitzwilliam Virginal Book, as well as numerous battle pieces scattered among the works of keyboard composers of the period. Heinrich Ignaz Franz Biber (1644–1704) also wrote Biblical sonatas, for violin and continuo; and the picturesque titles of Couperin's keyboard and orchestral works are part of this tradition.

The keyboard sonata

Ensemble Music

By the beginning of the eighteenth century Italian musical pre-eminence had been challenged by the achievements of the French clavecinists and the north German organists; but in the realm of instrumental chamber music, as in the opera and cantata, the Italians reigned as undisputed masters and teachers of Europe. The age of the great violin makers of Cremona—Niccolò Amati (1596–1684), Antonio Stradivari (1644–1737), and Giuseppe Bartolomeo Guarneri (1698–1744)—was also the age of great string music in Italy.

Violin made of maple, pine, and ebony by Antonio Stradivari (1644–1737) of Cremona. (Courtesy Metropolitan Museum of Art, Bequest of Annie Bolton Matthews Bryant, 1934)

The ensemble sonata

The word "sonata" appears fairly regularly on the title pages of Italian musical publications throughout the seventeenth century. In the earlier decades the term (like the parallel word, *sinfonia*) chiefly denoted instrumental preludes or interludes in predominantly vocal works; after 1630, though the earlier usage continued, *sonata* and *sinfonia* were used more and more often to designate separate instrumental compositions. The early stages of the emergence of the sonata from the canzona have been sketched in Chapter IX.

In the most general sense, the independent instrumental sonata of the Baroque period is a composition for a small group of instruments —usually two to four—having a basso continuo and consisting of several sections or movements in contrasting tempos and textures. Within this general scheme, of course, there may be any amount of diversity. Two main types or classes of sonatas begin to be clearly distinguished after about 1660: the *sonata da chiesa* (the church sonata, usually designated simply as "sonata"), the movements of which are not obviously in dance rhythms and do not bear the names of dances; and the *sonata da camera* (chamber sonata), which is a suite of stylized dances. So goes the definition, but in practice the two types do not always appear unmixed: many church sonatas end with one or more dance movements (not always so designated), while many chamber sonatas have an opening movement which is not a dance. The most common instrumentation after 1670 for both church and chamber sonatas is two treble instruments (usually violins) and bass, the harmonies to be completed by the continuo player. A sonata written in this way is called a *trio sonata*, even though for performance it requires four players (since the basso continuo line is doubled on a violoncello or similar instrument while the harpsichordist or organist fills in the implied harmonies). The texture exemplified in the trio sonata—two high melody lines over a bass—appears frequently in many other types of Baroque music, and persists even beyond the Baroque era.

Less numerous than trio sonatas in the seventeenth century, although more numerous after 1700, are sonatas for solo violin (or flute or gamba) with continuo (the so-called *solo sonata*). Larger groups, up to six or eight instrumental parts with continuo, are also used in the Baroque, and there are a few sonatas (or like pieces under a different designation) for a single stringed instrument without accompaniment.

The nomenclature, especially for works of the chamber sonata type, was fearfully and wonderfully various: sometimes the general title of a collection of these works was simply a list of names of the dances, or such a list followed by the words "da camera"; other titles were trattanimento, divertimento, concertino, concerto, ballo, balletto, and so on. Apparently no particular distinction as to musical forms and types was implied by these different titles. Furthermore, some composers in the second half of the seventeenth century used the word "sonata" or "sinfonia" to designate the introductory movement or movements of a suite of dance pieces.

With respect to its external form, the evolution of the canzonasonata in the seventeenth century may be summarized as a progressive reduction in the number of movements and a progressive increase in the length of each movement. The order of the movements did not become standard until toward the end of the seventeenth century. Traces of the cyclical plan of the old variation-canzona survived for a long time. Thus in one sonata for six instruments by Legrenzi, first published at Venice in 1663, there are three principal movements: (1) an Allegro in contrapuntal style, beginning somewhat like a canzona theme but going at once into the vigorously rhythmic instrumental style characteristic of the late Baroque; (2) a homophonic middle movement in fairly fast 3/2 (6/4) time, featuring interplay between two groups of instruments; and (3) a final Allegro, resembling in rhythm and general melodic outline the first Allegro, in quasi-contrapuntal texture but again contrasting the two instrumental groups, which are brought together for the final climax. The three movements are connected by brief adagio interludes in chordal style. Thematic similarity between movements is preserved in many sonatas of Giovanni Battista Vitali (*ca.* 1644–92), and survives in

HAM, NO. 220

some works of his son Tommaso Antonio Vitali (*ca.* 1665–1747). On the other hand, complete thematic independence of the various movements became increasingly the rule in the late seventeenth century.

The most important school of Italian chamber music in this period centered about the church of San Petronio in Bologna, where Maurizio Cazzati (*ca.* 1620–77), was director of music from 1657 to 1671. A sonata for solo violin and continuo by Cazzati, published in 1670, has the following order of movements: (1) Allegro, 12/8, *alla giga* (with the strange tempo mark *Largo e vivace*), in imitative style; (2) Grave, 4/4 ($\downarrow$. = $\downarrow$), constructed by close canonic imitation at the fifth and fourth; (3) Presto, 4/4 ($\downarrow$ = $\downarrow$), a strongly rhythmic theme treated in imitation; and (4) Prestissimo, 3/8 ($\downarrow$ = $\downarrow$.), likewise imitative but with a looser texture than the preceding movements, and broadening at the final cadence. A vague resemblance may be discerned among the themes of the four movements. Cazzati, unlike earlier Italian and contemporary German composers of solo sonatas, avoids showing off the player's technique or using any special trick effects on the violin; his restraint and serious approach are characteristic of the entire Bologna school.

In a more assured style, and with more contrast of texture between movements, is a trio sonata of 1669 by Cazzati's pupil, G. B. Vitali. The vigorous imitative opening Vivace in A minor is completed by a short homophonic coda (likewise marked Vivace); the ensuing Largo is a lyrical movement in sarabande rhythm with a broad hemiola cadence to the dominant E major; the final Vivace, beginning in C major but returning to A minor, is remarkable for the expertly handled close contrapuntal texture of the two violin parts. Vitali was one of the leaders in the restoration of counterpoint in the late seventeenth century; his *Artificii musicali* of 1689 is a veritable arsenal of canons and other musical experiments. Another Bolognese composer was Giovanni Battista Bassani (*ca.* 1657–1716), whose sonatas have many traits in common with those of Corelli.

It is significant that the trio sonata, not the solo sonata, was especially favored by Italian composers of the seventeenth century. The instrumentation of the trio sonata made possible an ideal balance of lyrical melody and limpid polyphony. The two high singing violins could interweave their contrapuntal patterns (in which the distant bass as well might join), but the texture, held together by the unobtrusive harmonies of the harpsichord, was sufficiently open so that there was no danger of obscuring the lines or making the sonority too thick. Also, the solo sonata was always prone to excesses of virtuosic display; but the trio sonata subordinated the individual to the ensemble in a regulated disposition of forces which directed attention to the substance rather than to the outward show of the music.

Italian chamber music

HAM, NO. 219

HAM, NO. 245

The perfect examples of the serene, classical phase of Baroque musical art are the violin sonatas of Arcangelo Corelli (1653–1713). Corelli was famous both as a composer and a performer. He studied four years at Bologna, and thoroughly assimilated the spirit of the Bolognese masters; most of his life after 1671 was passed tranquilly at Rome. His works were:

Arcangelo Corelli

Opus 1. Twelve trio sonatas (*sonate da chiesa*), first published in 1681.

Opus 2. Eleven trio *sonate da camera* and a chaconne, 1685.

Opus 3. Twelve trio sonatas, 1689.

Opus 4. Twelve trio *sonate da camera,* 1695.

Opus 5. Twelve solo sonatas (six *da chiesa,* five *da camera,* and one set of variations), 1700.

Opus 6. Twelve *concerti grossi,* published in 1714 but undoubtedly composed before 1700, some probably as early as 1682.

In his trio sonatas Corelli summed up the achievements of Italian chamber music in the late seventeenth century; in his solo sonatas and concertos he initiated developments that were followed for the next fifty years and more. He was exceptional among Italian composers of his time in that he apparently wrote no vocal music whatever; he transferred the national genius for song to the violin, the instrument that most nearly approaches the expressive lyric quality of the human voice. As if acknowledging this affinity, Corelli subjects the violins in his trio sonatas to deliberate technical limitations: nowhere does a player have to go beyond the third position, nor are the extreme low notes of the instrument much used; fast runs and difficult double stops are also avoided. The two violins are treated exactly alike, and the melodic lines are constantly crossing and interchanging. Suspensions, as effective with violins as with voices, are a constant feature, especially in slow movements, where they often occur in a series or chain, one on every strong beat for many measures in succession.

Corelli's trio sonatas

A fundamental technical device in all of Corelli's music is the sequence. It is no coincidence that Corelli, the first major Baroque composer to make extensive and systematic use of this means of construction, was also the first to write music in which we hear the full realization of the major-minor tonality practically free from any trace of modality. The sequence, whether carried out diatonically within one key or modulated downward in the circle of fifths, is one of the most powerful agents in establishing tonality. Corelli's modulations within a movement—most often to the dominant and (in minor keys) the relative major—are always logical and clear; he established the principles of tonal architecture which were elaborated and extended by Handel, Vivaldi, Bach, and all other composers of the next generation. Corelli's music is almost completely diatonic; chromaticism is limited virtually to a few diminished sevenths or an occasional flatted second (Neapolitan sixth) at a cadence.

Many of Corelli's trio church sonatas consist of four movements in the order slow–fast–slow–fast, analogous to the order of the four movements in the cantata of this period. The same order of movements was often used by other composers of the late seventeenth and early eighteenth centuries, so that some music historians regard it as "the" type of Baroque sonata—an over-simplified view, as there are so many exceptions to the general rule. Corelli's chamber sonatas, both trio and solo, usually begin with a *preludio,* which is followed by two or three of the conventional dances of the suite in the normal order; but the final gigue may be replaced by a gavotte.

It is typical of the seventeenth century that in the majority of Corelli's trio sonatas, all movements are in the same key. This is not true of his later works: all the solo sonatas that are in major keys (eight out of eleven) have one slow movement in the relative minor, and all the *concerti grossi* have a slow movement in a contrasting key. In general, movements are thematically independent, although rare instances occur of thematic similarity (such as the two slow movements of the trio sonata Opus 3, No. 7). There are no contrasting or "secondary" themes within a movement. The subject of the whole musical discourse to come is stated at once in a complete sentence with a definite cadence; from then on the music unfolds in a continuous expansion of this subject, with sequential treatment, brief modulations cadencing in nearby keys, and fascinating subtleties of phraseology. This steady unfolding or "spinning out" (the Germans call it *Fortspinnung*) of a single theme is highly characteristic of the late Baroque. It is not the same as the later Classical development of motives from a theme, but rather involves an unbroken and unconstrained flow of musical thoughts that seem to be generated spontaneously out of the original idea. Corelli sometimes combines this method with repetition of some preceding material, but his sonatas never have anything like the full recapitulation of the Classical sonata. Very often the last phrase of a movement will be stated twice, as though to avoid a too abrupt leavetaking. A favorite rhythmic device in triple meter is the hemiola cadence.

Two principal types of movements are found in Corelli's trio sonatas. The first is contrapuntal, in one section which is not repeated, with highly irregular phrase lengths. In slow tempo, this type is found mostly in the first movement of both the church sonatas and the chamber sonatas. The first Allegro of the church sonatas, and quite often the Allemande in the chamber sonatas, are in free fugal style, with the bass participating as a third contrapuntal line. This movement, the musical center of gravity of the Baroque church sonata, is the one which most obviously retains traits of the canzona, both in the use of imitative style and in the rhythmic character of

MM, NO. 39

the subject itself; in some sonatas (for instance, some of Purcell's) a movement like this is actually called "canzona." The second type of movement is homophonic, in two repeated sections and with somewhat more regular phraseology; it occurs most frequently in the dances of the chamber sonatas.

The terms "contrapuntal" and "homophonic" must be understood in a relative sense. Corelli's musical thinking, like that of all composers of his time, was essentially contrapuntal, but contrapuntal within a tonal harmonic framework that is clearly defined by the basso continuo. Thus the two manners of writing which we distinguish as contrapuntal and homophonic are combined in his work. Moreover, the theoretical distinction between church sonata and chamber sonata is not wholly valid in Corelli. For example, the third movement of a church sonata often is a lyrical cantilena in the rhythm of a sarabande, and the vivacious finale is very often a gigue in imitative style with two repeated sections; conversely, the serious character as well as the outward forms of the church sonata prevail in the first two movements of many of Corelli's chamber sonatas. In the first two movements of many of the latter we can detect a resemblance to the French overture: a slow introduction with persistent dotted rhythm followed by an imitative canzona-like Allegro. This combination of a slow introduction and fugal Allegro followed by a series of dances was common in the late Baroque.

Corelli's solo sonatas have the same order and character of movements as the corresponding types of trio sonatas, though in his solo sonatas an additional fast movement of contrasting texture is always coupled with one or the other of the regular two. Moreover, in the first Allegro, the three-part sonority of the trio sonata is simulated by the rich texture of the solo violin part, abounding in double stops. Naturally, the solo sonatas have a larger proportion of homophonic movements than do the trio sonatas. Corelli's most conspicuous innovation, however, is the technical treatment of the violin. Although the third position is never exceeded, there are difficult double and triple stops, fast runs, arpeggios, cadenzas, and étude-like movements in *moto perpetuo*.

Corelli's solo sonatas

All in all, these solo sonatas give us a comprehensive idea of what Corelli expected in the way of technique from his students. His teaching was the foundation of most of the violin schools of the eighteenth century; it was as influential on later generations of players as his music was on later generations of composers. Some of his contemporaries and many of his followers surpassed him in *bravura,* but none in the understanding of the *cantabile* qualities of his instrument nor in the good taste with which he avoided mere displays of virtuosity unjustified by musical content. His most difficult (at least as far as bowing technique is concerned) as well as his most enduringly popular composition is the masterly set of 24 variations which concludes his Opus 5. The theme is the *Follia* (or *Folia*, known also as *les Folies d'Espagne* and by other titles), a well-known tune of probably Portuguese origin dating from the early sixteenth century, with a bass similar to that of the romanesca (see Example IX–2), and like the romanesca a favorite subject for variations in the seventeenth century.

Performers in the Baroque era were always expected to add notes to those the composer had written. The realization of a figured bass, for example, was worked out by the player. Vocal and instrumental solo melodic lines were dependent on performers' skill, taste, and experience for their proper completion by means of ornaments. The practice in both these matters varied from country to country and from time to time, so that the restoration by modern scholars of all these vanished traditions of performance is a complex and delicate operation.

Improvisation in Baroque musical performance

Melodic ornamentation has a long history going back to the Middle Ages. Ornaments probably always originated in improvisation; and although they might at some later stage be partially or wholly written out, or else indicated by special signs (as in Example XI–2), still they always kept a certain coloring of spontaneity. For us, the word *ornamentation* is liable to carry misleading connotations, to suggest something unessential, superfluous, a mere optional adjunct to the melody. This was not the Baroque view. The ornaments were not merely decorative; they had a definite expressive function as means of conveying affections. Moreover, some of the more common ornaments—especially the trill and the appoggiatura —incidentally added a spice of dissonance, of which the notated version of the music gives no hint.

In general, there were two ways of ornamenting a given melodic line: (1) small melodic formulas (such as trills, turns, appoggiaturas, mordents) attached to one or two of the written notes. These were sometimes, though not always, indicated by special signs; and (2) longer ornaments, which included the smaller formulas and also scales, runs, leaps, arpeggios, and the like, by means of which the notes of a melody were broken down into a multitude of smaller notes to produce a free and elaborate paraphrase of the written line. The longer ornamentation (called *division, diminution, figuration, graces* and other names) was, of course, most appropriate to melodies in slow tempo. Graces for the slow movements of Corelli's solo sonatas have been preserved from an eighteenth-century edition (printed in HAM, No. 252), one of the few instances in Italian compositions where such ordinarily improvised decorations were written out. Whether or not the graces as we now have them are Corelli's own, they undoubtedly represent the general character of such melodic embellishments as practiced in the late Baroque.

Still another species of ornamentation, common in late Baroque opera and found also in some of the instrumental music of Corelli and his contemporaries, was the *cadenza,* an elaborate extension of the six-four chord of a final cadence. The cadenza at the end of the second movement of Corelli's solo sonata Opus 5, No. 3 is a fore-shadowing of the long cadenzas in the concertos of the Classical and Romantic periods.

Performers in the Baroque thus had the liberty to add to the composer's written score; they were equally free to subtract from it or change it in various other ways. Arias were omitted from operas, or different arias substituted, practically at the whim of the singers. Frescobaldi permitted organists to dismember his toccatas or end them at any point they pleased. Composers of variations, suites, and sonatas took it for granted that the players would omit movements *ad libitum.* Very many title pages of instrumental ensemble music collections allow not only for different kinds of instruments, but also for an optional number of them: for example, sonatas were issued for violin and basso continuo with an additional violin or two "if desired." Incidentally, most seventeenth-century Italian dance suites

Title page of the first violin part of Corelli's Opus 3: "Trio sonatas, [for] two violins, violone or archlute, with bass for the organ." The first edition, Rome 1689.

and chamber sonatas, including Corelli's, call for the bass to be played by a violone *or* clavier—one instrument playing both bass and harmonies—not two, as indicated or implied in most modern editions. The church sonatas, on the other hand, always specify the fuller sound of both violone and organ; in Corelli and other composers, the string bass is occasionally reserved to emphasize an entrance, or is given a faster, ornamental version of the keyboard bass, or even a partially independent melodic line.

Ensemble sonatas outside Italy

The Italian trio sonatas were imitated or adapted by composers in all countries. Their influence on the English composer Jenkins has already been noted. Purcell in his two sets of trio sonatas published in 1683 and 1697 "endeavor'd a just imitation of the most fam'd Italian masters"; some traces of French influence may be discerned in his rhythms and melodies, but many passages are profoundly English and Purcellian. The ninth sonata of the second set is popularly known, for some obscure reason, as the *Golden Sonata*. Another English composer, John Ravenscroft, published at Rome in 1695 a set of twelve trio sonatas in a style practically indistinguishable from Corelli's. Handel's trio sonatas are mostly in the same four-movement form and general style as those of Corelli.

In Germany, sonatas for trio or larger combinations were written by George Muffat (*Armonico tributo—A Harmonic Tribute;* 1682), Reinken (*Hortus musicus—The Garden of Music;* 1687), Buxtehude (1696), Fux, Caldara, Christoph Graupner, and others. The sonatas of Fux and Graupner contain some remarkable examples of intricate fugal writing which combines the German fondness for counterpoint with a form and style derived from Italian composers.

The earliest as well as the most important trio sonatas in France were those of Couperin. Some of these works were composed probably as early as 1692, although not published until many years later. A collection of 1726, entitled *Les Nations : Sonades et Suites de Simphonies en Trio,* contains four *ordres,* each consisting of a *sonata da chiesa* (the *sonade*) in several movements followed by a suite of dances (the *suite de simphonies*). The style, though obviously influenced in the *sonades* by that of Corelli and the other Italians, is distinguished throughout by the same refinement of melody and the same exquisite taste in ornaments that mark Couperin's clavecin pieces.

Couperin admired the works of both Lully and Corelli, and in the controversy which was then raging in France over the respective merits of French and Italian music he maintained a neutral position, affirming that the perfect music would be a union of the two national styles. In keeping with this ideal are two other trio suites, amusing examples of the clever sort of program music in which Couperin excelled, called respectively *Parnassus, or the Apotheosis of Corelli* and *The Apotheosis of Lully.* The rest of Couperin's chamber music comprises a series of twelve "concerts" (really suites; not concertos) for clavier and various combinations of instruments, each consisting of a prelude and a number of dance movements; the first four are generally known as the *Concerts royaux* (having been played before Louis XIV in 1714 and 1715), and the last eight were published in 1724 under the collective title *Les Goûts-réunis* (the united [French and Italian] styles).

Italian composers after Corelli, as well as those of other nationalities, wrote trio sonatas; in fact, there is an extensive literature in this form written from 1700 to around the middle of the century. But the main interest of the period was increasingly directed toward the solo sonata. *The solo sonata*

The solo violin sonata had always been a prime vehicle for experiments in special bowings, multiple stops, and all kinds of difficult passage work. This early Baroque tradition lived on in Germany in the works of Johann Jakob Walther (1650–1717?), whose collection of twelve sonatas published in 1676 under the tile *Scherzi* outdid in these respects anything previously known. Likewise a virtuoso player, but a composer of broader interests, was Heinrich Ignaz Franz Biber. Although Biber composed church music and instrumental ensemble works, he is remembered chiefly for his fifteen violin sonatas composed around 1675, which represent for the most part episodes in the life of Christ. These ingenuous examples of Baroque program music make considerable use of *scordatura,* unusual tunings of the violin strings to facilitate the playing of particular chords.

Both Walther and Biber often interspersed rhapsodic movements or sections analogous to a toccata in their sonatas, and both wrote many of their longer movements in the form of a theme and variations or a passacaglia. Biber's passacaglia for unaccompanied solo violin which is appended to the collection of Biblical sonatas is perhaps the most important precursor of Bach's great Chaconne in D minor. Most German violin composers after Biber and Walther came under the influence of the Italian schools and developed a cosmopolitan style on that foundation.

The solo sonata of the early eighteenth century lent itself readily to the new stylistic trends of the period, which were in the direction of homophonic texture, vivacious melodic rhythm, and an easy, quickly understandable flow of phrases. A sonata composed about 1725 by Corelli's pupil Giovanni Battista Somis (1686–1763) illustrates the way in which old and new factors were combined. It begins in the Corelli fashion with an introductory Adagio and a quasi-fugal Allegro in 4/4 time. A second Allegro in 3/4 time follows immediately and concludes the sonata. Both Allegros are in the two-part sectional form of Corelli's dance movements; in each, the second section begins with a transposition to the relative major of the *EE, NO. 35* opening measures of the movement, and includes both a literal recapitulation of the opening theme and a transposed recapitulation of the ending of the first section. (In the first Allegro also an episodic passage is repeated in the second section.) The approach to Classical sonata-form comes even closer in the second Allegro with the presence of two somewhat contrasting theme groups. The first Allegro, along with its simplified version of the traditional imitative style, uses and in fact abuses the Baroque device of the sequence: about two-thirds of the time it proceeds in stereotyped sequential patterns. The finale, on the other hand, continually exploits another mannerism, the echoed phrase: what with echoes and repetitions, 22 measures of music are inflated to 86; not a single new phrase, nor even a varied version of an old one, occurs after the double bar. All this repetition, of course, makes the music easy to grasp on first hearing; but this very fact, together with the somewhat perfunctory nature of the themes themselves, suggests the degree to which the serious character of Baroque music, as exemplified in Corelli, had gone out of date by 1725.

Another pupil of Corelli was Francesco Geminiani (1687–1762), who had a long career as virtuoso and composer in London. He published there, in 1751, a violin method which undoubtedly embodies the principles of technique and interpretation that were taught by Corelli and the other Italian masters of the early eighteenth century. Geminiani's solo sonatas and *concerti grossi* are founded on the style of Corelli, which is intermingled with progressive traits. Some characteristics of the Baroque still remain in the compositions of two other famous early eighteenth-century violinists, Francesco Maria Veracini (1690–*ca*. 1750) and Pietro Locatelli (1695–1764), the latter another Corelli pupil. Most celebrated of all the Italian virtuosi was Giuseppe Tartini (1692–1770); but his solo sonatas and concertos are predominantly in the pre-Classical style of the mid-eighteenth century.

The principal French composer of violin sonatas was Jean-Marie Leclair (1697–1764). His music seems to combine the Classical purity of Corelli with a peculiarly French grace and sweetness of melody, and perfect clarity of texture and form with abundant tasteful decoration; his rondeau movements have a particular charm.

Works for larger ensembles

The trio and solo instrumentations, although they were the most common, were not the only sonorities to be employed for sonatas (or similar pieces under whatever name) in the Baroque period. In Italy, from the days of Giovanni Gabrieli on through the first half of the seventeenth century, there was a steady production of canzonas, dance suites, sonatas, and sinfonias for groups of three or more melody instruments in addition to a basso continuo. Many Venetian sonatas of this period are similar to the contemporary Venetian opera overtures. The Bolognese composers and other Italians in the late seventeenth century also wrote many works for larger groups which in form and style resembled either the trio sonata or the concerto.

The sonata and more especially the suite for an ensemble of instruments had a particularly long life in Germany. The most notable (though not the most typical) works in this form after Schein's *Banchetto musicale* were the chamber sonatas of Johann Rosenmüller (*ca.* 1620–84), published in 1670. Each of the eleven sonatas in this collection consists of a sinfonia followed regularly by an allemande, courante, ballo (a short, light-humored, sharply rhythmic movement in 4/4 time), and sarabande. The instrumentation is for five strings ("or other instruments") and basso continuo. The sinfonias, which were evidently inspired by the Venetian opera overtures (Rosenmüller spent a large part of his life in Venice), are most remarkable: their principal section is a songful, expressive movement in moderate or slow triple meter, which is repeated da capo after a contrasting faster section. This movement has an introduction which may consist either of imposing block harmonies with dramatic pauses between the phrases, or of short vivid alternations of solemn Grave with agitated Allegro; and as a rule a brief recall of the impressive introductory material both follows the main movement and precedes its da capo repetition.

The national predilection for full sonority, combined with the prevailing conditions of musical life, encouraged the semipopular form of the ensemble sonata and suite in Germany in the seventeenth century. Music was cultivated not only in the courts and among the nobility, but by large numbers of the middle class as well. The *collegium musicum,* a society of citizens meeting to play and sing for their own pleasure, was a regular institution in many German towns, along with other musical organizations of a more or less public character. The town bands (*Stadtpfeifer*) and, in Lutheran regions, the church musicians were also closely associated with the life of the people. In some places, chorales or sonatas (called *Turmsonaten*) were played daily on wind instruments from the tower of the Rathaus or a church. The German musical tradition had a homely, direct quality; composers preferred relatively large ensembles, and liked the sound of wind instruments as well as strings.

Toward the end of the seventeenth century a generally recognized distinction of style began to be made between *chamber* music and *orchestral* music—that is, between ensemble music with only one instrument to a part and ensemble music with more than one instrument playing the same part. In a large proportion of seventeenth-century ensemble works it is not clear if composers had any preference in this regard; the choice could depend on circumstances. For instance, a trio *sonata da chiesa,* though presumably conceived for two solo violins, might be played in church by an orchestral ensemble

Orchestral music

if the size of the auditorium made it desirable or if the occasion were festive. Conversely, neither the designation "sinfonia" nor the presence of three, four, or more melodic parts above the bass necessarily called for an orchestral rather than a chamber group of players. When parts were to be reinforced the usual procedure in the seventeenth century was to increase the number of chord-playing instruments for the continuo and add more melody instruments on the soprano line. Beyond the use of the basso continuo and the predominance of the stringed instruments, there was no common standard that regulated either the makeup of an ensemble or the number of instruments to a part.

Opera houses of course maintained orchestras; consequently the opera overture in both Italy and France, as well as the numerous dances that formed an indispensable part of French opera, were always conceived as specifically orchestral music, and were written in a style suited to orchestral rather than chamber performance. The most famous orchestra in Europe was that of the Paris Opéra, which under the severe regime of Lully had been brought to a pitch of technical perfection hitherto unknown for so large a group of instrumental performers.

The orchestral suite

German disciples of Lully introduced French standards of playing, along with the French musical style, into their own country. One result was a new type of *orchestral suite* which flourished in Germany from about 1690 to 1740. The dances of these suites, patterned after those of Lully's ballets and operas, did not appear in any standard number or order. From the fact that they were always introduced by a pair of movements in the form of a French Overture, the word *ouverture* soon came to be used as a designation for the suite. Among the early collections of orchestral suites was Georg Muffat's *Florilegium* (1695 and 1698), the second part of which included an essay with much information about the French system of bowing, the playing of the *agréments,* and other matters. Another important collection was J. K. F. Fischer's *Journal de Printemps* (1695). *Ouverture* suites were written also by Fux, Telemann, and a host of other German composers, including J. S. Bach.

The concerto

A new kind of orchestral composition, the *concerto,* appeared in the last two decades of the seventeenth century, and became the most important type of Baroque orchestral music after 1700. The concerto was the synthesis in purely instrumental music of four fundamental Baroque practices: the *concertato* principle; the texture of a firm bass and a florid treble; musical organization based on the major-minor key system; and the building of a long work out of separate autonomous movements.

Three different kinds of concertos were being written around 1700. One, the *orchestral concerto* (also called *concerto-sinfonia* or *concerto-ripieno*), was simply an orchestral work of several movements in a style that emphasized the first violin part and the bass, and that usually avoided the more complex contrapuntal texture characteristic of the sonata and sinfonia. More numerous and important at this time were the other two types, the *concerto grosso* (grand concerto) and the *solo concerto,* both of which systematically contrasted sonorities: in the concerto grosso, a small group of solo instruments, in the solo concerto a single instrument, were set against the main mass of orchestral sound. The "orchestra" was almost always a string orchestra, usually divided into first and second violins, viola, violoncello, and violone, with basso continuo. The solo instruments also were usually strings: in the solo concerto, a violin; in the concerto grosso, as a rule two violins and continuo—though other solo string or wind instruments might be added or substituted. *Concerto grosso* originally signified the "large consort," that is, the orchestra, as opposed to the *concertino* or "little consort," the group of solo instruments. Later, the term *concerto grosso* was applied to the composition which used these opposed groups. In both the solo concerto and the concerto grosso, the usual designation for full orchestra is *tutti* (all) or *ripieno* (full).

The practice of contrasting solo instruments against full orchestra had been introduced into Baroque music long before the concerto as such made its appearance. Examples of concerto-like instrumentation are found throughout the seventeenth century in canzonas and other instrumental ensemble works. Lully inserted episodes for a trio of solo wind instruments in some of the dances of his operas. The tossing of short phrases back and forth between solo instruments and tutti was widespread in the late seventeenth century: it is found in overture-suites, church cantatas, and occasionally in sonatas and sinfonias. A predecessor of the concerto was the sinfonia or sonata for one or two solo trumpets with string orchestra, which was cultivated especially at Venice and Bologna. Various elements of the concerto also may be found in the Venetian opera overtures, which were occasionally played outside the opera house as independent instrumental sonatas.

The circumstances under which orchestral church music was presented were often such as to encourage the concerto style. The church of San Petronio in Bologna, for instance, maintained a small orchestra of expert instrumentalists; when large numbers of extra players were brought in for special occasions, the contrast between the modest technique of these outsiders and the accomplished virtuosity of the regular performers strongly suggested writing that could take advantage of the situation by providing an appropriately different kind of music for each group within the framework of a single composition—easy parts for the ripieno, more difficult parts for the soloists when heard alone.

Concertos, like sonatas and sinfonias, were played in church as "overtures" before Mass or at certain moments in the ceremony. For the Christmas Mass composers often added an optional movement in pastoral style; Corelli's *Christmas Concerto* (Opus 6, No. 8) contains the best known as well as one of the most beautiful of these pastorales. Other examples of pastorale movements in the late Baroque period are the *Sinfonia* at the beginning of the second part of Bach's *Christmas Oratorio* and the *Sinfonia pastorale* in the first part of Handel's *Messiah*.

The concerti grossi of Corelli, which are among the earliest examples of the form, employ the principle of solo-tutti contrast; but Corelli did not differentiate in style between the solos and the tutti portions, and these concertos are in effect merely church sonatas or chamber sonatas divided between a small and a larger group of instruments, although the comparative prominence of the first violin part occasionally suggests the texture of the later solo concerto. A similar dependence on the form and style of the sonata is evident in the earliest concerti grossi by German composers, for example those of Georg Muffat (1701), as well as in the concerti grossi of Alessandro Scarlatti. And well into the eighteenth century many concertos still exhibited at least one of the characteristic traits of the sonata, namely the fugal or quasi-fugal Allegro. The concerto grosso tended to be conservative for the reason that many composers (Geminiani, for example) shared Corelli's conception of the form as essentially a sonata with the musical substance divided on an equal basis between concertino and ripieno. When this conception changed, the change was due largely to the solo concerto, in which the newer ideas of rhythm, texture, and formal organization were first fully worked out.

Giuseppe Torelli

The composer who contributed most to the development of the concerto around the turn of the century was Giuseppe Torelli (1658–1709), the leading figure in the last years of the Bologna school. A significant stage of evolution is apparent in the violin concertos from Torelli's last publication (1709), a collection of six concerti grossi and six solo concertos. Most are in three movements (fast–slow–fast), an arrangement which became general with later concerto composers. The Allegros as a rule are in fugal style, while the middle movement is made up of two similar Adagios framing a brief Allegro. Torelli's vigorous, dynamic Allegro themes are characteristic of the early eighteenth century. Equally significant is the distinction in style between the tutti and the solo passages: the latter blossom forth with lively, diversified, idiomatic figuration, contrasting brightly with the solid thematic quality of the ripieno.

The most important achievement is the form of Torelli's Allegro movements: each begins with a complete exposition of the theme by the full orchestra; alternating with solo episodes, the material of this tutti exposition recurs once or twice, slightly modified and in different keys; the movement is rounded off and brought to a close with a final tonic tutti practically identical with the opening one. A tutti which recurs in this way in a concerto is called a *ritornello;* this structure is typical for all first and last movements of late Baroque concertos. The form is something like that of the rondeau, with the important exception that in a concerto all the ritornellos except the first and last are in different keys. The concerto therefore combines the principle of recurrence with the equally important principle of key relationship. An outline of the structure of the finale of Torelli's Opus 8, No. 8 illustrates the scheme:

HAM,
NO. 246

Ritornello I: Theme, C minor (10 measures) with sequential extension and cadence in the dominant minor (6 measures).

Solo I: 9½ measures with prominent sequential patterns, beginning in the dominant minor and modulating to the relative major.

Ritornello II: 8 measures, similar to Ritornello I, in the relative major, modulating to the subdominant.

Solo II: 12 measures, modulating to the tonic and concluding with four nonthematic measures of dominant preparation for:

Ritornello III: same as Ritornello I but cadencing in the tonic and with the last four measures repeated *piano* by way of coda.

A similar but slightly more complex scheme is found in the finale of Torelli's D minor Concerto Opus 8, No. 7. Here there are four ritornellos; the second is in the dominant, the third modulates from the subdominant to the relative major, and the last is, after four initial modulating measures, identical with the first. Each solo episode is in faster rhythm than the preceding one; this arrangement contributes markedly to a sense of growing animation as the movement proceeds. The first movement of this concerto uses a version of the chromatic passacaglia bass; the tutti intervenes briefly from time to time in the midst of the solo passages, a common practice in later concertos.

GMB,
NO. 257

The achievements of Torelli in the realm of the concerto were matched and extended by other Italian composers, especially the Venetian Tomaso Albinoni (1671–1750) and the Italian-German Evaristo Felice dall'Abaco (1675–1742). The concerti grossi of Geminiani and Locatelli are generally conservative, but Locatelli's solo concertos introduce virtuoso passages which foreshadow the importance of this element in the concertos of the Classical period. The greatest master of the Italian concerto of the late baroque was Antonio Vivaldi, whose works we shall study in the following chapter.

XII

Bach, Handel (most imp)

The Early Eighteenth Century

If there is such a thing as the march of history in music, it is certainly not a uniform movement; on the contrary, the more closely it is examined the more it is seen to be varied, tumultuous, and contradictory. There are always individuals and groups who are out of step: some drag back, some press forward ahead of the crowd, some move in other than what seems to be the prevailing direction. Moreover, each individual, if his work is of any significance at all, has something to say that is unique and that cannot be adequately subsumed under any general description of the period. One of the tasks of the historian is to appreciate this diversity, to resist the temptation of trying to make any comprehensive formula about an epoch hold more truth than it is capable of holding.

Looking at any given span of years, we may regard them either as a continuation of the past or as a presage of the future; we may see the individuals who lived then either as carrying on certain lines of development laid down by their predecessors or as laying down new lines of development that will be carried on by their successors.

The overlapping of style periods had seldom if ever been so extensive as in the first half of the eighteenth century. All around the late Baroque masters a new style of music was growing up. We have already discussed the first half of the eighteenth century under its aspect as a late stage of the Baroque; in the chapter that follows this one, we shall discuss it as an early stage of the Classical era. But the composers working during these years were not consciously, or at any rate not primarily, concerned with either the historical past or the possible historical future; they were living in the present. In this chapter we shall try to achieve a fuller understanding of the music of the first half of the eighteenth century by surveying the life and works of its four most important composers: Vivaldi, Rameau, Bach, and Handel.

All these four composers were successful and eminent in their own time; all wrote music which, by virtue of its craftsmanship, integrity, and imaginative content, is still significant today. All came to terms with the contemporary conflict between contrapuntal and homophonic styles; all were competent in both instrumental and vocal composition. All were aware of the new currents in musical thought, though none was a deliberate revolutionary in his own music. All worked within the established forms and styles of the late Baroque, and their originality consisted chiefly in doing the accepted things in a uniquely excellent way. Bach brought to consummation all forms of late Baroque music except opera. Vivaldi, Rameau, and Handel excelled in opera; Vivaldi, in addition, was a prolific master of the Italian Baroque concerto; Handel created—out of Baroque elements—a new kind of oratorio; and Rameau, in his theoretical writings, developed a new conception of harmony and tonality that proved valid not only for the music of his own time but also for that of many succeeding generations.

Pianoforte dated 1720, one of two instruments extant built by its inventor, Bartolomeo Christofori (1655–1731). (Courtesy Metropolitan Museum of Art, The Crosby Brown Collection of Musical Instruments, 1889)

Antonio Vivaldi

At the beginning of the eighteenth century Venice, although far declined in political power and headed for economic ruin, was still attracting travelers, and especially musicians, with the glamour of its colorful, exuberant life. It was a life set to music, like a perpetual opera. People sang on the streets and on the lagoons; the gondoliers had their own repertory of songs and declaimed the verses of Tasso to traditional, hauntingly oriental melodies. Men of the ruling class owned opera theatres; they themselves played and sang, and knew how to honor musicians. Public festivals, more numerous in Venice than elsewhere, were occasions of musical splendor. The chapel of St. Mark's was still famous. The city took pride in its tradition of being a center of music printing, of church music, of instrumental composition, and of opera. Never in the eighteenth century did Venice have fewer than six opera companies, which altogether played seasons totalling thirty-four weeks in the year. Between 1700 and 1750 the Venetian public absorbed new operas at the rate of ten or more annually, and this figure became even larger in the second half of the century. Private persons and academies frequently sponsored musical programs, and services in the churches on festival days were less like religious ceremonies than great instrumental and vocal concerts. The musical atmosphere of eighteenth-century Venice is well depicted in Dr. Charles Burney's *Present State of Music in France and Italy* (1771), and his observations are confirmed by those of other travelers throughout the century.

Antonio Vivaldi (1678–1741), son of one of the leading violinists of St. Mark's chapel, was educated both for music (under Legrenzi)

Vivaldi's career

and for the priesthood. He began his priestly duties in 1703, but because of ill health was excused from active service a year later and thenceforward devoted himself wholly to music. Such a combination of sacred office and secular profession was not uncommon in those days. Since Vivaldi had red hair he was always known as *il prete rosso* (the red-headed priest)—a nickname of the sort which the Italian public has always loved to bestow on its favorite artists. From 1704 to 1740 Vivaldi was continually employed as conductor, composer, teacher, and general superintendent of music at the Conservatory of the Pietà in Venice, with frequent leaves of absence to compose and conduct operas and concerts in other Italian cities and elsewhere in Europe.

The conservatories of eighteenth-century Naples and Venice were pious institutions founded originally to shelter orphans and illegitimate children—of whom there must have been a formidable number, if we are to believe some of the tales told by travellers.[1] The *noted for Instrumental & Concerto* organization of the conservatories was like that of a convent, but as a rule musical training formed an important part of the curriculum. The teaching was thorough and the results important for the musical life of the entire country. Instruction was efficiently organized and pursued without stinting either energy or expense. The resulting throng of enthusiastic young amateurs, their natural emulation spurred by special rewards in privileges and stimulated always by the presence of a few outstandingly gifted individuals, must have provided a highly favorable environment for any composer.

The concerts at the church of the Pietà, as well as at other fashionable places of worship in Venice, attracted large audiences. Travelers wrote of these occasions with enthusiasm not unmixed with amusement at the unusual spectacle of a choir and orchestra composed mainly of teenage girls. "They are reared at public expense and trained solely to excel in music. And so they sing like angels, and play the violin, the flute, the organ, the violoncello, the bassoon. . . . Each concert is given by about forty girls. I assure you there is nothing so charming as to see a young and pretty nun in her white robe, with a bouquet of pomegranate flowers in her hair, leading the orchestra and beating time with all the precision imaginable."[2]

A feature of the eighteenth century which is hard for us nowadays to appreciate, yet which was incalculably important, was the constant public demand for new music. There were no "classics," and few works of any kind survived more than two or three seasons. Bach had to provide new cantatas for Leipzig and Handel one or more new operas every year for London; and Vivaldi was expected to furnish new oratorios and concertos for every recurring festival at the Pietà. Such unceasing pressure accounts both for the prodigious output of many eighteenth-century composers and for the phenomenal speed at which they worked: Vivaldi perhaps holds the record with his opera *Tito Manlio,* said to have been completed in five days; and he prided himself on being able to compose a concerto faster than a copyist could copy the parts.

Like his contemporaries, Vivaldi composed every work for a definite occasion and for a particular company of performers. He was commissioned to write forty-nine operas, most of them for

[1] Thus Edward Wright, *Some Observations Made in Travelling through Italy* [etc.], London, 1730, I, 79 reports that the Pietà sometimes held as many as six thousand girls. It has been reliably estimated that this would have required a campus twice the size of Vassar.

[2] Charles de Brosses, *Lettres familières sur l'Italie,* Paris, 1885, I, 193–94. De Brosses's letter may be read in English in *Selections from the Letters . . .* tr. Lord Ronald Sutherland Gower, London, 1897, Ch. VII. (The translation is incorrect; the girls were not "nuns.")

Musicians singing in St. Mark's, Venice, 1766. A drawing by Antonio Canal, known as Canaletto. (Kunsthalle, Hamburg)

Venice, but a few also for Florence, Verona, Rome, and other Italian cities. His duties at the Pietà required him to write oratorios and church music, of which a large quantity survives in manuscript. Chiefly for the Pietà, also, he wrote concertos, the form of instrumental music commonly used at church festival services. About 450 concertos of his are extant, in addition to 23 sinfonias, 75 solo or trio sonatas, 49 operas, and many cantatas, motets, and oratorios.

Vivaldi is known today only as a composer of orchestral music; the only works printed during his lifetime (mostly at Amsterdam) were about forty sonatas and a hundred concertos. It would be a mistake, however, to ignore Vivaldi's achievements in opera, cantata,

Vivaldi's vocal works

motet, and oratorio. So little is known about the Italian opera of the early eighteenth century that it is impossible to estimate Vivaldi's merits in comparison with Scarlatti, Lotti, Gasparini, Albinoni, C. F. Pollarolo, Caldara, Handel, or others whose operas were produced at Venice during the first third of the century. But Vivaldi was certainly successful in his day; during the years in which he was writing operas (1713–39) the theatres of Venice staged more works of his than of any other composer, and his fame was by no means limited to his own city and country. The few accessible specimens of his church music show that in this realm also Vivaldi was a composer of real stature. The fact that many solo and choral passages in his works sound as though they might have been written by Handel proves merely that both composers used the international musical language of the early eighteenth century.

Vivaldi is remembered now chiefly for his instrumental music partly because compositions like sonatas and concertos are less attached than operas or oratorios to external conditions of performance and hence are less liable to fall out of circulation when performance conditions change. But it is also true that Vivaldi's instrumental works, and especially the concertos, are perennially attractive because of the freshness of their melodies, their rhythmic verve, their skilful treatment of solo and orchestral color, and the clarity of their form. Many of the sonatas, as well as some of the early concertos, are in the late seventeenth-century contrapuntal style of Corelli. However, in his first published collection of concertos (Opus 3, *ca.* 1712) Vivaldi already showed that he was fully aware of the modern trends toward distinct musical form, vigorous rhythm, and idiomatic solo writing exemplified by Torelli and Albinoni.

Vivaldi's concertos

About two-thirds of Vivaldi's concertos are for one solo instrument with orchestra—usually, of course, a violin, but with a considerable number also for violoncello, flute, or bassoon. In the concertos for two violins the soloists are usually given equal prominence, producing the texture of a duet for two high voices typical of the late Baroque; but many works that call for several solo instruments are in effect solo or duet concertos rather than genuine concerti grossi, in that the first violin or the first and second violins, and not infrequently the wind instruments—and even the mandolin—as well, are treated in a virtuoso manner that sets them markedly apart from the rest of the concertino. There are also a few important concertos for solo instruments with continuo, without the usual ripieno strings.

Vivaldi's usual orchestra at the Pietà probably consisted of twenty to twenty-five stringed instruments, with harpsichord or organ for the continuo; this is always the basic group, though in many of his concertos he also calls for flutes, oboes, bassoons, or horns, any of which may be used either as solo instruments or in ensemble combinations. The exact size and makeup of Vivaldi's orchestra varied, of course, depending on the players that might be available on a particular occasion. Vivaldi's writing is always remarkable for the variety of color he achieves with different groupings of the solo and orchestral strings; the familiar *Primavera* (*Spring*) concerto— first of a group of four concertos in Opus 8 (1725) representing programmatically the four seasons—is but one of many examples of his extraordinary instinct for effective sonorities in this medium.

Most of Vivaldi's concertos are in the usual eighteenth-century pattern of three movements: an Allegro; a slow movement in the same key or a closely related one (relative minor, dominant, or subdominant); and a final Allegro somewhat shorter and sprightlier than the first. Though a few movements are found in the older fugal style, the texture is typically more homophonic than contrapuntal —but homophonic in the late Baroque sense, with much incidental use of counterpoint and with particular emphasis on the two outer voices. Typical of the late Baroque, also, is Vivaldi's constant use of sequential patterns.

A page from one of Vivaldi's manuscripts—a tutti section from the finale of the Concerto in A for solo violin and four-part string ensemble.

Used the
ritornello a
lot.

The formal scheme of the individual movements of Vivaldi's concertos is the same as in Torelli's works: ritornellos for the full orchestra, alternating with episodes for the soloist (or soloists). Vivaldi differs from Torelli and all earlier composers not by virtue of any innovation in the general plan of the concerto but because his musical ideas are more spontaneous, his formal structures more clearly delineated, his harmonies more assured, his textures more varied, and his rhythms more impelling. Moreover, he establishes between solo and tutti a certain dramatic tension; he does not merely give the soloist contrasting idiomatic figuration (which Torelli had already done) but makes him stand out as a dominating musical personality against the ensemble as the solo singer does against the orchestra in opera—a relationship inherent in the ritornello aria (the precursor and model of the concerto form), but one which Vivaldi first brought to full realization in a purely instrumental medium. "The tutti announces the propositions that are to be debated in the course of the movement; and the arguments which these provoke give rise to a musical contest between soloist and orchestra, ending in a reconciliation or synthesis of emotions and ideas."[3]

As a rule, all the thematic motives appear in the tutti, though occasionally an important new theme may be announced in the opening solo, as in the first movement of the concerto for two violins in A minor, Opus 3, No. 8 (No. 6 in the London edition). Vivaldi's tutti may be analyzed as a rather loose series of related but separable musical ideas any of which can be selected for development in the course of the movement; this treatment represents a stage midway between the older Baroque practice of spinning out a single theme and the later Classical practice of developing contrasted themes.

Vivaldi's opening themes are so constructed as to define the tonality of the movement with the utmost precision: they consist of emphatically reiterated primary triads, triadic melodies, scales, or combinations of these elements. So stark a harmonic vocabulary could result in monotony; but this danger is avoided thanks to an unflagging vitality that drives the music onward in an ever varied but never ceasing rhythmic torrent from the beginning of a movement to its very last measure. Moreover, once the main tonality is firmly established, the harmony is varied not only by the usual cycle of modulations but also by devices such as the use of minor thirds and sixths in a major key, or of chromatic chords to signal the approach of a cadence. Triplet division of the beat is common. The phraseology of themes and sections is often irregular and sometimes quite subtle.

Vivaldi was the first composer to give the slow movement of a concerto equal importance with the two Allegros. His slow movement is usually a long-breathed expressive cantabile melody, like an adagio operatic aria or arioso, to which the performer was of course expected to add his own embellishments. The slow movements show a predeliction for minor keys, especially E minor. There is no standard formal scheme for these middle movements; many of them have particularly interesting sonorities in the accompani-

---

[3] C. R. Brijon, *Réflexions sur la musique et sur la vraie manière de l'exécuter sur le violon*, Paris, 1763, 2–3; paraphrased from the quotation in Pincherle, *Vivaldi*, I, 163.

ments, which usually are lightly scored in contrast to the two Allegros.

In his program music, such as the widely admired *Seasons* concertos and a dozen or so others of similar cast, Vivaldi shared the half-serious, half-playful attitude of the eighteenth century toward the naïve realism implied in such musical depictions. Although the pictorial intention doubtless often suggested particular effects of color or modification of the normal order of movements, the external program is completely absorbed into the standard musical structure of the concerto. The *Seasons* were among the first of many descriptive symphonic works in the eighteenth century which are the predecessors of Beethoven's "Pastoral" Symphony.

In Vivaldi's music one can find traces of all the different changes occurring in the first half of the eighteenth century. At the conservative extreme are some of the sonatas and concertos in the style of Corelli; at the progressive extreme are the solo concerto finales, the orchestral concertos (that is, those without solo instruments), and most of the twenty-three works which Vivaldi called *sinfonias.* As usual in this period, the terminology is imprecise, but the music, especially that of the sinfonias, clearly demonstrates that its composer is entitled to be reckoned among the earliest forerunners of the pre-Classic symphony: the conciseness of form, the markedly homophonic texture, the melodically neutral themes, the minuet finale, even many of the little mannerisms of style that were formerly thought to have been invented by German composers of the Mannheim school—all are found in Vivaldi.

Vivaldi's influence

Vivaldi's influence on instrumental music in the middle and later eighteenth century was equal to that of Corelli a generation earlier. Vivaldi was one of the most important figures in the transition from late Baroque to early Classical style; the assured economy of his writing for string orchestra was a revelation; his dramatic conception of the role of the soloist was accepted and developed in the Classical concerto; above all, the concise themes, the clarity of form, the rhythmic vitality, the impelling logical continuity in the flow of musical ideas, all qualities so characteristic of Vivaldi, were transmitted to many other composers, and especially directly to J. S. Bach. Bach copied at least ten of Vivaldi's concertos, arranging six of them for harpsichord, three for organ, and one (originally for four violins) for four harpsichords and string orchestra. Vivaldi's influence is apparent both in the general scheme and in the details of many of Bach's original concertos, as well as in those of his German contemporaries. Finally, Vivaldi, more than any other single composer, through his concertos impressed on the eighteenth century the idea of an instrumental sound in which the effect of solo-tutti contrast was important, an idea that prevails not only in concertos of the period but in much of the other orchestral music and keyboard music as well.

Jean-Philippe Rameau

Jean-Philippe Rameau (1683–1764), the foremost French musician of the eighteenth century, had a career unlike that of any other eminent composer in history. Practically unknown until the age of forty, he attracted attention first as a theorist and only afterward as a composer. He produced most of the musical works on which his fame depends between the ages of fifty and fifty-six. Attacked then as an innovator, he was assailed twenty years later even more severely as a reactionary; in favor with the French Court and reasonably prosperous during the later years of his life, he remained always a solitary, strict, and unsociable person, but a conscientious and intelligent artist.

Rameau's French School of Clarity Moderation Elegance Grace

From his father, an organist at Dijon, he received his first and, as far as we know, his only formal musical instruction. After a brief visit to Italy in 1701 and a term as organist at Clermont-Ferrand, he went to Paris and in 1706 published there a book of clavecin pieces. Soon after, apparently discouraged, he left the capital, and little is known about the next years of his life. Sometime after 1715, he returned to his former post at Clermont-Ferrand; here he wrote his famous *Traité de l'harmonie* (*Treatise on Harmony*), which was published at Paris in 1722.

Rameau's career French National apparent Champion of French music

In 1723 Rameau returned to Paris. The cultural life of France, unlike that of Germany and Italy, was concentrated in this one city. Neither success nor reputation counted unless it had been achieved in the capital; and the highroad for a composer, indeed the only road to real fame, was the opera. Rameau's prospects were poor: he had no money and no influential friends, and he was not endowed with the disposition of a good courtier. Worse still, his reputation as a theorist had preceded him. He was known as a *savant*, a *philosophe*. People would not believe that a man who discoursed so learnedly on intervals, scales, and chords could write music that anyone would hear with pleasure. Rameau himself, aware of his handicap, tried to combat it by emphasizing in a letter of 1727 that in his compositions he had "studied nature" and learned to reproduce her "colors and nuances" in appropriate musical expressions. Lacking better opportunities, he wrote airs and dances for three or four little musical comedies, pieces with spoken dialogue which were given at the popular theatres of Paris. He published some cantatas (1728) and two more books of clavecin pieces (1724 and *ca.* 1736); meanwhile, his reputation as a teacher and organist began to attract pupils. At length, in 1731, came a turn of fortune: Rameau was taken under the protection of La Pouplinière, the leading patron of music in France.

Competitor Was Rousseau—led back to nature movement Said if you put youngster on an island. – But wrote

Alexandre-Jean-Joseph Le Riche de la Pouplinière (1693–1762), descendant of an ancient and noble French family, had inherited an immense fortune which he further increased by speculation and

La Pouplinière

with the revenues of the lucrative post of tax collector (*fermier général*) which he held under Louis XV from 1721 to 1738. He maintained two or three residences in Paris as well as other houses in the country near by. His salon was a gathering place for a motley company of aristocrats, literary men (Voltaire and J. J. Rousseau), painters (Van Loo and La Tour), adventurers (Casanova), and above all musicians.

Eager for novelty, La Pouplinière sought out promising but obscure musicians and took pleasure in promoting their careers. At his chateau in Passy near Paris he maintained an orchestra of fourteen players, augmented by outside artists as needed; the weekly routine included a concert on Saturday, Mass in the private chapel with orchestra on Sunday morning, a large concert in the gallery of the chateau on Sunday afternoon, and a more intimate concert in the evening after supper—all this in addition to two or more concerts during the rest of the week. Altogether, La Pouplinière spent a sum equivalent to at least $50,000 annually on his musical interests, and many of the operas and most of the orchestral concerts of Paris were tried out before a select audience at the chateau before they were presented to the public. Rameau was La Pouplinière's organist, conductor, and composer-in-residence from 1731 to 1753. He had to compose or prepare music not only for concerts and church but also for balls, plays, festivals, dinners, ballets, and all sorts of special occasions. He gave lessons on the clavecin to Mme. La Pouplinière; his own wife, an accomplished clavecinist, frequently played his compositions at La Pouplinière's concerts.

Rameau's ambition to make a name as an opera composer was soon realized after La Pouplinière had taken matters in hand. A project of an opera on a libretto furnished by Voltaire remained uncompleted; then Rameau composed *Hippolyte et Aricie,* to a poem by a popular librettist, the Abbé Pellegrin, which was produced at Paris in 1733 when the composer was fifty years old. A more distinct success came in 1735 with *Les Indes galantes* (*The Gallant Indies*), an opera-ballet. Two years later followed the work which is usually regarded as Rameau's masterpiece, the opera *Castor et Pollux.* In 1739 he produced two new works: an opera-ballet, *Les Fêtes d'Hébé ou les Talents lyriques* and an opera, *Dardanus.*

Rameau's operas

From the first, Rameau's operas stirred up a storm of critical controversy. The intelligentsia of Paris, always eager for a battle of words, divided into two vociferous camps, one friendly to Rameau and the other attacking him as the subverter of the good old French opera tradition of Lully. The Lullists affected to find Rameau's music abstruse, difficult, forced, grotesque, thick, mechanical, and unnatural. It was of no use for Rameau to protest, in a foreword to *Les Indes galantes,* that he had "sought to imitate Lully, not as a servile copyist but in taking, like him, nature herself—so beautiful and so simple—as a model." As the quarrel of the Lullists and Ramists raged on, Rameau's increasing popularity was attested by the number of parodies of his operas that appeared in the theatres of Paris; a parody meant, at that time, not necessarily a travesty or caricature, but rather a lighthanded familiar imitation or adaptation of the original.

In 1745 Rameau scored a triumph with the comedy-ballet *La Princesse de Navarre,* performed at Versailles to celebrate the marriage of the Dauphin with the Infanta Maria Teresa. The king rewarded Rameau by paying the expenses of publication of the work and settling on the composer an annual pension, together with the honorary title of royal chamber music composer.

Rameau's later stage works were, for the most part, lighter in tone and less significant than the operas and opera-ballets of the 1730s; many were ephemeral pieces produced for special occasions. Exceptions were the comedy-ballet *Platée* (1745) and the serious opera *Zoroastre* (1749), the most important work of Rameau's later period. In the 1750s Rameau was embroiled, through no act of his own, in another critical battle, this time on the subject of the relative merits of French and Italian music. The celebrated War of the Buffonists (*guerre des bouffons*), as this quarrel came to be called, will receive more attention in the next chapter; for the present it is sufficient to note that Rameau, the most eminent living French composer, was exalted by one party as the champion of French music, and thus became the idol of the very faction which twenty years earlier had been decrying him because he did not write like Lully. At the head of the Italian party was Rousseau, who had always been one of the most trenchant critics of French music, along with some of the other *philosophes* who wrote articles on music in Diderot's *Encyclopédie.*

The closing years of Rameau's life were largely occupied with polemical writings and further theoretical essays. He died at Paris in 1764; indomitable to the end, and a perfectionist always, he found strength even on his deathbed to reproach the priest who came to administer the last rites for his bad chanting.

Throughout his life, Rameau was interested in the theory or, as it was called at that time, the "science" of music. In his numerous writings he sought to derive the fundamental principles of harmony from the laws of acoustics and formulated certain ideas which not only clarified musical practice of his time but also remained influential in music theory for the next two hundred years. Rameau considered the chord the primal element in music—not the single tone, not melodic lines or intervals. The major triad he eventually derived from the overtone series; he had more difficulty in accounting for the minor triad on "natural principles," though he did establish the so-called melodic minor scale. He posited the building

[handwritten margin notes:] this principals good for 200 yrs. 1. Chord - prime obtained from 2. Overtone series 3. Establish Maj. min. scale 4. Expands triads to chords of 9th, 9th. Rameau's theoretical works 5. Recognizes inversions 6. Tonic, Dom in & Sub, Dominant pillar of music 7. Functional thinking functional approach to theory

413

of chords by thirds (upward and downward), whereby the triad was expanded to a chord of the seventh or ninth. Rameau's recognition of the identity of a chord through all its inversions was an important insight, as was also the corollary idea of the *basse fondamentale,* or, as we would say, the root-progressions in a succession of harmonies. Moreover, Rameau established the three chords of the tonic, dominant, and subdominant as the pillars of tonality, and related other chords to these, thereby formulating the notion of functional harmony; he also stated the conception that modulation might result from the change of function of a chord (in modern terminology, a pivot chord). Less significant were his theory of the derivation of all melody from harmony (expressed or implied) and his views on the peculiar quality of specific keys.

Rameau's musical style

The entire development of French opera after Lully had been toward increasing the already large proportion of decorative elements—scenic spectacle and ballet, with descriptive orchestral music, dances, choruses, and songs. More and more the drama, even in works called *tragédies lyriques,* had deteriorated in both importance and quality, and eventually opera-ballet had frankly come to be nothing but ballet and spectacle on a huge scale with only the thinnest thread, or none at all, of continuity between the various scenes. Rameau's "heroic ballet" *Les Indes galantes* is a finished example of an opera-ballet: each of its four *entrées* or acts has a self-contained plot, and each takes place in a different quarter of the globe, thus giving opportunity for a variety of decorations and dances which gratified the early eighteenth-century French public's interest in exotic scenes and peoples. The *entrées* are entitled respectively "The Generous Turk" (the scene is laid in "an island of the Indian Ocean" and the plot is similar to that which Mozart later used for his *Abduction from the Seraglio*), "The Incas of Peru," "The Flowers, a Persian Festival," and "The Savages" (the locale is "a forest of America" and the plot introduces Spanish and French characters as well as Indians). Rameau's music, especially in the *entrée* of the Incas, is far more dramatic than the libretto would lead one to expect.

As far as musical features are concerned, Rameau's theatre works are obviously similar to Lully's. Both show the same minute interest in appropriate declamation and exact rhythmic notation in recitatives; both intermingle recitative with more formally melodic aria sections, choruses, or instrumental interludes; both follow the tradition of introducing frequent long *divertissement* scenes; and (in Rameau's early operas) the form of the overture is the same. But within this general frame, Rameau introduced many changes, so that in reality the resemblance between his music and Lully's is superficial rather than substantial.

Perhaps the most notable contrast is in the nature of the melodic lines. Rameau the composer constantly put into practice the doctrine of Rameau the theorist that all melody is rooted in harmony. Many of his melodic phrases are plainly triadic and none leave room for any uncertainty as to the harmonic progressions that must underlie them. Moreover, the harmony is of the eighteenth-century sort, with an orderly relationship, within the major-minor tonal system, of dominants, subdominants, and all secondary chords and modulations. Rameau uses purely harmonic means for expressive purposes in a way that is completely lacking in Lully's style. Rameau's harmonies are for the most part diatonic, but on occasion he uses chromatic and enharmonic modulations most effectively: in the trio of the Fates in the fifth scene of Act II of *Hippolyte et Aricie* (Example XII–1) he modulates rapidly by a descending chromatic sequence through five keys in as many measures, underlining the import of the words *Où cours-tu, malheureux? Tremble, frémis d'effroi!* (Where dost thou flee, miserable one? Tremble, shudder with terror!)

EXAMPLE XII–1 Modulations in *Hippolyte et Aricie,* Rameau

In his treatment of form also Rameau was an innovator. Even when he maintained Lully's pattern of the French *ouverture,* as he did in *Castor et Pollux* and *Les Indes galantes,* the second movement, particularly, was expanded and deepened. Some of the formal plans of the overtures are evidently experimental (for example, that of *Les Fêtes d'Hébé*) and in his last works Rameau freely adapted the three-movement form of the Italian sinfonia. Quite often his overture introduces a theme that is used later in the opera, and occasionally (as in *Zoroastre*) the overture becomes a kind of symphonic poem, depicting the course of the drama to follow.

As with Lully and other French composers, Rameau used less contrasting melodic styles for recitative and aria than did the Italian composers of this period. Rameau's vocal airs, despite their variety of dimensions and types, can for the most part be classified into two basic formal patterns: the relatively short two-part form *AB;* and the longer form with repetition after contrast, either *ABA* as in the Italian da capo aria or with more than one repetition as in the usual French rondeau. Nearly always, whatever their form or size, Rameau's airs preserve a certain coolness and restraint in contrast to the intensity and abandon of the early Italian opera aria. Elegance, picturesqueness, piquant rhythms, fullness of harmony, and melodic ornamentation by means of *agréments* are their outstanding traits.

This is not to say that Rameau's music lacks dramatic force; the opening scenes of Act I of *Castor et Pollux* and the closing scenes of Act IV of *Hippolyte et Aricie* have a grandeur not surpassed in eighteenth-century French opera. However, the most powerful effects in his operas are achieved not by solo voice, but by the joint use of solo and chorus. Choruses, which remained prominent in French opera long after they had passed out of use in Italy, are numerous throughout Rameau's works. The invocation to the sun (*Brilliant soleil*) in Act II of *Les Indes galantes* is an excellent example of the effectiveness of his predominantly homophonic choral writing.

On the whole, Rameau's most original contributions were made in the instrumental portions of his operas—the overtures, the dances, and the descriptive symphonies that accompany the stage action. In all these, his invention is inexhaustible; themes, rhythms, and harmonies have an incisive individuality and an inimitable pictorial quality. The French valued music especially for its depictive powers and Rameau was their leading tone-painter. His musical pictures range from graceful miniatures to broad representations of thunder (*Hippolyte*, Act I), tempest (*Les Surprises de l'Amour* [1757], Act III), or earthquake (*Indes galantes*, Act II). The pictorial quality of his music is often enhanced by novel orchestration. Rameau's use of the bassoons and horns, and in general the independence of the woodwinds in his later scores, are in accordance with the most advanced orchestral practice of his time.

Rameau's clavecin pieces have the fine texture, the rhythmic vivacity, elegance of detail, and picturesque humor that appeared also in the works of Couperin. In his third and last collection (*Nouvelle Suites de Pièces de clavecin, ca.* 1736), Rameau experimented with virtuoso effects in somewhat the same manner as Domenico Scarlatti. Rameau's only publication of instrumental ensemble music was a collection of trio sonatas entitled *Pièces de clavecin en concerts* (1741); in these, the harpsichord is not treated simply as accompaniment but shares equally with the other instruments in the presentation and working out of the thematic material.

Summary

The work of Rameau may be summed up under three aspects. In the heroic, grand style of his early operas and opera-ballets, he is a representative figure of the late Baroque, comparable to Bach and Handel. His heroic qualities are always accompanied, and sometimes supplanted, by the characteristic French traits of clarity, grace, moderation, and elegance, and by a constant striving toward the picturesque; in these respects he may be compared with his contemporary, Watteau. Finally, and equally typical of his country, he is a *philosophe* as well as a composer, an analyst as well as a creator; and in this respect he may be compared to his contemporary, Voltaire. These three aspects cannot be separated if we are to understand Rameau's achievements fully. He was one of the most complex as well as one of the most fecund musical personalities of the eighteenth century.

Johann Sebastian Bach

The uneventful external career of Johann Sebastian Bach (1685–1750) was similar to that of many successful musical functionaries of his time in Lutheran Germany. Bach served as organist at Arnstadt (1703–07) and Mühlhausen (1707–08); as court organist and later Concertmaster in the chapel of the Duke of Weimar (1708–17); as Music Director at the court of a prince in Cöthen (1717–23); and finally as Cantor of St. Thomas's school and Music Director in Leipzig (1723–50), a position of considerable importance in the Lutheran world. He enjoyed some reputation in Protestant Germany as an organ virtuoso and writer of learned contrapuntal works, but there were at least a half-dozen contemporary composers who were more widely known in Europe. He regarded himself as a conscientious craftsman doing a job to the best of his ability for the satisfaction of his superiors, for the pleasure and edification of his fellowmen, and to the glory of God. Doubtless he would have been astonished if he had been told that two hundred years after his death his music would be performed and studied everywhere and his name more deeply venerated by musicians than that of any other composer.

Bach's career

Johann Sebastian was one of a large family of Bachs stemming from the region of Thuringia in north central Germany, a family which in the course of six generations from 1580 to the nineteenth century produced an extraordinary number of good musicians and several famous ones. He received his earliest training from his father, a town musician of Eisenach, and, after his father's death in 1695, from his elder brother Johann Christoph, an organist and a pupil of Pachelbel. He studied the music of other composers through the customary method of copying or arranging their scores, a habit which he retained all through his life. In this way he became familiar with the styles of the foremost composers of France, Germany, Austria, and Italy, assimilating the characteristic excellences of each. Bach's musical development was controlled by five factors: the family tradition of craftsmanship, the laborious but fruitful method of assimilation from all sources by copying scores, the eighteenth-century system of patronage (whether by an individual, the church, or a municipality), his own religious conception of the function of art and the duties of an artist, and—underlying all the others— that inexplicable personal element which we call genius.

Bach composed in practically all forms of the late Baroque, with the exception of opera. Inasmuch as he wrote primarily in response to the requirements of the particular situation in which he was placed, his works may be grouped accordingly. Thus at Arnstadt, Mühlhausen, and Weimar, where he was employed to play the organ, most of his compositions were for that instrument. At Cöthen, where he had nothing to do with church music, the bulk of his works were for clavier or instrumental ensembles, music for instruction and for domestic or court entertainment. The most productive period for cantatas and other church music was the early years in Leipzig, though some of the most important mature compositions for organ and clavier also come from the Leipzig period. We shall survey Bach's compositions in the order in which each class of works occupied his attention as his career progressed.

Bach's Instrumental Music

Bach was trained as a violinist and organist, and organ music first attracted his interest as a composer. As a youth he visited *Bach's organ* Hamburg to hear the organists there, and while he was at Arnstadt *works* he made a journey on foot to Lübeck, where he was so fascinated by the music of Buxtehude that he overstayed his leave and was duly reproved by his superiors.

Bach's earliest organ compositions include chorale preludes, several sets of variations (partitas) on chorales, and some toccatas and fantasias which in their length, diffuseness, and exuberance of ideas recall the toccatas of Buxtehude. Then, while he was at the court of Weimar, Bach became interested in the music of Italian composers, and with his usual diligence set about copying their scores and making arrangements of their works; thus he arranged several of Vivaldi's concertos for organ or harpsichord, writing out the ornaments, occasionally strengthening the counterpoint, and sometimes adding inner voices. He also wrote fugues on subjects by Corelli and Legrenzi. The natural consequence of these studies was an important change in Bach's own style: from the Italians, especially Vivaldi, he learned to write more concise themes, to clarify and tighten the harmonic scheme, and above all to develop subjects by a continuous rhythmic flow into lucid, grandly proportioned formal structures. These qualities were combined with his own prolific imagination and his profound mastery of contrapuntal technique to make the style which we consider typically "Bachian," and which is in reality a fusion of Italian and German characteristics.

As has already been noted, one of the characteristics large musical structures of the late Baroque was the combination of a prelude (or toccata, fantasia) and a fugue. Most of Bach's important compositions in this form date from the Weimar period, though a few were written at Cöthen and Leipzig. Perfectly idiomatic to the instrument, technically difficult but never parading empty virtuosity, Bach's preludes and fugues sum up all the striving of the Baroque toward pure, balanced tonal architecture on a monumental scale.

Bach's preludes and fugues

The Toccata in D minor (?1709; BWV 565)[4] is an example of the form established by Buxtehude, in which the fugue is interspersed with sections of free fantasia. The Passacaglia in C minor (?1717; BWV 582) serves as prelude to a double fugue, one of whose subjects is identical with the first half of the passacaglia theme. Some of the preludes are extensive compositions in two or three movements; that of the great Fantasia and Fugue in G minor (Cöthen, 1720; BWV 542) glorifies the Baroque conception of a richly colored, passionately expressive fantasia or toccata with contrapuntal interludes. The variety of types and the incisive melodic and rhythmic outline of Bach's fugue subjects are especially remarkable; see Example XII–2.

From the later years of Bach's life comes the gigantic Prelude in E♭ major, and the Fugue ("St. Anne's") in the same key (BWV 552), published in 1739; these two are respectively the opening and closing sections of Part III of the *Clavier Übung* (literally, *Keyboard Practice,* an overall title that Bach used for four different collections of his keyboard pieces). The central portion of Part III of the *Clavier Übung* is a series of chorale preludes on the hymns of the Lutheran Catechism and Mass (Kyrie and Gloria, the so-called *missa brevis*). In symbolic recognition of the dogma of the Trinity, Bach writes for conclusion a triple fugue with a key signature of three flats; each of the three sections of the fugue has its own subject, with increasing rhythmic animation, and the first subject is combined contrapuntally with each of the other two. The multi-sectional fugue goes back to the practice of Buxtehude and other earlier masters; Bach had used it in his early Toccata in E major (BWV 566).

Less spectacular than the preludes and fugues, but equally important, are the six Trio Sonatas (BWV 525–530) which, according to Forkel, Bach wrote at Leipzig for his eldest son Wilhelm Friedemann. These works show the way Bach adapted the Italian ensemble trio sonata as a piece for a solo performer. They are written in a contrapuntal texture of three equal independent voices, one for each manual and one for the pedals, but the order of movements (mostly fast–slow–fast) and the general character of the themes

Bach's trio sonatas

[4] BWV stands for *Thematisch-systematisches Verzeichnis der musikalischen Werke von Johann Sebastian Bach (Thematic-Systematic List of the Musical Works of J. S. Bach),* Wolfgang Schmieder, ed., Leipzig, 1950. The abbreviation S. (for Schmieder) is sometimes used instead of BWV for referring to Bach's works.

EXAMPLE XII–2 Organ Fugue Subjects, J. S. Bach

show the influence of their Italian prototypes.

Bach, as an organist and a devout Lutheran, was naturally concerned with the chorale. Among the approximately 170 chorale settings which he made for the organ, all types known to the Baroque are represented; moreover, as with other forms of composition, Bach brought the organ chorale to a summit of artistic perfection. Short chorale preludes comprise the collection called the *Orgelbüchlein* (*Little Organ Book*), which Bach compiled at Weimar and during his first years at Cöthen. The arrangement and intention of this collection illustrate several things essential for an understanding of Bach. He originally planned to include settings for the chorale melodies required by the liturgy for the entire church year, 164 in all, though he actually completed only 45. However, the plan is characteristic of Bach's desire to fulfil thoroughly the potentialities of a given undertaking, to realize all the suggestions inherent in any musical situation. This is the reason that in the maturity of his life his compositions often are devoted to single aspects of one large unified design—for example, the complete circle of keys in *The Well-Tempered Clavier*, the cycle of catechism chorales in the *Clavier Übung*, the systematic order of the *Goldberg Variations*, the exhaustive working out of a single subject in *A Musical Offering*, or the exemplification of all types of fugue in *The Art of Fugue*.

Bach's chorale preludes

It was also characteristic of Bach to plan the chorale preludes of the *Orgelbüchlein* with the aim of teaching; the title page reads "Little organ book, in which a beginning organist is given guidance in all sorts of ways of developing a chorale, and also for improving his pedal technique, since in these chorales the pedal is treated as completely *obbligato* [essential, not optional]." Then is added a rhymed couplet which may be translated "To honor the Most High God alone, and for the instruction of my fellow-men." It is understandable that Bach, who all his life was a humble and diligent student, should have been a wise and kindly teacher. For both Wilhelm Friedemann and for his second wife Anna Magdalena he wrote books of little clavier pieces that teach technique and musicianship at the same time. The two-part *Inventions* and three-part *Sinfonie* are didactic musical works, as is also the first book of *The Well-Tempered Clavier*.

It is not surprising that Bach should dedicate a book of chorale preludes—church music—to "the Most High God," or that he should inscribe at the beginning of the scores of his cantatas and Passions the letters J. J. (*Jesu, juva*—Jesus, aid) and at the end S. D. G. (*soli Deo gloria*—to God alone be glory); but it may startle a modern reader to find the exercise-book of clavier pieces written for Wilhelm Friedemann beginning with the formula I. N. J. (*in nomine Jesu*—in the name of Jesus), or to learn that Bach defined the aim of thorough-bass as "to produce a well-sounding harmony to the glory of God and the permissible delight of the spirit." In short, he admitted no difference in principle between sacred and secular art, both alike being "to the glory of God"; he would sometimes use the same music for either sacred or secular words or for a purely instrumental work: the music of the "Osanna" in the B-minor Mass, for example, had previously been used in a serenade honoring Augustus II, Elector of Saxony and King of Poland, on one of his state visits to Leipzig.

All the numbers of the *Orgelbüchlein* are chorale preludes in which the tune is heard once through, generally in the soprano, in complete, continuous, and readily recognizable form; a few treat the melody in canon, and three present it with fairly elaborate *agréments*. Quite often the accompanying voices are not derived from motives of the chorale melody but each is constructed throughout on a single independent motive. In some instances the accompaniment exemplifies the practice—common to many composers of the Baroque, especially notable in Schütz, and carried out by Bach with surpassing poetic ingenuity—of recognizing, by means of pictorial or symbolic motives, the visual images or underlying ideas of the text of the chorale. Thus in *Durch Adams Fall ist ganz verderbt* (*In Adam's fall the world was lost*), the idea of *fall* is depicted by a jagged falling motive in the pedals, while the tortuous chromatic lines of the inner voices suggest at once the ideas of sin and sorrow and the sinuous writhing of the serpent (Example XII–3).

EXAMPLE XII–3   Chorale Prelude: *Durch Adams Fall,* J. S. Bach

Similar pictorial or symbolic suggestions abound in Bach's organ chorales, as well as, of course, in his vocal works; however, he never uses pictorial devices as mere superficial adornments, but always as a way to present the inner, musical significance of a passage. One of the finest examples of the poetic transfiguration of an external suggestion is the final cadence of the chorale prelude *O Mensch, bewein' dein' Sünde gross* (*O man, bewail thy grievous sin*) from the *Orgelbüchlein,* in which the long-drawn-out *adagissimo* reflects the word *lange* (long) in the closing phrase of the chorale text (see illustration, page 429).

Three collections of organ chorales were compiled during Bach's Leipzig period. The six *Schübler* chorales (BWV 645–650) are transcriptions of movements from cantatas. The *Eighteen Chorales* (BWV 651–668) that Bach collected and revised between 1747 and 1749 were composed at earlier periods of his life; they include all varieties of organ chorale settings: variations, fugues, fantasias, trios, and extended chorale preludes of various types. The catechism chorales in Part III of the *Clavier Übung* (BWV 669–689) are grouped in pairs, a longer setting requiring the organ pedals and a shorter one (usually fugal) for manuals only. This pairing has been sometimes regarded as a symbolic reference to the "longer" and "shorter" catechisms, but more probably the aim was only to offer prospective buyers the alternative of using either one or the other setting depending on what instrument was available. All the later organ chorales of Bach are conceived with larger proportions than those of the *Orgelbüchlein;* they also are less intimate and subjective, replacing with a more formal symbolism or a purely musical development of ideas the vivid expressive details of the earlier works. An example of the difference between Bach's early and late organ chorales may be found in two settings of *Wenn wir in höchsten Nöten sein (When we are in deepest need)*. In the *Orgelbüchlein* version (BWV 641) the melody appears with luxuriant ornamentations over an accompaniment whose principal motive is derived from the first four notes of the tune. In a later setting (BWV 668) the same melody is used with the title *Vor deinen Thron tret' ich hiermit (Before Thy throne I now appear)*; in this version Bach returns to the old Pachelbel form of chorale prelude. The melody is almost bare of ornaments, and each phrase is introduced by a short fugato on its leading motive in the three lower voices. Another example of the organ chorales of Bach's late period is a set of five canonic variations (BWV 679) on the Christmas hymn *Vom Himmel hoch (From high heaven)* which he wrote in 1747 on the occasion of his election to a learned musical society.

Bach's music for the clavier, like that for the organ, includes masterpieces in every form known to the late Baroque: preludes, fantasies, and toccatas; fugues and other pieces in fugal style; dance suites; and variations. In addition there are early sonatas and capriccios, miscellaneous short works (including many teaching pieces), and clavier concertos with orchestra. A large proportion of Bach's clavier music was written at Cöthen, although many important works were produced in the Leipzig period. In general, the clavier compositions—which were not bound, like the organ works, to a local German tradition or to a liturgy—show prominently the cosmopolitan or international features of Bach's style, the intermingling of Italian, French, and German characteristics.

Bach's clavier music

Among the most notable toccatas are those in F♯ minor and C minor (BWV 910, 911). Both begin with free running passages in improvisatory style. The former concludes with a fugue whose subject is derived by rhythmic transformation from the theme of the second movement—a reminiscence of the older variation ricercare. The C minor toccata leads into one of Bach's characteristic propulsive, driving fugues on a triadic concerto-like theme. The Chromatic Fantasia and Fugue in D minor (BWV 903) is Bach's greatest clavier work in this form, a worthy companion to the organ Fantasia and Fugue in G minor.

Undoubtedly the best known of Bach's clavier works is the famous set of preludes and fugues called *The Well-Tempered Clavier.*
Part I was completed at Cöthen in 1722, and Part II was collected at Leipzig around 1740. Each part consists of twenty-four preludes and fugues, one prelude and one fugue in each of the twelve major and minor keys. Part I is more unified in style and purpose than Part II, which includes compositions from many different periods of Bach's life. In addition to demonstrating the possibility, with the then novel tempered tuning, of using all the keys, Bach had particular didactic intentions in Part I. In most of the preludes a single specific technical task is given the player; thus they might be called, in the terminology of a later age, *études,* for which some of Bach's little preludes (BWV 933–943) as well as all the two-part inventions and the three-part sinfonias may be regarded as preliminary studies. The teaching aims of *The Well-Tempered Clavier* go beyond mere technique, however, for the preludes exemplify different types of keyboard composition of the late Baroque. The fugues, wonderfully varied in subjects, texture, form, and treatment, constitute a compendium of all the possibilities of concentrated, monothematic fugal writing. The ancient ricercare is represented (Book I, No. 4 in C♯ minor), as well as the use of inversion, canon, and augmentation (No. 8, E♭ minor), virtuosity in a fugue with a da capo ending (No. 3, C♯ major), and many other styles. In Part II, the Fugue in D major (No. 5) may be mentioned as a superlative example of concentrated abstract musical structure using the simplest materials, while the Prelude and Fugue in F♯ minor (No. 14) is outstanding for beauty of themes and proportions. As in the organ fugues, each subject in Bach's clavier figures is a clearly defined musical personality, of which the entire fugue is to be a logical development and projection.

Bach's clavier suites show the influence of French and Italian as well as of German models. There are three sets of six suites each: the
French and *English* Suites, composed at Cöthen, and the six Partitas published separately between 1726 and 1730 and then collected in 1731 as Part I of the *Clavier Übung.* Part II of the *Clavier Übung* also contains a large Partita in B minor, entitled "Overture in the French style for a harpsichord with two manuals."

The designations *French* and *English* for the suites composed at Cöthen are not Bach's own, and have no descriptive significance.

Mm. 21 (2d half)–24 (1st half), in Bach's autograph

Mm. 21–26, in Carl Czerny's edition

Mm. 22–24, in Hans Bischoff's edition

This passage from the first Prelude in Book I of Bach's The Well-Tempered Clavier *is shown in Bach's autograph manuscript and in two editions. Carl Czerny's edition (first published in the 1830s), evidently based on a copy made after Bach's death, incorporates an inauthentic extra measure after measure 22; elsewhere, Czerny adds phrasings, tempo and dynamic markings not present in Bach's manuscript (e.g. the* dimin. *in m. 21). Bischoff's edition (1883) attempts to give as accurate as possible a reproduction of the source—an ideal that, while not entirely unproblematic in practice, has generally been adhered to by modern scholars.*

The suites in both sets consist of the standard four dance movements (allemande, courante, sarabande, gigue) with additional short movements between the sarabande and gigue; each of the *English* Suites opens with a prelude. Some of these preludes illustrate particularly well the skill with which Bach transferred Italian ensemble forms to the keyboard: the prelude to the third suite, for example, is a concerto Allegro movement with alternating tutti and ritornellos. (An even more striking adaptation of the concerto form is the *Concerto in the Italian Style,* a harpsichord piece which utilizes the two manuals of the instrument to emphasize the tutti-solo contrasts.) The dances in the *English* suites are based on French models, and include several examples of the *double* or ornamented repetition of a movement. In the *French* suites, the second movement is more often an Italian corrente than a French courante.

Most of the dances, especially those in the partitas, are stylized to a high degree; they represent the ultimate in this Baroque form. The preludes of the partitas range through various forms and types of late Baroque keyboard music, as the titles indicate: Praeludium, Praeambulum, Sinfonia (in three movements), Fantasia, Ouverture, and Toccata.

In one clavier work Bach summarized another characteristic species of Baroque keyboard music, the theme and variations. The *Aria with* (thirty) *Different Variations,* published (probably) in 1742 as Part IV of the *Clavier Übung* and generally known as the *Goldberg Variations,* is organized in the monumentally complete fashion of many of the compositions from the latter part of Bach's life. The theme is a sarabande in two balanced sections, the essential bass and harmonic structure of which are preserved in all thirty variations. The form of the whole, therefore, is that of a chaconne or passacaglia. The variations are grouped by threes, the last of each group being a canon, with the canons at successive intervals from the unison to the ninth. The thirtieth and last variation, however, is a *quodlibet,* a mixture of two popular song melodies combined in counterpoint above the fundamental bass; and after this the theme is repeated da capo. The noncanonic variations are of many different types, including inventions, fughettas, a French *ouverture,* ornamental slow arias, and, at regular intervals, sparkling *bravura* pieces for two keyboards. The diverse moods and styles in these variations are unified by means of the recurring bass and harmonies and also by the symmetrical order in which the movements are arranged; the entirety is a perfectly organized structure of magnificent proportions.

Bach wrote six sonatas and partitas for violin alone (BWV 1001–1006), six suites for violoncello alone (BWV 1007–1012), and a sonata for solo flute (BWV 1013). In these works he demonstrated his ability to create the illusion of a harmonic and contrapuntal texture by means of multiple stops or single melodic lines which outline or suggest an interplay of independent voices—a technique going back to the lute composers of the Renaissance and related to the style of the French lutenists and clavecinists of the middle and late Baroque. The chaconne from Bach's solo violin Partita in D minor is one of the most famous works in this form.

In the ensemble forms of chamber music Bach's chief compositions include sonatas for violin and harpsichord (BWV 1014–1019), for viola da gamba and harpsichord (BWV 1027–1029), and for flute and harpsichord (BWV 1030–1035). Most of these works have four

Goldberg Variations

Works for solo violin and violoncello

Ensemble sonatas

movements in slow–fast–slow–fast order, like the *sonata da chiesa;*
and moreover, most of them are actually trio sonatas, since often the
right-hand part of the harpsichord is written as a single melodic
line which forms a duet in counterpoint with the melody of the
other instrument.

The amalgamation of Italian and German styles is most fully
exemplified in Bach's six concertos composed at Cöthen and dedicated to the Margrave of Brandenburg in 1721 (BWV 1046–1051).
In these, Bach adopted the usual three-movement, fast–slow–fast
order of the Italian concertos; the triadic themes, the steadily driving
rhythms, and the ritornello form of the Allegro movements are also
of Italian derivation. But Bach, as usual, transfigured all these
elements, and in addition provided his concertos with such wealth
of counterpoint and such variety of instrumental color as to make
them unique in the literature of this form.

Concertos

The four *Ouvertures* or orchestral suites (BWV 1066–1069) are
likewise masterly examples of this favorite type of Baroque composition, and contain some of Bach's most exuberant and attractive
music. The third and fourth suites, which have trumpets and drums
added to the strings and winds, were undoubtedly intended for performance out-of-doors. The piece popularly known as *Air for the G
String* is an arrangement of the slow movement of the third suite.

*Bach's
orchestral
suites*

The third and sixth Brandenburg concertos are ripieno concertos,
written without featured solo instruments; the others make use of
solo instruments in various combinations against the body of strings
and continuo, and hence are concerti grossi. Bach also wrote two
concertos for solo violin (and one for two violins) with orchestra, and
was probably the first composer to write (or arrange) concertos for
harpsichord. There are seven concertos for solo harpsichord with
orchestra, three for two harpsichords, two for three harpsichords, and
one for four harpsichords, this last an arrangement of a Vivaldi concerto for four violins. Most if not all of the harpsichord concertos,
in fact, are arrangements of violin compositions by Bach himself or
by other composers. Furthermore, Bach worked several movements
from his chamber and orchestral compositions into his Leipzig
cantatas: the prelude from the E-major solo violin partita (BWV
1006) was given a full orchestral setting as the sinfonia of Cantata
No. 29; the first movement of the third Brandenburg Concerto, with
two horns and three oboes added to the orchestra, became the
sinfonia of Cantata No. 174; no fewer than five movements from the
solo clavier concertos are found in cantatas; the opening chorus of
Cantata No. 110 is based on the first movement of the orchestral
Suite in D major (BWV 1069). Such transferring of musical material
from one medium to another was common in the early eighteenth
century; composers evidently felt that a good musical idea was
worth using more than once.

*Concertos for
solo
instruments
with orchestra*

Other works

Two late instrumental works of Bach are in a class by themselves: *Musikalisches Opfer* (*A Musical Offering*) and *Die Kunst der Fuge* (*The Art of Fugue*). The former is based on a theme proposed by Frederick the Great of Prussia on which Bach improvised when he was visiting that monarch at Potsdam in 1747. On returning to Leipzig, Bach wrote out and revised his improvisations, dedicating the finished work to the king. It contains a three- and a six-part ricercar for keyboard and a trio sonata in four movements for flute (King Frederick's instrument), violin, and continuo, together with ten canons. *The Art of Fugue*, composed in 1749–50 and left unfinished at Bach's death, is a systematic demonstration and summary of all types of fugal writing; it consists of eighteen canons and fugues in strictest style, all based on the same subject or one of its transformations, and arranged in a general order of increasing complexity, in the course of which the most difficult and abstruse contrapuntal devices are handled with masterful ease.

Bach's Vocal Music

Bach at Leipzig

In 1723, Leipzig was a flourishing commercial city with about 30,000 inhabitants, noted as a center of printing and publishing, and the seat of an ancient University. It had a good theatre and an opera house; the latter, which closed in 1729, had been a thorn in the side of Bach's predecessor at St. Thomas's, Kuhnau, who complained that it enticed away his best singers. There were five churches in Leipzig in addition to the University chapels; most important were the churches of St. Nicholas and St. Thomas, in which Bach was responsible for the music.

St. Thomas's school was an ancient foundation which took in both day and boarding pupils. It provided fifty-five scholarships for boys and youths who were obliged in return to sing or play in the services of four Leipzig churches as well as to fulfill other musical duties, and who consequently were chosen on the basis of musical as well as general scholastic ability. As Cantor of the school Bach ranked third in the academic hierarchy.

Appointment was in the hands of the City Council, subject to confirmation by the Consistory, the governing body for churches and schools. Bach was not the Council's first choice; the Consistory wanted a more "modern" musician. Both Telemann of Hamburg and Christoph Graupner of Darmstadt had been offered the position, but Telemann used the offer to wangle a raise in salary at Hamburg and Graupner was not able to obtain a dismissal from his master. Bach, having passed the usual examination and satisfied the Council about his theological soundness, was then unanimously elected, and assumed his post in May of 1723. His duties included

Bach's manuscript of the closing measures of the chorale prelude, O Mensch, bewein'.

four hours of teaching each day (he had to teach Latin as well as music), and also preparing music for the church services; and he bound himself, among other things, to lead an exemplary Christian life and not to leave town without permission from the Mayor. He and his family lived in an apartment in one wing of the school, where his study was separated by a thin partition from the home room of the second-year schoolboys.

The citizens of Leipzig did not suffer from any lack of opportunities for public worship. There were daily services in all the churches and special celebrations at festival times. The regular Sunday program of St. Nicholas's and St. Thomas's consisted of three short services in addition to the principal one which began at seven in the morning and lasted until about noon. At this service the choir sang a motet, a Lutheran Mass (Kyrie and Gloria only), hymns, and a cantata. The churches of St. Thomas and St. Nicholas presented the cantata on alternate Sundays. The Cantor directed the first choir at the church whose turn it was to hear the cantata while a deputy conducted the second choir in simpler music at the other church; at the same time the third and fourth choirs, made up of the poorest singers, took care of the more modest musical requirements in the two other churches. A note in Bach's hand (1730?) indicates the minimum requirements as twelve singers (three to each part) for each of the first three choirs and eight for the fourth choir.

Players for the orchestra which accompanied the first choir were recruited partly from the school, partly from the town musicians, and partly from the Collegium Musicum of the University, an extra-curricular musical society for the performance of contemporary music, which had been founded by Telemann in 1704 and of which Bach became director in 1729. The orchestra, according to Bach's requirements, consisted of two flutes (when needed), two or three oboes, one or two bassoons, three trumpets, kettledrums, and strings with continuo—a total of eighteen to twenty-four players. It seems probable, in view of the restrictions and difficulties under which he labored, that Bach never heard a really good performance of any of his works at Leipzig. Yet, on the other hand, conditions as a whole were such as to stimulate a composer's creative power: new compositions were required at regular intervals; singers and instrumentalists, however inadequate, at least were always on hand; and his position, with all its petty annoyances, was a secure and honorable one.

Altogether, the Leipzig churches required 58 cantatas each year, in addition to Passion music for Good Friday, Magnificats at Vespers for three festivals, an annual cantata for the installation of the City Council, and occasional music such as funeral motets and wedding cantatas for which the Cantor received an extra fee. Bach undertook to provide new works for the church services from his own pen as frequently as possible; for the first few years his production averaged about one cantata per month. Approximately 200 of his cantatas have been preserved—some of them newly written for Leipzig, others refashioned from earlier works. In the early cantatas the composer's poetic response to the changing affections and images of the text flows spontaneously in music of intense dramatic expression and unexpectedly varied forms; the later Leipzig cantatas are by comparison less subjective in feeling and more regular in structure. However, no generalized description can possibly suggest the infinite variety, the wealth of musical invention, technical mastery, and religious devotion in Bach's cantatas. Two or three examples will serve as an introduction to this vast treasure of music.

Bach's church cantatas

Cantata No. 21

Cantata No. 21,[5] *Ich hatte viel Bekümmernis (My heart was deeply troubled)*, probably composed at Weimar in 1713, consists of a sinfonia, four choruses on Biblical texts, three arias, two recitatives, and

[5] The numbering of the Bach cantatas follows the Bach Gesellschaft edition, which is also that of BWV. The order is not chronological.

a duet. The cantata is divided into two parts, one of which presumably was sung before the sermon and the other after. Part I depicts the sorrow and distress of the sinful soul, Part II its rejoicing in the salvation brought through Christ. The contrast of moods is announced in the first chorus by the sharply contrasted musical settings of the two phrases of text: "When the cares of my heart are many,/ Thy consolations cheer my soul" (Psalms, xciv: 19). The soul's distress is further depicted in a short soprano aria and in an eloquent accompanied recitative and aria for tenor. The texts of these numbers are typical examples of German Baroque religious poetry, with subjective feelings expressed in fervid—not to say extravagant— terms: the tenor aria likens the lost soul to a ship being driven to destruction in a storm, a favorite comparison in opera arias; and the music, a full da capo form in F minor, is no less operatic in the vehemence of its expression and the vividness of its pictorial details. Part I closes with a chorus of consolation: "Why art thou cast down, O my soul?" (Psalms, xlii:5), each phrase of which has its own musical motive, ending with a fugue on the words "my help and my God." The tonality throughout Part I is (except for the tenor aria) C minor.

Part II opens with a tender accompanied recitative for soprano and bass in E♭ major, leading into a duet in the same key. Here the soprano allegorically represents the soul and the bass the Saviour. The following chorus, in G minor, introduces the text "Return, O my soul, to thy rest; for the Lord has dealt bountifully with thee" (Psalms, cxvi:7) in a peacefully flowing stepwise theme in triple measure, which is developed contrapuntally in three voices. Against this background are intoned two stanzas from the chorale "If thou dost suffer God to guide thee." The chorale melody is heard in long notes, the first stanza in the tenor and the next in the soprano, with the stepwise theme in the other three parts always accompanying and furnishing interludes between the phrases of the chorale; the whole thus has the form of an extended organ chorale prelude, a form Bach often employed for choruses in his cantatas. A short cheerful tenor song in F major, with da capo, voices the soul's gladness, and the final chorus, in C major, brings the cantata to a stirring climax. This chorus begins with a setting of the words "Worthy is the Lamb that was slain" which is strikingly similar to Handel's setting of the same text in *Messiah;* equally Handelian is the brilliance of the choral writing in the concluding fugue, reinforced by the full orchestra with three trumpets and timpani on the words "Praise and honor and glory and power be to our God forever and ever, alleluia, amen." (Rev. v:12–13.) This chorus is to Bach's choral style what the early fugue in D major (BWV 532) is to his organ style: both show what he could do, when he chose, in the way of virtuosity and splendor of effect.

Cantatas No. 4 and No. 80

Bach used chorale melodies in a multitude of different ways in his cantatas. Cantata No. 4, *Christ lag in Todesbanden* (*Christ lay in death's dark prison*), refashioned from an earlier version and sung at Leipzig in 1724, is exceptional in that it goes back to the old form of chorale variations. A more usual scheme in the Leipzig cantatas is that used in No. 80, *Ein' feste Burg* (*A mighty fortress*), composed in 1715 and later (in 1724?) revised. The opening chorus in D major is a towering fantasia on the melody and words of the first stanza of the chorale. The vocal lines, freely adapted from the chorale tune, introduce each phrase in turn fugally, leading to a simple climactic statement of the phrase by the trumpet in its high "clarino" register, answered in strict canon by the bass instruments. In this way the melody, phrase by phrase, is expanded into a vast architectural structure of 223 measures. The next number is a duet, also in D, for soprano and bass. The soprano sings the words of the second chorale stanza to an ornate version of the tune while the bass, in an even more ornate but completely independent line, has a separate text appropriately commenting on that of the soprano; they are accompanied by a steady vigorous sixteenth-note figure in the strings *unisono* and the continuo bass moving in eighth notes. The texture is one of four independent contrapuntal parts, of which the highest, the soprano solo, is doubled and further embellished by the oboe. Then follow a recitative and arioso for bass and an aria (B minor) for soprano, both on inserted poetic texts. The third stanza of the chorale is set in the form of a chorale prelude, the tune being proclaimed by the chorus in unison while each phrase is introduced and accompanied by the full orchestra in an energetic 6/8 rhythm. A recitative-arioso for tenor and a quietly moving duet for tenor and alto (G major) follow, and the cantata is concluded by the fourth and final stanza of the chorale, now in a straightforward four-part harmonic setting for full chorus (in which the congregation also may have joined) with instruments doubling the vocal parts.

Cantatas like this one, beginning with an extended chorale fantasia and ending with the same chorale in simple four-part harmony, with possible references to, or other settings of, the chorale in the intermediate numbers, are numerous in Bach's Leipzig period. In both spirit and form they are intimately bound up with the church liturgy, but there is no uniform scheme that governs all. Many use more than one chorale; others have a chorale only at the end; still others use the full chorale text but with new music for some of the stanzas; and a few have no chorale. There are also a few solo cantatas from this period, among which No. 51 for soprano and No. 82 for bass are especially noteworthy.

Bach's secular cantatas

Bach's secular cantatas, most of which he titled "dramma per musica," were composed for various occasions, and not infrequently he used some of the same music for a sacred text: eleven numbers of the *Christmas Oratorio,* for example, appear also in secular cantatas. Among the best of the "musical dramas" are *Phoebus and Pan* (BWV 201) and *Schleicht, spielende Wellen (Glide gently, ye waters;* BWV 206) which was written to celebrate the birthday of Augustus III in 1733; the *Coffee Cantata* and the burlesque *Peasant Cantata* (BWV 211 and 212) are delightful specimens of Bach's lighter music.

The word *motet* at Leipzig in Bach's time signified a composition for chorus, generally in contrapuntal style, without obbligato instrumental parts, and with a Biblical or chorale text. The motets sung *Bach's motets* in the Leipzig churches were relatively short, and were used as musical introductions to the service; apparently they were chosen from a traditional repertoire of old works, and the Cantor was not expected to furnish new motets. The six surviving motets of Bach (BWV 225–230) were written either for particular occasions (such as funerals) or perhaps for special church services. They are long works, and four of them are for double chorus. The voice parts are always complete in themselves, but undoubtedly in Bach's time they were sung with instrumental doubling—as was also, for example, the opening chorus of Cantata No. 38, which is in motet style. Many of the motets incorporate chorale melodies; the five-voice *Jesu meine Freude (Jesus, my joy)* uses the chorale in six of its eleven movements.

The great Magnificat (BWV 243), for five-part chorus and orchestra, is one of Bach's most melodious works, more Italian in style than most of his church music. The *Christmas Oratorio* (BWV 248), produced at Leipzig in 1734, is in reality a set of six cantatas for the festivals of the Christmas and Epiphany season. The Biblical narratives (Luke ii:1–21; Matt. ii:1–12) are presented in recitative; appropriate arias and chorales are added to reflect or comment on the various episodes of the story. The designation of "oratorio" is justified by reason of the narrative element, which is not present in the usual cantata.

The culmination of Bach's work as a church musician was reached in his settings of the Passion according to St. John and St. Matthew. These two works, essentially similar in structure, are the crowning *Bach's* examples of the north German tradition of Gospel Passion settings *Passions* in oratorio style. For the *St. John Passion,* in addition to the Gospel story (St. John xviii and xix, with interpolations from St. Matthew) and fourteen chorales, Bach also borrowed words, with some alterations, for added lyrical numbers from the popular Passion poem of B. H. Brockes, adding some verses of his own. Bach's musical setting, which was, probably, first performed at Leipzig in 1724, was subjected later to numerous revisions.

The *St. Matthew Passion,* for double chorus, soloists, double orchestra, and two organs, first performed in 1729, is a drama of epic grandeur, "the most noble and inspired treatment of its subject in the whole range of music." The text is from St. Matthew's Gospel, chapters xxvi and xxvii; this is narrated in tenor solo recitative and choruses, and the narration is interspersed with chorales, a duet, and numerous arias, most of which are preceded by arioso recitatives. The "Passion Chorale" (see Example VIII–1) appears five times, in different keys and in four different four-part harmonizations. The author of the added recitatives and arias was C. F. Henrici (1700–64; pseudonym, Picander), a Leipzig poet who also provided many of Bach's cantata texts. As in the St. John Passion, the chorus sometimes participates in the action and sometimes, like the chorus in Greek drama, is an articulate spectator introducing or reflecting upon the events of the narrative. The opening and closing choruses of Part I are huge chorale fantasias; in the first, the chorale melody is given to a special ripieno choir of soprano voices.

Nearly every phrase of the *St. Matthew Passion* affords examples of Bach's genius for merging pictorial musical figures with expressive effects. Of the many beautiful passages in this masterpiece of music, four may be singled out for special mention: the alto recitative *Ah, Golgotha;* the soprano aria *In Love my Saviour now is dying;* the last setting of the Passion Chorale, after Jesus' death on the Cross; and the stupendous three measures of chorus on the words *Truly this was the Son of God.*

The *Passion According to St. Matthew* is the apotheosis of Lutheran church music: in it the chorale, the concertato style, the recitative, the arioso, and the da capo aria are united under the ruling majesty of the central religious theme. All these elements, save the chorale, are equally characteristic of Baroque opera. The dramatic, theatrical qualities of both the *St. Matthew* and the *St. John Passions* are obvious. While it is true that Bach never wrote an opera, nevertheless the language, the forms, and the spirit of opera are fully present in the Passions.

The Mass in B minor

The *Mass in B minor* is, necessarily, more general in content and more contemplative in viewpoint than the Passions, and hence less dramatic in detail. Choruses (mostly in five parts) take a far larger proportion of the work than they do in the Passions. The Kyrie and Gloria were presented in 1733 to Frederick Augustus, the Catholic King of Poland and Elector of Saxony, together with Bach's petition for an honorary appointment to the Electoral Chapel—a petition which was not granted until three years later. The remaining movements—some newly composed, others adapted—date from various periods in Bach's life; the work was not completed before 1747 or 1749. Bach probably never heard it performed in its entirety, though parts were sung at Leipzig, where an abbreviated form of the Latin Mass still had a place in the liturgy.

Several numbers of the B-minor Mass are rearrangements from cantatas, for example, the *Gratias agimus* and the *Dona nobis pacem* (both of which use the same music) from the first chorus of Cantata No. 29, and the *Crucifixus* from the first chorus of Cantata No. 12. This Mass is not liturgical music; it is too long and too elaborate to be used in any ordinary church service. It is rather a work which, like Beethoven's *Missa solemnis,* transcends denominational limits and rises to the height of a universal statement of Christian faith. Bach symbolized the continuity of the Christian tradition by using Gregorian *cantus firmi* in the Credo and in the *Confiteor* choruses. The *Crucifixus* is perhaps the most wonderful example in all music of the use of an ostinato bass. The music was written originally in 1714, to different words, as the opening chorus of a cantata. Bach altered the original ending to depict Christ's descent into the grave by the low register of the voices and at the same time, by a modulation to G major, to suggest the hope of the resurrection, which bursts forth in the next chorus like a dance of joy.

Burial and resurrection might serve in some degree to describe the history of Bach's music. Works published, or prepared by Bach for publication, during his lifetime include the *Clavier Übung,* the *Schübler* chorales, the variations on *Vom Himmel hoch,* the *Musical Offering,* and *The Art of Fugue.* Changed musical taste in the later eighteenth century led to a general neglect of Bach, but the eclipse was far from total. Although no complete large work of his was published between 1752 and 1800, some of the preludes and fugues from *The Well-Tempered Clavier* appeared in print and the whole collection circulated in innumerable manuscript copies. Haydn owned a copy of the *Mass in B minor.* Mozart knew *The Art of Fugue* and studied the motets on a visit to Leipzig in 1789. Citations from Bach's works are frequent in the musical literature of the time, and the important periodical, the *Allgemeine musikalische Zeitung,* opened its first issue (1798) with a Bach portrait. The full discovery of Bach, however, was the work of the nineteenth century. It was marked by the publication of the first important biography (by J. N. Forkel) in 1802; by Zelter's revival of the *St. Matthew Passion* and its performance at Berlin under Mendelssohn's direction in 1829; and by the foundation, in 1850, of the Bach society, whose collected edition of Bach's works was completed by 1900.

Summary

We can begin to understand the central position Bach has in the history of music when we realize, first, that he absorbed into his music the multiplicity of styles and forms current in the early eighteenth century and developed hitherto unsuspected potentialities in every one; and second, that in his music the opposed principles of harmony and counterpoint, melody and polyphony, are maintained in a tense but satisfying equilibrium found in no other composer. The continuing vitality of his music is not, of course, due to its historical significance as a summation of the late Baroque, but to the qualities of the music itself: the concentrated and individual themes, the copious musical invention, the balance between harmonic and contrapuntal forces, the strength of rhythm, the clarity of form, the grandeur of proportion, the imaginative use of pictorial and symbolic figures, the intensity of expression always controlled by a ruling architectural idea, and the technical perfection of every detail.

George Frideric Handel

Vivaldi represented the progressive Italian musical thought of his time; Rameau embodied the French tradition established from the days of Louis XIV; Bach, absorbing the achievements of both Italy and France, fused them with his own north German Lutheran heritage in an intense, uniquely personal synthesis. Handel (1685–1759), on the other hand, was a completely international composer; his music has German seriousness, Italian suavity, and French grandeur. These qualities were matured in England, the soil then most favorable to the development of such a cosmopolitan style; and England furthermore provided the choral tradition which made possible Handel's oratorios. Vivaldi's influence on the musical world was immediate (though he had died totally forgotten in 1741); Rameau's was felt more slowly, and then exclusively in the fields of opera and music theory; Bach's work lay in comparative obscurity for half a century. But Handel, unlike Bach, was internationally renowned in his lifetime; and unlike Rameau and Vivaldi, his fame was never eclipsed during succeeding generations.

Handel's career

There were no musicians in Handel's family, but the boy's talent was so pronounced that his father grudgingly allowed him to take lessons from Friedrich Wilhelm Zachow, composer, organist, and director of music in the principal church of Handel's native town of Halle in Saxony. Under Zachow's tuition, Handel became an accomplished organist and harpsichordist, studied violin and oboe, received a thorough grounding in counterpoint, and became familiar with the music of contemporary German and Italian composers by the usual and effective method of copying their scores. He matriculated at the University of Halle in 1702; at age eighteen he was appointed cathedral organist. Almost immediately, however, he determined to give up a musical career as cantor, for which he had been prepared under Zachow, in favor of opera. He went to Hamburg (then the principal center of German opera), where he remained from 1703 to 1706. There his principal musical acquaintances were Mattheson and Keiser. At the age of nineteen he composed his first opera, *Almira,* which was performed at the Hamburg opera house in 1705.

From some time in 1706 until the middle of 1710 Handel was in Italy, where he was soon recognized as one of the coming young composers and where he associated with the leading patrons and musicians of Rome, Florence, Naples, and Venice. He made the acquaintance of Corelli and the two Scarlattis; Domenico, the son, was exactly Handel's age. He also met Agostino Steffani, whose musical style, along with those of Corelli and Alessandro Scarlatti, was an important influence. Altogether, these Italian years were decisive for all Handel's later career. His chief compositions of the period were several Latin motets, an oratorio, a large number of Italian cantatas, and the opera *Agrippina,* which triumphed at Venice in 1709. The foundations of Handel's style were laid by the time he left Italy, at the age of twenty-five, to become Music Director at the Electoral Court of Hanover.

That appointment turned out to be only an episode. Almost immediately Handel was off on a long leave of absence, visiting London in the season of 1710–11, where he made a sensation with his opera *Rinaldo*. In the autumn of 1712, he was granted a second permission to go to London, on condition that he return "within a reasonable time." He had still not returned two years later when his master, the Elector of Hanover, was proclaimed King George I of England. For a while the truant Music Director hesitated to show his face at court. The legend is that Handel was restored to favor for having composed and conducted a suite of pieces for wind instruments to be played as a surprise for the King during a boating party on the Thames; these pieces, or at any rate some like them, were published in 1740 under the title of *Water Music*. Enjoying the patronage of the royal family, the Duke of Chandos, and other influential personages, Handel settled down to a long and prosperous career in London.

Handel at London

Italian opera was in fashion. About sixty noble and wealthy gentlemen had organized a joint stock company, called the Royal Academy of Music, to present operas to the London public. As composers they engaged Handel and two Italians, Attilio Ariosti (1666–ca. 1740) and Giovanni Bononcini (1670–1747); Bononcini, who had already produced many operas at Rome, Berlin, and Vienna, became for a time Handel's most serious rival in London. The Royal Academy of Music flourished from 1720 to 1728; for it Handel composed some of his best operas, including *Radamisto* (1720), *Ottone* (1723), *Giulio Cesare* (1724), *Rodelinda* (1725), and *Admeto* (1727). There were troubles with temperamental singers; a performance in 1727 was enlivened by a free fight on the stage between the two leading sopranos:

> . . . a great Disturbance happened at the Opera, occasioned by the Partisans of the Two Celebrated Rival Ladies, Cuzzoni and Faustina. The Contention at first was only carried on by Hissing on one Side, and Clapping on the other; but proceeded at length to Catcalls, and other great Indecencies: And notwithstanding the Princess Caroline was present, no Regards were of Force to restrain the Rudness of the Opponents.[6]

The popular success of *The Beggar's Opera* in 1728 showed that the English public was beginning to grow tired of Italian opera, and the Academy began to have financial difficulties. In 1729 the

---

[6] From the *British Journal* of June 10, 1727; quoted in Otto Erich Deutsch, *Handel, a Documentary Biography*, New York, 1955, p. 210.

Academy decided to give up its enterprise, and Handel with a partner took over the theatre in the dual role of composer and entrepreneur. However, a competing organization, the Opera of the Nobility, which featured the Neapolitan composer Nicola Porpora (1686–1768) and the highest-priced singers in Europe, so effectually divided the London public that by 1737 both companies were practically bankrupt. Handel's chief operas in this period were *Orlando* (1733) and *Alcina* (1735). The best of his later operas were *Serse* (1738) and *Deidamia* (1741), the former frankly comic and the latter subtly satirical. Neither was very successful at the time, though both are eminently worthy of revival today. Incidentally, the opening aria of *Serse* later became famous, usually in instrumental transcriptions, under the title "Largo from Xerxes."

Handel decided during the 1730s that opera, or at least his kind of opera, could no longer make its way in London. He therefore turned to a new kind of composition, the oratorio in English, which could be put on at less expense and for which moreover there was a potentially large middle-class public that had never felt at home with the aristocratic entertainment of opera in Italian. Handel had already experimented in oratorio-like forms with English words, of which the most notable examples were the serenata *Acis and Galatea* (*ca.* 1720), the oratorio *Esther* (first performed as a masque about 1720 and presented publicly in a revised version in 1732), and a setting of Dryden's ode, *Alexander's Feast,* in 1736. In 1739, the Handelian oratorio on a Biblical subject with choruses was established with two works, *Saul* and *Israel in Egypt.* After this time, Handel leased a theatre for annual Lenten oratorio performances, at which the composer, as an added attraction, improvised at the organ during intermissions. These concerts laid the foundation of Handel's immense popularity with the English public, a popularity which made his music the prevailing influence in British musical life for nearly a century. Of his 26 English oratorios the most notable, in addition to those already mentioned, were *Messiah,* first performed at Dublin in 1742; *Semele,* on a mythological text by Congreve (originally written in 1709 as an opera libretto); and the Biblical oratorios *Judas Maccabaeus* (1746) and *Jephtha* (1751).

Handel became a naturalized British subject in 1726. He has always been regarded by the English as a national institution, and with good reason: all his mature life was passed in London, and all the works for which he is remembered were written for British audiences; he was the most imposing figure in English music during his lifetime, and it was the English public that nourished his genius and remained loyal to his memory. His body was buried with public honors in Westminster Abbey. His imperious, independent nature made him redoubtable in everything with which he was concerned, and not only in matters strictly professional: the opposition represented by the Opera of the Nobility, for example, was as much political as musical. He was satirized as a glutton and a tyrant, but the rougher aspects of his personality were balanced by a sense of humor and redeemed by a nature generous, honorable, and fundamentally pious.

Handel's instrumental music is least important in his production and least in quantity, although it must be remembered that the organ and harpsichord improvisations for which he was so famous have naturally not been preserved. Unlike the operas and oratorios, most of the instrumental compositions cannot be accurately dated, since the published collections included pieces that had been composed many years before the date of publication.

Handel's instrumental music

Handel's keyboard works include three sets of concertos for harpsichord or organ, two collections of suites for harpsichord published respectively in 1720 and 1733, and a number of miscellaneous pieces. The suites contain not only the usual dance movements but also specimens of most of the keyboard forms of the time. The popular set of variations called *The Harmonious Blacksmith* (the title was bestowed in the nineteenth century) is the air (with variations) from the fifth Suite of the first collection. Handel composed 19 solo sonatas and an equal number of trio sonatas, for various chamber music combinations. In most of these the dominant influence is obviously that of Corelli, but the sophistication of the harmonies and the smooth, easy assurance of the musical movement (particularly in the Allegros) mark a later stage of the Italian style.

Handel's suites and sonatas

The most significant of Handel's instrumental works are those for full orchestra, including the overtures to his operas and oratorios, the two suites known as the *Fireworks Music* (1749) and the *Water Music* (?1717), and above all the concertos. There are six concertos for woodwinds and strings, usually called the "oboe concertos," and twelve *Grand Concertos* Opus 6, composed in 1739.

Handel's concertos

On the whole, the concertos of Opus 6 show a combination of retrospective and modern elements, with the former predominating. The ruling conception is the same as that in Corelli's work, namely, a *sonata da chiesa* for full orchestra. The framework is the usual order of four movements (slow–fast–slow–fast), with one of the Allegros fugal; but this scheme is usually expanded by an additional movement or two, which may be in dance rhythm. The common designation of *concerto grosso* does not strictly suit these works, since as a rule the solo parts are not markedly set off from the tuttis: in fact, in a majority of the movements the concertino strings either merely play throughout in unison with the ripieno or else appear by themselves only for brief trio-like interludes; and when there are extended passages for the solo violins, these usually differ neither in thematic material nor in style from the tutti passages. Only rarely and, as it were, incidentally, does Handel imitate Vivaldi in giving decorative figuration to a solo violin (as in Nos. 3, 6, and 11). Moreover, the serious, dignified bearing and the prevailingly full contrapuntal texture of this music are less characteristic of the 1730s than of the earlier part of the century when Handel was forming his style in Italy. But, conservative or no, the concertos are fascinating music, original and abundantly varied.

The sixth, in G minor, may serve as an example of the range of Handel's orchestral writing. An opening *Larghetto e affettuoso* of serenely Classical mould is followed by a vigorous fugal Allegro, a fine specimen of an orchestral or ripieno concerto movement. The second slow movement, in E♭, is a broad pastoral landscape in the form of a *musette en rondeau.* The next Allegro begins with a solidly constructed tutti and continues in the manner of Vivaldi with the first violin featured in independent solo figuration. There is a short final Allegro of minuet-like character, with spare three-voice homophonic texture, and in the usual bisectional dance form, like the finale of a sinfonia. Most of the other concertos of Opus 6 are equally variegated; the individual quality of the themes, the inexhaustible flow of invention, and the grandeur of proportion have assured these works a permanent place in the repertory.

Handel's operas

To the general public, Handel has long been known almost exclusively as a composer of oratorios; nonetheless, for thirty-five years of his life his principal occupation was composing and conducting operas—and his operas contain as large a proportion of memorable music as do his oratorios. He was no revolutionist, like Monteverdi or Wagner; his achievement was simply that in an age when opera was the main concern of ambitious musicians, Handel excelled all his contemporaries. His operas were heard not only in London but also quite frequently in Germany and Italy during his lifetime. Today, after a long period of neglect, they are beginning to come back into favor. Many of them have proved successful in modern revivals, a practice which started in Germany in the 1920s and by now has extended to England, America, and other countries. How far it is necessary or allowable to "adjust" Handel's operas (as well as those of other Baroque composers) for performance in the present-day theatre is currently a live issue among musicologists and conductors.

The subjects of these operas are the usual ones of the time: tales of magic and marvelous adventure, or, more often, episodes from the lives of heroes of antiquity, freely adapted to get the maximum number of intense dramatic situations. The musical scheme is likewise that of the early eighteenth century: development of the action in *recitativo secco,* interrupted periodically by solo da capo arias. Each aria is intended to give musical expression to a single specific mood or effect, so that the opera as a whole consists of a series of arias strung like pearls on the thread of the plot.

These operas were written so that every singer had arias that favorably displayed the scope of his vocal and histrionic powers; furthermore, the arias had to be distributed according to the importance of each member of the cast. Within the limits of these requirements the composer might work with as much freedom as he chose or as his inventive powers allowed. Handel, like most eighteenth-century composers, could turn out an opera any time that would be good enough to satisfy expectations and enjoy the usual brief success; but he could also on occasion create a masterpiece like *Ottone,* which teems with beautiful melodic writing. His scores are remarkable for the wide variety of aria types, a variety that eludes strict classification. Arias range from brilliant virtuoso coloratura effects to sustained, sublimely expressive pathetic songs, such as the *Cara sposa* in *Rinaldo* or *Se pietà* in *Giulio Cesare;* arias of Baroque grandeur with rich contrapuntal accompaniments alternate with simple folk-like melodies or arias *all'unisono,* in which the strings play in unison with the voice throughout; still other songs are in dance rhythms, and others (especially in *Serse* and *Deidamia*) in the fashionable light melodic manner of the Italian school. The pastoral scenes are especially noteworthy examples of eighteenth-century musical nature painting. Not all of Handel's arias are in da capo form, and occasionally he presented two contrasted affects in the same aria.

Transcending all mastery of technique is Handel's power of incarnating in music the essence of a mood or affect, with overwhelming poetic depth and suggestiveness. This is a quality that cannot be adequately analyzed or described in words, but can only be sensed from the experience of the music itself. It is because of this power that some of the personages in Handel's operas loom as figures of heroic grandeur, like the great characters in the tragedies of Corneille and Racine.

In addition to the ordinary *recitativo secco* Handel sometimes, for scenes of particular poignancy or rapidly shifting affects, used the more weighty and more melodic *recitativo accompagnato.* For these accompanied recitatives—as indeed for many other features of his operas—Handel found models in the works of Alessandro Scarlatti. Sometimes both types of recitative are freely combined with short arias or ariosos (short songs flexible in form and rhythm, syllabic in style, and without text repetition) to make large scene-complexes that recall the freedom of seventeenth-century Venetian opera and at the same time foreshadow the methods of Gluck and other composers of the later eighteenth century. Examples of such scene-complexes occur in *Orlando* (end of Act II) and, on a smaller scale, in *Giulio Cesare* (Act I, Scene 7, and Act III, Scene 4) and elsewhere.

Handel's operas, typically for his time, consist almost entirely of solo singing. There are occasional descriptive sinfonias and, in a few works, ballets. Ensembles larger than duets are rare, as are also choruses, most of which, strictly speaking, are ensembles in chordal style with only one singer to a part.

The Italian Baroque oratorio was hardly anything other than an opera on a sacred subject, presented in concert instead of on the stage. This conception is an essential element of Handel's oratorios. Most of the arias in these works differ in no important respects— neither in form, musical style, nature of the musical ideas, nor technique of expressing affects—from the arias in his operas. As in the operas also, the mood of each aria is usually prepared, and the aria introduced, by a preceding recitative. But there are alterations and additions which transform the oratorios into something different from the conventional eighteenth-century opera.

Fundamental is the fact that Handel's oratorio librettos were in English. The Italian used in opera undoubtedly had snob appeal for London listeners most of whom, if pressed, could hardly have translated a dozen words of that language without help. The use of English was gratifying to the middle class; it also meant that at least some of the absurdities and conceits which were part of the tissue of the usual opera libretto must be renounced, since they could no longer be decently concealed under the cloak of a foreign tongue. Even more important, a new kind of subject matter had to be found. Classical mythology and ancient history were all very well for upper-class audiences who, whatever the actual state of their education, felt obliged to pretend some acquaintance with such matters.

The entire storehouse of both history and mythology known to middle-class Protestant England in the eighteenth century was the Bible, or, more accurately, the Old Testament, including the apocryphal books. All of Handel's sacred oratorios, and especially his most popular ones, were based on Old Testament stories (even *Messiah* has more text from the Old than from the New Testament, except in its third part). Moreover, such subjects as *Saul, Israel in Egypt, Judas Maccabaeus,* and *Joshua* had an additional appeal based on something besides familiarity with the ancient sacred narratives: it was impossible for English audiences in an era of prosperity and expanding empire not to feel a kinship with the chosen people of old whose heroes triumphed by the special favor of Jehovah. Handel more than once was chosen to be the official musical spokesman on occasions of national moment, as with his four anthems for the coronation of George II (1727), the Funeral Anthem for Queen Caroline (1737), the *Te Deum* in thanksgiving for an English military victory at Dettingen in 1743, and the *Fireworks Music* of 1749 celebrating the Peace of Aix-la-Chapelle; the oratorio *Judas Maccabaeus* (1747), like the *Occasional Oratorio* of the preceding year, was designed to honor the Duke of Cumberland for his victory over the Jacobite rebels at Culloden. But even where there was no immediate connection with a particular occasion, many of Handel's oratorios struck a responsive patriotic note with the British public.

The oratorios are not to be regarded as church music. They are intended for the concert hall, and are much closer to the theatre than to the church service. Not all are even on sacred subjects: some, like *Semele* and *Hercules* (1744), are mythological; others, like *Alexander's Feast,* the *Ode for St. Cecilia's Day* (1739), and Handel's last composition, *The Triumph of Time and Truth* (1757), are allegorical. The arrangement of the libretto varies: *Susanna* (1748), *Theodora* (1749), and *Joseph* (1743) are practically straight operas; most of the Biblical oratorios stay close to the original narrative, but the Biblical text was rewritten in recitatives (sometimes prose, sometimes rhymed verse), arias, and choruses; *Israel in Egypt,* on the other hand, tells the story of the exodus of the Israelites entirely in the words of scripture. *Messiah* also has a purely Scriptural text, but is the least typical of all Handel's oratorios in that it tells no story; it is a series of contemplations of the Christian idea of redemption, starting with Old Testament prophecies and going through the life of Christ to His final triumph.

Beyond question the most important innovation in the oratorios was Handel's use of the chorus. To be sure, the chorus had had its place in the Italian oratorios of Carissimi, and Handel's early training had made him familiar with the Lutheran choral music of Germany as well as with the characteristic combination of the chorus with orchestra and soloists in the southern German Catholic centers; but the English choral tradition impressed him most profoundly. His conquest of this English musical idiom was fully achieved in the *Chandos* anthems, written for the Duke of Chandos between 1718 and 1720—masterpieces of Anglican Baroque church music from which the composer frequently borrowed in his later works.

The monumental character of Handel's choral style was particularly appropriate to oratorios in which emphasis is on communal rather than individual expression as in the opera aria. Handel often used choruses in the oratorios where in opera an aria would appear —that is, as appropriate commentary or reflection on a situation that has arisen in the course of the action. Inevitably the collective nature of the choral group tends to endue such places with a certain impersonality, a quality akin to the choruses of Greek drama: one of the best of many examples from the Handel oratorios is the chorus *How dark, O Lord, are Thy decrees* in *Jephtha*. Handel's chorus also participates in the action, for instance in *Judas Maccabaeus;* is an element in incidental scenes, as in *Solomon;* or even narrates, as in *Israel in Egypt,* where the choral recitative *He sent a thick darkness* is remarkable equally for its unusual form, its strange modulations, and its pictorial writing.

Handel's choral style

Pictorial and affective musical symbolism is one of the most conspicuous and endearing features of Handel's choral writing. Of course word painting and descriptive figures—the musical language

Handel's autograph manuscript of I know that my Redeemer liveth *from* The Messiah. *(The Royal Music Library, British Museum)*

of the affections—were universal in the Baroque, but Handel often used these devices in especially felicitous ways. Many examples may be found in *Israel in Egypt:* the somewhat literal representation of frogs, flies, lice, hail, and the other plagues of Egypt is amusing rather than impressive; but the profound and moving symbolism of *The people shall hear* lifts this chorus to an eminence hardly equalled elsewhere even by Handel himself. In *Messiah* there is a half-playful use of word painting, the appositeness of which is surprising in view of the fact that the music, up to the last few measures, was adapted from a rather frivolous Italian duet of Handel's composed shortly before. The chorus in *Messiah* sings: "All we like sheep have *gone astray* [diverging melodic lines]; we have *turned* [a rapidly twisting, turning figure that never gets away from its starting point] every one *to his own way"* [stubborn insistence on a single repeated note]; but the point is revealed suddenly, with incomparable dramatic force, at the solemn coda: "and the Lord hath laid on Him the iniquity of us all." A parallel though less striking dramatic contrast is heard in the chorus *For unto us a child is born.* This music is taken from another part of the same Italian duet; the carefree roulades that celebrate the birth of the Redeemer lead up to the mighty Handelian hammerstrokes on the words "Wonderful, Counsellor, the Mighty God."

Passages such as these reveal Handel the dramatist, the unerring master of grandiose effects. He is one of the great composers who know how to write well for a chorus. His style is simpler than Bach's, less finely chiseled, less subjective, less consistently contrapuntal. He alternates passages in open fugal texture with solid blocks of harmony, sets a melodic line in sustained notes against one in quicker rhythm. Everything is planned so as to lie well within the most effective range of the voices; at points where he designs the maximum fullness of choral sound, especially, Handel brings the four parts tightly together, the basses and tenors high, the sopranos and altos in the middle register. This grouping is often used in the characteristically Handelian closing cadences: an *allegro* chorus climaxing on an inconclusive chord; a tense moment of silence; and then the final cadential chords in three or four splendid sonorous *adagio* harmonies, in which the chorus, in one great outburst of sound, gathers up the whole meaning of everything that has come before.

Handel, like most eighteenth-century composers, occasionally incorporated in his compositions themes, sections, or even whole movements from other works, sometimes literally but more often with changes and improvements. Most of his borrowings were from his own earlier works, but a considerable number were from other composers; three duets and eleven of the 28 choruses of *Israel in Egypt,* for example, were taken in whole or in part from the music of others, while four choruses were arrangements from earlier works by Handel himself. Further borrowings, although not on such an extensive scale, have been traced in many of Handel's compositions written after 1737. It has been conjectured that he resorted to this as a means of overcoming the inertia that sometimes afflicted him when he was beginning a new work, particularly after 1737, when he had suffered a paralytic stroke and nervous collapse. However that may be, Handel is not to be criticized as a modern composer might be for plagiarism. Borrowing, transcribing, adapting, rearranging, parodying (in the same sense as in the Parody Mass of the sixteenth century) was a universal and accepted practice in the Baroque. When Handel borrowed, he more often than not repaid with interest, clothing the borrowed material with new beauty and preserving it for generations that otherwise would scarcely have known of its existence.[7]

Handel's borrowings

[7] Apropos the question of originality in art are these words of William Ivins. He is speaking particularly of drawing, but his conclusions are equally relevant to music: " 'Originality' in art is very much like originality in sin, for we should always bear in mind that 'original sin' is the sin, or at least the kind of sin, about which we poor mortals can do nothing at all. We have it simply because we are descended from Adam and Eve. In the same way, draughtsmen who are original are so no matter how much they may attempt to copy or emulate something that someone else has done before them. . . . 'Copies' and imitations made by men who have this ineradicable quality of originality are infinitely more original than 'original drawings' made by men who lack it . . . The best way to find out how much originality a man has is to see what he can do with another man's idea. I believe it is something of this kind that explains why the great masters—the most original men, that is—have always come out of long lineages of other great artists, on whose shoulders and triumphs they stand." William M. Ivins, Jr., "Some Disconnected Notes about Drawing," *Harper's Magazine*, December, 1949, 84–85. Quoted by permission of the publishers. See also F. B. Zimmerman, "Musical Borrowings in the English Baroque," *MQ* 52 (1966), 483–95.

XII. The Early Eighteenth Century

Summary

Handel's greatness and historical significance rest on two achievements: his contribution to the musical treasure of the late Baroque and his anticipation of many elements that became important in the new style of the mid-eighteenth century. As a choral composer in the grand style he is without peer. He is a consummate master, not only in choral music but in all fields, of the basic Baroque principle of contrast. At the same time, Handel's emphasis on melody and harmony, as compared to the more strictly contrapuntal style of Bach, links him with the progressive elements of his time. His deliberate appeal to a middle-class audience in the oratorios was one of the first manifestations of a social change which continued throughout the latter half of the century, and which had far-reaching effects on music. In some details it might be said that Handel anticipated even the Romantics—the descriptive music of the pastoral scenes in *Giulio Cesare;* the dramatic scene-painting in the "Witch of Endor" episode in *Saul;* the use of clarinets in *Tamerlano* (antedating Rameau by twenty-five years); or the four horns in *Giulio Cesare.* The vast intellect of this lord of music seems to have embraced both past and future in one superb and comprehensive grasp.

XIII

‖‖‖

Sources of Classical Style: The Sonata, Symphony, and Opera in the Eighteenth Century

The Background

In 1776 Dr. Charles Burney published at London the first volume of his *General History of Music,* which contains the following statement: "Music is an innocent luxury, unnecessary, indeed, to our existence, but a great improvement and gratification of the sense of hearing." Less than a hundred years earlier Andreas Werckmeister had called music "a gift of God, to be used only in His honor."[1] The contrast between these two statements illustrates the change in thought that had taken place during the eighteenth century, affecting every department of life.

The complex movement known as "the Enlightenment" began as a revolt of the spirit: a revolt against supernatural religion and the

[1] A. Werckmeister, *Der Edlen Music-Kunst, Würde, Gebrauch und Missbrauch* (*The Worthiness, Use, and Abuse of the Noble Art of Music*), Frankfurt, 1691, preface.

447

XIII. The Sonata, Symphony, and Opera in the Eighteenth Century

The
Enlightenment

church, in favor of natural religion and practical morality; against metaphysics, in favor of common sense, empirical psychology, applied science, and sociology; against formality, in favor of naturalness; against authority, in favor of freedom for the individual; and against privilege, in favor of equal rights and universal education. The temper of the Enlightenment was thus secular, skeptical, empirical, practical, liberal, equalitarian, and progressive. Its early leaders were Locke and Hume in England, Montesquieu and Voltaire in France. The initial phase of the Enlightenment was primarily negative; but the vacuum left by destructive criticism was soon filled by a new idea: that nature and the natural instincts or feelings of man were the source of true knowledge and right action. Rousseau was the chief apostle of this phase of the Enlightenment, which became conspicuous after about 1760 and which influenced the poet-philosophers Lessing and Herder and the literary movement in Germany described as *Sturm und Drang* (storm and stress).

The two basic ideas of eighteenth-century thought—faith in the efficacy of applied experimental knowledge and faith in the value of common natural feeling—were at one in regarding the individual as both the starting point of investigation and the final criterion of action. Religion, philosophical systems, science, the arts, education, the social order, all were to be judged by how they contributed to the well-being of the individual. "The individual revelling in his own inner life . . . is the characteristic phenomenon of the age of the Enlightenment."[2] The consequences of this viewpoint were evident in many ways, as for example in the ethical systems characteristic of the eighteenth century, which either declared the highest good to be the harmonious development of the innate capacities of the individual, or else, as with the Utilitarians, found the ethical ideal in the formula of "the greatest happiness of the greatest number." The effects of this individualistic bias on the arts, and on music in particular, we shall examine presently.

Life was not guided by the philosophers in the eighteenth century any more than in any other period; systems of thought are responsive to, and influenced by, the conditions of life fully as much as they themselves influence those conditions. Thus, doctrines about the rights of the individual as opposed to the rights of the state, doctrines some of which are incorporated in the American Declaration of Independence and Constitution, grew out of criticism of the terrible inequalities between the common people and the privileged classes on the continent of Europe. This social criticism was particularly sharp in France in the years before the Revolution. Advances in the application of scientific discoveries came hand in hand with the beginnings of the industrial revolution; the rise of the philosophy of feeling and the glorification of the "natural" man

2 W. Windelband, *A History of Philosophy*, tr. J. H. Tufts, New York, 1923, p. 500.

coincided with the rise of the middle class; and so on.

Four aspects of eighteenth-century life and thought are especially important for understanding the music of this period. In the first place, the eighteenth century was a *cosmopolitan* age. National differences were minimized in comparison with the common humanity of men. Foreign-born rulers abounded: German kings in England, Sweden, and Poland, a Spanish king in Naples, a French duke in Tuscany, a German princess (Catharine II) as empress of Russia. The Frenchman Voltaire sojourned at the French-speaking court of Frederick the Great of Prussia, and the Italian poet Metastasio at the German imperial court in Vienna; equally typical were the German symphony composers at Paris and the Italian opera composers and singers in Germany, Spain, England, Russia, and France. Quantz, writing at Berlin in 1752, postulates as the ideal musical style one made up of the best features of the music of all nations: "A music that is accepted and recognized as good not by one country only . . . but by many peoples . . . must, provided it is based as well on reason and sound feeling, be beyond all dispute the best."[3] Chabanon, in 1785, declared "Today there is but one music in all of Europe . . . this universal language of our continent."[4] The eighteenth century was receptive to influences from distant ages as well as distant places: the Classical movement took inspiration and example from the art and literature of the ancient world; toward the end of the century, with the beginnings of Romanticism, attention was turned to the Middle Ages, while musicians and poets alike began to take an interest in folk song.

Aspects of eighteenth-century life

The Enlightenment was *humanitarian* as well as cosmopolitan. Rulers not only patronized arts and letters but also busied themselves with programs of social reform. The eighteenth century was the age of enlightened despots: Frederick the Great of Prussia, Catharine the Great of Russia, Joseph II of Austria, and (in the early part of his reign) Louis XVI of France. Humanitarian ideals, longings for universal human brotherhood, were embodied in the movement of Freemasonry, which spread rapidly over Europe in the eighteenth century and numbered among its adherents kings (Frederick the Great), poets (Goethe), and composers (Mozart). Mozart's *Magic Flute,* Schiller's *Ode to Joy,* and Beethoven's Ninth Symphony were among the outgrowths of the eighteenth-century humanitarian movement.

With the rise of a numerous middle class to a position of influence, the eighteenth century witnessed the first steps in a process of *popularization* of art and learning. A new market was appearing for the productions of writers and artists, and not only the subject matter but also the manner of presentation had to be shaped to the

---

[3] J. J. Quantz, *Versuch,* XVIII, in SR, 597–98 (SRC, 23–24).
[4] Michel Paul Gui de Chabanon, *De la musique considerée en elle-même et dans ses rapports* [etc.], Paris, 1785, p. 97.

Concert at Vauxhall Gardens *(1786), by Thomas Rowlandson. Opened in 1736, this popular place of amusement in London offered concerts every summer. Among its "resident composers" was Thomas Augustine Arne. (Prints Division, New York Public Library, Astor, Lenox, and Tilden Foundations)*

new demands. Philosophy, science, literature, and the fine arts all began to take account of a general public instead of a select group of experts and connoisseurs. Popular treatises were written to bring culture within the reach of all, while novels and plays began to depict everyday people with everyday emotions. Even manners and costumes were affected: at the beginning of the century the bourgeoisie aped the aristocracy; by 1780 the aristocracy aped the lower classes. The popularizing trend found powerful support with the growth of the "back to nature" movement and the exaltation of sentiment in literature and the arts.

Music was affected along with everything else. Patronage was on the wane and the modern musical public was coming into being. Public concerts designed for mixed audiences began to rival the older private concerts and academies; at Paris, a series of public concerts was founded in 1725; another series begun by J. A. Hiller at Leipzig in 1763 was continued after 1781 as the famous *Gewandhaus* concerts; similar concert organizations were founded at Vienna in 1771 and at Berlin in 1790; concert societies had flourished in London sporadically since 1672, and a popular new series began in 1765. Music printing increased enormously; the bulk of the publication was directed at amateurs, and much music was issued in periodicals. An amateur public naturally demanded and bought music that was easy to understand and to play, and the same public was interested in reading about and discussing music. Musical journalism began; after the middle of the century magazines sprang up which were devoted to musical news, reviews, and criticism. The first histories of music were written and the first collection of medieval musical treatises published.

Finally, the Enlightenment was a *prosaic* age. Its best literature was prose, and it valued in all the arts the virtues of good prose writing: clarity, animation, good taste, proportion, and elegance. Rational rather than poetic, the age had little liking for Baroque mysticism, gravity, massiveness, grandeur, and passion, and its critical temper inhibited great poetry in large forms. Early eighteenth-century esthetics held that the task of music, like that of the other arts, was to imitate nature, to offer to the listener pleasant sounding images of reality. Music was supposed to imitate not the actual sounds of the world of nature, but rather the sounds of speech, especially as these expressed the sentiments of the soul; according to Rousseau and some others, it should imitate a mythical primitive speech-song, assumed to be the natural language of man; or again, music might in some way imitate the feelings themselves, not necessarily by imitating speech. Only toward the end of the century did theorists gradually come to think that music might move the feelings directly through the beauty of sounds and that a work of music might develop in accordance with its own nature, independent of any model. But even then the idea of imitation persisted; music was an imitative, hence a decorative art, "an innocent luxury," as Dr. Burney called it.

Moreover, music of the Enlightenment is supposed to meet the listener on his own ground, and not compel him to make an effort to understand what was going on. It will overwhelmingly favor the major mode. It must please (by agreeable sounds and rational structure) and move (by imitating feelings), but not too often astonish (by excessive elaboration) and never puzzle (by too great complexity). Music, as "the art of pleasing by the succession and combination of agreeable sounds,"[5] must eschew contrapuntal complexities, which could only be appreciated by the few learned in such abstruse matters. Not all writers went so far in this respect as Rousseau, who defined musical composition as "the art of inventing tunes and accompanying them with suitable harmonies" and declared that "to sing two melodies at once is like making two speeches at once in order to be more forceful"[6]; but Quantz felt that "the old composers were too much absorbed with musical 'tricks' [contrapuntal devices] and carried them too far, so that they neglected the essential thing in music, which is to move and please."[7] Burney criticised J. S. Bach as having in his organ works "been constantly in search of what was

[5] Burney, "Essay on Musical Criticism," introducing Book III of his *General History of Music.*
[6] *Dictionnaire de musique,* s.v. "composition," "mélodie," "unité de mélodie."
[7] Quantz, *op. cit.*, Introduction, §16.

new and difficult, without the least attention to nature and facility"
and regretted that that master could not have learned to sacrifice "all
unmeaning art and contrivance" in his compositions and write "in
a style more popular, and generally intelligible and pleasing."[8]
Burney here is implying as an esthetic norm "nature," that great
catch-word of the Enlightenment, a term of many vague and frequently contradictory meanings.[9] It is only fair to mention that
Burney later achieved a better understanding of Bach's music; but
the opinions expressed above were shared by most critics in the
1780s, and the expressive qualities of eighteenth-century music are
often sentimental and childlike, bound up as they are with this artificial striving for naturalness.

The ideal music of the middle and later eighteenth century, then,
might be described as follows: its language should be universal, not

*The ideal
eighteenth-
century music*

limited by national boundaries; it should be noble as well as entertaining; it should be expressive within the bounds of decorum; it
should be "natural," in the sense of being free of needless technical
complications and capable of immediately pleasing any normally
sensitive listener. The music that most fully realized these ideals
was written in the Classical period, approximately the years 1770
to 1800, and its masters were Gluck, Haydn, Mozart, and the young
Beethoven.

This formula is not advanced as an explanation of all eighteenth-
century music, but only as a summary of the general aims which
seem to have more or less consciously governed the minds of both
composers and audiences, particularly in the last thirty years of the
century. No formula could possibly comprehend the manifold
aspects of all the music composed between 1700 and 1800. The
Baroque yielded only gradually to new styles, and the old and the
new existed side by side. Works typical of the new era—Pergolesi's
comic opera *La serva padrona* and Sammartini's first symphonies,
for example—were being written in the 1730s at the same time as
Bach's B-minor Mass, and earlier than Handel's *Messiah* and Bach's
Goldberg Variations. Yet after about 1740 the change of style was
generally noticeable.

The eighteenth-century was a cosmopolitan age; nonetheless,
lively arguments about the relative merits of various national musical
styles were carried on up to the eve of the French Revolution;
moreover, after 1750 in every country new national forms of opera
were coming to the fore, harbingers of the Romantic era. The
eighteenth-century stream of humanitarian idealism did not mark-

8 Burney, *op. cit.*, Book IV, Ch. 10.

9 On the sixty-odd distinct meanings attached to the words "nature" and
"natural" by different writers from the seventeenth to the nineteenth centuries,
see references in the index of Arthur O. Lovejoy's *Essays in the History of Ideas*,
New York, 1955.

edly affect music until the time of the French Revolution, and may even be considered, like the rise of national opera and the growth of interest in folk song, as a pre-Romantic trait.

Because Gluck, and more especially Haydn and Mozart, overshadow their predecessors and contemporaries in much the same way that Bach and Handel overshadow theirs, it is easy to fall into the error of viewing the late seventeenth-century composers merely as the forerunners of Bach and Handel, and the mid-eighteenth century composers merely as the forerunners of Gluck, Haydn, and Mozart. It is especially easy in the latter instance because comparatively little is known about early eighteenth-century opera or the origins of the Classical symphony. The fallacy of this "mere forerunner" conception is undoubtedly due to a confused notion that progress occurs when old things are superseded by new; we are prone to imagine that in the same way that the automobile superseded the horse and buggy, the symphonies of Mozart superseded those of Stamitz. To deny this is not to deny that Mozart was a greater composer than Stamitz, but only to assert that the idea of progress is not the only possible way to approach a comparison of the two. It is the historian's task to judge any work of music according to its intrinsic qualities and its significance for its own time, as well as to discern in it those features for which the composer was indebted to his predecessors and those which in turn proved useful or stimulating to his successors.

Instrumental Music: Sonata and Symphony

Two general styles or manners can be distinguished within the so-called pre-Classical period beginning around 1720: the *rococo* and the *expressive*. The former was cultivated especially in France, and the French term *style galant* (gallant style) is often used as a synonym for rococo. The expressive style, which arose somewhat later and was chiefly associated with German composers, is often designated by the equivalent German phrase *empfindsamer Stil* (literally, sensitive style). Both may be regarded as outgrowths of the Baroque tendency to concentrate all musical interest in the two outer voices; but in these newer styles the bass loses all vestiges of leadership and contrapuntal independence, and becomes simply an underpinning for the melody, while the inner voices are mere harmonic fillers.

Rococo and expressive styles

The rococo or *galant* style arose in courtly, aristocratic circles; it was elegant, playful, easy, witty, polished, and ornate. *Rococo* originally described the elaborately ornamental decoration of interiors and furnishings fashionable in France during the age of the Regency; *galant* was a catch word of the same period, applied to

Chamber Music in a Garden Salon *(1769), by Daniel Nikolaus Chodowiecki; an engraving for a 1770 textbook.*

everything that was thought to be modern, smart, chic, smooth, easy, and sophisticated. The rococo is Baroque decorativeness without grandeur. The expressive style, on the other hand, was an affair of the middle class; it was the *style bourgeois*. Instead of being ornate, it is sometimes ostentatiously plain. It domesticates the Baroque affections, turning them into sentiments of the individual soul. The ease and elegance of the rococo, as well as some of its decorative charm, were combined with the expressive quality of the *style bourgeois* in most compositions by the middle of the eighteenth century, and both styles are completely absorbed into the music of the Classical period.

New concepts of melody and harmony

The change from Baroque to the new kind of eighteenth-century music included among other things a change in the conception of melody and melodic development. The normal Baroque technique had been to announce the theme of a movement—the melodic-rhythmic subject embodying the basic affection—at the outset; this material was then spun out, with relatively infrequent and usually inconspicuous cadences, and with sequential repetition of phrases as the principal articulating device within periods. The result was a highly integrated movement without sharp contrasts, or else (as in Vivaldi's concertos) a formal pattern of contrasts between thematic tutti and nonthematic solo sections; but in either case, the phrase structure was usually so irregular that there was no marked feeling of periodicity, of antecedent-and-consequent phrases. The new composers of the eighteenth century, while retaining the late Baroque method of constructing a movement on the basis of related keys, gradually abandoned the older idea of the one basic affection and began to introduce contrasts between the various parts of a movement or even within the theme or themes themselves. Moreover, instead of the Baroque continuity and spinning-out technique, the melodies came to be articulated into distinct phrases, typically two or four measures in length (but also frequently three, five, or six measures), resulting in a periodic structure and thereby raising the problem how to achieve continuity under this new condition—a problem that was not fully solved until the time of Haydn and Mozart. The melodic substance itself might be simply chord figurations, decorated perhaps by passing tones, turns, appoggiaturas, and the like; or a vivacious *parlando* of swiftly interchanged or echoed phrases, a type of melody borrowed from the Italian *opera buffa;* or sometimes a singing allegro, derived perhaps from the style of serious opera arias. Melodies in a major key were sometimes colored by momentary shifts to the minor mode. For a long time all melodies, but especially slow ones, kept a certain amount of ornamentation; as C. P. E. Bach wrote in 1753, "Probably no one has ever doubted the necessity of embellishments." The graceful, lyric charm which we ordinarily call "Mozartean" is not peculiar to Mozart, but is part of the common musical language of the second half of the century.

The harmonic vocabulary and tonal system of the middle and late eighteenth century were substantially the same as those of the late Baroque, but the harmonic rhythm of most of the new music is slower and the harmonic progressions less weighty than in the older style. A great deal of bustling activity goes on over relatively slow-moving and conventional harmonies, and important harmonic changes almost always coincide with the strong accents indicated by the barlines. The subordination of the bass and harmonies to the role of mere accompaniment to the melody is symbolized by one of the most widely used devices of mid-eighteenth-century keyboard music, the *Alberti bass,* named for the Italian composer, Domenico Alberti (*ca.* 1710–40). This device consists in breaking each of the underlying chords into a simple pattern of short notes incessantly repeated, thus producing a discreet undulation in the background which sets off the melody to advantage. The Alberti bass was extremely useful; it was not disdained by Haydn, Mozart, and Beethoven, and lasted well into the nineteenth century.

The chief Italian keyboard composer of the eighteenth century, and one of the most original geniuses in the history of music, was Domenico Scarlatti (1685–1757). Son of the famous Alessandro Scarlatti, born in the same year as Bach and Handel, Domenico Scarlatti produced no works of lasting importance before his first collection of harpsichord sonatas (called on the title page *essercizi*

Domenico Scarlatti

455

—exercises or diversions) which was published in 1738. In 1720 or 1721 Scarlatti left Italy to enter the service of the King of Portugal. When his pupil the Infanta of Portugal was married to Prince Ferdinand of Spain in 1729, Scarlatti followed her to Madrid, where he remained for the rest of his life in the service of the Spanish courts and where he composed most of his 550 sonatas.

Scarlatti's music is idiomatic for the harpsichord as Chopin's or Debussy's is for the piano. Every imaginable shading of harpsichord sonority, every resource of harpsichord technique, may be found in the sonatas. Some are virtuoso pieces of formidable difficulty, others quiet pastorale-like movements; variegated moods, reminiscences of popular song and of Italian, Portuguese, and Spanish dance rhythms pervade them. A basic two-voice homophonic texture is alternately filled and thinned, sometimes with sudden contrasts of key or texture but always with an infallible ear for the shape of the phrase and the right sound on the instrument. Rhythmic vitality is combined with an exuberant flow of thematic invention. Because his sonatas absorb and transfigure so many of the sounds and sights of the world, and because he treats texture and harmony freely with a view to sonorous effect, Scarlatti's music may be termed "impressionistic"; but it has none of the vagueness of outline that we are apt to associate with that word.

All the Scarlatti sonatas are organized by means of tonal relationships into the standard late Baroque and early Classical binary pattern used for dance pieces and other types of composition: two sections, each repeated, the first cadencing in the dominant or relative major (rarely some other key), the second modulating further afield and then returning to the tonic. This is the basic scheme which underlies much instrumental and solo vocal music in the eighteenth century. In Scarlatti's sonatas the closing part of the first section invariably returns, but in the tonic key, at the end of section two. Within each section there is a contrast between the tense, rapidly modulating central portion and the broad, relaxed, cadential closing periods. This placing of the point of highest tension toward the middle of the movement rather than toward the end (as was usual in the late Baroque style) became one of the important features of the Classical sonata of the late eighteenth century.

The majority of Scarlatti's sonatas after 1745 are arranged in pairs, each pair, in effect, a sonata of two movements, always in the same key (though one may be major and the other minor), sometimes similar in mood, sometimes contrasted. Sonatas in two movements were written by Alberti and many other Italian composers of the eighteenth century, though there is no evidence that they took the idea from Scarlatti. In fact, as Scarlatti seems to have created his own keyboard idiom without models, so he apparently had no successors, with the possible exception of a few Portuguese and Spanish composers. The *essercizi* of 1738 and a few other sonatas were known and admired in England in the eighteenth century, but very little of Scarlatti's music circulated in France and practically none of it was known in Germany or Italy.

Italian composers of the middle and late eighteenth century produced a large amount of music for harpsichord which is not yet as widely known as it deserves to be, and which is perhaps underrated because it is less familiar than the works of C. P. E. Bach and other German composers. Italians and Germans were equally active in experimenting with formal organization in the keyboard sonatas of the eighteenth century.[10] Some of their forms are related to the late Baroque concerto grosso, others to the dance forms of the Baroque suite. No single type emerges as predominant until well after the middle of the century.

The Classical sonata (likewise the symphony and most kinds of chamber music), as found in Haydn, Mozart, and Beethoven, is a composition in three or four (sometimes two) movements of contrasting mood and tempo. Typically the first movement, and often the slow movement and the finale, exemplify what is known as *sonata form* or *first movement form*, the essential outlines of which are:[11] (1) division into two distinct sections, the first being usually and the second not always repeated; (2) in the first section, establishment of a tonic, modulation to the dominant (or relative major), and close on a cadence in the new key; (3) beginning with the second section, further modulations with increasing tension to a point not more than half way through this section, at which comes (4) a strongly marked return to the tonic, coinciding with a recognizable (not necessarily literal) restatement of the opening material of section one and constituting the principal climax of the movement; then (5) continuation in the tonic with "reinterpretation" of the material from section one—especially that material which had there been heard in the dominant—and proceeding to a final resolution on the tonic. Underlying all the foregoing are certain general characteristics: (6) periodic structure of melodies in a variety of rhythms and textures, with continuity achieved by means of (a) transitions from one to another rhythm, texture, key, or dynamic level and (b) recall of or allusion to melodies, phrases, and motives previously heard; (7) an over-all movement from tension (modulation away from the tonic) to resolution (return to the tonic), the climactic points of tension and resolution being clearly signalized as dramatic "events" within a symmetrical structure; and (8) unity, arising from the continual recurrence of the tension–resolution process at every level from the single phrase up to the entire movement.

The Classical Sonata

The above outline of sonata form is partially represented in the well-known "textbook" definition, which posits: (1) an *exposition*

---

10 See analysis in Appendix, pp. 765.

11 For this outline of sonata form, I am much indebted to the excellent book of Charles Rosen, *The Classical Style: Haydn, Mozart, Beethoven,* New York, 1971.

(usually repeated), incorporating a first theme or group of themes in the tonic, a second more lyrical theme in the dominant or relative major, and a closing theme also in the dominant or relative major—the different themes being connected by appropriate transitions or bridge passages; (2) a *development* section, in which motives or themes from the exposition are presented in new aspects or combinations, and in the course of which modulations may be made to relatively remote keys; (3) a *recapitulation,* where the material of the exposition is restated in the original order but with all themes now in the tonic; following the recapitulation there may be a *coda.*

The full textbook definition of sonata form appeared only in the late 1830s. It was not intended as a historical summation of what the classical composers did, but as a prescription of what composers of sonatas ought to do. Obviously it is an abstraction, made by dwelling exclusively on the key scheme and the melodic-thematic elements of sonata form. So understood, it will fit a good many sonata movements of the late Classical period and the nineteenth century; but there are many more (including most of Haydn's) which it will fit only awkwardly if at all. For example: many other elements besides "themes" are important for defining a form; themes themselves are not always melodies of definite contour; there may be no "second theme," or if there is one it may not differ in character from the "first theme"; new themes may be introduced anywhere; development may occur in any part of the movement, including the coda; or there may be no coda. Nevertheless, despite its shortcomings one needs to know about the textbook definition. It is tacitly assumed in many discussions of classical music, and its terminology has perfectly legitimate uses; but the structure it purports to describe must not be regarded as either an ideal of perfection or a goal of evolution. A sonata that brings back the opening material in the dominant at the start of the second section (as many early Classical sonatas do) instead of recapitulating it in the tonic further on, or one that altogether avoids any formal restatement of the opening material (as most of Scarlatti's do) is not on such account to be thought imperfect or "primitive." Many different composers in the eighteenth century, with different kinds of musical ideas, made use of a common, loosely-defined pattern, modifying or expanding or adding to it as their own inventiveness and the nature of their musical material required.

In the matter of recapitulation, one difference between the Classical sonata and the Baroque concerto should be pointed out. The ritornellos of a concerto do of course recapitulate the main thematic material of the movement. They say, in effect, "this is the subject we are discussing," and the subject has essentially the same meaning at every recurrence. In the Classical sonata, on the other hand (most clearly with Haydn and Beethoven), the subject at each recurrence, whether literal or modified, takes on a different meaning; the musical idea undergoes a continual, dynamic change in the course of the movement. This particular dynamic quality—one might call it a product of musical *dialectic,* if the term could be divested of irrelevant Hegelian and Marxist overtones—is one of the essential contrasts between the Baroque and the Classical musical styles.

Both keyboard sonatas and orchestral compositions of similar form of the early part of the eighteenth century were influenced by the Italian opera overture (*sinfonia*), which about 1700 assumed a structure of three movements in the order fast–slow–fast, that is, an Allegro, a short lyrical Andante, and a finale in the rhythm of some dance, such as a minuet or a gigue. Inasmuch as such overtures as a rule had no thematic or other connection with the opera to follow, they could be played as independent pieces in concerts. Hence it was natural, around 1730, for Italian composers to begin to write concert symphonies using the general plan of the opera overtures—though the earliest such symphonies are equally if not more indebted to the tradition of the late Baroque concerto and trio sonata for details of structure, texture, and thematic style. One of the first symphonists was G. B. Sammartini (1701–75) of Milan. Other Italians whose works were important in the history of the symphony were the opera composers Rinaldo di Capua (*ca.* 1710–*ca.* 1780), Baldassare Galuppi (1706–85), and Niccolò Jommelli (1714–74). Composers in Germany, Austria, and France soon followed the lead of the Italians, so that from about 1740 the symphony gradually replaced the concerto as the leading form of concerted instrumental music.

Pre-Classical symphonies and chamber music

Chamber music in this new style did not begin to have a separate history until after the middle of the eighteenth century; many works called "trios" and "quartets" in the pre-Classical era could be performed by either solo instruments or full orchestra. The trio sonatas attributed to G. B. Pergolesi (1710–36), written in 1732–33, exemplify the new formal principles, which often appear side by side with the fugal and ostinato bass patterns of the late Baroque; the melodies are cheerful, sensitive, and imbued with a lyrical quality which resembles that of vocal arias. The violin concertos and sonatas of Giuseppe Tartini (1692–1770) indicate that the new style gradually penetrated and transformed these types of composition also in the mid-eighteenth century. From then on, partly due to the growth of public concerts, orchestral and chamber music styles gradually became more clearly differentiated.

The entrance of the expressive style (*empfindsamer Stil*) into instrumental music toward the middle of the century, though not exclusively the achievement of German composers, may be most clearly illustrated in their works. Two of the sons of J. S. Bach are important in this connection. The eldest, Wilhelm Friedemann (1710–84), was a gifted organist and composer whose life ended in failure and poverty because he was not able to adjust himself to the contemporary requirements for a successful musical career.

The empfindsamer Stil

459

Some of his works are conservative in style, like those of his great father and teacher; others pay tribute to the fashionable *style galant;* but the outstanding features of his music are a certain freedom, even capriciousness, in the details of harmony, melody, and rhythm; sudden contrasts of mood; and, on occasion, an intensely personal, almost Romantic emotion, which presages the nineteenth century. A kindred spirit to W. F. Bach was Johann Schobert (*ca.* 1720–67), one of the many German musicians resident in Paris around the middle of the eighteenth century. Schobert is credited with having introduced orchestral effects into keyboard writing, a technique which was taken up by later composers.

C. P. E. Bach

Carl Philipp Emanuel Bach (1714–88), one of the most influential composers of his generation, has been called the founder of Classical style. Trained in music by his father, he was in service at the court of Frederick the Great in Berlin from 1740 to 1768 and then became music director of the five principal churches in Hamburg. His compositions include oratorios, songs, symphonies, and chamber music, but most numerous and important are his works for clavier. In 1742 he published a set of six sonatas (the *Prussian* sonatas) and in 1744 another set of six (the *Württemberg* sonatas). These sonatas, especially those of 1742, were quite new in style, and exerted a strong influence on later composers. Bach's favorite keyboard instrument was not the harpsichord but the softer, more intimate clavichord, with its capacity for delicate dynamic shadings. The clavichord enjoyed a spell of renewed popularity in Germany around the middle of the eighteenth century before both it and the harpsichord were gradually supplanted by the pianoforte; the last five sets of Emanuel Bach's sonatas (1780–87) were written for the pianoforte, as were many of the later keyboard pieces of Friedemann Bach.

The principal technical characteristics of the *empfindsamer Stil,* of which C. P. E. Bach was one of the chief representatives, may be summarized as follows: the aim to express feeling naturally was realized through two devices, used either separately or in combination: the melodic *sigh,* a motive ending *portamento* on a weak beat —usually the resolution of an appoggiatura and often including also an anticipation of the note of resolution; and *chromaticism,* which might affect both melody and harmony. These two devices are amply illustrated in the *cantabile* movement of the third sonata from Bach's first collection of *Sonatas for Connoisseurs and Amateurs* (*für Kenner und Liebhaber*) published in 1779. This piece is typical in its union of sentiment and *galanterie,* and is interesting furthermore because it uses the Baroque chromatic passacaglia bass and has withal a quite Baroque unity of mood and rhythm.

Simplicity or naturalness must be understood in the eighteenth-century sense: the ideal did not by any means preclude ornamentation, but composers did endeavor to keep the ornaments within proportion and to assimilate them into the entire expressive content of a passage. The expressive style often exploited the element of surprise, with abrupt shifts of harmony, strange modulations, unusual turns of melody, expectant pauses, changes of texture, sudden *sforzando* accents, and the like. The subjective, emotional qualities of the *Empfindsamkeit* reached a climax during the 1760s and 1770s; the style is sometimes described by the same term *Sturm und Drang*—storm and stress—which is applied to German literature of the same period. The Classical composers later brought this emotionalism under control by imposing unity of content and form. The entire development will be traced in the discussion of Haydn, in the following chapter.

Emanuel Bach introduced in his instrumental works sections of musical dialogue and passages of recitative. Audiences reportedly were deeply stirred by his keyboard improvisations, the character of which is doubtless preserved to some degree in his fantasias. These works recall the fantasies of J. S. Bach and at the same time point toward the piano fantasies of Mozart and the improvisatory passages in the sonatas of Beethoven.

Movements in sonata form in Emanuel Bach's works often do not have two distinct themes; even when two themes are present, there is seldom a real contrast in character between them. As is usual with the north German composers, Bach's ruling ideal is unity of mood and material; consequently, themes usually begin to be developed as soon as they have been stated; and the section immediately after the double bar, the development section of the standard Classical symphony, is relatively short. In this concept of thematic unity within sonata form, as well as in his general musical language, Bach is closer to Haydn than to Mozart. Most of his sonatas have three movements—Allegro (or Allegretto), Andante, Allegro—though in some of the later ones the Andante was shortened to a mere bridge between the two fast movements. Some of Bach's most ingenious and charming music is found in the rondos which alternate with the sonatas and fantasias of the last five sets of the *Sonatas for Connoisseurs* published from 1780 to 1787.

Not the least of his contributions to music was Bach's *Essay on the True Art of Playing Keyboard Instruments* (1753–62), the most important treatise on ornamentation in the middle eighteenth century and a work which, like Quantz's essay on flute playing, includes much information about the musical thought and practice of the period.

The principal German centers of symphonic composition from 1740 onward were Mannheim, Vienna, and Berlin. The founder of the Mannheim school was Johann Stamitz (1717–57); under his leadership the Mannheim orchestra became renowned all over Europe for its virtuosity (Burney called it "an army of generals"), for its hitherto unknown dynamic range from the softest *pianissimo*

German symphonic composers

461

to the loudest *fortissimo,* and for the thrilling sound of its crescendo. The growing use of crescendo and diminuendo around the middle of the century was one symptom of a trend toward attaining variety within a movement by means of gradual transitions; Baroque movements had either kept to a uniform dynamic level or else introduced distinct contrasts, as in the concerto. The same desire for flexibility of musical effects was responsible for the eventual replacement of the harpsichord by the pianoforte.

Stamitz was one of the first composers regularly to use a contrasting, lyrical second theme in his Allegro movements in sonata form and to expand the symphony from three movements to four (the standard number in most of Haydn's and Beethoven's symphonies) by adding a fast finale after the minuet, which earlier had often served as the closing movement. Despite such anticipations, however, his music, like that of all the early German symphony composers, is still in the rococo-expressive style of the middle eighteenth century; at the hands of his successors many of his tricks of style degenerated into mannerisms. One of the best of the later Mannheim symphonists was Christian Cannabich (1731–98).

The Vienna school is of especial interest because it was the immediate background of the work of Haydn, Mozart, and Beethoven. Georg Matthias Monn (1717–50) was one of the earliest of the Viennese composers, but a more important figure was Fux's pupil Georg Christoph Wagenseil (1715–77). In his music, as also in that of the later Austrian composers Florian Leopold Gassmann (1729–74) and Michael Haydn (1737–1806), we find the pleasant, typically Viennese lyricism and good humor that is such an important feature in Mozart's style. The Viennese composers for the most part favored contrasting theme-groups in their movements in sonata form.

The principal symphonic composers of the Berlin or north German group were Johann Gottlieb Graun (1703–71) and C. P. E. Bach. The north Germans were conservative, in that they held consistently to three-movement structure for the symphony and were chary of introducing sharp thematic contrasts within a movement. On the other hand, it was they chiefly who initiated the technique of thematic development in a dynamic, organically unified, serious, and quasi-dramatic style, and at the same time enriched symphonic texture with contrapuntal elements.

An important composer of symphonies, as well as of chamber music, keyboard music, and operas, was Johann Christian Bach (1735–82), youngest of the sons of Johann Sebastian Bach. Trained in music by his father and his elder brother Emanuel Bach, Johann Christian made his way to Milan at the age of twenty. He studied with the celebrated theorist, teacher, and composer Padre Giambattista Martini (1706–84) of Bologna; in 1760 he was appointed organist of the Cathedral at Milan. After two of his operas had been successfully produced at Naples, he moved in 1762 to London, where he enjoyed a long career as composer, performer, teacher, and impresario. His music was dominated by the *galant,* pleasantly melodious Italian manner of his time. His symphonies were widely popular and had a strong influence on the development of symphonic style in the Classical period.

Paris became an important center of composition and publication toward the middle of the eighteenth century; a considerable number of German and other foreign composers lived there. Works of the French school included symphonies and, particularly after 1770, a form known as the *symphonie concertante,* that is, a symphonic work employing two or more solo instruments in addition to the regular orchestra. One of the most noted composers of symphonies in France was a Belgian, François Joseph Gossec (1734–1829), who came to Paris in 1751 and who afterwards succeeded Rameau as conductor of La Pouplinière's orchestra. Gossec published his first symphonies in 1754 and his first string quartets in 1759. Later he turned to writing comic operas; he was one of the most popular composers of the Revolutionary period and one of the first directors of the Paris Conservatoire. Among the many composers of *symphonies concertantes* was Giovanni Giuseppe Cambini (1746–1825), an Italian living at Paris; and a large number of native French composers also participated in the extraordinary flowering of this type of composition in the last quarter of the eighteenth century.

Another noteworthy eighteenth-century composer of symphonies was the Englishman, William Boyce (1710–79). His symphonies are conservative in form, but fresh and engaging in their melodies and rhythms.

In the last quarter of the eighteenth century the symphony and other forms of ensemble music gradually discarded the basso continuo as all the essential voices were taken over by the melody instruments. With the final disappearance of the harpsichord from the symphony orchestra, toward the end of the century, the responsibility of conducting the group fell on the leader of the violins.

The eighteenth-century symphony orchestra was much smaller than the orchestra of today. In 1756 the Mannheim orchestra consisted of twenty violins, four each of violas, violoncellos, and double-basses, two each of flutes, oboes, and bassoons, four horns, one trumpet, and two kettledrums; but this was an exceptionally large group. Haydn's orchestra from 1760 to 1785 rarely had more than twenty-five players, including strings, flute, two oboes, two bassoons, two horns, and a harpsichord, with trumpets and kettledrums occasionally added. Even in the 1790s the orchestras at Vienna normally had not more than thirty-five players.

The symphony orchestra

In the symphonies of the middle eighteenth century the usual orchestration gave all the essential musical material to the strings, and used the winds only for doubling, reinforcing, and filling in the harmonies. Sometimes in performance woodwinds and brasses might be added to the orchestra even though the composer had written no parts for them. Later in the century the wind instruments came to be entrusted with more important and more independent material.

The types of chamber music in the 1770s and 1780s included the sonata for clavier and violin, with the violin usually in a subsidiary role; but the principal medium eventually became the string quartet. A distinguished composer of chamber music was Luigi Boccherini (1743–1805), whose output includes about 140 string quintets, 100 string quartets, and 65 string trios, besides other chamber and orchestral music.

Chamber music

A different type of music, designed primarily for out-of-doors or for informal occasions, was the Viennese serenade, which like the divertimento, cassation, and notturno was an intermediate form between the Baroque orchestral suite and the Classical symphony; it consisted usually of five or more movements, many of them in dance rhythms, but in no regularly prescribed order. Such pieces were written for wind instruments alone, or strings alone, or a combination of the two; they kept a certain popular flavor in their tunes and rhythms, and were not without influence on the style of the Viennese Classical symphony. Historically, they were important because they accustomed composers to the sound of ensemble music without basso continuo, the elimination of which was an essential step in the evolution of the Classical string quartet.

Opera, Song, and Church Music

As with the sonata and symphony, so with the opera: new forms and styles were emerging from and gradually supplanting the old during the first quarter of the eighteenth century. The French *tragédie lyrique* was resistant to change in this period, and the general style of Venetian Baroque opera maintained itself for a long while in Germany; but a strong progressive current was emanating from Italy. The new Italian opera that eventually dominated the stages of Europe in the eighteenth century was a product of the same forces that were reshaping all other forms of music in the age of the Enlightenment. It aimed to be clear, simple, rational, faithful to nature, of universal appeal, and capable of giving pleasure to its audiences without causing them undue mental fatigue. The artificialities which it soon acquired, and for which it was roundly condemned by critics in the latter part of the century, were in part merely outmoded conventions of an earlier period and in part accidental accretions.

The Italian *opera seria* was given its standard formulation by the Italian poet, Pietro Metastasio (1698–1782), whose dramas were set to music hundreds of times by composers in the eighteenth century. These works as a rule presented a conflict of human passions in an action based on some story from an ancient Greek or Latin author; they made use of the conventional cast of two pairs of lovers and subordinate personages, and quite often brought in a favorite eighteenth-century character, the "magnanimous tyrant." The course of the action gave occasion for introducing varied scenes —pastoral or martial episodes, solemn ceremonies, and the like— and the resolution of the drama often turned on a deed of heroism or sublime renunciation by one of the principal characters. There were three acts, cast almost unvaryingly in the form of alternating recitatives and arias; the action was developed in dialogue in the recitatives, while each aria represented what might be called a dramatic soliloquy, in which a principal actor of the preceding scene would give expression to appropriate feelings or comments about the particular situation then existing. There were occasional duets but few larger ensembles, and very few, quite simple choruses.

Italian opera seria

Except for the overture the orchestra had not much to do but accompany the singers. Ordinary recitative was of relatively little musical importance and was accompanied only by the harpsichord and a sustaining bass instrument. Accompanied recitatives, reserved for the most important dramatic situations, used voice and orchestra in free interchange. With these exceptions, the musical interest of the Italian opera was centered in the arias, which were created by eighteenth-century composers in astounding profusion and variety. The most common form in the earlier part of the century was the da capo aria, a basic scheme that permitted infinite variation in detail. After about the middle of the century it became more common to write arias in a single movement, usually an expanded version of the first part of a da capo aria, with a key-scheme like that of the sonata and with orchestral ritornellos as in a concerto.

The aria

Some idea of the different forms and types of the aria in eighteenth-century opera may be obtained from four examples in the general collections:

1. HAM, No. 262: a small da capo aria with accompaniment by continuo only from Giovanni Bononcini's *Astianatte* (London, 1727). The principal section has the usual cadence in the relative major (m. 10); the middle section, slightly contrasting, is in the dominant minor.

2. HAM, No. 290: a short aria in one movement, with ritornellos, from a masque (?) *The Fall of Phaeton* (London, 1736) by Thomas Augustine Arne (1710–78), the most eminent English composer of this era. The second section (from m. 11) may be regarded as the middle part of a da capo aria, after which the repetition of part

one is merely suggested by repeating the four measures of orchestral introduction.

3. GMB, No. 298: a full-scale, fiery da capo aria from the opera *Merope* (Rome and Florence, 1743) by the excellent composer Domingo Terradellas (1713–51), a Spaniard who studied and worked in Italy and whose style was thoroughly Italian. The normal introductory ritornello is omitted in order not to break the connection with the preceding accompanied recitative; its place is taken by the impressive twofold announcement (mm. 1–16) of the theme by voice and orchestra in alternation. The principal section is in full sonata form with recapitulation (p. 452, m. 3); the short *B* section in the relative minor uses the same motives as part *A*. The written melodic line would of course have been embellished by the singer; cadenzas would have been inserted at the end of the middle section and probably at the two places marked by fermate in the principal section.

4. HAM, No. 282: a *cavatina, i.e.,* an aria without da capo, from *Montezuma* (Berlin, 1755), by the Italianate German composer Karl Heinrich Graun (1704–59), on a libretto by his patron, King Frederick the Great. Notable details are the simple transparent harmonic texture, the minuet movement, and the division of a beat according to Lombardic rhythm (the figure ♪.), which is almost a trademark of mid-eighteenth-century style.

Concentration upon the aria as almost the only significant musical ingredient in opera opened the way to abuses. The scheme of regularly alternating recitatives and arias came to be treated too rigidly. Singers, including the famed Italian *castrati* (male sopranos and altos), made arbitrary demands on the poets and composers, compelling them to alter, add, and substitute arias without respect for dramatic or musical propriety. Moreover, the melodic embellishments and cadenzas which the singers added at will were all too often mere tasteless displays of vocal acrobatics. A famous satire on the opera and everything connected with it, entitled *The Fashionable Theatre* (*il Teatro alla moda*), was published anonymously by Benedetto Marcello in 1720, but not until about 1745 did Italian composers attempt any important reforms. The beginning of operatic reform coincided with the rise of the expressive style, and, like that style, was a sign of the growing influence of middle-class ideas on the narrowly aristocratic standards of the early part of the century.

Among the leading composers of Italian opera were Handel, Pergolesi (whose serious operas, however, were unsuccessful and practically without influence), Nicola Porpora (1686–1768)—and a German, Johann Adolph Hasse (1699–1783). Hasse was for most of his life director of music and opera at the court of the Elector of Saxony in Dresden, but he spent many years in Italy, married an Italian wife (a celebrated soprano, Faustina Bordoni), and became thoroughly Italian in his musical style. His music is the perfect complement to Metastasio's poetry; the great majority of his eighty operas are on librettos of Metastasio, some of which he set two and even three times. He was the most popular and successful opera composer of Europe around the middle of the century, and Burney's remarks about his music reveal the qualities that endeared him to the connoisseurs:

> . . . the most natural, elegant, and judicious composer of vocal music . . . now alive; equally a friend to poetry and the voice, he discovers as much judgment as genius, in expressing words, as well as in accompanying those sweet and tender melodies, which he gives to the singer. Always regarding the voice, as the first object of attention in a theatre, he never suffocates it, by the learned jargon of a multiplicity of instruments and subjects; but is as careful of preserving its importance as a painter, of throwing the strongest light upon the capital figure of his piece.[12]

When certain Italian composers began seriously to try to bring the opera into harmony with changing ideals of music and drama, their efforts were directed toward making the entire design more "natural"—that is, more flexible in structure, more deeply expressive in content, less laden with coloratura, and more varied in other musical resources. The da capo aria was not abandoned but it was modified, and other forms were used as well; arias and recitatives were alternated more flexibly so as to carry on the action more rapidly and realistically; greater use was made of accompanied recitative; the orchestra became more important both for its own sake and for adding harmonic depth to accompaniments; choruses, long disused in Italian opera, reappeared; and there was a general stiffening of resistance to the arbitrary demands of the solo singers.

Beginnings of opera reform

Two of the most important figures in the movement of reform were Niccolò Jommelli and Tommaso Traetta (1727–79). The fact that both these Italian composers worked at courts where French taste predominated—Jommelli at Stuttgart and Traetta at Parma—naturally influenced them toward a cosmopolitan type of opera. More in the purely Italian tradition were the twelve operas of Johann Christian Bach, which included *Alessandro nell'Indie* (*Alexander in India*), on a libretto by Metastasio (Naples, 1762); *Orione* (London, 1763); and *La clemenza di Scipione* (*The Mercy of Scipio*; London, 1778).

The consummation of the international style of opera was the work of Christoph Willibald Gluck (1714–87). Born in Bohemia, Gluck studied under Sammartini in Italy, visited London, toured in Germany as conductor of an opera troupe, became court com-

Christoph Willibald Gluck

---

[12] Burney, *The Present State of Music in Germany*, London, 1775, I, 238–39. Dr. Burney's—or his editor's—punctuation has been preserved.

poser to the Emperor at Vienna, and triumphed in Paris under the patronage of Marie Antoinette. He began by writing operas in the conventional Italian style, but was strongly affected by the movement of reform in the 1750s. Spurred on by the more radical ideas of the time, he collaborated with the poet Raniero Calzabigi (1714–95) to produce at Vienna *Orfeo ed Euridice* in 1762 and *Alceste* in 1767. In a dedicatory preface to the latter work Gluck summarized his aims: to remove the abuses that had hitherto deformed Italian opera, "to confine music to its proper function of serving the poetry for the expression and the situations of the plot" without regard either to the outworn conventions of the da capo aria or the desire of singers to show off their skill in ornamental variation; furthermore, to make the overture an integral part of the opera, to adapt the orchestra to the dramatic requirements, and to lessen the contrast between aria and recitative. "I believed that my greatest effort should be directed to seeking a beautiful simplicity . . . and there is no accepted rule that I have not thought should be gladly sacrificed in favor of effectiveness."

The beautiful simplicity which Gluck professed to seek is exemplified in the celebrated aria *Che farò senza Euridice?* (What shall I do

A stage setting for Gluck's Alceste, *as produced in Paris in 1776; drawing by François-Joseph Bélanger.*

without Euridice?) from *Orfeo,* and in other airs, choruses, and dances of the same work. *Alceste* is a more monumental opera, in contrast to the prevailingly pastoral and elegiac tone of *Orfeo.* In both, the music is plastically molded to the drama, with recitatives, arias, and choruses intermingled in large unified scenes. Gluck achieved his mature style in these operas, assimilating Italian melodic grace, German seriousness, and the stately magnificence of the French *tragédie lyrique.* He was ready for the climax of his career, which was ushered in with the production of *Iphigénie en Aulide (Iphigenia at Aulis)* at Paris in 1774.

The musical atmosphere of the French capital was such that this event awakened extraordinary interest. Long-simmering critical opposition to the old-fashioned, state-subsidized French opera had erupted in 1752 in a verbal battle known as the *guerre des bouffons* (War of the Buffonists), so called because its immediate occasion was the presence in Paris of an Italian opera company which for two seasons enjoyed sensational success with performances of Italian comic operas *(opere buffe).* Practically every intellectual and would-be intellectual in France had taken part in the quarrel—partisans of Italian opera on one side and friends of French opera on the other. Rousseau, one of the leaders of the former faction, published an article in which he argued that the French language was inherently unsuitable for singing and concluded "that the French have no music and cannot have any; or that if they have, it will be so much the worse for them." Rousseau and his friends, despite the foolish extremes to which they occasionally strayed in the heat of argument, represented advanced opinion in Paris. As a result of their campaign the traditional French opera of Lully and Rameau soon lost favor; but nothing had appeared to take its place before Gluck arrived on the scene. Gluck cleverly represented himself, or was represented by his supporters, as wanting to prove that a good opera could be written to French words; he professed himself desirous of having Rousseau's aid in creating "a noble, sensitive, and natural melody . . . music suited to all nations, so as to abolish these ridiculous distinctions of national styles." He thus appealed at the same time to the patriotism and the curiosity of the French public.

Iphigénie en Aulide, with a libretto adapted from Racine's tragedy, was a tremendous success. Revised versions of *Orfeo* and *Alceste* (both with French texts) swiftly followed. In a mischievously instigated rivalry with the popular Neapolitan composer Niccolò Piccinni (1728–1800), Gluck composed in 1777 a five-act opera, *Armide,* on the same libretto of Quinault that Lully had set in 1686. Gluck's masterpiece, *Iphigénie en Tauride (Iphigenia in Tauris),* was produced in 1779. It is a work of large proportions, having an excellent balance of dramatic and musical interest, and utilizing all the resources of opera—orchestra, ballet, solo and choral singing—to produce a total effect of Classical tragic grandeur.

Gluck's operas were models for the works of his immediate followers at Paris, and his influence on the form and spirit of opera was transmitted to the nineteenth century through such composers as his erstwhile rival Piccinni, Luigi Cherubini (1760–1842), Gasparo Spontini (1774–1851), and Hector Berlioz (1803–69) in *Les Troyens*.

Comic opera

The term *comic opera* denotes works that are lighter in style than serious opera; they present familiar scenes and characters rather than heroic or mythological material, and require relatively modest performing resources. Comic opera took different forms in different countries, although everywhere it represented an artistic revolt against the *opera seria*, the "serious" or tragic Italian opera. Comic opera librettos were always in the national tongue, and the music likewise tended to accentuate the national musical idiom. From humble beginnings the comic opera grew steadily in importance after 1760, and before the end of the century many of its characteristic features had been absorbed into the main stream of operatic composition. Its historical significance was twofold: it responded to the universal demand for naturalness in the latter half of the eighteenth century, and it was the principal early channel of the movement toward musical nationalism which became prominent in the Romantic period.

ITALY

An important type of Italian comic opera was the *intermezzo,* so called because it originated in the custom of presenting short comic musical *intermezzi* between the acts of a serious opera. An early master was Pergolesi, whose *La serva padrona* (*The Maid as Mistress,* 1733) is still popular. Written for only bass and soprano (there is a third character who is mute) with a string orchestra, the music is a paragon of the nimble, spirited comic style at which Italian composers surpass the rest of the world.

One of the achievements of Italian comic opera was its exploitation of the possibilities of the bass voice, either in straight comedy or in burlesque of other styles. In the comic operas of Nicola Logroscino (1698–*ca.* 1765) and Baldassare Galuppi another feature appeared, the *ensemble finale:* for the ending of an act all the characters are gradually brought on to the stage while the action continues with growing animation until it reaches a climax in which every singer in the cast takes part. These ensemble finales were unlike anything in the serious opera, and in writing them composers were forced to follow the rapidly changing action of the scene without losing coherence in the musical form. The challenge was well met by two Neapolitan composers, Piccinni and Giovanni Paisiello (1740–1816), but complete success in this difficult task was reserved for Mozart.

Meanwhile, beginning about the middle of the century, largely owing to the Italian dramatist Carlo Goldoni (1707–93), a refinement of the comic opera libretto took place; plots of a serious, sentimental, or pathetic character began to appear, as well as the traditional comic ones. Conforming to this change, the older designation *opera buffa* was replaced by *dramma giocoso*—literally a jocular but more accurately a pleasant or cheerful, that is a non-tragic, drama. An example of this new type was Piccinni's *La buona figliuola* (*The Good Girl*) of 1760, adapted by Goldoni from Richardson's novel *Pamela* which had appeared twenty years before. Paisiello's *Barbiere di Siviglia* (*The Barber of Seville;* 1782), from Beaumarchais's drama, was a semiserious treatment of current political issues, while his *Nina* (1789) had an out-and-out sentimental plot. All in all, the *opera buffa* came a long way, both dramatically and musically, in the course of the century; Mozart made good use of its mingled heritage of comic, serious, and sentimental drama and live, flexible, and widely acceptable musical style.

The national French form of light opera was known as *opéra comique.* It began around 1710 as a lowly form of popular entertainment, and until the middle of the century relied almost entirely on popular tunes (*vaudevilles*), or simple melodies in imitation of such tunes, for its music. The visit of the Italian buffonists to Paris in 1752 stimulated the production of *opéras comiques* in which original airs (called *ariettes*) in a mixed Italian-French style were introduced along with the old vaudevilles; gradually the ariettes replaced the vaudevilles until by the end of the 1760s the latter were completely discarded and the entire score was newly composed. One of the composers in this transitional decade was Gluck, who arranged and composed a number of *opéras comiques* for the entertainment of the court at Vienna. Rousseau in 1752, one year before he declared that "the French cannot have any music," had composed a charming little opera with airs and recitatives, called *Le Devin du village* (*The Village Soothsayer*).

FRANCE

The French *opéra comique,* like all the national forms of light opera except the Italian, used spoken dialogue instead of recitative. Following the general European trend in the second half of the century, the *opéra comique* took on a romantic tinge, and some of the librettos furthermore dealt quite boldly with the burning social issues that were agitating France during the pre-Revolutionary years. The principal composers were François André Danican-Philidor (1726–95; also famous as a chess master), Pierre-Alexandre Monsigny (1729–1817), and above all the Belgian-born André Ernest Modeste Grétry (1741–1813), whose *Richard Coeur-de-Lion* (*Richard the Lion-Hearted;* 1784) was a forerunner of numerous "rescue" operas around the turn of the century—Beethoven's *Fidelio* was one—in which the hero, after lying for two and a half acts in imminent danger of death, is finally saved through the devoted heroism of a friend. Grétry's music in his fifty or more operas is never profound, but it is melodious, singable, and quite effective, with occasional moments of moving dramatic expression. The *opéra comique,* with its alternation of spoken dialogue and musical numbers, was extremely popular in France. It flourished through the Revolution and the Napoleonic era and took on even greater musical significance during the Romantic period.

ENGLAND

The English *ballad opera* rose to popularity after the extraordinary success of *The Beggar's Opera* at London in 1728. This piece broadly satirized the fashionable Italian opera; its music, like that of the early *opéra comique,* consisted for the most part of popular tunes —ballads—with a few numbers parodied from familiar operatic airs. The immense popularity of ballad operas in the 1730s was one sign of a general reaction in England against foreign opera, that "exotic and irrational entertainment," as Dr. Johnson called it—a reaction which, as we have already noticed, had among its consequences that of turning Handel's energies from opera to oratorio in the latter part of his life. The only notable composer of English opera in the eighteenth century was Thomas Augustine Arne; many comic operas on sentimental or romantic subjects were produced by him and lesser composers throughout the century.

GERMANY

In Germany a form of comic opera called the *Singspiel* arose about the middle of the eighteenth century. The first singspiels were adaptations of English ballad operas, but the librettists soon turned for their material to translations or arrangements of French comic operas, for which the German composers provided new music in a familiar and appealing national melodic vein. Many of the eighteenth-century singspiel tunes found their way into German song collections and thus in the course of time have become practically folk songs. The principal early singspiel composer was Johann Adam Hiller (1728–1804) of Leipzig. In northern Germany, the singspiel developed along romantic lines, its history eventually merging with that of early nineteenth-century German Romantic opera. In the south, particularly at Vienna, the fashion was for farcical subjects and treatment, with lively music in popular style, influenced to some extent by the idioms of the Italian comic opera. A typical Viennese singspiel composer was Carl Ditters von Dittersdorf (1739–99), who was also notable for his instrumental music. The German singspiel was as important as the Italian *dramma giocoso* in the historical background of Mozart's works for the theatre.

The Lied

Solo songs, cantatas, and other types of secular vocal music outside opera were produced in every country during the eighteenth century, but special artistic importance attaches to the rise of the new German *Lied*. The first important collection of *Lieder* was published at Leipzig in 1736 under the title *Die singende Muse an der Pleisse* (*The Muse of Song on the [River] Pleisse*). The songs in this collection were parodies, in the eighteenth-century sense of the term; that is, the words were written to fit music already existing. In this instance, the musical originals were little clavier pieces, mostly in

EXAMPLE XIII–1   Lied: Erlkönig, J. F. Reichardt

*Who rides so late through night and wind? It is the father with his
child. He has the boy within his arm, he holds him fast, he keeps him
warm. "My son, why do you hide your face in fear?" . . . "You dear
child, come, go with me; lovely games I'll play with you."*

dance rhythms. Other collections of similar songs, some parodied and some with original music, appeared subsequently. The principal center of song composition after the middle of the century was Berlin, with J. J. Quantz (1697–1773), K. H. Graun, and C. P. E. Bach the chief composers. The professed ideals of the Berlin school required that *Lieder* should be in strophic form with melodies in a natural, expressive style like folksong, having but one note to a syllable; only the simplest possible accompaniments, held completely subordinate to the vocal line, were permitted. These principles, which were in accord with the philosophy of the expressive style, were generally accepted in the eighteenth century; but their effect eventually was to impose artificial restrictions on the Lied, and composers of imagination gradually transcended them, particularly in the direction of making the form more varied and giving more significance to the accompaniment. The leading Berlin composers toward the end of the century were Johann Abraham Peter Schulz (1747–1800) and Johann Friedrich Reichardt (1752–1814); the latter's 700 *Lieder* included many on poems by Goethe (see Example XIII–1).

Over 750 collections of *Lieder* with keyboard accompaniment were published in Germany during the second half of the century, and this figure does not include the numerous singspiels of the same period, which consist for the most part of songs exactly similar to *Lieder*. Practically all composers of singspiels, in fact, also wrote *Lieder* in large quantities. The production continued steadily into the nineteenth century; when Schubert began composing songs in 1811 he was entering into a long and rich tradition, which his own work carried to new heights.

Church music

The secular, individualistic temper of the eighteenth century had the effect of bringing sacred music into conformity with the style of secular music, particularly that of the theatre. A few composers in the Catholic countries ably carried on the ancient tradition of Palestrina or the polychoric style of Benevoli; among such may be mentioned the Spanish master Francisco Valle (1665–1745) of Barcelona and the Roman, Giuseppe Ottavio Pitoni (1657–1743). But the dominant trend was to introduce into the church the musical idioms and forms of opera, with orchestral accompaniment, da capo arias, and accompanied recitatives. The list of the leading eighteenth-century Italian church composers is almost identical with the list of leading opera composers of the same period. Even more than the Mass and motet, the oratorio in Italy grew to be almost indistinguishable from opera. At the same time some composers, particularly in northern Italy and southern Germany and Austria, effected a compromise between conservative and modern elements, and this mixed style—influenced also by the instrumental symphonic forms of the Classical period—was the background of the sacred compositions of Haydn and Mozart.

Lutheran church music rapidly declined in quality and importance after the death of J. S. Bach. The principal achievements of the
north German composers were in the half-sacred, half-secular form
of the oratorio; oratorios written after 1750 show some reaction
against the excesses of operatic style. The best oratorios of this period
were those of C. P. E. Bach. Karl Heinrich Graun's *Der Tod Jesu*
(*The Death of Jesus*), a mediocre work which was first performed at
Berlin in 1755, remained popular in Germany up to the end of the
nineteenth century.

In England, the overpowering influence of Handel operated to
discourage originality, and the generally low level of church music
is relieved only by the works of a few composers such as Maurice
Greene (1695–1775) and Samuel Wesley (1766–1837). Wesley, incidentally, was one of the first musicians of his time to recognize
the greatness of J. S. Bach and did much to stimulate performance
of Bach's organ music in England. The latter half of the eighteenth
century was not by any means a period of musical stagnation in
England; there was an active concert life, and much intelligent
appreciation of foreign musicians, notably Haydn, who wrote several
of his most important symphonies for London audiences.

XIV

<hr/>

The Late Eighteenth Century

Many times, two nearly contemporary famous composers have become linked as representatives of a particular era: Leonin and Perotin, Dufay and Binchois, Obrecht and Josquin, Palestrina and Lasso, Bach and Handel, and, in more recent times, Liszt and Wagner, Brahms and Bruckner, Debussy and Ravel. The better we know the music of any of these pairs of composers, the more we become aware of the ways in which they differ; yet both differences and likenesses are important if we are to understand the style common to the period in which they both worked.

The two outstanding composers of the late eighteenth century are Haydn and Mozart. Together they represent the Classical period in much the same sense that Bach and Handel represent the late Baroque, using the accepted musical language of their time and creating in that language works of unsurpassed perfection. Haydn and Mozart have much more in common than mere contemporaneity and similarity of idiom; they became personal friends, and each admired and was influenced by the music of the other. Haydn was born in 1732, Mozart in 1756; Mozart died in 1791 at the age of 35, Haydn in 1809 at the age of 77. Haydn's growth to artistic maturity was much slower than Mozart's, who was a child prodigy. Had Haydn died at 35 he would hardly be remembered today; in fact, many of his best known works were not produced until after Mozart's death. In personality the two men were utterly different: Mozart was a precocious genius, of roving disposition and unsettled habits, a born showman, a virtuoso pianist, a consummate musical dramatist, but helpless in most of the practical affairs of life; Haydn was largely self-taught, a patient and persistent worker, modest, an excellent conductor but no virtuoso soloist (though he occasionally played viola in string quartets), precise and regular in the conduct of his affairs, and one who on the whole lived contentedly under the patronage system—the last eminent composer to do so.

Franz Joseph Haydn

Haydn was born of poor parents at Rohrau, a little town in the eastern part of Austria near the Hungarian border. He received his first musical training from an uncle with whom he went to live at the age of six. Two years later he became a choirboy at the Cathedral of St. Stephen in Vienna, where he acquired a great deal of practical musical experience but was given no systematic instruction in theory. Dismissed when his voice changed, the boy supported himself precariously with odd jobs and teaching. He mastered counterpoint by himself, using Fux's *Gradus ad Parnassum;* meanwhile he gradually made himself known to influential persons in Vienna and received a few lessons in composition from Nicola Porpora, the famous Italian composer and singing teacher. In 1759 or earlier, he obtained the position of music director of the chapel of Count von Morzin, a Bohemian nobleman, for whose orchestra Haydn wrote his first symphony. The year 1761 was momentous in Haydn's life: he was taken into the service of Prince Paul Anton Esterházy, head of one of the wealthiest and most powerful Hungarian noble families, a man devoted to music and a bountiful patron of the art.

In the service of Paul Anton and his brother Nicholas, called "the Magnificent," who succeeded to the title in 1762, Haydn passed nearly thirty years under circumstances well-nigh ideal for his development as a composer. From 1766, Prince Nicholas lived for the most of the year on his remote country estate of Eszterháza, the palace and grounds of which had been constructed to equal the splendor of the French Court at Versailles. There were two theatres, one for opera and one for marionette plays, as well as two large and sumptuously appointed music rooms in the palace itself. Haydn was obligated to compose whatever music the prince demanded, to conduct the performances, to train and supervise all the musical personnel, and to keep the instruments in repair. He built up the orchestra from ten to about twenty-five players, and there were a dozen or so singers for the opera as well; all the principal musicians

Haydn's career

477

were recruited from the best talent available in Austria, Italy, and elsewhere. Two operas and two long concerts were presented each week. In addition there were special operas and concerts for notable visitors, as well as almost daily chamber music in the prince's private apartments, in which the prince himself usually joined. He played the baryton, a complicated instrument like a large viola da gamba

The Esterházy Palace at Eisenstadt. Engraving by János Beckeny after Szabo. (Hungarian National Museum, Budapest)

with an extra set of resonating metal strings; Haydn wrote—on command—nearly 200 pieces for the baryton, mostly in a trio combination with viola and violoncello.

Although Eszterháza was isolated, the constant stream of distinguished guests and artists, together with occasional trips to Vienna, enabled Haydn to keep abreast of current developments in the world of music. He had the inestimable advantages of a devoted, highly skilled band of singers and players and an intelligent patron whose requirements, it is true, were burdensome, but whose understanding and enthusiasm were at most times an inspiration. As Haydn once said, "My prince was pleased with all my work, I was commended, and as conductor of an orchestra I could make experiments, observe what strengthened and what weakened an effect and thereupon improve, substitute, omit, and try new things; I was cut off from the world, there was no one around to mislead and harass me, and so I was forced to become original."

Haydn's contract with Prince Paul Anton Esterházy forbade him to sell or give away any of his compositions; but this provision was later relaxed, and as Haydn's fame spread in the 1770s and '80s he filled many commissions from publishers and individuals all over Europe. He remained at Eszterháza until the death of Prince Nicholas in 1790, when he moved to Vienna and settled in his own house. Then followed two strenuous but productive and profitable seasons in London (January, 1791 to July, 1792 and February, 1794 to August, 1795), mostly under the management of the impresario Johann Peter Salomon. Here Haydn conducted concerts and wrote a multitude of new works, including the twelve *London* symphonies. Returning home, he resumed his service with the Esterházy family, living now, however, most of the time in Vienna.

The new prince, Nicholas II, cared less for Haydn's music than for the glory that accrued to himself from having such a famous man in his employ; the principal works Haydn wrote for him were six Masses in the years 1796 to 1802. Since Haydn's other duties were by now nominal, he was able to devote himself to the composition of quartets and his last two oratorios, *The Creation* and *The Seasons*. *The Creation* was performed at Vienna in 1798 and *The Seasons* in 1801, both with resounding success. Haydn's last composition was the String Quartet Op. 103, which he began in 1803, but of which he completed only two movements.

It is impossible to determine exactly how many compositions Haydn wrote. No reliable catalogue was made during his lifetime and the new modern critical edition of his works is as yet incomplete. Publishers in the eighteenth century brought out many compositions which they falsely attributed to Haydn because they knew his name would attract buyers. Some 150 such false attributions of symphonies and 60–70 of string quartets have been detected. The *Toy* Symphony, for example, which has so often been cited as typifying Haydn's naive, childlike nature, has recently been held spurious (it may have been written by Leopold Mozart). The task of establishing a corpus of authentic Haydn works is still engaging the efforts of scholars. Provisionally, the list of his authenticated compositions includes 106 symphonies and 68 string quartets; numerous overtures, concertos, divertimentos, serenades, baryton trios, string trios, piano trios, and other chamber works; 60 piano sonatas; songs, arias, cantatas, Masses and other settings of liturgical texts; between 20 and 25 operas (of which only 15 are extant), and 4 oratorios. Most important are the symphonies and quartets, for Haydn was above all an instrumental composer and the symphonies and quartets are his finest achievements in this field. Of his vocal music before 1790 the most important works are the *St. Caecilia* Mass from the early seventies, the *Mariazeller* Mass of 1782, the Stabat Mater in G minor, and the oratorio *The Return of Tobias* (1775). Better known are the last six Masses and the two oratorios *The Creation* and *The Seasons;* all these last are permeated to some extent by the spirit and techniques of the symphony, with which Haydn had been so intensively concerned in the early 1790s.

The symphonies up to No. 92 were written before 1788, most of them of course for Prince Esterházy's orchestra; Nos. 82–87 were composed on commission in 1785–86 for a concert series in Paris (and hence are known as the *Paris* Symphonies); Nos. 88–92 were commissioned by private individuals. No. 92 is called the *Oxford* Symphony because it was played on the occasion when Haydn received the honorary degree of Doctor of Music from Oxford University in 1791. Many of the other symphonies (as well as many of the quartets) have been given special names for one reason or another, but hardly any of these designations are the composer's.

Very many of Haydn's earliest symphonies are in the preclassical three-movement form derived from the Italian opera overture (*sinfonia*); these consist typically of an allegro followed by an andante in the parallel minor or subdominant key, ending with a minuet or a rapid gigue-like movement in 3/8 or 6/8 (examples: Nos. 9, 19).[1] Other symphonies from the early period recall the baroque *sonata da chiesa* in that they begin with a slow movement and continue with (usually) three other movements in the same key, the typical order being andante–allegro–minuet–presto (examples: Nos. 21, 22). Soon, however, the normal type becomes that represented by Symphony No. 3, in G major, which apparently was written not later than 1762. It has the standard classical division into four movements: I. Allegro; II. Andante moderato; III. Minuet and Trio; IV. Allegro —departing from the usual pattern only in that the slow movement is in the parallel minor key instead of the more common subdominant or dominant. The wind instruments (here two oboes and two horns) have considerable independence, a feature that was to become even more marked in some of the later symphonies. The first movement is a good example of Haydn's freedom of phrase structure; both this movement and the finale exhibit his way of softening the rigidity of eighteenth-century four-measure phrases by some recall of the Baroque "spinning-out" method for developing musical ideas. The Andante of No. 3, for strings alone, is in a type of sonata form frequently employed by Haydn for his slow movements: two parts (each repeated), with modulation to the relative major (alternatively, to the dominant) in part one; in part two, further modulations and a sequence, followed by a return to the tonic with modified recapitulation of part one. A good deal of the writing in this symphony is contrapuntal: the minuet is canonic; the finale combines fugal form with classical instrumental figuration and Haydn's characteristic rhythmic drive.

Minuet and Trio is a movement found in almost every Classical symphony. The Minuet is always in a two-part $|: a :|: á (a) :|$ form; the Trio has a similar form and is usually in the same key as

---

[1] Numbering is according to the catalogue in Appendix I of H. C. Robbins Landon's *Symphonies of Joseph Haydn* and A. van Hoboken's *Thematisches-bibliographisches Werkverzeichnis*.

the Minuet (possibly with change of mode), but is shorter and has lighter orchestration; after the Trio the Minuet returns da capo without repeats. Haydn's minuets with their trios contain some of his most charming music. It is remarkable what a wealth of musical ideas, what happy traits of harmonic invention and instrumental color he was able to infuse into this modest form; he said once that he wished someone would write "a really new minuet," but he himself succeeded admirably in doing so nearly every time he wrote one. The frequent conspicuous use of wind instruments in Haydn's minuets suggests the dance origin of this classical symphonic third movement as well as its relation to the contemporary divertimento and cassation.

Certain exceptional features appear in three symphonies (Nos. 6, 7, and 8) which Haydn composed soon after entering the service of Prince Esterházy in 1761. He gave them the semi-programmatic titles *Le Matin, Le Midi,* and *Le Soir (Morning, Noon, Evening)*, without further explanation. All have the normal four movements of the Classical symphony. The first movements are, as usual with Haydn, in sonata form with the customary modulations but without strongly marked secondary themes. Nos. 6 and 7 have brief adagio introductions. That to *Le Matin* is undoubtedly meant to depict a sunrise, and may be regarded as a predecessor of the lovely passage of musical landscape-painting that opens the third part of *The Creation.* The slow movements of these two symphonies are irregular: *Le Matin* has a stately dance-like movement in moderately slow tempo (Andante), framed by two Adagios; in *Le Midi* there are two slow movements, coupled together in the guise of a *recitativo accompagnato* followed by an aria—or rather, a duet for solo violin and violoncello, complete with cadenza and decorated by ornamental flute passages. The "recitative," in which a solo violin represents the vocal line, is a remarkably passionate outpouring, with far-ranging modulations.

Occasional *concertante* use of solo instruments, the concerto-like alternating tutti-solo sections in some of the allegros, divertimento-like use of the wind instruments, occasional Corelli-like adagio passages with chains of suspensions, and the constant underlying tendency toward compromise between preclassical articulated phrasing and Baroque *Fortspinnung*—all are ways in which Haydn, even from his earliest works, was enriching the language of the Classical symphony by the fusion of new and old elements. His orchestration retains another Baroque feature, the employment of the harpsichord and the doubling of the bass line (by the bassoon along with the violoncellos and double basses) for a basso continuo. The harpsichord is an essential instrument in Haydn's symphonies until about 1770, and it or the piano was used even in his later ones in eighteenth-century performances, since at that time the orchestra was usually conducted from the keyboard instrument.

Of all the four movements, it was the finale which eventually came to be the crowning glory of a Haydn symphony. The Classical symphony generally aims to get through its more serious business in the first two movements. The Minuet provides relaxation, since it is shorter than either of the two preceding movements, is written in a more popular style, and has a form easy for the listener to follow. But the Minuet does not make a satisfactory closing movement: it is too short to balance the preceding two, and moreover, the spirit of relaxation which it induces needs to be balanced by a further climax of tension and release. Haydn soon came to realize that the 3/8 or 6/8 *Presto* finales of his earliest symphonies were inadequate to accomplish this, as well as being too light in form and content to produce a satisfying unity of effect in the symphony as a whole. He therefore developed a new type of closing movement which begins to make its appearance in the late 1760s: an Allegro or Presto in 2/4 or ¢, in sonata or rondo form or a combination of the two, shorter than the first movement, compact, swiftly moving, overflowing with high spirits and nimble gaiety, abounding in little whimsical tricks of silence and all sorts of impish surprises. This kind of finale is found in Symphonies Nos. 35 and 38 (the latter as well with a virtuoso oboe part almost like a solo concerto); but the big important finales of the mature Haydn begin with Symphony No. 82.

Many of the symphonies of the 1760s are experimental. No. 31 (*With the Horn Signal*) is divertimento-like in its conspicuous use of the winds (four horns instead of the customary two) and in the theme-and-variations form of the finale. This "hunting" symphony has successors in Haydn's later works, for example the chorus *Hark, the mountains resound* from *The Seasons*. In general, Haydn's symphonies after 1765 progress toward more serious and meaningful musical content (No. 35) and more subtle use of form (finale of No. 38). The symphonies in minor keys (Nos. 26, 39, and 49, all from 1768) have an intensity of feeling that is a harbinger of the music written in the years 1770–72, the first great culmination of Haydn's style. No. 26 (*Passio et lamentatio*) incorporates a melody from an old plainsong Passion drama as thematic material in the first movement and a liturgical chant from the *Lamentations* in the second.

The *symphonies of 1771–74*

The works of 1771–72 show Haydn as a composer of ripe technique and fervent imagination, with a quality analogous to the type of emotion expressed in the literary monument of the *Sturm und Drang*. As representative symphonies from these years we may take Nos. 44, 45, and 47. All are on a larger scale than the symphonies of the previous decade. Themes are more broadly laid out, those of the fast movements often beginning with a bold unison proclamation followed immediately by a contrasting idea, with the whole theme then restated. Development sections, which use motives from the themes, become more propulsive and dramatic. Dramatic also are

Henry Fuseli, The Nightmare *(ca. 1781–2). Friend and teacher of William Blake, Fuseli rejected the gay elegance of the style galant and turned his attention to the macabre and fantastic subjects that characterized the* Sturm und Drang *in art. (Goethe Museum, Frankfurt)*

the unexpected changes from *forte* to *piano,* the crescendos and *sforzati* that are a part of this style. Counterpoint appears, not as a foreign element contrasting with homophonic texture, but as a natural concomitant of the musical ideas. The harmonic palette is richer than in the early symphonies; modulations range more widely and the harmonic arches are broader.

The slow movements have a romantically expressive warmth. Symphony No. 44, in E minor, known as the *Trauersinfonie (Symphony of Mourning)*, has one of the most beautiful Adagios in all Haydn's works. Most of the slow movements are in sonata form, but with such leisurely, freely drawn out progression of the thought that a listener is hardly conscious of the structure. The slow movement of No. 47, however, is a theme with variations, a favored form for slow movements in Haydn's later works; the first period of the theme is constructed in double counterpoint at the octave, so that the last period of the theme (and of each of the four variations) is the same as the first but with the melody and the bass interchanged. Another contrapuntal device is exhibited in the Minuet of No. 44, which is in canon at the octave. (A second canonic Minuet occurs in Haydn's Quartet Op. 76, No. 2.) The Minuet of No. 47 is written *al rovescio* —that is, the second section of the Minuet, and also of the Trio, is the first section played backward.

Symphony No. 45 is called the *Farewell* Symphony. According to one well-known story, Haydn wrote it as a hint to Prince Esterházy that it was time to move back to town from his summer palace and give the musicians an opportunity to see their wives and families again; the final Presto breaks off into an Adagio, in the course of which one group of instruments after another concludes its part and the players get up and leave until only two first violins remain to play the closing measures. The *Farewell* Symphony is unusual in several other respects: the first movement introduces a long new theme in the course of the development section—an experiment which Haydn never repeated; both the second movement and the final Adagio use the extended harmonic vocabulary characteristic of Haydn's works in this period. The key of this symphony, F♯ minor, is exceptional for the eighteenth century, but such remote tonalities are one of the marks of Haydn's style at this time (see also Symphony No. 46 in B major and No. 49 [*La Passione,* 1768] in F minor); characteristically, he departs from the minor mode in the Adagio (A major) and Minuet (F♯ major) of the *Farewell* Symphony, and although the Presto is in F♯ minor, the closing Adagio begins in A major and ends in F♯ major. This slow ending, of course, is exceptional, and due to reasons not purely musical. Symphonies 44 and 47 have presto finales in monothematic sonata form, but the latter introduces so many recurrences of the theme as almost to give the impression of a Baroque concerto allegro with ritornellos.

The quartets of 1760–81

Haydn's string quartets of the time around 1770 testify as strongly as do the symphonies to his arrival at full artistic stature. His earliest quartets, which were probably composed in 1757–58, are like divertimentos, with five movements (a minuet on each side of the slow movement), written in the light pre-Classical style of the middle eighteenth century; they may have been intended for either a string orchestra or a quartet of soloists. The six quartets of Op. 3² are of dubious authenticity and in any case show few significant traces of Haydn's later manner. With Op. 9 (*ca.* 1770), we come into a different style. The dramatic opening movement of No. 4 of this group, in D minor, reveals a new mood of seriousness, as well as some measures of genuine motivic development after the double bar. The proportions of this movement—two repeated sections of nearly equal

---

2 Haydn's string quartets are identified by the familiar Opus numbers, which correspond to the numbering in Group III of van Hoboken's catalogue as follows:

"Opus"	Hoboken	"Opus"	Hoboken
3	13–18	50	44–49
9	19–24	54, 55	57–62
17	25–30	64	63–68
20	31–36	71, 74	69–74
33	37–42	76	75–80
42	43	77	81–82
		103	83

length—clearly illustrate the relationship of Classical sonata form to the Baroque suite movements; the development is brief and the recapitulation so condensed (nineteen measures as against thirty-four of the exposition) that these two parts together are only seven measures longer than the exposition. This quartet, like all those of Op. 9 (also all those of Op. 17 and a good half of those in Opp. 20 and 33), places the Minuet before the slow movement instead of after it, as is usually done in the symphonies. The final Presto, in 6/8 time, has something of the dynamic energy of a Beethoven scherzo.

In the Quartets Opp. 17 and 20, composed respectively in 1771 and 1772, Haydn achieved a union of all stylistic elements and a perfect adaptation of form to expressive musical content. These works definitely established both Haydn's contemporary fame and his historical position as founder of the Classical string quartet. Rhythms are more varied than in the previous quartets; themes are expanded, developments become more organic, and all the forms are treated with assurance and finesse. The four instruments have individuality and equality; particularly in Op. 20, the violoncello begins to be used as a melodic and solo instrument. The texture is free from any suspicion of dependence on a basso continuo; at the same time, counterpoint rises to importance. Three of the finales in Op. 20 are called "fuga," a term which may be somewhat misleading. These movements are not fugues in the Bach sense; technically, they are essays in invertible counterpoint with two, three, or four parts. In fact, everywhere in these quartets contrapuntal writing enriches the texture, as in the symphonies of this same period. Movements in sonata form approach the full three-part structure, with development sections enlarged so that all three parts—exposition, development, and recapitulation—are more nearly equal in length than they are in the quartets of Op. 9; moreover, development of the announced themes is spread over the entire movement, a procedure typical of Haydn's later works in sonata form. One of Haydn's favorite "effects" makes its appearance in the first movement of Op. 20, No. 1: the opening theme pops up, in the tonic key, in the midst of the development section, as though the recapitulation had already begun—but this is a deception, for the theme is only a starting point for further development and the real recapitulation comes later. This device, sometimes called a *fausse reprise* or false recapitulation, may be regarded historically as a vestige of the Baroque concerto form. There is much variety of mood in the quartets of Op. 20, from the sombre F minor of No. 5 to the serene joyousness of No. 4 in D major. Marks of dynamics and expression are frequent and explicit, showing the composer's care for details of interpretation.

Haydn's piano sonatas follow in general the same lines of style development as the symphonies and quartets. Notable among the sonatas of the late 1760s are Nos. 19 (30)[3] in D major and 46 (31) in A♭, both evidencing the influence of C. P. E. Bach on Haydn at this time; the great sonata in C minor, No. 20 (33), composed in 1771, is a tempestuous work very characteristic of Haydn's so-called romantic period.

The symphonies of 1774–88

Immediately after 1772 Haydn entered into a new period of craftsmanship—emerging, as it seems, from a critical phase in his development as a composer. The rather striking change is most evident, perhaps, in the symphonies Nos. 54 and 57, both composed in 1774: the minor keys, the passionate accents, the experiments in form and expression of the preceding period now give way to a smooth, assured, and brilliant exploitation of orchestral resources in works of predominantly cheerful, robust character. The transformation may be attributed in part to Prince Esterházy's injunction to write "not so much for learned ears"; also, after 1772, Haydn began to be busied more and more with the composition of comic operas, and this doubtless affected his symphonic style. Symphony No. 56 (1774) is one of Haydn's twenty symphonies in C major. All but the very earliest of the symphonies written in that key form a special group, many of them possibly having been composed for particular celebrations at Eszterháza. They are generally festive in spirit, and require the addition of trumpets and drums to the normal Haydn orchestra.[4] The first movement of No. 56 gains additional pomp from the timbre of the high horns and trumpets. The Minuet is in Haydn's best popular, hearty vein, while the finale sounds like a brilliant, capricious tarantella, with sharp dynamic contrasts and tremendous rhythmic energy. Each of the fast movements of this symphony is in sonata form and has a contrasting second theme, something by no means common with Haydn.

Symphony No. 73 (*ca.* 1781) is typical of the smooth craftsmanship of this period; its rollicking 6/8 finale, taken over from an opera *La fedeltà premiata* (*Fidelity Rewarded*), is entitled *La Chasse*. The finale of No. 77 (1782) is one of the earliest examples in Haydn's work of the sonata-rondo form, which combines features of the sonata (key scheme, systematic development of motives) with those of the rondo (multiple recurrence of the principal theme). This form was frequently used for finales in Haydn's subsequent works, and was a favorite with Beethoven.

The six quartets of Op. 33, known as the *Russian* quartets, were composed in 1781. These quartets are on the whole lighter in mood

---

[3] The sonatas are numbered according to van Hoboken's catalogue and (in parentheses) the excellent three-volume edition by Christa Landon, Universal Edition 13337–39.

[4] The most important C-major symphonies are Nos. 48, 50, 56, 69, 82, 90, and 97. See Forewords to pocket score editions by H. C. Robbins Landon (Universal Edition).

than those of 1772, less romantic, but more witty and popular. Only the first movements are in sonata form; the finales (except that of No. 1) are either rondos or variations. The Minuets, although entitled "scherzo" or "scherzando" (whence the alternative name *Gli Scherzi* for this set), are not essentially different from Haydn's other minuets except that they require a slightly faster tempo in performance. The finest of this group is No. 3, in C major, known as the *Bird* quartet from the trills in the trio of the Minuet. In the Adagio, Haydn wrote out the repeat of the first section in order to vary the melodic ornaments—a device possibly borrowed from C. P. E. Bach, whose ideas on music had influenced Haydn over many years. The finale is an excellent specimen of Haydnesque humor.

The piano sonatas Nos. 21–26 (36–41), a set of six written in 1773 and dedicated to Prince Esterházy, show a general relaxation and lightening of style comparable to that in the symphonies and quartets of the same period. Most interesting from the middle and late 70s are the two sonatas No. 32 (47) and 34 (53), respectively in B and E minor.

The six *Paris* symphonies (No. 82–87) of 1785 and the five next following (Nos. 88 to 92) of 1787–88 introduce the culmination of Haydn's symphonic achievements. No. 85 (called *La Reine* and said to have been especially loved by Queen Marie Antoinette) is a model of Classical style; Nos. 88 and 92 (*Oxford*) are two of the most popular of Haydn's symphonies. All the works of this period have ample dimensions, incorporating significant and expressive musical ideas in a complex but thoroughly unified structure and making always appropriate use of many different and ingenious technical resources.

One feature[5] of the first movements of these symphonies is the slow introduction, themes of which are sometimes related to those of the following Allegro. Haydn still avoids or at least minimizes contrasting subjects in movements in sonata form; thematic development, instead, pervades all parts of the movement. Many of the slow movements have a quiet introspective coda featuring the woodwind instruments and using colorful chromatic harmonies (as in No. 92). The wind instruments are prominent also in the trios of the minuets; indeed, Haydn gives to the winds in all his symphonies much more responsibility than the average listener is likely to realize, for the large size of the string section in a modern symphony orchestra tends to overwhelm the sound of the flutes, oboes, and bassoons and thus destroy the balance of timbres that the composer intended.

The finales of Symphonies Nos. 82–92 are either in sonata form

---

[5] Already anticipated in some earlier symphonies, e.g. Nos. 6, 7, 53, 64.

or, more characteristically, sonata-rondo form. Unlike Haydn's earlier finales, these make great use of contrapuntal texture and contrapuntal devices—for example, the canon in the last movement of No. 88. By such means Haydn perfected closing movements that at the same time had popular appeal and sufficient weight to balance the rest of the symphony; the finale of No. 88 is a particularly fine example.

The quartets of the 1780s

The quartets of the late 1780s are on an equally high level of inspiration with the symphonies. The opus numbers are 42 (one quartet, 1785), 50 (the six *Prussian* quartets, 1787), 54, 55 (three each, 1789) and 64 (six quartets, 1790). Technique and forms are like those of the symphonies of the same period, except that the first movements do not have a slow introduction. There are many fascinating details in Haydn's handling of first-movement sonata form, as well as some unusual features, such as the recapitulation in the tonic major of Op. 50, No. 4, the fusing of development and recapitulation in Op. 54, No. 6 (at measure 108), or the "purple patch" apparently in F major before the cadence on A at measures 38–48 of Op. 50, No. 6. Many of the slow movements have the form of theme and variations, and among these we find some special types: the Andante of Op. 50, No. 4 is a set of double variations, using two themes in alternation, one in major and the other in minor, so that the pattern becomes A (in major) B (in minor) $A'B'A''$. In the slow movements of Op. 54, No. 3 and Op. 64, No. 6, the variation technique is combined with a broad lyric three-part form (ABA'); similar patterns emerge in Nos. 3 and 4 of Op. 64, except that in these the B section is either a variant of, or clearly derived from, A. The slow movement of Op. 55, No. 2 (in this instance the first movement of the quartet) is a full set of double variations, alternately minor and major, with a coda. The double variation form was frequently employed by Haydn in his later works, as in the Andante of Symphony No. 103 (*Drum Roll*) and the beautiful pianoforte Variations in F minor, composed in 1793.

The London symphonies

Haydn, like most composers of his time, usually wrote his music to order for specific occasions and for players and singers whom he knew; when he accepted a commission for a work to be performed elsewhere than at Eszterháza he was always careful to inform himself as fully as possible of the circumstances under which it would be produced and to adapt the music to those circumstances to the best of his ability. The invitation from Salomon in 1790 to compose and conduct six, and later six more, symphonies for the cosmopolitan and exacting audiences of London spurred him to supreme efforts. Hailed by the British as "the greatest composer in the world," he was determined to live up to what was expected of him. The *London* symphonies are consequently the crown of his achievements. Everything he had learned in forty years of experience went into them.

While there are no radical departures from his previous works, all the elements are brought together on a grander scale, with more brilliant orchestration, more daring conceptions of harmony, and an intensified rhythmic drive.

Haydn's shrewd awareness of the tastes of the London musical world is evident in little things as well as great ones. The sudden *fortissimo* crash on a weak beat in the slow movement of Symphony No. 94 which has given this work its nickname (*Surprise*) was put there because, as he later acknowledged, he wanted something novel and startling to set people talking about his concerts and take their minds off those of his pupil and rival Ignaz Pleyel (1757–1831), which had begun a week earlier. Similar in intention perhaps, but of a higher order of musical cleverness, are such devices as the "Turkish" instruments (triangle, cymbals, bass drum) and the trumpet fanfare in the Allegretto of the *Military* Symphony (No. 100); and the ticking accompaniment in the Andante of No. 101 (the *Clock*). Some very characteristic examples of folksong melodies among the themes of the *London* symphonies (for example, the first, second, and fourth movements of No. 103; finale of No. 104) evidence Haydn's desire to make the basis of appeal in these works as broad as possible. He always aimed to please both the ordinary music lover and the expert; and it is one of the measures of his greatness that he succeeded.

The orchestra of the *London* symphonies includes trumpets and timpani, which (contrary to Haydn's earlier practice) are used in most of the slow movements as well as in the others. Clarinets make their appearance in all but No. 102 of the second set of *London* symphonies. Trumpets sometimes have independent parts instead of doubling the horns as previously, and likewise the violoncellos are now more often used independently of the basses. In several of the symphonies solo strings are featured against the full orchestra. Woodwinds are treated even more independently than hitherto, and the whole sound of the orchestra achieves a new spaciousness and brilliance.

Even more striking than the orchestration, however, is the expanded harmonic range of the *London* symphonies and other works of the same period. Between the various movements, or between Minuet and Trio, the mediant relationship is sometimes exploited instead of the conventional dominant or subdominant; examples occur in Symphonies 99 and 104, and similar contrasts of tonality may be found in the three quartets of Op. 74, which were composed in 1793. Within the single movements there are sudden shifts (sometimes one can hardly call them modulations) to remote keys, as at the beginning of the development section of the Vivace of Symphony No. 97; or wide-ranging modulations, as in the recapitulation of the same movement, where the music passes quickly through E♭, A♭,

D♭, and F minor to reach the dominant of the principal key, C major.[6] An illustration of Haydn's expansion of the harmonic frontiers, a foretaste of Romantic harmony, is found in the Adagio, entitled *Fantasia,* of the Quartet Op. 76, No. 6 (1797), which begins in B major and wanders through C♯ minor, E major and minor, G major, B♭ major and minor, back to B major (Example XIV–1), then through C♯ minor, G♯ minor, and A♭ major, finally settling down in B major for the second half of the movement. Typical illus-

EXAMPLE XIV–1 Adagio (*Fantasia*), Quartet Op. 76, No. 6, Haydn

b♭: N6=I⁶ in B:

trations of Haydn's late Classical chromaticism may be heard in the Andante of Symphony No. 104 or the first movement (*Andante grazioso*) of his last Quartet, Op. 103.

Harmonic imagination is an important factor also in the slow introductions to the first movements of Haydn's *London* symphonies. These opening sections have a portentous quality, a purposive dramatic suspense which prepares the listener for the Allegro to follow; they are either in the tonic minor of the Allegro (as in Symphony No. 104), or else gravitate toward the minor mode as a foil for the forthcoming major of the fast movement. The first movements in sonata form usually have two distinct themes, but the second one is apt to appear only toward the close of the exposition as a closing element, while the function of the "textbook" second theme is taken over by a varied repetition, in the dominant, of the first theme. The slow movements are either in the form of theme and variations (Nos.

6 No. 97, the finest of all Haydn's symphonies in C, may have been in the back of Beethoven's mind when he wrote the first movement of his *Eroica:* the triadic outline of the principal theme of Haydn's first movement, the opening of his development section, the fast triple meter, the rhythmic figure ♪♪♪ ♪, the displaced accents at the unison triplet passage in both exposition and recapitulation—all are suggestive.

94, 95, 97, 103) or in a free adaptation of sonata form; one common feature is a contrasting minor section. The minuets are no longer courtly dances, but rather *allegro* symphonic movements in minuet-and-trio pattern; like the corresponding movements of the late quartets, they are already scherzos in everything but name. Some of the finales are in sonata form with two themes, but the favored pattern is the sonata-rondo—a general formal concept that admits the utmost variety and ingenuity in actual practice.[7]

Some of the quartets of Haydn's last period have already been mentioned. Altogether they include Opp. 71, 74 (three each, 1793), 76 (six, 1797), 77 (two, 1799, of which the second is probably Haydn's greatest work in this form), and the two-movement torso, Op. 103 (1803). Of the relatively familiar late quartets, a few details should be mentioned: the interesting modifications of sonata form in the first movement of Op. 77, No. 1 and the wonderful coda of the slow movement; the lovely variations on Haydn's own melody, the Austrian national hymn, in the slow movement of Op. 76, No. 3; the romantic character of the Largo (in F♯ major) of Op. 76, No. 5; and the apotheosis of the Haydn finale in all these quartets, especially perhaps in Op. 76, Nos. 4 and 5 and Op. 77, No. 1.

The last quartets

We have said nothing about Haydn's other chamber music or his concertos because the essential steps in the evolution of his style as well as the best illustrations of his genius are to be found in the symphonies, sonatas, and quartets. Among the late Haydn sonatas, special attention should be called to No. 49 (59) in E♭, which was composed in 1789–90; all three movements are of full Classical dimensions, and the Adagio, Haydn himself declared, has "deep significance." From the London period there are three sonatas, Nos. 50–52 (60–62), dating from 1794–95, of which the last, in E♭, is the best; its slow movement is in the remote key of E major (prepared for by a passage in that key in the development of the first movement), and has an almost Romantic quality with its Chopinesque ornaments.

Haydn's Vocal Works

In 1776 Haydn was asked to contribute an autobiographical sketch to an Austrian encyclopedia; he responded with a modest article in which he named as his most successful works three operas, an Italian oratorio (*The Return of Tobias*, 1774–75) and a setting of the *Stabat mater*—a work which was famous in Europe in the 1780s. Not one word did he think it worthwhile to mention about the

---

[7] For some details, see Eugene K. Wolf, "The Recapitulations in Haydn's London Symphonies," MQ 52 (1966), 71–89.

sixty-odd symphonies he had written up to that time, and all he had to say about his chamber music was to complain that the Berlin critics sometimes dealt too harshly with it. In part, his reticence may have been due simply to Haydn's knowledge that the symphonies, which required the presence of the composer for their performance, were little known outside Eszterháza; and it may be also that he did not fully realize the significance of his symphonies and string quartets until the success of the *Paris* and *London* symphonies showed him how much more highly the world regarded his instrumental works than his vocal ones.

Posterity, on the whole, has endorsed this verdict. Few people since the eighteenth century have ever heard a Haydn opera, but they were very successful in their day. Opera occupied a large part of Haydn's time and energy at Eszterháza. Besides his own works, he arranged, prepared, and conducted some 75 operas by other composers there between 1769 and 1790; Eszterháza was, in fact, despite its remote situation, an international center for opera fully comparable in importance to Vienna in this period.[8] Haydn himself wrote six little German operas for marionettes and at least fifteen regular Italian operas. Most of the latter were of the *dramma giocoso* variety, with music abounding in the frank humor and high spirits characteristic of the composer. Haydn also wrote three serious operas, the most famous of which was the "heroic drama" *Armida* (1784), remarkable for its dramatic accompanied recitatives and arias on a grand scale. Still, he must have come eventually to realize that his future as a composer lay elsewhere. In 1787, he declined a commission to compose an opera for Prague on the ground that he was not familiar with the conditions there and that in any event "scarcely any man could stand comparison with the great Mozart"—who by that time had written *Figaro* and *Don Giovanni*.

Haydn's songs for solo voice with clavier accompaniment, especially the twelve to English words which he composed in 1794, are an unpretentious but valuable portion of his work. In addition to original songs, Haydn, with the help of his pupils, arranged about 450 Scottish and Welsh airs for various English publishers.

Of Haydn's church music written before the 1790s, two works deserve special mention. The *Mass of Mariazell* of 1782 combines

Haydn's church music

Baroque and newer style elements: the Kyrie is in a kind of sonata form with slow introduction; there is an exciting fugue at the end of the Gloria, and the *Incarnatus* and *Crucifixus* portions of the Credo are particularly impressive. About 1786 Haydn wrote on commission for the Cathedral of Cadiz an introduction and seven orchestral "sonatas," all adagios lasting about ten minutes each, with a concluding "earthquake" movement. These pieces were written to

8 Dénes Bartha, "Haydn's Opera Repertory at Eszterháza Palace" in W. W. Austin, ed., *New Looks at Italian Opera*, Ithaca, 1968, pp. 172–219.

serve as instrumental interludes between short sermons on the Seven Last Words of Christ on the Cross, and in the original version each "sonata" was preceded by a baritone recitative declaiming the Word in question. To compose seven adagios in succession, and to maintain throughout a single basic mood yet offer sufficient variety to avoid monotony was, as Haydn remarked, "no easy matter"; but the work was so successful that two years later the composer arranged the *Seven Last Words* for string quartet, and in 1799 published another rearrangement of the whole work as an oratorio with a suitable Passion text.

Haydn wrote no Masses for fourteen years after 1782, partly no doubt because an imperial decree in force from 1783 to 1792 restricted the use of orchestrally accompanied music in the churches. The last six Masses, composed for Prince Nicholas II Esterházy between 1796 and 1802, show the influence of Haydn's recent preoccupation with the symphony. All are on the large scale of festival Masses, using orchestra, chorus, and four solo vocalists. Haydn's Masses, like those of Mozart and most other South German composers of the eighteenth century, have a certain flamboyant character that goes well with Austrian Baroque church architecture. The fact that these Masses employ a full orchestra, including drums and trumpets, and are written in a musical idiom not unlike that of the opera and the symphony does not mean that they are either insincere or inappropriate. Haydn was occasionally criticized for writing music that was too cheerful for church; he replied that at the thought of God his heart "leaped for joy" and he did not think God would reproach him for praising Him "with a cheerful heart."

True to the Viennese tradition, in his late Masses Haydn interchanged solo voices with chorus; what is new in these Masses is the leading position given to the orchestra, and the pervasion of the entire work by symphonic style and even by symphonic principles of form. Yet traditional elements are retained: the generally contrapuntal style of the writing for solo voices, for instance, and the customary choral fugues at the conclusion of the Gloria and the Credo. Probably the best known of Haydn's late Masses is the *Missa in angustiis,* known also as the *Lord Nelson* or *Imperial* Mass, in D minor, composed in 1798. Among the many impressive features of this work, the beautiful setting of the *Incarnatus* and the electrifying close of the *Benedictus* are moments of particularly high inspiration. On an equal level with the *Nelson* Mass are the *Missa in tempore belli (Mass in Time of War;* also known as the *Paukenmesse,* or kettledrum Mass) of 1796, the *Theresienmesse* of 1799, and the *Harmoniemesse (Wind-band Mass)* of 1802.

One important consequence of Haydn's sojourn in London was that he became acquainted with Handel's oratorios. At a performance of *Messiah* in 1791 at Westminster Abbey, Haydn was so deeply

Haydn's oratorios

moved by the Hallelujah Chorus that he burst into tears and exclaimed "He is the master of us all." The results of Haydn's discovery of Handel are apparent in all the choral parts of his late Masses, and above all in his oratorios *The Creation* and *The Seasons.*

The text of *The Creation* is based on the book of Genesis and Milton's *Paradise Lost;* that of *The Seasons* is distantly related to James Thomson's poem of the same name, which had been published between 1726 and 1730. Both oratorios are ostensibly religious in concept; but the God of *The Creation,* in accordance with eighteenth-century ideas, seems more like a craftsman than a Creator in the Biblical sense, while *The Seasons,* though beginning and ending in religion, turns into something like a singspiel the rest of the time.

Opening measures of The Depiction of Chaos, *from Haydn's* The Creation; *autograph manuscript in the Austrian National Library.*

A large part of the charm of both works consists in their naïve and loving depiction of Nature and of man's innocent joy in the simple "natural" life. The various instrumental introductions and interludes are among the finest examples of late eighteenth-century program music. The *Depiction of Chaos* at the beginning of *The Creation* introduces Romantic harmonies that foreshadow Wagner, while the transition in the following recitative and chorus, climaxed by the superb choral outburst on the C-major chord at the words "and there was light," is one of Haydn's great strokes of genius. The choruses *The Heavens are telling*, and *Achieved is the glorious work* from *The Creation* and the chorus *But who shall dare these gates to pass?* at the end of *The Seasons* have a Handelian breadth and power. No music more perfectly captures the mood of pure delight in nature than the arias *With verdure clad* and *Rolling in foaming billows* from *The Creation,* or the mood of awe before nature's grandeur than the choruses *Behold on high he mounts* and *Hark the deep tremendous voice* from *The Seasons.* The accompanied recitative *Straight opening her fertile womb* in *The Creation,* describing the creation of the animals, is a charming example of humorous musical depiction, while the chorus *Joyful the liquor flows* and the air and chorus *A wealthy lord, who long had loved* from *The Seasons* reflect Haydn's sympathy with the pleasures of simple people. As in the Masses, in these two oratorios Haydn effectively combines solo voices with the chorus. These works are among the most extraordinary instances in history of a composer's manifestation, at an advanced age, of unimpaired youthful freshness and vigor.

Summary

In forming an estimate of Haydn's historical position, it is necessary to avoid extremes. In the first place, he is not the naïve, amiable composer of pretty tunes that the nickname "Papa Haydn" has unfortunately connoted to so many generations; nor, on the other hand, is he a devout mystic like Bach, or a heaven-storming Titan like Beethoven. Least of all is he a mere forerunner of Beethoven or of Romanticism. His achievement was original and complete. His personal development was long and laborious, marked by emotional and stylistic crises of which the severest was that of 1770–72. He assimilated the past, enriching the spare mid-century style with elements of the late Baroque, absorbing the romantic impulses of the *Empfindsamkeit* and the "storm-and-stress" movements, fusing all finally in that singular blend of sophistication and second naïveté which is the special quality of his compositions after 1790. The perfected Classical style of the late eighteenth century owes more to Haydn than to anyone else. His art is characterized by the union of sophistication with honest craftsmanship, humility, purity of intention, and a never failing spiritual contact with the life of the common people from whom he had sprung.

Wolfgang Amadeus Mozart

Mozart (1756–91) was born in Salzburg, a city then situated within the territory of Bavaria (now in western Austria). Salzburg was the seat of an archbishopric, one of the numerous quasi-independent political units of the German Empire; it had a long musical tradition and in Mozart's time was a lively provincial center of the arts. His father, Leopold Mozart, was a member of the archbishop's chapel and later became its assistant director; he was a composer of some ability and reputation, and the author of a celebrated treatise on violin playing. From earliest childhood Wolfgang showed such a prodigious talent for music that his father dropped all other ambitions and devoted himself to educating the boy—and to exhibiting his accomplishments in a series of journeys that eventually took them to France, England, Holland, and Italy, as well as to Vienna and the principal cities of Germany.

Young Mozart was thus on tour and on show over half of his time between the ages of six and fifteen. By 1762 he was a virtuoso on the clavier, and soon became a good organist and violinist as well. His public performances as a child included not only the playing of prepared pieces, but also reading concertos at sight and improvising variations, fugues, and fantasias. Meanwhile he was composing: he produced his first minuets at the age of six, his first symphony just before his ninth birthday, his first oratorio at eleven, and his first opera at twelve. His more than 600 compositions are listed and numbered in the thematic catalogue first compiled by L. von Köchel in 1862 and periodically since brought up to date in new editions incorporating the results of modern research; the Köchel or "K." numbers are universally used to identify a Mozart composition.

Thanks to his father's excellent teaching, and even more to the many trips made during his formative years, young Mozart was brought into contact with every kind of music that was being written or heard in contemporary western Europe. He absorbed all that was congenial to him with uncanny aptitude. He imitated, but in imitating he improved on his models; and the ideas that influenced him not only were echoed in his immediate productions but also continued to grow in his mind, sometimes bearing fruit many years later. His work thus came to be a synthesis of national styles, a mirror in which was reflected the music of a whole age, illumined by his own transcendent genius. In this particular cosmopolitan quality Mozart differs from Haydn, whose background was more exclusively Austrian.

Mozart's own musical style is related to a trait which we may call *absolute musicality*. This expression requires some qualification. A good deal of the music of Beethoven, as well as that of some Romantic composers like Berlioz and Chopin, is in a sense autobiographical.

Mozart's music is much less so. It is hard to find in it any specific traces of all the hardships and disappointments which he underwent during his life, particularly in his last ten years. It is even harder to draw from it any definite conclusions about his attitude toward Nature, or toward the greatest historical event of his time, the French Revolution (to which he never alludes in any surviving document), or toward the widely prevalent new ideas associated with that movement. All these influences were undeniably there, but Mozart's music reflects them only as sublimated, transformed into measured Classic beauty. Like all great artists, but to a greater degree than with many composers, Mozart lived his real life in the inner world of his music, to which his everyday existence often seems only a troubled and shadowy parallel.

Mozart did not have to struggle with composing. He had been trained systematically and thoroughly from infancy, and he learned instantaneously from each new musical impression. Haydn always found composition a labor, and he was always experimenting with the machinery. He set himself to compose at regular hours; when ideas did not come at once he prayed for them, and when they came he worked them out with conscious and unremitting industry. One cannot imagine Mozart having to pray for musical ideas: they were always superabundantly there. Usually he worked them out first in his mind, with intense and joyous concentration, complete to the last detail. Writing them down then consisted only in transferring to music paper a structure which was already, so to speak, before his eyes; hence he could laugh and joke and carry on conversation while "composing." There is a touch of the miraculous, something both childlike and godlike, about all this; and although recent research has revealed in some cases more of labor and revision in Mozart's creative processes than used to be thought, nevertheless the aura of miracle remains. It was perhaps this that made him, rather than Haydn, the musical hero of the early Romantic generation.

One monumental study of Mozart distinguishes in his life and work no fewer than thirty-five style periods. For our purposes a broader and simpler division will suffice: (1) childhood and early youth, to 1774; (2) the period of the first masterworks, 1774–81; and (3) the years in Vienna, 1781–91.

Mozart's Childhood and Early Youth

The first period may be considered Mozart's apprentice and journeyman years. During all this time he was under the tutelage of his father—completely as far as practical affairs were concerned, and to a considerable extent also in musical matters. The relation between

497

Mozart's early works

father and son is an interesting one. Leopold Mozart fully recognized and respected the boy's genius, and his major efforts soon went into furthering young Wolfgang's career and trying to secure for him a worthy permanent post, in which aim he failed; his conduct toward his son was that of a devoted mentor and friend, and was on the whole remarkably free from selfish motives. The childhood journeys of Mozart were rich in musical experiences. In June of 1763 the whole family—father, mother, Wolfgang, and his talented elder sister Marianne ("Nannerl")—embarked on a tour that included lengthy sojourns in Paris and London. They returned to Salzburg in November, 1766. On this trip, while they were in Paris, young Mozart became interested in the music of Johann Schobert, an interest which was immediately reflected in his own clavier compositions.

Another important and lasting influence was that of Johann Christian Bach, whose acquaintance the boy made when he was in London. His influence was immediately apparent in the symphonies which Mozart began to compose at London and in the clavier compositions of the same period; moreover, the spirit of Italian music and especially the Italian style in opera, to which Mozart was first introduced by Bach, became a fundamental and permanent factor in his work.

A visit to Vienna in 1768 led, among other things, to the composition by the precocious twelve-year-old of an Italian *opera buffa, La finta semplice (The Pretended Simpleton;* not performed until the next year at Salzburg) and the attractive German singspiel *Bastien und Bastienne.* The years 1770 to 1773 were largely occupied with travels in Italy, from which Mozart returned more thoroughly italianized than ever and profoundly discontented with his limited prospects in Salzburg. The chief events in these years were the production of two *opere serie* at Milan in 1770 and 1772, and some studies in counterpoint with Padre Martini at Bologna. Mozart's first string quartets also date from these Italian years. The influence of the Italian symphonists—for example, Sammartini—on Mozart may be discerned in his symphonies written from 1770 to 1773, especially K. 81, 95, 112, 132, 162, and 182; but a new influence, that of Joseph Haydn, becomes apparent in some other symphonies of this period, particularly K. 133 (composed in July, 1772). Another sojourn at Vienna in the summer of 1773 brought Mozart a renewed understanding and feeling for the characteristic qualities of southern German music; from this time onward Haydn's works became an increasingly important factor in Mozart's creative life, and after 1781, their influence was reinforced by personal friendship with the older composer.

One of the characteristics of the European musical scene in the eighteenth century was the existence of distinct national styles; in the latter part of the century, many theorists and composers consciously endeavored to bring these diverse styles into a common, supranational musical language. The two most important national idioms after 1760 were those of Italy and Germany; that of France was influential chiefly in the field of opera. Italy was still the homeland of music and the Mecca of every aspiring student of composition; yet the four principal composers of the second half of the eighteenth century—C. P. E. Bach, Gluck, Haydn, and Mozart—were all of northern extraction, and two of them—Bach and Haydn—never set foot in Italy. The cosmopolitan aim of the late eighteenth century was realized most fully in the works of Gluck and Mozart; but Gluck was significant only as a composer of opera, whereas Mozart fused Italian and German styles in every domain of music.

What were the differences at this time between Italian and German music? These may be summed up as follows: the bulk of Italian music aimed at entertainment and the best German music at expression; hence, on the whole, Italian music was light and German music serious. The Italians' natural medium was vocal and their natural forms the opera and cantata; the Germans' natural medium was instrumental and their natural forms the symphony and the sonata. The natural Italian musical texture was homophony, the German polyphony; to charm and please through melody was the Italian goal, whereas the Germans were not averse to some display of the science of counterpoint. All these statements, of course, are over-simplifications, for neither in theory nor in practice were the two styles so utterly different; and although the Italians were little disposed to learn from the Germans, the latter were strongly influenced by the Italian style. Haydn expressed an enlightened view and at the same time uttered a profound judgment of Mozart's genius when he said to Leopold Mozart: "Before God and as an honest man I tell you that your son is the greatest composer known to me either in person or by name. He has taste and, what is more, the most profound knowledge of composition." Those were the two essentials: taste, the instinct for what is appropriate, the awareness of limits; and knowledge, the technique to say what one has to say fully, clearly, and persuasively. Broadly speaking, taste was the specialty of the Italians and knowledge that of the Germans. Mozart combined the two in his own style.

Mozart's First Masterworks

Late in 1773 and early in 1774, Mozart composed two symphonies which were his first masterworks in this form. The one in G minor (K. 183) is a product of the mood of *Sturm und Drang* which was finding expression in the contemporary symphonies of Haydn. It

Mozart's Italian and German traits

Imp. Page ✱

Heavy philosoph- ille approach to music.

is remarkable not only for its intense, serious quality but also for its thematic unity and for the expansion of the entire form as compared with Mozart's earlier symphonies. Similar dimensions and formal characteristics are found in the A-major Symphony (K. 201), the mood of which is robust and cheerful; the finale has a particularly long and well worked out development section. On the whole, Mozart was much less adventurous than Haydn in the matter of formal experiments. His themes seldom give the impression, as Haydn's sometimes do, of having been invented with a view chiefly to their possibilities for motivic development; on the contrary, a theme of Mozart usually is complete in itself, and his invention is so profuse that sometimes he will dispense with a formal development section altogether and in its place write a completely new theme (as in the first movement of the String Quartet K. 428). Again unlike Haydn, Mozart nearly always has a contrasting, lyrical second theme (or themes) in his allegro movements in sonata form, though he is apt to conclude the exposition with a reminiscence of the opening subject; and, once more unlike Haydn, he seldom surprises the listener by making extensive changes in the order or treatment of his materials in the recapitulation.

Piano and violin sonatas

From 1774 to 1781, Mozart lived chiefly at Salzburg, where he became more and more impatient with the narrowness of provincial life and the lack of musical opportunities. In a fruitless attempt to better himself he undertook, in September, 1777, in company with his mother, another journey, this time to Munich, Augsburg, Mannheim, and Paris. All his hopes for a good position in Germany came to nothing, and prospects for a successful career at Paris likewise ended in failure. The stay in Paris was further saddened by his mother's death in July, 1778, and Mozart returned to Salzburg early in 1779 more discontented than ever. Nonetheless, he was steadily growing in stature as a composer. Among the important works of this period are the piano sonatas K. 279–284 (Salzburg and Munich, 1774–75), K. 309 and 311 (Mannheim, 1777–78), K. 310 and 330–333 (Paris, 1778), and several sets of variations for piano, including those on the French air *Ah, vous dirais-je maman* (K. 265; Paris, 1778). The variations were probably intended for pupils, but the sonatas were played by Mozart himself as part of his concert repertoire. His custom in the earlier years had been to improvise such pieces as needed, so that few very early Mozart solo piano compositions have survived.

The sonatas K. 279–284 were undoubtedly designed to be published together: there is one in each of the major tonalities in the circle of fifths from D to E♭, and the six works show a wide variety of form and content. The two Mannheim sonatas have brilliant and showy Allegros and tender and graceful Andantes. The Paris sonatas are among Mozart's best-known compositions in this form:

the tragic A-minor sonata (K. 310), its light counterpart in C major (K. 330), the A-major sonata with the variations and the *rondo alla turca* (K. 331), and two of the most characteristically Mozartean sonatas, those in F major and B♭ major (K. 332 and 333).

Mozart's piano sonatas are closely related to his sonatas for piano and violin; in his early years the latter had been, in accordance with the eighteenth-century custom, really no more than piano pieces with violin accompaniment *ad libitum*. The first of Mozart's works in which the two instruments begin to be treated on a basis of equality are the sonatas written at Mannheim and Paris in 1777 and 1778 (K. 296, 301–306), of which the one in E minor (K. 304) may be singled out for the exceptional emotional intensity of its first movement and the one in D major (K. 306) for its brilliant concerto-like style.

Of the chamber music from this middle period we may mention the Flute Quartet in D major (K. 285), composed in December, 1777, an excellent example of the light, charming Mozart style; and the Oboe Quartet (K. 370), an equally representative but more serious work dating from the early part of 1781.

Most of Mozart's music was composed either on commission or for a particular occasion; even in those works that do not seem to have been intended for an immediate performance, he had in mind a definite type of potential performer or audience, and considered their preferences. Like all his contemporaries, he was a "commercial composer" in that he not merely hoped but expected as a matter of course that his music would be performed, that it would please, and that he would make money from it. There are, of course, some compositions of his that have little significance outside their immediate social or commercial occasion—for instance, the many sets of dances that he turned out for balls at Vienna during the last four years of his life. But there are other works which, though produced only with the modest aim of furnishing background music or light entertainment for some ephemeral occasion, have greater musical importance than their original purpose deserved.

Of this sort are the pieces, dating for the most part from the 1770s and early 1780s, which Mozart composed for garden parties, serenades, weddings, birthdays, or home concerts for his friends and patrons, and which he called usually either serenade or divertimento. Some are like chamber music for strings with two or more added wind instruments; others, written for six or eight wind instruments in pairs, are music for out-of-doors; still others approach the style of the symphony or concerto. All have in common a certain unaffected simplicity of both material and treatment, an informal charm which is appropriate to their purpose. Examples of the pieces similar to chamber music are the Divertimento in F (K. 247) for strings and two horns, composed at Salzburg in June, 1776, its

Serenades

Mozart's autograph manuscript of the first page of the Serenade in B♭, K. 361. (Library of Congress)

companion divertimentos in B♭ (K. 287) and D (K. 334), and the Septet in D (K. 251). The pieces for wind instruments are illustrated by the short divertimentos from Salzburg (for example, K. 252), and three larger and more sophisticated serenades written at Munich and Vienna in 1781 and 1782: K. 361 in B♭, K. 375 in E♭, and the rather enigmatic Serenade in C minor (K. 388)—enigmatic because both the tonality and the serious character of the music (including a canonic Minuet) seem inconsistent with the sort of occasion for which this type of piece was usually written. The most familiar of Mozart's serenades is *Eine kleine Nachtmusik* (K. 525), a work for small string orchestra, originally in five movements, composed in 1787 but for what occasion (if any) is not known. Elements of the concerto appear in the three Salzburg serenades in D (K. 203, 204, 320), each of which has interpolated two or three movements where the solo violin is featured. The *Haffner Serenade* of 1776 is the clearest example of the concerto-symphonic style, and the *Haffner Symphony* (1782) was originally written as a serenade with an introductory and closing march and an additional Minuet between the Allegro and the Andante.

Among the notable compositions of Mozart's second period are the violin concertos K. 216, 218, and 219, in G, D, and A respectively, all from the year 1775, the piano concerto in E♭, K. 271 (1777) <u>Violin</u> ~~concertos~~ with its romantic slow movement in C minor, and the expressive Symphonie Concertante, K. 364 in E♭, for solo violin and viola with orchestra. The violin concertos are works of great beauty; nowhere is the Mozartean blend of crystalline clarity with sensuously luxuriant sound more potent than in the Adagio of the G major concerto, or the Mozartean verve and humor more evident than in the rondo finale of the same work. These three violin concertos are, with one possible exception,[9] the last of Mozart's works in this form. The piano concerto K. 271, on the other hand, is but the first in a long series that reaches a climax in the concertos of Mozart's Vienna period.

In view of his father's official position in the archiepiscopal chapel and his own appointments at Salzburg—first as concertmaster and later as organist—it was natural that Mozart should compose for the *Vocal music* Church fairly regularly from an early age. With few exceptions, however, his Masses, motets, and other settings of sacred texts are not to be counted among his major works. His Masses, like those of *First evidence* Haydn, are for the most part in the symphonic-operatic idiom of the *of 12 tone shown* period, intermingled with counterpoint at certain places in ac- *in Mozarts* cordance with the current custom, the whole for chorus and soloists *technique.* in free alternation, with orchestral accompaniment. An example is the *Coronation* Mass in C (K. 317), composed at Salzburg in 1779. The finest of his Masses is the one in C minor (K. 427), which *Mozart* Mozart wrote as fulfillment of a vow at the time of his marriage in *Extensive* 1782. Though the Credo and Agnus Dei were never completed, this *Just played He had* Mass nevertheless is one of the few works of its kind in the eighteenth *it in him.* century worthy to be named along with the B-minor Mass of Bach. It is noteworthy that Mozart wrote it not on commission, but apparently to satisfy an inner need. Equally devout, equally profound, though brief and in simple homophonic style, is another church com- *Beethoven* position, the motet *Ave verum* (K. 618, 1791). In connection with *Intensive* the vocal church music may be mentioned Mozart's seventeen *Epistle* *—very structured* *Sonatas*—short pieces for organ and orchestra which he wrote to be *& organized.* played in the Salzburg Cathedral.

Mozart's last important composition before he moved to Vienna was the opera *Idomeneo*, first performed at Munich in January of 1781. *Idomeneo* is the best of Mozart's *opere serie*. The music, despite the rather clumsy libretto, is dramatic and pictorial. Numerous accompanied recitatives, conspicuous use of the chorus, and the presence of spectacular scenes show the influence of Gluck and the French *tragédie lyrique;* but the ruling conception of the work, in which the music wholly dominates and embraces the dramatic movement, is Mozart's own.

---

[9] K. 271a, which, if authentic, has survived in a form that is probably not Mozart's original version.

The Vienna Period

When in 1781 Mozart decided, against his father's advice, to quit the service of the Archbishop of Salzburg and settle in Vienna, he was sanguine about his prospects. The first years there were, in fact, fairly prosperous. His singspiel, *Die Entführung aus dem Serail* (*The Abduction from the Seraglio*, 1782) was performed repeatedly; he had all the distinguished pupils he was willing to take, he was the idol of the Viennese public both as pianist and composer, and for four or five seasons he led the bustling life of a successful freelance musician. But then the fickle public deserted him, pupils fell off, commissions were few, family expenses mounted, his health declined, and, worst of all, no permanent position with a steady income came his way, except for a trifling honorary appointment in 1787 as Chamber Music Composer to the Emperor with a salary less than half that which Gluck, his predecessor in the post, had received. The most pathetic pages in Mozart's correspondence are the begging letters written between 1788 and 1791 to his friend and brother Mason, the merchant Michael Puchberg of Vienna. To Puchberg's honor, he always responded to Mozart's appeals.

Most of the works which make Mozart's name immortal were composed during the last ten years of his life, in Vienna, when the wonderful promise of his childhood and early youth came to fulfillment between the ages of twenty-five and thirty-five. The perfect synthesis of form and content, of the *galant* and the learned styles, of polish and charm on the one hand and of textural and emotional depth on the other, was finally achieved, and equally in every kind of composition. The principal influences on Mozart in this period came from his continuing study of Haydn and his discovery of the music of J. S. Bach. The latter experience he owed to Baron Gottfried van Swieten, who during his years as Austrian ambassador to Berlin (1771–78) had become an enthusiast for the music of northern German composers. Van Swieten was the Imperial Court Librarian and a busy amateur of music and literature; he later wrote the librettos of Haydn's last two oratorios. At van Swieten's home, in weekly reading sessions during 1782, Mozart became acquainted with Bach's *Art of Fugue, The Well-Tempered Clavier,* the trio sonatas, and other works. He arranged several of Bach's fugues for string trio or quartet (K. 404a, 405), and another immediate result of this new interest was his own fugue in C minor for two pianos (K. 426). The influence of Bach was deep and lasting, it is manifested in the increasing use of contrapuntal texture throughout Mozart's later works (for example, in his last piano sonata, K. 576) and in the profoundly serious moods of *The Magic Flute* and the *Requiem.*

Of the piano solo compositions of the Vienna period, the most important is the Fantasia and Sonata in C minor (K. 475 and 457). The fantasia in its melodies and modulations foreshadows Schubert, while the sonata is clearly the model for Beethoven's *Sonate Pathétique*. Other keyboard works of this period are the Sonata in D major for two pianos (K. 448, 1781) and the finest of all Mozart's four-hand sonatas, the one in F major (K. 497, 1786). For chamber music ensembles of various kinds there is an impressive number of masterpieces, of which the following must be mentioned: the Violin Sonata in A major (K. 526), the Piano Trios in B♭ (K. 502) and E major (K. 542), the Piano Quartets in G minor (K. 478) and E♭ major (K. 493), the String Trio (K. 563), and the Clarinet Quintet (K. 581).

In 1785, Mozart published six string quartets dedicated to Joseph Haydn as a token of his gratitude for all that he had learned from the older composer. These quartets were, as Mozart said in the dedicatory letter, "the fruit of a long and laborious effort"; indeed, the manuscript bears evidence of this in the unusually large number of corrections and revisions. Mozart had earlier been impressed by the quartets Opp. 17 and 20 of Haydn, and had sought to imitate them in the six quartets (K. 168–173) which he composed at Vienna in 1773. Since those were written, Haydn's *Russian* quartets (Op. 33) of 1781 had fully established the technique of pervasive thematic development with complete equality of the four instruments. Mozart's six *Haydn* quartets (K. 387, 421, 428, 458, 464, 465) show his mature capacity to absorb the essence of Haydn's achievement without becoming a mere imitator.

The Haydn *quartets*

Closest to Haydn in mood and themes are the opening and closing movements of the Quartet in B♭ (K. 458), while the Adagio has harmonies that may be called Romantic (Example XIV–2a). The D-minor quartet (K. 421) expresses a gloomy, fatalistic mood. The striking cross-relations in the slow introduction to the first movement of the C-major Quartet (K. 456) have given this work its name of the *Dissonance* Quartet (Example XIV–2b).

All the *Haydn* quartets are remarkably unified and concentrated. There are no merely transitional or filling passages; every measure is alive with thematic significance. Contrapuntal texture is ever present, though never obtrusive. Moreover, even in the Allegros the themes always sing; the instrumental melodies have a vocal allure that reflects the Italian heritage in Mozart's training. Mozart never surpassed these six quartets in his later works for the same medium, which include the *Hoffmeister* Quartet (K. 499) and three others of a projected set of six for the King of Prussia (K. 575, 589, 590). Unlike Haydn and Beethoven, Mozart most fully revealed his genius as a chamber music composer not in his quartets, but rather in his quintets. The best of these are the string quintets in C major (K. 515) and G minor (K. 516), both composed in the spring of 1787, works comparable only with Mozart's last two symphonies,

EXAMPLE XIV–2   Themes from Quartets, Mozart

(a) Mozart: Adagio from Quartet K. 458

(b) Mozart: Introduction of Quartet K. 465
Adagio

which are in the same keys. Another masterpiece is the Clarinet Quintet in A (K. 581), composed at about the same time as the opera buffa *Così fan tutte,* and similar to it in mood.

Mozart's Vienna symphonies include the *Haffner* Symphony (K. 385), the *Prague* Symphony in D major (K. 504), the charming *Linz* Symphony in C major (K. 425), and his last and greatest works in this form, the Symphonies in E♭ (K. 543), G minor (K. 550), and C major (the *Jupiter,* K. 551). These three symphonies were composed within a space of six weeks in the summer of 1788. It is not known for what occasion Mozart intended them or indeed whether he ever heard them played at all. Each has its own character; each is a complex but distinct personality, a personality which is defined perfectly by the music but which completely eludes verbal formulation. To say that the E♭ Symphony is one of tender cheerfulness and grace, the G minor of melting sadness and inexorable fatalism, or the *Jupiter* the expression of victory, strength, and wisdom—to use these or any similar phrases is only to demonstrate the impossibility of translating the language of music into the language of words. The three works must be viewed as a summation, unusually complete and clear, of three fundamental aspects of Mozart's musical being and consequently of the whole Western musical world of the late eighteenth century.

A very important place among the productions of Mozart's Vienna years must be assigned to the seventeen concertos for piano and orchestra. All were written in order to provide brand-new works for concerts, and the rise and fall of Mozart's popularity in Vienna may be roughly gauged by the number of new concertos he found it necessary to supply for each year: three in 1782–83, four in each of the next two seasons, three again in 1785–86, and only one for each of the next two seasons; after that no more until the last year of his life, when he played a new concerto (K. 595) in a concert organized by another musician.

The concertos for piano and orchestra

The first three Vienna concertos (K. 414, 413, 415) were, as Mozart wrote to his father,[10] "a happy medium between what is too easy and too difficult . . . very brilliant, pleasing to the ear, and natural, without being vapid. There are passages here and there from which connoisseurs alone can derive satisfaction; but these passages are written in such a way that the less learned cannot fail to be pleased, though without knowing why." The next concerto (K. 449, in E♭), originally written for a pupil, was later played by Mozart with "unusual success," as he reported. Then follow three magnificent concertos, all completed within a month of one another in the spring of 1784: K. 450 in B♭, K. 451 in D (both, in Mozart's words, "concertos to make the player sweat"), and the more intimate, lovely K. 453 in G. Three of the four concertos of 1784–85 are likewise works of first rank: K. 459 in F, K. 466 in D minor (the most dramatic and most frequently played of Mozart's concertos), and K. 467 in C, spacious and symphonic. During the winter of 1785–86, when he was at work on *The Marriage of Figaro*, Mozart turned out three more concertos, of which the first two (K. 482 in E♭ and K. 488 in A) are in comparatively lighter mood, while the third (K. 491, C minor) is one of his great tragic creations, one of his most "Beethovenish" works. The big C-major concerto of December, 1786 (K. 503) may be regarded as the triumphal counterpart of K. 491. Of the two remaining concertos, one is the popular *Coronation* Concerto in D (K. 537), so called because Mozart played it (and probably also K. 459) at a concert in Frankfurt in 1790 during the coronation festivities for the Emperor Leopold II. K. 595, in B♭, Mozart's last concerto, was completed on the fifth of January, 1791; it is a work of serene, transcendent beauty, the testament of a musician who must have felt himself to be already beyond the passions, the struggles, and the triumphs of this life.[11]

The concerto, particularly the piano concerto, was more important in Mozart's work than in that of any other composer of the second half of the eighteenth century. In the realm of the

---

10 Letter dated December 28, 1782; pr. in *The Letters of Mozart and his Family*, Emily Anderson, ed., London, 1938, III, No. 476.
11 A. Einstein, *Mozart*, 314.

symphony and the quartet Haydn is his peer, but Mozart's concertos are incomparable. Not even the symphonies reveal such wealth of invention, such breadth and vigor of conception, such insight and resource in the working out of musical ideas. The Classical concerto, in the form definitively established by Mozart in the 1780s, resembles the concerto of Vivaldi in its general scheme of three movements in fast–slow–fast order, and in the relatively greater length and weight of the first movement as compared with the other two. But Mozart's concerto differs from that of Vivaldi and indeed of all preceding composers (including C. P. E. Bach and J. C. Bach) in respect to the relation between the solo instrument and the orchestra: since the piano is fully on a par with the orchestra in range and flexibility, the two are treated as equal protagonists in a symphonic texture, a conception that considerably modifies the older idea of regular alternation of distinct tutti and solo sections. Yet, naturally, the traditional scheme is not wholly discarded. A first movement in one of Mozart's concertos is typically constructed somewhat as follows:

1. Preliminary exposition by the orchestra of some of the principal themes, centering for the most part about the tonic key.
2. Fuller exposition by orchestra and piano, usually introducing additional themes, expanding the transitions and cadences, and modulating to the dominant (or relative major) as in the first movement of a symphony.
3. Codetta-like extension of the previous cadence by the orchestra.
4. Development section (as in a symphony), for piano and orchestra.
5. Recapitulation, piano and orchestra (Mozart here displays great variety in the order and combination of themes.)
6. Second codetta for orchestra, which comes to a pause on a tonic six-four chord.
7. Cadenza for piano, improvised by the soloist-composer in Mozart's own performances, and at any rate always in improvisatory style, using at will thematic material from the preceding sections together with free figurations, ending with a . conventional trill on the supertonic over a dominant seventh and cadencing on the tonic chord.
8. Coda, for orchestra without piano (exceptions: K. 271, K. 491).

Of course this general plan can be modified in all sorts of ways; one of the most fascinating features of Mozart's concertos is the way in which he achieves a balance within the movement by carefully spacing the recurrence of themes—for example, making the final coda a condensed summary of the opening orchestral tutti. As can be easily seen, the pattern outlined combines the sonata form (the symphonic first movement), the aria form with orchestral ritornellos (Nos. 1, 3, 6, 8 in the above outline), and the cadenza.

The second movement of a Mozart concerto is like a lyrical aria, with a tempo of andante, larghetto, or allegretto; it may be in the subdominant of the principal key, or (less often) in the dominant or the relative minor; its form, although extremely variable in details, is most often a kind of modified sonata scheme without development, and less commonly a three-part (*ABA*) form, as in the *Romanza* of K. 466. The finale is typically a rondo or sonata-rondo on themes with a popular character, which are treated in scintillating virtuoso style with opportunity for one or more cadenzas. Although these concertos were show pieces, intended to dazzle an audience, Mozart never allowed the element of display to get out of hand; a healthy balance of musical interest between the orchestral and the solo portions is always maintained, and Mozart's ear was infallible for the myriad combinations of colors and textures that arise from the interplay of the piano with the orchestral instruments. Moreover, the immediate public purpose of his concertos did not prevent his using the form as a vehicle for some of the most profound expressions of his musical thought.

After *Idomeneo* Mozart wrote no more *opere serie*, with the exception of *La clemenza di Tito* (*The Mercy of Titus*), which was commissioned for the coronation of Leopold II as King of Bohemia *Mozart's operas* at Prague and composed in haste during the summer of 1791. The chief dramatic works of the Vienna period were the singspiel, *Die Entführung aus dem Serail* (*The Abduction from the Seraglio,* 1782), three Italian operas, *Le nozze di Figaro* (*The Marriage of Figaro,* 1786), *Don Giovanni* (*Don Juan;* Prague, 1787), and *Così fan tutte* (*Thus Do They All,* 1790)—all three on librettos by Lorenzo da Ponte (1749–1838)—and the German opera *Die Zauberflöte* (*The Magic Flute,* 1791).

Figaro is the epitome of Italian eighteenth-century comic opera, with its lively and amusing libretto, beautiful arias, and masterly ensembles; but it is *opera buffa* transformed from the stock antics of type figures into profound human comedy, in which the characters are real three-dimensional persons, thanks to Mozart's psychological penetration and his genius for characterization in music. It is remarkable that the character delineation takes place not only in solo arias but more especially in duets, trios, and larger ensembles; and the ensemble finales combine realism with ongoing dramatic action and superbly unified musical form.

Figaro had only moderate success in Vienna, but its enthusiastic reception at Prague led to the commission for *Don Giovanni,* which was given in that city the next year. *Don Giovanni* is a *dramma giocoso* of a very special sort. The medieval legend on which the plot is based had been treated often in literature and music since the early seventeenth century; but with Mozart, for the first time in opera, Don Juan himself was taken seriously—not as an incongruous mixture of figure of farce and horrible blasphemer, but as a romantic hero, a rebel against authority and a scorner of vulgar morality, a supreme

The second scene of Don Giovanni, *as staged by the Metropolitan Opera. Don Giovanni tries to placate Donna Elvira, while Donna Anna and Don Ottavio wonder which of the two to believe. (Photograph courtesy Louis Mélançon)*

individualist, bold and unrepentant to the last. It was Mozart's music rather than Da Ponte's libretto that raised the Don to this eminence and defined his lineaments for all succeeding generations. The daemonic quality of the opening measures of the overture, intensified by the sound of the trombones in the cemetery scene and at the apparition of the statue in the finale, appealed especially to the Romantic musical imagination of the nineteenth century.

Cosi fan tutte is an *opera buffa* in the best Italian tradition, with a brilliant libretto glorified by some of Mozart's most melodious music. The fashion of reading into Mozart's works everything from autobiography to romantic irony, neo-Freudian psychology, and crypto-revolutionary sentiments has been extended even to this sparkling opera, where all such nonsense seems to be quite superfluous.

The plot of *Die Entführung* is a romantic-comic story of adventure and rescue, set against the popular eighteenth-century oriental background; its subject had been treated by Rameau, Gluck, Haydn, and many lesser composers before Mozart. With this work, Mozart at one stroke raised the German singspiel into the realm of great art without altering any of its established features.

Die Zauberflöte is a different matter. Though outwardly a singspiel —with spoken dialogue instead of recitative, and with some characters and scenes appropriate to popular comedy—its action is full of symbolic meaning and its music so rich and profound that *Die Zauberflöte* must be regarded as the first and one of the greatest of modern German operas. The solemn mood of much of its music is probably due in part to the fact that Mozart created a relationship between the action of this opera and the teachings and ceremonies of Freemasonry; his Masonic affiliation meant much to him, as is obvious from allusions in his correspondence and especially from the serious quality of the music which he wrote for Masonic occasions in 1785 (K. 468, 471, 477, 483, 484) and the Masonic cantata of 1791 (K. 623), his last completed composition. *Die Zauberflöte* gives the impression that Mozart desired to weave into new designs the threads of all the musical ideas of the eighteenth century: the vocal opulence of Italy; the folk humor of the German singspiel; the solo aria; the *buffo* ensemble, which is given new musical meaning; a new kind of accompanied recitative applicable to German words; solemn choral scenes; and even (in the duet of the two armed men in Act II) a revival of the Baroque chorale prelude technique, with contrapuntal accompaniment.

In the *Requiem*—Mozart's last work, left unfinished at his death —Baroque elements are still more prominent. The double fugue of the Kyrie has a subject that had been used by both Bach and Handel —also by Haydn in his Quartet Op. 20, No. 5—and the movement is definitely Handelian in flavor; even more so are the dramatic choral outbursts of the *Dies irae* and *Rex tremendae majestatis*. But the *Recordare* is pure Mozart, the German composer who understood and loved the musical tradition of Italy and interpreted it in his own perfect way.

XV

Ludwig van Beethoven (1770-1827)

The Man and His Music

On July 14th, 1789, a Paris mob stormed the Bastille, liberated seven prisoners, and paraded the streets carrying the heads of the murdered guards on pikes. Within three years France was proclaimed a republic and her citizen armies were rallying against invaders to the strains of a new patriotic song called *La Marseillaise*. A few months later Louis XVI was guillotined and an obscure lieutenant of artillery, Napoleon Bonaparte, had begun his rise to dictatorship.

In 1792 George Washington was President of the United States; Goethe, at Weimar, was directing the ducal theatre and publishing studies in the science of optics; Haydn was at the height of his fame, and Mozart's body was lying in an unmarked pauper's grave in a Vienna cemetery. Early in November of 1792, an ambitious young composer and pianist named Ludwig van Beethoven, then just under twenty-two years of age, travelled from the city of Bonn on the Rhine to Vienna, a journey of some five hundred miles which took a week by stage coach. He was short of money in Vienna and for a while kept a detailed account of his finances. One of the entries in his notebook records an expenditure of twenty-five groschen for "coffee for Haidn and me."

Haydn had stopped off at Bonn on his way to London in December of 1790; and doubtless having heard some of Beethoven's compositions, he urged the latter's master, the Archbishop Elector of Cologne, to send the young man to Vienna for further study. It is not certain how much Beethoven learned from his lessons with Haydn, but at all events the lessons continued until Haydn again left Vienna for London in 1794. Meanwhile, Beethoven also received help from Johann Schenk (1753–1836), a popular Viennese composer of singspiels. After 1794, Beethoven studied counterpoint for a year or so with Johann Georg Albrechtsberger (1736–1809), one of the leading teachers of his day and the author of a famous treatise on composition published in 1790. Beethoven also received some informal lessons in vocal composition from the Italian opera composer Antonio Salieri (1750–1825), an erstwhile pupil of Gluck who had been living at Vienna since 1766. Beethoven's musical education had begun with his father, a singer in the Chapel at Bonn, who forced the boy's progress in the hope of making a second Mozart of him; he had also had lessons at Bonn from Christian Gottlob Neefe (1748–98), the Court organist, who had attained a modest renown as a composer of singspiels and songs. On a brief visit to Vienna in 1787 Beethoven had played for Mozart, who prophesied a bright future for him.

Beethoven came on the scene at a favorable moment in history. He inherited from Haydn and Mozart a style and certain musical forms which were well developed but still capable of further growth. He lived at a time when new and powerful forces were abroad in human society, forces which strongly affected him and made themselves felt in his work. Beethoven, like Napoleon and Goethe, was a child of the tremendous upheaval which had been fermenting all through the eighteenth century and had burst forth in the French Revolution. Historically, Beethoven's work is built on the achievements of the Classical period. Through external circumstances and the force of his own genius he transformed this heritage and became the source of much that was characteristic of the Romantic period. But he himself is neither Classic nor Romantic; he is Beethoven, and his figure towers like a colossus astride the two centuries.

Beethoven's character

His works include 9 symphonies, 11 overtures, incidental music to plays, a violin concerto and 5 piano concertos, 16 string quartets, 9 piano trios and other chamber music, 10 violin sonatas and 5 violoncello sonatas, 30 large piano sonatas and many sets of variations for piano, an oratorio, an opera (*Fidelio*), and two Masses (one the *Missa solemnis* in D), besides arias, songs, and numerous lesser compositions of different sorts. There is an obvious disparity when these figures are compared with the output of Haydn and Mozart: 9 symphonies, for example, to Haydn's 100 or Mozart's 50. A partial explanation, of course, is that Beethoven's symphonies are longer; but a more important reason is that Beethoven wrote music with

great difficulty. Probably no other composer ever habitually subjected himself to longer or more severe criticism. Beethoven kept
notebooks in which he jotted down plans and themes for compositions, and thanks to these sketchbooks we can sometimes follow the
progress of a musical idea through various stages until it reaches the
final form (Example XV–1).[1] The sketches for the Quartet Op. 131

EXAMPLE XV–1   Sketches for Theme of Adagio of Ninth Symphony,
Beethoven

[1] See also sketches for the Fifth Symphony in the edition of that work prepared by Elliott Forbes, New York, 1971, 117–28. For a detailed study of some
aspects of Beethoven's compositional processes, see Lewis Lockwood, "The Autograph Score of the First Movement of Beethoven's Sonata for Violoncello and
Pianoforte, Opus 69," *The Music Forum* II (1970) 1–109 and facsimile of the
autograph, with introduction by Lockwood, New York, 1970, part of which is
reproduced on p. 534.

✗ *Scribbled notes by Beethoven for the third movement of the Fifth Symphony.*

cover three times as many pages as the finished copy of the work.

Beethoven's music, more than that of any composer before him, gives the impression of being a direct outpouring of his personality. To understand the music, therefore, it is helpful to know something about the man himself. Sir Julius Benedict described his first sight of Beethoven (1823) in these words:

> . . . a short, stout man with a very red face, small, piercing eyes, and bushy eyebrows, dressed in a very long overcoat which reached nearly to his ankles . . . notwithstanding the high color of his cheeks and his general untidiness, there was in those small piercing eyes an expression which no painter could render. It was a feeling of sublimity and melancholy combined. . . . The wonderful impression his first appearance made on me was heightened every time I met him. When I first saw him at Baden, his white hair flowing over his mighty shoulders, with that wonderful look—sometimes contracting his brows when anything afflicted him, sometimes bursting out into a forced laughter, indescribably painful to his listeners—I was touched as if *King Lear* or one of the old Gaelic bards stood before me.[2]

The "indescribably painful" sound of Beethoven's laughter may have been due to his deafness. This most dreadful of all afflictions for a musician began to manifest itself as early as 1798, and grew steadily worse until by 1820 it was practically total. In the autumn of 1802 Beethoven wrote a letter, now known as the "Heiligenstadt testament," intended to be read by his brothers after his death; in

[2] Quoted in Thayer, *Life of Beethoven,* III, 138–39.

it he describes in moving terms how he suffered when he realized that his malady was incurable:

> I must live almost alone like one who has been banished, I can mix with society only as much as true necessity demands. If I approach near to people a hot terror seizes upon me and I fear being exposed to the danger that my condition might be noticed. Thus it has been during the last six months which I have spent in the country . . . what a humiliation for me when someone standing next to me heard a flute in the distance and *I heard nothing,* or someone heard a *shepherd singing* and again I heard nothing. Such incidents drove me almost to despair, a little more of that and I would have ended my life—it was only *my art* that held me back. Ah, it seemed to me impossible to leave the world until I had brought forth all that I felt was within me. . . . Oh Providence—grant me at last but one day of *pure joy*—it is so long since real joy echoed in my heart . . .[3]

—yet the same man who thus cried out of the depths had, during that same half year in the country, written the exuberantly joyful Second Symphony!

It was Beethoven's habit to compose out-of-doors, often while taking long walks. He said:

> You will ask me whence I take my ideas? That I cannot say with any degree of certainty: they come to me uninvited, directly or indirectly. I could almost grasp them in my hands, out in Nature's open, in the woods, during my promenades, in the silence of the night, at the earliest dawn. They are roused by moods which in the poet's case are transmuted into words, and in mine into tones, that sound, roar and storm until at last they take shape for me as notes.[4]

His friend Schindler tells about a visit to Beethoven in 1819, while he was at work on the Mass in D:

> Towards the end of August . . . I arrived at the master's home in Mödling [a suburb of Vienna]. It was 4 o'clock in the afternoon. As soon as we entered we learned that in the morning both servants had gone away, and that there had been a quarrel after midnight which had disturbed all the neighbors, because as a consequence of a long vigil both had gone to sleep and the food which had been prepared had become unpalatable. In the living-room, behind a locked door, we heard the master singing parts of the fugue in the *Credo*—singing, howling, stamping. After we had been listening a long time to this almost awful scene, and were about to go away, the door opened and Beethoven stood before us with distorted features, calculated to excite fear. He looked as if he had been in mortal combat with the whole host of contrapuntists, his everlasting enemies. His first utterances were confused, as if he had been disagreeably surprised at our having overheard him. Then he reached the day's happenings and . . . he remarked: "Pretty doings, these! Everybody has run away and I haven't had anything to eat since yesternoon!" . . . He complained about the wretched state of his domestic affairs, but . . . there was nothing to be done. Never, it may be said, did so great an art work

---

[3] *Thayer's Life of Beethoven,* rev. & ed., E. Forbes, Princeton, 1967, I, 304–06.
[4] *Ibid.* II, 851, 852.

as the *Missa Solemnis* see its creation under more adverse circumstances.[5]

The outstanding characteristic of Beethoven's music, in comparison with that of his predecessors, is the quality of daemonic energy which such glimpses of the man reveal. It is a quality that is felt most starkly in passages like the close of the first movement of the Fifth Symphony, the coda of the finale of the Sonata Op. 57, or the finale of the Quartet Op. 59, No. 3. The energy breaks forth also as humor —not the playfulness of Haydn nor the grace and gaiety of Mozart, but something more robust and hearty, something which in certain cases may be understood as "romantic irony."[6] Examples are: the anxious antics of the double basses in the trio of the Scherzo of the Fifth Symphony, the stuttering halts in the rhythm after the double bar; the metronomic Allegretto of the Eighth Symphony; the apparently premature entrance of the horn in the first movement of the Third Symphony, just before the recapitulation; or the exquisitely comic passage in the coda of the finale of the Eighth Symphony where the entire orchestra starts chasing off after the theme like a puppy after a stick in the impossibly remote key of F♯ minor—and then, once safely returned home to F, proceeds presently to reassure itself by sounding the major third F–A down and back through five octaves of the woodwinds. (Note incidentally, as an example of Beethoven's customary long-range planning, how we have been prepared for this F♯-minor episode from the very beginning of the movement: the stubborn dominant C♯ of measures 374–79—appearing first as D♭ in measure 372—refers us back to the solitary, apparently totally arbitrary, and quickly abandoned *fortissimo* C♯ in measure 17.)

Characteristics of Beethoven's music

Beethoven's music is not always volcanic and exuberant; it may melt into tenderness (second movement of the Sonata Op. 90) or sadness (Adagio of the Quartet Op. 59, No. 1). Abrupt contrasts of mood occur: the Sonata Op. 57 opens with an ominous theme, builds up suspense, hesitates, pauses tentatively, then bursts out in sudden fury, recedes, sighs, and finally soars into a beautiful singing melody in A♭, which is subtly akin to the first theme (Example XV–2).

EXAMPLE XV–2   First Movement from Sonata Op. 57, Beethoven

[5] *Ibid.*, II, 735.
[6] See R. M. Longyear, "Beethoven and Romantic Irony," MQ 56 (1970) 647–64; reprinted in P. H. Lang, ed., *The Creative World of Beethoven*, New York, 1971, 145–62.

An even more striking contrast occurs in the development section of the first movement of the Third Symphony: after a long, fiercely dissonant *fortissimo* with off-beat *sforzandos,* we hear what seems to be a completely new theme, of tender melancholy, in the strangely foreign key of E minor.[7] Perhaps the most overwhelming of Beethoven's sudden changes of mood, however, is found in the finale of the Ninth Symphony, at the words "vor Gott." Full chorus and orchestra have reached a stupendous climax on a unison tonic A, to which at the last moment a strident and surprising F♮ has been added; this climax has been preparing steadily for over ninety measures, and it leaves the hearer breathless. What can possibly follow? A very strange thing indeed: after a few apparently random grunts and thumps, all the wind instruments, together with triangle, cymbals, and bass drum, go into a "Turkish March," a little 6/8 tune grotesquely caricaturing the main theme. Beethoven thus introduces a moment of comic relief, just as Shakespeare does with the entrance of the sleepy porter after Duncan's murder in *Macbeth;* but, also as with Shakespeare, the comic moment shades rapidly over into a new aspect of the prevailing mood: a heroic tenor solo followed by an intricately worked-out double fugue, all dominated by the new 6/8 rhythm, which continues to underlie the next big choral statement of the principal theme.

It is customary to divide Beethoven's works into three periods, on the basis of style and chronology. Vincent d'Indy[8] calls them the periods of Imitation, Externalization, and Reflection. Needless to say, the dividing lines are not sharp, but they run approximately as follows: the first period, of Imitation, goes to about 1802, and includes the six string quartets Op. 18, the first ten piano sonatas (through Op. 14), and the first two symphonies. The second period, of Externalization, runs to about 1816, and includes the symphonies III to VIII, the incidental music to Goethe's drama *Egmont,* the *Coriolan* overture, the opera *Fidelio,* the piano concertos in G and E♭, the violin concerto, the quartets of Opp. 59 (the *Rasumovsky* quartets), 74, and 95, and the piano sonatas through Op. 90. The last period, of Reflection, includes the last five piano sonatas, the *Diabelli* variations, the *Missa solemnis,* the Ninth Symphony, the quartets Opp. 127, 130, 131, 132, 135, and the *Grosse Fuge (Grand Fugue)* for string quartet (Op. 133, originally the finale of Op. 130).

---

[7] Neither the theme nor the key are as new and foreign as they seem. See R. B. Meikle, "Thematic Transformation in the First Movement of Beethoven's *Eroica* Symphony," *The Music Review* 32 (1971) 205–18.

[8] *Cobbett's Cyclopedic Survey of Chamber Music,* "Beethoven," London, 1926.

First Style Period

The works of the first period naturally show most clearly Beethoven's dependence on the Classical tradition. The first three sonatas published at Vienna (Op. 2, 1796) contain some passages reminiscent of Haydn, to whom they are dedicated; the Adagio of No. 1, for example, is quite Haydnesque both in themes and treatment. But these sonatas all have four movements instead of the usual Classical three; moreover, in the second and third sonatas the Classical minuet is replaced by the more dynamic Beethoven scherzo, a practice to which the composer held fairly consistently throughout his later works. The choice of F minor as the key of the first sonata was undoubtedly suggested by the F-minor sonata of C. P. E. Bach, which served as Beethoven's model; but this tonality is not common in the Classical period. The extensive use of the minor mode and the bold modulations in Beethoven's first three sonatas are also individual traits; in the second sonata, for example, the second theme of the first movement begins in the dominant minor, E, and immediately modulates, over a rising bass line, through G major and B♭ major to a climactic diminished seventh before settling down into the "proper" key of E major for the closing part of the exposition. Some of the harmonic characteristics in these early works, as well as the frequent use of octaves and the thick full texture of the piano writing, may have been suggested to Beethoven by the piano sonatas of Muzio Clementi (1752–1832). Among other possible influences here are the piano sonatas of the Bohemian-born Jan Ladislav Dussek (1760–1812).

The sonatas

The sonata in E♭ (Op. 7), published in 1797, is especially characteristic of Beethoven in the theme of the Largo with its eloquent pauses and in the mysterious *minore* trio of the third movement. Op. 10, No. 1, in C minor (1798) is a companion piece to the *Sonate Pathétique,* Op. 13, which was published in the following year. Each is in three movements, of which the outer two have the stormy, passionate character associated with the key of C minor, not only in Beethoven but in Haydn and Mozart as well; and each has a calm, profound, and richly scored slow movement in A♭. The Adagio of Op. 10, No. 1 has a typical retrospective coda; in the *Pathétique,* the twofold recurrence of the Grave introduction in the first movement and the obvious resemblance of the theme of the finale to one of the themes of the first movement foreshadow some of the formal innovations of Beethoven's later works.

The Quartets of Op. 18 (composed 1798–1800) demonstrate how well Beethoven had learned from Haydn's example the art of developing motives and animating the texture by means of counterpoint; yet these quartets are no mere imitations, for Beethoven's individ-

The quartets

uality is evident in the character of the themes, the frequent unexpected turns of phrase, the unconventional modulations, and some subtleties of formal structure. Thus the Adagio of the G-major quartet (No. 2) is a three-part ABA structure in C major; its middle section is an Allegro in F, consisting entirely of a development of a little motive from the closing cadence of the Adagio; and this motive, moreover, is related to conspicuous motives in the opening themes of the other three movements (Example XV–3).

EXAMPLE XV–3   Related Motives from Quartet in G Major Op. 18, No. 2, Beethoven

Beethoven's other chamber music of the first period includes the three Piano Trios, Op. 1; three Violin Sonatas, Op. 12; two Violoncello Sonatas, Op. 5; and the Septet in E♭ for strings and winds, Op. 20, which was played for the first time at a concert in 1800 and soon became so popular that Beethoven grew to detest it.

The First Symphony

The First Symphony was composed in 1799; it was first played at a concert in April, 1800, on a program that included also a symphony of Mozart, an aria and a duet from Haydn's *Creation,* a piano concerto and the septet by Beethoven, and improvisations by Beethoven at the piano. The First is the most Classical of the nine symphonies. Its spirit and many of its technical features stem from Haydn; all four movements are so regular in form that they might serve as textbook models. Beethoven's originality is evident not in the large formal outlines but in the details of his treatment, and also in the unusual prominence given to the woodwinds, in the character of the third movement—a scherzo, though labeled a minuet—and especially in the long and important codas of the other movements. The frequent marking *cresc.* $<$ p is but one example of the careful attention to dynamic shading that is an essential element in Beethoven's style.

The Adagio introduction to the first movement of this symphony is especially noteworthy. The key of the symphony is C, but the introduction begins in F, modulates to G at the fourth measure, and avoids a definitive cadence in C for the next eight measures, or until the first chord of the Allegro itself; Beethoven thus converges on the tonic from two opposite sides, the subdominant and the dominant. The short introduction to the finale is a joke in the manner of Haydn: the theme is introduced, as Tovey says, by a process of "letting the cat out of the bag."

With the Second Symphony in D major (composed in 1802) we are on the verge of Beethoven's second style period. The long Adagio that introduces the first movement announces a work conceived on a scale hitherto unknown in symphonic music. The introduction is broadly laid out in three divisions: (a) eight measures in D major; (b) sixteen measures of modulation, first to B♭ then gradually back to the dominant of D; (c) ten measures of dominant preparation, cadencing on the tonic at the beginning of the Allegro. The rest of the symphony has correspondingly large dimensions, with a profusion of thematic material held together in perfect formal balance. The Larghetto is especially remarkable for the large number of themes, and for its rich *cantabile* character. The scherzo and finale, like the first movement, are full of Beethovenian energy and fire. The finale is written in an enlarged sonata form, with suggestions of rondo in extra recurrences of the first theme, one at the beginning of the development section and one at the beginning of the coda; the coda itself is twice as long as the development section, and introduces a new theme.

The Second Symphony

Second Style Period

Within a dozen years after his coming to Vienna Beethoven was acknowledged throughout Europe as the foremost pianist and composer for the piano of his time, and as a symphonist who ranked equally with Haydn and Mozart. Such adverse criticisms as were uttered were directed against his eccentricity, his "frequent daring shifts from one motive to another, by which the organic connection of a gradual development of ideas was put aside. Such defects often weaken his greatest compositions, which spring from a too great exuberance of conception. . . . The singular and the original seemed to be his main object in composition." These are the words of J. V. Tomášek, pianist and composer, a slightly younger contemporary of Beethoven, who heard him improvise at Prague in 1795; they are typical of many later criticisms. Tomášek's opinions show that some of the ideas in even the early works of Beethoven, which now we accept as natural because they have become a part of our common musical language, disturbed an intelligent musician of the 1790's, for whom the ideal composers were presumably Haydn and Mozart. Haydn himself was not particularly sympathetic with all of Beethoven's innovations, and sometimes referred humorously to his brash young former pupil as the "great Mogul."

Beethoven may have cultivated his eccentricities of speech and manner as a social asset. He was received on terms of friendship by the highest noble families of Vienna. He had devoted and generous patrons, but his relations with them were different from Haydn's and Mozart's with their patrons: for most of his life Haydn wore a servant's uniform, and Mozart was once thrown out of the house by an Archbishop's secretary. Beethoven did not cringe before princes to seek their favor; instead he treated them with independence and occasionally with extreme rudeness, to which they responded with delighted offers of financial support. As Beethoven once remarked, "It is well to mingle with aristocrats, but one must know how to impress them." He drove hard bargains with his publishers and he was not above an occasional bit of sharp practice in business dealings. All in all, he managed to leave a comfortable estate at his death, and what is more important, he never in his life had to write music at anyone else's command and seldom had to meet a deadline. He could afford, as he said, to "think and think," to revise and polish a work until it suited him. It was because he wrote for himself—that is to say, for an ideal universal audience and not for a patron or an immediate particular function—that his music seems so strongly personal, so much the direct expression of himself, and of his historical epoch as he interpreted it.

The Eroica *Symphony*

The Third Symphony in E♭, composed in 1803, is one of the most important works of Beethoven's second period. This symphony bears the title *Eroica,* the "heroic symphony." There is a long-standing legend that Beethoven idealized Napoleon as the hero who was to lead humanity into the new age of liberty, equality, and fraternity, and dedicated the symphony to him. When he heard that Napoleon had had himself proclaimed Emperor, Beethoven, in his disappointment at finding that his idol was only another ambitious human being on the way to becoming a tyrant, angrily tore up the title page containing the dedication. It is apparently impossible to determine just how much exaggeration there is in this legend, but the fact seems to be that the symphony was originally entitled *Bonaparte* (not dedicated to him), and that the title was changed by Beethoven himself. His anger at Napoleon's being proclaimed Emperor is quite in keeping with Beethoven's beliefs and character, and it is equally characteristic of him that any resentment he may have felt was not permanent; at any rate, he conducted the symphony at a concert in

Title page of the manuscript of Beethoven's Third Symphony, the Eroica, *with the name of Napoleon Bonaparte erased.*

Vienna in 1809 at which Napoleon was to have been present, and in 1810 he apparently considered dedicating his Mass in C (Op. 86) to Napoleon.

Whatever the truth about its dedication, the Third Symphony stands as an immortal expression in music of the ideal of heroic greatness. It was a revolutionary work, of such unprecedented length and complexity that audiences at first found it difficult to grasp. In place of the usual slow movement it has a funeral march in C minor with a contrasting section in C major, of tragic grandeur and pathos. The finale is a set of variations with fugally developed episodes and coda, in an extremely complex but thoroughly logical form. The first movement begins, after two introductory chords, with one of the simplest imaginable themes on the notes of the E♭-major triad, a theme which Beethoven subjects to endless variation and development in the course of the movement. Five other themes are presented in the exposition, and the development section brings in still another, which recurs in the coda. Most remarkable, however, in this movement, as in all of Beethoven's, is neither the formal pattern nor the abundance of ideas, but the way in which all the material is propelled constantly along, one theme seeming to unfold out of another in a steady dynamic growth which mounts from one climax to the next, driving with a sense of utter inevitability to the end. This capacity to organize a large amount of contrasting material into a unified musical whole is one of the chief marks of Beethoven's greatness.

XV. Ludwig van Beethoven (1770–1827)

Fidelio

The opera *Fidelio* was composed at about the same time as the Third Symphony and is similar to it in character. As far as the libretto is concerned, *Fidelio* is a rescue opera of the kind that was so popular at the turn of the century (its libretto, in fact, is actually borrowed from a French revolutionary-era rescue opera). Beethoven's music, however, transforms this conventional material, making of the chief character Leonore (after whom the opera was originally named) a personage of sublime courage and self-abnegation, an idealized figure. The whole last part of the opera is in effect a celebration of Leonore's heroism and the great humanitarian ideals of the Revolution. This opera gave Beethoven more trouble than any other of his works. The first performances of the original three-act version took place in November of 1805, just after the French armies had marched into Vienna; rearranged and shortened to two acts, the opera was brought out again the following March, but immediately withdrawn. Finally, in 1814, a third version, with still more extensive revisions, was successful. In the course of all these changes Beethoven wrote no fewer than four different overtures for the opera. The first was never used, being replaced at the performances of 1805 by the overture now called *Leonora No. 2;* this one in turn was replaced by *Leonora No. 3* for the revival in 1806; and for the final version of the opera in 1814 Beethoven wrote still another, now known as the *Fidelio* overture. (*Leonora No. 3* is the one most often heard now in concerts.)

Not only the overture, but practically everything else in *Fidelio* was rewritten time and again. The introduction to the recitative and aria at the beginning of Act II, for example, was revised at least eighteen times before Beethoven was finally satisfied. The difficulties were not merely like those he had to overcome in his instrumental compositions; his problems were further complicated by the presence of a text. Beethoven knew well enough how to write for voices, but his thought moved habitually on such a lofty plane that he found it exceedingly difficult to make music for a text which, like the usual opera libretto, is concerned with the small doings of individuals in particular situations. Therefore, in those parts of *Fidelio* that are like any ordinary *opéra comique* or singspiel, Beethoven is ill at ease; only when the words suggest grander emotions and universal ideas does he speak with all his natural power. He never wrote another opera, chiefly because he could not find another libretto to suit him. It is a pity that he never composed music for Goethe's *Faust,* a project which he considered at various times.

The
Rasumovsky
quartets

The three quartets of Op. 59 are dedicated to Count Rasumovsky, the Russian Ambassador to Vienna. Rasumovsky was the patron of a quartet of string players said to be the finest in Europe, in which he himself played second violin. As a compliment to the Count, Beethoven introduced a Russian melody as the principal theme of the finale of the first quartet, and another in the third movement of the second quartet. These three quartets, composed in the summer and autumn of 1806, occupy a position in Beethoven's work similar to that of the Quartets Opp. 17 and 20 in Haydn's: they are the first to exemplify the composer's mature style and characteristic manner of expression in this medium. They are indeed full of the emotional fire, boldness of formal treatment, and striking originality that characterize Beethoven's second period. So great was their novelty that musicians were slow to accept them. When Count Rasumovsky's players first tried over the Quartet in F (No. 1 of the set), they were convinced that Beethoven was playing a joke on them. Clementi, the brilliant London pianist whom Mozart had once described as a "mere mechanician," reported that he had said to Beethoven "Surely you do not consider these works to be music?" to which the composer, with unusual self-restraint, answered, "Oh, they are not for you, but for a later age." The Allegretto movement of the F-major Quartet in particular gave rise to charges of "crazy music." It took some time for musicians and audiences to realize that Beethoven's innovations were logical, that the nature of his musical ideas compelled modification of the traditional language and forms.

In the quartets of Op. 59 as well as in the *Eroica Symphony,* the sonata form is expanded to unheard-of proportions by the multitude of themes, the long and complex developments, and the extended codas which take on the dimensions and significance of a second development section. Along with this expansion, Beethoven intentionally conceals the formerly clear dividing lines between the various parts of a movement: recapitulations are disguised and varied, new themes grow imperceptibly out of previous material, and the progress of the musical thought has a dynamic, propulsive character that toys with, if not actually scorns, the neat, symmetrical patterns of the Classical era. These developments continue throughout the whole of Beethoven's second period, but the change is more radical in the quartets and piano sonatas than in the less intimate symphonies and overtures. The two quartets Op. 74 (1809) and Op. 95 (1810) show Beethoven on the way toward the dissolution of traditional form that later marked the last quartets of the third period.

Among the other chamber works of Beethoven's second period, special mention should be made of the Violin Sonatas Op. 47 (the *Kreutzer* sonata) and Op. 96, and the Trio in B♭, Op. 97. The two Sonatas for Violoncello and Piano, Op. 102 (1815), belong stylistically to the third period.

The Fourth, Fifth, and Sixth Symphonies were all composed between 1806 and 1808, a time of exceptional productivity. Beethoven seems to have worked on the Fourth and Fifth Symphonies at the same time; the first two movements of the Fifth, in fact, were already in existence before the Fourth was completed. The two works contrast, as though Beethoven wished to express simultaneously

The Fourth to Eighth Symphonies

525

two opposite poles of feeling. Joviality and humor mark the Fourth Symphony, while the Fifth has always been interpreted as the musical projection of Beethoven's resolution "I will grapple with Fate; it shall not overcome me." The progress through struggle to victory, as symbolized in this symphony by the succession C minor to C major, has been an implicit subject of many symphonies since Beethoven's, but none other has so caught the popular imagination. The first movement is dominated by the four-note motive so impressively announced in the opening measures, and the same motive recurs in one guise or another in the other three movements as well. The transition from minor to major takes place in an inspired passage which leads without a break from the scherzo into the finale, where the entrance of the full orchestra with trombones on the C major chord has an electrifying effect. This is said to have been the first use of trombones in a symphony, although they had been used by both Gluck and Mozart in operas. The finale of the Fifth Symphony also employs a piccolo and a contra-bassoon, in addition to the trombones and the normal complement of strings, woodwind, brass, and kettledrums.

The Sixth (*Pastoral*) Symphony was composed immediately after the Fifth and the two were first played on the same program in December, 1808. Each of the five movements bears a descriptive title suggesting a scene from life in the country. Beethoven adapts his descriptive program to the usual Classical symphonic form, merely inserting after the scherzo (*Merrymaking of the Peasants*) an extra movement (*Storm*) which serves to introduce the finale (*Thankful feelings after the storm*). In the coda of the Andante (*Scene by the brook*), flute, oboe, and clarinet join harmoniously in imitating bird calls—the nightingale, the quail, and, of course, the cuckoo. All this programmatic apparatus is subordinate to the expansive, leisurely musical form of the Symphony as a whole; the composer himself warns that the descriptions are not to be taken literally: he calls them "expression of feelings rather than depiction." The *Pastoral Symphony* is one of hundreds of works from the eighteenth and early nineteenth centuries that aimed to portray natural scenes or suggest the moods aroused by the contemplation of such scenes (*cf.* Vivaldi's *Seasons* concertos); its enduring appeal testifies not to the accuracy of its landscape painting but to the way in which the emotions of a lover of nature have been captured in great music.

The Seventh and Eighth Symphonies were both completed in 1812. The Seventh, like the Second and Fourth, opens with a long slow introduction with remote modulations, leading into an Allegro dominated throughout by the rhythmic figure ♪♩♪ . The second movement, in the parallel minor key of A, was encored at the first performance and has always been a favorite with audiences. The scherzo (not so labeled) is in F major, the lower submediant of the principal key of the symphony; it is unusual furthermore in that the trio (D major) recurs a second time, thus expanding this movement to a five-part form (*ABABA*). The finale, a large sonata-form with coda, "remains unapproached in music as a triumph of Bacchic fury."[9] By contrast with the huge scale of the Seventh Symphony, the Eighth appears miniature—or would, if it were not for the long coda of the first movement and the still longer one of the finale. This is the most mercurial of all the nine symphonies, but its humor is sophisticated and its forms extremely condensed. The second movement is a brisk Allegretto, while the third, by way of compensation, is a deliberately archaic Minuet instead of the usual Beethoven Scherzo.

Related in style to the symphonies are Beethoven's orchestral overtures, which usually take the form of a symphonic first movement. The *Leonore* Overtures have already been mentioned. The other most important overtures are *Coriolan* (1807), inspired by a tragedy of the same name by H. J. von Collin which was performed occasionally at Vienna after 1802; and *Egmont,* composed, together with songs and incidental music, for a performance of Goethe's drama in 1810.

The piano sonatas of the second period show a wide range of styles and forms. Among the earliest, dating from about 1802, are the Sonata in A♭ with the funeral march, Op. 26, and the two sonatas of Op. 27, each designated as "quasi una fantasia"; the second is the one popularly known as the *Moonlight Sonata*. The first movement of the D-minor Sonata Op. 31, No. 2 has an introductory *largo* phrase which recurs at the beginning of the development section and again at the beginning of the recapitulation, each time in expanded form and with increased musical significance; its last appearance leads into an expressive instrumental recitative, of the kind that Beethoven afterward used with effect in some of his later works. The finale of this sonata is an exciting *moto perpetuo* in sonata-rondo form.

The sonatas and concertos

Outstanding among the sonatas of the second period are Op. 53 in C major (called the *Waldstein Sonata* after Beethoven's patron, to whom it is dedicated) and Op. 57 in F minor, commonly called the *Appassionata*. Both were composed in 1804. These two works illustrate what happened to the Classical sonata at Beethoven's hands. Each has the usual Classical three movements in the order fast–slow– fast; each exhibits the patterns of sonata-form, rondo, or variations, with appropriate key-schemes. But their formal order has, as it were, been expanded from within by the resistless force of Beethoven's musical imagination, expressed in themes of elemental power that require a structure of hitherto unknown tension and concentration to support their natural development and completion. When we

[9] D. Tovey, *Essays in Musical Analysis,* New York, 1935, I, 60.

listen to a sonata by Mozart we rejoice in the composer's constant and willing submission to an accepted order of things musical; when we listen to one of Beethoven's sonatas we rejoice that the revolutionist submits only where he pleases, and that elsewhere he creates a new order, one growing out of the old but resembling it only in externals.

After the *Waldstein* and the *Appassionata*, there were no more sonatas from Beethoven for five years. To the year 1809 belong both the Sonata in F♯, Op. 78, which Beethoven once declared to be his favorite, and the quasi-programmatic Sonata Op. 81a. The latter was inspired by the departure from and return to Vienna of the Archduke Rudolph, one of his patrons; its three movements are entitled *Farewell, Absence,* and *Return.* The Sonata Op. 90 (1814) is a work bordering on Beethoven's third period; it has two movements, an Allegro in E minor in concise sonata form and a long, leisurely sonata-rondo Andante in E major, which is one of Beethoven's happiest lyric inspirations.

As a concert pianist Beethoven naturally composed concertos for his own use. His first three piano concertos date from the early years in Vienna (No. 1 in C, No. 2 in B♭, No. 3 in C minor). The two largest works in this form are the Concerto in G major Op. 58, composed in 1805–06 and the one in E♭, known as the *Emperor Concerto,* which was composed in 1808–09 and first performed at Vienna in 1812 by Carl Czerny. (Czerny [1791–1857] as a young man had studied piano with Beethoven, and subsequently had a successful teaching career at Vienna; he was the composer of many studies and other works for the piano.)

The concertos of Beethoven are related to those of Mozart much as are the symphonies of these two composers: Beethoven retained the division of the concerto into three movements and the general outline of the Classical form; but he expanded the framework, and intensified the content. The virtuosity of the solo part is more marked than in Mozart's concertos, but is not excessive in view of the expanded dimensions. In Beethoven's magnificent Violin Concerto, Op. 61 in D major (composed 1806), the solo part is ideally interwoven with the orchestra.

Third Style Period

The years up to 1815 were, on the whole, peaceful and prosperous for Beethoven. His music was much played in Vienna, and he was celebrated both at home and abroad. Thanks to the generosity of patrons and the steady demand from publishers for new works, his financial affairs were in good order, despite a ruinous devaluation of the Austrian currency in 1811; but his deafness became a more and more serious trial. As it caused him to lose contact with others, he retreated into himself, becoming morose, irascible, and morbidly suspicious even toward his friends. Family troubles, ill health, and unfounded apprehensions of poverty were also plaguing Beethoven, and it was only by a supreme effort of will that he continued composing amidst all these troubles. The last five piano sonatas were written between 1816 and 1821; the *Missa solemnis* was completed in 1822, the *Diabelli* variations in 1823, and the Ninth Symphony in 1824, each after long years of labor; and the last quartets, Beethoven's musical testament, followed in 1825 and 1826. At his death in 1827 he had plans for a tenth symphony and many other new works.

By 1816, Beethoven had accepted the decree of Fate that for him the only possible source of happiness was to be the soundless world of tones that existed in his mind. His compositions of the third period more and more come to have a meditative character; the former urgent sense of communication is replaced by a feeling of assured tranquillity, passionate outpouring by calm affirmation. The language becomes more concentrated, more abstract. Extremes meet: the sublime and the grotesque side by side in the Mass and the Ninth Symphony, the profound and the apparently naïve side by side in the last quartets. Classical forms remain as the former features of a landscape remain after a geological upheaval—recognizable here and there under new contours, lying at strange angles underneath the new surface.

One of the characteristics—a concomitant of the meditative quality—in Beethoven's late works is the deliberate working out of themes and motives to the utmost of their potentialities. This is in part a continuation of his earlier technique of motivic development, which he now carries to its limits; more especially, it reflects a new conception of the possibilities of thematic *variation*.

Characteristics of Beethoven's late style

The principle of variation is one of repeating a given theme in new guises while recognizably preserving the essential structure of the entire theme in each repetition. It differs from development in that it involves an entire theme, not just fragments or motives. Variation is a method of writing that may be practiced at any level of technical ability; Mozart, for example, often gave a beginning pupil in composition the assignment of writing variations on a theme, and when pianists like Mozart and Beethoven improvised in public a standard feature of their performance would be to improvise variations on a theme. In the works of Haydn, Mozart, and Beethoven, variation occurs in three kinds of situations: (1) as a technique within a larger formal plan, as when in a rondo each recurrence of the principal theme is varied, or in a sonata form the first theme is varied in the recapitulation; (2) a theme-and-variations as an independent composition; and (3) a theme-and-variations as one of the movements of a symphony or sonata. Examples of the first use in Beethoven's late

Beethoven's manuscript of the theme of the variation movement from the Piano Sonata Op. 109. (Library of Congress)

works are the slow movements of the Sonata Op. 106, the Quartet Op. 132, and the Ninth Symphony; the finale of this symphony also begins (after the introduction) as a set of variations.

As for independent compositions in variation form, in all Beethoven wrote twenty sets of these for piano, the majority of them on favorite tunes from contemporary operas; from the last period there is only one independent set, but it is a work that surpasses anything in this form since Bach's *Goldberg Variations:* the *Thirty-three Variations on a Waltz by Diabelli,* Op. 120, which were completed and published in 1823. These differ from other variations of the late eighteenth or early nineteenth centuries in that they are made up not of comparatively straightforward alterations in the physiognomy of the theme, but of transformations in its very character. Diabelli's commonplace little waltz, taken by Beethoven as if contemptuously to show what could be made of it, surprisingly expands into a world of variegated moods—solemn, brilliant, capricious, mysterious— ordered with due regard for contrast, grouping, and climax. Each variation is built on motives derived from some part of the theme, but altered in rhythm, tempo, dynamics, or context so as to produce a new design. The *Diabelli* variations were the model for Schumann's

Symphonic Etudes, Brahms's *Variations on a Theme of Handel,* and many other works in this form in the nineteenth century. Other examples of variations, like the Diabelli set but more concentrated, are the slow movements in Beethoven's Sonata Op. 111 and in the Quartets Opp. 127 and 131. In these, as it were, we overhear the composer while he meditates on his theme, finding with each meditation new depths of insight, and gradually leading us into a realm where the music takes on a luminous and transcendent quality of mystical revelation.

Another feature of Beethoven's late style is a continuity he achieved by intentionally blurring dividing lines: within a musical sentence, by making cadential progressions terminate on a weak beat, by delaying the progression of the lower voices, placing the third or the fifth of the tonic chord in the upper voice at such a resolution, or by otherwise concealing the cadential effect (first theme of the slow movement of the Ninth Symphony); within a movement, by interpenetration of Introduction and Allegro (first movements of Sonata Op. 109 and Quartets Opp. 127, 130, 132) or making the Introduction a part of the Allegro (first movement of the Ninth Symphony); even within a complete work, by interpenetration of movements (Adagio and Fuga in the Sonata Op. 110; recall of the first movement theme after the Adagio of Op. 101). A feeling of vastness comes also from the wide-spaced harmonic arches and the leisurely march of the melodies in such movements as the Adagio of the Quartet Op. 127 or the *Benedictus* of the Mass in D. At times all motion pauses for long moments of reflection; such passages have the character of improvisation, and may give us some idea of the actual improvisations of Beethoven at the piano which so impressed his hearers. (Similar examples are the slow movement of the Sonata Op. 101 and the Largo introduction to the finale of the Sonata Op. 106; this style was forecast in the slow movement of the *Waldstein Sonata,* Op. 53.) Sometimes these improvisatory passages culminate in instrumental recitative, as in the Adagio of the Sonata Op. 110, and also the recitatives in the Quartets Op. 131 and Op. 132 and the finale of the Ninth Symphony.

The abstract, suprapersonal quality of Beethoven's late style is symbolized by the increased extent and importance of contrapuntal textures in the compositions of the third period. This increase was in part the fruit of his lifelong reverence for the music of J. S. Bach, but it was also a necessary consequence of the nature of his musical thought in the last ten years of his life. It is apparent in the numerous canonic imitations and generally contrapuntal voice-leading of all the late works; it is evidenced specifically by fugatos incorporated in development sections (as in the finale of Op. 101) and by complete fugal movements, such as the finales of the Sonatas Opp. 106 and 110, the first movement of the Quartet in C♯ minor, Op. 131, the gigantic

Grosse Fuge for String Quartet Op. 133, the fugues at the end of the Gloria and Credo of the Mass in D, and the two double fugues in the finale of the Ninth Symphony.

Another, incidental consequence of the abstract quality of Beethoven's last works was the invention of new sonorities: as the former habits of vertical tone combination were modified by the rigorous logic of contrapuntal lines, or as new ideas required new alignments of sound for their realization, he produced unaccustomed effects. The widely spaced piano sonorities at the end of the Sonata Op. 110, the partition of the theme between the two violins (on the principle of the medieval hocket) in the fourth movement of the C♯-minor Quartet, and the extraordinary dark coloring of the orchestra and chorus at the first appearance of the words "Ihr stürzt nieder" in the finale of the Ninth Symphony are instances of such new sonorities. Some of the experiments seem to be unsuccessful. Critics have held that in his late works Beethoven went too far in subjugating euphony and considerations of practicability to the demands of his musical conceptions, and some attribute this alleged fault to his deafness. There are places—the finale of the Sonata Op. 106, the first section of the *Grosse Fuge*, the B-major cadenza of the four soloists in the last movement of the Ninth Symphony, the *Et vitam venturi* fugue in the Mass—that almost require a miracle to make them "sound" in performance. The ideas seem too big for human capabilities to express; but whether one approves or condemns these passages, there is not the slightest reason to suppose that Beethoven, even had his hearing been perfect, would have altered a single note, either to spare tender ears among his auditors or to make things easier for the performers.

As with Classical texture and sonority, so with Classical form in the instrumental works of Beethoven's third period: two of the last quartets and two of the last sonatas retain the external scheme of the usual four movements, but the rest dispense with even this obeisance to tradition. The Sonata Op. 111 has only two movements, an Allegro in compact sonata form and a long set of variations, Adagio molto, so eloquent and so perfect that nothing further seems to be required. The Quartet Op. 131 has seven movements: (1) A fugue in C♯ minor, adagio, 4/4. (2) Allegretto molto vivace, D major, 6/8, in something vaguely like sonata form. (3) Eleven measures, allegro moderato, in the spirit of a recitativo accompagnato, functioning as an introduction to the following movement and modulating from B minor to E major, which becomes the dominant of (4) Andante, A major, 2/4: theme of two double periods, with six variations and a seventh variation incomplete, merging with a coda which itself embodies still one more variation of the first and fourth periods of the theme. (4) Presto, ¢ , E major: four themes, rapidly chasing one another around in the order AbcdAbcdAb̄cdA.

(6) Adagio, G♯ minor, 3/4: 28 measures in the form *ABB* with coda, introducing (7) Allegro, C♯ minor, ₵ , sonata form. All this could be forcibly equated with the Classical sonata scheme by calling 1 and 2 an introduction and first movement, 3 and 4 an introduction and slow movement, 5 a scherzo, and 6 and 7 an introduction and finale; a similar arbitrary adjustment would also be possible with the Quartet Op. 132, but not with Op. 130, which in the number and order of movements is more like a serenade than anything else. In any event, in all Beethoven's late sonatas and quartets both the musical material and its treatment are so different from those of Haydn and Mozart that resemblances to Classical patterns are at most incidental.

The most imposing works of the last period are the Mass in D (the *Missa solemnis*) and the Ninth Symphony. The former is, with the possible exception of Bach's Mass in B minor, the worthiest musical interpretation of this text that exists. Beethoven himself regarded it as his greatest work. It is a deeply personal and at the same time universal confession of faith. The score incorporates historic musical and liturgical symbols to an extent far greater, and in a manner far more detailed, than an uninformed listener can be aware of.[10] Like Bach's Mass, Beethoven's is too long and elaborate for ordinary liturgical use; it is rather a huge vocal and instrumental symphony using the text of the Mass as its fabric. Yet it is more than merely a "setting" of the words; one might better call it a *representation,* both pictorial and symbolic, of the whole liturgy of the Mass.

The Mass in D

The choral treatment owes something to Handel, whose music Beethoven revered equally with that of Bach; one theme of the *Dona nobis pacem* is adapted from Handel's melody to the words "And He shall reign forever and ever" in the Hallelujah Chorus, and the lofty style of the whole is quite in the spirit of Handel. The form, however, is different. Handel's oratorios and Bach's Mass were conceived, in accordance with the Baroque practice, as a series of independent numbers, without interconnecting themes or motives and usually without any very definite plan of musical unity in the work as a whole. Beethoven's Mass is a planned musical unit, a symphony in five movements, one on each of the five principal divisions of the Ordinary of the Mass. In this respect it is like the late Masses of Haydn, and like them also it freely combines and alternates solo voices and chorus in each movement. Beethoven's attention to requirements of musical form occasionally leads him to take liberties with the liturgical text, such as the repetition of the opening sentence "Gloria in excelsis Deo" at the end of the second movement,

---

[10] See the important article by Warren Kirkendale, "New Roads to Old Ideas in Beethoven's *Missa solemnis*," MQ 56 (1970) 665–710; reprinted in P. H. Lang, ed., *The Creative World of Beethoven*, New York, 1971, 163–99; in a somewhat fuller version in *Sitzungsberichte der Oesterreichischen Akademie der Wissenschaften,* Bd. 271 (Vienna, 1971) 121–58.

XV. Ludwig van Beethoven (1770–1827)

Mm. 36–38, in Beethoven's autograph

The top line is the cello part, to be read in bass clef; the second and third lines are the piano part, in treble and bass clefs, respectively; a key signature of A major is assumed.

Mm. 35–38 in the Schirmer edition

Mm. 34–37 in the Henle edition

A passage from the first movement of Beethoven's cello sonata in A major, Op. 69, as it appears in the composer's autograph and in two editions. In measure 35, Beethoven wrote a C♮ for the piano, but in measure 36 a C♯ for the cello. Until the recent Henle publication, all editions, from the first (published by Breitkopf and Härtel in 1809) have given the cello a C♮ in measure 36. The 1905 Schirmer edition shown here is one of the many (including the 19th-century Gesamtausgabe of Beethoven's works, and that edited by Donald Francis Tovey) that have perpetuated this misreading, which evidently arose from Beethoven's hurried proofreading of the first edition, in which the cello and piano parts were printed separately, rather than in score—and thus probably proofread separately by the composer.

or the rondo-like recurrences of the word "Credo" with its musical motive in the third movement; but these and similar liberties are found in Masses by other composers both before and since Beethoven.

Within the frame of the symphonic structure there is abundant variety of detail. Beethoven seizes every phrase, every single word that offers him a possibility for dramatic musical expression; to realize the contrast in this respect between Beethoven's treatment of the text and that of Bach, one should compare their respective settings of the words "judicare vivos et mortuos" (to judge both the quick and the dead) in the Credo. (Beethoven's effective pause after the word "et," here and elsewhere in the Credo, had been anticipated in Haydn's *Missa in tempore belli*.) The threefold interruption of the *Dona nobis pacem*—the "prayer for inward and outward peace," as Beethoven headed it—by ominous orchestral interludes with martial flourishes in the trumpets and drums is a feature likewise anticipated by Haydn as well as many earlier composers. It is a superbly theatrical touch, but neither this nor any of the other vivid details of the score is theatrical in a bad sense; all are absorbed into and made part of the vast and wonderfully organized structure of the work.

The Ninth Symphony was first performed on May 7, 1824, on a program with one of Beethoven's overtures and three movements of the Mass (the Kyrie, Credo, and Agnus Dei). The large and distinguished audience applauded vociferously after the symphony. Beethoven did not turn around to acknowledge the applause because he could not hear it; one of the solo singers "plucked him by the sleeve and directed his attention to the clapping hands and waving hats and handkerchiefs. . . . he turned to the audience and bowed."[11] The receipts at the concert were large, but so little remained after expenses had been paid that Beethoven accused his friends who had managed the affair of having cheated him. A repetition two weeks later before a half-full house resulted in a deficit. Thus was the Ninth Symphony launched into the world.

The Ninth Symphony

Its most striking novelty is the use of chorus and solo voices in the finale. Beethoven had had the thought as early as 1792 of composing a setting of Schiller's *Ode to Joy*, but his decision to make a choral finale on this text for the Ninth Symphony was not reached before the autumn of 1823. It is significant of Beethoven's ethical ideals that in choosing the stanzas to be used he selected those that emphasize two ideas: the universal brotherhood of man through joy, and its basis in the love of an eternal heavenly Father. Beethoven was troubled by the apparent incongruity of introducing voices as the climax of a long instrumental symphony. His solution of this esthetic difficulty determined the unusual form of the last movement: a brief tumultuous dissonant introduction; a review and rejection (by instrumental recitatives) of the themes of the preceding movements; suggestion of the joy theme and its joyful acceptance; orchestral exposition of the theme in four stanzas, *crescendo*, with

[11] Thayer-Forbes, *op. cit.*, II, 909.

coda; again the tumultuous dissonant opening measures; bass recitative: "O friends, not these tones, but let us rather sing more pleasant and joyful ones"; choral-orchestral exposition of the joy theme in four stanzas, varied (including the Turkish March), and with a long orchestral interlude (double fugue) before a repetition of the first stanza; new theme, orchestra and chorus; double fugue on the two themes; and a complex, gigantic coda, in which the "heaven-descended flame" of Joy is hailed in strains of matchless sublimity. The first three movements of the symphony are on a comparably grand scale. The scherzo, in particular, is an outstanding example of Beethoven's ability to organize an entire movement in sonata form around a single rhythmic motive.

Beethoven and the Romantics

Only a few of his contemporaries understood Beethoven's late works, which in any event were so personal that they could hardly be imitated. His influence on later composers came mostly from the works of the middle period, especially the *Rasumovsky* Quartets, the Fifth, Sixth, and Seventh Symphonies, and the piano sonatas. Even in these works it was not the Classical element in Beethoven's style— not the overruling sense of form, unity, and proportion that always dominated even his most subjective creations, nor yet the painstaking craftsmanship to which the sketchbooks bear such constant witness—but rather the revolutionary element, the free, impulsive, mysterious, daemonic spirit, the underlying conception of *music as a mode of self-expression,* that chiefly fascinated the Romantic generation. As E. T. A. Hoffmann wrote, "Beethoven's music sets in motion the lever of fear, of awe, of horror, of suffering, and awakens just that infinite longing which is the essence of romanticism. He is accordingly a completely romantic composer. . . ."[12] Hoffmann was not unaware nor unappreciative of the importance of structure and control in Beethoven's music, nor in that of Haydn and Mozart— whom he also called "romantic." (One gets the impression that he used the word mainly as a general term of approbation.) Romantic or not, Beethoven was one of the great disruptive forces in the history of music. After him, nothing could ever be the same again; he had opened the gateway to a new world.

[12] From an essay on "Beethoven's Instrumental Music," 1813; in SR, 777 (SRRo, 37).

XVI

‖‖

The Nineteenth Century: Romanticism; Vocal Music

Classicism and Romanticism

The names of historical periods in music always have a double meaning: they denote certain styles of music and also certain segments of time during which those styles are dominant. For example, in ordinary usage, the same adjective "classical" applies to the style of Haydn, Mozart, and Beethoven and also the period 1770 to 1800 or 1830 when that style flourished. In principle, the two meanings coincide. In principle, it is always possible to define a style (or a complex of significantly related styles) in general terms and to fix more or less precisely the dates of its beginning and ending. In practice, of course, the more we learn about the music of any particular time, place, or composer, the more clearly we begin to see that the generalized style descriptions are inadequate and the period boundaries somewhat arbitrary. Nothing is easier than to criticize them on such grounds. Nevertheless, the division of music history into style periods has its uses. Periodization is a means of doing justice to both principles—continuity and change—in history. Rough and imprecise as the labels may be, they can serve as points of orientation, directions from which to approach the actual music. They will serve that purpose best if we remember that they are labels; they no more pretend to describe all the music subsumed under them than the label on a box pretends to describe in detail all the contents. Once we have opened the box we can discard the label if we choose, or make a better one if we can.

The terms "classic" and "romantic" as descriptions of style periods are especially troublesome, for two reasons. In the first place, both words, as used in literature and the fine arts and in general history, have a much greater variety of meaning than those we usually attach to them in music history. "Classic" suggests something finished, perfect, exemplary, a standard against which later production may be measured. The works of certain ancient authors are known as "the classics," and in somewhat the same sense Palestrina's music has been called classic; but for the nineteenth and twentieth centuries, it was the music of Haydn, Mozart, and Beethoven that became the classic ideal. As for "romantic," the word is constantly being used to mean so many different things that it is quite useless for describing a musical style until it has been especially defined for that purpose.

The second reason why the traditional antithesis classic-romantic causes confusion in music history is that it is not a total antithesis. The continuity between the two styles is more fundamental than the contrast. It is not merely that one can find romantic traits in music of the eighteenth century and classical ones in that of the nineteenth; it is rather that the great bulk of the music written from about 1770 to about 1900 constitutes a single style period, with a common limited stock of usable musical sounds, a common basic vocabulary of harmonies, common basic principles of harmonic progression, rhythm, and form, and a common intention, namely to communicate meaning exclusively through music without extraneous symbolism from composer to performer to listener, starting from an exact and complete notation. From Mozart to Mahler, all tentative departures, individual modifications, experiments, developments along special lines—all take place within one tradition and with reference to one common basic set of principles. If Mozart could have heard Mahler's music he might or might not have liked it, but he would not have found it utterly strange. The experience for him would have been more like flying from Vienna to Peking than from Vienna to the moon.

We shall now attempt to define, or suggest, the meaning of Romanticism with reference to the music of the nineteenth century. The adjective *romantic* comes from *romance,* which had an original literary meaning of a medieval tale or poem treating heroic personages or events and written in one of the Romance languages —that is, one of the vernacular languages descended from Latin ("Roman"). The medieval poems dealing with King Arthur were called the Arthurian romances, for example. Hence, when the word *romantic* first came into use around the middle of the seventeenth century it carried the connotation of something far off, legendary, fictitious, fantastic, and marvelous, an imaginary or ideal world which was contrasted with the actual world of the present. This connotation is the basis of Walter Pater's definition of Romanticism as "the addition of strangeness to beauty," and is hinted in Lord Bacon's dictum that "there is no excellent beauty that hath not some strangeness in the proportion." In the early part of the eighteenth century, the dawn of the romantic spirit was manifest in the beginning of appreciation for wild and picturesque natural scenery and in the widespread popularity of the "English garden," that is a garden giving the impression of primitive natural growth instead of cultivation and formal arrangement. Another sign, from about the middle of the century, was the gradual transformation of "Gothic" from a term of abuse to one of praise; people began to find beauty in medieval cathedrals, to admire them for their irregularity and complexity of detail, so different from the symmetry and simplicity of classical architecture. Associated with this change of taste was the rise of the so-called Gothic novel, beginning in 1764 with Walpole's *Castle of Otranto*.

In a very general sense, all art may be said to be Romantic; for, though it may take its materials from actual life, it transforms them and thus creates a new world which is necessarily to a greater or lesser degree remote from the everyday world. From this point of view, Romantic art differs from Classic art by its greater emphasis on the qualities of remoteness and strangeness, with all that such emphasis may imply as to choice and treatment of material. Romanticism, in this general sense, is not a phenomenon of any one period, but has occurred at various times in various forms. It is possible to see in the history of music, and of the other arts, alternations of Classicism and Romanticism—or, as Curt Sachs calls them, cycles of *ethos* and *pathos;* thus the *ars nova* may be considered Romantic in comparison with the *ars antiqua,* or the Baroque in comparison with the Renaissance, in somewhat the same way that the nineteenth century is Romantic in comparison with the Classicism of the eighteenth century.

Traits of Romanticism

Another fundamental trait of Romanticism is boundlessness, in two different though related senses. First, romantic art aspires to transcend immediate times or occasions, to seize eternity, to reach back into the past and forward into the future, to range over the expanse of the world and outward through the cosmos. As against the classic ideals of order, equilibrium, control, and perfection within acknowledged limits, Romanticism cherishes freedom, movement, passion, and endless pursuit of the unattainable. And just because its goal can never be attained, Romantic art is haunted by a spirit of longing, of yearning after an impossible fulfillment.

Second, the Romantic impatience of limits leads to a breaking down of distinctions. The personality of the artist tends to become merged with the work of art; Classical clarity is replaced by a certain intentional obscurity, definite statement by suggestion, allu-

Preliminary sketch for The Raft of the "Medusa," *by Théodore Gericault (1791–1824). Romantic art aspired to an extravagant portrayal of man's struggles and of nature in its wilder aspects.*

sion, or symbol. The arts themselves tend to merge; poetry, for example, aims to acquire the qualities of music, and music the characteristics of poetry.

If remoteness and boundlessness are Romantic, then music is the most Romantic of the arts. Its material—ordered sound and rhythm —is almost completely detached from the concrete world of objects, and this very detachment makes music most apt at suggesting the flood of impressions, thoughts, and feelings which is the proper domain of Romantic art. Only instrumental music—pure music free from the burden of words—can perfectly attain this goal of communicating emotion. Instrumental music, therefore, is the ideal Romantic art. Its detachment from the world, its mystery, and its incomparable power of suggestion which works on the mind directly without the mediation of words, made it the dominant art, the one most representative, among all the arts, of the nineteenth century. "All art constantly aspires towards the condition of music," wrote Pater. Schopenhauer believed that music was the very image and incarnation of the innermost reality of the world, the immediate expression of the universal feelings and impulses of life in concrete, definite form. That all music had trans-musical content was one of the cherished, if not always acknowledged, beliefs of the nineteenth century.

At this point we come upon the first of several apparently opposing conditions that beset all attempts to grasp the meaning of *The Romantic* *Romantic* as applied to the music of the nineteenth century. We *dualities* shall endeavor to deal with this difficulty by summarizing the con-

540

flicting tendencies that affected the music of the time and noting in what way the musicians sought to harmonize these oppositions in their own thought and practice.

The first opposition involves the relation between music and words. If instrumental music is the perfect Romantic art, why is it that the acknowledged great masters of the symphony, the highest form of instrumental music, were not Romantics, but were the Classical composers, Haydn, Mozart, and Beethoven? Moreover, one of the most characteristic nineteenth-century forms was the Lied, a vocal piece in which Schubert, Schumann, Brahms, and Hugo Wolf attained a new and intimate union between music and poetry. Even the instrumental music of most Romantic composers was dominated by the lyrical spirit of the Lied rather than the dramatic spirit of the symphony, as exemplified in the later works of Mozart and Haydn and above all in Beethoven. Furthermore, a large number of leading composers in the nineteenth century were extraordinarily articulate and interested in literary expression, and many leading Romantic novelists and poets wrote about music with deep love and insight. The novelist E. T. A. Hoffmann was a successful composer of operas; Weber, Schumann, and Berlioz wrote distinguished essays on music; Wagner was a poet, essayist, and philosopher (of sorts) as well as a composer.

Music and words

The conflict between the ideal of pure instrumental music as the supremely Romantic mode of expression on the one hand, and the strong literary orientation of nineteenth-century music on the other, was resolved in the conception of *program music*. Program music, as the nineteenth century used the term, was instrumental music associated with poetic, descriptive, or even narrative subject matter—not by means of rhetorical-musical figures (as in the Baroque era) or by imitation of natural sounds and movements (as sometimes in the eighteenth century), but by means of imaginative suggestion. Program music aimed to absorb and transmute the imagined subject, taking it wholly into the music in such a way that the resulting composition, while it includes the "program," nevertheless transcends it and is in a certain sense independent of it. Instrumental music thus becomes a vehicle for the utterance of thoughts which, though they may be hinted in words, are ultimately beyond the power of words to express. A second way in which the Romantics reconciled music with words is reflected in the importance they placed on the instrumental accompaniment of vocal music, from the *Lieder* of Schubert to the symphonic orchestra that enfolds the voices in Wagner's music dramas.

The starting point for nineteenth-century program music was Beethoven's *Pastoral* Symphony. The composers most explicitly committed to program music up to the middle of the century were Mendelssohn, Schumann, Berlioz, and Liszt, while its chief representatives at the end of the century were Debussy and Richard Strauss. But practically every composer of the era was, to a greater or lesser degree, writing program music, whether or not he publicly acknowledged it; and one reason why it is so easy for listeners to connect a scene or a story or a poem with a piece of Romantic music is that often the composer himself, perhaps unconsciously, was working from some such idea. Writers on music projected their own conceptions of the expressive function of music into the past, and read Romantic programs into the instrumental works not only of Beethoven but also of Mozart, Haydn, and Bach.

The crowd and the individual

Another area of conflict involved the relationship between the composer and his audience. The transition from relatively small, homogeneous, and cultured audiences for music to the huge, diverse, and relatively unprepared middle-class public of the nineteenth century had begun already a hundred years before. The disappearance of individual patronage and the accelerated growth of concert societies and musical festivals in the early part of the nineteenth century were signs of this continuing change. Composers, if they were to succeed, somehow had to reach the vast new audience; their struggle to be heard and understood had to occur in an incomparably larger arena than at any previous epoch in the history of music. Yet it is just this period more than any other that offers us the phenomenon of the unsociable artist, one who feels himself to be separate from his fellow-men and who is driven by isolation to seek inspiration within himself. These musicians did not compose, as did their eighteenth-century forebears, for a patron or for a particular function, but for infinity, for posterity, for some imaginable ideal audience which, they hoped, would some day understand and appreciate them; either that, or they wrote for a little circle of kindred spirits, confessing to them those inmost feelings considered too fragile and precious to be set before the crude public of the concert halls. This is the basis for the contrast, so typical of the time, between the grandiose creations of Meyerbeer, Berlioz, Wagner, Strauss, or Mahler on the one hand and the intimate lyrical effusions of Schumann's *Lieder* or Schubert's, Mendelssohn's, and Chopin's short piano pieces on the other.

The gulf between the mass audience and the lonely composer could not always be bridged. Facile musicians with a knack for pleasing the public turned out reams of trivial or bombastic salon music, but conscientious artists despised such vulgarity. Partly in sheer self-defense, as compensation, they were driven to the conception of the composer as an exalted combination of priest and poet, one to whom it was given to reveal to mankind the deeper meaning of life through the divine medium of music. The artist was a "genius" who wrote under "inspiration," a prophet even though his message might be rejected.

In the third part of Novalis's novel *Heinrich von Ofterdingen* (1802), there is a story that illustrates the Romantic ideal of the artist: a humble young woodsman secretly weds a princess, and a child is born to them. They come with trepidation to seek reconciliation with the king, the princess' father. The king receives them and their child with joy, amid the approving shouts of the populace. Undoubtedly the climax of this tale represents allegorically the public acceptance and triumph which the Romantic artist always longed for but did not always obtain. If his will and energy were sufficient he might come to dominate the popular imagination, as Beethoven had done, as Berlioz struggled to do, and as Liszt and Wagner did on an unprecedented scale. It is remarkable that the great virtuoso performers of the nineteenth century were dominating, heroic individuals—for example, Paganini and Liszt. They were instrumental soloists, as opposed to the typical eighteenth-century virtuoso, the operatic singer, who was the most conspicuous member of a group, and the typical twentieth-century virtuoso, the conductor, who is the dictator of a group. This accent on the individual is present everywhere in Romanticism: the best vocal music of the century is for solo voice, not for chorus. This conception of the composer as a prophet, a lone, heroic figure struggling against a hostile environment, also served to lend the music a quality of excitement, an emotional tension by means of which the audience was stimulated and uplifted.

A related contrast in the classic-romantic period was that between professional and amateur performers. The distinction between experts (the *Kenner*) and amateurs (the *Liebhaber*), already marked in the eighteenth century, grew sharper as professional standards of performance improved. At one extreme was the great spell-binding virtuoso before his rapt audience in the concert hall; at the other, the neighborhood instrumental or vocal ensemble or the family gathered around the parlor piano to sing favorite airs and hymns. Family music-making, almost unknown now since the coming of the phonograph and television, was a constant, if unpublicized feature of the nineteenth- and early twentieth-century musical background.

Professional and amateur music-making

Partly because of the industrial revolution, the population of Europe increased tremendously during the nineteenth century. Most of the increase occurred in cities: the populations of both London and Paris quadrupled between 1800 and 1880. Consequently, the majority of people, including the majority of musicians, no longer lived in a community, a court or town, where everybody knew everybody else and the open countryside was never very far away; instead, they were lost in the huge impersonal huddle of a modern city.

Man and nature

But the more man's daily life became separated from Nature, the more he became enamoured of Nature. From Rousseau onward, Nature was idealized, and increasingly so in its wilder and more picturesque aspects. The nineteenth century was an age of landscape painting. The musical landscapes of Haydn's *Seasons* and Beethoven's *Pastoral* Symphony were succeeded by Mendelssohn's overtures, Schumann's *Spring* and *Rhenish* Symphonies, the symphonic poems of Berlioz and Liszt, and the operas of Weber and Wagner. However, for the Romantic composer Nature was not merely a subject to be depicted. A kinship was felt between the inner life of the artist and the life of Nature, so that the latter became not only a refuge but also a source of strength, inspiration, and revelation. This mystic sense of kinship with Nature, counterbalancing the artificiality of city existence, is as prevalent in the music of the nineteenth century as it is in the contemporary literature and art.

Science and the irrational

The nineteenth century saw a rapid expansion in exact knowledge and scientific method. Simultaneously, as though in reaction, the music of that period is constantly thrusting beyond the borders of the rational into the unconscious and the supernatural. It takes its subject material from the dream (the individual unconscious), as in Berlioz's *Symphonie fantastique,* or from the myth (the collective unconscious), as in Wagner's music dramas. Even Nature itself is haunted in the Romantic imagination by spirits and is fraught with mysterious significances. The effort to find a musical language capable of expressing these new and strange ideas led to extensions of harmony, melody, and orchestral color.

Materialism and idealism

The nineteenth century was in the main a secular and materialistic age, though there was an important movement of revival in the Catholic church with musical results which we shall examine later. But the essential Romantic spirit, once again in conflict with an important trend of its time, was both idealistic and nonchurchly. The most characteristic nineteenth-century musical settings of liturgical texts were, like Beethoven's *Missa solemnis,* too personal and too big for ordinary church use: the gigantic *Requiem* and the *Te Deum* of Berlioz and the *Requiem* of Verdi. The Romantic composers also gave expression to generalized religious aspiration in nonliturgical settings, such as the *German Requiem* of Brahms, Wagner's *Parsifal,* and Mahler's Eighth Symphony. Furthermore, a great deal of Romantic music is infused with a kind of idealistic longing that might be called "religious" in a vague pantheistic sense.

Nationalism and internationalism

Another area of conflict in the nineteenth century was political: it was the conflict between the growth of nationalism and the beginning of supranational socialist movements outlined by the *Communist Manifesto* of Marx and Engels (1848), and Marx's *Capital* (1867). Nationalism was an important influence in Romantic music. Differences between national musical styles were accentuated and folk song came to be venerated as the spontaneous expression of the national soul. Musical Romanticism flourished especially in Germany, not only because the Romantic temper was congenial to German ways of thinking, but also because in that country national sentiment, being for a long time suppressed politically, had to find vent in music and other forms of art. Supplementary to the concentration on national music was a delight in exoticism, the sympathetic use of foreign idioms for picturesque color. The music of the great Romantic composers was not, of course, limited to any one country; what it had to say was addressed to all humanity. But its idioms were national as compared with the eighteenth-century ideal of a cosmopolitan musical language in which national peculiarities were minimized.

The Romantic movement had from the beginning a revolutionary tinge, with a corresponding emphasis on the virtue of originality in art. Romanticism was seen as a revolt against the limitations of Classicism, although at the same time music was regarded as exemplifying the prevalent conception that the nineteenth century was an era of progress and evolution.

Tradition and revolution

Composers up to the end of the eighteenth century had written for their own time, for the present; by and large they were neither much interested in the past nor much concerned about the future. But the Romantic composers, feeling the present unsympathetic, took an appeal to the judgment of posterity; it is not altogether coincidence that two of Wagner's essays on music were entitled *Art and Revolution* (1849) and *The Art-Work of the Future* (1850). With respect to the immediate past, however, the revolutionary aspect was overshadowed by the conception of Romanticism as the fulfillment of Classicism. The *empfindsamer Stil* and *Sturm und Drang* tendencies of the 1770s, which from our vantage point we can see as early manifestations of the Romantic movement, were not much regarded; but Beethoven and, to some extent, Mozart also were viewed by the Romantic composers as having marked out the path which they themselves were to follow. Thus arose the concept of music as an art that had a history—moreover, a history which was to be interpreted, in accord with the dominant philosophical ideas of the time, as a process of evolution.

The past was manifested by the persistence of the Classical tradition. Composers still wrote in the Classical forms of sonata, symphony, and string quartet; the Classical system of harmony was still the basis of their music. Moreover, not all composers went the whole way in adopting Romantic innovations; there were conservatives and radicals within the general movement. Mendelssohn, Brahms, and Bruckner were conservative; Berlioz, Liszt, and Wagner were more radical. Conservative and radical tendencies existed side by side in Schumann.

One aspect of the Romantic movement was its preoccupation with music of the distant as well as of the immediate past. The music histories of Burney and Hawkins in the eighteenth century, and the publication of sacred works by Byrd, Gibbons, Purcell, and other composers in the three volumes of *Cathedral Music* edited by William Boyce (1760, 1768, 1778), show that this tendency, like others in Romanticism, had important English antecedents. Bach and Palestrina were particularly congenial to the Romantics. Bach's *Passion According to St. Matthew* was revived in a performance at Berlin under Mendelssohn's direction in 1829; this performance was one conspicuous example of a general interest in Bach's music, which led in 1850 to the beginning of the publication of the first complete edition of his works. A similar edition of Palestrina's works was begun in 1862. The rise of historical musicology in the nineteenth century was another outgrowth of the Romantic interest in the music of former ages, while the discoveries of musicologists further stimulated such interest. The Romantics, of course, romanticized history; they heard in the music of Bach, Palestrina, and other older composers what it suited them to hear, and adopted such things as they wanted for their own purposes. It was not the least of the many contradictions within the movement that its subjectively motivated reach into the past should have opened the way to the objective discipline of historical research in music.

Sources and Characteristics of the Romantic Style

The meaning of *Romantic* as applied to the music of the nineteenth century is not to be found in any single statement. Romanticism was a style, or rather a complex of many individual styles having elements in common, developed by musicians who had to resolve certain basic conflicts between their art and their environment. Similar conflicts may have existed in earlier periods, but now for the first time composers were forced publicly and continuously to come to grips with them. The nature of the issues, the urgency of the challenge, and the character of the response were peculiar to the nineteenth century.

Haydn's *Creation* and *Seasons*, Mozart's *Don Giovanni* and *Magic Flute,* and Beethoven's Fifth and Ninth Symphonies were the immediate sources of musical Romanticism. From Haydn came its pleasure in depicting the world of nature, from Mozart its preoccupation with the inner life of the individual human being, and from Beethoven its Faustian aspirations and storming assaults on the Ideal.

A few general observations may be made about the technical differences between Romantic and Classical music. On the whole, Romantic rhythms are less vital and less varied than those of the earlier period; interest is directed rather to lyrical melody. Long sections, even entire movements (as for example Chopin's études or the finale of Schumann's *Symphonic Études*) may continue in one unbroken rhythmic pattern, with the monotony and—when successful—the cumulative effect of an incantation. Highly developed Classical forms, like the symphony or sonata, are handled less satisfactorily by the Romantics. A piano sonata by Chopin or Schumann, for example, is like a novel by Tieck or Novalis—a series of picturesque episodes without any strong bond of formal unity within the work. Quite often, however, a Romantic symphony or oratorio aimed at achieving a new kind of unity by means of using the same themes—identical or transformed—in different movements. The Romantic treatment of shorter forms is usually quite simple and clear.

Romantic and Classical music

The most remarkable achievements of the nineteenth century lay in the development of harmonic technique and instrumental color. Chromatic harmonies, chromatic voice leading, distant modulations, tonal ambiguity, complex chords, freer use of nonharmonic tones, and a growing tendency to avoid distinct cadences, all operated to extend and eventually to blur the outlines of tonality. Romantic harmony as a means of expression went hand in hand with an ever-expanding palette of color. New sonorities were discovered in piano music; new instruments were added to the orchestra, and older instruments were redesigned to be more sonorous and more flexible; above all, new combinations of instruments in the ensemble were invented to produce new color effects. A sign of the times was the appearance in 1844 of Berlioz's *Treatise on Instrumentation and Orchestration*, the first textbook of any importance on this subject that had ever been published. Harmony and color were the principal means whereby the nineteenth-century composers sought to express in music the Romantic ideals of remoteness, ardor, and boundless longing.

The Lied

Romantic traits had begun to appear in the German Lied by the end of the eighteenth century. An important composer of that time was Johann Rudolf Zumsteeg (1760–1802), who excelled in a new type of song, the *ballad*. This poetic genre was cultivated in Germany in imitation of the popular ballads of England and Scotland, and rose quickly to favor after the publication of G. A. Bürger's *Leonore* in 1774. One of the most prolific composers of ballads

The ballad

was Carl Loewe (1796–1869). Most ballads were fairly long poems, alternating narrative and dialogue in a tale replete with romantic adventures and supernatural incidents; at the same time, the poets sought to preserve something of the forthright quality of the old folk ballads on which they were modeled (as did Coleridge, for example, in his *Ancient Mariner*).

Composers eagerly seized on a form so well adapted for musical setting. Obviously, Romantic ballads demanded a quite different kind of musical treatment from the short, idyllic, strophic Lied of the eighteenth century. Their greater length necessitated greater variety of themes and textures, and this in turn required some means of imposing unity on the whole; moreover, the contrasts of mood and the movement of the story had to be captured and enhanced by the music. The influence of the ballad thus worked to expand the concept of the Lied, both in its form and in the range and force of its emotional content. The piano part rose from being simply an accompaniment to the position of being a partner with the voice, sharing equally in the task of supporting, illustrating, and intensifying the meaning of the poetry. By the early nineteenth century the Lied had become a vehicle fit for the utmost powers of any composer.

Franz Schubert

Franz Peter Schubert (1797–1828) came of a humble family. His father, a pious, strict, but kindly and honorable man, was a schoolmaster in Vienna. The boy's formal training in music theory was not systematic, but his environment, both at home and in school, was saturated with music-making. Although educated to follow his father's profession, his heart was elsewhere, and after three years of school teaching (1814–17) he retired to devote himself entirely to composition. His pitifully short life, like Mozart's, illustrates the

Moritz von Schwind: A Schubert evening at the home of Joseph von Spaun. *Schubert is at the piano accompanying the singer Vogl.*

tragedy of genius overwhelmed by the petty necessities and annoyances of everyday existence. Without wide public recognition, sustained only by the love of a few friends, constantly struggling against illness and poverty, he composed ceaselessly. "I work every morning," he said. "When I have finished one piece I begin another." In the year 1815 alone he wrote one hundred and forty-four songs. He died at the age of thirty-one, and on his tombstone was inscribed "Music has here buried a rich treasure but still fairer hopes." One may also think of William Drummond's words: "Nor is that musician most praiseworthy who hath longest played, but he in measured accents who hath made sweetest melody."

Schubert's works include nine symphonies, 22 piano sonatas and a multitude of short piano pieces for two and four hands, about 35 chamber compositions, six Masses, 17 operatic works, and over 600 *Lieder*. The songs reveal Schubert's supreme gift for making beautiful melodies, a power which few even of the greatest composers have possessed so fully. Many of his melodies have the simple artless quality of folk song (*Heidenröslein, Der Lindenbaum, Wohin?, Die Forelle*); others are suffused with an indescribable romantic sweetness and melancholy (*Am Meer, Der Wanderer, Du bist die Ruh'*); still others are declamatory, intense, and dramatic (*Aufenthalt, Der Atlas, Die junge Nonne, An Schwager Kronos*); in short, there is no mood or nuance of Romantic feeling but finds spontaneous and perfect expression in Schubert's melody. This wonderful melodic stream flows as purely and as copiously in the instrumental works as in the songs.

Schubert's Lieder

Along with melody went a sensitive feeling for harmonic color. Schubert's modulations, often far-flung and complex, sometimes embodying long passages in which the tonality is kept in suspense, powerfully underline the dramatic qualities of a song text. Striking examples of harmonic boldness may be found in *Gruppe aus dem Tartarus* and *Das Heimweh;* the latter also illustrates one of Schubert's favorite devices, that of hovering between the major and minor forms of the triad (*Ständchen* and *Auf dem Wasser zu Singen* also illustrate this trait). Masterly use of chromatic coloring within a prevailing diatonic sound is another characteristic of Schubert's harmony (*Am Meer, Lob der Thränen*). His modulations tend characteristically to move from the tonic toward flat keys, and the mediant or submediant is a favorite relationship. These are but a few of the procedures and a few instances, out of hundreds that might be cited both from the songs and the instrumental works, of the inexhaustible harmonic richness of Schubert's music.

Equally diverse and ingenious are the piano accompaniments in Schubert's *Lieder*. Very often the piano figuration is suggested by some pictorial image of the text (as in *Wohin?* or *Auf dem Wasser zu Singen*). Such pictorial features are never merely imitative, but are designed, in the best Romantic fashion, to contribute toward the mood of the song. Thus the accompaniment of *Gretchen am Spinnrad*—one of the earliest (1814) and best of the *Lieder*—suggests not only the whirr of the spinning wheel but also the agitation of Gretchen's thoughts as she sings of her lover. The pounding octave triplets of *Erlkönig* depict at the same time the galloping of the horse and the frantic anxiety of the father as he rides "through night and storm" with his frightened child clasped in his arms. This song, composed in 1815, is one of Schubert's relatively few ballads. Goethe's poem is more compact than the usual early Romantic ballad, and is all the more effective because of the speed of its action. Schubert has characterized in an unforgettable manner the three actors in the drama—the father, the wily Erlking, and the terrified child with his cries rising a tone higher at each repetition; the cessation of movement and the final line in recitative make a superbly dramatic close. An entirely different style of accompaniment is found in another of Schubert's Lieder, *Der Doppelgänger:* here are only long, somber chords, with a recurrent sinister melodic motif in low triple octaves, below a declamatory voice part which rises to an awesome climax before sinking in a final despairing phrase. Nothing could better suggest the ghostly horror of the scene than the heavy, obsessive dark chords, revolving fatally about the tonic of B minor except for one brief, lurid flash of D♯ minor near the end.

Many of Schubert's *Lieder* are in strophic form, with either literal repetition of the music for each stanza (*Litanei*) or repetition with slight variation (*Du bist die Ruh'*). Others, particularly those on longer texts, alternate between declamatory and arioso style, the whole unified by recurring themes and evidencing a carefully planned scheme of tonalities (*Fahrt zum Hades, Der Wanderer*). The form, however complex, is always suited to both poetic and musical requirements. Schubert drew on the works of many different poets for his texts; from Goethe alone he took fifty-nine poems, and he wrote five different solo settings for *Nur wer die Sehnsucht kennt* from *Wilhelm Meister*. (It is interesting, incidentally, to compare Schubert's settings of these verses with those by Beethoven, Schumann, Tchaikovsky, and Hugo Wolf—the most important of some 80 composers who wrote music for these words in the nineteenth century.) Some of the finest of Schubert's *Lieder* are found in the two cycles on poems by Wilhelm Müller, *Die schöne Müllerin* (1823) and *Winterreise* (1827). The *Schwanengesang* (1828), not intended as a cycle but published as such posthumously, includes six songs on poems by Heinrich Heine. On the whole, Schubert's texts are excellent material for musical treatment, though naturally uneven in literary quality; but his music is able to glorify even commonplace poetry.

Lieder were written by most of the Romantic composers, but the first important successor of Schubert in this field was Robert Schumann (1810–56). Schubert, though his music is Romantic in its lyrical quality and harmonic color, nevertheless always maintained a certain Classical serenity and poise. With Schumann we are in the full restless tide of Romanticism. His first collection of songs appeared in 1840, all his previously published works having been for piano. Although his melodic lines are warm and expressive, Schumann's *Lieder* lack the spontaneous charm of Schubert's; the accompaniments, however, are of unusual interest. Indeed, many of Schumann's *Lieder* are really duets for voice and piano. The musical phrase may be divided between the two (as in *Der Nussbaum*); the piano may, as it were, comment or reflect on what the voice has sung (as in *Liebeslied,* Op. 51, No. 5). The preluding piano phrases, the interludes, and especially the sometimes quite extended postludes (as in the *Dichterliebe* cycle) often seem to sum up in concentrated and poignant form the essence of an entire song.

Schumann's Lieder

An excellent example of perfect union between voice and piano is found in the beautiful *Mondnacht* (1840), on words by J. von Eichendorff, one of Schumann's favorite poets. With simpler accompaniment, but equally permeated with the quintessence of Romantic feeling and harmony, is the setting of Heine's *Die Lotosblume* (1840). Schumann's most famous song of the ballad type is *Die beiden Grenadiere* (1840), which incorporates the melody of *La Marseillaise* at the climax. Some of the finest of Schumann's *Lieder* are the love songs; in 1840, the year of his long-delayed marriage to his beloved Clara Wieck, he produced over one hundred *Lieder,* including the two cycles *Dichterliebe* (Heine) and *Frauenliebe und Leben* (A. von Chamisso). In these works the Romantic genius of Schumann appears to perfection.

Lesser composers of *Lieder* were Peter Cornelius (1824–74) and Robert Franz (1815–92), whose well-known *Widmung* is typical of the simplicity and melodic grace of his style. *Lieder* constitute a relatively unimportant part of the work of Mendelssohn. Liszt's songs, though not so widely known as his orchestral and pianoforte compositions, include some beautiful settings of poems by Heinrich Heine, especially a very dramatic treatment of *Die Lorelei* (revised version, 1856).

The principal successor to Schumann, however, was Johannes Brahms (1833–97), for whom the Lied was a congenial medium and whose works in this form (over 260 altogether) come from every period of his life. He made arrangements of many German folk songs, including a set of 14 published in 1858 (dedicated to the children of Robert and Clara Schumann) and 49 published in 1894. The simplicity of these songs, the care taken never to detract from the tune by intricate or harmonically inappropriate accompaniment, is all the more striking in a composer who was a master, when occasion demanded, of most sophisticated musical constructions. Brahms

Brahms's Lieder

declared that his ideal was the folk song, and many of his own songs, as for example the familiar *Wiegenlied,* are exactly in this style. A similar folk-like, popular appeal is evident in the two sets of *Liebeslieder* waltzes for quartet of solo voices (optional, in the first set) with four-hand piano accompaniment.

Schubert was Brahms's model in song writing, and a considerable proportion of his *Lieder* are, like Schubert's, in a more or less freely treated strophic form. Among them are *Vergebliches Ständchen,* one of the few Brahms songs of a humorous and outrightly cheerful nature (*Tambourliedchen* and *Der Gang zum Liebchen* are also cheerful songs). For the most part, however, Brahms's tone is serious. His music is Romantic in harmony and texture, but it has not the soaring, ardent, impulsive character of Schumann's; restraint, a certain classic gravity, an introspective, resigned, elegiac mood are predominant. This quality is well exemplified by one of Brahms's best known *Lieder,* the *Sapphische Ode,* which incidentally illustrates a frequently recurring mannerism of this composer, namely the building of a melodic line on or around notes of the triad, sometimes with the omission of the root (see Example XVI–1). Within the fundamentally reflective style of Brahms there is room for the expression of passion, expression all the more effective because it avoids excess and is felt to be always under control. Among all German *Lieder* there are no finer love songs than some of the Romances of the *Magelone* cycle (Op. 33) on poems by Ludwig Tieck, or such songs as *Wie bist du meine Königin* and *Meine Liebe ist grün.*

EXAMPLE XVI–1   Melodic Figures, Brahms

The essential elements of Brahms's *Lieder* are the melody and bass, the tonal plan and form. The accompaniments are rarely pictorial, and there are not many of the instrumental preludes and postludes which are so important in Schumann's songs. Yet the piano parts are marvelously varied in texture, frequently using extended arpeggio figuration (*O wüsst' ich doch den Weg zurück*) and syncopated rhythms. Perhaps the greatest—certainly the most typically Brahmsian—of the *Lieder* are those concerned with reflections on death. *Feldeinsamkeit, Immer leiser wird mein Schlummer, Auf dem Kirchhofe,* and *Der Tod, das ist die kühle Nacht* are examples, as well as the *Vier ernste Gesänge,* the "four serious songs" (Op. 121, 1896) on Biblical texts, the supreme achievement of Brahms's last years.

Choral Music

In considering the choral music of the nineteenth century, it is necessary to make a distinction between works in which the chorus is used as a part of a larger apparatus and those in which the choral writing is intended to be a principal focus of interest. To the former category belong the numerous and extensive choruses in operas, choral movements in symphonies, and some of the big choral-or-chestral works of Berlioz and Liszt. It is significant that the two composers of the Romantic period who best understood how to write idiomatically for chorus—Mendelssohn and Brahms—were precisely the two who were most strongly resistant to the extreme tendencies of Romanticism. The chorus is less suited to express typically Romantic sentiments than the symphony orchestra, and indeed, many nineteenth-century composers treated the chorus primarily as a division of the orchestra, to supply picturesque touches and supplementary colors.

Nineteenth-century choral music is of three main classes: (1) part songs (that is, songs in homophonic style for a small vocal ensemble, with the melody in the topmost voice) or other short choral pieces, usually on secular words, to be sung either *a cappella* or with accompaniment of piano or organ; (2) music on liturgical texts or intended for use in church services; (3) works for chorus (often with one or more solo vocalists) and orchestra, on texts of dramatic or narrative-dramatic character, but intended for concert rather than stage performance. The nomenclature within this third class is not definitely established: a long, elaborate composition on a sacred or otherwise edifying subject is generally styled an oratorio; works that are shorter or less dramatic or on a secular subject are sometimes called (whether by the composer, the publisher, or the historian) cantatas—but there is no consistent usage of this term.

The composition of part songs, which had begun before the end of the eighteenth century, received impetus in the Romantic period from the rise of national sentiment and the awakening of interest in folk song. The example of the popular festivals in France of the Revolutionary period, along with the multiplication of singing societies and the institution of music festivals in France and Germany during the first half of the nineteenth century were a further stimulus to choral composition. Weber's settings for men's voices (1814) of stanzas from Körner's *Leier und Schwert (The Lyre and*

Part songs and cantatas

the Sword) were among the first of thousands of similar patriotic effusions. Schubert, Mendelssohn, Schumann, Gounod, Liszt, and practically every other composer in Europe produced part songs and choruses for men's, women's, or mixed voices, accompanied and unaccompanied, on patriotic, sentimental, convivial, and every other imaginable kind of verse. This music served its purpose and has been for the most part forgotten. Of more permanent interest are some of the Romantic cantatas, such as Mendelssohn's *Erste Walpurgisnacht* (1832, revised 1843) and Schumann's *Paradise and the Peri* (1843) and *Scenes from Goethe's "Faust"* (1844–53). The master in this field was Johannes Brahms, whose works include many short, usually unaccompanied songs for women's, men's, or mixed voices, as well as a number of larger compositions for chorus with orchestra. Among these are some of the most beautiful choral works, not only of the nineteenth century but of all time—the *Rhapsody* for alto solo and men's chorus (1870), the *Schicksalslied* (*Song of Fate,* 1871) and *Nänie* (song of lamentation on verses by Schiller, 1881) for mixed chorus, and *Gesang der Parzen* (*Song of the Parcae, i.e.,* the Fates; 1883), for six-part mixed chorus.

Church music

The nineteenth century was not one of the great ages of church music. Toward the middle of the century an agitation for musical reform—later called the Cecilian movement after St. Cecelia, the patron saint of music—arose within the Roman Catholic Church. The Cecilian movement was in part stimulated by Romantic interest in music of the past, and it worked to some effect for a revival of the supposed a cappella style of the sixteenth century and the restoration of Gregorian Chant to its pristine form; but it stimulated little significant new music from the composers who dedicated themselves to these ideals. The best Catholic church music in the early part of the century came from Luigi Cherubini at Paris and Franz Schubert at Vienna. Schubert's Masses in A♭ and E♭ (D. 678, 950) are among the finest settings of this text in the nineteenth century. On the Protestant and Anglican side, the psalms of Mendelssohn and the anthems of Samuel Sebastian Wesley (1810–76) may be mentioned. In Russia, Dimitri Bortniansky (1751–1825), director of the Imperial Chapel at St. Petersburg after 1796, was the first of a long line of composers who in the nineteenth century developed a new style of church music; this derived its inspiration from the modal chants of the Orthodox liturgy, had a free rhythm, and used a wide range of unaccompanied voices in single or double choruses of four to eight or more parts, with effective octave doublings in a rich and solemn texture. The Masses and other sacred music of the Parisian Charles Gounod (1818–93) were highly regarded in their time, but his peculiar blend of piety and mild Romanticism had the misfortune to be so assiduously (though unintentionally) parodied by later composers that it has lost whatever validity it may have possessed. Gounod's most famous Mass, the *St. Cecilia* (1885) has been condemned also on liturgical grounds because of the insertion of words not normally part of the sung text in the last movement.

A dazzling conflagration was set off by the collision of Romantic musical energy with sacred themes in the *Grande Messe des Morts* (*Requiem*) and the Te Deum of Hector Berlioz (1803–69). These are magnificent religious works, but they are not music for the church service. Their nature is wholly original and Romantic. They are dramatic symphonies for orchestra and voices which use poetically inspiring texts that happen to be liturgical. The tradition to which they belong is not ecclesiastical but secular and patriotic; their historical forebears are the great musical festivals of the French Revolution. The *Requiem* was first performed in 1837, the Te Deum in 1855. Both works are of vast dimensions—vast not only in length and number of performers, but in grandeur of conception and brilliance of execution. Too much has been said about the orchestra of one hundred and forty players, the four brass choirs, the four tam-tams, ten pairs of cymbals, and sixteen kettledrums that Berlioz requires for the *Tuba mirum* chorus of the *Requiem*—and too little about the superb musical effect he obtains in the comparatively few places where all these are sounding. Berlioz's orchestra, like the Emperor Gordianus's twenty-two concubines,[1] is "designed for use rather than ostentation." There are a hundred other strokes of genius in the orchestration of the *Requiem:* one may take for examples the chords for flutes and trombones alternating with men's chorus in the *Hostias,* and the further development of this kind of sonority at the beginning of the Agnus Dei; the stark lines of the English horns, bassoons, and low strings in combination with unison tenor voices in the *Quid sum miser;* or the return of the wonderful long tenor melody of the Sanctus, where the five-measure responsive phrases of soloist and chorus are punctuated by *pianissimo* strokes of the bass drum and cymbals. The Te Deum is less replete with striking orchestral experiments than the *Requiem,* but it is in a more mature style, and its final number (*Judex crederis*) is certainly one of the most thrilling movements ever written for chorus and orchestra.

What Berlioz did outside the church Franz Liszt (1811–86) tried to do within it. His Festival Mass for the consecration of the cathedral at Gran (Esztergom), Hungary, in 1855, as well as his Mass for the coronation of the King of Hungary in 1867, are on a scale and in a style corresponding to Liszt's own ideal of Romantic sacred music, which he expressed thus in 1834:

Other music on liturgical texts

> For want of a better term we may call the new music Humanitarian.
> It must be devotional, strong, and drastic, uniting on a colossal scale

[1] E. Gibbon, *The Decline and Fall of the Roman Empire,* Book I, Ch. VII.

the theatre and the church, at once dramatic and sacred, splendid and simple, ceremonial and serious, fiery and free, stormy and calm, translucent and emotional.[2]

This duality of aim is never quite welded into unity of style in Liszt's church music. He comes closest in some shorter works, such as his setting of Psalm XIII (*How long wilt thou forget me, O Lord?*) for tenor solo, chorus, and orchestra (1855) and—in a different way, with many passages of "experimental" harmony—in the *Via Crucis (Stations of the Cross)*, a large work for soloists, chorus, and organ, completed in 1879 but not published or publicly performed during Liszt's lifetime.

Two Italian composers, Gioacchino Rossini (1792–1868) and Giuseppe Verdi (1813–1901), made important contributions to church music in the nineteenth century. It is fashionable nowadays to stigmatize Rossini's *Stabat Mater* (1832, 1841) as operatic and therefore meretricious. It is true that the theatrical style in which this work is written was expressly forbidden in 1903 by the famous encyclical *Motu proprio* of Pope Pius X; but the standards there set forth would also exclude from church use the Masses of Haydn, Mozart, Beethoven, Schubert, and Bruckner, not to mention those of Berlioz, Liszt, and Verdi. Rossini's *Stabat Mater* is a serious and well-made composition, containing some excellent choral writing (especially in the opening and closing numbers) along with the objectionable operatic arias; but the style of these arias was not felt by either the composer or the public of his time to be flippant or inappropriate.

Verdi's *Requiem* (1874) was composed in memory of Alessandro Manzoni (1785–1873), author of *I promessi sposi,* the most famous Italian novel of the nineteenth century. The *Requiem* is an immense work, deeply moving, vividly dramatic, and at the same time thoroughly Catholic in spirit—unlike the *Requiem* of Berlioz, to which Verdi's is musically indebted in many respects.

The most important church composer of the later nineteenth century was Anton Bruckner (1824–96), whose choral and symphonic compositions are now at last beginning to be generally known outside the Germanic countries of Europe. A solitary, simple, profoundly religious soul, thoroughly schooled in counterpoint, organist of the Cathedral at Linz and from 1867 Court Organist at Vienna, Bruckner succeeded as no one before him in uniting the spiritual and technical resources of the nineteenth-century symphony with a reverent and liturgical approach to the sacred texts. His Masses and his symphonies have many qualities and even some musical themes in common.

The Mass in D minor was composed in 1864, that in F minor

---

2 Reprinted in Liszt, *Gesammelte Schriften*, Leipzig, 1881, II, 55–57.

(the larger of the two) in 1867; like all Bruckner's works, they were subjected to numerous revisions before being published. The influence of the Cecilian movement is apparent in some of Bruckner's motets, for example the strictly modal Gradual *Os justi* (1879) for unaccompanied chorus; a unique work of neo-medieval quality is the short Mass in E minor (1866; published 1890) for eight-part chorus and fifteen wind instruments (paired oboes, clarinets, bassoons, and trumpets, four horns, three trombones). The only church compositions of the late nineteenth century that can be compared with this Mass are Brahms's a cappella motets Opp. 74 and 110, which bear much the same relation to the Lutheran chorale that Bruckner's Masses do to Roman plainsong. The last of Bruckner's sacred compositions were the Te Deum in C major (1884) and Psalm CL (1892), both for soloists, chorus, organ, and full orchestra.

The Romantic oratorio, which flourished chiefly in the Protestant countries of England and Germany, developed along lines laid down in the eighteenth century. It may be defined as a drama, usually on a Biblical or other sacred subject; but as a drama free from the limitations of actual staging, it may have an epic and contemplative breadth that would not be possible in opera. Thus an oratorio can aspire to such themes as are treated in *The Last Judgment* (1826) by Ludwig Spohr (1784–1859), or in Liszt's *Christus* (1856), César Franck's *Beatitudes* (1879), or Gounod's *Redemption* (1882) and *Mors et vita* (*Death and Life;* 1885); both of these last were written for festival performances at Birmingham, England. More straightforwardly dramatic and pictorial are Mendelssohn's two popular oratorios *St. Paul* (1836) and *Elijah* (1846; also written for Birmingham) and Liszt's *Legend of St. Elizabeth* (1857–1862). Berlioz, as usual, stands apart from the rest with his *Enfance du Christ* (*The Childhood of Christ;* 1854), which is charming and picturesque rather than churchly.

The Romantic oratorio

The main strength of the nineteenth-century oratorio lay in its use of the chorus, and in this respect its descent from the form established by Handel is obvious. Mendelssohn, like Handel, could write choral music that "sounds"—for instance, the *Baal* choruses or the exquisite *He watching over Israel* from *Elijah.* Unfortunately most of his many imitators in England and his successors on the continent lacked this gift; or if they did possess it, they lacked Mendelssohn's imagination and good taste. The choral writing of Gounod, Liszt, and Franck is too uniformly homophonic to be always effective, and the only composers of first rank who equalled Mendelssohn in technique were Bruckner and Brahms.

Brahms's *German Requiem* (1868), for soprano and baritone solos, chorus, and orchestra, has for its text not the liturgical words of the Latin Requiem Mass but Biblical passages of meditation and solace in German, admirably chosen by the composer himself.

Brahms's music, like that of Schütz and Bach, is inspired by a deep concern with man's mortal lot and his hope of Heaven; but in the *German Requiem* these solemn thoughts are expressed with the peculiar intensity of Romantic feeling and clothed with the opulent colors of nineteenth-century harmony, regulated always by spacious formal architecture and guided by an unerring judgment for choral and orchestral effect.

XVII

‖‖

The Nineteenth Century: Instrumental Music

The Piano

The piano of the nineteenth century was quite a different instrument from the one for which Mozart had written. Reshaped, enlarged, and mechanically improved, it had been made capable of producing a full, firm tone at any dynamic level, of responding in every way to demands for both expressiveness and overwhelming virtuosity. The piano was the supreme Romantic instrument.

At the beginning of the century there were two distinct schools of piano playing: one emphasized clarity of texture and fluency of technique, and was represented by Mozart's talented pupil, Johann Nepomuk Hummel (1778–1837). The other school, to which Beethoven certainly belonged, emphasized fullness of tone, wide dynamic range, orchestral effects, dramatic execution, and abundance of technical power. Both styles are present in the works of the influential Italian composer, pianist, teacher—and, from 1799 in London, manufacturer of pianos—Muzio Clementi. Clementi's famous *Gradus ad Parnassum*, published 1817–26, consists of one hundred études "in strict and free style," that is, contrapuntal and virtuoso studies; his many sonatas were highly regarded by Beethoven.

As technical requirements became constantly more exacting and new styles of piano music developed in the nineteenth century, several important schools of playing and composition emerged.

Elegance and sentiment, brightness and clarity, were the goals of Clementi's pupil John Field (1782–1837), Hummel's pupil Adolf von Henselt (1814–99), and (for the most part) Chopin, whose early works in particular show the influence of Hummel's style. Other pianists aimed rather at impressiveness, audacity, and showmanship. The most conspicuous figures here were Friedrich Kalkbrenner (1785–1849), Sigismund Thalberg (1812–71), and the exotic American, Louis Moreau Gottschalk (1829–69)—all successful display pianists but, as composers, decidedly of second rank. A third group were the great virtuosos of the nineteenth century, outstanding for both technical and interpretive gifts, the "Titans of the piano": Franz Liszt, Anton Rubinstein (1829–94), Hans von Bülow (1830–94), and Karl Tausig (1841–71). Of these, Liszt and Rubinstein were also important as composers and von Bülow as a conductor.

The best composers and players of piano music in the nineteenth century made constant efforts to avoid the two extremes of sentimental salon music and pointless technical display. Among those whose style and technique were primarily determined by the musical substance, without superfluous ornament or bravura, were Schubert, Schumann, Clara Wieck Schumann (1819–96), and the composer-pianists Mendelssohn and Brahms.

Much Romantic piano music was written in dance forms or as short lyrical pieces. The latter had a great many names and nearly always were suggestive of some romantic mood or scene, which was sometimes specified in a title. The principal longer works were concertos, variations, fantasias, and sonatas, although many of the last may well be regarded as collections of mood pieces rather than as sonatas in the Classical sense.

Music for Piano

The early Romantic composers

The piano works of Carl Maria von Weber (1786–1826) include four sonatas, two concertos, and the better known *Concertstück* in F minor for piano and orchestra (1821), as well as many short pieces of which the *Invitation to the Dance* (1819) has been played by several generations of pianists. Weber's style is rhythmic, picturesque, full of contrast, and technically brilliant, but without profound content.

A distinctive school of pianists and composers flourished in Bohemia in the early nineteenth century. Jan Ladislav Dussek was known throughout Europe especially for his sonatas, some passages of which contain notable examples of early Romantic harmony. Jan Václav Tomášek (1774–1850) and his pupil Jan Hugo Voříšek (1791–1825) wrote short lyrical piano pieces with titles such as *eclogue, rhapsodie,* or *impromptu*. Voříšek is also remarkable for his

Piano Sonata Op. 20 and a fine Symphony in D major (1821); he lived in Vienna after 1813 and his music exerted considerable influence on Schubert.

Schubert wrote for the piano, in addition to innumerable marches, waltzes and other dances, fourteen short pieces to which he gave the modest titles of *impromptu* or *moment musical*. His most important larger works for the piano are the eleven completed sonatas and a Fantasia in C major (1822) on a theme adapted from his song, *Der Wanderer*. Important also are his many duets, particularly the *Grand Duo* (D. 812), the Fantasia in F minor (D. 940), and the Rondo in A major (D. 951). He wrote no concertos. The six *moments musicaux* (D. 789) and the eight Impromptus (D. 899, 935) are for the piano what his *Lieder* are for the voice. Abounding in Schubertian melodies and harmonies, perfect in form and detail, each one quite distinctive in mood, these works became the model for every subsequent Romantic composer of brief, unpretentious, intimate piano pieces. The *Wanderer* fantasia (D. 760) stands almost alone among Schubert's piano compositions in making considerable demands on the player's technique. It is in four movements like a sonata; the movements are linked together and the whole is centered around the Adagio and Variations, the theme of which also appears, variously transformed, in the other three movements of the work.

Franz Schubert

In his sonatas Schubert seems to have been influenced more by Haydn and Mozart than by Beethoven. Their external form never departs from the standard Classical patterns, but their atmosphere is more lyric than dramatic; instead of concentrated thematic development or surging Romantic emotions Schubert gives us expansive melodies and shimmering harmonic progressions. Some of the slow movements might well have been published as impromptus or *moments musicaux*—for example, those of the sonatas in B major Op. 147 (D. 575) and A major Op. 120 (D. 664). The three sonatas of 1825–26, in A minor, D major, and G major (Opp. 42, 53 and 78 = D. 845, 850, 894), are on a bigger scale than the earlier ones, but not radically different in character; Schumann wrote "we must call all three of these sonatas of Schubert 'masterly,' but the third seems to us his most perfect one, both in form and spirit."

In his last three piano sonatas of 1828 Schubert was obviously conscious of Beethoven, as witness the stormy first movement of the Sonata in C minor (D. 958) and the opening of the finale of the Sonata in B♭ (D. 960), which begins like the finale of Beethoven's Quartet Op. 130. But these are superficial similarities; Schubert is nowhere more independent, more the incomparable lyric master, than in these sonatas, and above all in the last one (B♭), which is undoubtedly his greatest work for the piano. A long singing melody begins the first movement; hovering modulations are featured in the subsidiary theme section and the development; the sonorities are perfectly spaced throughout. The slow movement is in C♯ minor (the enharmonic lowered mediant key), with a middle section in A major; the delicately varied ostinato rhythm of this movement is typical of Schubert, as are also the expressive harmonic suspensions and the unexpected shifts between major and minor in the coda.

Felix Mendelssohn-Bartholdy (1809–47) was himself a virtuoso pianist. His piano music requires a fluent technique, but in general the style is elegant and sensitive, not given to violence or excess bravura. Mendelssohn's musical ancestors are Mozart and Domenico Scarlatti. His larger compositions for piano comprise two concertos, one of which, the Concerto in G minor (1831), was long a favorite with pianists, three sonatas, preludes and fugues, variations, and fantasias. The preludes and fugues are one evidence of Mendelssohn's interest in the music of J. S. Bach.

Felix Mendelssohn-Bartholdy

Mendelssohn's finest large work for piano is the *Variations sérieuses* in D minor, Op. 54 (1841). A certain elfin lightness and clarity in scherzo-like movements, a quality unique in Mendelssohn's music, is evident in the familiar *Andante and Rondo Capriccioso,* Op. 14, which was probably written at the age of fifteen; in similar vein but more brilliant is the *Capriccio* in F♯ minor, Op. 5 (1825). The most popular piano works of Mendelssohn were the 48 short pieces issued at intervals in six books under the collective title *Songs without Words* (the names now attached to the separate pieces were for the most part supplied by publishers). The title itself is typical of the Romantic period. Here, along with a few tunes that now seem faded and sentimental, are many distinguished examples of the Romantic short piano piece and of Mendelssohn at his best: the *Gondola Song* in A minor (Op. 62, No. 5), the delightful little *Presto* in C major known as the *Spinning Song* (Op. 67, No. 4), the *Duetto* in A♭ (Op. 38, No. 6), or the tenderly melancholy B-minor melody of Op. 67, No. 5. Mendelssohn's harmony has few of the delightful surprises that one encounters in Schubert, nor do his melodies, rhythms, and forms introduce many unexpected features. His music, like his life, flowed serenely and harmoniously; it is essentially Classical in outline, imbued with Romantic color and sentiment but never more than lightly touched with Romantic pathos or passion.

Mendelssohn's three preludes and fugues and six sonatas for organ are among the few distinguished contributions of the Romantic period to the literature of that instrument. Most of the movements of the sonatas were first written as separate Voluntaries and only later brought into their present arrangement. Notable features in the sonatas are the frequent fugal writing and the use of Lutheran chorale melodies, particularly in the first movement of the Third Sonata and the first two movements of the Sixth Sonata.

Robert Schumann, after University studies in law, devoted himself with enthusiasm to becoming a concert pianist. An injury to his right hand cut short this career; he then turned his energies wholly to composition and to work on the Leipzig *Neue Zeitschrift für Musik* (*New Journal of Music*), of which he was editor from 1834 to 1844. His essays and reviews were an important progressive force in the Romantic movement; he was one of the first to recognize the genius of Chopin and Brahms. All of Schumann's published compositions (Opp. 1–23) up to 1840 were for piano, and these include most of his important works for that instrument with the exception of his one concerto (1845). This concerto, the Fantasia in C major Op. 17 (1836), and the set of variations entitled *Symphonic Études* (1834) are his chief longer works for piano, though he also wrote several other sets of variations and three sonatas. The remainder of his production consists of short character pieces, which he often grouped in loosely organized cycles with names such as *Papillons, Carnaval, Fantasiestücke, Kinderscenen, Kreisleriana, Novelletten, Nachstücke, Faschingsschwank aus Wien.* Attractive little pieces for children are gathered in the *Album for the Young* (published 1848).

Robert Schumann

The titles of both the collections and the separate pieces suggest that Schumann intended his music not only to be considered as patterns of sound but in some manner to suggest extra-musical poetic fancies or the taking over into music of literary forms. This is a typical Romantic attitude and its significance is not at all diminished by the fact that Schumann, on his own admission, usually wrote the music before he thought of the title. His music embodies more fully than that of any other composer the depths, and the contradictions and tensions of the Romantic spirit; it is by turns ardent and dreamy, vehement and visionary, whimsical and learned. In his writings and in the *Davidsbundlertänze* the different facets of his own nature were personified in the imaginary figures of Florestan, Eusebius, and Raro, members of the *Davidsbund,* a League of David set to oppose the Philistines of music—Florestan the impulsive revolutionist, Eusebius the youthful dreamer, and Raro the wise mature master. Musical sketches of the first two appear in *Carnaval.* One might say that Florestan speaks in the fiery finale of the *Symphonic Études,* Eusebius in the *Aria* of the F♯ minor sonata (based on the melody of an early song), and Raro in the *Canonic Studies* for pedal piano Op. 56 and the fugues of Opp. 60, 72, and 126, as well as in the subtly contrapuntal inner voices and fugal passages of many of Schumann's other piano works.

The influence of Bach on Schumann's style is especially noticeable after 1842. Schumann was constantly studying the music of Beethoven and Bach, and constantly advising other composers to do likewise. One of his counsels to young musicians was: "Diligently play fugues of good masters, especially those of Johann Sebastian Bach.

Let the *Well-Tempered Clavier* be your daily bread and you will certainly become a fine musician." Schumann's piano music, while far from easy to play, never aims to impress the listener by a sheer bravura. It is thoroughly idiomatic for the instrument, and the virtuoso element is always subordinate to the poetic idea.

Frédéric Chopin

The compositions of Frédéric Chopin (1810–49) are almost exclusively for piano. The principal works are: two concertos and a few other large pieces for piano with orchestra, three sonatas, 27 études, four scherzos, four ballades, 24 preludes, three impromptus, 19 nocturnes, numerous waltzes, mazurkas and polonaises, a *Barcarole* in F♯, a *Berceuse* in D♭, and a *Fantasia* in F minor.

Although Chopin lived in Paris from 1831, he never ceased to love his native Poland or to be afflicted by her misfortunes. His mazurkas, impregnated with the rhythms, harmonies, forms, and melodic traits of Polish popular music (though usually without any direct quotation from Polish folk themes) are among the earliest and best examples of Romantic music inspired by national idioms. In particular, the "Lydian" raised fourth, characteristic of Polish folk music, is present from the earliest works of Chopin. To some extent his polonaises may also be regarded a national manifestation. Inasmuch as this particular Polish form had come into western European music as early as the time of Bach, it had inevitably, in the course of more than a century acquired a conventional character; but some of

Last page of the autograph manuscript of the Chopin Barcarole.

Chopin's polonaises blaze anew with the knightly and heroic spirit of his native land—particularly those in A♭ (Op. 53) and F♯ minor (Op. 44).

Most of Chopin's pieces have an introspective character and, within clearly defined formal outlines, contrive to suggest the quality of improvisation. Although he was a concert pianist, he was not an overwhelming, theatrical performer, and it is probable that other virtuosos have projected the heroic side of his music more emphatically than he himself was able to do, and perhaps more emphatically than he would have desired. All his works, however, demand of the player not only a flawless touch and technique but also an imaginative use of the pedals and a discreet application of *tempo rubato,* which Chopin himself described as a slight pushing or holding back within the phrase of the right-hand part while the left-hand accompaniment continues in strict time.

The nocturnes, impromptus, and preludes are Chopin's most intimate works. Both the name and the general idea of the nocturnes were taken from the Irish pianist and composer John Field, those of the impromptus presumably from Schubert. The Nocturne in D♭ (Op. 27, No. 2) and the Impromptu in F♯ (Op. 36) are examples of Chopin's *cantabile* melodic style—influenced probably by the Italian opera composer, Bellini—his sensitive use of widely spaced accompaniment figures (an expansion of the old Alberti bass technique), and his inimitable creative fancy in pianistic ornamentation, by means of which he produces some effects that forecast Impressionism. Such piano sonorities had been unknown before Chopin. The preludes were composed at a time when Chopin was immersed even more deeply than usual in the music of Bach. Like the preludes in the *Well-Tempered Clavier,* these brief, sharply defined mood pictures go through all the major and minor keys, though the succession Chopin uses is by the circle of fifths (C major—A minor—G major E minor, and so on). Chopin's music was an important source of later developments in harmony; his extraordinary genius for chromatic harmonies and modulations is evident in many of the preludes, most notably perhaps in Nos. 2, 4, 8 and the middle sections of Nos. 14 and 24.

The fundamental traits of Chopin's style are displayed on a larger canvas in the ballades and scherzos. He was apparently the first composer to use the name *ballade* for an instrumental piece; his works in this form (especially Op. 23 in G minor and Op. 52 in F minor) capture the Romantic charm and fire of the narrative ballads of the great nineteenth-century Polish poet, Adam Mickiewicz, combining these qualities with that indefinable spontaneity, those constantly fresh turns in the harmony and form, that are a distinctive mark of Chopin. The principal scherzos are those in B minor (Op. 20) and C♯ minor (Op. 39). Chopin's scherzos have no trace of this form's original connotation of playfulness; these are wholly serious, virile, and passionate works, organized—as are the ballades—in compact forms that grow naturally out of the musical ideas. On an equally large scale but even more varied in content is the great *Fantasia* in F minor (Op. 49), a worthy companion to the like-named works of Schubert and Schumann. The *Polonaise-Fantasie* (Op. 61), Chopin's last large work, has an even freer form; it and the Violoncello Sonata (Op. 65) point toward directions he would have explored, had he lived longer.

Chopin's études (twelve in each of Opp. 10 and 25 and three without opus numbers) are important landmarks in the history of piano music. An *étude* is, as the name indicates, a study primarily for the development of technique; consequently each single étude as a rule is devoted to a specific technical desideratum and is based on a single musical motive. Of the thousands of piano études written in the nineteenth century those of Chopin were the first which fully realized the potential of combining this practical aim with conceptions of the highest musical significance; Liszt and Brahms followed Chopin's lead in this respect. Chopin's études are transcendent studies in technique and at the same time intensely concentrated tone poems; they are all the more definite in meaning because the composer carefully avoided any clues that could serve as a pretext for attaching descriptive labels.

The *Berceuse* (Op. 57) is like a florid nocturne on unchanging tonic-dominant harmonies, while the *Barcarole* (Op. 60) is a treatment in large form of lyrical themes with high-wrought ornamentation. The sonatas in B♭ minor (Op. 35) and B minor (Op. 58) are sonatas in the Romantic sense—unconventional in formal aspects, with considerable stylistic diversity among the movements, but dramatic and moving works. The concertos in E minor (Op. 11) and F minor (Op. 21) are comparatively early works (1830 and 1829 respectively). They contain some beautiful pianistic writing, especially in the slow movements, but the orchestration is undistinguished and the total effect is of a piano solo with orchestral accompaniment and interludes rather than of equal partnership.

Franz Liszt

The life of Franz Liszt was one of the most brilliant of the Romantic era. Born in Hungary, the son of an official in the service of Prince Nicholas Esterházy, he studied piano under Carl Czerny at Vienna and at the age of eleven began a dazzling career as concert virtuoso that with few interruptions lasted until 1848. During most of this time he made his home in Paris. From 1848 to 1861 he was Court Music Director at Weimar, where he powerfully encouraged the Romantic movement by conducting performances of many important new works, among them Wagner's *Lohengrin* in 1850. To his fame as pianist, conductor, and composer was added the glamour of several well-publicized love affairs with ladies of high position and of honors showered upon him by cities and sovereigns all over Europe. From 1861 until about 1870 Liszt resided chiefly at Rome,

Joseph Dannhauser's painting of Liszt and his friends exemplifies the Romantic attitude towards the artist. Kneeling beside Liszt at the piano is Madame D'Agoult; seated behind him are George Sand and Alexandre Dumas, père. Standing in the background are Victor Hugo, Paganini and the host, Rossini. Notice the bust of Beethoven which dominates the scene.

where he took minor orders in the Church; the remainder of his life was divided among Rome, Weimar, and Budapest.

Liszt's cosmopolitan career was matched by the eclecticism of his music. Many diverse factors entered into the formation of his style. The first was his Hungarian heritage, manifest not only in his compositions based on or inspired by national melodies, but also in his fiery, dynamic, and impulsive temperament. Superimposed on this background were his early German training at Vienna and the strong influence of Parisian literary Romanticism and its ideal of program music as represented by Berlioz. Nearly everything Liszt wrote either has an explicit programmatic title or can easily be imagined to have one. His piano style was based on Chopin's, from whom he took the latter's repertoire of pianistic effects—adding new ones of his own—as well as his lyrical melodic qualities, his manner of *rubato* playing, and his harmonic innovations, which Liszt further extended. Some of the late works, in particular, contain strikingly advanced chords and modulations.

At Paris Liszt came under the spell of one of the most hypnotic figures, as well as one of the greatest artists, of nineteenth-century music, the Italian violinist Niccolò Paganini (1782–1840). Stimulated by Paganini's fabulous technical virtuosity, Liszt determined to accomplish similar miracles with the piano, and pushed the technique of the instrument to its furthest limits both in his own playing and in his compositions. His technical innovations, however, were not all for mere display, but went hand in hand with the development of Romantic musical rhetoric to heights previously unimagined. There is a curious duality about Liszt, a duality we have already mentioned in connection with his sacred music and one that is perhaps characteristic of the Romantic temperament: he was a grandiloquent virtuoso, not without a touch of bombast; but he was also a generous, warm-hearted friend of other artists, and he had a vein of religious sentiment that must be accepted as genuine however inconsistent it may appear with some of the unconventional episodes of his life.

A considerable proportion of Liszt's piano music consists of transcriptions or arrangements—fantasies on operatic airs, transcriptions of Schubert's songs and Berlioz's and Beethoven's symphonies, Bach's organ fugues, excerpts from Wagner's music dramas, and the like. The usefulness these pieces had in their day should not be underrated. They made important music known to many people who had little or no opportunity to become acquainted with the original works; furthermore, Liszt's transference of orchestral idioms to the piano demonstrated new possibilities for that instrument. A second category of Liszt's piano music includes compositions which make free use of national tunes; chief among these are the nineteen *Hungarian Rhapsodies*—though by "Hungarian" Liszt and other nineteenth-century composers did not understand genuine Hungarian folk tunes, but rather the gypsy music which until recent times was thought to represent authentic folk elements.

For piano and orchestra Liszt wrote two concertos (E♭ major, A major), a *Hungarian Fantasia* (expanded from the 14th Rhapsody), and the *Totentanz (Dance of Death)*, a paraphrase on the plainsong *Dies irae*. His piano studies include the formidable 12 *Études d'exécution transcendante,* published in their finally revised version in 1852 with titles (No. 4 is the frequently played *Mazeppa*); six studies transcribed from Paganini's caprices for solo violin, published in final shape in 1851 (among them *La Campanella*); and three *Études de concert* (1848).

The variety of Liszt's poetic imagination is displayed in many of his short separately published piano pieces and in several collections of tone pictures, of which the chief are *Années de pèlerinage* (three books; the first two composed before 1850 and the third in 1867–77), *Consolations* (1850), and *Harmonies poétiques et religieuses* (1852). These collections contain some of his best compositions, which negate the all too common impression of Liszt as concerned only with bravura effects. An important large work is the Sonata in B minor (1853), in which four themes are worked out in one extended movement, although with subdivisions analogous to the sections of a Classical sonata movement. The themes are transformed and combined in an apparently free rhapsodic order which, however, is perfectly suited to the thematic material and the intentions of the composer; the entire sonata, one of the outstanding piano compositions of the nineteenth century, is a successful adaptation of the principle of cyclic development characteristic of the symphonic poem.

In some of his late works Liszt experimented with harmonies that surprisingly anticipate late nineteenth-century developments in the direction of impressionism.[1] He was one of the first composers to make much use of augmented triads; the first theme of the *Faust* Symphony, for example, is derived entirely from this chord (see Example XVII–4, page 588), which is also prominent in the B-minor Sonata and many other of Liszt's works. Example XVII–1 shows the ending of a short piano piece *Nuages gris* (Gray Clouds) composed in 1881. The descending succession of augmented triads over the B♭–A ostinato in the bass has already been heard in the first part of the piece; now, in a broken texture it accompanies a slowly rising melody in octaves, covering fourteen steps of the chromatic scale in

EXAMPLE XVII–1   Ending, *Nuages gris,* Liszt

[1] For details see Bengt Johnsson, "Modernities in Liszt's Works," *Svensk Tidskrift för Musikforskning* 46 (1964) 83–118; late piano pieces are published in *Franz Liszt, the Final Years,* G. Schirmer Library, Vol. 1845.

a rhythm which is an augmentation of that of the initial theme of the work. The tonality of G major is affirmed at the final cadence chiefly by the slowing down of the movement and the full-measure pause before the appoggiatura-like F♯–G in the melody. The lowest notes A–E in the penultimate chord may be said to "represent" the dominant; their effect in the closing chord is the coloristic one of an unresolved dissonance. In fact, in that chord these two notes are almost lost to hearing as distinct entities—first, because they remain unchanged from the previous measure, so that our attention is diverted to the melodic line resolving upward to the tonic; and second, because the diminuendo and the slow upward arpeggiation of the two final chords tend still further to veil, both acoustically and psychologically, the sound of these lower notes.

Liszt wrote about a dozen works for organ, the most important of which are a big *Fantasia and Fugue* (1850) on a chorale theme (*Ad nos, ad salutarem undam*) from Meyerbeer's opera *Le Prophète*, and a Prelude and Fugue on the name of Bach—that is, on a theme beginning with the chromatic motif *B* (the German symbol for B♭), *A, C, H* (the German symbol for B♮).

Johannes
Brahms

The piano style of Brahms has neither the elegance of Chopin nor the brilliance and romantic rhetoric of Liszt. Its models are Schumann and Beethoven. Technically it is characterized by fullness of sonority, broken chord figuration, frequent doubling of the melodic line in octaves, thirds, or sixths, and considerable use of cross-rhythms. It has the harmonic richness and emotional warmth of Romanticism, but the language is governed by basic conceptions that are essentially more Classical than Romantic. Brahms's works for the piano include two concertos, three sonatas, several sets of variations, and some 35 shorter pieces with titles such as ballade, rhapsody, capriccio, or intermezzo. Chief among the larger works are the concertos, the Sonata in F minor (1853), the *Variations and Fugue on a Theme of Handel* (1861), and the difficult étude-like *Variations on a Theme of Paganini* (1863). The importance of the variation form for Brahms—not only in piano music but in other media as well—is one evidence of his inclination toward Classical principles of construction. Even in his shorter piano pieces the forms are purely outgrowths of the musical material. Brahms avoids the descriptive titles used by Schumann and Liszt; his attitude is unsympathetic to the Romantic ideal of program music and to the extreme tendencies of Romanticism in general. Brahms, in short, is the great conservative of the Romantic era. A direct link with the past is found in his eleven chorale preludes for the organ, written during the last years of his life—the finest compositions in this form since Bach.

Among the piano music of Brahms's contemporaries must be noted Mussorgsky's *Pictures at an Exhibition* (1874), Balakirev's *Islamey*

and *Sonata in B♭ minor,* and three works by the Belgian César
Franck (1822–90), namely a *Prelude, Chorale, and Fugue* (1884), a
Prelude, Aria, and Finale (1887) and the *Symphonic Variations* for
piano and orchestra (1885). Franck studied in Paris and made his
home there after 1844; like Brahms, he sought to incorporate the
achievements of Romanticism in an essentially Classical framework,
with a harmonic idiom influenced to some extent by the chromaticism of Liszt and Wagner. His compositions for organ include
several sets of short pieces and three so-called *Chorales* (1890), which
actually are richly developed fantasias on original themes. He was
the founder of a new school of organ music in France, and indeed
the fountainhead of the whole movement that gave renewed vitality
to French musical education and composition beginning with the
establishment of the *Société nationale de musique française* (National Society for French Music) in 1871.

Chamber Music

The style of chamber music was not congenial to many Romantic
composers; on the one hand it lacked the intimate personal expressiveness of the solo piano piece or the Lied and on the other the
glowing colors and overpowering sound of orchestral music. It is
therefore not surprising that the arch-Romantics Berlioz, Liszt, and
Wagner contributed nothing to chamber music, nor that the best
works in this medium in the nineteenth century came from those
composers who had the closest affinity with the Classical tradition—
Schubert and Brahms pre-eminently, Mendelssohn and Schumann to
a lesser degree.

Schubert's first quartets, modeled after Mozart and Haydn, were
written primarily for the pleasure of his circle of friends. The
Quartet in E♭ (D. 87, 1813) is a work of Classical purity; in the
E-major Quartet of 1816 (D. 353) Schubert's own style, combining
warmth of sonority with clarity of line, is established. The most
popular work from his earlier period is the *Forellen* or *Trout*
Quintet for piano and strings (1819), so called because between the
scherzo and the finale there is an additional movement (*andantino*)
consisting of variations on his own song *Die Forelle*. Schubert's
mature period in chamber music begins in 1820 with an Allegro in
C minor (D. 703), intended as the first movement of a string quartet
that was never completed. Three important works followed—the
quartets in A minor (D. 804, 1824), D minor (D. 810, 1824–26), and
G major (D. 887, 1826).

The A-minor quartet is an outpouring of sadness, elegiac in the
first movement and minuet, full of Schubertian melody and beautiful modulations. The theme of the Andante occurs also in an

entr'acte of Schubert's incidental music to *Rosamunde* and the same theme served him later for the piano Impromptu Op. 142, No. 3. At the opening of the minuet is a quotation from Schubert's setting of a stanza by Schiller (D. 677) beginning with the words "Lovely world, where art thou?" The finale of this quartet is an Allegro in Hungarian style, in a cheerful mood contrasting rather sharply with the preceding three movements.

The Quartet in D minor is more grimly serious and more consistent in feeling. It is built around the second movement, a set of variations on Schubert's own song, *Death and the Maiden*. Within the sustained unity of the quartet as a whole each movement offers variety of thematic ideas, developed with great skill and contrapuntal ingenuity. The G-major quartet is on a larger scale than either of the other two; its form is as perfect as that of the D-minor quartet, but it is even more abundant in musical content. It opens with one of the most remarkable instances of Schubert's device of alternating major and minor forms of the triad, reversed and differently colored at the recapitulation (see Example XVII–2), and the whole is full of harmonic boldness.

EXAMPLE XVII–2   First movement, Quartet in G major (D.887), Schubert

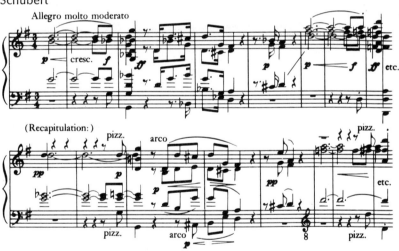

The Octet in F major (D. 803, 1824) is a gay, relaxed work, written for string quartet, double bass, clarinet, horn, and bassoon. Its form, obviously patterned after Beethoven's Septet Op. 20, is that of a suite or divertimento, in six movements. The Andante is a set of variations on the melody of a duet from one of Schubert's singspiels, *Die Freunde von Salamanka* (1815). Two Piano Trios, in B♭ and E♭ respectively (D. 898, 929), are attractive but uneven chamber works.

Undoubtedly Schubert's masterpiece of chamber music is the String Quintet in C major (D. 956), written during the last year of his life. As in Boccherini's quintets, the added instrument is a second violoncello, and Schubert obtains from this combination some of the most exquisite sound effects in all Romantic music. The Quintet has the profound lyricism, the unobtrusive contrapuntal mastery, the long melodic lines (for example, the first fifteen measures of the Adagio), and the wealth of harmonic invention that characterize the late piano sonatas. The finale, like that of the Quartet in A minor, is in a more popular style, relaxing the tension built up by the first three movements.

Mendelssohn's published chamber music comprises six string quartets, two quintets, an octet, a sextet for piano and strings, and

Mendelssohn's autograph of the second page of the scherzo from the String Octet Op. 20. (Library of Congress)

*Mendelssohn's
chamber music* two piano trios, as well as a sonata for piano and violin, two sonatas for piano and violoncello, and a few lesser works and arrangements. Very few of these pieces are as interesting as his symphonic productions. Mendelssohn writes smoothly, if diffusely, in the Classical forms; but his Romantic feeling for descriptive tone color finds relatively little scope in the medium of chamber music. An exception, however, is the early Octet (1825), particularly the scherzo, which is a fine example of Mendelssohn's inimitable style in this type of movement; other examples are the scherzos of the Piano Trio in C minor and the String Quartet in A minor. Of the string quartets the best are probably the two in E♭ Opp. 12 and 94 and the late Quartet in F minor, Op. 80 (1847). The two piano trios (D minor, Op. 49 and C minor, Op. 66) are among the most popular of Mendelssohn's chamber works and well display both the excellences and the weaknesses of the composer in this field—tuneful, attractive themes, vigorous idiomatic writing, but occasional looseness of form and repetitiousness in the development of the material.

*Schumann's
chamber music*
Schumann's principal chamber music works were composed in 1842. In that year he wrote three string quartets, a piano quartet, and a piano quintet. The string quartets reveal the influence of Beethoven not only in general aim but also in some details: developments are frequently contrapuntal, and the *Andante quasi variazoni* of the second Quartet, a movement in A♭ major, is reminiscent of the Adagio of Beethoven's Op. 127. Schumann's third quartet, in A major, is a deeply Romantic work, with a particularly beautiful slow movement. The Piano Quartet, Op. 47, is less successful than the Piano Quintet, Op. 44, which is a splendid example of the mature style of this most romantic of all the Romantic composers. Less important in Schumann's chamber music are the three piano trios, though special mention should be made of the poetic slow movement of the Trio Op. 63 and also of the slow movement of the F major Trio Op. 80, in which the D♭ major melody of the violin sings above a secondary theme in strict canon between pianoforte and violoncello.

*Brahms's
chamber music*
Brahms is the giant among composers of chamber music in the nineteenth century, the true successor of Beethoven in this field as in that of the symphony. Not only is the quantity of his production impressive—24 works in all—but it includes at least a half-dozen masterpieces of the first rank. His first published chamber work was a Piano Trio in B (Op. 8, 1854), which he issued again in a thoroughly rewritten version in 1891. Two string sextets—Op. 18 in B♭ (1862) and Op. 36 in G (1867)—make an interesting contrast. The B♭ Sextet is a hearty work of ample dimensions, combining humor and Classical poise; the slow movement is a set of variations in D minor and the finale is a Haydn-like rondo form with a big coda. The Sextet in G has a more serene mood, with widely spaced transparent sonorities in the opening Allegro and a quietly vivacious finale; the second

movement, labeled Scherzo, is a semiserious moderate Allegro in 2/4 time in G minor—a type of movement that Brahms also employed, with modifications, in his symphonies—and the Adagio, in the form of a theme in E minor with five variations, may be considered an epitome of some of Brahms's most individual harmonic and rhythmic procedures.

Two piano quartets, Op. 25 in G minor and Op. 26 in A major, date from the late 1850s. The first is one of the most original and most popular of Brahms's chamber works with its mysterious romantic second movement (called Intermezzo) and lively Hungarian rondo finale on a theme of three-measure phrases. These two quartets contrast with each other much as do the first two string sextets. The third Piano Quartet (Op. 60, C minor) was given its final form in 1874; it is a grandly tragic composition, with the concentration of material characteristic of Brahms's later works. The slow movement is in E major, and thus has the same mediant relationship to the main tonality of the work as the slow movement of the First Symphony.

The "climax of Brahms's first maturity" is the great Piano Quintet in F minor, Op. 34A. Brahms originally composed this in 1862 as a

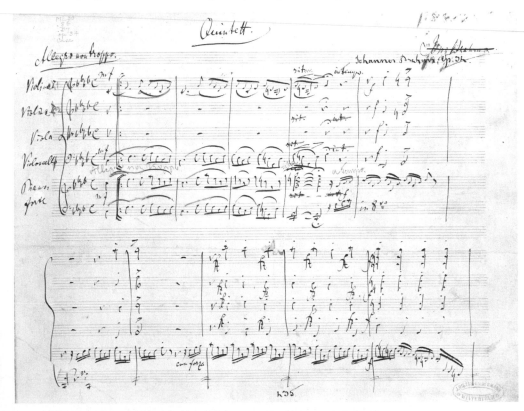

Brahms's autograph of the first page of the Piano Quintet Op. 34. (Library of Congress)

string quintet with two violoncellos; he later arranged it effectively for two pianos, and then, still unsatisfied, combined the string and pianoforte sonorities for the final version (1864). The first movement is a powerful, closely knit Allegro in sonata form, with a second theme group in C♯ minor, a well integrated development section, and a coda that begins *pianissimo* with a quiet contrapuntal improvisation on the principal theme above a tonic pedal and then rises to end in the stormy mood of the beginning. The slow movement (A♭) is a beautiful Schubertian three-part *Andante un poco adagio* with a middle section in E major. Both the spirit and the themes of the Scherzo recall those of the corresponding movement in Beethoven's Fifth Symphony. The rousing Finale is preceded by a broad *poco sostenuto* which is like a sketch for the even broader introduction to the last movement of Brahms's First Symphony. Some idea of the intricate relationships among themes and motives in this Quintet may be gathered from Example XVII–3. Throughout, and especially

EXAMPLE XVII–3   Themes and Motives from the Piano Quintet in F minor Op. 34a, Brahms

in the first and last movements, we may admire equally Brahms's skill in counterpoint and the good judgment with which he subordinates this technique to the general design of the work.

The Trio Op. 40 for piano, violin, and Waldhorn (the natural horn, without valves) is another successful example of the union of a sonorous, expressive Romantic idiom with forms well grounded in Classical practice. The Trio was composed in 1865; it brings to an end what may be called, by analogy with Beethoven, Brahms's second period. After a pause of eight years came the two string quartets in C minor and A minor, Op. 51; then in 1876 (the year of the First Symphony) the String Quartet in Bb, Op. 67. The eloquent *Grave ed appassionato* of the String Quintet in F major, Op. 88 (1882) is combined with the scherzo in a single movement—a device used by César Franck seven years later in his Symphony.

Outstanding among Brahms's later works are the two piano trios Op. 87 in C major (1882) and Op. 101 in C minor (1886), the String Quintet in G major Op. 111 (1890), and the profound Clarinet Quintet in B minor, Op. 115 (1891). All these have something of the same character as Beethoven's late quartets and piano sonatas: the musical ideas are pure, with a purity that is sometimes thoughtlessly called abstract because it is so concretely musical as to be undefinable in any other medium; textures are smoothly contrapuntal; and forms are handled with a freedom that is the result of logic in movement and conciseness in statement.

A special category of Brahms's chamber music consists of sonatas for a single instrument with piano. There are three such sonatas for violin, two for violoncello, and two for clarinet. All except the first violoncello sonata (1862–65) are late works. The first two violin sonatas (G major, Op. 78, 1878; A major, Op. 100, 1886) contain some of Brahms's most lyric and melodious writing; the third (D minor, Op. 108, 1887) is on a more symphonic scale. The clarinet sonatas Op. 120 (F minor and Eb major), written in 1894, may be grouped with the piano pieces Opp. 116–119, the Clarinet Quintet, the *Four Serious Songs*, and the organ chorale preludes as among the ripest achievements of the composer whose music demonstrated, more clearly than that of any other nineteenth-century composer, that the flower of Romanticism had deep roots in the Classical tradition.

The founder of modern French chamber music was César Franck; his chief works in this field are a Piano Quintet in F minor (1897), a String Quartet in D major (1889), and the well-known Violin Sonata in A major (1886). All these works employ cyclical themes— that is, themes that recur identically or transformed in two or more different movements. This nineteenth-century principle of structure, exemplified perhaps unintentionally in Beethoven's *Sonate Pathétique* but quite explicitly in Schubert's *Wanderer Fantasie*, had attracted Franck as early as 1840, when he used it in his first Piano

César Franck's chamber music

Trio in F♯ minor. Cyclical themes are most effective in his mature chamber works, as well as the Symphony in D minor (1888).

Music for Orchestra

The history of nineteenth-century symphonic music indicates most clearly that the composers developed along two roads, both of which stemmed from Beethoven. One of the roads started from the Fourth, Seventh, and Eighth Symphonies, and led in the direction of absolute music in standard Classical forms; the other started from the Fifth, Sixth, and Ninth Symphonies, and diverged toward program music in unconventional forms. Common to both were the Romantic character of their musical expression and the acceptance of contemporary advances in harmony and tone color. The one road may be called conservative, the other radical—a distinction useful for purposes of historical analysis although actually of course the two tendencies were always intermingled. Furthermore, the distinction cannot be simply equated with a distinction between absolute music and program music, for in the nineteenth century there was no really definite boundary line between these two. Generally speaking, the conservative composers were those whose musical imagination worked naturally within the formal structures, themes, harmonies, and orchestrations that had been inherited from the Classical period; if these composers gave descriptive titles to their works they did so incidentally and without emphasis. The radicals were those whose creative imagination was less apt to be stimulated by a strictly musical idea than by a literary or some other extra-musical impulse; and precisely because the impulse came from outside the conventional domain of music, the resulting composition was likely to be unconventional in some respects—in form, for instance—although in other respects it might adhere to Classical usage. Radical composers published their symphonies with a descriptive title or programmatic commentary, not in order to explain or justify what they had written—they knew as well as anyone that a work of art has to be its own justification—but because the program was part of the idea of the symphony in the same way that the text is part of the idea of a song.

By and large the lineup of symphonic composers in the first half of the nineteenth century is already familiar: Schubert, essentially Classical and untroubled by inner conflicts; Mendelssohn, Classical and gentle by disposition but with a special gift for Romantic scene painting; Schumann, torn between conservative and radical tendencies and trying to mediate between the two; Berlioz and Liszt each, in his own way, radical. After about 1860 two opposing schools appeared: Romantic Classicism, represented by Brahms, and a special kind of Romantic radicalism, represented by Wagner. (The latter school is sometimes called "realism," but the word is so nearly meaningless in this context that it is best avoided.) Here again, however, the issues between the two are not simple. The plainest example of the conservative-radical antithesis would be the contrast between the late chamber works of Brahms and the contemporary early orchestral tone poems of Richard Strauss; but in the symphonies of Bruckner and César Franck conservative and radical traits are mingled in a very complex way.

The foregoing general observations will be clarified by a survey of the principal symphonic compositions of the Romantic period.

The most important symphonies of Schubert—the *Unfinished* in B minor of 1822 and the great C major Symphony of 1828— exemplify the harmonic originality which has already been noted as a feature of his style. A new element, related to Schubert's harmonic sensitivity, is his feeling for orchestral tone color: the quietly moving figure in the strings beginning at measure nine of the first movement of the *Unfinished* Symphony; the violoncello melody of the G major second theme with its syncopated accompaniment for violas and clarinets over the pizzicato of the doublebasses; in the slow movement, the middle section in C♯ minor and D♭ major, with the clarinet solo and the dialogue of clarinet and oboe over a shimmering magic carpet of Schubertian modulations. The *Unfinished* may be called the first truly Romantic symphony. In the C-major Symphony Schubert has expanded his material almost to the breaking point; the "heavenly length" which Schumann admired in this work would be less heavenly if it were not for the beauty of Schubert's melodies. This symphony also illustrates Schubert's felicitous treatment of orchestral color: the unison theme for two horns at the opening; the *pianissimo* trombones (then a novel effect) in the codetta of the first movement; the repeated *g'* of the horns against the changing harmonies of antiphonal strings just before the return of the principal theme in the slow movement; and the somewhat similar passage at the recapitulation in the finale, with the low chords for bassoons, horns, and trombones.

In addition to these two, Schubert had written six earlier symphonies and made a complete sketch for another. As in his chamber music, the chief formative influences were from Haydn, Mozart, Cherubini, and early Beethoven. Another influence, that of Rossini, may be detected in some of the symphonies and the orchestral concert overtures, especially the two "in Italian style" (D. 556, 590) from 1817. All Schubert's symphonies have regular Classical forms, and not one of them—not even No. 4 in C minor, which he called the *Tragic*—can reasonably be considered programmatic. They are Romantic solely by virtue of the music—its lyricism, its fascinating harmonic excursions, and its enchanting colors.

Schubert's symphonies

With Mendelssohn we enter the realm of Romantic landscapes. His two most important symphonies carry geographical subtitles— the *Italian* (1833) and the *Scotch* (1842). In these works Mendelssohn records some typical German Romantic impressions of the south and the north: the south, sunny and vibrant, a procession of chanting pilgrims trudging along the road, and people in the city squares dancing the spirited *saltarello;* the north, gray and somber, with the skirling of bagpipes and sound of the old heroic ballads. In both symphonies Mendelssohn's writing is, as always, impeccable, and he has skilfully fitted his melodious themes into the regular Classical forms. The four divisions of the *Scotch Symphony* are linked by the use of portions of the slow introduction to the first movement as introductions to the following two movements, as well as by subtle similarities of melodic outline among many of the themes throughout the work. The four movements are directed to be played without pause.

Mendelssohn's peculiar genius for musical landscapes is especially evident in his overtures *The Hebrides* (or *Fingal's Cave;* 1832) and *Calm Sea and Prosperous Voyage* (1828–32), while *Melusine* (1833) is a symphonic incarnation of the early Romantic spirit of the fairy tale. Among his incidental music for plays, the overture for Victor Hugo's *Ruy Blas* (1839) is excelled only by the incomparable *Midsummer Night's Dream* overture, written at the age of seventeen —a work that set the standard for all subsequent concert overtures of the Romantic period. All this music, while it may be called programmatic (in the same sense as Beethoven's *Pastoral Symphony*), and while it is certainly Romantic in the quality of its imagination and its treatment of the orchestra, is nonetheless Classical in outline (most of the overtures, for example, are in sonata form), and Classical moreover in that it avoids extremes of feeling and never allows the extra-musical inspiration to disturb the musical balance. The program is no more than a faint mist about the structure, lending charm to the view but not obscuring the outlines. Essentially the qualities of Mendelssohn's symphonies and overtures are not different from those of his Violin Concerto (1844), one of his masterpieces and one of the greatest of all violin concertos—a work as Romantic as the *Italian* Symphony or the *Hebrides Overture,* but one to which not the slightest suggestion of a program has ever been attached.

Schumann's first two published symphonies were composed in 1841 —his symphony year, as 1840 was the *Lieder* and 1842 the chamber music year. The first, in B♭ major, is called the *Spring Symphony.* It was the composer's intention at one time to prefix a descriptive title to each movement—the first, for example, was to have been called "Spring's Awakening" and the Finale, "Spring's Farewell." The name is appropriate, for the music is fresh, spontaneous, teeming with Romantic themes and driven along with exhaustless rhythmic energy.

Much the same can be said of the Symphony in D minor, first composed in 1841 but published only ten years later after extensive revisions; in consequence this symphony, though second in order of composition, was fourth in order of publication, and is so numbered. Schumann once thought of calling the revised version a symphonic fantasia. We do not know whether he had any program in mind, but the fantasia element is present in the irregular form of the first Allegro and in the fact that each movement contains themes derived from motives announced in the slow introduction to the first. As with Mendelssohn's *Scotch* Symphony, the four movements (in the 1851 version) are to be played without a break; they are joined either by means of skillful harmonic coupling or—before the finale —by a transitional passage similar to the one at the corresponding place in Beethoven's Fifth.

Schumann's Second Symphony (again, the second to be published), in C major (1846), is the most severely Classical of his symphonies, but except for the Adagio its musical interest is less than that of the two earlier works. The Third or *Rhenish* Symphony in Eb (1850) is vaguely programmatic and contains some characteristically vigorous themes, though on the whole it is less spontaneous than the First Symphony. Most remarkable is the interpolated slow fourth movement, which Schumann at first inscribed "in the manner of an accompaniment to a solemn ceremony"; it is said to have been inspired by the enthronement of a Cardinal Archbishop in the Cathedral at Cologne.

Apart from the symphonies and the piano concerto, Schumann's chief orchestral work is the overture from his incidental music to Byron's *Manfred* (1849). His orchestral style in general has been criticized as pianistic, and it is true that he was not so good a judge of orchestral effects as were Schubert and Mendelssohn. In his symphonies, despite the incidental pictorial suggestions, he wished to write absolute music and his ideal was Beethoven; but on the whole he failed to achieve the long lines and the organic unity of Classical symphonic style. The beauty of Schumann's symphonies lies in their details and in the ardor of their Romantic spirit.

The diffused scenic effects in the music of Mendelssohn and Schumann seem pale indeed when compared with the feverish and circumstantial drama which is commonly supposed to constitute the story of Berlioz's *Symphonie fantastique* (1830). Because his imagination always tended to run in parallel literary and musical channels, Berlioz once subtitled this work "Episode in the Life of an Artist" and provided a program for it which was in effect a piece of romantic autobiography. In later years he conceded that if necessary, when the

Berlioz's symphonies

Sketch of introduction and beginning of first movement of Schumann's First Symphony.

symphony was performed by itself in concert, the program need not be given out to the audience, since he hoped that the music would "of itself, and irrespective of any dramatic aim, offer an interest in the musical sense alone." But it was natural for Berlioz, as it was for his eighteenth-century compatriots Rameau and Couperin, to associate music with images, and the *Symphonie fantastique* is descriptive just as the music of an opera is descriptive. The work is a musical drama without words. As Berlioz wrote, "The program should be regarded in the same way as the spoken words of an opera, serving to introduce the musical numbers by describing the situation

Page 1 of the autograph score of Schumann's First Symphony. (Library of Congress)

that evokes the particular mood and expressive character of each."
The literary influences in the program are too numerous to be
detailed (De Quincey's *Confessions of an English Opium Eater* and
Goethe's *Faust* are conspicuous among them), and the supposed
situations are depicted in the perfervid prose of a young and sensitive
Romantic.

There is nothing revolutionary about the main formal outlines of
the *Symphonie fantastique*. The principal novelty is the recurrence
of the opening theme of the first Allegro (the *idée fixe,* the obsessive
image of the hero's beloved, according to the program) in all the

The Symphonie
fantastique

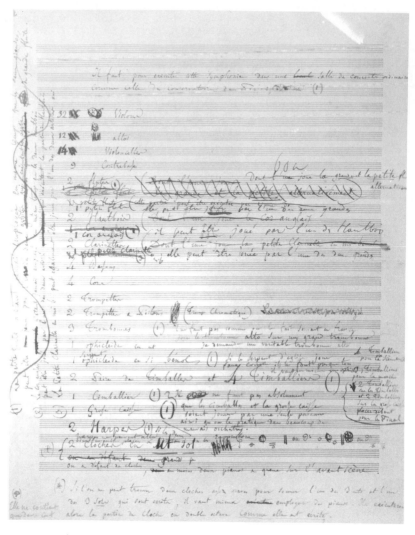

Berlioz's concern with the most minute details of orchestration is demonstrated on the title page of the autograph manuscript of the Symphonie fantastique. *(Collection André Meyer)*

other movements. The first movement (*Reveries and Passions*) consists of a slow introduction followed by an Allegro in modified sonata form; the second is a waltz, corresponding to the Classical scherzo; the third is a pastorale, an Adagio in large two-part form; a fourth movement (*March to the Scaffold*) is inserted, as in Beethoven's Sixth Symphony; and the finale, an introduction and Allegro, uses a transformation of the *idée fixe* and two other themes—one of them the melody of the *Dies irae*—first singly then in combination (as is done in the finale of Beethoven's Ninth Symphony).

The true originality of the *Symphonie fantastique* lies in its musical substance. It is partly a matter of details—melodies, harmonies, rhythms, phrase structures—and partly Berlioz's astounding ability to express the many shifting moods, the essential emotional content of his drama, in music of precision and communicative power. Moreover, the symphony as a whole has a unity achieved not by the artificial device of a recurring theme, but by the organic development of the dramatic idea through the five movements; it is the same kind of unity as that in Beethoven's Third and Fifth Symphonies. A salient aspect of Berlioz's originality is his orchestration; he had no textbooks and few models to help him, but his vivid aural imagination and his inventiveness in the realm of orchestral sonorities are evident in practically every measure of the *Symphonie fantastique*. To mention but one example: in the coda of the Adagio there is a passage for solo English horn and four kettledrums intended to suggest "distant thunder"—a marvelously poetic and evocative twenty-two measures, and no more an example of realism (if by that word is meant mere literal imitation of natural noises) than the bird songs in the slow movement of the *Pastoral Symphony*.

Berlioz's second symphony, *Harold in Italy* (1834), is a set of four scenes suggested by his reading of Lord Byron's *Childe Harold*. As with the *Symphonie fantastique,* the movements are in a conventional Classical order. There is a connecting recurrent theme, given chiefly to a solo viola, and this instrument is featured throughout somewhat in the manner of a concerto; but the soloist is less dominant than in an ordinary concerto—it is said that Paganini refused to play the work because it did not give him enough opportunity to be heard—and in fact much of the symphony is scored so lightly as to suggest chamber music. In each movement the viola melody is contrapuntally combined with the other themes, and the solo instrument, in every sort of idiomatic figuration, is continually blended with different orchestral groups in a ravishing display of sonorities.

Five years after *Harold in Italy* Berlioz produced his "dramatic symphony," *Romeo and Juliet,* for orchestra, soloists, and chorus, in seven movements. In adding voices to the symphonic orchestra, he was following the example of Beethoven; but in this work the voices enter in the first movement (after an instrumental introduction) and are used in three of the remaining ones as well, so that the entire symphony, although the scheme of the Classical order of movements can still be traced, begins to approach the form of the "dramatic legend" which the composer later perfected in his *Damnation of Faust* (1864). Nonetheless, *Romeo and Juliet* is essentially a symphonic work, and may be understood as an extension of the idea of the *Symphonie fantastique:* the program is explicitly announced in the Prologue, and words help to create the mood of the scene in the garden and of Juliet's funeral. Only the finale is decidedly operatic in character.

Berlioz's other symphonic works

The *Queen Mab* Scherzo from this symphony is another of Berlioz's *tours de force* of imagination and deft orchestration. For the most passionate and tragic parts of the play—the love scene and the death scene—Berlioz uses the orchestra without voices: "the very sublimity of this love," he writes in his preface to the score, "makes the musical interpretation of it such a dangerous undertaking for the composer that he must of necessity have more freedom than the specific character of words will permit; hence he must have recourse to the language of instrumental music, a language richer, less limited, and by its very indefiniteness incomparably more powerful for his purpose."

Among Berlioz's other symphonic works are several overtures (including the familiar *Roman Carnival*, 1844) and the *Funeral and Triumphal Symphony*, composed for a national ceremony in 1840. But his importance for the history of nineteenth-century instrumental music rests chiefly on his first three symphonies, especially the *Symphonie fantastique*. Even though his conception of the relation between music and program was widely misunderstood, these works made Berlioz the first leader of the radical wing of the Romantic movement, and all subsequent composers of program music—including Strauss and Debussy—were indebted to him. His orchestration initiated a new era: by example and precept he was the founder of modern orchestral conducting; he enriched Romantic music with new resources of harmony, color, expression, and form; and his use of a recurrent theme in different movements (as in the *Symphonie fantastique* and *Harold in Italy*) was an important impulse toward the development of the cyclical symphonic forms of the later nineteenth century.

Liszt's symphonic poems

The foremost composer of program music after Berlioz was Franz Liszt, twelve of whose symphonic poems were written between 1848 and 1858; a thirteenth was written in 1881–82. The name *symphonic poem* is significant: these works are symphonic but Liszt did not call them symphonies, presumably because they are relatively short and are not divided into separate movements in a conventional order. Instead, each is a continuous form with various sections more or less contrasting in character and tempo, and a few themes which are developed, repeated, varied, or transformed in accordance with the particular design of each work. *Poem* in the designation may refer simply to the root meaning of the word—something "made," invented—or perhaps to the poetic content in the sense of the program of each work; for the content and form in every instance are suggested by some picture, statue, drama, poem, scene, personality, thought, impression, or other object not identifiable from the music alone; it is, however, identified by the composer's title and usually also by a prefatory note. Thus *The Battle of the Huns* is related to a painting, *Mazeppa* to a poem, *Hamlet* to Shakespeare's hero,

Prometheus to the myth and also to a poem by Herder, and so on. The nature of the relationship is the same as in Berlioz; the program does not tell the story of the music, but runs parallel with it—an evocation, in a different medium, of analogous ideas and similar states of feeling.

Les Préludes was said by Liszt to be "after Lamartine," but the fact is that he wrote the music first as an overture to a choral work; only later, when he decided to publish it separately, did he cast about for a program, and eventually he made one up which consisted of a condensation of the ideas of one of Lamartine's *Méditations poétiques.* In *Die Ideale,* the score of which is liberally interspersed with quotations from Schiller's poem of that title, Liszt did not hesitate to change the order of Schiller's passages to make them conform with his own musical plan and to add an "apotheosis" of his own at the end. The best of the symphonic poems are probably *Orpheus* and *Hamlet. Les Préludes,* the only one of them that is still much played, is well designed, melodious, and effectively scored; but its idiom, like that of some of Liszt's other compositions, seems rhetorical, in a bad sense. It impresses most listeners nowadays as being filled with extravagant theatrical gestures, and as lavishing excessive emotion on ideas that do not seem sufficiently important for such displays of feeling. But *Les Préludes* did not so impress its contemporaries; the Romantics did not care much for that prudent economy of the emotions which is conventional in our time, and Liszt's symphonic poems were widely influential in the nineteenth century. The form was imitated by such composers as Smetana (*Má Vlast*), Franck (*Psyché*), Saint-Saëns (*Le Rouet d'Omphale, Danse macabre*), and Tchaikovsky (*Francesca da Rimini*), and their bold chord constructions and chromatic harmonies also contributed to the formation of Wagner's style after 1854.

Liszt's two symphonies are as programmatic as his symphonic poems. His masterpiece, the *Faust* Symphony (1854), was dedicated to Berlioz; it consists of three movements entitled respectively *Faust, Gretchen,* and *Mephistopheles,* with a finale (added later) which is a setting, for tenor soloist and chorus of men's voices, of the *chorus mysticus* which closes Goethe's drama. The first three movements correspond to the Classical plan: introduction and Allegro (in sonata form), Andante (three-part form), and Scherzo (three-part form, followed by a long additional development and coda). The first *Faust* theme illustrates Liszt's use of one of his favorite chords—the augmented triad, here transposed sequentially downward through four chromatic steps so as to comprise all twelve notes of the chromatic scale (Example XVII–4). Themes are interchanged among the movements and transformed in accordance with the program; the *Mephistopheles* part, for example, is largely made up of sinister caricatures of the *Faust* themes (a device also used in the finale of

EXAMPLE XVII–4   First theme, *Faust* Symphony, Liszt

Berlioz's *Symphonie fantastique*), and the *Gretchen* melody is used as the principal theme of the finale. In this symphony Liszt most successfully combined a grandiose and momentous program with music of great inspiration, substance, and passion, in a form whose huge dimensions are justified by the scope and power of the generating ideas. The *Dante Symphony* (1856) is altogether a less inspired work. It is in two movements (*Inferno* and *Purgatorio*) with a quiet concluding section for women's voices on the text of the *Magnificat*.

It is a far journey from Liszt's seething Romanticism to the Olympian realm of Brahms's four symphonies. The Classical reaction of the second half of the nineteenth century is epitomized in these works. Brahms, through no fault of his own, had come to be regarded as the representative of the party opposed to the Liszt-Wagner school. Naturally conscientious, severely self-critical, he approached the composition of a symphony with much care and deliberation, oppressed by what he felt to be his responsibility not to fall below Beethoven's achievements in this form. His only earlier orchestral pieces were two Serenades (D major, Op. 11, 1858; A major, Op. 16, 1860) and the masterly *Variations on a Theme of Haydn* (Op. 56A, 1873). The First Symphony, in C minor, was finished after many years of work in 1876, when the composer was forty-three; the second, in D major, appeared in 1877, while the last two (F major and E minor) were composed in 1883 and 1885 respectively. Brahms's other works for orchestra were the *Academic Festival Overture* (1880) and the *Tragic Overture* (1881); also, to the two piano concertos already mentioned are to be added the Violin Concerto in D major (1878), which ranks with Beethoven's concerto in the literature of this instrument, and the Double Concerto in A minor for violin and violoncello, Op. 102 (1887).

The Brahms symphonies are Classical in several respects: they are laid out in the customary design of four movements, each of which has a form recognizably close to the Classical pattern; they make use of the Classical techniques of counterpoint and motivic development; and they have no specified program—that is, they are absolute music in the same sense as Brahms's chamber works. At the same time, the symphonies are Romantic in their harmonic idiom, in their full, multicolored orchestral sound, and in other general features of their musical language. Yet they are no mere

Brahms's symphonies

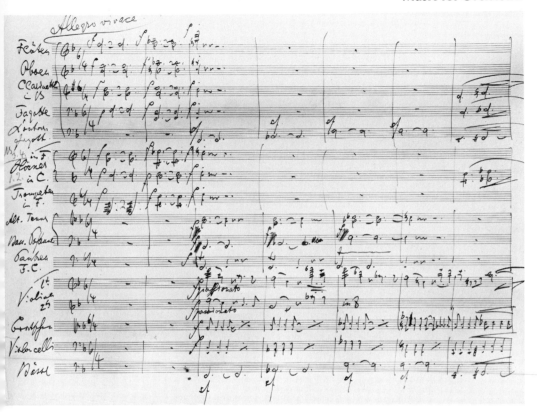

First page of the autograph score of Brahms's Third Symphony. (Library of Congress)

synthesis of Classicism and Romanticism; Brahms's style is consistent and individual, and various elements may be distinguished within it—among them a profound Schubertian, lyrical breadth of melodic line, a ballad-like quality of Romantic strangeness, and a fundamental respect for tradition as against the individualistic approach to music of Berlioz and Liszt. For Brahms, inspiration was not enough: ideas had to be soberly thought out and brought to a finally perfect form. He was concerned to avoid the pitfalls of Romanticism—false rhetoric, empty display of virtuosity, and above all what must have seemed to him (as it did to many of his contemporaries) the formlessness of music that apparently was held together only by an unguided stream of associated ideas in the mind of the composer. Brahms's control of his inspirations, and the consequent thought-out character of all his compositions account for the feeling of repose that sets his music apart from the more impulsive, impetuous Romantic compositions of 1830 to 1860. Brahms, whether he realized it or not, was responding to a general tendency of his time. The childlike freshness and the youthful ardor of Romanticism were alike spent by the middle of the century, and the wild oats period was over; a return to discipline, a revival of order and form, is apparent in the late works of Schumann and Berlioz, and even in those of Liszt and Wagner. Brahms's symphonies illustrate the trend even more clearly.

The First is the most Romantic. In key and general construction it takes its departure from Beethoven's Fifth; it is the only one of Brahms's symphonies which uses the Romantic formula of struggle (in minor) leading to triumph (in major). Other Romantic features are the key scheme (C minor–E major–Ab and B major–C minor and major); the recurrence of the opening chromatic theme in the second and fourth movements; the two portentous slow introductions, out of which the outlines of the themes to follow gradually emerge like mountains when the clouds lift; the emotional pathos of the slow movement, with an irruption of minor harmonies within the theme; and, in the introduction to the last movement, the romantic C-major melody played by horns and flutes over a mysteriously undulating accompaniment, and the solemn four-measure chorale phrase for trombones and bassoons which appears once more fortissimo at the climax of the Allegro.

The Second Symphony, in contrast to the First, has a peaceful, pastoral character, though not without serious undertones. Its third movement (like the corresponding movement in the First and Third Symphonies) has the lyrical rhythmic grace of an intermezzo rather than the intensity of the Beethoven scherzo; it is of the type that Brahms had created in the G major Sextet of 1867.

The Third Symphony has been called Brahms's *Eroica*. Its opening measures afford a particularly good illustration of one characteristic trait in his harmonic usage, the cross-relation of the minor and major forms of the tonic triad (see Example XVII–5); the rising

EXAMPLE XVII–5   Outline of First Theme of Third Symphony, Brahms

F–Ab–F motive of the bass is conspicuous again in the last movement of this symphony, which begins in F minor and does not settle in F major until the coda.

The Andante of the Fourth Symphony is one of Brahms's balladesque movements, the mood being suggested by the modal (Phrygian) tinge of the introduction and principal theme. The finale of this work is written in a form unusual in a symphony: a passacaglia or chaconne, consisting of 32 variations and a brief coda on an ostinato eight-measure theme. We have already mentioned Brahms's fondness for the variation form, one of the oldest types of musical structure, which embodies *par excellence* the twofold principle of unity and variety in composition. The nineteenth century had produced many sets of variations, some based on the older Classical techniques (Schubert and Mendelssohn), others in the style of the character variation which Beethoven had established with his *Diabelli* set—notably the *Symphonic Études* of Schumann and Brahms's *Handel Variations* for piano and *Haydn Variations* for orchestra. The *Symphonic Variations* of César Franck were the first important example of another, freer type. The revival of the Baroque ostinato variation in the Fourth Symphony is one more illustration of Brahms's feeling of spiritual kinship with the past; but he imbues the ancient form with Romantic color and passion. The diversity of figuration and mood among the variations is balanced by a feeling of continuous, controlled movement throughout. Superimposed on the passacaglia pattern is a suggestion of broad three-part form, the middle section consisting of four quiet variations in 3/2 meter (in effect, a tempo twice as slow as the preceding and following 3/4).

César Franck's only symphony (1888) shows some trace of Liszt in its chromatic harmonies and cyclical treatment of themes. But it is nonprogrammatic, and its stylistic elements are welded into a highly individual work, the influence of which was acknowledged by the following generation of composers in France.

Franck's symphony

Bruckner, like Brahms, had to reconcile the conflicting forces of Romanticism and Classicism in his symphonies, but his solution was fundamentally different. His First Symphony—preceded, however, by two experimental ones which he refused to publish—was composed in 1865–66; the finale of his Ninth was left uncompleted by his death in 1896. Bruckner, who tended to be overly sensitive to others' criticism, was constantly revising his symphonies, with the result that most of them exist in two or more different versions of his own and some also in still other, unauthorized versions made by conductors and editors. All are in the conventional four movements and none in explicitly programmatic, though the composer did at one time furnish a few descriptive tags for the Fourth (*Romantic*) Symphony—after its composition, however. There were no striking changes in Bruckner's style comparable to those which took place in Beethoven's; his symphonies are essentially alike in conception and technique, though undoubtedly the last three are the summit of his achievement in this form.

Bruckner's symphonies

The connection between Bruckner's symphonies and his sacred choral works has already been mentioned. The symphonies may perhaps best be understood as the expression of a profoundly religious spirit, revealed not so much by quotation of religious themes from the Masses and the *Te Deum* as by the prevailing serious, weighty mood of the symphonies as a whole; this is especially evident in the combination of mystic ecstasy and tonal splendor of the chorale-like themes that are the climaxes of his finales (and sometimes also of the first movements). Certain influences are obvious in Bruckner's musical language: his idol Wagner's particularly in the general harmonic idiom, the great length of the symphonies, the sequential repetitions of entire passages, and the huge size of the orchestra—the Wagner tubas are used in the slow movements and finales of the last three symphonies. From Beethoven's Ninth Bruckner derived his grandiose conception of symphonic form, some technical formal procedures, the type of thematic contrast in the Adagio of the Seventh Symphony, and the citation of themes from the previous movements in the introduction to the finale of the Fifth Symphony. That Bruckner was an organist is evident from his orchestration. The various instruments or instrumental groups are brought in, opposed, and combined like the contrasting registers or manuals of an organ; moreover, the expansion of thematic material is often effected by piling up massive blocks of sound in a way strongly suggestive of an organist's improvisation.

Bruckner's symphonies typically begin, like Beethoven's Ninth, with a vague agitation in the strings—a *nebula,* as one writer happily describes it,[2] out of which the theme gradually condenses and then builds up in a crescendo. These first themes have what may be called an elemental character; they begin with conspicuous emphasis on the notes of the tonic triad, extended usually over an octave or more, and set the tonality of the movement in most positive terms; the favorite rhythmic formula is the pattern $\left(\begin{smallmatrix}4\\4\end{smallmatrix}\right)$ ♩ ♩ ♩♩♩ . The finales open in the same way and usually with the same[3] kind of theme, which may even so closely resemble that of the first movement as to suggest cyclical recurrence. The first-theme complex is followed by the "song-theme group" (as Bruckner called it), and this in turn by a broad, closing section in which a chorale-like theme may be introduced. The movement continues with what would be called, in orthodox sonata form, development and recapitulation (sometimes merged), and a final section which often presents a grand apotheosis of the preceding themes. Both the first and last movements, though in allegro tempo, give the effect of moving slowly because of their long-breathed harmonic rhythm and spacious structure. The slow movements, usually cast in a broad sonata-like form with extended coda, are devout and solemn; those of the last three symphonies are especially impressive. The Scherzos reveal a different aspect of

2 Robert Simpson, *The Essence of Bruckner,* London 1967, 20.

Bruckner's musical personality. Their energy is like Beethoven's, but the melodies and rhythms of their trios reflect the spirit of Austrian popular songs and rustic dances.

Bruckner had the misfortune to live in Vienna under the shadow of Brahms and to be continually attacked by critics as a disciple of Wagner. His symphonies received little acclaim during his lifetime; for many years only two of them—the Fourth and Seventh—were played often outside Vienna and a few other European centers. No doubt their cathedral-like proportions and their monumental character were obstacles to popular acceptance; they seemed to lack both Classical clarity and easy Romantic appeal. Recent changes in taste, however, are bringing the Bruckner symphonies into deserved favor with a growing international public.

The only remaining symphonists to be mentioned are the Bohemian Antonín Dvořák (1841–1904) and the Russian Peter Ilyich Tchaikovsky (1840–93). They have a place in this chapter because, although their music is in some respects an outgrowth of nationalist ideas, their symphonies are essentially in the line of the German Romantic tradition. Of Dvořák's nine symphonies, the best is usually said to be No. 7[3] in D minor (1885), a work copious in thematic ideas and in a prevailingly tragic mood relieved only by the G-major trio of the scherzo. More relaxed in mood, with fresh folklike melodies and rhythms and many fine touches of orchestration, are the Symphonies No. 6 in D major and No. 8 in G major (1889). Most familiar is No. 9 (*From the New World*), which Dvořák wrote in 1893 during his first sojourn in the United States. This symphony, according to the composer, uses themes suggested by American Indian melodies and especially by Negro spirituals which Dvořák had heard sung at New York by Harry T. Burleigh. Among Dvořák's other orchestral music is a fine Concerto for violoncello; his string quartets are among the most attractive chamber music works of the late nineteenth century.

Other composers

Tchaikovsky's principal orchestral works include his last three symphonies (No. 4, F minor, 1877; No. 5, E minor, 1888; No. 6 [*Pathétique*], B minor, 1893). The immense popularity of these symphonies is due to their tunefulness, brilliant orchestration, and somewhat theatrical exhibition of Romantic emotion. The Fourth is probably the best example of a union of programmatic features

[3] References are to the now standard chronological numbering of Dvořák's symphonies. Relation between old and new numbering:

New	Old
5	3
6	1
7	2
8	4
9	5

with firm symphonic construction along fairly conventional lines. Other well-known orchestral works of Tchaikovsky are the symphonic poem *Francesca da Rimini* (1877), the overture-fantasia *Romeo and Juliet* (1867, 1880), the First Piano Concerto in B♭ minor (1875), and the Violin Concerto (1878). Less pretentious, and thoroughly charming, are the ballets, particularly *Swan Lake* (1876), *The Sleeping Beauty* (1890), and *The Nutcracker* (1892).

XVIII

‖‖

The Nineteenth Century: Opera and Music Drama

France

The combined influences of Gluck, the Revolution, and the Napoleonic Empire made Paris the operatic capital of Europe during the first half of the nineteenth century, and favored the rise there of a certain type of serious opera that is exemplified in *La Vestale* (1807). The composer of this work was the Empress Josephine's favorite musician, Gasparo Spontini (1774–1851), an Italian who had come to Paris in 1803 and who had a second career after 1820 as Court Music Director at Berlin. In *La Vestale* Spontini united the heroic, statuesque character of the late Gluck operas with the heightened dramatic tension of the then popular rescue plot, and clothed the whole in a grand display of solo, choral, and orchestral magnificence. Spontini's principal colleagues at Paris were Luigi Cherubini, whose opera, *Les deux Journées* (*The Two Days*, 1800; known also by the German title *Der Wasserträger, The Water Carrier*) was one of the models for Beethoven's *Fidelio;* and Étienne Nicolas Méhul (1763–1817), remembered now chiefly for his Biblical opera, *Joseph* (1807).

With the rise of a numerous and increasingly powerful middle class after 1820, a new kind of opera came into being, designed to appeal to the relatively uncultured audiences who thronged the theatres in search of excitement and entertainment. The leaders of this school of *grand opera,* as it came to be known, were the librettist

Grand opera

595

Eugène Scribe (1791–1861), the composer Giacomo Meyerbeer (1791–1864), and the director of the Paris Opera Theatre, Louis Véron (1798–1867). Two operas by Meyerbeer definitely established the style: *Robert le diable* (*Robert the Devil,* 1831) and *Les Huguenots* (1836).

Grand opera, following the fashion that had prevailed in France ever since the time of Lully, was as much an affair of spectacle as of music; librettos were designed to exploit every possible occasion for ballets, choruses, and crowd scenes. Meyerbeer's music was thoroughly eclectic and included the most popular elements of both the Italian and the French styles. It differed from Spontini's *Vestale* and other operas of the Napoleonic period not so much in externals as in the efficiency with which it set about achieving its main purpose, which was to give people what they wanted. For a public which presumably cared above all for sentiment and sensationalism, librettists and composers seemed willing to sacrifice both dramatic and musical integrity wherever necessary to produce an effect. The inevitable result was a style which, in spite of occasional beautiful and appropriate individual numbers, was as a whole vitiated by a too facile yielding to the temptation of immediate popular success. This judgment does not preclude recognition of the fact that Meyerbeer was an expert craftsman, or that his treatment of the orchestra, in particular, influenced Verdi and many other later composers; and it must also be acknowledged that some of his works —notably his two later grand operas *Le Prophète* (1849) and *L'Afri-caine* (first performed in 1865)—were less beset by the artistic shortcomings that marred *Robert* and *Les Huguenots.* Other composers of grand opera around 1830 were Auber (*La Muette de Portici, The Dumb Girl of Portici* [also known as *Masaniello*]; 1828), Rossini (*Guillaume Tell;* 1829) and Jacques Fromental Halévy (1799–1862), whose masterpiece, *La Juive* (*The Jewess;* 1835) deservedly outlasted Meyerbeer's works. *La Juive* and *Guillaume Tell* are the best of the grand operas of this period because they best incorporate the essential grandeur of the form—grandeur of structure and of style—in music that effectively serves more than the externals of the action. The French ideal of grand opera remained alive, though with diminishing vigor, throughout the nineteenth century; it was an influence in the work of Bellini (*I Puritani*), Verdi (*Las Vêpres siciliennes, Aïda*), and Wagner. Wagner's *Rienzi* is grand opera pure and simple, and certain features of that style are apparent in some of his later works, particularly *Tannhäuser, Lohengrin,* and even *Götterdämmerung.* The grand-opera tradition survives also in such twentieth-century works as Milhaud's *Christophe Columb* and Barber's *Antony and Cleopatra.*

Side by side with the grand opera in France, the *opéra comique* pursued its course during the Romantic period. As in the eighteenth century, the technical difference between these two was that the *opéra comique* used spoken dialogue instead of recitative. Apart from this, the principal differences were those of size and subject matter. The *opéra comique* was less pretentious than grand opera, required fewer singers and players, and was written in a much simpler musical idiom; its plots as a rule presented straightforward comedy or semiserious drama instead of the huge historical pageantry of grand opera. Two kinds of *opéra comique* may be distinguished in the early part of the nineteenth century, namely the romantic and the comic; it is not possible to maintain this distinction too rigidly, however, since many works possessed characteristics of both types. Predominantly romantic in plot, melodious, graceful, and sentimental in music, was the extremely popular *La Dame blanche* (*The White Lady*) by François Adrien Boieldieu (1775–1834), which was first performed at Paris in 1825. Similarly romantic *opéras comiques* were *Zampa* (1831) and *Le Pré aux clercs* (*The Field of Honor,* 1832) by Ferdinand Herold (1791–1833).

A more mordant Parisian style is evident in the work of Daniel François Esprit Auber (1782–1871), who in *Fra Diavolo* (1830) and his many other comic operas mingled romantic and humorous elements in tuneful music of considerable melodic originality. A new genre, the *opéra bouffe* (not to be confused with the 18th-century Italian *opera buffa,* despite the identity of name), which emphasized the smart, witty, and satirical elements of comic opera, appeared at Paris in the 1860s. Its founder was Jacques Offenbach (1819–80), whose *Orphée aux enfers* (*Orpheus in the Underworld;* 1858) and *La Belle Hélène* (1864) may be taken as typical. Offenbach's work influenced developments in comic opera elsewhere: the operettas of Gilbert and Sullivan in England (*The Mikado,* 1885) and those of a Viennese school whose best known representative is Johann Strauss the Younger (*Die Fledermaus* [*The Bat*]; 1874).

The perennial charm of nineteenth-century comic opera owes much to spontaneous elements of melody and rhythm; the simple textures and harmonies, the conventional formal patterns, and the deceptively naïve air should not mislead anyone into underrating this music. In the Romantic period, comic opera sheds a ray of sunshine over an otherwise distressingly humorless musical landscape.

The romantic type of *opéra comique* developed toward a form for which the designation "lyric opera" seems appropriate. Lyric opera lies somewhere between light *opéra comique* and grand opera. Like the *opéra comique,* its main appeal is through melody; its subject matter is romantic drama or fantasy, and its general scale is larger than that of the *opéra comique,* although still not so huge as that of the typical grand opera.

A favorite lyric opera was *Mignon* (1866) by Ambroise Thomas (1811–96), but by far the most famous example of this genre is

Gounod's *Faust,* which was first given in 1859 as an *opéra comique* (that is, with spoken dialogue) and later arranged by the composer in its now familiar form with recitatives. Gounod wisely restricted himself to Part One of Goethe's drama, dealing chiefly with the tragic love affair of Faust and Gretchen, for which his musical gifts were adequate. The result is a work of just proportions, in an elegant lyric style, with attractive melodies, sufficiently expressive but without Romantic excess. Gounod's other works for the stage include the opera *Roméo et Juliette* (1867) and a number of tuneful *opéras comiques.* Among the followers of Gounod may be mentioned Camille Saint-Saëns (1835–1921), of whose dramatic productions the Biblical opera *Samson et Dalila* (1877) is the most important.

A landmark in the history of French opera was Georges Bizet's (1838–75) *Carmen,* first performed at Paris in 1875. Like the original version of *Faust, Carmen* was classified as an *opéra comique* because it contained spoken dialogue (later set in recitative by another composer); but the fact that this stark, realistic drama could ever be called *"comique"* is simply an indication that by this time the distinction between opera and *opéra comique* had become a mere technicality. Bizet's rejection of a sentimental or mythological plot was significant of a narrow but important anti-Romantic movement toward realism in late nineteenth-century opera. In its Spanish setting and Spanish musical atmosphere, however, *Carmen* exemplifies a trait that runs through the whole Romantic period, namely exoticism—a trait equally evident in some of Bizet's earlier works (for example, the incidental music to Daudet's play *L'Arlésienne*) and in other French operas and ballets of the period. The music of *Carmen* has an extraordinary rhythmic and melodic vitality; it is spare in texture and beautifully orchestrated, obtaining the utmost dramatic effect always with the most economical means.

Hector Berlioz

Hector Berlioz contributed more than any other composer to the glory of French Romantic opera. His *Damnation of Faust* may be included here, although strictly speaking it is not an opera and is not intended for stage performance. The title page calls it a "dramatic legend." It incorporates, with revisions, an earlier work, *Eight Scenes from Goethe's Faust* (1828). In the final version (1846) the *Damnation* consists of twenty scenes, and requires three soloists, chorus, and orchestra. Its basic conception is like that of the *Symphonie fantastique* and *Romeo and Juliet,* namely a symphonic drama of which the connecting plot is assumed to be already known, so that the composer sets to music only those particular scenes which he finds most suitable for such treatment—in this way assuring the maximum of variety with the greatest possible compactness. Unlike the two earlier works, however, *The Damnation of Faust* has no lingering resemblance to the formal structure of the Classical symphony. Its unity is a function of Berlioz's own musical style and is dependent hardly at all on the few instances of recurring themes or motives. Altogether, this is one of the most diversified and most inspired of Berlioz's works; the familiar orchestral excerpts (including the Hungarian *Rákóczy* March) give but a partial impression of its riches.

The opera *Benvenuto Cellini* (1838) is another example of this composer's new way with traditional forms. Its general plan is, like that of *The Damnation of Faust,* a chain of broadly conceived episodes rather than a plot minutely developed. The score is notable for the vigor and variety of its music and for the treatment of the crowd scenes, which foreshadow those of Wagner's *Meistersinger.* Berlioz's two-act *opéra comique, Beatrice and Benedict,* was produced at Baden in 1862. The crown of Berlioz's dramatic works is the great five-act opera *Les Troyens,* composed in 1856–58. Its first part, *La Prise de Troie (The Capture of Troy),* was never staged until 1890; the second part, *Les Troyens à Carthage (The Trojans at Carthage),* had a few performances at Paris in 1863. It is only within recent years that this masterpiece has begun to receive the appreciation it deserves, and it has yet to make its way into the repertoire of established opera houses. *Les Troyens* is unlike any other opera. The text, by Berlioz himself, is based on the second and fourth books of Vergil's *Aeneid;* as with *Cellini* and *Faust,* only the essential stages of the action are presented, in a series of mighty scene-complexes. The narrative is condensed, and various appropriate occasions are used for the introduction of ballets, processions, and other musical numbers. Although the outward form and the use of a historical (or legendary) subject make *Les Troyens* apparently resemble a grand opera of the 1830s, in actuality nothing could be further from the meretricious glitter of a work like Meyerbeer's *Huguenots.* The drama preserves the antique, suprapersonal, epic quality of Vergil's poem, and the music speaks in the same accents. Not a note is there for mere effect; the style is severe, almost ascetic by comparison with some of Berlioz's earlier works. At the same time every passion, every scene and incident, are brought to life intensely and on a heroic scale. *Les Troyens* is the Romantic consummation of the French opera tradition in the line of descent from Rameau and Gluck.

Italy

The history of Italian opera in the nineteenth century may be understood as the orderly evolution of an established tradition, healthily grounded in the life of the nation. Italy was less susceptible than northern countries to the seductions of the Romantic movement, and her composers were therefore less quickly tempted to try new and radical experiments. Romantic elements permeated Italian opera only gradually, and never to the same degree as in Germany and France. Moreover, opera was the only important Italian musical outlet in this period, so that the genius of the nation was largely concentrated on this one form; and such a situation also tended to encourage a conservative attitude.

The distinction between *opera seria* and *opera buffa* was quite clearly maintained until well into the new century; then, in the serious opera, signs of change first appeared. Although Gluck's theories had little effect in Italy, the influence of the French opera began to be felt shortly after 1800 in the expansion of orchestral color by increased use of woodwinds and horns, greater importance of the orchestra as a whole, and more extensive use of choruses. The founder of the nineteenth-century style of Italian serious opera was Johann Simon Mayr (1763–1845), a German by birth who, like Hasse before him, lived most of his life in Italy, and who was able through his works to promote general acceptance of many of the changes which Jommelli had advocated a generation earlier.

Gioacchino Rossini

Gioacchino Rossini (1792–1868), the principal Italian composer of the early nineteenth century, was endowed with a pronounced gift for melody and a flair for stage effect that brought him quick success. Between the ages of eighteen and thirty he produced in Italy 32 operas and two oratorios, in addition to a dozen cantatas, two symphonies, and a few other instrumental works. Among his best serious operas were *Tancredi* (Venice; 1813), *Otello* (Naples; 1816), and *La donna del lago* (Naples; 1819), though the Romantic libretto of the last (adapted from Scott's *Lady of the Lake*) was not approved by the public.

Comic opera was congenial to Rossini, and many of his works in this genre sound as fresh today as when they were first written —for example, *La Scala di seta* (*The Silken Ladder,* Venice; 1812), *L'Italiana in Algeri* (*The Italian Woman in Algiers,* Venice; 1813), *La Cenerentola* (*Cinderella,* Rome; 1817), and *La Gazza ladra* (*The Thieving Magpie,* Milan; 1817). His masterpiece, *Il Barbiere di Siviglia* (*The Barber of Seville,* Rome; 1816), ranks with Mozart's *Figaro* and Verdi's *Falstaff* among the supreme examples of Italian comic opera.

Rossini's style combines an inexhaustible flow of melody with pungent rhythms, clear phraseology, well-shaped and sometimes quite unconventional structure of the musical period, a spare texture, clean and discriminative orchestration, and a harmonic scheme which, though not complex, is by no means always unoriginal. He shares with other early nineteenth-century composers a fondness for bringing the mediant keys into close juxtaposition with the tonic. Above all, he is a master of comic delineation, both of characters and situations—comic, not merely witty, for at his best he is able, like Mozart and Verdi, to make us feel the hint of pathos that underlies all high comedy. Rossini's ensembles, that type of scene so characteristic of comic opera, are managed with sparkle and gusto. A simple but effective device, in ensembles and elsewhere, is the crescendo: building up excitement by means of many repetitions of a phrase, each time louder and at a higher pitch (for instance, in the aria *La calunnia* from *Il Barbiere*). Rossini was no revolutionary, though he did encourage certain reforms; he sometimes replaced the piano in *recitativo secco* with orchestral accompaniment (first in *Otello*), and he attempted to bridle the excesses of improvised embellishment by writing out the coloratura passages and cadenzas.

After the comparative failure of his serious opera *Semiramide* at Venice in 1823, Rossini accepted an invitation to London; then, in 1824, he settled in Paris. Here he brought out new versions of two of his earlier works (adapting them to the French taste by giving greater importance to chorus and orchestra), and composed an *opéra comique, Le Comte Ory* (1828) and the grand opera *Guillaume Tell* (1829). In the remaining forty years of his life he wrote only sacred music, songs, and "albums" of piano pieces. *Tell* was Rossini's nearest approach to Romanticism, and his natural antipathy to the new Romantic doctrines may be one reason why he voluntarily ended his operatic career at that point; but his figure dominated Italian opera through the first half of the century. As far as the bulk of his work is concerned, Rossini represented the deep-rooted Italian conviction that an opera is in essence the highest manifestation of an intensely cultivated art of song, and that its primary purpose is to delight and move the hearer by music that is melodious, unsentimental, spontaneous, and, in every sense of the word, popular. This national ideal was important in the Romantic period as a counterbalance to the different conceptions of opera that were held in France and Germany.

One of the most prolific Italian composers of the second quarter of the century was Mayr's pupil, Gaetano Donizetti (1797–1848), who in addition to some 70 operas composed about 100 songs, *Gaetano* several symphonies, oratorios, cantatas, chamber music, and church *Donizetti* music. His most enduring works were the serious operas *Lucrezia Borgia* (1833), *Lucia di Lammermoor* (1835), and *Linda di Chamounix* (Vienna; 1842); the *opéra comique, La Fille du régiment* (*The Daughter of the Regiment,* Paris; 1840); and the buffo operas *L'elisir d'amore* (*The Elixir of Love;* 1832) and *Don Pasquale* (1843). Donizetti had some of Rossini's instinct for the theatre and his talent for melody, and in *Don Pasquale* he created a work that can well endure comparison with *Il Barbiere*. On the whole his comic operas stand the test of time better than his serious ones. The rough, primitive, impulsive character of his music is well adapted to the

A scene from the second act of Don Pasquale *by Donizetti as it was depicted in the contemporary press of 1843 when it was first performed at the* Théâtre Italien *in Paris.*

representation of crude, melodramatic situations, but his works—composed for the most part very rapidly and with a view to immediate success—are all too often marred by monotony of harmony, rhythm, and orchestration; yet much of *Lucia* and *Linda,* and some scenes in his other operas must be excepted from this criticism. Donizetti was the immediate historical precursor of Verdi; the two had in common an implicit reliance on the taste and judgment of the Italian public, and their work is deeply rooted in the life of the people.

Vincenzo Bellini (1801–35), by comparison, may be called the aristocrat of his period. Of his ten operas (all serious) the chief are *La Sonnambula* (*The Sleepwalker;* 1831), *Norma* (1831), and *I Puritani e i Cavalieri* (*The Puritans and the Cavaliers*; Paris, 1835). The style is one of utmost lyric refinement; the harmony is sensitive, and the intensely expressive melodies have a breadth, a flexibility of form, a certain elegance of curve, and an elegiac tinge of feeling that are often reminiscent of Chopin's nocturnes. Bellini is a master of psychological expression in recitative, of which a splendid

Vincenzo Bellini

example is afforded by the opening number of the second act of *Norma*. His treatment of the chorus and the orchestra evinces a corresponding care for detail; some of his choral scenes (notably in *La Sonnambula*) have a peculiarly classic repose and breadth.

Some influences of Romanticism in general and of French opera in particular may be discerned in both Donizetti's and Bellini's works with the appearance of another genre, the *opera semiseria*—a serious plot leavened by Romantic scenery and sentiment, in a manner analogous to the lyric opera of France; Donizetti's *Linda di Chamounix* and Bellini's *Sonnambula* are of this sort. Material for such operas was drawn increasingly from Romantic instead of from ancient classic literary sources, as in the eighteenth-century *opera seria*. French grand opera furnished the model for pseudo-historical subjects treated on a huge scale, as in Bellini's *Puritani* and to a certain extent also in *Norma*. Romantic influence is more marked in the Italian librettos of this period than in the music itself; there is hardly a trace of it in the scores of the extrovert Donizetti, and with Bellini it is manifested in the generally subjective quality of the sentiment rather than in particular details.

The career of Giuseppe Verdi (1813–1901) practically constitutes the history of Italian music for the next fifty years after Donizetti. Except for the *Requiem* and a few other settings of sacred texts, a few songs, and a string quartet, all Verdi's works were written for the stage. The first of his 26 operas was produced in 1839, the last in 1893. At no point did Verdi break with the past or experiment radically with new theories; his evolution was toward refinement of aim and technique, and in the end he brought Italian opera to a point of perfection never since surpassed.

Giuseppe Verdi

Such an orderly development, so different from the course of musical affairs in the northern countries, was possible because Italy possessed a long, unbroken operatic tradition which was understood and loved by a whole people; the conflict between the individual artist and society—and, indeed, most of the other contradictions that underlay the Romantic attitude in Germany and France—did not exist in Italy. The only basic Romantic issue that much affected Italian music was nationalism, and in this respect Verdi was uncompromising. He believed wholeheartedly that each nation should cultivate the kind of music that was native to it; he maintained a resolute independence in his own musical style and deplored the influence of foreign (especially German) ideas in the work of his younger compatriots. Many of his early operas contain choruses that were thinly disguised inflammatory appeals to the patriotism of his countrymen struggling for national unity and against foreign domination during the stirring years of the *Risorgimento;* and Verdi's popularity was further increased when his name became a patriotic symbol and rallying-cry: *"Viva Verdi!"*

to Italian patriots stood for *"Viva Vittorio Emanuele Rè D'Italia!"* —Long live Victor Emanuel, King of Italy.

A more profoundly and essentially national trait in Verdi was his unswerving adherence to an ideal of opera as human drama— in contrast to the emphasis on romanticized Nature and mytho- logical symbolism in Germany—to be conveyed primarily by means of simple, direct, vocal solo melody—in contrast to the orchestral and choral luxuriance of French grand opera. His independence was not, of course, absolute. Apart from the genial influence of Beethoven, whom he revered above all composers, and the obvious indebtedness to his predecessors Donizetti, Bellini, and Rossini, Verdi learned much from the harmony and orchestration of Meyer- beer; but he never accepted anything without having first fully assimilated it and made it part of his own language.

Verdi's creative life may be divided into three periods, the first culminating with *Il Trovatore* and *La Traviata* (1853), the second with *Aïda* (1871), and the last comprising only *Otello* (1887) and *Falstaff* (1893). With the exception of *Falstaff* and one unsuccess- ful early work, all Verdi's operas are serious. Their subjects for the most part were adapted by his librettists from various Romantic authors—Schiller (*Giovanna d'Arco, I masnadieri, Luisa Miller, Don Carlos*), Victor Hugo (*Ernani* and *Rigoletto*), Dumas the Younger (*La Traviata*), Scribe (*Les Vêpres siciliennes, Un Ballo in Maschera*), or Spanish dramatists (*Il Trovatore, La Forza del Destino, Simon Boccanegra*); from Shakespeare, in addition to *Macbeth,* came the librettos of the last two operas, skillfully arranged by Verdi's friend, the poet and composer Arrigo Boïto (1842–1918); *Aïda* was developed from a plot sketched by a French Egyptologist, A. F. F. Mariette, when Verdi was commissioned to compose an opera to celebrate the opening of an opera house in Cairo.

Verdi's main requirements of a libretto were strong emotional situations, contrasts, and speed of action; plausibility was no object. Consequently most of the plots are violent blood-and-thunder melo- dramas, full of improbable characters and ridiculous coincidences, but with plenty of opportunity for the exciting, lusty, ferocious melodies and rhythms which are especially characteristic of Verdi's early style. Certain features about the construction are common to many of Verdi's operas. Typically, each has four main divisions —either four acts, or three acts with a prologue, or three acts sub- divided into scenes in such a way as to approximate a fourfold division; the second and third divisions have important ensemble finales, there is usually a big duet in the third, and the fourth com- monly opens with a *preghiera* (prayer scene) or similar meditation for a soloist (preferably the heroine), often accompanied by chorus. That this scheme was a dependable one for purposes of the theatre is proved by the fact that Verdi not only adopted it in his early works but retained it without essential alteration even in *Aïda* and *Otello*.

Many of the early operas are notable for their choruses; *Nabucco* (1842), probably the best of the very early works, has excellent choral writing, as do also *I Lombardi* (1843), *Giovanna d'Arco* (1845), and the occasional opera, *La Battaglia di Legnano* (*The Battle of Legnano;* 1849). Many of the features of the early period are summed up in *Il Trovatore* (*The Troubadour,* 1853), one of Verdi's most popular works. But a change began to be evident in *Luisa Miller* (1849); here, and increasingly henceforward, personages are depicted with finer psychological distinction, and emotion in the music becomes less raw than in the early operas. Characterization, dramatic unity, and melodic invention unite in the masterpiece *Rigoletto* (1851). The famous quartet—a companion piece to the sextet in Donizetti's *Lucia*—the aria *Caro nome,* the storm music in Act III, and the effective recall of the tenor aria *La donna è mobile* in the closing scene, are a few of the high points of this work. *La Traviata* (*The Lost One;* 1853) is in a more intimate vein than heretofore, and is remarkable for the appearance of a new kind of melody, a flexible, expressive, semideclamatory arioso which Verdi developed still further in *Otello.* *Early works*

Two experiments in grand opera were *Les Vêpres siciliennes* (*The Sicilian Vespers;* 1855) and *Don Carlos* (1867), both of which were first performed at Paris. *Don Carlos* is the more successful of the two; its revised version (1884) contains powerful dramatic scenes, as well as some interesting orchestral and harmonic effects typical of Verdi's late style. Throughout the second period the operas appeared at less frequent intervals than formerly; Verdi was indulging in a certain amount of cautious experimentation. Solo, ensemble, and chorus are more freely combined in the dramatic scheme (for example, the finale of Act I of *Simon Boccanegra,* 1857), harmonies become more venturesome, while the orchestra is treated with greater care and originality. Comic roles are introduced in *Un Ballo in Maschera* (*A Masked Ball;* 1859) and *La Forza del Destino* (*The Power of Destiny,* 1862; revised, 1869). Both these operas also make use of a device fairly common in the nineteenth century and one with which Verdi had experimented already in *Rigoletto* and elsewhere: the recurrence of one or more distinctive themes or motives at crucial points which serves to produce both dramatic and musical unity. All the advances of the second period are gathered up in *Aïda* (1871), which unites the heroic quality of grand opera with sound dramatic structure, vivid character delineation, pathos, and a wealth of melodic, harmonic, and orchestral color.

Sixteen years elapsed before Verdi came before the public with another opera. During this interval a number of important new works of music had appeared—among them Verdi's own *Requiem,* *Late works*

Bizet's *Carmen,* all four of Brahms's symphonies, Bruckner's Seventh Symphony, and Wagner's *Ring* (in its first complete performance) and *Parsifal.* For all his deliberate isolation Verdi was sensitive to new currents, and *Otello,* produced at Milan in 1887, was his response to the changed musical situation. Yet it was a response determined no more by Verdi's reaction to outside forces than by his own inner evolution. Externally, *Otello* seems to differ from the earlier operas chiefly in the more nearly complete continuity of the music within each act. But closer inspection reveals that the traditional scheme of Italian opera with solos, duets, ensembles, and choruses is still present; the continuity is achieved by subtle transitions, a plastic flow of melody, and the connective power of the orchestra. The libretto, incomparably the best that Verdi had ever had, sets forth a powerful human drama which the music penetrates, sustains, and glorifies at every turn. The harmonic language and the orchestration are fresh and vital, yet transparent, never usurping the expressive function of melody or obscuring the voices. A summary idea of these features, as well as of the evolution of Verdi's style in general, can be obtained by comparing the beautiful love duet at the end of the first act of *Otello* with some duets from his earlier operas: *Nabucco* (Act III, *Donna, chi sei?*), *Rigoletto* (end of Act II, *Piangi, fanciulla*), and *Aïda* (end of Act IV, *O terra addio*).

Otello was the consummation of Italian tragic opera, *Falstaff* (1893) of comic opera. In both, the timeless essence of Italian opera, of the long tradition extending from Monteverdi through Steffani, Scarlatti, Hasse, Mozart, and Rossini, was fulfilled and at the same

Backstage at the Paris Opera, 1894: Verdi and the baritone Victor Maurel who created the role of Iago in Otello. *(Courtesy Opera News)*

time enriched with new elements derived from Romanticism—but Romanticism purified by Verdi's clear intellect and sensitive discrimination. As *Otello* transfigured dramatic lyrical melody, so *Falstaff* transfigured that characteristic element of *opera buffa,* the ensemble. Carried along over a nimble, fine-spun, endlessly varied orchestral background, the comedy speeds to its climaxes in the great finales of the second and third acts. At times Verdi seems to be satirizing the entire Romantic century, himself included. The last scene culminates in a fugue to the words "tutto nel mondo è burla"—"all the world's a joke, all men are born fools."

In all Verdi's operas, from *Nabucco* to *Falstaff,* one trait is constant: a combination of primitive, earthy, elemental emotional force with directness, clarity, and—beneath all its refinement of detail— *Summary* fundamental simplicity of utterance. Verdi is essentially more Classical than Romantic in spirit; his Classicism is attained not by triumphing over Romanticism, as Brahms did, but rather by almost ignoring it. His relation to the Romantic movement might be suggested by the contrast between his attitude and that of the northern Romantics toward Nature. The depiction of the natural background in Verdi's operas is concise, suggestive, almost formalized, like the landscapes in Renaissance Italian paintings—the storm music in *Rigoletto* and *Otello,* for example, or the exotic atmosphere in *Aïda.* His attitude toward Nature is completely unsentimental. All his interest is in humanity; Nature is there to be used, not worshiped. Verdi is the only eminent composer in history who was also a successful farmer.

German Romantic Opera

One of the distinguishing marks of the nineteenth century, as we have seen, was the strong mutual influence between music and literature. The composite art form of opera is well adapted to display the effects of such influences; and since Germany was the country in which Romanticism flourished most intensely, some of the most far-reaching developments and ramifications of the whole movement are exhibited in German opera. Germany had no such long-established operatic tradition as did Italy, and this circumstance also tended to favor experimentation. The immediate background of German Romantic opera was the singspiel, exemplified at its best by Mozart's *Magic Flute.* In the early nineteenth century the singspiel, partly owing to the influence of the French opera of the period, became increasingly imbued with Romantic elements, at the same time retaining and even intensifying its specific national features. Both trends are illustrated by two operas produced in 1816: *Undine,* by the distinguished author and musician E. T. A. Hoffmann (1776–1822), and *Faust,* by Ludwig Spohr (1784–1859), a famous violinist, composer of oratorios, symphonies, concertos, and chamber music, and the leading minor German composer of the early Romantic era. The definitive work that established German Romantic opera, however, was Weber's *Der Freischütz,* first performed at Berlin in 1821.

Weber

Carl Maria von Weber was familiar with the theatre from early childhood. His principal music teachers were Michael Haydn and Georg Joseph Vogler (1749–1814), generally known as Abbé or Abt Vogler, one of the most bizarre characters in the history of music—an organist, organ builder, theorist, composer of operas and church music, teacher of many famous pupils (including Meyerbeer), and subject of one of Browning's poems. Weber became director of the Opera at Prague in 1813 and at Dresden in 1816. His chief dramatic compositions besides *Der Freischütz* were *Euryanthe* (Vienna; 1823) and *Oberon* (London; 1826).

The characteristics of German Romantic opera, as exemplified in *Der Freischütz* and similar works, may be summarized as follows: plots are drawn from medieval history, legend, or fairy tale; in conformity with contemporary trends in literature, the story involves supernatural beings and happenings, lays stress on a background of wild and mysterious Nature, but frequently also introduces scenes of humble village or country life. Supernatural incidents and natural background are treated not as incidental decorative fantasy, but seriously, as intertwined with the fate of the human protagonists. Human characters are regarded not merely as individuals, but in some sense as agents or representatives of supernatural forces, whether good or evil, so that the eventual victory of the hero becomes also the triumph of angelic over demonic powers. This victory itself is often interpreted in terms of salvation or redemption—a concept, with its vaguely religious connotation, which is perhaps an extension of the rescue motif so prominent in the opera of the early years of the century. In the importance given to the physical and spiritual background, German opera differs strongly from contemporary French and Italian opera. Its musical style and forms naturally have much in common with the opera of other countries, but a new element is the use of simple folklike melodies of a distinctly German national cast. Of even more importance is the strong reliance on harmony and orchestral color for dramatic expression. This emphasis on the inner voices of the texture (in contrast to the Italian concentration on melody) may be regarded as a musical counterpart of the emphasis in the German libretto on the mood, setting, and occult significance of the drama.

Reference to certain details of *Der Freischütz* will serve to illustrate these generalizations. There is no intelligible brief English equivalent for the title. The story revolves about a situation common in folklore and immortalized in Goethe's *Faust:* a man has sold his soul to the devil in return for earthly favors—in this instance, for some magic bullets which will enable him to win a contest of marksmanship and with it the hand of the lady he loves. As usual, the devil is cheated; the hero is redeemed by his lady's pure love from the consequences of his bargain, and all ends well. The sombre forest background is depicted idyllically by the melody for horns at the beginning of the overture and diabolically in the eerie midnight "Wolf's Glen" scene of the casting of the magic bullets (finale of Act II). Rustic choruses, marches, dances, and airs mingle in the score with full-bodied arias in Italian style. The quintessence of mysterious Romantic suggestion through orchestration and harmony is in the twelve measures at the end of the Adagio introduction to the overture; likewise, it is the orchestration and the strange harmonic scheme (contrast of F$\sharp$ minor and C minor) that chiefly contribute to the musical effectiveness of the Wolf's Glen scene, a model of Romantic depiction of supernatural horror. Another feature of this opera is the use of recurrent themes: for example, the melody of the last part of the big soprano aria in Act II (at the words *All' meine Pulse schlagen*) has already been heard as one of the themes of the overture, and will appear once more at the end of the opera; other themes from the overture recur in a tenor aria in Act I (at *Doch mich umgarnen finstre Mächte*) and in the finale of Act II. The overture to *Der Freischütz* is not, like so many opera overtures of the early nineteenth century, a simple medley of tunes; rather, like the overtures of Beethoven, it is a complete symphonic first movement in sonata form with a slow introduction.

The immense popular success of *Der Freischütz*—a success based on its appeal to national sentiment as well as on the beauty of the music—was not repeated either by Weber's later works or by those of his immediate followers. *Euryanthe,* Weber's only opera that does not contain spoken dialogue, is on a scale approaching grand opera; it is unified to an even greater degree than *Der Freischütz* by its continuous musical texture and consistent use of contrasting harmonic styles to characterize the opposing forces of the drama, as well as by the recurrence and transformation of musical themes. This device of recurring themes in opera may be likened to the cyclical principle in symphonic music used by Liszt, Franck, and other composers. It was not altogether new in nineteenth-century opera—indeed, we find it as far back as Monteverdi's *Orfeo*—but it was the nineteenth-century composers who first made extensive and systematic use of it; it represents a rather radical departure from the older principle of complete thematic independence of the various divisions of an opera or a symphony. Weber's procedures in *Euryanthe* represent one stage in a process that reached its logical culmination in Wagner.

Oberon, Weber's last opera, is weakened by an insignificant and rambling libretto; by way of compensation, however, the score contains some of his most sophisticated passages of orchestral color, along with some good examples of Romantic tone-painting.

Other German opera composers

Most of Schubert's operas and singspiels—a half dozen of each, and several others uncompleted—never reached the stage during his lifetime, and have remained without influence, though they contain a great deal of excellent music. In his best opera, *Fierrabras* (1823), there are some interesting anticipations of the leitmotif technique.

German opera for twenty years after Weber was carried on by a number of estimable second-class composers, chief of whom were Heinrich Marschner (1795–1861) and Albert Lortzing (1801–51). Marschner specialized in Romantic singspiels of a semipopular sort; his most important work, *Hans Heiling* (1833), derives from Weber and at the same time looks forward to Wagner in both its plot and its musical style. Lortzing's *Zar und Zimmermann* (*Czar and Carpenter;* 1837) is a good example of the comic genre in which he excelled. Other German composers of comic opera were Otto Nicolai (1810–49) and Liszt's disciple, Peter Cornelius; the latter's *Barbier von Bagdad* (*The Barber of Bagdad;* 1858) is a witty and original work. Schumann's romantic opera *Genoveva* (1850), despite critical esteem for the quality of its music, obtained no success in the theatre. Along with the growth of national opera in the period from 1830 to 1850, the French *opéra comique* was popular in Germany; serious opera on historical subjects was represented by the late works of Spontini and Meyerbeer.

Richard Wagner: The Music Drama

Richard Wagner

The outstanding composer of German opera, and one of the crucial figures in the history of nineteenth-century music, was Richard Wagner (1813–83). Wagner's significance is threefold: he brought German Romantic opera to its consummation, in much the same way that Verdi brought Italian opera; he created a new form, the *music drama;* and the harmonic idiom of his late works carried to the limit the Romantic tendencies toward dissolution of Classical tonality, becoming the starting point for developments still continuing to the present day. In addition, Wagner's writings had considerable influence on nineteenth-century thought, not only about music, but also about literature, drama, and even political and moral issues.

For Wagner, the function of music was to serve the ends of dramatic expression; his only important compositions are those for the theatre. His first triumph came with *Rienzi,* a five-act grand opera performed at Dresden in 1842. In the following year, also at Dresden, appeared *Der fliegende Holländer* (*The Flying Dutchman*), a Romantic opera in the tradition of Weber and Marschner. The success of these two works led to Wagner's being appointed director of the Opera at Dresden, thus putting an end (temporarily) to a long period of wandering and struggle in his life. In *Der fliegende Holländer* the lines of development that Wagner was to follow in his later works are established. The libretto—written, like those of all his operas, by the composer himself—is based on a legend; the action takes place against a background of the stormy sea, and the drama is resolved with the redemption of the hero through the unselfish love of the heroine Senta. Wagner's music is most vivid in the depiction of the storm and of the contrasted ideas of curse and salvation, which are clearly set forth in the central number of the opera, Senta's ballad. The themes of the ballad are also those of the overture, and they recur elsewhere throughout the opera, although this technique was not so thoroughly and systematically applied as it was in Wagner's later works.

Tannhäuser (Dresden; 1845) is a brilliant adaptation of the substance of the German Romantic libretto to the framework of grand opera. The music, like that of *Der fliegende Holländer*, evokes the opposite worlds of sin and blessedness, but with greater emotional fervor and more luxuriant resources of harmony and color. The display numbers—the Venusberg ballet, the Pilgrims' choruses, the Song Contest—are plausibly connected with the course of the drama, and effective use is made of thematic recurrence. A new kind of flexible, semideclamatory vocal melodic line, such as Wagner later employed regularly, is heard in Tannhäuser's narrative in Act III (*Inbrunst im Herzen*).

Lohengrin, first performed under Liszt's direction at Weimar in 1850, is the last important German Romantic opera and at the same time embodies several changes prophetic of the music dramas of Wagner's next period. The sources of the story are medieval legend and folklore, but the treatment is more generalized and symbolic than in the preceding operas: Lohengrin himself, for example, may represent divine love descending in human form, and Elsa the weakness of humanity unable to receive with faith the proffered blessing. Such a symbolic interpretation is suggested by the Prelude, which depicts the descent of the Holy Grail and its return to Heaven.

The orchestration of *Lohengrin* is at once fuller and more subdued than that of *Tannhäuser;* the music flows more continuously, with less marked traces of division into separate numbers; the well-written choruses are combined with solo singing and orchestral background into long, unified musical scenes. Greater use is made of the new style of declamatory, arioso melody (as in Lohengrin's *In fernem Land*, Act III). The technique of recurring themes is further developed and refined, particularly with respect to the motifs associated with Lohengrin and the Grail and the motif of the "forbidden question" (first at the words *Nie sollst du mich befragen,* Act I). As with Weber, tonality becomes important in dramatic as well as musical organization: Lohengrin's key is A major, Elsa's A♭ or E♭, and that of the evil personages F♯ minor. The style on the whole is diatonic, with modulations usually toward the mediant keys.

As a result of the political troubles of 1848–49, Wagner emigrated to Switzerland, and this country became his home for the next ten years. Here he found leisure to formulate his theories about opera and to publish them in a series of essays, the most important of which is *Opera and Drama* (1851). At the same time he was writing the poems of a cycle of four dramas with the collective title *Der Ring des Nibelungen* (*The Ring of the Nibelung*). The music of the first two—*Das Rheingold* (*The Rhine Gold*) and *Die Walküre* (*The Valkyrie*)—and part of the third, *Siegfried,* was finished by 1857; the entire cycle was completed with *Götterdämmerung* (*The Twilight of the Gods*) in 1874, and the first complete performance took place two years later in a theatre especially built according to Wagner's specifications at Bayreuth. In the meantime he had composed *Tristan und Isolde* (1857–59) and *Die Meistersinger von Nürnberg* (*The Mastersingers of Nuremberg,* 1862–67). His last work was *Parsifal* (1882).

The Ring

Wagner's conception of the music drama is illustrated most clearly in the *Ring.* Its subject matter is drawn not from legend or fairy tale, but from Norse mythology; Wagner regarded the myths as suitable not only because they offer plentiful opportunities for effective theatre but also because they embody, in a concentrated, poetic fashion, certain philosophical issues that are of fundamental importance in human life. The ruling ideal of Wagner's form is the absolute oneness of drama and music; the two are organically connected expressions of a single dramatic idea—unlike conventional opera, in which song predominates and the libretto is mainly a framework for the music. The action of the drama is considered to have an inner and an outer aspect; the former is the province of instrumental music, that is, of the orchestra, while the sung words make clear the particular events or situations that are the outer manifestations of the action. Consequently, the orchestral web is the primary factor in the music and the vocal lines are part of the polyphonic texture, not arias with accompaniment. The music is continuous throughout each act, not formally divided into recitatives, arias, and other set numbers; in this respect Wagner carried to its logical end a steadily growing tendency in the opera of the first half of the nineteenth century. Even so, the continuity is not completely unbroken; broad scene divisions remain, and within the scenes a distinction is still evident between recitative-like passages

EXAMPLE XVIII–1   Leitmotifs from the *Ring,* Wagner

I. a. The Rhine   *b. Erda*

c. Twilight of the Gods

II. a. The Rhine gold   *b. Woe*   *c. Fate*

d. Death Song   *e. Wanderer*   *f. Hagen*

III. a. Alberich's curse

b. Siegfried

c. Redemption

with orchestral punctuation and others of arioso melody with continuous orchestra. Moreover, the unfolding of the drama is occasionally interrupted, or adorned, with interwoven scenes of
decidedly operatic character that are not always strictly necessary
to the plot.

Within the general continuity of the action and music Wagner
uses two principal means for achieving articulation and formal
coherence. The first is the leitmotif. A leitmotif is a musical theme
or motive associated with a particular person, thing, or idea in the
drama. The association is established by sounding the leitmotif
(usually in the orchestra) at the first appearance or mention of the
object of reference, and by its repetition at each subsequent appearance or mention. Thus the leitmotif is a sort of musical label—but it
is more than that: it accumulates significance as it recurs in new contexts; it may serve to recall the thought of its object in situations
where the object itself is not present; it may be varied, developed,
or transformed in accord with the development of the plot; similarity
of motifs may suggest an underlying connection between the objects
to which they refer (see Example XVIII–1); motifs may be contrapuntally combined; and, finally, repetition of motifs is an effective

The leitmotif

613

means of musical unity, as is repetition of themes in a symphony. Theoretically, there is complete correspondence between the symphonic web of leitmotifs and the dramatic web of the action; in practice, however, Wagner sometimes introduces certain motifs for what seem to be purely musical reasons, without any obvious necessary connection with the dramatic situation of the moment (though a connection can usually be discovered if one is sufficiently determined to find it).

About twenty leitmotifs appear in all four of the *Ring* dramas; some thirty others are also used quite extensively. A similar system prevails in *Tristan, Die Meistersinger,* and *Parsifal.* Wagner's use of the leitmotif principle differs from that of such composers as Verdi and Weber. First, Wagner's motifs themselves are for the most part short, concentrated, and (in intention, at least) so designed as to characterize their object at various levels of meaning: the motifs associated with Loki, for example, not only depict the flickering of flames but also suggest the unstable, slippery character of Loki who (as the German version of his name, Loge, suggests) is the god of lies and deceitful cleverness, as well as of fire. Another and more important difference, of course, is that Wagner's leitmotifs are the essential musical substance of the work; they are used not as an exceptional device, but constantly, in intimate alliance with every step of the action.

A system of leitmotifs, however ingeniously applied, cannot of itself produce musical coherence. To this end, Wagner wrote his *Formal structure* acts in sections or "periods," each of which is organized in some recognizable musical pattern, most often *AAB* (*Bar* form) or *ABA* (three-part, or *Bogen* [arch] form). This structural framework, is must be said, is revealed only by analysis. The forms are not intended to be obvious to the listeners, and their essential outlines are modified by transitions, introductions, codas, varied repetitions, and many other devices. Periods are grouped and related so as to form a coherent pattern within each act, and each act in turn is a structural unit in the shape of the work as a whole. This formidable complex of forms within forms was perhaps not entirely a matter of deliberate planning on the composer's part, but it exists nevertheless. In its largest aspects, the form of the music dramas depends on key relationships: the entire *Ring,* according to Lorenz, is organized around the tonality of D♭, *Die Meistersinger* around C. *Tristan* is a peculiar case: it begins in A minor and ends in B major so that its tonality of E (which actually is heard very little in the score) is, as it were, polarized, held between its subdominant and dominant. (Compare the way Beethoven establishes C major at the beginning of his First Symphony.) One should add that these extremely long-range concepts of tonality in Wagner are, for the majority of listeners at any rate, more intellectual constructs than conscious audible experiences. Still, in *Die Meistersinger* the unity is clearly enough heard, the key of C being emphasized not only by the tonal identity of the overture and the last act finale but also by the fact that the finale itself, from the entrance of the Meistersinger, is an extended and varied reprise of the overture.

Tristan und Isolde is in many respects the quintessence of Wagner's mature style. Few works in the history of Western music have so potently affected succeeding generations of composers. The system of leitmotifs is happily subordinated to a flow of inspiration, an unbroken intensity of emotion, that effectively conceals and transcends mere technique. In contrast to the tragic gloom and the extremely chromatic idiom of *Tristan* are the sunny human comedy and predominantly diatonic harmony of *Die Meistersinger*. Here Wagner succeeded most fully in fusing his conceptions of the music drama with the forms of Romantic opera, and in combining a healthy nationalism with universal appeal. *Parsifal*, by comparison, is somewhat less assured, less unified both in content and musical form, but abounds (as does *Die Meistersinger*) in beautiful choral scenes and instrumental numbers.

Late works

A contemporary production of Tristan und Isolde *(Act I) at the Metropolitan Opera House. (Photograph courtesy Louis Mélançon)*

In the harmony of his later works, especially in *Tristan* and the prelude to the third act of *Parsifal*, Wagner carried out an evolution in his personal style that had been stimulated by his acquaintance in the 1850s with the chromatic idiom of Liszt's symphonic poems.

Isolde's costume for the original production of Tristan und Isolde *at Munich in 1865.*

The complex chromatic alterations of chords in *Tristan,* together with the constant shifting of key, the telescoping of resolutions, and the blurring of progressions by means of suspensions and other non-harmonic tones, produces a novel, ambiguous kind of tonality, one that can be explained only with difficulty in terms of the harmonic system of Bach, Handel, Mozart, and Beethoven. This departure from the Classical conception of tonality in such a conspicuous and musically successful work can today be viewed historically as the first step on the way toward new systems of harmony which marked the development of music after 1890. The evolution of harmonic style from Bruckner, Mahler, Reger, and Strauss to Schoenberg, Berg, Webern, and later twelve-tone composers can be traced back to the *Tristan* idiom.

Wagner's influence

Wagner's work affected all subsequent opera. His peculiar use of mythology and symbolism could not be successfully imitated; but his ideal of opera as a drama of significant content, with words, stage setting, visible action, and music all working in closest harmony toward the central dramatic purpose—the ideal, in short, of the *Gesamtkunstwerk* or universal art-work—was profoundly influential. Almost equally influential was his technical method of continuous music (endless melody) which minimized divisions within an act and assigned to the symphonic orchestra the function of maintaining continuity with the help of leitmotifs while the voices sang in free, arioso lines rather than in the balanced phrases of the traditional aria. As a master of orchestral color Wagner had few equals, and in this respect also his example was fruitful. Above all, his music impressed itself on the late nineteenth century because it was able, by its sheer overwhelming power, to suggest or arouse or create in its hearers that all-embracing state of ecstasy, at once sensuous and mystical, toward which all Romantic art had been striving.

XIX

The End of an Era

The late nineteenth and early twentieth centuries witnessed the last stages of Romanticism and the transformation of the late Romantic idiom into a new musical language. This movement took place chiefly in Germany, which after the Franco-Prussian War of 1870–71 became a united empire and rose rapidly to the position of a first-class power. The formerly dominant musical position of Germany was being challenged by two forces, however. One was a surgent nationalism, first strongly evident in Russia and Bohemia but soon spreading to the Baltic and Scandinavian countries, to Spain, Italy, Hungary, England, and America. The second was the rise of a new school of composition in France. The conflicting influences of late Romanticism, nationalism, and the French school are the essential factors in the history of music from 1870 to 1910. The last thirty years of the nineteenth century were relatively peaceful and stable in Europe; the beginning of the twentieth century was marked by increasing social unrest and international tension, culminating in the catastrophe of the First World War. Similar unrest and tension in the musical realm were manifested by various radical experiments; and in these years not only the Classic-Romantic period ended, but also the whole concept of tonality as the eighteenth and nineteenth centuries had understood it.

Post-Romanticism

Wagner exercised an enormous fascination over European musicians in the last quarter of the nineteenth century. All composers came under his spell, although at the same time most of them were consciously struggling not to imitate him. One of the characteristic features of this period in Germany was a revival of interest in the *Märchenoper*, the fairytale opera. The principal work of this type was *Hänsel und Gretel* (1893) by Engelbert Humperdinck (1854–1921), which rather incongruously combined Wagnerian orchestral polyphony and the use of leitmotifs with simple and charming folklike melodic material. The influence of Wagnerian harmony in the symphonies of Bruckner has already been mentioned.

Another Wagner enthusiast was Hugo Wolf (1860–1903). Wolf's compositions include piano pieces, choruses, symphonic works, one completed opera (*Der Corregidor*, 1896), a string quartet, and the *Italian Serenade* for small orchestra (1892; originally composed as a string quartet movement in 1887); but he is chiefly important for his 250 *Lieder*, which ably continue the German Romantic tradition of the solo song with piano accompaniment, bringing to it as well certain elements which may be ascribed largely to the influence of Wagner. Most of Wolf's songs were produced in short periods of intense creative activity during the ten years from 1887 to 1897. They were published in six principal collections, each devoted to a single poet or group of poets, as follows: 53 on poems of Eduard Mörike (1889); 20 of Eichendorff (1889); 51 of Goethe (1890); the *Spanisches Liederbuch* (1891), 44 songs on German translations of Spanish poems; the *Italienisches Liederbuch* (Part I, 1892; Part II, 1896), 46 settings of translations from the Italian; and three poems by Michelangelo in German translation (1898)—a projected additional three of this set having never been completed, owing to the onset of the insanity that afflicted the composer in the last years of his life.

Hugo Wolf

Wolf's literary taste in the selection of texts was more uncompromising than that of earlier German song writers. He concentrated on one poet at a time, and placed the name of the poet above that of the composer in the titles of his collections—indicating a new conception of the relation between words and music in the Lied, derived from Wagner's music dramas, an ideal of a particular kind of equality between poetry and music, and of particular technical means for achieving such equality. Wolf had no use for the folksong type of melody and little use for the strophic structures that were so characteristic of Brahms. Precedents for his *Lieder* are the five songs that Wagner composed in 1857–58 on poems of Mathilde Wesendonck. (It is incidentally interesting that Wolf made orchestral arrangements of the piano parts of a few of his own *Lieder*.) But his piano accompaniments, even in the most "symphonic" of his songs, seldom suggest either an orchestral texture or the predominance of instrumental over vocal sound which is common in Wagner. Likewise, the singer's line, though it often is written in a declamatory or arioso style rather than being organized into periodic melodic phrases, always preserves a truly vocal character. In short, Wolf adapted Wagner's methods with discrimination; the fusion of voice and instrument is achieved without sacrificing either to the other.

A good illustration of such balance is *Auf einer Wanderung* (Mörike), in which the typical extended piano introduction, interludes, and postlude have an important poetic role. *Anakreons Grab* (Goethe) is equally characteristic of a more lyric vein. Some of the Goethe *Lieder* successfully stand comparison with Schubert's settings of the same words—*Kennst du das Land?* for example, or the three great songs *Prometheus, Ganymed,* and *Grenzen der Menschheit.* The Spanish and Italian *Lieder* are for the most part shorter, more relaxed in feeling and at the same time more concentrated in style —exquisite miniatures such as *In dem Schatten meiner Locken* or *Und willst du deinen Liebsten sterben sehen.* The utmost intensity and concentration is found in one of the last songs, *Alles endet, was entstehet,* from the Michelangelo collection.

Some passages in Wolf's songs are clearly inspired by the idiom of *Tristan* with its chromatic voice-leading, appoggiaturas, and rapid modulations (Example XIX–1); but equally beautiful effects are obtained in a sensitive diatonic style, for example in *Nun wand're Maria,* one of the Spanish songs. Wolf's treatment of pictorial images is always restrained but at the same time highly poetic

EXAMPLE XIX–1   *Anakreons Grab,* Hugo Wolf

What grave is this which all the gods have planted and adorned with life?

and original; one instance among many is the suggestion of distant bells in the piano part of *St. Nepomuks Vorabend* (Goethe). It is impossible to convey an adequate idea of the infinite variety of fine psychological and musical details in Wolf's songs. Study of the scores brings continuous discovery of new delights.

The last of the great German post-Romantic symphony composers was the Austrian Gustav Mahler (1860–1911). An eminent interpreter as well as composer, Mahler served as director of the Vienna Opera from 1897 to 1907 and conductor of the New York Philharmonic Society from 1909 to 1911. His works, composed for the most part in the summer between busy seasons of conducting, include nine symphonies (a tenth remained uncompleted) and five song-cycles for solo voices with orchestra, of which the chief is *Das Lied von der Erde* (*Song of the Earth,* composed in 1908). All but the last three symphonies and the *Song of the Earth* were frequently revised, and it is likely that these also would have undergone revision had Mahler lived longer The earlier published versions did not incorporate all the composer's emendations, but this is now being done in the new Collected Edition which was begun in 1960.

Gustav Mahler

Mahler's symphonies are typical post-Romantic works: long, formally complex, programmatic in nature, and demanding enormous performing resources. Thus the Second Symphony, first performed in 1895, requires, along with a huge string section, 4 flutes (two interchangeable with piccolos), 4 oboes, 5 clarinets, 3 bassoons and a contrabassoon, 6 horns and 6 trumpets (plus four more of each, with percussion, in a separate group), 4 trombones, tuba, 6 kettle-drums and numerous other percussion instruments, 3 bells, 4 or more harps, and organ, in addition to soprano and alto soloists and a chorus. The Eighth, composed in 1906–07 and popularly known as the *Symphony of a Thousand,* calls for an even larger array of players and singers. But the size of the orchestra is not the whole story. Mahler is one of the most adventurous and most fastidious of composers in his treatment of instrumental combinations, comparable in this respect perhaps only with Berlioz; his natural genius for orchestration was reinforced by his constant activity as a conductor, which gave him opportunity to perfect details of scoring in the light of practical experience. Instances of his felicity in orchestral effects, ranging from the most delicate to the most overwhelmingly gigantic, occur abundantly in all the symphonies (compare, for example, the ending of the third movement of the First Symphony or the beginning of the second movement of the *Song of the Earth* with the tremendous opening of the Eighth Symphony). Mahler's instrumentation, as well as his extremely detailed indications of phrasing, tempo, and dynamics and his occasional use of unusual instruments (such as the mandoline in the Seventh and Eighth Symphonies and the *Song of the Earth*), are not mere displays of ingenuity, but are intrinsically part of the composer's musical

Mahler's symphonies

A cancelled page from the autograph orchestral score of the third movement of Mahler's Ninth Symphony, corresponding to the first 11 measures of page III/35 of the score sketch facsimile published by Universal Edition; this section does not appear in the final version. (Private collection, New York)

ideas. For instance, the *scordatura* solo violin—all the strings tuned one full tone higher than normally—in the scherzo of the Fourth Symphony is intended to suggest the sound of the medieval *Fiedel* (fiddle) in a musical representation of the Dance of Death, a favorite subject in old German paintings.

The programmatic content is not always expressly indicated in Mahler's symphonies. With the first four he gave out rather detailed programs, somewhat in the manner of Berlioz or Liszt; but these were later suppressed. No such definite clues exist for the Fifth, Sixth, or Seventh Symphonies (composed between 1901 and 1905), but certain quotations from or references to some of Mahler's songs, the presence of many obviously pictorial details, and the total plan of each of these works all irresistibly suggest that the composer had in mind generalized extra-musical ideas similar to those illustrated in the Third and Fifth Symphonies of Beethoven. Thus Mahler's Fifth and Seventh move steadily from funereal gloom to triumph and joy; the Sixth, on the contrary, is his "tragic" symphony, culminating in a colossal finale in which heroic struggle seems to end in defeat and death. The Ninth, Mahler's last completed symphony (composed 1909–10), flows in a mood of resignation, of indescribably strange and sad farewell to life, symbolized by deliberate reference to the *Lebe wohl* (Farewell) theme of the opening of Beethoven's Sonata Op. 81a. This motif, or reminiscences of it, pervades the first and last movement (both in slow tempo) of the Ninth Symphony, as well as that other "farewell" work of Mahler's last years, the *Song of the Earth* (Example XIX–2).

Mahler the symphonist cannot be separated from Mahler the song composer. Themes from his early *Lieder eines fahrenden Gesellen (Songs of a Wayfarer;* composed 1883–84) appear in the opening and closing movements of the First Symphony; the Second, Third, and Fourth Symphonies incorporate melodies from the cycle of twelve songs on folk poems from the early nineteenth-century

EXAMPLE XIX–2   "Farewell" Motives

d. Dark is life, is death. e. The lovely earth everywhere blossoms in the new green of spring.

collection *Des Knaben Wunderhorn* (*The Boy's Magic Horn*) which Mahler composed between 1888 and 1899. Following the example of Beethoven, Berlioz, and Liszt, Mahler uses voices as well as instruments in four of his symphonies. The last movement of the Fourth has a soprano soloist, while soprano and alto soloists join with women's and boys' choruses in the fourth and fifth movements of the Third. The most extensive use of singing, however, occurs in the Second and Eighth Symphonies.

The Second, one of Mahler's most frequently played works, is known as the *Resurrection Symphony*. Like Beethoven, Mahler brings in voices for the final climax of the work. After a long, agitated, and highly developed first movement there follows an Andante in the easy, swinging, folksong-like rhythm of an Austrian *Ländler*, or slow waltz. The third movement is a symphonic adaptation of one of the *Wunderhorn* songs, and the brief fourth movement is a new setting, for contralto solo, of still another poem from this collection. This serves to introduce the finale which, after a vivid and dramatic orchestral section depicting the day of Resurrection, leads to a monumental setting for soloists and chorus of a Resurrection ode by the eighteenth-century German poet, Klopstock. The Eighth Symphony consists of two huge choral movements, on the texts respectively of the plainsong hymn *Veni creator spiritus* and the whole closing scene of Part II of Goethe's *Faust*. The second movement is practically a complete secular oratorio in itself, resembling in many ways Liszt's *Faust* Symphony and *St. Elizabeth,* or Wagner's *Parsifal*.

The Song of the Earth

The *Song of the Earth* is based on a cycle of six poems translated from the Chinese by Hans Bethge under the title *The Chinese Flute*. The texts alternate between a frenzied grasping at the fleeting dream-like whirl of life and a resigned sadness at imminent parting from all its joys and beauties. As Mahler called on the human voice in the symphonies to complete his musical thought with the language of words, so here he calls on the orchestra to sustain and supplement the tenor and contralto solos with all its resources, both in accompaniment and in extensive connecting interludes. The exotic atmosphere of the words is lightly suggested by details of instrumental color and the use of the pentatonic scale. The *Song of the Earth* is deservedly Mahler's best-known work, one that epitomizes all the traits of his genius. Nowhere else did he so perfectly define and bring into balance that peculiar dualism of feeling, that ambivalence of ecstatic pleasure underlaid with deadly foreboding, that seems to characterize not only the composer himself but also the whole autumnal mood of late Romanticism. At no other time in history, perhaps, could the insistently recurring phrase "Dark is life, dark is death" (Example XIX–2d) have been given such poignant musical expression.

The most general clue to Mahler's style is just this dualism, which extends to every feature of his work. In his symphonies he attempted—not always with success—to join sophistication with simplicity, to juxtapose the most lofty, wide-ranging cosmic conceptions and struggles with lyricism, Austrian folk song, nature painting, popular dance rhythms, chorale themes, marches, elements of parody, the spooky, and the grotesque. In his own phrase, each symphony was to be "a world." In this Faustian striving to be all-inclusive, Mahler was at one with the Romantic spirit, which he embodied most clearly in the Second Symphony. The Third, on the other hand, suffers from a too apparent dichotomy of styles. A vast, full-blown symphonic first movement is followed by five relatively short ones, diverse in character: a minuet with trio, a *scherzando* based on one of Mahler's early songs and featuring a posthorn, a contralto solo on a text from Nietzsche's *Zarathustra,* a soprano solo with boys' and women's chorus on a merry song from *Des Knaben Wunderhorn,* and, for conclusion, a broadly expressive orchestral adagio. The Fourth Symphony likewise mirrors a variegated "world," but one better unified in musical form, shorter, more lightly orchestrated, and altogether more easily accessible; this symphony and the Second have always been more popular than any of Mahler's works except the *Song of the Earth.*

Summary

In nearly all the symphonies Mahler freely transfers motives from one movement to another, though never to the extent of suggesting a cyclical scheme. Notable also is his practice, stemming from Mahler's feeling for the symphonic significance of the various tonalities, of ending a symphony in a different key from the one in which it began (IV, G major–E major; V, C♯ minor–D major; VII, B minor–E major–C major; IX, D major–D♭ major). Mahler owes to Bruckner's influence his "chorale" themes, his fondness for motives based on the intervals of the fourth and fifth, his introductions (especially the opening of the Second Symphony), and the adagio movements of the Third and Ninth Symphonies. The three middle symphonies (the Fifth, Sixth, and Seventh) approach most closely the Classical forms, but on a colossal scale and in an impassioned Romantic idiom, with prominent pictorial features and sharp contrasts of mood and style. Even such a device as the shift from the major to the minor triad, which Mahler may have learned from Schubert or Dvořák, is used with symbolic intent to portray in typically Romantic fashion the change from optimism to despair (the Sixth Symphony). The Eighth Symphony is the climax of Mahler's second period and the extreme point in his work of the post-Romantic exaggeration in the size of the performing forces.

With the composition (1900–04) of ten songs for solo voice and small orchestra on poems of Friedrich Rückert, Mahler had forecast the change of style which is evident in his Ninth and (unfinished) Tenth Symphonies and the *Song of the Earth*. The typically full, crowded textures of the earlier works were often replaced by a more austere idiom, with clearer contrapuntal lines in an instrumentation of almost chamber-music style and proportions. At the same time, some of Mahler's techniques contributed to the steadily weakening sense of traditional tonal organization and furnished suggestions of procedure which later composers took up and developed. Mahler was thus, in a way to which there seems to be no real parallel in previous musical history, a transitional composer. He fell heir to the whole Romantic tradition—Berlioz, Liszt, Wagner—and particularly to the Viennese branch—Beethoven, Schubert, Brahms, and above all Bruckner. Restlessly experimenting, all-devouring in his interests, he expanded the Romantic Symphony and symphony-oratorio to their point of final dissolution; still experimenting, he foreshadowed a new age and became a prime influence on the later Viennese composers, Schoenberg, Berg, and Webern.

Richard Strauss

A quite different historical significance must be assigned to the most famous of the German post-Romantic composers, Richard Strauss (1864–1949). Strauss, like Mahler, was a celebrated conductor; trained under Hans von Bülow, he held positions in the opera houses of Munich, Weimar, Berlin, and Vienna, and in the course of numerous tours he conducted most of the great orchestras of the world. He received many official honors both at home and abroad, and was universally recognized as the dominant figure in German musical life during the first part of the present century.

Strauss's piano pieces, chamber music, and choral works are of minor interest. He wrote some 150 *Lieder,* of which not more than a dozen or so—mostly from his early period—are commonly known outside Germany and Austria; but songs such as *Allerseelen* (1883), *Ständchen* (1887), and the wonderfully evocative *Traum durch die Dämmerung* (1895) prove that Strauss is one of the masters of the nineteenth-century Lied. He is important mainly, however, for his symphonic poems and operas. Most of the symphonic poems were produced before 1900, while all but one of the operas came after that date.

Mahler, despite his inclusion of many programmatic and even operatic elements, had held essentially to the Classical idea of a symphony as a work in several distinct movements in a form primarily determined by principles of musical architecture, to which the extra-musical factors are considered subordinate; he was, in fact, the last of the line of German symphonists extending from Haydn through Mozart, Beethoven, Schubert, Schumann, Brahms, and

Bruckner. Strauss, on the contrary, attached himself at once (after a few youthful experiments) to the more radical Romantic line of the symphonic poem, where his chief models were Berlioz and Liszt.

There are two kinds of program for a symphonic poem: one, which we may call the "philosophical," lies in the realm of general ideas and emotions, unattached to particular incidents; Liszt's *Les Préludes,* and most of his other symphonic poems, have a program of this sort. The other, which we may call the "descriptive" type of program, requires the composer to render or attempt to illustrate in music particular nonmusical events; most of Berlioz's programs are of this kind. The two types cannot be strictly set apart, since philosophical programs often include descriptive elements and descriptive programs usually have also a more general significance; the distinction rests only on the relative conspicuousness of the descriptive details. Music lends itself quite well to the philosophical type of program, which indeed may be known or suspected to exist behind many compositions that are not acknowledged to be program music at all, such as Beethoven's Fifth Symphony, Schumann's Third, the symphonies of Bruckner generally, and the purely instrumental symphonies of Mahler. Description, on the other hand, is more difficult to reconcile with the nature of the language of music. Obviously, the more definite the event to be described, and the more prosaic (that is, incapable of being immediately felt as symbolic of some general idea or emotion), the greater the danger to the composer of producing something that is a mere curiosity, an excrescence without significance in the musical structure. His skill is shown, in such cases, by his ability to absorb the imitated events and sounds into the musical whole by subjecting them to the procedures of absolute music. Successful examples are the bird songs of Beethoven's *Pastoral* Symphony, the distant thunder in the third movement of Berlioz's *Symphonie fantastique,* and the depiction of Resurrection day in the finale of Mahler's Second Symphony.

Strauss wrote symphonic poems to both philosophical and descriptive programs. His best works of the former type are *Tod und Verklärung (Death and Transfiguration;* 1889) and *Also sprach Zarathustra (Thus Spake Zarathustra;* 1896); of the latter, *Till Eulenspiegels lustige Streiche (Till Eulenspiegel's Merry Pranks;* 1895) and *Don Quixote* (1897). His other principal orchestral works are: the symphonic fantasia *Aus Italien (From Italy;* 1886), musical sketches like those of Mendelssohn's *Italian Symphony* but in the then revolutionary musical idiom of Strauss; *Don Juan* (1889), after a poem by Nikolaus Lenau, Strauss's first completely mature work— vividly scenic and descriptive music of tremendous verve, with brilliant orchestration; *Macbeth* (1886, revised version 1891); *Ein Heldenleben (A Hero's Life;* 1898), the program of which is autobiographical, a mocking and defiant challenge to Strauss's critics

Strauss's symphonic poems

whom he caricatures in cacophonous passages while glorifying his own deeds and triumphs with citations from his early works—a climax of post-Romantic gigantism in style and orchestration; the *Sinfonia domestica* (1903), also autobiographical but idyllic rather than epic, a picture on an overly broad canvas of the family life of the composer; and the *Alpensymphonie (Alpine Symphony;* 1915), romantic pictorial program music in a simpler, less chromatic style than the previous works.

Tod und Verklärung embodies a program similar to that of many symphonies and operas of the nineteenth century: the progress of the soul through suffering to self-fulfillment. This is a general, philosophical program, though Strauss later admitted that he had had in mind certain descriptive details. These were elaborated, after the work was written, by Alexander Ritter in a poem now prefixed to the score. The music is worked out with genuine warmth of emotion in themes and harmonies of spontaneous power, with strong dramatic contrasts. Its musical form can best be understood as an Allegro in free sonata form with a slow introduction and a hymnlike epilogue; the principal themes occur in cyclical fashion in all three parts. Dissonances, which so shocked some of Strauss's contemporaries, are freely used here as in his other works for the expression of violent feeling. Many of his novel harmonic and orchestral effects have been so often copied that by now we are likely to underestimate the real originality of Strauss in his own day. But in *Tod und Verklärung,* at least, there are no traces of the occasional tendency to make effects for their own sake, or of mere perverse pleasure in startling the listener, that taint with vulgarity some passages of *Ein Heldenleben* and the *Sinfonia domestica.*

The program of *Zarathustra* is philosophical in a double sense: the work is a musical commentary on the celebrated prose-poem by the brilliant, erratic Friedrich Nietzsche, whose doctrine of the superman was agitating all Europe at the end of the century (a choice of subject typical of Strauss's highly developed sense for the value of publicity). Although a part of Nietzsche's prologue stands at the head of the score and the various divisions are furnished with titles from the book, the music cannot be regarded as an attempt to depict a philosophical system in tones; Nietzsche's ideas served merely as a stimulus to Strauss's musical imagination. The only obviously artificial touch is the construction of a fugue theme which uses all twelve notes of the chromatic scale (Example XIX–3) to symbolize the all-embracing but dark and cloudy realm of *Wissenschaft* (science, learning, knowledge)—the symbolism being reinforced by the low-lying thick sound of the fugal exposition, which is given to the double-basses and violoncellos, each divided in four parts. It is not such incidental matters, but rather the length (30–35 minutes) of this one-movement symphonic poem, its dense polyphonic texture, its free-fantasia form, and its apparently capricous diversity of moods that make *Zarathustra* difficult for the unprepared listener to follow. Its musical content is rich and original and, like all of Strauss's works, it is full of expertly contrived orchestral effects. One unifying feature is the motive *C–g–c* (first measure of Example XIX–3), a "nature" motive like those of Bruckner which announces the "sunrise" at the opening of the work and is heard recurrently throughout, even in the final cadence; another consistent feature is the constant play of contrast between the tonalities of C and B, a contrast that remains unreconciled even in the closing measures where, under the sustained B-major chords of the woodwinds and high strings, the unresolved appoggiatura C♮ still sounds in the pizzicato of the double basses and violoncellos. *Zarathustra* is also remarkable for Strauss's first use of a waltz, a genre which he employed frequently in his later works.

EXAMPLE XIX–3   Fugue subject from *Also sprach Zarathustra,* Strauss

In *Till Eulenspiegel,* the popular favorite among his symphonic poems, Strauss developed a comic program in music of unfading freshness and melodic attractiveness. The realistic details of Till's adventures (specified by a few marginal notes that the composer added to the printed score) are so thoroughly blended with the musical flow that the work could easily be heard simply as a character sketch of a particularly appealing rascal, or even more simply as a piece of unmediated musical humor, reminiscent of Haydn. A further suggestion of Haydn lies in Strauss's indication that *Till* is "in rondo form." Rondo it is not in the Classical sense, but rondo-like by reason of the many recurrences of the two *Till* themes, which appear in an endless variety of guises, enlivened by shrewd touches of instrumentation. In no other work does Strauss seem so unconstrained, so spontaneously himself, as in this merry musical tale.

The realism of *Don Quixote* is of a rather more dubious order. Ten adventures of the knight of the sorrowful countenance and his stolid squire, Sancho Panza, are recounted in the form of ten "fantastic variations on a knightly theme" (really a triple theme). Windmills, the bleating of sheep, the ride through the air, and other details are depicted with wit and orchestral virtuosity, but the effects, unlike those in *Till,* remain external to the music; one cannot understand them without knowing the incidents they are meant to describe. More poetically conceived are the conversations between the knight and squire, each of whom is distinguished by his own themes and also by his own instruments—Don Quixote chiefly by solo violoncello, Sancho by solo viola or bass clarinet and tenor tuba. The death of Don Quixote, like that of Till Eulenspiegel, is occasion for a tender and sympathetic epilogue to a score otherwise largely dominated by the spirit of irony and satire.

Strauss wrote one unsuccessful opera, *Guntram,* in 1893. In 1901 *Feuersnot* (*The Fire Famine*) had a moderate but not long-continued success. He leaped into fame as an opera composer first in 1905 with *Salome* and from that time on the powers of depiction and characterization that had formerly gone into symphonic poems were utilized almost exclusively in opera. Like Beethoven, Berlioz, Liszt, Wagner, and Mahler, Strauss came to feel the need of words to supplement the language of music. At the same time, the necessity of creating a musical counterpart to subjects, actions, and emotions different from any that had been previously attempted in opera stimulated him to create harmonically complex and dissonant idioms that were of considerable influence for the later growth of expressionism and the dissolution of tonality in German music of the first half of the twentieth century.

Strauss's operas

Strauss accepted the Wagnerian principles of continuous music, the primacy of the polyphonic orchestra, and the systematic use of leitmotives; but, after *Guntram,* he renounced any desire to make opera an instrument of propaganda for philosophic or religious doctrines as Wagner had done in the *Ring* and *Parsifal. Feuersnot* is an odd mixture of medieval legend, eroticism, farce, parody, and satire, with a corresponding welter of musical styles. *Salome* is a setting of Oscar Wilde's one-act play in German translation. Strauss illumined this decadent version of the Biblical story with music which by its orchestral splendor, novel rhythms, and keenly descriptive harmonies captures with such expressive force the macabre tone and atmosphere of the drama as to lift it to a plane where artistry prevails over perversion. *Elektra* (1909) began the long and fruitful collaboration between Strauss and the Viennese dramatist, Hugo von Hofmannsthal (1874–1929). For Hofmannsthal's rather one-sided version of Sophocles' play, which dwells throughout its long single act on the emotions of insane hatred and revenge, Strauss conceived music that in sharpness of dissonance and apparent harmonic anarchy outdid anything previously known.

The anarchy is only apparent. In spite of *Tristan,* audiences in 1905 still expected chords that sounded like dominants to resolve to a tonic, which Strauss's seldom do. The prevailing post-Romantic chromatic harmony is offset by some dissonant polytonal passages, as well as by others in a pure diatonic tonal style. The sound of the harmony may be considered as emanating from a single germinal chord (Example XIX–4a). Strauss thus anticipates a technique used by some later twentieth-century composers. The score is further uni-

fied by the use of leitmotives and by the association of certain keys
with particular characters or situations: B♭ with Agamemnon, E♭
with Chrysothemis, and a C–E complex with Elektra's triumph.
Chord relationships at the interval of a tritone are frequently exploited, as in the motive associated with Elektra (Example XIX–4b).
Dissonances most often occur as the result of contrapuntal movement of lines, but occasionally are used deliberately for shock effect.

EXAMPLE XIX–4   Examples of Strauss's Harmony

a. The Germinal Chord of *Elektra*

b. *Elektra* motive

Salome and *Elektra* scandalized the respectable public of the
1900s, the former chiefly by its subject and the latter by its music.
Time has tempered the critcisms, and the once fearful dissonances
sound common enough. What remains, and is to be esteemed, is
Strauss's amazing virtuosity in the invention of musical ideas and
instrumental sonorities to characterize both persons and actions.

Der Rosenkavalier (*The Rose Cavalier,* 1911), on an excellent
libretto in three acts by von Hofmannsthal, takes us into a sunnier
world, a world of elegant, stylized eroticism and tender feeling, the

Alfred Roller's design for the original 1911 Vienna production of
Strauss's Der Rosenkavalier. *The caption reads: "Stage setting for the
3rd Act: Private room in a small inn." (Reproduced by permission
of Boosey & Hawkes, Inc.)*

aristocratic wig-and-powder milieu of eighteenth-century Vienna. *Der Rosenkavalier* is Strauss's operatic masterpiece. The sultry harmonies of *Salome* and the cacophonies of *Elektra* are softened to a mature synthesis of the elements in the earlier operas and symphonic poems. The ultra-Romantic, sensuous melodic curves, the sophisticated chromatic harmonies (see Example XIX–5), the magical orchestral colors, tumultuous rhythms, lively sense of comedy, and speciously simple diatonic style derived from South German dances and folk songs, are held together in poise and given depth of meaning by an overruling humane sympathy that never quite slips over the verge into irony. Consistent with this turn toward Classicism, in *Der Rosenkavalier* the human voice once again becomes prominent; woven into the orchestral background and alternating with much cleverly wrought *parlando* dialogue are melodious arias, duets, trios—not really separate numbers as in the Classical opera, but still significant as departing from the Wagnerian (and earlier Straussian) rule of purely declamatory or, at most, arioso singing subordinated to the orchestra. The whole score, with its mingling of sentiment and comedy, is pervaded with the lighthearted rhythms and melodies of Viennese waltzes.

EXAMPLE XIX–5   Introduction, mm. 69–74, *Der Rosenkavalier*, Strauss

Ariadne auf Naxos (*Ariadne at Naxos,* 1912) was originally set, with other incidental music, in the framework of von Hofmannsthal's adaptation of Molière's *Bourgeois gentilhomme.* It has survived in revised form (1916) as an independent work, half *opera buffa* and half mythological drama. Its delightful music, in a modernized Mozartean idiom and using a small orchestra, includes recitatives, ensembles, and arias in Classical forms; it is, in short, a model of neo-Classical chamber opera.

In his subsequent operas, Strauss remained comparatively unaffected by the progressive currents of his time, preferring to continue along the lines he had laid down in *Der Rosenkavalier* and *Ariadne*. Of special interest are the comic opera *Intermezzo* (1924), in which Strauss exploits a technique of treating nearly all the dialogue in realistic speech-recitative above the bustling accompaniment of a chamber orchestra which also plays lyrical interludes; and the lyrical comedy, *Arabella* (1933), the last of Strauss's seven operas on librettos by von Hofmannsthal. The instrumental *Metamorphoses* (1945), for 23 solo stringed instruments, is notable as an example of the neo-Classical tendencies in Strauss's late works.

Brief mention must suffice for two other German composers of the post-Romantic period. Max Reger (1873–1916), a spiritual descendant of Brahms rather than of the radical Romantics, possessed a prodigious contrapuntal technique and a copious imagination, together with a facility that tended to lead him, in his more ambitious compositions, to inordinate length and unrelieved fullness of texture. Reger's harmony is for the most part a complex post-Wagnerian style of extreme chromaticism and restless modulation. His best and most characteristic large works are those in which the flood of late Romantic sound is confined within the bounds of Baroque or Classical strict forms, such as the fugue, the chorale prelude, or the theme and variations. Typical are the orchestral *Variations and Fugue on a Theme of J. A. Hiller* (1907) and a similar work (1914) on the theme of the first movement of Mozart's piano sonata K. 331. Reger's compositions for the organ are noteworthy, especially the chorale preludes and fantasias, which range from the simplest to the most elaborate settings of the traditional Lutheran melodies. He wrote no operas and practically no program music. His many songs, piano pieces, and choral and chamber works, though highly esteemed in Germany, are almost completely unknown to the public in other countries. Hans Pfitzner (1869–1949), the leading conservative German composer of the post-Romantic generation, is remembered—though only in his own country—chiefly for his operas, especially *Palestrina* (1917), though he also composed songs, chamber music, and a notable Violin Concerto in B minor (1925).

Reger and Pfitzner

Nationalism, Old and New: Russia

Nationalism was an important force in nineteenth-century music. A distinction must be made, however, between early Romantic nationalism and the nationalism which appeared after 1860. The results of the early nineteenth-century German folk song revival were so thoroughly absorbed into the fabric of German music as to become an integral part of its style, which in that period was the nearest thing to an international European musical style. Thus, although Brahms, for instance, made arrangements of German folk songs and wrote melodies that resemble folk songs, and although Debussy called him the most Germanic of composers, we still do not think of him as any more a "nationalist" composer than Haydn, Schubert, Strauss, or Mahler, all of whom likewise more or less consciously made use of folk idioms. In similar fashion, the national qualities of the nineteenth-century French and Italian music were assimilated to a firmly established tradition in each country. And as for the Polish elements in Chopin, or the Hungarian-Gypsy ones in Liszt and Brahms, these are for the most part only exotic accessories to a style fundamentally cosmopolitan.

The new nationalism, in contrast to the old, flourished largely in countries that had no great or unbroken musical tradition of their own but had long been musically dependent on other nations, chiefly Germany. Nationalism was one of the weapons by which composers in those countries sought to free themselves from the domination of foreign music. As a movement, it was self-conscious, and sometimes aggressive. It underlies such externals as the choice of national subjects for operas and symphonic poems, the collecting and publishing of folk songs, and the occasional quoting of folk tunes in compositions; but a more important consequence was the rise of new styles through fertilization of orthodox Germanic music by tonal, melodic, harmonic, rhythmic, and formal characteristics of the national idioms. This development took place earliest in Russia.

Until the nineteenth century, secular art music in Russia was to a great extent in the hands of imported Italian, French, or German composers. Both they and their Russian contemporaries made considerable use of folksong in their works, but so far as the average Western listener is concerned, the history of Russian music begins in 1836 with the performance of the patriotic opera *A Life for the Tsar* by Michael Glinka (1804–57). This work gave impetus to a movement that gained momentum with Glinka's second opera, *Russlan and Ludmilla* (1842) and the opera *Russalka* (1856) by Alexander Dargomizhsky (1813–69). The principal Russian nationalists were a group of composers known as "the mighty handful": Mily Balakirev (1837–1910), Alexander Borodin (1833–87), Modest Mussorgsky (1839–81), and Nicolas Rimsky-Korsakov (1844–1908).

All these men save Balakirev were amateurs—a fact important in the growth of Russian music. Some eminent Russians in the nineteenth century from choice remained fundamentally western, using national idioms only incidentally if at all. One such was Anton Rubinstein (1829–94), a celebrated pianist and the first director of the Conservatory at St. Petersburg; some of his operas, symphonies, and piano pieces remained in favor up to quite recent times. Tchaikovsky's two most popular operas, *Eugen Onegin* (1879) and *The Queen of Spades* (1890), seem to have been modeled after Meyerbeer, Verdi, and Bizet, though national subjects and a few traces of national musical idioms occur in both these and, much more conspicuously, in some of his less familiar works for the theatre. In their fight to create an all-Russian style of music, the nationalist composers' comparative ignorance of conventional harmony and counterpoint became a positive asset: it forced them to discover their own ways of doing things, and in the process they used the materials nearest at hand, namely folk songs. Their frequent use of actual or imitated folk material for the generating themes of a work "has literary parallels in the borrowing by Pushkin and Gogol of folk-tales as the bases of so many of their most characteristic stories."[1]

Balakirev, the only member of the "mighty handful" who was a professional musician, made effective use of folksong melodies in his symphonic poem *Russia* (1887) and his piano fantasia *Islamey* (1869). Borodin, though by profession a chemist, was a significant musical figure. After his early interest in Mendelssohn had been turned by the persuasions of Balakirev to Russian music, he became an ardent nationalist. His principal works are the Second Symphony in B minor (1876), the second String Quartet in D major (1885), a symphonic sketch *In Central Asia* (1880), and the four-act opera *Prince Igor,* completed after Borodin's death by Rimsky-Korsakov and Glazunov and first performed in 1890.

Borodin seldom quotes folk tunes but his melodic style is permeated with their spirit. His symphonies and quartets are evidence of the determination of the Russian nationalists to compete with foreign composers in absolute music. Although, compared to Beethoven or Brahms, Borodin is only a minor master of symphonic development, he succeeded by reason of the individuality of his themes, his transparent orchestral texture (derived from Glinka), his delicate, modally tinged harmonies, and his original method of spinning out an entire movement from a single pregnant thematic idea announced at the beginning (for example, the first movement of the Second Symphony). The key schemes of both his symphonies are typical of the Russian fondness for unusual tonal relationships: the First Symphony, in E♭, has its third (slow) movement in D, with a middle section in D♭; the four movements of the Second Symphony are respectively in B minor, F major, D♭ major, and B major. Borodin's talent, like Mendelssohn's, was primarily lyrical and descriptive, and *Prince Igor* is less a drama than a series of picturesque tableaux. The familiar *Polovetsian Dances,* which occur in Act II of the opera, illustrate the iridescent harmonies, bright colors, graceful melodic lines, and the refined, exotic oriental flavor that characterize much Russian music after Glinka's *Russlan.*

[1] G. Abraham, *A Hundred Years of Music,* 145.

Modest
Mussorgsky

Mussorgsky, the greatest of the "mighty handful," was also the one least well-equipped with the techniques of composition. A militant nationalist, he earned a painful living as a clerk in the civil service, and received most of his musical training from Balakirev. His principal works were: a symphonic fantasy *Night on Bald Mountain* (1867); the set of piano pieces *Pictures at an Exhibition* (1874); the song cycles *Without Sun* (1874), *Songs and Dances of Death* (1875), and *The Nursery* (1872); and the operas *Boris Godunov* (first performed in 1874) and *Khovanshchina,* which was completed by Rimsky-Korsakov and privately performed in 1886, but not produced publicly till 1892. Mussorgsky's individuality is evident in every aspect of his music. His treatment of texts was based on the methods of Dargomizhsky, and aims at the closest possible adherence to the accents of natural speech; hence in his vocal music he generally avoids lyrical melodic lines and symmetrical phrasing. His songs are among the finest of the nineteenth century. Although Mussorgsky only occasionally quotes actual folk tunes (as in the Coronation Scene or *Boris*), it is evident that Russian folk song is rooted in his musical nature even more deeply than in Borodin's.

The Coronation Scene from Boris Godunov, *as staged by the Bolshoi Opera in Moscow. George London appears in the title role. (Photo courtesy Edgar Vincent Assoc.)*

Russian folk tunes tend to move within a narrow range and to be made up either of obsessive repetition of one or two rhythmic motives or of phrases in irregular rhythm constantly sinking to a cadence, often by the interval of a descending fourth. Another prominent feature of Russian folk songs, and of Mussorgsky's melodies, is their modal character, and this modality affected Mussorgsky's harmonic style, as well as that of all the Russian nationalists. Brahms had used modal chords and progressions, but it was the Russians first of all who were responsible for introducing modality into the general musical language of Europe, and their influence in this respect on the music of the early twentieth century is important. In his harmony Mussorgsky is one of the most original and indeed revolutionary of all composers. Unfettered by traditional habits of thought and unpracticed in the manipulation of standard formulas, he was obliged to work out laboriously at the piano his "bold, new, crude, but curiously 'right' harmonies"[2]—for which, as well as for his rhythms, he may have been indebted to his memories of polyphonic folk singing. His harmonic vocabulary is seldom advanced (except for some use of the whole-tone scale, in which Glinka and Dargomizhsky had anticipated him), but his apparently simple progressions convey precisely the effect he wants, and often resist any attempt made to explain them by analysis on normal textbook principles (see Examples XIX–6, 7).

The realism that is such a prominent trait in nineteenth-century Russian literature is exemplified in the music of Dargomizhsky's opera *The Stone Guest* (1872) and also finds some echo in Mussorgsky —not only in the sense of imitating the spoken word, but in the lifelike musical depiction of gestures (*Boris,* end of Act II), the sound and stir of people in crowds (choral scenes in *Boris* and *Khovanshchina*), and even paintings (*Pictures at an Exhibition*). The psychological insight evidenced on a miniature scale in the songs is applied with equal mastery to depicting the character of the Czar Boris in the opera. Like other Russian composers, Mussorgsky builds his effects by the repetition and accumulation of single impressions, not by thematic development to a climax. Even *Boris Godunov,* one of the great tragic operas of the nineteenth century, is not a continuously developed action but a series of episodes welded together partly by the epic nature of the scenes and the central figure of Boris, but chiefly by the sheer dramatic energy of Mussorgsky's music. His art owes little or nothing to Wagner; his use of leitmotifs is unimportant and his orchestra, while it most effectively supports the drama, never assumes independent symphonic life.

The work of Rimsky-Korsakov forms a link between the first generation of nationalists and the Russian composers of the early twentieth century. Abandoning an early career in the navy, he served from 1871 as professor of composition at the St. Petersburg

Rimsky-Korsakov

[2] Abraham, *op. cit.,* 151.

EXAMPLE XIX–6

a. Folk Song from the collection 30 Chants populaires russes *harmonized by Balakirev.*

Oĭ, u - tu - shka mo - ĭa lu - go - va - ĭa oĭ, u - tu - shka

mo - ĭa lu - go - va - ĭa oĭ _____ lu - go - va - ĭa

oĭ _____ lu - go - va - ĭa.

a. Oh, duckling my meadow, oh, duckling my meadow, oh, meadow, oh meadow!

b. Folk Song, idem.

Kak pod le - som, pod ____ le - soch - kom, shel - ko - va tra -

va, _____ Oĭ - li,* Oĭ - li, oĭ - li, oĭ liu - shën' - ki

shel - ko - va tra - va!

* Oili is a stock folk song syllable, like fa la la or tra la la.
Liushën′ki is a diminutive of another stock syllable: liuli.

b. Now near the wood, near the wood, silky grass.

c. Melody from the Prologue of Boris Godunov, *Mussorgsky.*

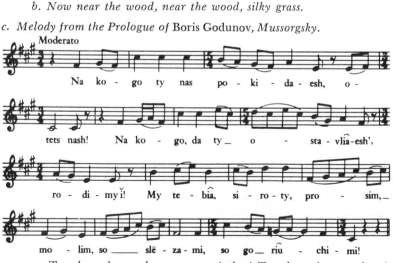

Moderato

Na ko - go ty nas po - ki - da - esh, o -

tets nash! Na ko - go, da ty ____ o - sta - vlia - esh',

ro - di - my ĭ! My te - bĭa, si - ro - ty, pro - sim, ____

mo - lim, so ____ slë - za - mi, so go ____ riu - chi - mi!

c. To whom do you leave us, our father! To whom do you abandon us, dear ones! We are orphans, we beg you, we implore you with tears, with scalding tears.

Conservatory and was also active in Russia as a conductor. To supplement his rather sketchy early musical training under Balakirev he undertook a course of counterpoint by himself. He took the lead in a new movement among Russian musicians in the 1880s away from the extreme nationalism of the Balakirev circle toward a style based on broader, more eclectic methods and resources, though one still strongly impregnated with national idioms. His abiding interest in national music was shown not only in the characteristics of his own melodies and harmonies and in the frequent use of folk melodies in his compositions, but also by his arranging and editing collections of folk songs.

EXAMPLE XIX–7   End of Act II, *Boris Godunov*, Mussorgsky

Lord! You do not wish the death of a sinner. Forgive the soul of guilty Tsar Boris!

Rimsky-Korsakov's compositions include symphonies, chamber music, choruses, and songs, but his principal works are symphonic poems and operas. His music, in contrast to the intense dramatic realism of Mussorgsky's, is distinguished by lively fantasy and bright orchestral colors. The *Capriccio espagnol* (1887), the symphonic suite *Scheherazade* (1888), and the *Russian Easter* Overture (1888) are outstanding manifestations of his genius for orchestration; his teachings on this subject were systematized in a treatise published in 1913. In the two most important of his fifteen operas—*Sadko* (1897) and *The Golden Cockerel* (first performed in 1909)—he alternates a diatonic, often modal style with one lightly chromatic, fanciful, and most apt at suggesting the fairytale world in which the action of these pieces takes place.

Rimsky-Korsakov's leading pupils were Alexander Glazunov (1865–1936), the last of the Russian nationalists and a minor master of the symphony; and Igor Stravinsky (1882–1971), whose early works, especially the ballet *The Fire Bird* (1910), are continuations of Rimsky-Korsakov's style and orchestral technique.

Of some interest is Sergei Rachmaninov (1873–1943), a distinguished pianist whose compositions, like those of Tchaikovsky, mingle some national traits with a late Romantic idiom. Apart from numerous songs and piano pieces his most notable works are the Second Piano Concerto (1901), the Third Piano Concerto (1909), and a symphonic poem *The Isle of the Dead* (1907).

A quite unclassifiable Russian composer of the post-Romantic period, one whose music has no connection whatever with the nationalist movement, was Alexander Scriabin (1872–1915). A concert pianist, Scriabin began by writing nocturnes, preludes, études, and mazurkas in the manner of Chopin. Influenced by the chromaticism of Liszt and Wagner, and to some extent also by the methods of Impressionism, he gradually evolved a complex harmonic vocabulary peculiar to himself; the growth of this language can be followed step by step in his ten piano sonatas, of which the last five, composed 1912–13, dispense with key signatures and attain a harmonic vagueness amounting at times to atonality. Traditional tonal structures were replaced by a system of chords built on unusual intervals (particularly fourths, with chromatic alterations; see Example XIX–8); traditional formal articulations were dissolved in a

Alexander Scriabin

EXAMPLE XIX–8   Chord Forms, Alexander Scriabin

stream of strange, colorful, and sometimes magnificent sound. All this was intended to express vast conceptions of an extraordinary, mysterious, theosophical cast; Scriabin eventually deleveped a theory of an ultimate synthesis of all the arts for the sake of inducing states of unutterable mystic rapture.

Scriabin's most typical compositions, apart from the late sonatas, are two orchestral works, the *Poem of Ecstasy* (1908) and *Prometheus* (1910); for the latter the composer wished the concert hall to be flooded with colored light during the playing of the music. Scriabin's style and methods were too personal, and his aesthetic aims too much bound up with post-Romantic ideas, to become the basis of a school. Except for a few unimportant Russian composers he had no direct disciples, though his harmonic idiom, a radical example of early twentieth-century antitonal tendencies, doubtless indirectly influenced composers of the period.

Other Nations

Bedřich Smetana (1824–84) and Antonín Dvořák were the two principal Czech composers of the nineteenth century. (Dvořák has already been mentioned in connection with the symphonic and chamber music of the Romantic period.) Bohemia had for centuries been an Austrian crown land, and thus, unlike Russia, had always been in contact with the main stream of European music; her folk songs do not differ from those of western nations nearly so much as do the Russian. Nor was the Czech nationalist movement marked from the outset, as was the Russian, by self-conscious efforts to avoid western influence. The nationalism of Smetana and Dvořák is chiefly apparent in the choice of national subjects for program music and operas, and in the infusion of their basic musical language (Smetana's derived from Liszt, Dvořák's more like Brahms's) with a melodic freshness and spontaneity, a harmonic and formal nonchalance, together with occasional traces of folklike tunes and popular dance rhythms—for example, in the movements based on the *dumka* or the *furiant* in Dvořák's symphonies and chamber music. The most prominent national traits of both composers are found in some of their operas—Smetana's *Bartered Bride* (1866) above all, but also in his later opera *The Kiss* (1876)—and in some works in small forms, such as Dvořák's *Slavonic Dances*.

Czech composers

A Czech composer with thoroughly national tendencies was Leoš Janáček (1854–1928), a more important figure in early twentieth century music than his as yet limited fame would indicate. Unlike Smetana and Dvořák, Janáček after 1890 consciously renounced the styles of western Europe. Like Bartók but even earlier, he was a diligent scientific collector of folk music, and his own mature style grew out of the rhythms and inflections of Moravian peasant speech and song. Recognition came late, beginning only with the performance of his opera *Jenufa* (1903) at Prague in 1916. Janáček's creative power continued unabated to the end of his life. Later operas were *Kát'a Kabanová* (1921), *The Cunning Little Vixen* (1924), *The Makropulos Case* (1925), and *From a House of the Dead* (1928). Janáček composed much choral music, among which the *Glagolitic Mass* of 1926, on a text in Old Slavic, is an outstanding work. His chamber music includes two quartets and a violin sonata; for orchestra the chief works are the symphonic rhapsody *Taras Bulba* (1918) and a *Sinfonietta* (1926).

Nationalism in Norway is represented by Edvard Hagerup Grieg (1843–1907), whose best works are his short piano pieces, songs, and incidental orchestral music to plays. (The two suites that Grieg arranged from his music for Ibsen's *Peer Gynt* [1875, reorchestrated 1886] include only eight of the original 23 numbers.) Among his larger compositions are the well-known Piano Concerto in A minor (1868, revised 1907), a piano sonata, three violin sonatas, a violoncello sonata, and a string quartet (1878) that apparently provided Debussy with a model for his own work in the same form fifteen years later.

NORWAY

The weaknesses in these works arise from Grieg's tendency to think always in two- or four-measure phrases and his inability to achieve rhythmic continuity and formal unity in long movements; such national characteristics as they possess are superimposed on an orthodox style which Grieg learned in youthful studies at the Leipzig Conservatory. His essential nationalism is more clearly apparent in the songs on Norwegian texts, the choruses for men's voices Op. 30, the four Psalms for mixed chorus Op. 74, many of his *Lyric Pieces* for piano (ten collections), the four sets of piano arrangements of folk songs, and especially the *Slåtter* (Norwegian peasant dances arranged by Grieg for the piano from transcripts of country fiddle playing). His piano style, with its delicate grace notes and mordents, owes something to Chopin, but the all-pervading influence in his music is that of Norwegian folk songs and dances; this is evidenced particularly in modal turns of melody and harmony (Lydian raised fourth, Aeolian lowered seventh, alternative major-minor third), frequent drone basses (suggested by old Norwegian stringed instruments), and such details as the fascinating combination of 3/4 and 6/8 rhythm in the *Slåtter*. These national characteristics blend with Grieg's sensitive feeling for harmony in a personal, poetic music that has not lost its freshness.

Nationalist composers in some other countries of Europe can only be briefly mentioned. Most important in Poland was Stanislaw Moniuszko (1819–72), creator of Polish national opera with *Halka* (1848, expanded to four acts 1858) and notable also for his songs, which display marked national qualities in both texts and music. In Denmark, Carl August Nielsen (1865–1931) composed songs, operas, piano and chamber music, concertos, and symphonies. His best known work, the Fifth Symphony (1922) is unconventional in form and orchestration and original in its adaptation of tonality to a sometimes very dissonant harmonic idiom. Contemporary with Nielsen was the outstanding nineteenth-century Netherlands composer, Alfons Diepenbrock (1862–1921), whose music, influenced first by Wagner and Palestrina and later by Debussy, includes sacred works for chorus and orchestra, songs, and incidental music for stage plays.

Musical nationalism in the European countries could be defined as the rise of an important body of art music under the impetus of patriotic feeling, in a style whose distinctive features result from the composers' more or less conscious use of folk elements as material or inspiration for compositions. In this sense there was no continuity of musical nationalism in the United States of America in the nineteenth century. The material, to be sure, lay ready in profusion—old New England hymnody, rural revival-meeting songs, tunes from the urban popular minstrelsy of Stephen Foster (1820–94) and James Bland (1854–1911), Indian tribal melodies, above all the great body of black folk spirituals with their unique fusion of African and Anglo-American elements—but to no avail. All the "serious" music the American public could take was imported—Italian opera, English oratorio, German symphony—while Gottschalk's piano pieces in Creole rhythms were looked down on and dismissed as claptrap. Dvořák's enthusiastic interest in the American musical heritage suggested to a few composers the possibility of using national materials in symphonic works; but the composers of this group—among them Arthur Farwell (1872–1952) and Henry Gilbert (1868–1928), who were chiefly active in the first two decades of the twentieth century—lacked both the genius and the social encouragement to do for the United States what Glinka, Balakirev, and Mussorgsky had done for Russia.

UNITED STATES

Specific national traits are not prominent in the music of the two most celebrated American composers of the post-Romantic era. Horatio Parker (1863–1919), whose output included songs, choruses, and two prize-winning operas, is best known for his cantatas and oratorios, especially the oratorio *Hora novissima* (1893). Edward MacDowell (1861–1908) lived and studied for ten years in Germany, where he became known as a pianist and where many of his compositions were first played and published. From 1896 to 1903 he held the first professorship of music at Columbia University. His compositions include songs, choruses, symphonic poems, orchestral suites, many piano pieces and studies, four piano sonatas, and two piano concertos. His best large works are the Second Piano Concerto, in D minor, and the last Piano Sonata (the *Keltic,* dedicated to Grieg).

MacDowell's melodies have a peculiar charm; his harmony, late Romantic in color but without modality, is handled in a distinctly personal way. A fine sensitiveness for the sonorous effects of spacing and doubling is evident in his short piano pieces, which are his most characteristic works. Most of them were issued in collections— *Woodland Sketches,* the *Sea Pieces,* the *New England Idyls*—and the individual pieces are furnished with titles or poems suggesting musical moods and pictures of the sort common in Grieg, to whose general style MacDowell's bears some resemblance. One of his finest works, and the only one that uses American folk material (Indian melodies), is the second (*Indian*) suite for orchestra.

The first important distinctively American composer was the New Englander, Charles Ives (1874–1954), a pupil of his father and of Horatio Parker. Like the early Russian nationalists, Ives was not a musician by profession. Public recognition of his achievements came only in the 1930s, many years after he had, in isolation and without models, created works that anticipated some of the most radical developments of twentieth-century music (dissonance, polytonality, polyrhythm, and experimental form). His compositions, most of which were written between 1890 and 1922, include some 200 songs, five violin sonatas and other chamber music, two piano sonatas, five symphonies, and other orchestral music. Conventional and unconventional elements stand side by side in his works, or are mingled— in John Kirkpatrick's phrase—"with a transcendentalist's faith in the unity behind all diversity"; fragments of folk songs, dance tunes, or gospel hymns emerge from a complex, rhapsodic, uniquely ordered flow of sound. The many movements based on hymn tunes offer a parallel to the use of Lutheran chorales by German composers.

Ives's technical procedures, which he would have scorned to designate as a system, were dictated by an uncompromising idealism in the pursuit of his artistic aims, coupled with an extraordinary musical imagination and a mordant sense of humor. His work has been of incalculable importance to younger generations of American musicians.

FINLAND

The great Finnish composer Jean Sibelius (1865–1957) is nationalistic only in a limited sense. His mind was steeped in the literature of his country, particularly the *Kalevala,* the Finnish national epic, from which he chose texts for vocal works and subjects for symphonic poems; and it is easy to imagine much of his music—"somber," "bleak," and "elemental" are favorite adjectives for it—as having been inspired by his profound love of nature and the particular aspects of nature characteristic of northern countries. On the other hand, he does not quote or imitate folk songs and there is small evidence of direct folksong influence in his works, the best of which depend little, if at all, on qualities that can be concretely defined as national. His music was for a long time extremely popular in England and the United States but hardly known in Continental western Europe. Unlike Grieg and MacDowell, who were essentially miniaturists, the natural genius of Sibelius is best revealed in his symphonies and symphonic poems; his numerous compositions in other forms, with the exception of the Violin Concerto (1903) and one string quartet (Op. 56 in D minor, 1909), are for the most part of secondary value and many indeed are merely facile though attractive salon pieces.

Although Sibelius lived until 1957, he published no important works after 1925. The first of his seven symphonies appeared in 1899, the last in 1924. Three symphonic poems—*En Saga, The Swan of Tuonela,* and the familiar *Finlandia*—were works of the 1890s (all revised about 1900); the principal later symphonic poems were *Pohjola's Daughter* (1906) and *Tapiola* (1925). The programs of these poems, except for *Pohjola's Daughter,* are very general; the symphonies have no expressed programmatic suggestions.

Traces of Tchaikovsky in the Violin Sonata and of Tchaikovsky, Grieg, and Borodin in the first two symphonies disappeared as Sibelius developed his personal style, one in which intense (but never autobiographical) emotion is tautly controlled within unified but unconventional formal structures in a spare, clean-lined orchestral texture. His originality is not of a sensational order. Except in the Fourth Symphony, his conception of tonality and his harmonic vocabulary are close to common practice; he makes no conspicuous use of chromaticism or dissonances, though modality is a basic factor. Sibelius remained aloof from the disturbing experimental movements in European music in the first quarter of the century, and in his late works, particularly the Seventh Symphony and *Tapiola,* he arrived at a final synthesis in a style of Classical tranquillity.

His originality consists partly in the free use he makes of familiar chords, partly in his orchestration (emphasizing low registers and unmixed colors), but above all in the nature of his themes, his technique of thematic development, and his treatment of form. Instead of full periodic melodies, a theme may be built of short motives that, first sounded separately, gradually coalesce into a complete entity (as in the third movement of the Fourth Symphony). Motives from one theme may be transferred to another, or themes dissolved and their motives recombined in such a way that the original theme is gradually transformed by the replacing of its motivic units one by one until a new structure results (first movement of the Third Symphony). One or two basic motives may recur throughout an entire movement or even an entire symphony (the Sixth Symphony).

Though movements can usually be analyzed with reference to Classical formal schemes, such schemes—particularly so as Sibelius's style evolves in his later works—are felt to be wholly subordinate, incidental to the organic development of the musical ideas. The acme of formal unity is the Seventh Symphony, which is in one continuous movement. Long ostinato passages, sometimes in the form of a subdued agitato rustling of strings under fragments of solo woodwind melody, are a common connective device; pauses, brief ejaculatory phrases, sudden contrasts of timbre, are incidental features. The Second and Fifth Symphonies are the ones most frequently played, but the Fourth is the quintessence of Sibelius—a model of concision, intensity, and thematic unity, exploiting in every

EXAMPLE XIX–9   Some Thematic Transformations in the Fourth Symphony, Sibelius

© 1912 by Breitkopf and Hartel; renewed 1940 by Breitkopf and Hartel; used by permission of Associated Music Publishers, Inc. New York. (Reproduced by permission of Boosey & Hawkes, Inc.)

movement the tritone interval C–F♯ of the opening phrase (Example XIX–9).

Nationalism in English music came comparatively late. Sir Edward Elgar (1857–1934) was the first English composer in more than two hundred years to obtain wide international recognition; but his music is not in the least touched by folk song nor has it any technical characteristics that seem to derive from the national musical tradition. Yet it "sounds English." It has been suggested that this may be due to the resemblance between Elgar's typical melodic line (wide leaps and a falling trend; see Example XIX–10) and the intonation patterns of British speech. Certainly he is English in that he wrote effectively for chorus and that a large proportion of his output consisted of cantatas and oratorios. The oratorio *The Dream of Gerontius* (1900) is the most important among these. Elgar also composed a number of excellent orchestral works, including two symphonies, the *Enigma* Variations (1899), the overture *Cockaigne* (1901), and the "symphonic study," *Falstaff* (1913). His musical speech is that of late Romanticism. From Brahms and Wagner he derived his harmonic style, from Wagner the system of leitmotifs in his oratorios and perhaps also his persistent technique of sequential repetition. Some of his music is, to present taste, pretentious; the direction *nobilmente* occurs often in his scores. But at his best, as in the *Enigma* Variations, Elgar is impressive, combining solid craftsmanship with genial poetic imagination.

ENGLAND

EXAMPLE XIX–10   The Melodic Line in the *Enigma* Variations, Elgar

The English musical renaissance signalized by Elgar took a nationalist turn in the twentieth century. Folksong collections by Cecil Sharp (1859–1924), Ralph Vaughan Williams (1872–1958), and others led to the use of these melodies in compositions such as Vaughan Williams's *Norfolk Rhapsodies* for orchestra (1907) and the *Somerset Rhapsody* by Gustav Holst (1874–1934). These two composers became the leaders of a new English school which will be dealt with in the following chapter.

In Spain a nationalist revival somewhat like the English was initiated by Felipe Pedrell (1841–1922) with his editions of sixteenth-century Spanish composers and his operas, chief of which was *Los Pirineos* (*The Pyrenees;* composed 1891). Further nationalist impetus came from the works of Isaac Albéniz (1860–1909), whose piano suite *Iberia* (1909) used Spanish dance rhythms in a colorful virtuoso style. The principal Spanish composer of the early twentieth century,

SPAIN

Manuel de Falla (1876–1946), collected and arranged national folk songs, and his earlier works—for example, the opera *La Vida breve* (*Life is Short;* composed 1905) and the ballet *El Amor Brujo* (*Love, the Sorcerer;* 1915)—are imbued with the melodic and rhythmic qualities of Spanish popular music. *Nights in the Gardens of Spain,* three "symphonic impressions" for piano and orchestra (1916), testify both to national sources and the influence of Debussy. Falla's finest mature works are the concerto for harpsichord with five solo instruments (1926) and the little stage piece *Master Peter's Puppet Show* (1923), based on an episode from *Don Quixote.* Both are profoundly Spanish in inspiration, but the specific national elements are transmuted into a translucent, delicately colored musical fabric of classic serenity.

Summary

The musical nationalism of the late nineteenth century took different forms in different countries. Nowhere else did it have the exclusive, intensely patriotic character that marked the early stage of the movement in Russia. Composers like Elgar and MacDowell were national only in the sense that they were natives of their respective countries. Grieg, Ives, and Sibelius were isolated figures, not founders of schools. Everywhere, even in Russia after the first generation, nationalism came to terms with the mainstream of European music in one way or another; but it diversified that stream, enriched it with new idioms and new technical procedures, and so originated many of the new currents that were to flow in the music of the twentieth century.

New Currents in France

The French musical renaissance is usually dated from 1871, with the foundation at the end of the Franco-Prussian War of the National Society for French Music. The Society's purpose was to encourage native composers, specifically by giving performances of their works; one effect was a marked rise, both in quantity and quality, of symphonic and chamber music. The entire movement that was symbolized by the Society was at the outset nationalistic, both in that it was motivated by patriotism and that it consciously sought to recover the characteristic excellences of the national music. It sought inspiration, however, not only in folk song but also in the revival of the great music of the past—signalized by editions and performances of Rameau, Gluck, and the sixteenth-century composers. The Schola Cantorum, founded at Paris in 1894, introduced broad historical studies in music, in contrast to the narrow technical training emphasizing opera that had prevailed at the older Conservatory ever since its foundation at the time of the Revolution. The outcome of all these and similar activities was to raise France in the first half of the twentieth century once more to a leading position in music among the nations of the world. Thus the French revival, begun with aims similar to those of nationalistic movements in other countries, ended by producing results of prime importance for music everywhere.

Three main lines of development—interdependent, naturally— may be traced in the history of French music from 1871 to the early years of the twentieth century. Two of these are best defined by their historical background: first, the cosmopolitan tradition, transmitted through César Franck and carried on by his pupils, especially d'Indy; and second, the specifically French tradition, transmitted through Saint-Saëns and continued by his pupils, especially Fauré. The third development, later in inception but more fundamental and far-reaching in its influence, was rooted in the French tradition and was carried to unforeseen consequences in the music of Debussy.

Franck worked mainly in the regular instrumental forms (symphony, symphonic poem, sonata, variations, chamber music) and oratorio; his style preserved the basic orthodox ways of shaping and developing themes, and his texture was essentially homophonic although enriched to some extent by contrapuntal features. Underlying all his work was a warm religious idealism and a belief in the serious social mission of the artist. His music evidences a certain anti-Romantic logic in the working out of ideas and a pointed avoidance of Romantic extremes of expression, together with some mildly chromatic innovations in harmony and a systematic application of the cyclical principle.

The cosmopolitan tradition

Franck's leading pupil, Vincent d'Indy (1851–1931), held faithfully to the ideals and methods of his master. D'Indy's principal compositions are: the First Symphony, "on a French mountain air" (1886), the Second Symphony, in B♭ (1903), the symphonic variations *Istar* (1896), the symphonic poem *Summer Day on the Mountain* (1905), the Violin Sonata (1904), and the opera *Fervaal* (1897). The First Symphony is exceptional for a French work because it uses a folk song as its principal subject; both this and the Second Symphony exhibit to the highest degree the process of cyclical transformation of themes that d'Indy learned from Franck. The quasi-programmatic *Istar* variations are remarkable as an inversion of the usual plan: the set begins with the most complex variation and progresses to the simple statement of the theme at the end. *Istar* and the First Symphony are the most spontaneous and attractive of d'Indy's compositions. He is sometimes liable to overload melodies with contrapuntal elaboration and this tendency, together with a relentless employment of the cyclical technique, emphasizes unduly the intellectual structure of his music. The fascination that Wagner exercised over many of the best minds of France in the last quarter of the nineteenth century is evident in *Fervaal*, both in the poem (which d'Indy wrote himself) and, to a more limited extent, in the music. Yet many of its pages, and especially the beautiful closing choral scene, in which is incorporated the melody of the plainsong hymn *Pange lingua,* testify to the poetic power and the profound religious faith of the composer.

The French tradition

The specifically French tradition is something essentially Classical: it rests on a conception of music as sonorous form, in contrast to the Romantic conception of music as expression. Order and restraint are fundamental. Emotion and depiction are conveyed only as they have been entirely transmuted into music. That music may be anything from the simplest melody to the most subtle pattern of tones, rhythms, and colors; but it tends always to be lyric or dance-like rather than epic or dramatic, economical rather than profuse, simple rather than complex, reserved rather than grandiloquent; above all, it is not concerned with delivering a Message, whether about the fate of the cosmos or the state of the composer's soul. A listener will fail to comprehend such music unless he is sensible to quiet statement, nuance, and exquisite detail, able to distinguish calmness from dullness, wit from jollity, gravity from portentousness, lucidity from emptiness. This kind of music was written by two French composers as remote in time and temperament as Couperin and Gounod. Berlioz did not write such music; and Berlioz was not a success in France.

In Camille Saint-Saëns this French inheritance was coupled with high craftsmanship, facility in managing Classical forms, and the ability to adopt at will any of the fashionable tricks of Romanticism. This eclectic, hedonistic trait also runs through the many successful operas of Jules Massenet (1842–1912), chief of which were *Manon* (1884), *Werther* (1892), *Thaïs* (1894), and *Le Jongleur de Notre Dame (Our Lady's Juggler;* 1902). His operas also exhibit Massenet's talent for suave, sensuous, charming, and often sentimental melody, a talent that has always been appreciated in France. (As Paul Henry Lang has remarked, "There is a bit of Massenet in every Frenchman of whatever generation.")[3] The music of Gustave Charpentier's opera *Louise* (1900) is in a style not greatly different from Massenet's.

Gabriel Fauré

Gabriel Fauré (1845–1924) was one of the founders of the National Society for French Music and first president of the Independent Musical Society which branched off from the parent association in 1909. After studying composition under Saint-Saëns from 1861 to 1865, Fauré held various posts as an organist; he became professor of composition at the Paris Conservatory in 1896 and its director from 1905 to 1920, when he was obliged to resign on account of deafness.

Fauré's refined, highly civilized music embodies the aristocratic qualities of the French tradition. Except for a few songs,[4] his works

[3] P. H. Lang, *Music in Western Civilization,* New York, 1941, 1021.
[4] He is not the composer of *The Palms.* That song was perpetrated by Jean-Baptiste Faure (1830–1914).

have never become widely popular, and many foreigners, even musicians, cannot understand why he is so highly regarded in France. Primarily a composer of lyric pieces and chamber music, his few compositions in larger form include the *Requiem* (1887), incidental music to Maeterlinck's *Pelléas et Mélisande* (1898), and the operas *Prométhée* (1900) and *Pénélope* (1913). His music is not remarkable for color; he was not skilled at orchestration, and published no symphonies or concertos. His characteristics are most fully revealed in his nearly one hundred songs, of which we may note particularly *Lydia, Après un rêve* (both 1865), *Clair de lune* (1887), *Au cimetière* (1889), the *Cinq mélodies* (1890) to poems of Verlaine, and especially the cycles *La Bonne Chanson* (Verlaine; 1892), *La Chanson d'Ève* (Charles van Lerberghe; 1907–10), and *L'Horizon chimérique* (Jean da la Ville de Mirmont; 1922). Fauré's piano pieces, like the songs, were written during all periods of his creative life; they include impromptus, preludes, 13 barcarolles, 13 nocturnes, and a few larger works. The principal chamber compositions are three late works: the second Violin Sonata (1917), the second Piano Quintet (1921), and the String Quartet (1924).

Fauré began with songs in the manner of Gounod, and piano salon pieces deriving from Mendelssohn and Chopin. In some respects he never changed: lyrical melody, with no display of virtuosity, remained always the basis of his style, and small dimensions were always congenial to him. But in his maturity, from about 1885, these small forms began to be filled with a language that was new. Aside from a steadily growing power to create living, plastic melody, there were innovations in harmony. Fauré was familiar with plainchant from his early schooling and later studies, and this may have been one source for the modality that is so prominent in his harmonic idiom. Equally prominent is the free succession of seventh chords, usually associated with suspensions and other nonharmonic tones; sequential passages may involve enharmonic modulations (illustrated in Example XIX–11), but with all his darting excursions into remote keys Fauré never allows us to lose the sense of a definite tonal center. His apparently Wagnerian chromatic progressions are determined (or suggested) by the melodic movement of the several voices of each chord. They lack the feeling of emotional unrest that Wagner's progressions have because they lack the tension resulting from a constantly felt pull toward diatonic resolution; they are like the evolutions of a dance without the sense of strain that would result if we were made to feel that every step and gesture was achieved by a struggle against some force trying to make them different from what they are. The combination of chromaticism and repose is very characteristic of Fauré. His music has been often described as "Hellenic" in recognition of the qualities of clarity, balance, and serenity that recall the spirit of ancient Greek art. Such

651

EXAMPLE XIX–11   Enharmonic Modulations in the Eleventh Nocturne, Fauré

Permission for reprint granted by Durand et Cie., Paris, France, © owners; Elkan-Vogel Co., Inc., Philadelphia, Pa., agents.

qualities are evident not only in the more intimate works, but also in *Pénélope* (where, of course, they are particularly appropriate) and in the *Requiem*. After 1910 Fauré's style became even more concentrated, his textures more austere (*L'Horizon chimérique,* the Tenth Barcarolle), and his lines more contrapuntal (Second Quintet, Thirteenth Nocturne).

Fauré is worthy of remembrance for more than the beauty of his music; he set an example of personal and artistic integrity by holding to tradition, logic, moderation, and the poetry of pure musical form in an age when these ideals were not generally valued. His harmonic language may have offered some suggestions to Debussy, though on the whole his style of lyrical, continuously developing melody and clear textural lines is antithetic to impressionism. But his influence on his immediate pupil Ravel, and, through the famous teacher Nadia Boulanger, on countless later composers, is one of the important factors in the history of twentieth-century music.

Claude Debussy

One of the greatest of French composers, and one of the most potent influences on the course of music in the twentieth century, was Claude-Achille Debussy (1862–1918). One aspect of his style—an aspect which sometimes is over-emphasized—is summed up in the term "impressionism." This word was first applied to a school of French painting which flourished from about 1880 to the end of the century; its chief representative is Claude Monet (1840–1926). In relation to music, the word is thus defined in Webster's Dictionary: "A style of composition designed to create descriptive impressions by evoking moods through rich and varied harmonies and timbres." Impressionism is thus a kind of program music. It differs from most Romantic program music in that, first, it does not seek to express feeling or tell a story, but to evoke a mood, an "atmosphere," with the help of suggestive titles and occasional reminiscences of natural sounds, dance rhythms, characteristic bits of melody, and the like; second, impressionism relies on allusion and understatement instead of the more forthright or strenuous methods of the Romantics; and third, it employs melodies, harmonies, colors, rhythms, and formal principles which, in one way and another, contribute to making a musical language radically different from that of the German Romantic tradition.

One element in that language is color: color not only in the narrow sense of timbre, but in the broader sense as rising from harmonic, melodic, and rhythmic factors as well. Melodies are likely to be short motives of narrow range, freely combined to make a musical mosaic of irregular, varicolored pieces. Pentatonic, whole-tone, or pseudo-modal scales may furnish the material of melodies and chords. Rhythm, in the kind of music one most often thinks of as "impressionistic," is nonpulsatile, vague, concealed by syncopations and irregular subdivisions of the beat. Outlines of phrases and the formal structure as a whole may be deliberately blurred and indistinct, though in many impressionistic pieces a general three-part (*ABA*) form is discernible.

The principal means by which Debussy achieved his color effects was harmony. One basic factor in his harmonic idiom is the use of chords in a largely "nonfunctional" manner: that is, chords are not used to shape a phrase by tension and release through a conventional series of progressions and resolutions; instead, each chord is conceived as a sonorous unit in a phrase whose structure is determined more by melodic shape or color value than by the movement of the harmony. Such a procedure does not negate tonality, which indeed Debussy sometimes maintains in ways that Franck or Schoenberg thought too simple—by pedal points, for example, or frequent returns to the primary chords of the key; but the tonal relationships within the phrase may be so complex or willful that it is impossible to hear a given chord or series of chords as being in the key of the phrase in which they occur. The structure of chords is also veiled by abundance of figuration and, in the piano works, by the blending of sounds with the use of the damper pedal. The chords employed are chiefly sevenths and ninths (often with chromatic alterations and nonharmonic tones), sometimes triads, augmented fifths, or irregular types built on fourths or seconds. A very common device is the "chord stream," a succession of chords with organum-like parallel movement of all the voices.

Debussy's harmony

Instances of all these devices may easily be found in Debussy's piano music, which—along with Ravel's—constitutes the most important addition made to the literature of that instrument in the early twentieth century. No mere listing of technical features can suggest the coruscating play of color, the ravishing pianistic effects, the subtle poetic fancy these pieces reveal. The principal impressionistic piano works of Debussy occur in collections published between 1903 and 1913: *Estampes,* two books of *Images,* and two books of *Préludes.*

As we have already indicated, "impressionism" is only one aspect of Debussy's style; in many of his compositions there is little or no trace of it—for example (among the piano music), the early *Suite Bergamasque* (1893), the suite *Pour le piano* (1901), and the delightful *Children's Corner* (1908), which in the midst of the *Golliwog's Cake Walk* introduces a satirical quotation from Wagner's *Tristan* and with *Dr. Gradus ad Parnassum* pokes fun at Czerny. The String Quartet (1893) fuses Debussy's harmonic and coloristic traits with classical forms and cyclic treatment of themes. Far from "impressionistic" are his late works, in particular the ballet *Jeux* (1912), the four-hand piano *Épigraphes antiques* (1914), the piano *Études* (two books, 1915), the suite *En blanc et noir* for two pianos (1915), and the *Sonates pour divers instruments* (violoncello and piano; flute, viola, and harp; piano and violin) of 1915–17.

Debussy's most celebrated orchestral work is the *Prélude à l'après-midi d'un faune* (1894), based on a poem of Mallarmé; this was followed by the *Nocturnes* (1899) and the symphonic sketches, *La Mer* (1905). Debussy's orchestration, like his piano writing, is admirably suited to the musical ideas. A large orchestra is required, but it is seldom used to make a loud sound. Strings are frequently divided and muted; harps add a distinctive touch; among the woodwinds, the flute (especially in the low register), oboe, and English horn are featured in solos; horns and trumpets, also often muted, are heard in short pianissimo phrases; percussion of many types— kettledrums, large and small drums, large and small cymbals, tam-tams, celesta, glockenspiel, xylophone—is still another source of color. The orchestral technique is well illustrated in the *Nocturnes:* in the second (*Fêtes*), the clarity of the full ensemble; in the first (*Nuages*) and third (*Sirènes*), the magic of rich, subdued instrumentation, supplemented in *Sirènes* by a wordless chorus of women's voices. With this music an enchanted world seems to rise before us —far-off, antique, misty with distance or bright with the inexplicable colors of a dream.

Debussy's only completed opera is his setting of Maeterlinck's symbolist play *Pelléas et Mélisande* (1902). The veiled allusions and images of the text are perfectly matched by the strange (often modal) harmonies, subdued colors, and restrained expressiveness of the music. The voices, in plastic recitative, are supported but never dominated by a continuous orchestral background, while the instrumental interludes connecting the scenes carry on the mysterious inner course of the drama. Debussy's other vocal works include songs

Pelléas et
Mélisande

The first page of the original manuscript of Prélude à l'après-midi d'un faune. *The dedication in the upper right-hand corner is to Gaby Dupont, to whom Debussy gave the manuscript in 1899.*

—notably two sets of *Fêtes galantes* to poems of Paul Verlaine (1892, 1904), the *Chansons de Bilitis* of Pierre Louys (1897), and *Trois Ballades* (1910) of the fifteenth-century poet François Villon—the early cantata *La Demoiselle élue* (1888, on a partial French translation of Rossetti's *Blessed Damozel*), and incidental music (1911) both choral and orchestral to the mystery play *Le Martyre de Saint-Sébastien* by Gabriele d'Annunzio.

Various early influences contributed to the formation of Debussy's style. The immediate background included César Franck, Saint-Saëns, and the witty and original Emmanuel Chabrier (1841–94);

but it is likely that contemporary French painters and poets were at least as much in Debussy's mind as these musicians. His admiration for Wagner was coupled with revulsion against the latter's magniloquent rhetoric and his attempts to expound philosophy in music— an example of the detested German *profondeur*. Russian music, especially Mussorgsky's *Boris* and his songs, revealed to Debussy potential new directions; the influence of Grieg has been previously mentioned; after 1900 that of Ravel is conspicuous, especially in the piano music. Debussy's national bent for musical exoticism was strengthened when he heard a Javanese *gamelan* orchestra at the Paris exposition in 1889, and it may be that his imaginative use of percussion and the many gong effects in his piano pieces were consequences of this experience. Spanish local color, inspired in part by Chabrier's *España* and Ravel's *Habanera,* is evident in the *Soirée dans Grenade* (No. 2 of *Estampes*) and the *Iberia* movement of the orchestral *Images* (1912).

Precedents for some of the technical features of the impressionist style existed in Chopin's works (end of the Db-major Nocturne) and Liszt's (*The Fountains of the Villa d'Este* in the third set of *Années de Pèlerinage,* and some of the late piano works). From the French tradition Debussy inherited his fine sensibilities, his aristocratic taste, and his anti-Romantic conception of the function of music; and in his last works he turned with renewed conviction to the heritage of Couperin and Rameau.

The changes that Debussy introduced, especially those in the harmonic system, made him one of the great seminal forces in the history of music. To name the composers who at one time or another came under his influence would be to name nearly every distinguished composer of the early and middle twentieth century. Such a list, in addition to Ravel, Messiaen, and all others of French nationality, would include Scriabin, Reger, Strauss, Falla, Puccini, Janáček, Stravinsky, Bartók, Berg, Webern, Hindemith, and Orff, as well as others in whose music the methods of impressionism were relatively more conspicuous or lasting, such as the Alsatian-born American, Charles Martin Loeffler (1861–1935), the Swiss-American, Ernest Bloch (1880–1959), the American, Charles Griffes (1884–1920), the Pole, Karol Szymanowski (1882–1937), the Englishman, Arnold Bax (1883–1935), the Italian, Ottorino Respighi (1879–1936), and the German, Franz Schreker (1878–1934).

Erik Satie

An anti-impressionist (not altogether anti-Debussy) movement in France was spearheaded on the literary and theatrical side by Jean Cocteau and on the musical side by the eccentric genius Erik Satie (1866–1925). Some of Satie's early piano pieces (for example the three *Gymnopédies* of 1888) anticipated the unresolved chords and quasi-modal harmonies of impressionism in an ostentatiously plain texture. By 1891 he was writing chords in parallel motion built on perfect fourths. His piano works between 1900 and 1915 specialized in caricature, which took the outward form of surrealistic titles: *Trois morceaux en forme de poire (Three Pieces in the Form of a Pear), Embryons desséchés (Dehydrated Embryos)*, and the like, with a running commentary and directions to the player in the same style: *pp en un pauvre souffle* (pianissimo, short of wind), *avec beaucoup de mal* (with much difficulty), all printed along with the music, satirizing some of the impressionistic titles and directions of Debussy. But the comic spirit lives also in the music itself—notated without barlines, spare, dry, capricious, brief, repetitive, parodistic, witty in the highest degree.

The curtain painted by Pablo Picasso for the Diaghilev production of Parade *in Paris, 1917. The ballet, with music by Satie, is a satire on the activities of a small French touring company. The instru-mentation includes sirens and typewriters.*

Among Satie's works for other media than the piano are the stylized "realistic ballet" *Parade* (1917) on a scenario by Cocteau with scenery and costumes by Picasso; and the "symphonic drama" *Socrate* (1920)—three songs for soprano voice and a small orchestra on texts translated from Plato—which, particularly in the last scene, *The Death of Socrates,* attains a poignancy which is intensified by the very monotony of the style and the studied avoidance of direct emotional appeal. Satie's biting, antisentimental spirit, economical textures, and severity of harmony and melody made his influence felt in France in the music of Milhaud and, to a lesser extent, Honegger, Poulenc, and others.

The next important French composer after Debussy was Maurice Ravel (1875–1937); the titles of his first two and last compositions for piano—*Menuet antique* (1895), *Pavane pour une Infante défunte* (*Pavane for a Deceased Infanta;* 1899), and *Le Tombeau de Couperin* (1917)—give a hint of the direction in which his work diverged from that of Debussy. Although Ravel adopted some of the impressionist technique, this never overcame his basic affinity for the clean melodic contours, distinct rhythms, and firm structures of Classicism. Moreover, his harmonies, while complex and sophisticated (as in the *Valses nobles et sentimentales* for piano, 1911), are functional, not only pictorial and impressionistic like some of Debussy's. Ravel's Classical orientation is most clearly apparent, of course, in such works as the piano *Sonatine* (1905) and the chamber music, which includes a Quartet (1903), a Piano Trio (1914), a sonata for violin and violoncello (1922), and one for violin and piano (1927). His most markedly impressionistic works for piano are the *Jeux d'eau* (1901), the five pieces entitled *Miroirs* (1905), and the three entitled *Gaspard de la nuit* (1908). Impressionist also to some extent are the orchestral suite *Rapsodie espagnole* (1907) and the ballet *Daphnis et Chloé* (1909–11).

Ravel, like Debussy, was a brilliant colorist, and made orchestral versions of several of his piano pieces. He also was able to absorb ideas from everywhere, adapting them to his own use with as much assurance as he adapted impressionism. He used Viennese waltz rhythms in the "choreographic poem" *La Valse* (1920), jazz elements in the piano *Concerto for the Left Hand* (1930), and Spanish idioms in the *Rapsodie,* the comic opera *L'Heure espagnole* (1910), and the rousing *Bolero* (1928), which became the musical equivalent of a best-seller. One of his most charming works is *Ma Mère l'Oye* (*Mother Goose*), a set of five little piano duets written in 1908, children's music comparable to Mussorgsky's *Nursery* songs and Debussy's *Children's Corner.* Equally perceptive and compassionate, although written with a different object and in a different technique, is the "lyrical fantasie," *L'Enfant et les sortilèges* (*The Child and the Sorceries;* 1925).

Among Ravel's songs are many settings of folk melodies from various countries; his important original songs are the five humorous and realistic characterizations of animal life in the *Histoires naturelles* (1906) and the *Chansons madécasses* (*Songs of Madagascar;* 1926), for voice, flute, violoncello, and piano; and three poems of Mallarmé set for voice, piano, string quartet, two flutes and two clarinets (1913), suggested to Ravel by Schoenberg's *Pierrot Lunaire.*

Three other French composers of the early twentieth century deserve special mention. Paul Dukas (1865–1935) belongs in the Franck-d'Indy line. His most popular work was *The Sorcerer's Apprentice* (1897), a symphonic poem like those of Franck and

Saint-Saëns. His one opera, *Ariane et Barbe-bleue* (*Ariadne and Bluebeard;* 1907) was a serious if belated attempt to combine the symphonic drama of Wagner and d'Indy with some features suggested by the music of Debussy. Florent Schmitt (1870–1958), the one French composer of this period who seems to have some kinship with the German post-Romantics, is notable for a symphonic poem *La Tragédie de Salomé* (1907 as a mimodrama; rewritten 1910). A composer whose significance extends beyond the first decade of the century is Albert Roussel (1869–1937), who studied at the Schola Cantorum under d'Indy. In his three symphonic *Évocations* (1911) and the opera-ballet *Padmâvatî* (composed 1914, first performed 1923) he carried to new heights the French Romantic musical treatment of exotic subjects; both these works depict scenes and impressions of India and make use of Hindu scales. Roussel's later works show the contemporary trend toward neo-Classicism, evident particularly in the orchestral *Suite in F* (1926), the Third Symphony, in G minor (1930), and the *Sinfonietta* for string orchestra (1934).

Peripheries

One of the lesser musical "isms" of the late nineteenth century was *verism* (*verismo*) in Italian opera. The word means literally "truthism"; it is sometimes translated as "realism" or "naturalism." *Italian opera* Its first sign is the choice of a libretto that presents everyday people in familiar situations acting violently under the impulse of primitive emotions. Its second sign is a musical style appropriate to such a libretto. The veristic opera is the innocent grandfather of the television and cinema shock drama. It was just as typical of the post-Romantic period as dissonance, hugeness, and the other musical devices which were used to titillate jaded sensibilities. The veristic operas par excellence are *Cavalleria rusticana* (*Rustic Chivalry;* 1890) by Pietro Mascagni (1863–1945) and *Pagliacci* (*The Clowns;* 1892) by Ruggiero Leoncavallo (1858–1919). Verism was shortlived, though it had some parallels or repercussions in France and Germany.

The most important Italian opera composer of the late nineteenth and early twentieth centuries was Giacomo Puccini (1858–1924), like Massenet a successful eclectic whose works reflect in turn the late Romantic taste for sentiment (*Manon Lescaut;* 1893), sentiment with realism (*La Bohème;* 1896), verism (*Tosca;* 1900), and exoticism (*Madama Butterfly,* 1904; *Turandot,* 1926) in music of lyric intensity, discreetly incorporating modern touches of harmony, and managed with a marvelous flair for theatrical effect.

Not much has been said here about the correspondence between music and the other arts in the post-Romantic era. Prominent among

Theatrical poster created by Adolfo Hohenstein for the opera Tosca *by Giacomo Puccini, 1899.*

Summary

the tendencies that influenced music were realism in the novel (Zola) and impressionism and its later offshoots in painting and literature (Monet, Mallarmé, Cézanne, Picasso, Cocteau). Among other "isms" briefly fashionable in music of the early twentieth century were barbarism or primitivism and futurism or *bruitisme* (use of noise-making instruments). The earliest modern experiments in microtones and other unorthodox divisions of the octave also took place in the 1900s. Two tendencies beginning in this period but not attaining their full development until after the First World War—neo-Classicism and the work of Schoenberg and his school—will be covered in the next chapter.

The unity of the Western musical world, maintained since the fifteenth century under the successive hegemony of the Netherlands, Italy, and Germany, seems to have been definitely if not permanently broken by 1900. In this respect the twentieth century may prove to have had the same relationship to the previous five as the fourteenth century had to the Middle Ages. The period from 1900 to 1920 was one of separate, largely independent movements without any generally acknowledged central standard to which they could be referred. Running through all the movements was the steady trend toward the dissolution of Classical tonality, a trend already perceptible in Schubert and Chopin, continued in Liszt and Wagner, accentuated with the harmonic experiments of Mussorgsky, Mahler, Strauss, Fauré, Debussy, and Ravel, and climaxed to a certain point in the prewar works of Scriabin, Ives, Schoenberg, Bartók, and Stravinsky. Chromaticism, complex and unorthodox chords, national folk song, exoticism, modality, the use of pentatonic, whole-tone, or other non-Classical scales, chord-streams, polytonality—all had a part. To a large extent composers in the first half of the twentieth century were occupied with endeavors to work out new concepts of, or find an adequate substitute for, tonality and to reconcile with new harmonic idioms the other musical elements of instrumentation, counterpoint, rhythm, and form.

XX

The Twentieth Century

Introduction

In this final chapter we shall survey the work of a few composers who were leading figures in music from about 1910 to 1950 and give some account of various movements that have arisen since the latter date. Some of the composers to be mentioned were already active before 1910, others rose to prominence only after the Second World War; the career of one, Stravinsky, spanned the entire period 1910 to 1970. We shall still be concerned in this chapter with the momentous first decade of the century—not, now, in its aspects as the end of the Classic-Romantic age but as the beginning of a new era.

The interwar period was marked by a continually increasing state of international tension and the establishment of dictatorships in *General features* Russia, Italy, and Germany. Coinciding with the onset of a world-wide economic depression and the rise of fascism at about 1930, the social history of the time may be divided into two periods: postwar and prewar. Postwar society was characterized by rebellion and unshackled experimentation, prewar by the beginning, or attempted beginning, of new adjustments toward moral, political, social, and economic questions. The music of this era may be correspondingly divided. The radically experimental nature of many works written between 1910 and 1930 caused them to be designated as "the new music"—an expression which we have met before, with *ars nova* of the fourteenth century and the *nuove musiche* of 1602. "New," as the word was used with reference to much of the music written between 1900 and 1930, reflected an emphasis on features that seemed to involve an almost total rejection of the accepted principles regulating tonality, rhythm, and form. Between 1930 and 1950 the gap between the old and the new music seemed to be narrowing as composers worked hopefully towards some kind of synthesis of the two. Government censorship in both Russia and Germany after 1930 undertook to shield the public from the deleterious effects of the "new music," which was condemned in the one country as bourgeois decadence and in the other as "cultural Bolshevism." On the other hand, special efforts were made throughout the interwar period in all countries to bring contemporary music to more people: *Gebrauchsmusik* (workaday music, for use by school groups or other amateurs) in Germany and similar projects elsewhere; "proletarian" music in Russia; and film background music by first-rate composers in all countries were some of the efforts.

Since 1950, however, the gulf between old and new music has widened and the reconciliation once longed for seems ever less likely to be realized, at least in any form that we can now imagine. The new music of the '50s and '60s is more radically new than was that of the *ars nova,* the *nuove musiche,* or the 1920s. We may regard it, if we like, as another stage in the evolution of the art of music— but only if we recognize that evolution sometimes has a way of turning off at a sharp angle instead of proceeding steadily in a straight line.

Some new social and technological factors have played a part in the twentieth century. The phonograph, radio, television, and magnetic tape have been responsible for an unparalleled increase in the size of the audience for many kinds of music (as well as for a decrease in opportunities for ordinary performers). These inventions have brought about a widespread dissemination of the standard repertoire of pieces from Bach to Prokofiev, and of other "serious" music from the more remote past and the up-to-date present. They have also furthered the growth of a huge body of "popular" music —using this word for the moment to include blues, jazz, rock and their commercialized versions, as well as so-called folk and country music, various blends of watered-down romantic idioms, hybrids of all sorts, the occasionally interesting singing commercials, the ceaseless lukewarm gush of Muzak, and so on. Popular music as such, of course, is no modern phenomenon; such music has always flourished along with the art music with which the present book deals, and has affected that music in various ways, in the past as well as now. Peculiar to the present age is the existence of an enormous population in which almost everyone can easily hear the kinds of music he likes and (usually) avoid the kinds he dislikes, so that every kind has its devotees and every new kind may quickly attract a following. One result of this situation is that novelties in both the popular and the serious field proliferate rapidly while factions among composers and hearers arise, increase, and continually diverge: in this respect the present musical universe, like the galactic universe, seems to be perpetually expanding.[1]

The closer we are to events the more difficult it is for us to see any consistent historical pattern in them. The classifications we shall adopt for considering the music of the present century are necessarily loose and tentative; other schemes would be possible. Future historians, with a longer perspective on the period, will doubtless find more settled ways of organizing its history.

Three main directions or tendencies may be traced in the music of the first half of the twentieth century, which correspond roughly to the three main lines of development in the preceding period: first, the continuing growth of musical styles which employed significant elements from national folk idioms; second, the rise of various movements, including neo-Classicism, in the interwar years, which aimed at incorporating the new discoveries of the early part of the century into musical styles having more or less overt connection with principles, forms, and techniques of the past (especially, in some cases, the pre-nineteenth-century past); and third, the transformation of the German post-Romantic idiom into the *dodecaphonic* or twelve-tone styles of Schoenberg, Berg, and Webern. Cutting across all these tendencies, participating to some extent in one or more of them but not classifiable under any one of them, is the work of two extraordinary composers, Messiaen and Stravinsky, whom we must consider independently.

The three directions or tendencies mentioned are not "schools": except for the group around Schoenberg, none of these movements acknowledged a single central authority; all overlapped in time; each included many diverse practices, and more than one of them often were evident in a single composer or even a single composition; moreover, traces of Romanticism, exoticism, impressionism, and other influences were often mingled with them in one way or another.

Musical Styles Related to Folk Idioms

Consistent with the diversity of the musical scene in the first half of the twentieth century, national differences continued to be emphasized; indeed, speedier communication at first only accentuated

[1] "The universe as we know it today is . . . moving outward at a uniform rate with no favorite direction, no center, and no edge . . . a universe in which we are . . . one of a huge crowd of spectators at the single performance of a great evolutionary show beginning in a blaze of light and ending with the dilute galaxies spread far out toward an endless dark horizon." (From a paper by Philip Morrison read at a meeting of the American Academy of Arts and Sciences in December, 1971). Some idea of the comparably expanding musical microcosm may be gained by browsing through the last third of the book *Contemporary Composers on Contemporary Music*, E. Schwartz and B. Childs, eds., New York, 1967.

contrasts between cultures. The nationalist musical activities of the twentieth century differed in several respects from those of the nineteenth. The study of folk material was undertaken on a much wider scale than previously, and with rigorous scientific method. Folk music was collected not by the clumsy process of seeking to transcribe it in conventional notation but with the accuracy made possible by the use of the phonograph; and collected specimens were analyzed objectively, by techniques developed in the new discipline of ethnomusicology, so as to discover the actual character of folk music instead of ignoring its "irregularities" or trying to adjust them to the rules of art music, as the Romantics had often done. More realistic knowledge led to greater respect for the unique qualities of folk music. Composers, instead of trying to absorb folk idioms into more or less traditional styles, used them to create new styles, and especially to extend the realm of tonality.

Central Europe was the scene of some of the earliest extensive scientific study of folk music. Janáček's pioneer work in the Czecho-Slovak region was soon followed by that of two Hungarian scholar-composers, Zoltán Kodály (1882–1967) and Béla Bartók (1881–1945).

Bartók's importance is threefold. He published nearly two thousand folk tunes, chiefly from Hungary and Rumania, these being only a part of all that he had collected in expeditions ranging over Central Europe, Turkey, and North Africa. He wrote five books and innumerable articles on folk music, made settings of or based compositions on folk tunes, and developed a style in which he fused folk elements with highly developed techniques of art music more intimately than had ever been done. Second, he was a virtuoso pianist and a teacher of piano at the Budapest Academy of Music from 1907 to 1934; his *Mikrokosmos* (1926–37)—153 piano pieces in six books of graded difficulty—is not only a work of great pedagogical value but also a summary of Bartók's own style and of many aspects of the development of European music in the first half of the twentieth century. Third and finally, he was one of the four or five composers active between 1910 and 1945 whose music is likely to endure for several generations to come.

Béla Bartók

The earliest works that begin to manifest Bartók's individual style were composed about 1908, shortly after he had become interested in Hungarian, Rumanian, and other folksongs. Compositions of this period include the First Quartet (1908), the one-act opera *Duke Bluebeard's Castle* (1911), and the *Allegro barbaro* for piano. The last is frequently cited as an example of "primitivism," that is, the stylized imitation of primitive music by means of pounding frenetic rhythms, limited melodic range with much repetition of motives, and pungent percussive harmonies. Bartók, like many twentieth-century composers, often treats the piano more as an instrument of percussion, in a class with the celesta or xylophone, than

Autograph manuscript of the first page of the Finale of Bartók's Concerto for Orchestra. (*Library of Congress*)

as a producer of cantabile melodies and arpeggiated chords, as the Romantics had conceived it. By 1917, the influences from late Romanticism and impressionism had been thoroughly absorbed into the characteristic rhythmic vigor, exuberant imagination, and elemental folk qualities of Bartók's style; in that year he wrote the Second Quartet. Compositions of the next ten years show him pushing toward the limits of dissonance and tonal ambiguity, reaching the furthest point with the two violin sonatas of 1922 and 1923. Other works of this decade were the pantomime *The Miraculous Mandarin* (1919), the *Dance Suite* for orchestra (1923), the Piano Sonata (1926), the first Piano Concerto (1926), and the Third Quartet (1927).

The later works of Bartók are the most widely known. In the *Cantata profana* (1930), for tenor and baritone soloists, double chorus, and orchestra, is distilled the spirit of all Bartók's many vocal and instrumental works specifically based on folksongs or folklike themes. A second Piano Concerto dates from 1931. The Violin Concerto (1938) and the *Concerto for Orchestra* (1943) are masterpieces in large form. Other works of the late period are the Fifth and Sixth Quartets (1934, 1939), the *Divertimento* for string orchestra (1939), the *Mikrokosmos,* the *Music for Strings, Percussion, and Celesta* (1936), the *Sonata for Two Pianos and Percussion* (1937), and the Third Piano Concerto (1945; his last completed composition).

Bartók's ideal was to express, in twentieth-century terms, Bach's texture of contrapuntal fullness, Beethoven's art of thematic development, and Debussy's discovery of the sonorous (as distinct from the functional) value of chords. The elements of his style are: melodic lines derived or sublimated from East European folk music; powerful "motoristic" rhythms, characteristically subtilized by irregular meters and offbeat accents; an intense expressionistic drive, regulated by strong formal control embracing everything from the generation of themes to the comprehensive design of an entire work. His textures may be prevailingly homophonic or be made up of contrapuntal lines carried on with secondary regard for vertical sonorities *(linear* counterpoint). The polyphony may include free use of imitative, fugal, and canonic techniques (No. 145 of the *Mikrokosmos,* the first movement of the *Music for Strings, Percussion, and Celesta,* or the two outer movements of the *Concerto for Orchestra*); and frequently one or more of the interweaving lines is enriched by parallel-moving voices in chord streams.

Bartók's harmony is partially an incidental result of the contrapuntal movement; it grows out of the character of the melodies, which may be based on pentatonic, whole-tone, modal, or irregular scales (including those found in folk music) as well as the regular diatonic and chromatic scales. All kinds of chords appear, from triads to combinations built on fourths (quite frequent) and other constructions more complex. Bartók often gives pungency to a chord by adding dissonant major or minor seconds (as in the final Ab triad of the *Allegretto pizzicato* movement of the Fourth Quartet: see Example XX–1a); sometimes seconds are piled up in tone clusters (as in the Piano Sonata, the first Piano Concerto [Example XX–1b], or the slow movement of the Second Concerto). But on the whole, especially in the Quartets, both the construction and the progressions of chords are extremely complex and difficult to analyze. Bartók's music, although it is essentially Western, not exotic, nonetheless has a great deal of the strange, unpredictable violence of barbaric impulses in its harmonies as well as in its rhythms.

Most of his music is tonal in the sense that a fundamental key

Bartók's harmony

EXAMPLE XX–1   Examples of Chords with Seconds and Tone Clusters, Béla Bartók

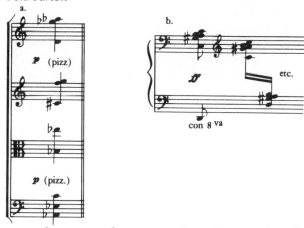

center is recurrently present, though it may be effectually obscured for considerable stretches either by modal or chromatic means, or both at once. Occasionally, and especially in the works of the nineteen-twenties, Bartók writes on two or more simultaneous harmonic planes (so-called *polytonality*), but he does not aim systematically at negating tonality. Moreover, though he sometimes writes a theme that includes up to twelve different tones in a row (as in the first movement of the Violin Concerto, measures 73–75 and finale at 129–34), or otherwise uses all the notes of the chromatic scale in a single phrase (opening of the Third and Fourth Quartets), he never uses a technique systematically based on this device. In some of Bartók's late works tonality is defined by relatively familiar procedures—particularly so in the third Piano Concerto, the *Concerto for Orchestra,* and the Violin Concerto. More commonly, however, the tonal field is less definite and the relations within it harder to grasp. In the Quartets, tonality is

> . . . handled so freely that one is justified only in saying that they are "on"—not "in"—this or that tonality. So the First and Second Quartets are on A, the Third on C♯, the Fourth on C, the Fifth on B♭, and the Sixth on D. By this it is understood that these key-notes serve as orientation points: that the music is organized around them, modally or chromatically, freely fluctuating, using the key-notes as points of departure and points of repose, effecting modulations from and back to them.[2]

In the *Music for Strings, Percussion, and Celesta* the main tonality of the first and last movements is A with an important secondary center at the augmented fourth D♯ (substituting for the conventional dominant E); the second movement is in C, with a similar

---

[2] Halsey Stevens, *The Life and Music of Béla Bartók,* 172. Quoted by permission of the publishers, Oxford University Press.

tritonic subcenter on F♯; the Adagio is indeterminate, fluctuating in the region C–F♯ (the two keys equidistant on either side from the principal tonality of the work). Some of the principal themes and all of the final cadences bring out clearly this tritone relationship (Example XX–2), which is common in Bartók, Schoenberg, and many other twentieth-century composers.

Bartók is as individual in his treatment of form as in his harmony. Typically, themes are evolved out of two or three germinal motives (first movement of the Second Quartet), and often the same motives serve to generate themes in more than one movement of a work

Bartók's form

EXAMPLE XX–2   *Music for Strings, Percussion, and Celesta*, Béla Bartók

(Fourth Quartet, *Music for Strings, Percussion, and Celesta*). With all this unification of material, however, Bartók usually maintains the principle of contrast, and most movements are articulated in distinct sections. In the main, the formal outlines are those of the Classical tradition; but in some of the late works a symmetrical arch pattern is superimposed, as in the Violin Concerto, where the first and third movements correspond in both thematic materials and formal structure. A similar pattern occurs in the Adagio of the *Music for Strings, Percussion, and Celesta:* of the six sections, the first and sixth correspond, while the fifth is a variant of the second but in the sonorities of the third, so that the fourth becomes the keystone of the arch.

Brilliant, imaginative sonorities are amply evident in any of Bartók's scores: examples are the colorful orchestration of *The Miraculous Mandarin,* the *Dance Suite,* and the *Concerto for Orchestra.* The percussive piano style is tranfigured and etherealized in the *Music for Strings, Percussion, and Celesta,* and virtuosity in the treatment of percussion is especially notable in the *Sonata for Two Pianos and Percussion.* The Quartets are full of arresting sonorities, in some of which multiple stops, glissandos, different types of pizzicato, *col legno,* and the like play a part.

The range of Bartók's style is summarized not only in the *Mikrokosmos* but also—and even more thoroughly—in the Quartets, which constitute the most important large addition to the repertoire of this medium since Beethoven. The guiding thread through all Bartók's work is the variety and skill with which he integrated the essence of folk music with the highest forms of Western art music. Bartók was not primarily an innovator; rather, like Handel, he gathered up the achievements of the past and present in an individual synthesis and expressed them eloquently. It is a sign of the difference between their worlds—and particularly of the changed relationship between composer and public—that, unlike Handel, Bartók was very little understood during his lifetime.

No composer other than Bartók so perfectly exemplifies the integration of folk and art styles in the twentieth century. The music of Kodály, more narrowly national, is less thoroughgoing in this respect, though his singspiel *Háry János* (1926) and his most famous composition, the *Psalmus hungaricus* for tenor soloist, chorus, and orchestra (1923), are thoroughly estimable works. In Germany, Carl Orff (born 1895) achieved an attractive, deceptively simple idiom —somewhat indebted in spirit and rhythm to folksong and in some aspects of sonority to Stravinsky's *Les Noces*—for his *Carmina burana* (1936) and other settings of Latin and German poetry for voices with orchestra. His operas *Der Mond* (*The Moon;* 1939) and *Die Kluge* (*The Wise Woman;* 1943) are based on fairy tales from Grimm; their stylized neo-primitive rhythmic declamation with

Other composers

sparse orchestral accompaniment in brightly percussive color combinations was further developed in the operas *Antigonae* (1949) and *Oedipus der Tyrann* (1959).

A distinctive and important work by Orff is his *Music for Children* (1950–54, in revised form), a carefully graded collection for use in schools which has won acceptance among enlightened music educators in many countries. It involves movement, singing, and playing on suitable instruments (mostly percussive in the early stages) and leads children in a natural way, by means of their own experiences, through a great variety of scales and rhythms to a broadly based understanding of music.

Russian folksongs and rhythms appear to some extent in the early compositions of Stravinsky. National influences of various sorts are of course prominent in much Soviet music, as for example the cantata *Alexander Nevsky* (1938) and the opera *War and Peace* (1941) by Sergei Prokofiev (1891–1953), the folksong quotations in the opera *Lady Macbeth* (1934) by Dmitri Shostakovich (born 1906), and the same composer's Seventh Symphony, inspired by the heroic defense of Leningrad against the German armies in 1941. The large amount of film music, mass choruses, and similar popular music by Soviet composers may also be related to nationalistic aims.

Neither Prokofiev nor Shostakovich, however, is a nationalist in the narrower meaning of the word. Prokofiev lived outside Russia from 1918 to 1934, and his compositions of these years are only sporadically touched by national influences. The *Scythian Suite* for orchestra (1916) represents an early nationalistic stage in his music. The *Classical Symphony* (1918), the third Piano Concerto (1921), and some of the music from the opera *The Love of Three Oranges* (1921) are the best known of his early works; the symphonic suite *Lieutenant Kije* (1934; arranged from music for a film), the "symphonic fairy tale" *Peter and the Wolf,* for narrator and orchestra (1936), and the ballet *Romeo and Juliet* (1938) have become widely popular. Prokofiev's other works include chamber music, piano sonatas and other piano pieces, operas, ballets, concertos, and symphonies, among which the second Violin Concerto (1935) and the Fifth Symphony (1944) are outstanding. In general, Prokofiev's style is spiced by a sufficient admixture of national and modern features to save it from banality without endangering its chances for wide popular acceptance. The music of Shostakovich, whose principal compositions, in addition to those already noted, are the Fifth Symphony (1937) and the Piano Quintet (1940), assimilates the national heritage (coming largely through Tchaikovsky) to the main European tradition, with particular influences from Mahler and Hindemith; but although it is undeniably Russian in sound, it shows few traces of specific folksong elements.

England

The foremost English composer in the first half of the twentieth century was Ralph Vaughan Williams, whose productions include nine symphonies and other orchestral pieces, songs, operas, and a great many choral works. Amid all the variety of dimensions and forms, Vaughan Williams's music was constantly motivated from sources both national and cosmopolitan—English folksong, hymnody, and literature on the one hand, and the European tradition of Bach and Handel, Debussy and Ravel on the other. But the essential quality of his music is deeper than any enumeration of influences can suggest; his works exemplify his own saying that "the composer must not shut himself up and think about art, he must live with his fellows and make his art an expression of the whole life of the community"[3]—meaning here not only the English nation but the whole community of English-speaking peoples on both sides of the Atlantic.

From 1904 to 1906 Vaughan Williams served as musical editor of the new English Hymnal; concerning this experience he wrote long afterward in his *Musical Autobiography:* "Two years of close association with some of the best (as well as some of the worst) tunes in the world was a better musical education than any amount of sonatas and fugues." He modestly neglected to add that he himself composed a half dozen new tunes, one of which was the well-known *Sine nomine* for the hymn *For all the Saints* (Example XX–3a).

Editorial work on the Hymnal, the collection *Songs of Praise* (1925), and the *Oxford Book of Carols* (1928) manifested his unaffected lifelong interest in the democratic sharing of music; another manifestation was the annual Leith Hill Music Festivals in which, from 1909 to 1953, he conducted local amateur singers and players in performances of the music of Bach and other great composers, and for which he wrote a number of choral works, among them the *Benedicite* (1930). Similar examples of music for use by amateurs are his *Household Music* (1941) for string quartet or "almost any combination of instruments," a Concerto Grosso for triple string orchestra (1950) in which the third section may consist of "those players who prefer to use only open strings," and many choral settings of folksongs, including the cycle *Folk-Songs of the Four Seasons* written for a choir festival in 1950. Works for particular occasions are the *Serenade to Music* (1938) for sixteen

---

[3] From an essay, "Who Wants the English Composer?", 1912, pr. in Hubert Foss, *Ralph Vaughan Williams,* 200.

solo singers with orchestra and *A Song of Thanksgiving* (1945) for speaker, soprano soloist, choruses, and orchestra; and here may be mentioned also the music for films (beginning in 1940), particularly that for *Scott of the Antarctic* which was later transformed into the *Sinfonia antartica* (1952).

These activities and works of Vaughan Williams emphasize the fact that the profoundly national quality of his symphonies and all other compositions, large or small, was not a matter of quoting or imitating British folk tunes or writing "modal harmonies" after the manner of the Elizabethans; they were simply an expression of his natural way of life. His early studies under two composers who were among the heralds of the English musical renaissance, C. H. H. Parry (1848–1918) and Sir Charles Villiers Stanford (1852–1924), were supplemented by work at Berlin and, for three months in 1909, at Paris with Ravel. A trace of impressionism may be sensed in the song cycle *On Wenlock Edge* for tenor, piano, and string quartet (1909, to poems of A. E. Housman), but the chief thing Vaughan Williams learned from Ravel was orchestration, "how to orchestrate in points of color rather than lines." How well the lesson was learned shows in the *London Symphony* (1914; revised 1920), a loving evocation of the sounds and atmosphere of the city, a program symphony in the same sense as Mendelssohn's *Italian* or Schumann's *Rhenish*. It has the regular four movements —the third is called *Scherzo (Nocturne)*—and dies away at the end in an Epilogue on the theme of the lento introduction to the first movement. Similar epilogues are found in the later symphonies, and many of Vaughan Williams's large compositions end pianissimo. The *London* was his second symphony. The first, the *Sea Symphony* (1910) for orchestra and voices on texts from Walt Whitman, is less important than another early work, the *Fantasia on a Theme of Thomas Tallis* (1909) for double string orchestra and string quartet, in which are heard the antiphonal sonorities and the rich texture of ascetic triads in parallel motion within a modal framework that also characterized many of his later compositions.

Vaughan Williams's style

The *Pastoral Symphony* (1922) is less definitely programmatic than the *London*. A single mood prevails throughout; there are few strong contrasts of melodic character, dynamics, or tempo among the four movements, but many changing instrumental colors. A wordless melisma in unbarred free rhythm for solo soprano is heard at the beginning and (in shortened form) the close of the last movement (Example XX–3b); it exemplifies a type of melody with gapped scales (here of pentatonic character) that often occurs in Vaughan Williams's music. Equally characteristic and folksong-like is the trumpet tune in the trio of the third movement (Example XX–3c). Especially effective use is made of the chord-stream texture in this symphony (Example XX–3d).

EXAMPLE XX–3   Examples of Themes by Vaughan Williams

Used by permission of the composer and J. Curwen & Sons, Ltd.

Other works nearly contemporary with the *Pastoral Symphony* are the neo-modal Mass in G minor (1922) for small a cappella chorus, one of Vaughan Williams's few liturgical compositions; *Flos campi* (1925) for solo viola, small wordless chorus, and chamber orchestra, each of the five movements headed by a quotation from the Song of Solomon, the whole a marvel of sensuous musical imagery; and the oratorio *Sancta Civitas* (*The Holy City;* 1925) for two soloists, three choruses, and orchestra, on English texts (despite the Latin title) from the book of Revelation—one of the composer's "mystical outpourings," of which other examples are the *Five Mystical Songs* of 1911 on poems of George Herbert, the "morality" *The Pilgrim's Progress* (1949), and *Job* (1931), a "Masque for Dancing" based on the drawings of William Blake.

The Fourth Symphony in F minor (1934) has a dissonant idiom and a vehemence in strong contrast to the *Pastoral*. The F-minor Symphony and its two successors in D major (1943) and E minor (1947) have been interpreted as reflecting Vaughan Williams's concern with world events—the Fourth as prophesying the war, the Sixth as describing the nature of war, and the Fifth as a vision of peace—although no warrant for a programmatic interpretation of any kind is given by the composer himself. On the other hand, each movement of the *Sinfonia antartica* has a brief superscription that suggests its underlying reference; the symphony is a tribute to the heroism of Captain Scott and his men and, by extension, to all men's in the struggle against overwhelming forces of nature.

Vaughan Williams was on the whole a conservative composer, sharing the Englishman's typical distrust of theories, especially theories pushed to extremes in practice. Even his most dissonant passages never outrage the national instinct for euphonious sound present also in the *Sumer* canon and the works of Dunstable and Byrd; and although his field of tonality is broad, as befits a composer of the twentieth century, it does not extend to regions of obscurity. Fundamental simplicity, a sense of humor, and a horror of Romantic rhetoric are compatible with strong ethical, even mystical, emotions.

The principal English contemporary, as well as close friend, of Vaughan Williams was Gustav Holst (1874–1934), whose music was influenced not only by English folksong but also by Hindu mysticism. The latter comes out in his choice of texts (*Choral Hymns from the Rig-Veda*, 1912), occasional peculiarly static passages of harmony (*The Hymn of Jesus*, for double chorus and orchestra, 1917), and details of exotic harmony and color as in the last movement (*Neptune*) of the orchestral suite *The Planets* (1916), Holst's best known work. He shares with Vaughan Williams the habit of practical, direct musical expression and fine imaginative sensitiveness to texts. His setting of Walt Whitman's *Ode to*

Other English composers

Death (1919) is an outstanding example, as is also, on a smaller scale, the *Dirge for Two Veterans* (1914)—another Whitman poem— for men's voices, brass, and drums.

Outstanding among Holst's later music is an orchestral piece *Egdon Heath* (1927) which the composer considered to be his best work. Inspired by a sentence in Thomas Hardy's *Return of the Native,* this is no mere descriptive tone poem but rather a sugges- tion of the mood of a somber, bleak landscape. Spare-textured, with some passages apparently influenced in the orchestration by Sibelius, its harmonic structure is indefinitely tonal, emphasizing especially the augmented-fourth relationship, as in the superposition of har- monies in G and D♭. More overtly polytonal are the prelude and scherzo *Hammersmith* (1930), originally written for military band and later rewritten for orchestra, and six canons (1932) for unac- companied equal voices.

Another English composer of our period is Sir William Walton (born 1902), whose production includes symphonic and chamber music, a fine Viola Concerto, a large oratorio *Belshazzar's Feast* (1931) and the opera *Troilus and Cressida* (1954).

Benjamin Britten (born 1913), the most prolific and most famous English composer of the mid-twentieth century, is distinguished especially for his choral works *(A Boy Was Born,* 1935; *A Ceremony of Carols,* 1942; *Spring Symphony,* 1947), songs, and operas, of which the most important are *Peter Grimes* (1945) and *The Turn of the Screw* (1954). Britten's *War Requiem* (1962) received worldwide acclaim following its first performance at Coventry Cathedral. It is an impressive large work for soloists, chorus, boys' choir, and or- chestra on the Latin text of the Requiem Mass alternating with verses by Wilfred Owen, a young English soldier who was killed in France in 1918. The music, while incorporating many modern features in a very individual way, is not essentially radical in its language. The work takes its place in the long European musical tradition and particularly—like Britten's other vocal works—in the great English tradition of choral music. Somewhat more venture- some in style is the *Children's Crusade* (1969) for children's voices on poems by Bertolt Brecht.

The United States

Nationalism has played only a subsidiary part in the musical scene of twentieth-century United States of America. The com- poser who hoped to bridge the gulf between popular music and the concert hall audience in the 1920s was George Gershwin (1898– 1937), whose *Rhapsody in Blue* (1924) was an attempt to combine the languages of jazz and Lisztian Romanticism. More spontaneous expression of his natural gifts came in the musical comedies (*Of Thee I Sing;* 1931) and especially in the "folk opera" *Porgy and Bess* (1935).

An example of integration of national American idioms in the music of a composer of high endowment and thorough technical training is found in the work of Aaron Copland (born 1900). Copland was the first of many American composers of his generation who studied at Paris under Nadia Boulanger. Jazz idioms and dissonance are prominent in some of his earlier works, such as the *Music for the Theater* (1925) and the Piano Concerto (1927). These were followed by a number of compositions of a more reserved and harmonically complex style, represented by the Piano Variations of 1930. The felt need to appeal to a larger audience motivated a turn toward simplicity, diatonic harmonies, and the use of folksong material—Mexican folksongs in the brilliant orchestral suite *El Salón México* (1936), cowboy songs in the ballets *Billy the Kid* (1938) and *Rodeo* (1942). The school opera *The Second Hurricane* (1937) and scores for a number of films (including *Our Town,* 1940) are examples of music specifically "for use" in this period. The apex of this trend was reached in *Appalachian Spring* (1944), first written as a ballet with an orchestra of thirteen instruments but better known in the arrangement as a suite for symphony orchestra. *Appalachian Spring* is in Copland's work what the *Pastoral* Symphony is in Vaughan Williams's. Unlike the English composer, Copland incorporates an actual folk tune (the Shaker hymn *The Gift to Be Simple*) as well as suggestions of folk dance music; but the material is subtly transfigured and its essence absorbed in a work that sincerely and simply expresses the pastoral spirit in authentically American terms.

On the technical side, Copland sometimes uses any or all notes of the diatonic scale for vertical combinations: the opening chord of *Appalachian Spring,* with its derivations and amplifications, serves as a unifying device, a characteristic sonority with divided strings and soft woodwinds that returns from time to time throughout the work (see Example XX–4).

Aaron Copland

EXAMPLE XX–4　Chord Forms in *Appalachian Spring,* Copland

A new synthesis on a large scale appeared with the Third Symphony (1946), which has no overt programmatic significance (though some of its tunes are suggestive of folksongs), and well exemplifies Copland's characteristic combination of "leanness and grandiosity."[4] A more finely-wrought chamber music idiom, a further evolution from the style of the Piano Variations, is found in the Piano Sonata (1941). In the songs on *Twelve Poems of Emily Dickinson* (1950), and more markedly in the Piano Quartet (1950), the Piano Fantasy (1957) and the orchestral *Inscape* (1967), Copland adopts some features of the twelve-tone technique. Despite the various influences reflected in the range of styles in his works, Copland retains an unmistakable personal quality. His music preserves the sense of tonality, though not always by traditional means; his rhythms are live and flexible, and he is adept at obtaining new sounds from simple chords by instrumental color and spacing. His work and counsel have influenced many younger American composers.

Other American composers

A more self-conscious nationalist was Roy Harris (born 1898), whose music at its best (as in the Third Symphony, 1939) suggests something of the rugged simplicity of Walt Whitman; some of his works embody actual folk themes, as for example the choral *Folk Song Symphony* (1941). Likewise incorporating specifically American idioms (blues) is the *Afro-American Symphony* (1931) of William Grant Still (born 1895). A neo-primitive episode in American music is represented by Virgil Thomson (born 1896) in his opera *Four Saints in Three Acts* (1934) on a libretto by Gertrude Stein, and in many of his symphonic and choral works.

The genuinely national element in this country's music is not easily isolated or defined, blended as it is with cosmopolitan style features which it shares with European music of the period. One obvious external sign, of course, is the choice of American subjects for operas, cantatas, or symphonic poems, as for example in some of the compositions of William Schuman (born 1910); but in much of the music itself nationalism is a more subtle ingredient; it may be detected, perhaps, in a certain forthright, optimistic character, or in a feeling for flowing, unconstrained color and melody as in Ulysses Kay's (born 1917) *Serenade for Orchestra* (1954) and *Umbrian Scene* (1964)—or again, in a fast-driving rhythmic energy, such as that of Robert Palmer's (born 1915) Piano Quartet (1947). Some eminent American composers wrote habitually in a language that cannot be called national in any limiting sense of the word. Howard Hanson (born 1896) was an avowed neo-Romantic with a style influenced by Sibelius; the chamber music and symphonies of Walter Piston (born 1894) are in a sturdy and sophisticated neo-Classical idiom. The music of Roger Sessions (born 1896) is more intense, dissonant, and chromatic, receptive to influences from his teacher Ernest Bloch

4 Arthur Berger, *Aaron Copland*, 40.

and, to a lesser degree, from Arnold Schoenberg, but nonetheless stoutly individual (Third Symphony, 1957; the opera *Montezuma,* 1962; the cantata *When lilacs last,* 1971). An equally personal style, with notable innovations in the treatment of rhythm and form, is evident in the compositions of Elliott Carter (born 1908), particularly the *Variations for Orchestra* (1955), the second String Quartet (1959), and the Double Concerto for piano and harpsichord (1961); still further innovations characterize his more recent Piano Concerto and *Concerto for Orchestra.*

The principal representatives of nationalism in Latin American music were Heitor Villa-Lobos (1887–1959) of Brazil and Carlos Chávez (born 1899) of Mexico. Villa-Lobos's best known works are a series of compositions for various vocal and instrumental combinations under the general designation *choros,* which make use of Brazilian rhythms and sonorities. Chávez is particularly notable for the *Sinfonia India* (1936) and the Piano Concerto (1940). Significant among more recent Latin-American composers is the Argentinian Alberto Ginastera (born 1916), whose opera *Bomarzo* made a strong impression at its first performances in 1967.

Neo-Classicism and Related Movements

The effects of experiments begun in the earlier part of the century continued to be felt in the interwar decades. Many composers (including most of those mentioned in the foregoing section) endeavored, in various ways and to varying extents, to absorb the new discoveries without losing continuity with tradition; they held to some recognizably familiar features of the past—tonal centers (defined or alluded to often in quite new ways), melodic shape, goal-oriented movement of musical ideas, for example—while incorporating fresh and unfamiliar elements. Two composers of this era in France were Arthur Honegger and Darius Milhaud.

Honegger (1892–1955), of Swiss parentage but born in France and resident in Paris after 1913, excelled in music of dynamic action and graphic gesture, expressed in short-breathed melodies, strong ostinato rhythms, bold colors, and dissonant harmonies. The French composer to whose style his is most nearly related is Florent Schmitt. Honegger's "symphonic movement," *Pacific 231,* in which he aimed not to imitate the sound, but to translate into music the visual and physical impression, of a speeding locomotive, was hailed as a sensational piece of modernistic program music in 1923. His principal orchestral works are the five symphonies (1931–51).

Honegger became world famous after the appearance in concert form (1923) of his oratorio *King David,* which had been first presented in an original stage version two years before. This work marks the beginning of the rise of an important new form in the second quarter of the twentieth century, a compound of oratorio and opera. *King David* has become popular because the choruses are easy to sing (they were written in the first place for amateurs), the rhythmic and formal patterns are conventional, the few harmonic audacities are mingled with familiar consonant diatonic writing, and the unified action—the scene connections, in the concert version, being effected by means of a narrator—is illustrated by music of pictorial vividness and spontaneous melody.

On a grander scale—with five speaking parts, five soloists, mixed chorus (which both sings and speaks), children's chorus, and large orchestra—is *Jeanne d'Arc au Bûcher* (*Joan of Arc at the Stake;* 1938), an elaborate oratorio-drama by Paul Claudel, with music in which Gregorian chant, dance tunes, and modern and medieval folksongs are mingled with Honegger's dissonant, highly colored idiom; this work is held together more by dramatic power than by musical architecture.

Darius Milhaud

Darius Milhaud (born 1894) was a native of Aix in Provence. He created a gracious memorial of his native region in the *Suite Provençale* for orchestra (1937), which incorporates melodies of the early eighteenth-century composer André Campra. Milhaud has produced an immense quantity of music. He seems to compose with a facility rare in the twentieth century, which recalls the days of Haydn and Mozart. His works include piano pieces, chamber music (the eighteen string quartets are especially notable), suites, sonatas, symphonies, film music, ballets, songs, cantatas, and operas. There is a contrast between the frivolity, the mockery and satire of the ballets *Le Boeuf sur le toit* (*The Ox on the Roof;* 1919) or *Le Train bleu* (*The Blue Train;* 1924) and the cosmic earnestness of the opera-oratorio *Christophe Colomb* (1928) or the religious devotion of the music for the Jewish *Sacred Service* (1947). Milhaud is an artist of Classical temperament, not given to theories or systems, but infinitely receptive to many kinds of stimuli which are spontaneously converted to musical expression: Brazilian folk melodies and rhythms, for example, in the orchestral dances (later arranged for piano) *Saudades do Brasil* (*Souvenirs of Brazil;* 1920–21); saxophones, ragtime syncopations, and the blues third in the ballet *La Création du monde* (*The Creation of the World;* 1924). Milhaud's music is essentially lyrical in inspiration, blended of ingenuousness and ingenuity, clear and logical in form, and addressed to the listener as objective statement, not personal confession.

One technical device which appears recurrently in Milhaud as well as in many other composers contemporary with him (for example, the Netherlander Willem Pijper, 1894–1927) is *polytonality* —one of those terms that are easier to use than to define. Of course we can say that polytonality is the property of music written in two or more keys at once. But is it really possible to *hear* more than one tonality at a time? If it is not, we must conclude that "polytonal" music means no more than music in which one can discern by analysis (usually visual) that two or more lines of melody or planes of harmony, each in a distinct and different key, are sounding simultaneously. A simple instance is given in Example XX–5a.

Extension of the polytonal principle produced the complex dissonances of *Christophe Colomb* and of the closing scene of the opera *Les Euménides* (1924); in the latter Milhaud builds up to six simultaneous different keys, reduces them gradually to two, and finally resolves on the single key of C major. A similar piling up of tonalities occurs in the first movement of the Fourth Symphony (1948). Of course no listener hears the two tonalities B major and G major in Example XX–5a. What he hears is G major with a few dissonant notes which he probably interprets as passing tones or nonresolving appoggiaturas; in *Les Euménides* and similar passages, he hears a mass of undifferentiated dissonance in which the direction of the musical movement is defined by rhythms and melodic lines, while the arrival at the final goal is made climactic by the resolution of dissonance into consonance. Milhaud offers a simple explanation of his use of polytonal chords: "The sound of them satisfied my ear; a polytonal chord when soft is more subtly sweet and when forceful is more violent than the normal kind." And he adds that he used such chords "only to support a diatonic melody" —an important qualification, to which another may be added, namely that the various polytonal planes are distinguished by different instrumental timbres in orchestral writing, and this incidentally diminishes their dissonant effect.

EXAMPLE XX–5   Polytonality in Works of Milhaud

a. Saudades do Brasil, I, No. 4 (Copacabana)

b. String Quartet No. 12, second movement

Coda

Excerpt of the String Quartet No. 12 by Darius Milhaud used by permission of
Editions Salabert, publishers and © owners. Saudades do Brasil, © 1922, renewed
1950, by Editions Max Eschig.

To illustrate this aspect of Milhaud's style, we may take (Example XX–5b) two passages from the slow movement of the Twelfth Quartet (1945). The opening motives of the movement, exploiting the sonority of seconds and thirds against a dominant pedal in A major, form the subject of the coda: two polytonal measures (A–G–D–E♭) followed by a diatonic passage in A with the Lydian sharped fourth, and final cadence with momentary clash of minor and major third.

The gamut of Milhaud's style is disclosed in his operas. In addition to the music for Claudel's translations of three plays from Aeschylus (composed between 1913 and 1924), these include *Les Malheurs d'Orphée (The Misfortunes of Orpheus,* 1924), *Le Pauvre Matelot (The Poor Sailor,* 1926) on a libretto by Jean Cocteau; three *opéras minutes,* running about ten minutes each, on parodies of classical myths (1927); the huge oratorio-opera *Christophe Colomb* (1928; text by Paul Claudel); the formally more conventional *Maximilien* (1930), *Médée* (1938), and *Bolivar* (1943); and the Biblical opera *David,* commissioned to celebrate the 3,000th anniversary of Jerusalem as the capital of David's kingdom, and first performed in concert version at Jerusalem in 1954. All Milhaud's operas, in contrast to the symphonic music dramas of Wagner, are organized in distinct scene complexes with arias and choruses, and the singing voices are the center of interest rather than the orchestra.

The compositions of Francis Poulenc (1899–1963) were for the most part in small forms. He combined the grace and wit of the Parisian popular *chansons* with a gift for satirical mimicry—of *Francis Poulenc* Puccini, Massenet, and Debussy in his comic opera *Les Mamelles de Tirésias (The Breasts of Tiresias;* 1940), for example—and natural fluent melody with an ingratiating harmonic idiom. By no means were all his works frivolous. His *Concert champêtre (Pastoral Concerto)* for harpsichord or piano and small orchestra (1928) is neo-Classical in the spirit of Rameau and Domenico Scarlatti; among his compositions are a Mass in G for chorus a cappella (1937), several motets, and other choral works. He is very highly regarded as a composer of songs. His three-act serious opera *Dialogues des Carmélites (Dialogues of the Carmelites;* 1956) is a most effective setting of an unusually fine libretto by Georges Bernanos.

The leading German composer of the first half of the twentieth century was Paul Hindemith (1895–1963). He is notable not only as a composer but also as a theorist who undertook to formulate a *Paul Hindemith* general system of composition, hoping to establish a basis on which the divergent practices of the time might find common ground for further progress. His work as a teacher—at the Berlin School of Music 1927–37, Yale University 1940–53, and the University of Zurich after 1953—was also important.

Hindemith was first of all a practical musician. An experienced solo, orchestral, and ensemble player on the violin and viola, he learned to play many other instruments as well. Younger than Schoenberg, Bartók, and Stravinsky, he did not go through any early important Romantic or impressionist stage but plunged at once with his first published compositions into the confused and confusing world of the new music in Germany of the 1920s. It is noteworthy that in the light of changed conceptions of tonality the composer some twenty-five years later revised the three principal large works of this decade. These were a song cycle for soprano voice and piano on poems of R. M. Rilke, *Das Marienleben* (*The Life of Mary*, 1923), the tragic expressionist opera *Cardillac* (1926), and the comic opera *Neues vom Tage* (*News of the Day;* 1929). Four string quartets and a large quantity of other chamber music are also among Hindemith's works of this period.

In the late 1920s and early 1930s, Hindemith, disturbed by the cleavage between composers and an increasingly passive public, undertook the works that caused his name to be associated with *Gebrauchsmusik*—that is, music for use, as distinguished from music for music's sake. Among such works were a musical playlet for children entitled *Wir bauen eine Stadt* (*Let's Build a Town;* 1930) and a number of pieces of the sort known in Germany as *Sing- und Spielmusik,* a term for which there is no convenient English equivalent. It means "music for singing and playing" by amateurs who do it for fun; it is "play" music in a double sense of the word. It is of necessity not too difficult, and must be attractive for the performers without being vulgar. *Spielmusik* occupies an important place both in Hindemith's works and in his teachings about the social obligations of a composer.

Less dissonant linear counterpoint, more systematic tonal organization, and a new quality of almost Romantic warmth became evident in the 1930's (compare a. and b. of Example XX–6). Compositions of this decade include the opera *Mathis der Maler* (*Matthias the Painter;* 1934), based on the life and works of the sixteenth-century German artist Matthias Grünewald; the orchestral suite of excerpts from this opera is probably the best known of all Hindemith's works. Also from this time come the three Piano Sonatas (1936); a sonata for piano four hands (1938); the ballets *Nobilissima visione* (1938; on St. Francis of Assisi) and *The Four Temperaments* (1940); and the Symphony in E♭ (1940).

Much of Hindemith's music was composed for use in the sense that it was written for particular players, or to add to the repertoire of certain instruments for which little literature existed: among his numerous sonatas are some for such comparatively neglected solo instruments as the viola d'amore, horn, trumpet, English horn, double bass, and tuba, as well as the more usual ones (flute, oboe, clarinet, viola, violin, organ). There are concertos for or-

EXAMPLE XX–6   Examples of Hindemith's Harmony

a. Quartet No. 4, slow movement (1923)

b. Mathis der Maler, *Scene 7 (1934)*

Quartet No. 4, ⓒ 1924, renewed 1952, by B. Schott's Soehne, Mainz. *Mathis der Maler,* ⓒ 1935 by B. Schott's Soehne, Mainz.

chestra and various instrumental groups (string quartet with piano, brass, and two harps; woodwinds and harp; trumpet, bassoon, and strings) and for solo instruments (piano, violin, violoncello, clarinet, organ); and there is a *Symphony for Concert Band* (1951).

Another kind of music for use was written for teaching purposes. The title *Klaviermusik: Übung in drei Stücken (Piano Music: Three Practice Pieces;* 1925) is reminiscent of Bach's *Clavier Übung.* Analogous to *The Well-Tempered Clavier* is Hindemith's *Ludus tonalis (Game of Tonalities;* 1942) for piano: subtitled "Studies in Counterpoint, Tonal Organization, and Piano Playing," it consists of twelve fugues (one in each key) with modulating interludes, a Prelude (C → F♯), and Postlude (F♯ → C).

Compositions after 1940 include the Fifth and Sixth Quartets (1943, 1945), the *Symphonic Metamorphoses* on themes of Weber (1943), a "requiem" on words of Whitman (*When lilacs last in the dooryard bloom'd*), and other choral works; the new version of the *Marienleben* (1948); and the opera *Die Harmonie der Welt* (*The Harmony of the Universe*). Hindemith had begun writing this opera in the 1930s, but laid it aside when he came to the United States because there seemed no chance of getting such a work performed at that time. In 1952 he made a three-movement orchestral symphony out of some of the music and then continued work on the opera, which was finally presented at Munich in 1957. Among Hindemith's last works were an Octet for clarinet, bassoon, horn, violin, two violas, violoncello, and double bass; several fine madrigals;[5] an unpretentious one-act opera, *The Long Christmas Dinner* (after Thornton Wilder; 1961), and a Mass for chorus a cappella, first sung at the Piaristenkirche in Vienna in November of 1963.

Hindemith's musical philosophy is set forth in *A Composer's World*. Four elements are necessary for an understanding of his music and his historical position in the twentieth century.

Hindemith's musical philosophy

Communication: "Music, as we practice it, is, in spite of its trend toward abstraction, a form of communication between the author and the consumer of his music." The composer "can do nothing better than to reach a mutual understanding with the consumers on their inarticulate desires and his ability of wisely and honestly gratifying them."[6] Thus he is obligated not only to organize his material perspicuously but also to consider the needs and capacities of the audience for whom he writes, as well as such factors as the place in which the music is to be heard and the technical ability of the performers.

Craftsmanship: All musical theorizing must be done in connection with musical practice. Essential to a composer's training is familiarity through constant practical experience with instruments and with the processes of making music, especially in groups. Almost everyone has musical inspirations at one time or another, but only the composer knows how to bring his vision of a work into communicable form through labor controlled by broad and detailed knowledge of his technique and tools. The craftsmanship which Hindemith proposed was intended to serve composers for music in all styles, not merely his own.

Tonality: For Hindemith, tonality in music was as inevitable as the law of gravity in the physical world, and he held that attempts to ignore it not only are ineffective but result in chaos. The various

---

[5] See the score and analysis of one of these madrigals in Austin, *Music in the Twentieth Century*, 408–16.

[6] Hindemith, *A Composer's World,* 65, 209.

possible combinations of intervals within the twelve tones of the scale have a naturally ordered relationship both to each other and to fundamental central tonalities, and such natural relationships must be observed in all musical composition. Hindemith's statement does not imply a return to the particular method of tonal organization that prevailed in the eighteenth and nineteenth centuries, but is a much more inclusive synthesis. In Book I of his *Craft of Musical Composition* (1937) Hindemith made the most important attempt so far in the present century to establish a system of tonality intended to be generally valid for contemporary use.

A practical result of his theories was the 1948 revision of the *Marienleben* songs, which involved, among other things, changes in the vocal line to integrate the melodies more closely with the harmony, and the introduction of a general scheme of precise tonal interrelationships serving expressive or symbolic purposes. Some typical changes of detail are illustrated in Example XX–7, the first eight measures of the second song. Hindemith altered both the passacaglia bass theme and the vocal melody, and the result is a line that is more natural to sing and more consistent with the harmony (for instance, the circled nonchord tones resolve downward by step), while the phrase as a whole is tonally more clearly organized around C, with a climax of tension (most remote keys) at measures five to seven. It must be noted, incidentally, that not all critics agreed with the composer in regarding the changes in *Das Marienleben* (likewise those in *Cardillac* and *Neues vom Tage,* which were made at about the same time) as improvements.

Symbolism. After 1940 Hindemith increasingly embraced the idea that the order within a musical composition is symbolical of a higher order within the moral and spiritual universe—a conscious return to the medieval doctrine expressed by St. Augustine and others. The most thorough exemplification of the doctrine in Hindemith's music occurs in the *Harmonie der Welt*. The poem is (like that of *Mathis*) by the composer himself; it deals with the life of the early seventeenth-century astronomer Johannes Kepler, the title of whose treatise *Harmonices mundi* (1619) Hindemith adopted for his opera. In the new version of the *Marienleben* there is a symbolical relationship of tonalities: the principal key of E is associated with Christ, the dominant B with His earthly nature, the subdominant A with His heavenly nature, and other keys with other ideas in an order conforming to their degree of nearness to the central tonality of E.

Hindemith's work was as versatile and nearly as large in amount as Milhaud's. He was a mid-twentieth-century representative of the German cosmopolitan line of Schumann, Brahms, and Reger; additional influences in his work came from Debussy as well as from Bach, Handel, Schütz, and the German sixteenth-century Lied composers. Hindemith was a "natural musician" like Bach,

EXAMPLE XX–7   Changes Made in *Das Marienleben,* Hindemith

a. Version of 1923

b. Version of 1948

Marienleben (old version) © 1924, renewed 1951, by B. Schott's Soehne, Mainz.
Marienleben (new version) © 1948, Schott & Co., Ltd. London.

producing music as a tree produces fruit. Although his efforts to establish a common basis for all musical composition in the twentieth century were not successful, his music retains its vitality. Several of his compositions—*Mathis der Maler,* the Violin Concerto of 1939, the *Nobilissima Visione,* the *Symphonic Metamorphoses*—are still among the most frequently performed works in concerts, while his numerous sonatas for brass and other wind instruments are staples in the repertoire of players.

Messiaen

An influential, unique, and quite unclassifiable figure in music around the middle of the twentieth century was Olivier Messiaen. Born at Avignon in 1908, Messiaen studied organ and composition at Paris and became professor in the Conservatoire there in 1942. His many distinguished pupils included Pierre Boulez and Karlheinz Stockhausen, who became leaders among the new musical movements of the 1950s and '60s, as well as the Italian Luigi Nono, the Netherlander Ton de Leeuw, and many other important composers of that generation.

It is a tribute to the quality of Messiaen's teaching that not one of his pupils has merely imitated his style; each, while acknowledging a debt to the instruction received, has gone his own way. Thus Messiaen was not the founder of a school of composition in the ordinary sense of the word. His own compositions of the 1930s, especially those for the organ, attracted favorable attention everywhere; his works of the '40s and '50s are less widely known. In his music after 1960 he continued to cultivate a highly personal idiom, which diverged more and more from the main "progressive" currents of the second half of the century. An intricate system of verbal and grammatical equivalences pervades his *Meditations on the Mystery of the Holy Trinity* for organ, composed in 1969.

Characteristic of Messiaen's music from the beginning is a complete integration of wide-ranging emotional expressiveness, deeply religious in tone, with minutely organized means of intellectual control. To these he brings continuous discoveries of new sounds, new rhythms and harmonies, and new modes of relation between music and life—life in both the natural and the spiritual (supernatural) realms, which Messiaen views as wholly continuous or interlocked. His musical language shows traits of such diverse ancestors as Debussy, Scriabin, Wagner, Rimsky-Korsakov, Monteverdi, Josquin, and Perotin. In addition, he is a poet (writing his own texts for vocal works), a student of Greek poetry, and an accomplished amateur ornithologist.

Besides numerous works for piano and his own instrument, the organ, Messiaen's principal compositions include a *Quatuor pour la fin du temps* (*Quartet for the End of Time*) for violin, clarinet, violoncello, and piano, first performed by the composer and three fellow-prisoners at a German military prison camp in 1941; *Trois petites liturgies pour la présence divine* (*Three Short Liturgies of the Divine Presence*) for unison chorus of women's voices and small orchestra (1944); a symphony *Turangalîla* in ten movements for large orchestra (1948); *Cinq rechants (Five Refrains)* for unaccompanied chorus of mixed voices (1949); and *Chronochromie* (literally, *Time-Color*) for orchestra (1960).

Within a prevailingly rich homophonic texture, Messiaen's music has a peculiar personal quality which results in part from certain special technical features:

(1) Scales or "modes" of eight tones to the octave, constructed on the plan of alternating whole- and half-steps in various combinations, for example:

(2) "Rhythmic pedals," that is, a repeating pattern of rhythm made up of various duration-values, and usually overlapping the melodic-harmonic pattern in a way similar to the overlapping of *talea* and *color* in some medieval isorhythmic motets. This device is used systematically in a highly developed form in *Chronochromie*.

(3) On occasion, avoidance of regular beats by means of (a) "added values" resulting in rhythmic figures such as ♩ ♩ ♩ ♩, ♩ ♩. ♩ ♩, and others much more complex; (b) rhythmic "palindromes," rhythmic patterns that read the same forward and backward, for example:

♩ ♩. ♪. ♪ ♩.   ♪ ♪. ♩. ♩

(c) augmentation (or diminution) of a melodic line otherwise than by multiples of two: for example, ♩ ♫ becoming not ♩ ♩ ♩ but (perhaps) ♩. ♫. ; (d) use of rhythms derived from Greek meters or Hindu *talas*.

(4) Extremely complex vertical sound-aggregations (chords) incorporating the higher harmonics of a fundamental tone and typically used to lend what Messiaen calls a "rainbow" or "stained-glass window" effect to the notes of a sometimes clearly tonal melodic line.

(5) A multitude of melodic decorative figures derived from bird songs—stylized, of course, idealized—in great variety and profusion, with sometimes many sounding simultaneously in a crowded, complex texture.

(6) Other new sound resources, such as the choral "orchestration" by means of consonant and vowel sound-effects in *Cinq rechants;* or the imaginative use of the piano, the distinctive colors of the vibraphone and *Ondes Martenot,* and the variety of percussion instruments in orchestral combinations.

Bird songs and other natural sounds always interested Messiaen; decorative bird-like figurations appear in the *Quatuor* of 1941 and increasingly in subsequent compositions. The *Oiseaux exotiques* for piano (1958) are entirely devoted to them, and they make up practically the entire melodic-harmonic substance of *Chronochromie*. This devotion exemplifies one way in which Messiaen conceived music as related most intimately to Nature and, through Nature, to all of life. In this sense, all his music is programmatic—not only imitative or descriptive but also symbolical. One can best comprehend this from reading some of his explanatory "program notes" to his own works.

In a piano piece entitled *Mode de valeurs et d'intensités* (1949) Messiaen systematically organized the different elements of musical sound in such a way that every tone of the chromatic scale—now in one, now in another of three different octave registers—was always associated with a certain fixed duration, loudness, and way of playing (legato, staccato, etc.). This work is chiefly interesting as having anticipated (and stimulated) the "total serialism" of some younger European composers in the 1950s.

Stravinsky

We come now to a composer whose works exemplify nearly every significant musical tendency of the first half of the twentieth century, whose career might almost by itself serve as an epitome of that changeful epoch, and whose influence on three generations of composers has been as great as, if not greater than, Wagner's influence between 1870 and 1910: Igor Stravinsky. Born in Russia in 1882, he came to Paris in 1911, lived in Switzerland after 1914, in Paris again after 1920, in California after 1940, and in New York from 1969 until his death in 1971. Stravinsky's principal early compositions were three ballets commissioned by Sergei Diaghilev (1872–1929), the founder and director of the Russian Ballet, which for twenty years after its first season at Paris in 1909 was a European institution that attracted the services of the leading artists of the time. For Diaghilev and Paris, Stravinsky wrote *The Fire Bird* (1910), *Petrushka* (1911), and *Le Sacre du printemps* (*The Rite of Spring*, subtitled *Pictures of Pagan Russia;* 1913). *The Fire Bird* stems from the Russian nationalist tradition, and has the exotic orientalism and rich sensuous orchestration of Stravinsky's teacher, Rimsky-Korsakov. *Petrushka* brings a touch of *verismo* in its circus scenes and characters, while the alert rhythms, bright raw orchestral colors, and leaner contrapuntal texture indicate realms that later were further explored by Stravinsky. The *Sacre* is undoubtedly the most famous composition of the early twentieth century; it had the effect of an explosion that so scattered the elements of musical language that they could never again be put together as before. Its first performance provoked a famous riot at Paris, though in the long run this

Early works

work, along with *The Fire Bird* and *Petrushka,* has enjoyed more public favor than Stravinsky's later compositions.

The *Sacre* was the culminating point of primitivism; Cocteau called it "a pastorale of the pre-historic world." Its novelty consisted not only in the rhythms but even more in the hitherto unheard orchestral effects and chordal combinations, and in the ruthless logic and elemental power with which all these were combined.

1913–1923 The forced economy of wartime, together with Stravinsky's inner impulsion toward new goals, led to a change of style that became evident in the years 1913 to 1923. Compositions of this period include chamber music, short piano pieces, and songs; the ballets *L'Histoire du Soldat* (*The Soldier's Tale;* 1918), *Les Noces* (*The Wedding;* 1917–23), and *Pulcinella* (1919); and the Octet for Wind Instruments (1923). The first feature of the new style which strikes one is the replacement of a large orchestra by small combinations:

The title page of Stravinsky's piano arrangement of Ragtime (*J. & W. Chester, London, 1919*), *designed by Picasso.*

for *L'Histoire,* solo instruments in pairs (violin and double bass, clarinet and bassoon, cornet and trombone) and a battery of percussion—seven players in all; for *Les Noces,* four pianos and percussion; for *Pulcinella,* a small orchestra with strings divided into concertino and ripieno groups. The *Ragtime* and *Piano Rag Music* were early examples (followed by some others, such as the *Ebony Concerto* of 1945) of his interest in jazz, an interest reflected also in the instrumentation and rhythms of *L'Histoire. Pulcinella* is a prelude to Stravinsky's neo-Classical period, of which the Octet is an example convenient for study. The Octet was followed by a Concerto for Piano and Wind Instruments (1924), a Piano Sonata (1924), and the *Serenade in A* for piano (1925).

Neo-Classical is the tag usually attached to Stravinsky's style from the time of the Octet to that of the opera *The Rake's Progress* (1951). The word may more broadly also designate a general tendency of this period, one best exemplified perhaps in Stravinsky and largely inspired by him, but evident also to a greater or lesser degree in the majority of other contemporary composers (including Schoenberg). In this sense neo-Classicism may be defined as adherence to the Classical principles of balance, coolness, objectivity, and absolute (as against Romantic program) music, with the corollary characteristics of economy, predominantly contrapuntal texture, and diatonic as well as chromatic harmonies; it sometimes involves also imitation or quotation of, or allusion to, specific melodies or style traits of older composers—as in Stravinsky's *Pulcinella,* which is built on themes supposedly from Pergolesi, or the ballet *Le Baiser de la Fée* (*The Fairy's Kiss;* 1928), based on themes from Tchaikovsky.

Stravinsky's neo-Classicism

Of course the idea of renewing an art by turning to principles and models of an earlier time was not new; it was one of the basic ideas of the Renaissance, and composers of all periods have on occasion deliberately made use of older styles. But the neo-Classicism of the twentieth century had two special features: first, it was a symptom of a search for principles of order, for some way other than Schoenberg's out of the pitfalls of Romanticism and the seeming chaos of the years between 1910 and 1920; and second, composers as never before had a detailed knowledge of many past styles and were aware of the uses they were making of them. The aim was not to revive archaic idioms, but to acknowledge tradition in the sense that Stravinsky defined it: "a living force that animates and informs the present. . . . Far from implying the repetition of what has been, tradition presupposes the reality of what endures. It appears as an heirloom, a heritage that one receives on condition of making it bear fruit before passing it on to one's descendants."[7]

It was difficult for critics and the public, who thought of Stravinsky as the revolutionary composer of the *Sacre,* to comprehend the apparent reversal implied by *L'Histoire, Pulcinella,* and the Octet. With our perspective we can see that the change was not so radical as it at first seemed. However, each new work by Stravinsky continued to cause some reaction of surprise, because in each he

[7] Stravinsky, *Poetics of Music,* 58–59.

elaborated a particular generative idea in forms, timbres, and harmonies appropriate to that idea and to no other. Merely to label all of his compositions written between 1923 and 1951 as neo-Classical would be—as always with classifications but especially so here—to overlook the variety in these productions, the individuality of each composition, and the continuity that underlies not only this period but the whole of his work from *The Fire Bird* on.

Stravinsky contributed two large compositions to choral literature: the opera-oratorio *Oedipus rex* (*Oedipus the King;* 1927) on a Latin translation of Cocteau's adaptation of Sophocles, for soloists, narrator, men's chorus, and orchestra; and the *Symphony of Psalms* (1930) for mixed chorus and orchestra on Latin texts from the Vulgate. Stravinsky used Latin because the language's being conventionalized, like a ritual, left him free to concentrate, as he said, on its "phonetic" qualities. *Oedipus* is statuesque, static, blocklike, intense within its stylized form. The *Symphony of Psalms* is one of the great works of the twentieth century, a masterpiece of invention, musical architecture, and religious devotion.

In line with Stravinsky's attraction to Classical subjects are the ballet *Apollon musagète* (*Apollo, Leader of the Muses;* 1928) and the ballet-melodrama *Perséphone* (1934), the former for string orchestra and the latter for a normal orchestra with reciter, tenor soloist, mixed chorus, and children's chorus. Chamber music works include, besides the Octet, a *Duo Concertant* for violin and piano (1932), a Concerto for Two Pianos (1935), the *Dumbarton Oaks Concerto* in E♭ (1938), and the *Basle Concerto* in D (1946), both for chamber orchestra. Normal orchestral forces are employed in the *Capriccio* for piano and orchestra (1929) and the Violin Concerto (1931). The Symphony in C (1940) is a model of neo-Classical clarity and compact form. The *Symphony in Three Movements* (1945) is more agitated and dissonant, and recalls some features of the *Sacre*.

The subject of the opera *The Rake's Progress* was suggested by Hogarth's engravings; the libretto is by W. H. Auden and Chester Kallman. In this work Stravinsky adopts the eighteenth-century division into recitatives, arias, and ensembles, organizes the entire opera on the basis of key relationships, and achieves in the final scenes a climax of pathos without sentimentality.

Stravinsky's late works

A setting of the Mass (1948) for mixed chorus with double wood-wind quintet and brasses exhibits an austere "neo-Gothic" style that places this work transitionally between the *Symphony of Psalms* and the *Canticum sacrum* for tenor and baritone soloists, chorus, and orchestra, composed "in honor of St. Mark" and first sung in St. Mark's Cathedral at Venice in 1956. In parts of the *Canticum sacrum* and other compositions of the 1950s (including the Septet, 1953; the song *In memoriam Dylan Thomas*, 1954; the ballet *Agon*, 1954–57; and *Threni*, 1958, for voices and orchestra on texts from the Lamentations of Jeremiah), Stravinsky, very gradually and judiciously but most effectively, adapted for his own purposes the techniques of the Schoenberg-Webern school—techniques that he explored still further in *Movements* (1959) and the *Orchestra Variations* (1964).

An analysis of Stravinsky's style that would do justice to both the diversity of its manifestations and the unity that underlies it throughout would require a book. Here we can only call attention to a few characteristic features, emphasizing as we do that Stravinsky's rhythms, harmonies, colors, and all other details are inseparate from a living body of music; the student should hear and study these features in their context, in the works themselves, and in so doing he will sharpen his perception for all the details in Stravinsky's music.

Stravinsky's style

Rhythm: One of the steps of the present century was the liberation of rhythm from the "tyranny of the barline," that is, from the regularity of constant two- or three-unit groups of strong and weak accents in which the strong accents regularly coincide with changes of harmony. Stravinsky often denies the barline by introducing an irregular pattern of rhythm after a regular one has been established, and by returning to the regular pattern from time to time (Example XX–8a). The regular beat may be maintained in one part against a conflicting irregular pattern in another (Example XX–8b); or two different rhythms may be combined (Example XX–8c). A rhythmic motif may be shifted from place to place in the measure (Example XX–8d). The rhythm at the beginning of the last movement of the *Sacre* looks very irregular but sounds orderly; as a matter of fact it is organized rather symmetrically around the motive ♪♫♫ which appears eight times (Example XX–8e). Patterns of the subtlety of Example XX–8f may be found in practically any of Stravinsky's compositions of the neo-Classical period. Particularly fascinating is the way in which he thickens and then opens out the harmonies, dislocates and relocates the rhythms, in a long pulsation of tension and release before an important cadence: the endings of the Octet, the third and fourth movements of the Symphony in C, and the Sanctus in the Mass.

Another detail in Stravinsky's rhythm is his use of silences— sometimes merely a lift between chords, sometimes a breath on the downbeat before the beginning of a phrase, sometimes a rhetorical pause that accumulates tension in the progress toward a climax (the Interlude between the second and third movements of the *Symphony in Three Movements* and many places elsewhere in this symphony, the Symphony in C, and other works).

Harmony: Stravinsky's music is organized around tonal centers. Ambiguous chords like the one in the second movement of the *Sacre* (Example XX–9a) and the notorious bitonal C–F♯ in *Petrushka* (Example XX–9b), however they may be explained, are certainly not to be interpreted in their context as atonal. One type of am-

EXAMPLE XX–8   Stravinsky Rhythms

a. *Sacre (Augures printaniers)*

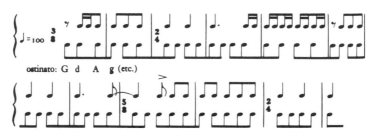

b. *Histoire du Soldat*, Scene 1

ostinato: G d   A   g (etc.)

c. *Petrushka*, Pt. I

d. *Symphony of Psalms*, last movement

e. *Sacre (Danse sacrale)*

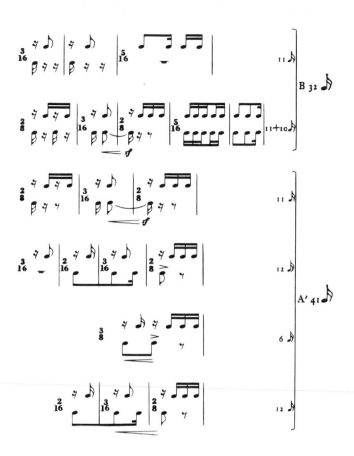

f) Symphony in C major, second movement

biguity common in Stravinsky's work results from his use of both the major and minor third of a triad either simultaneously or in close juxtaposition (Examples XX–9c and d; in the latter example, other degrees of the scale are also present in simultaneously conflicting forms).

A more subtle use of the major-minor third relationship is shown in Example XX–9e: here the conflict between the keys of C and E♭ major (the minor third of C) is resolved to C major at measure seven. This chord marks at the same time a resolution of the tonal

EXAMPLE XX–9   Examples of Stravinsky's Harmony

Symphony of Psalms, © Edition Russe de Musique, revised version © 1948 by Boosey & Hawkes Inc., reprinted by permission.

tendencies of the two preceding movements which centered respectively on the notes E and E♭, the major and minor thirds of C.

The diatonic passage in A major (with a chromatic F♮) of Example XX–10a contrasts with the more linear texture of Example XX–10b (notice the motive marked by brackets). This passage is in D and predominantly modal (Dorian). It is an instrumental phrase that recurs identically twice as a ritornello; at the end (Example XX–10c) Stravinsky takes B♯ = C♮ as a pivot note for a modulation back from the dominant A, then recapitulates in condensed form the harmonies of the ritornello and adds a cadential echo, using only modal tones and leaving the seventh of the mode (C♮) with its fifth (G) unresolved in the final chord.

Orchestration: A high proportion of Stravinsky's works is written for unusual groups of instruments. This is another respect in which each new composition is a law to itself; the particular color is part of the particular musical conception in each instance. The odd combination of *L'Histoire* is ideally suited to—is inseparable from—the kind of music that the piece is; so equally are the serene strings of *Apollon musagète,* the dark solo woodwinds at the opening of the *Sacre,* and the Mozartean clarity of the orchestra of the Symphony in C.

The piano is used conspicuously and effectively in *Petrushka;* it contributes to the orchestral color (usually in conjunction with the harp) in many later works, notably *Oedipus,* the *Symphony of Psalms, Perséphone,* and the *Symphony in Three Movements.* Several works of the years around 1920 use no stringed instruments (*Rag-Time, Les Noces,* Octet, Piano Concerto, *Symphonies of Wind Instruments*); it is as though Stravinsky distrusted their color as associated with sentimentality. The warm tones of the violins, violas, and clarinets are avoided in the *Symphony of Psalms.* In some of the

699

EXAMPLE XX–10   Examples of Stravinsky's Harmony

a. *Symphony in Three Movements*

b. Agnus Dei from *Mass:* beginning

c. Agnus Dei from *Mass:* conclusion

Mass, © 1948 by Boosey & Hawkes, Inc.; reprinted by permission.

late works the instruments are grouped antiphonally. In the Mass two oboes, English horn, and two bassoons are balanced against two trumpets and three trombones; the instrumentation of the *Canticum sacrum* is similar though somewhat larger (seven woodwinds and eight brasses), and harp, organ, violas, and double basses are also added to the antiphony. The tenor voice in the Dylan Thomas song is accompanied sparely by solo strings with short ritornellos for string quartet, and the song is framed by a prelude and postlude in which the strings alternate with a quartet of trombones in chorale-like dirge canons.

Of innumerable special orchestral effects in Stravinsky we cite: the ravishing duet and trio combinations with their arabesques and open-work accompaniment in the first and last sections of the slow movement of the Symphony in C; the heterophony of the strings in the finale of the same symphony; the accompaniment of upward-rushing scales at the *Divum Jocastae caput* monologue in *Oedipus Rex* (compare the opening of the *Symphony in Three Movements*);

and the device of doubling a legato melodic line by another instrument playing staccato, which gives a peculiar percussive accent to each note (finale of the *Symphony in Three Movements*).

Stravinsky clearly defined his attitude toward composition in the *Poetics of Music* as the acceptance of limits as a means to freedom:

Stravinsky's esthetic

> The creator's function is to sift the elements he receives from [imagination], for human activity must impose limits on itself. The more art is controlled, limited, worked over, the more it is free.
>
> As for myself, I experience a sort of terror when, at the moment of setting to work and finding myself before the infinitude of possibilities that present themselves, I have the feeling that everything is permissible to me. . . .
>
> Will I then have to lose myself in this abyss of freedom? To what shall I cling in order to escape the dizziness that seizes me before the virtuality of this infinitude? . . . Fully convinced that combinations which have at their disposal twelve sounds in each octave and all possible rhythmic varieties promise me riches that all the activity of human genius will never exhaust . . . I am always able to turn immediately to the concrete things that are here in question. I have no use for a theoretic freedom. Let me have something finite, definite— matter that can lend itself to my operation only insofar as it is commensurate with my possibilities. And such matter presents itself to me together with its limitations. I must in turn impose mine upon it. . . .
>
> My freedom thus consists in my moving about within the narrow frame that I have assigned myself for each one of my undertakings.
>
> I shall go even farther: my freedom will be so much the greater and more meaningful the more narrowly I limit my field of action and the more I surround myself with obstacles. Whatever diminishes constraint diminishes strength. The more constraints one imposes, the more one frees oneself of the chains that shackle the spirit.[8]

Schoenberg and His Followers

The movement which because of its radical nature attracted most attention in the first half of the twentieth century grew out of the music of post-Romanticism in Germany. The earliest important work of Arnold Schoenberg (1874–1951), the string sextet *Verklärte Nacht* (1899), is in a chromatic idiom clearly derived from that of *Tristan*, while the symphonic poem *Pelleas und Melisande* (1903) is reminiscent of Strauss. With the huge symphonic cantata *Gurre-Lieder* (*Songs of Gurre*) for five soloists, narrator, four choruses, and large orchestra (1901, orchestration finished 1911) Schoenberg outdid even Mahler and Strauss in size and complexity of the score and Wagner in Romantic violence of expression.

A new direction is evident in the works of Schoenberg's second period, which include the first two Quartets (D minor and F♯ minor,

[8] *Ibid.*, Lesson Three: "The Composition of Music". Quoted by permission of the publisher, Harvard University Press.

Autograph manuscript of the opening page of Opus 16, Five
Orchestral Pieces *(1909) by Schoenberg. (C. F. Peters Corp.)*

1905 and 1908), the first *Kammersymphonie (Chamber Symphony;*
1906) for fifteen instruments, the *Five Orchestral Pieces,* Op. 16
(1909), two sets of short piano pieces (Op. 11, 1908 and Op. 19, 1911),
a cycle of songs with piano accompaniment, *Das Buch der hängenden
Gärten (Book of the Hanging Gardens;* 1908), a mono-drama for
soloist and orchestra *Erwartung (Expectation;* 1909), and a dramatic
pantomime *Die glückliche Hand (The Lucky Hand;* 1911–13). In
these works Schoenberg turns away from post-Romantic gigantism
either to small instrumental combinations or, if he uses a large
orchestra, to soloistic treatment of instruments or swift alternation
of colors (as in the *Five Orchestral Pieces* and *Erwartung*) rather
than massive blocks of sound. Concurrent with this is an increasing
rhythmic and contrapuntal complexity and fragmentation of the
melodic line, together with greater concentration: for example, the
First Quartet, which is in a one-movement cyclical form, evolves all

its themes from variations and combinations of a few germinal motives and uses hardly any material, even in the subsidiary voices, that is not derived from the same motives. Historically significant also is the fact that between 1905 and 1912 Schoenberg moved from a chromatic style on a tonal basis to something that is commonly called *atonality*.

Atonal means literally "not tonal." Roughly speaking, atonal music is music in which the person who is using the word cannot hear tonal centers. More precisely, atonal music is that in which the composer systematically avoids reference to tonal centers by avoiding harmonic and melodic formulas—for instance, dominant-tonic progressions and melodic phrases implying such progressions, or diatonic scales and triads or even voice-leading from other intervals to octaves—which suggest the traditional system of chords organized about a fundamental tonic or key note. In theory, it is questionable whether atonality is really possible, since any combination of sounds can be referred to a fundamental root; some theorists contend that the effect of atonality results from progressions in which the fundamentals are so difficult to define, or are obscured by such complex dissonances, or change so rapidly, or succeed one another in a manner so unlike that of traditional harmony, that the ear is unable to grasp the tonal relationships that may exist. Whatever the theory, it is unfortunate that the negative term has become fixed in usage instead of Schoenberg's own word *pantonal,* meaning "inclusive of all tonalities." But since *atonal* seems to be permanently lodged in the musical vocabulary, we shall use it, bearing in mind that, like *dissonance,* it is a relative term and that its exact signification varies with the context.

Atonality

To illustrate: the phrase of Example XX–11a is from a piece by Schoenberg that is always called atonal. The atonal effect in this instance is due partly to the obscurity of the roots and partly to the "illogical" root movements; but the impression of atonality is reinforced by three factors that are not part of the harmonic scheme at all, namely, the fast tempo, the subdivision of beats, and the octave displacement of two melody and two bass notes. If we slow down the pace, smooth out the rhythm, and bring most of the notes within a single octave range, we obtain a phrase that could conceivably— if irrelevantly—be analyzed as shown in Example XX–11b. The atonal quality of Webern's Symphony Op. 21 (see Example XX–15) is much more pronounced, owing partly to the numerous major and minor seconds in the harmony and the conspicuous melodic leaps of a minor ninth, as well as to the discontinuous lines and the distribution of the melody notes among different instruments.

Much late Romantic music, especially in Germany, had been unconsciously tending toward atonality. Chromatic melody lines and chord progressions, even in Wagner, had resulted in passages in which no tonal center could be perceived; but these passages had

EXAMPLE XX–11   Possible Harmonic Analysis of Passage of Op. 23, No. 5, Schoenberg

been exceptional, relatively short, and anchored within a tonal context.

The close relationship between the late Romantic and the Schoenbergian melodic styles may be seen in Example XX–12; extreme ranges and wide leaps are characteristic of both. Schoenberg explored the extreme possibilities of chromaticism within the limits of tonality in the *Gurre-Lieder* and *Pelleas*. After that, it was a natural move to cut loose altogether from a key center and treat all twelve notes of the octave as of equal rank instead of regarding some of them as chromatically altered tones of a diatonic scale. Corollary to this was another step—already foreshadowed by the nonfunctional harmonies of Debussy—which Schoenberg called "the emancipation of the dissonance," meaning the freedom to use any combination of tones whatever as a chord not requiring resolution. The change from tonality obscured by extreme chromaticism to atonality with free dissonance was a gradual process with Schoenberg. The piano pieces

EXAMPLE XX–12   Relationships of style between Schoenberg and Late Romantic Composers

a. Wagner—*Tristan*

b. Bruckner—Ninth Symphony

c. Strauss—*Heldenleben*

d. Mahler—Tenth Symphony

e. Schoenberg—*Gurre-Lieder*

f. Schoenberg—*Pierrot Lunaire*

g. Schoenberg—Fourth Quartet

Schoenberg—*Fourth Quartet*

Op. 11 are in a transitional style; the last movement of the Second Quartet (except for the final cadence in F♯) and the piano pieces of Op. 19 are more nearly atonal.

Pierrot Lunaire (*Moonstruck Pierrot;* 1912), Schoenberg's best-known composition of the prewar era, is a cycle of twenty-one songs on rather decadent surrealist French poems in German translation, for woman's voice with a chamber ensemble of five players and eight instruments: flute (interchangeable with piccolo), clarinet (bass clarinet), violin (viola), violoncello, and piano. Each song is accompanied by a different instrumental combination in textures of crystalline clarity. One feature of *Pierrot Lunaire* which accentuates the atonal impression is the use of *Sprechstimme* (speaking voice): the voice, instead of singing tones of fixed pitch, only suggests the pitches and then immediately moves away from them. This stylized musical declamation partakes of the character of both speaking and singing. The rhythm is notated strictly, while the approximate or initial pitch is indicated by the sign ♩; this conspicuous notational innovation was carried still further in later works, where a single line takes the place of the conventional five-line staff. Schoenberg's masterly contrapuntal technique, evident in all his works from the earliest onward, is especially notable in *Pierrot Lunaire*. The intricate canons of Nos. 17 and 18 suggest that the composer was searching for some other means in addition to the text to assure unity in compositions which, because they lack defined tonality, cannot depend, as older music did, on key and chord relationships to supply unification.

Expressionism

Schoenberg and his pupil Alban Berg are the chief representatives in music in a movement called *expressionism*. This word, like *impressionism,* was first used in connection with painting. Expressionism emphasized a contrasting approach, however; whereas impressionism sought to represent objects of the external world as perceived at a given moment, expressionism, proceeding in the opposite direction, sought to represent *inner* experience, using whatever means seemed best suited to the purpose. By virtue of its subjective starting point expressionism is an outgrowth of Romanticism; it differs from Romanticism in the kind of inner experience it aims to portray, and in the means chosen to portray it. The subject matter of expressionism is man as he exists in the modern world and is described by twentieth-century psychology: isolated, helpless in the grip of forces he does not understand, prey to inner conflict, tension, anxiety, fear, and all the elemental irrational drives of the subconscious, and in irritated rebellion against established order and accepted forms.

Hence, expressionistic art is characterized both by desperate intensity of feeling and revolutionary modes of utterance: both characteristics are illustrated by Schoenberg's *Erwartung*, which has tremendous emotional force and is written in a dissonant, rhythmically atomistic, melodically fragmentary, strangely orchestrated, nonthematic musical idiom. *Erwartung, Die glückliche Hand,* and *Pierrot Lunaire* are all expressionist works. They are devoted, down to the last detail, not to being either pretty or realistic, but to using the most penetrating means imaginable, no matter how unusual—subject, text, scene design and lighting (in the operas), as well as music—to communicate the particular complex of thought and emotion which Schoenberg wanted to express. Form, of course, they must have. At this period of his development Schoenberg was depending mostly on the text to establish unity in long works; the early atonal piano pieces of Op. 19 are so short—models of concise, epigrammatic style—that the difficulties of formal unity inherent in long instrumental compositions are avoided.

By 1923, after six years during which he published no music, Schoenberg had formulated a "method of composing with twelve tones which are related only with one another." The essential points of the theory of this *twelve-tone* (dodecaphonic) technique may be summarized as follows. The basis of each composition is a *row* or *series* consisting of the twelve tones of the octave arranged in any order the composer decides. The tones of the series are used either successively (as melody) or simultaneously (as harmony or counterpoint), in any octave and with any desired rhythm. The row may also be used in inverted, retrograde, or retrograde inverted form, and in transpositions of any of the four forms. No note may be used in the composition that does not occur in a succession identical with that of one or another of the forms of the row. The style is thus chromatic—not like Wagner's, in which chromatic passages are always to be understood with reference to a diatonic basis, but chromatic in a new and radical way.

Dodecaphony

In practice, all sorts of modifications, refinements, complications, and compromises are made. Stated baldly, the theory may sound like a recipe for turning out music by machine. Actually, when applied mechanically it will not work; and moreover, it no more necessarily inhibits a composer's spontaneity than do the rules for composing a tonal fugue, provided the technique has been mastered. Using the same tone row for an entire composition is a means of unity analogous to using one main key for a composition in tonal style; at the same time the technique permits and indeed requires much variety of rhythm, texture, dynamics, and timbre. In a sense, a work using this method may be called a perpetual variation of the basic row.

The first works in which Schoenberg deliberately used tone rows were the five piano pieces Op. 23 (1923), of which however only the last has a complete row of twelve tones (see Example XX–11). The technique was perfected over the next few years in some works which are often designated as neo-classic (Serenade, Op. 24; Suite for Piano, Op. 25; Wind Quintet, Op. 26) and the twelve-tone method appears completely developed in the Third Quartet (1926) and the *Variations for Orchestra* (1928). It is employed also for most of the works Schoenberg wrote after coming to America in 1933, particularly the Violin Concerto (1936) and the Fourth Quartet (1937). "In olden [and tonal] style" he wrote a Suite for String Orchestra (1934). In the *Ode to Napoleon* and the Piano Concerto (both 1942), he approached a synthesis of his own system with some elements of orthodox tonality; but these works are less characteristic than the String Trio (1946) and the *Fantasy for Violin and Piano* (1949).

In 1931–32 Schoenberg composed the first two acts of a three-act opera for which he had written his own libretto, entitled *Moses and Aaron*. The music was never completed, and the score remains a magnificent torso. Against the Old Testament background Schoenberg presents the tragic conflict between Moses as mediator of the word of God and Aaron as Moses's interpreter to the people: conflict, because Moses is unable himself to communicate his vision, and Aaron, who can communicate, cannot rightly understand; tragic, because the flaw of separation is intrinsic and not to be overcome by good will, being rooted in the nature of the philosopher-mystic on the one hand and the statesman-educator on the other. (Aaron says to Moses [Act III, Scene 1], "I was to discourse in images, you in concepts; I to the heart, you to the mind.") Symbolically, Moses speaks (*Sprechstimme*) but does not sing: the Word is not incarnate in music save for one moment only (Act I, Scene 2) as Moses warns Aaron, "Purify your thought: set it free from earthly things, dedicate it to Truth." The solemn alliteration of the German text is reminiscent of Wagner (see Example XX–13) and throughout Schoenberg employs vowel and consonant sounds in symbolic connection with the music and the dramatic ideas.

Moses and Aaron is as much oratorio as opera. The choruses of the people of Israel have a large part in the action; a group of six solo voices (in the orchestra, not on the stage) represents the Voice of God—again, like Moses himself, in *Sprechstimme* with orchestral accompaniment. Undoubtedly the most picturesque part of the score is the complex of solos, choruses, and dances in the big scene of the worship of the Golden Calf (Act II), where rhythm, instrumental color, and sudden contrasts combine in a spectacle of oriental gorgeousness and dramatic effect. The entire opera is based on a single tone row, one form of which is represented in Example XX–13. In *Moses and Aaron* a profound philosophical conception embodied in appropriate dramatic form unites with the penetrating expressive power of the music and a towering unity of construction to make this work its composer's masterpiece and to give it, along with Berg's *Wozzeck,* a place among the great operas of its time.

Moses and
Aaron

EXAMPLE XX–13   *Moses and Aaron,* Act I, Scene 2, Schoenberg

Rei - ni - ge dein Den-ken, lös es von Wert-lo - sem, wei - he es

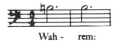

Wah - rem:

Schoenberg has exercised a far-reaching and profound influence on the music of the twentieth century, not only through his compositions but also through his work as a teacher and his intellectual stature as a philosopher and interpreter of the age. From 1920 to about 1950, the revolutionary nature of atonality and the twelve-tone method was much discussed, not always in good temper; opinions of advocates and opponents tended to polarize. Two opposing extreme views, the one erring on the side of superficiality and the other on the side of dogmatic assertion, were either that the productions of Schoenberg and his followers were a mere anarchic divagation without permanent significance; or that Schoenberg had "swallowed up the past" and shown the only possible valid way for the future evolution of music.

Schoenberg's influence

Undoubtedly for many listeners the mere sound of most music written in accordance with these principles was—and for some still is—a formidable initial barrier. The difficulties are due mostly to four factors: dissonance, the absence of a tonal center, the compression of style, and the feeling that this kind of music is cerebral, that is, mechanically constructed and without emotional significance.

Schoenberg or his disciples might have replied to these objections somewhat as follows: a revolution in musical style consists in the acceptance as normal of something which has hitherto been exceptional—for example, polyphony in the twelfth century and melody with chordal accompaniment in the beginning of the seventeenth century. "Dissonance" is a relative term, the definition of which changes from age to age: chords that would have been unthinkable in the sixteenth century were accepted easily at the end of the nineteenth century. The "emancipation of the dissonance" was therefore a logical evolutionary step, and new combinations of sounds that at first seem incomprehensible will gradually come to be accepted and their laws understood. Similarly, pantonality was a logical move forward from a situation in which the possibilities of the older tonal system had manifestly been exhausted. Compression of style only imposes the necessity for more attentive listening, since all superfluous elements have been deleted. As to the charge of dry intellectualism, this is flatly denied: twelve-tone music is not necessarily more cerebral than other kinds, since all styles in art must

709

conform to some analyzable system of structure; the significance of what is produced within any system, whether tonal or atonal, depends wholly on the ability of the composer to conceive and communicate significant musical ideas. The era of tonal harmony, it might be said, corresponds to the era of Newtonian physics. As modern physics contradicts commonsense notions with regard to matter, so the work of Schoenberg and his school contradicts hitherto received notions with regard to music; but this circumstance does not mean that the new systems are either invalid or incapable of furnishing material for poetic treatment.

To all this it might be rejoined, first, that the theory of evolution, however useful in the realm of biology, is irrelevant when uncritically applied to justify styles in art; such styles must justify themselves by (at least eventually) convincing competent judges of their value. Second, it might be said that the absence of clear distinction between consonance and dissonance, and of clear gradation among dissonances, as well as the absence of tonal centers, deprives music of one fundamental means of coherence through the alternation of harmonic tension and release, of dynamic and static moments. To these objective considerations might be added others of a more subjective nature, namely, that the devices introduced to compensate for lack of tonal organization tended sometimes to give the music an artificial aspect: unnatural wide leaps in the melodic line, overcomplicated rhythmic constructions, monotony of constant dissonance. Paradoxically, the use by Schoenberg, in some of his earlier twelve-tone compositions, of traditional forms and other familiar features tended for some listeners to exacerbate the situation—to make the *Variations for Orchestra,* Op. 31, for example, sound like Brahms with all the notes wrong.

Such matters aside, however, it remains undoubtedly true that the work of Schoenberg is on the boundary of the Western musical tradition. The continuity of his thought (and, in many respects, his practice) with that of Bach, Mozart, Beethoven, Brahms, and Wagner is genuine, but the radical break is equally a fact: what Schoenberg did in music could not be repealed—any more than could the achievements of James Joyce in literature.

Expressionism, and atonalism as a musical style closely associated with it, were in tune with a state of mind prevalent in western Europe in the 1920s, and are therefore significant as a social phenomenon of the period. The Schoenberg followers must be regarded, as far as the first half of the twentieth century is concerned, as a school existing side by side with others which still maintain an allegiance to Classical tonal principles. The music of Berg, some of the late works of Schoenberg, and experiments by other composers with serial methods indicate a potential synthesis which, however, could be only individual, not communal.

Schoenberg's famous pupil Alban Berg (1885–1935) adopted most of his master's methods of construction, but he used them with freedom and often chose tone rows that allowed for tonal-sounding chords and progressions in the harmony. Moreover, Berg combined the technique with a warmth of Romantic feeling so that his music is more readily accessible than that of many twelve-tone composers. His chief works are a *Lyric Suite* for string quartet (1926); a Violin Concerto (1935); and two operas, *Wozzeck* (composed 1917–21, first performed 1925) and *Lulu* (composed 1928–35, the orchestration not quite completed at Berg's death).

Alban Berg

Wozzeck is the outstanding example of expressionist opera as well as an impressive historical document. The libretto, arranged by Berg from fragments of a drama by Georg Büchner (1813–37), presents the soldier Wozzeck as a symbol of "wir arme Leut'" ("we poor people"), a hapless victim of his environment, despised, betrayed in love, driven finally to murder and suicide. The music is continuous throughout each of the three acts, the changing scenes (five in each act) being connected by orchestral interludes as in Debussy's *Pelléas*. Berg's music is unified partly by the use of a few leitmotifs but chiefly by being organized in closed forms adapted from those of Classical music (suite, rhapsody, song, march, passacaglia, rondo, symphony, inventions) and by other subtle means. In the vocal parts Berg flexibly alternates ordinary speech and *Sprechgesang* with conventional singing. The many passages of stylized realism (snoring chorus, gurgling of water, a tavern orchestra with an out-of-tune piano caricaturing a waltz motive from Strauss's *Rosenkavalier*) are skilfully employed for expressionistic purposes. The grim, ironical, symbolical action, the wealth of musical invention, the ever-varied, ingenious, and appropriate orchestration, the formal clarity and concentration, the pictorial quality and dramatic force of the music cumulate in an effect of unforgettable poignancy.

Lulu is a more abstract, complex opera, equally expressionistic but with more involved symbolism than *Wozzeck;* its music is organized more strictly on twelve-tone lines, though not without some tonal implications. The *Lyric Suite* and the Violin Concerto, like the two operas, are typical of Berg's constant tendency to show the connection between the new style and that of the past. Both the Suite and the Concerto are partially written according to the twelve-tone method; both display Berg's inventive genius and his easy mastery of contrapuntal technique. The basic row of the Concerto is designed in such a way that tonal combinations become practically inevitable (Example XX–14); in the finale also the tone row forms a link to introduce the melody of a chorale that Bach had harmonized to the words of the hymn *It is Enough* (Cantata No. 60)—an allusion to the death of Manon Gropius, to whose memory the Concerto is dedicated.

EXAMPLE XX–14   Tone Row in Alban Berg's Violin Concerto

Berg represents the Romantic potential of Schoenberg's teaching; Schoenberg's other celebrated pupil, Anton Webern (1883–1945) represents the Classical potential—atonality without Romanticism. Webern wrote no opera and he never used the device of *Sprechstimme*. The ruling principles in his work are economy and extreme concentration. In his mature style each composition is evolved by imitative counterpoint (often strictly canonic); he uses devices such as inversion and rhythmic shifts, but avoids sequences and (for the most part) repetitions. The melodic outline of the generating "cells" usually involves intervals like major sevenths and minor ninths which exclude tonal implications. Textures are stripped to bare essentials; rhythmic patterns are complex, often based on simultaneous duple and triple divisions of all or a part of the measure; and the sound, with all its fine gradation of dynamics, seldom rises above the level of a forte.

Anton Webern

Most remarkable is Webern's instrumentation. A melodic line may be distributed among different instruments somewhat in the manner of medieval hocket, so that sometimes only one or two—seldom more than four or five—successive tones will be heard in the same timbre. The result is a texture made up of sparks and flashes of sound blending in a unique balance of color (see Example XX–15). A good illustration of this kind of orchestration applied to a more familiar kind of music is Webern's arrangement of the Ricercare from Bach's *Musical Offering*. Special effects—pizzicato, harmonics, tremolo, muting, and the like—are common in all of Webern's music. His sensitiveness for color and clarity often leads him to choose unusual combinations, as in the Quartet Op. 22 for violin, clarinet, tenor saxophone, and piano, or the three songs Op. 18 for soprano, Eb clarinet, and guitar.

It is natural that in a style of such concentration the compositions should be short. Not all are so brief as the *Six Bagatelles* for string quartet, Op. 9, or the Five Pieces for Orchestra, Op. 10 (both 1913), which average respectively about 36 and 49 seconds for each movement (No. 5 of Op. 10 runs only 19 seconds); but even "larger" works like the Symphony (1928) and the String Quartet (1938) take only eight or nine minutes' playing time, so intensely compressed is the language. This compression, together with the unfamiliarity of the idiom, requires an unusual degree of attention from the listener. With respect to dissonance (the effect of which is largely mitigated by skilful use of contrasting timbres) and harmonic complexity in general, Webern's music is considerably easier to hear than that of Schoenberg, Berg, and many other twentieth-century composers.

In his development, Webern, like Schoenberg, passed through the stages of late Romantic chromaticism, free atonality, and organization by tone rows, the last beginning with the three songs of Op. 17 (1924). With few exceptions his works are in chamber style; they are about equally divided between instrumental and vocal compositions. The principal instrumental works are the Symphony Op. 21, the String Quartet Op. 28, the Concerto for nine instruments Op. 24 (1934), and the Piano Variations Op. 27 (1936). For voices there are numerous collections of solo songs—some with piano, others with different small ensembles—and a few choral pieces, notably *Das Augenlicht* (*Light of the Eyes;* 1935) and two cantatas (1939, 1943) for soloists, chorus, and orchestra. These cantatas, and also the Variations for Orchestra Op. 30 (1940), are in a somewhat more relaxed and expressive style than Webern's previous works; in them he applied the serial technique but included homophonic as well as contrapuntal texture.

The Symphony Op. 21 is for nine solo instruments. It is in two movements, the first in sonata form and the second a theme with seven variations. Some idea of Webern's use of the serial technique may be obtained from Example XX–15, the beginning of the first movement. What may be called the "original" form of the tone row is designated by the numbers 1, 2, etc. (note that the second half of the row is the retrograde of the first half and that consequently the retrograde form of the entire row is a duplicate of its original form); the numbers 1', 2', etc. designate an inversion (or a retrograde inversion) of the original form, beginning a major third lower; 1'', 2'', etc. designate an inversion (or retrograde inversion) beginning at the original pitch. The C♯ in measure four begins a statement of the original form of the row (or its retrograde) transposed a major third upward. To be noted also in this example is the characteristically spare, open texture, the numerous rests in all the parts; thus every single note counts, and the ensemble becomes a succession of tiny points or wisps of sound.

Webern's output was small: his complete works (excepting the recently discovered early music) have been recorded on eight long-playing record sides. Though his achievement received hardly any acclaim during his lifetime, recognition of his work grew steadily in the years after the Second World War, and his music launched important new developments in Italy, Germany, France, and the United States.

After Webern

The first half of the twentieth century witnessed a progressive breakup of the system of music which had prevailed over the pre-

EXAMPLE XX–15   First Movement, Symphony Op. 21, Anton Webern

ceding two hundred years, roughly from Bach to Richard Strauss. Schoenberg, at first intuitively and later methodically with his twelve-tone rows, had introduced a new conception of musical structure and with his "emancipation of the dissonance" had in effect simply abolished the traditional distinction between consonance and dissonance. Stravinsky had participated, in turn, in all the movements of the time, arriving in the 1950s as his own version of dodecaphony. Many other composers had by 1950 accepted in prin-

715

ciple the twelve-tone system, modifying it in details and adapting it to their own purposes. It was Webern, however, who more than anyone else anticipated and stimulated a movement which came to be associated with a group of young composers centered about the "holiday courses for new music" at Darmstadt. These courses had begun immediately after the end of the war, in 1946. At a memorial concert of his works at Darmstadt in 1953, Webern was hailed as the father of the new movement. The two principal composers of the Darmstadt group, both pupils of Messiaen, were Pierre Boulez (born 1925) of Paris and Karlheinz Stockhausen (born 1928) of Cologne. Darmstadt was important in that many of the ideas fostered there spread through the world and stimulated experiments on the part of composers everywhere, including, eventually, the countries of eastern Europe. But every composer worked independently, striking out in new directions, cultivating his own language, his own style, his own special techniques. There was no allegiance to one consistent body of principles, no well defined "common practice" as in the eighteenth and nineteenth centuries.

We shall not attempt to deal with the work of every composer individually, but rather try to summarize the most general common features and mention a few of the most notable individual achievements of the period since 1945. It is most important to remember that all the features we are about to discuss came into prominence almost simultaneously; all were evident, to different extents and in varying degrees and combinations, in the new music of the third quarter of the present century.

One of the first developments, beginning even before 1950, was the rise of "total serialism," that is, the extension of the principle *Serialism* of Schoenberg's rows to elements of music other than pitch. If the twelve tones of the chromatic scale could be serialized, as Schoenberg had done, so also could the factors of duration, intensity, timbre, texture, silences, and so on. But whereas in the eighteenth and nineteenth centuries all these elements—particularly those involving melody, rhythm, and harmony—had been conventionally interdependent (being combined in certain accepted ways), now all could be regarded as simply interchangeable. Thus a series of pitches could be combined with a series of one or more of the other factors—as Messiaen had shown with his *Mode de valeurs et d'intensités* and Milton Babbitt (born 1916), in a different formulation, with his *Three Compositions for Piano* (1948). The different series might be conceived independently, or all might be derived in one way or another from a single arithmetical series; in either case the various series could intersect, all proceeding simultaneously, to a point of "total control" over every detail of a composition. Naturally this could not be done just by arbitrarily or mechanically selecting the various series and their combinations. Their relationship had to be a musically rational, not merely mathematical one; otherwise the application of total control in this sense would produce music which gave the effect of total randomness. Especially for an unaccustomed ear, that impression could not easily be avoided even in works constructed by the most musically sensitive composers working with the technique.

One reason for such an impression was that music based on these principles was typically *athematic:* that is, it had no themes in the classical sense of readily perceived melodic-rhythmic-harmonic entities and recognizable extensions, derivations, and developments of those. Concomitant with this was the typical absence of a distinct rhythmic pulse and—even more important—the absence of any sense of progression, of movement toward definite foreseeable points of climax culminating toward the end of the work, such as had been characteristic of the symphony, for example, from the time of Haydn through the nineteenth century. Instead, one was aware only of successive, unrepeated, and unpredictable musical "events." Such events might take the form of minute "points" of sound—color, melody, rhythm—intertwining, dissolving into one another in an apparently random fashion. Of course, when a work was well constructed the totality of the events would form a logical pattern, but it might be a very complex one which only became perceptible after much study and repeated hearings.

The rigidities of total serialism were soon relaxed. The pointillist style is fused with sensitive musical realization of a text in one of the most famous avant-garde pieces, Boulez's *Le Marteau sans maître* (The Masterless Hammer; 1954, revised 1957). This is a setting of verses from a cycle of surrealist poems by René Char, interspersed with instrumental "commentaries," in nine short movements. The ensemble (a different grouping in each movement) comprises alto flute, xylorimba, vibraphone, guitar, viola, and a variety of light percussion instruments; it produces a translucent tissue of sound, all in the middle and high registers, with effects often suggestive of Balinese music. The contralto vocal line, with wide melodic intervals, glissandos, and occasional use of *Sprechstimme,* is often the lowest voice in the texture, and is related in a quasi-systematic way to particular instruments in the ensemble.

One of the most conspicuous features of the new music was the immense number of new sounds that were found acceptable for use. Earlier examples of such new sounds were the "tone clusters" on the piano, introduced by the American Henry Cowell (1897–1965) in the 1920s, and the "prepared piano" of John Cage (born 1912) in the 1940s. Other examples include a great many hitherto unexploited uses of conventional instruments: for example, new harmonics and increased use of the flutter-tongue technique and other special effects on wind instruments; glissandos; dense chromatic clusters or

New timbres

717

"bands" of sound for strings or voices, a frequent recourse of the Greek composer Yannis Xenakis (born 1922), the Polish Krzysztof Penderecki (born 1933), and the Italian Luigi Nono (born 1924); spoken and whispered sounds (words, syllables, letters, noises) in vocal pieces—and required also occasionally of instrumentalists. New instruments, such as the vibraphone and the Ondes Martenot, appeared in the orchestra. Especially noteworthy throughout the whole period was the tremendously expanded percussion group (often including instruments borrowed from or suggested by Asian or African musics) and the greatly increased importance of percussive sounds in ensembles of all kinds.

Decisive for recognition of the importance of timbre in the new music was the work of Edgard Varèse (1883–1965). For Varèse, sounds as such were the essential structural components of music, more basic than melody, harmony, or rhythm. In his *Ionisation* (1933), written for a huge battery of percussion instruments (including piano and bells) along with chains, anvils, and sirens, Varèse created a form which could be said to be defined by contrasting blocks and masses of sound. Some of his late works (*Déserts*, 1954; *Poème électronique,* 1958) utilized new sound resources that became available soon after the middle of the century.

The Philips Pavilion, Brussels World Fair, 1958. Composer Edgard Varèse collaborated with architect Le Corbusier when he wrote his Poème électronique, *commissioned for performance in this building during the Fair. (Photo courtesy of* Architectural Forum)

No development after 1950 attracted more public attention or held greater potential for new structural and other far-reaching changes in the world of music than the use of electronically produced or manipulated sounds. This began with the *musique concrète* of the early 1950s; the raw material consisted of musical tones or other natural sounds which after being transformed in various ways by electronic means were assembled on tape to be played back. The next step was to replace or supplement sounds of natural origin by sounds generated electronically in a studio. One of the most familiar early electronic compositions, Stockhausen's *Gesang der Jünglinge (Song of the Young Men;* 1956),[9] as well as many of his later works in this medium, used sounds from both sources.

Electronic resources

The consequences of the new discovery were immense, and have not yet been anywhere near completely explored. In the first place, it freed the composer from all dependence on a performer, enabling him to exercise complete, unmediated control over the sound of his compositions (except for the unavoidable uncertainties about acoustical conditions in the place where the music was to be heard). Already much of the new music demanded minute shadings of pitch, intensity, and timbre which could be only approximately notated in a score, as well as complexities of "irrational" rhythms which were hardly realizable by performers; and since absolute accuracy of performance was necessary, the practical requirements of specially qualified personnel and lengthy rehearsal time[10] were additional obstacles. But in the electronic studio every detail could be accurately calculated and recorded. Moreover, a whole new realm of possible sounds now became available—including an infinitude of sounds not producible by any "natural" means. Different acoustical effects could be attained by placing the loudspeakers in various positions relative to the audience. Composers in Europe, America, and Japan industriously exploited all these advantages. Further possibilities (and problems) were revealed by the use of tape recordings in combination with live performers. One ingenious example of such combination was Milton Babbitt's *Philomel* (1964), for soprano soloist with tape which incorporates an altered recording of the voice together with electronic sounds.

Electronics did not by any means supersede live music. A good many of the new composers, among them Boulez, did not work at all, or to any important extent, with electronic media. Undoubtedly, however, the electronic sounds stimulated the invention of new

---

9 The reference is to Dan. III: 12 and the aprocryphal insertion after v. 23.

10 With experienced conductor and performers "less than a dozen rehearsals" would be needed for Boulez's *Marteau sans maître*, "a very modest figure" (Hodeir, *Since Debussy*, p. 154); but the expense, even with only eight musicians involved, would hardly be a "modest figure."

sound effects to be obtained from voices and conventional instruments; this is especially noticeable in the music of the Hungarian György Ligeti (born 1923).

In both electronic and live music many composers worked with the idea of dispersing the various sound sources and thereby incorporating space as, so to speak, an additional dimension of music. This, of course, was not altogether a new discovery. Antiphonal singing of plainchant, the *cori spezzati* of the sixteenth-century Venetians, the *Requiem* of Berlioz, had exemplified the same principle—as had also Vaughan Williams's *Fantasia on a Theme of Thomas Tallis* of 1909 and Bartók's *Music for Strings, Percussion, and Celesta* of 1936. But in the latter half of the century, composers began to use space with more calculation and inventiveness than ever before. Thus, two or more groups of instruments might be placed on different parts of the stage; loudspeakers or performers might be located at the sides or back of the hall, above or below the level of the audience, or even in the midst of the audience. Varèse's *Poème électronique,* featured at the Brussels Exposition in 1958, was projected by 425 loudspeakers ranged all about the interior space of Le Corbusier's pavilion while moving colored lights and projected images accompanied the music. By such means as these, direction in space became a potential factor for defining the form of a work.

The pitch continuum

From the end of the seventeenth century, all Western music had utilized a set of twelve equidistant semitones systematically controlling the space of an octave. Proposals at one time or another for including more tones in the octave came to no practical result. Now, however, the very conception of distinct pitches and intervals (including the octave itself) came to be supplemented by the conception of pitch as a *continuum,* an unbroken range of sound from the lowest to the highest audible frequencies, without distinguishing separate tones of fixed pitch. Of course in practice some sounds of shifting pitch had always been used, for example glissandos in singing and on stringed instruments; also sounds outside the twelve semitones of the tempered scale, as in minute adjustments by string players or specified quarter-tones (or other microtones) such as Berg required in his *Chamber Concerto* (1925). Unspecified shifting pitch characterized the *Sprechstimme* of Schoenberg and Berg. The sirens in Varèse's *Ionisation* and similar electronic sounds in his later works, the glissandos of the Ondes Martenot in Messiaen's *Turangalîla,* the frequent glissando effects on traditional instruments in the music of Penderecki and others, are striking examples of use of the pitch continuum. Related to this is the use of complex or unpitched non-musical sounds, from whatever source, as elements in composition.

Throughout the history of Western music since the Middle Ages, there has been continual interaction between composer and performer, between those factors (such as pitch and relative duration) which the composer could specify by notation and those which were left to the performer, either by convention or of necessity through lack of adequate notational signs. Examples of conventional freedom were: option of voices or instruments in most polyphonic music up to the end of the sixteenth century; optional instrumentation in the seventeenth century; the Baroque basso continuo, where the harpsichordist played what he thought best over the bass line of the score; unspecified ornaments of a melodic line in the seventeenth and eighteenth centuries; and addition of unspecified trumpets and drums to the symphony orchestra in the eighteenth century.

Freedom due to inadequate notation is exemplified in the field of dynamics: despite the increased number of signs for different levels and gradations of loudness in the nineteenth century, indications were still only approximate and relative. Instrumentation by this time had come to be strictly specified; but slight fluctuations of tempo (rubato), use of the damper pedal of the piano, relative prominence of different parts of the texture, and many other details were matters in which performers for the most part had to use their own judgment. The existence of different "interpretations" of the same symphony by different conductors is a standard example of the way in which authority and freedom came to an adjustment in the nineteenth century.

In the twentieth century, multiplication of detailed indications for dynamics, manner of attack, tempo (frequent metronome marks), pauses, and rhythms (changing time signatures, minute and complex subdivisions of the beat) evidenced the aim of composers to exercise total control over performance; but total control became possible, or nearly possible, only in the case of all-electronic works, where the performer was totally eliminated. Roughly contemporary with this step (though not as a consequence of it) arose the characteristic twentieth-century forms of the control-freedom polarity.

Basic to all these is the fact that the limits of control (determinacy) and freedom (indeterminacy[11]) are planned and can hence be planned differently for each composition. The indeterminate features do not originate either from established conventions of choice, as in the sixteenth century, or accidentally out of imprecision of notation, as in the nineteenth century. In practice, indeterminacy

---

[11] Indeterminacy (John Cage's term) is used here in preference to the more restricted term "aleatory" (from the Latin *alea* = dice), to cover everything from improvisation within a fixed framework to situations where the composer gives only the minimum of directions to the performer or exercises only the minimum of choice in composition.

operates primarily in the area of performance; it is applicable to either live or electronic performances or to combinations of the two. It may occur as indeterminate sections (somewhat like improvisation) within a composition otherwise fixed by the score; or it may occur as a series of distinct musical "events," each one of which the composer specifies more or less exactly while leaving the order in which they are to occur partly or wholly indeterminate, thus making what is sometimes called "open" form. In such works the performer (soloist, member of a group, or conductor) may either determine the order of the events simply by his own choice, or be led by means of certain devices into an apparently chance or random order. Or he may also, both within an event and in choosing the order of events, be guided by his reactions to what other in the group (or even members of the audience) are doing. In short, the possibilities of indeterminacy—the possible modes of interaction between freedom and authority, the extent to which "chance" can be "controlled"—are limitless.

The composer who has worked most consistently in this domain is Stockhausen. Reference to two of his compositions may help to clarify some of the procedures. The score of *Klavierstück* (piano piece) *XI* (1956) consists of nineteen short segments of notation displayed on a large sheet (about 37 by 21 inches); these segments can be put together in various ways as the player's eye happens to light on one after another; certain directions are given as to the manner of linking the segments played; not all need be played, and any may be repeated. When in the course of his performance the pianist finds he has repeated any one segment twice, the piece ends.

The setup in Stockhausen's *Opus 1970* is a little more complicated. This piece is performed by four players (piano, electric viola, electronium, and tam-tam) and four loudspeakers.

> Material is obtained from a regulating system (radio short waves), selected freely by the player and immediately developed . . . spread, condensed, extended, shortened, differently colored, more or less articulated, transposed, modulated, multiplied, synchronized. . . . The players imitate and vary, adhering to the sequence of development specified by the score. . . . As regulating system each of the four players has a magnetophone [tape recorder] on which, for the whole of the recording period, a tape, prepared differently for each of the players, continuously reproduces fragments of music by Beethoven. The player opens and shuts the loudspeaker control whenever he wishes.[12]

A new element here is the incorporation of fragments (transformed but immediately recognizable) from Beethoven. Stockhausen had already used borrowed material in similar ways in some of his earlier works, notably the *Gesang der Jünglinge,* the *Telemusik* (1966), and

[12] Wilfried Daenicke: from the record jacket DGG 139-461-SLPM.

the *Hymnen* (1967). *Hymnen* incorporates words and melodies of many different national anthems in a performance combining electronic sounds with voices and instruments. The intention in every instance is, in Stockhausen's words, "not to interpret, but to hear familiar, old, preformed musical material with new ears, to penetrate and transform it with a musical consciousness of today." This represents a quite new mode of relating music of the present to that of the past.[13]

One by-product of indeterminacy is the variety of new kinds of notation. "Scores" range all the way from fragments of conventional staff-notes through purely graphic suggestions of melodic curves, dynamic ranges, rhythms, and the like to even more impressionistic and meager directives.

Naturally, one main consequence of indeterminacy is that no two performances of the "same" piece will be the same. The difference, whether small or great, between one performance and another will not be merely a matter of interpretation but a substantive difference in musical content and order of presentation. (Recordings of such works can be only of one particular performance.) The meaning of "a composition" thus becomes quite unlike the traditional meaning. In effect, a composition does not exist as such, but only as a performance, or as the inconceivable totality of possible performances.

Indeterminacy may be applied to the act of composition as well as to performance; this is the case when some or all of the pitches, durations, intensities, timbres, and so on of the notated score have been decided by chance—by casting dice, tossing coins, using tables of random numbers, and similar means. And finally, indeterminacy in composition may be combined with indeterminacy in performance. When the indeterminacy is practically total on both sides the result evidently is no longer a work of art in the normal sense of the word, that is, something *made.*

Indeterminacy, random techniques of all kinds, tended to focus attention on radically new ideas about the nature and purposes of music, ideas which came into prominence especially in America around the middle of the century. As we have already noted, the

"Anti-art"

[13] The psychology of quotation in literature is analogous to that in music: "Even if a text is wholly quotation, the condition of quotation itself qualifies the text and makes it so far unique. Thus a quotation from Marvell by Eliot has a force slightly different from what it had when Marvell wrote it. Though the combination of words is unique it is read, if the reader knows his words either by usage or dictionary, with a shock like that of recognition. The recognition is not limited, however, to what was already known in the words; there is a perception of something previously unknown, something new which is a result of the combination of the words, something which is literally an access of knowledge. Upon the poet's skill in combining words as much as upon his private feelings, depends the importance or the value of the knowledge." (R. P. Blackmur, *Form and Value in Modern Poetry*, 184; quoted in Leonard B. Meyer, *Music, the Arts, and Ideas,* 201.)

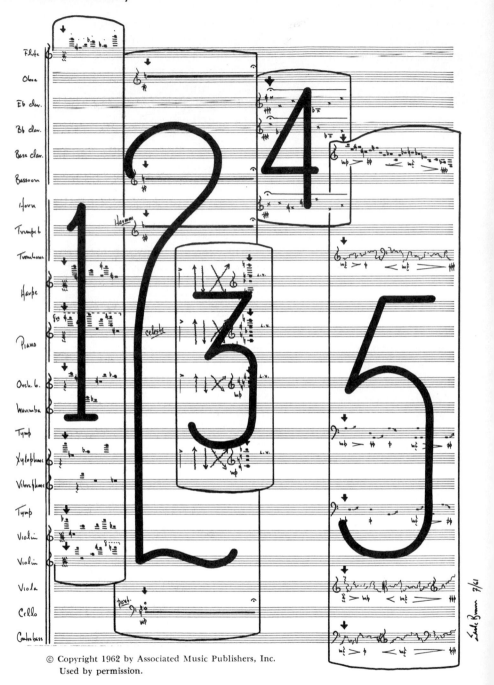

A page from Earle Brown's Available Forms I *(1961). The five numbered areas, or "events" may be played in any succession specified by the conductor, whose downbeat also implies the relative speed and intensity.*

music of total serialism and its offshoots, and even more the music of indeterminacy, is heard as a succession of discrete musical events, no one of which apparently grows out of its predecessors nor apparently sets up any situation from which the hearer can anticipate (let alone predict) what is to follow. Nevertheless, throughout all this the composer maintains some degree of control, even if only the slightest; both he and the performer make choices, and the consequent result is a musical form, even though (with indeterminacy) that form may be different every time the music is heard. The principle of cause (the choices) and effect (the form) is still operative.

Now, however, let us suppose that one extends spontaneity to a point where all choice is voluntarily abandoned. Whether as composer, performer, or listener, one decides to accept what happens without regard to his own preferences as to what *ought* to happen. As listener, he simply hears sounds as sounds, enjoying each as it comes, not trying to connect one sound with preceding or following ones, not expecting the music to communicate feelings or meanings of any kind. The sounds may not even be only intentional ones; any mistake, any accidental noise from anywhere that happens in the course of a performance, is perfectly acceptable. Value judgments are therefore irrelevant and musical time becomes simply duration, something that can be measured with a clock.

However strange such an esthetic may seem—and however vulnerable in practice to sheer dilettantism—it has a tenable philosophic basis; but the philosophy in question, though familiar in the Orient and to some Western mystics, is fundamentally different from the main line of Western philosophy which has come down unbroken from the time of ancient Greece and whose ideas are so ingrained in our thinking that most of us never imagine it possible to question them. The chief proponent of this "new" philosophy is the enigmatic John Cage, who has been in the forefront of most new musical developments in both America and Europe since the late 1930s. His influence in Europe has been greater than that of any other American composer. Since 1956 he has worked more and more toward total openness in every aspect of composition and performance, constructing his scores by wholly random methods and offering to performers such options as in his *Variations IV* (1963): "for any number of players, any sounds or combinations of sounds produced by any means, with or without other activities." The "other activities" might well include dance and theater. All this is consonant with Cage's personal interest in Zen Buddhism. More important, it is consonant with what is probably a growing tendency for Western artists—and for Western civilization generally—to become more open to the ideas and beliefs of other great world cultures.

Conclusion

If we recall the four basic characteristics of Western music which began to take shape in the eleventh century (see Ch. III, pp. 75–76), we can see that some developments in the twentieth century have altered three of them almost out of recognition. *Composition,* in the sense of existence of a work of music apart from any particular performance, has in some quarters given way to controlled improvisation (which was the practice in antiquity and the early Middle Ages). As to *notation,* the score in many cases is now no longer a definitive set of directions; the performer, instead being only a mediator between composer and audience, has become himself to a great extent the composer (again, as in the early Middle Ages). *Principles of order* have changed—arguably, the change is greater than any within the whole previous eight hundred years; and, if we think of total indeterminacy, principles of order have simply ceased to exist. Only *polyphony* remains. In view of all this, it seems not too much to say

Composer-conductor Pierre Boulez during a discussion period at a New York Philharmonic "Encounter" concert in the New York Shakespeare Festival Theatre. In the background, the American composer Charles Wuorinen. (Whitestone Photo)

that the twentieth century has witnessed a musical revolution in the full sense of the word.

It is a revolution, however, that has affected only a few people. This is not to say that those few are unimportant. Even the total audience for all "serious" music (that is, art music of a certain complexity which requires some effort to understand) has never at any time been more than a minute fraction of the population. Now that audience is still relatively small, and within it the audience for the new and experimental is even smaller. This too is normal. Composers who write in a difficult, unfamiliar idiom cannot expect a large popular following. Meanwhile, who cares if they listen?[14] The revolution may go on; if it does, no one knows what directions it may take.

We have been concerned in this section exclusively with the new techniques and ideas in recent Western music, but we should keep in mind that a good deal of the music of the past—and more of it all the time—is still very much alive and meaningful to many people. So also—though some advocates of "new" styles do not accept it—is a great deal of music written by composers of the present (Britten, for example) who deliberately refuse to go all the way with the new discoveries. Efforts in this century toward reconciling old and new in one common great musical culture have come to naught. What of the future?

Let us resist the temptation to prophesy, and leave the last word with Schoenberg: "Contemporaries are not final judges, but are generally overruled by history."[15]

---

[14] Distortion (non-electronic) of the provocative title of a wise essay "Who Cares if You Listen?" by Milton Babbitt in *High Fidelity* VIII, 2 (February 1958), reprinted in E. Schwartz and B. Childs, *Contemporary Composers on Contemporary Music*, 243–50.

[15] From "Composition with Twelve Tones" (1941), in *Style and Idea*, 103.

Glossary

Accidental. A sign used to change the pitch of a note by raising it one semitone (sharp, ♯), lowering it one semitone (flat, ♭), or cancelling the effect of a previous sharp or flat (natural, ♮).

Aleatory, see *Indeterminacy.*

Alteration. Changing the pitch of a note by means of an accidental (♯, ♭, or ♮) to raise or lower it by one semitone from its normal pitch in the scale.

Appoggiatura. A nonharmonic tone, sounded on a strong beat and resolved (regularly by step) to a harmonic tone on a following weaker beat (see also *suspension*).

Athematic. Property of music which does not use themes as structural units of composition.

Atonality (atonal). The absence of tonality.

Bar. (1) A vertical line (barline) through the staff(s) marking the division into measures; (2) a measure (not used in this sense in this book); (3) a form, *AAB,* common in medieval monophonic music, polyphonic ballads of the fourteenth century, Lutheran chorales, and other music.

Cadence. The melodic and/or harmonic formula that marks the end of a musical phrase, section, or composition. The most common harmonic final cadence is the progression Dominant-Tonic (V-I).

Canon, canonic imitation. (1) Exact imitation, continued for more than one phrase, of the melody of one voice by another voice or voices: the imitating voice(s) may begin on the same note as the leading voice (canon at the unison), or on another note (canon at the fifth above, at the fourth below, etc.); (2) a rule or direction specifying the way in which such imitation is to be carried out; (3) a composition in which two or more voices proceed throughout in canonic imitation (see also *round*).

Chord. A simultaneous combination of three or more notes of different pitch forming an entity that can be used for the analysis of harmony (see also *triad*).

Chromaticism (chromatic). (1) The use of tones not in the regular diatonic scale of the composition or passage in which such tones occur; (2) a quality of harmonic style marked by the frequent use of such tones (see also *Twelve-tone music*).

Circle of fifths. The arrangement of keys by ascending fifths (C–G–D, etc.), each key having one more sharp or one less flat in its signature; or by descending fifths (C–F–B♭, etc.), each key having one more flat or one less sharp in its signature. *Circle* refers to the fact that at the twelfth step the series returns to its point of beginning: in the equal-tempered tuning B♯ or D♭♭ = C.

Clavier. A keyboard instrument of the harpsichord or clavichord type.

Clavier music. Music for harpsichord, clavichord, or pianoforte.

Cluster (tone cluster). On the piano, the effect obtained by striking a number of adjacent keys with the flat of the hand or with the forearm; also, similar effects by other instruments.

Coda. A concluding section of a composition, particularly of a fugue or a movement of a sonata or symphony.

Codetta. Literally, a "small coda"; particularly, the closing passage of one section of a piece, for example, of the exposition of a movement in sonata form.

Color. (1) The quality of a musical sound (as the color of the clarinet tone) or of sounds in combination (as the color of Debussy's orchestration); (2) the quality of the sound of a composition or passage (see also *texture, timbre*).

Consonance (consonant). An interval or chord which produces an agreeable or satisfactory effect, or an effect of repose.

Contrary motion. Movement of two simultaneous voices in opposite directions, one upward and the other downward.

Counterpoint (contrapuntal). A musical texture consisting predominantly of two or more simultaneous melodic lines, with or without additional material.

Cross-relation. The use of a note and its chromatic alteration in different voices, either simultaneously or in immediate or close juxtaposition.

Diatonic. (1) Pertaining to a major, minor, or modal scale of eight tones to the octave; (2) the quality of music marked by infrequent use of chromatic tones.

Dissonance (dissonant). An interval or chord which produces a disagreeable ("discordant") or unsatisfactory effect, or an effect which requires completion (see also *resolution*).

Dodecaphonic (dodecaphony), see *Twelve-tone music*.

Dominant. In harmonic practice, the fifth degree or note of the scale (see also *cadence*).

Drone. (1) A note or notes, usually in the bass, sustained throughout an entire piece or section; (2) a string, pipe, or mechanism for producing such notes (see also *ostinato*).

Duet, duo. A composition, or section of a composition, having two equally important melodic lines, with or without accompaniment; or a composition written for two performers of equal importance, on the same or different instruments.

Enharmonic. In Greek music, intervals less than a semitone; in Western music, notes which are identical in sound in the equal-tempered scale (as F♯-G♭).

Equal temperament. A method of tuning in which the octave is divided into twelve equal semitones.

Form patterns. The arrangement of material within a composition. In this book form patterns are designated by italic letters thus: *aba*, *ABA*, etc. The mark ′ after a letter (*A′*) indicates a modified repetition of the formal unit.

Free rhythm. Rhythm in which the durations of the notes and rests are not fixed fractions or multiples of a common unit of duration (see *metrical rhythm*).

Fuga (Latin, "flight"). In medieval and renaissance usage, a canon; after 1600, the meaning is usually the same as *fugue*.

Fugato. A short fugal passage or fugal exposition.

Fughetta. A short fugue.

Fugue (*fugal*). A type or style of contrapuntal composition based on the development of (usually) a single short theme or *subject* in imitation.

Harmonic. (1; adj.) A musical texture consisting predominantly of chords or of melody accompanied by chords; (2; noun) a high flute-like tone produced by lightly touching the string of a violin at 1/2, 1/3, etc. of its length. (3) sounds produced by analogous means on other instruments.

Harmonic rhythm. The movement of music as marked by the succession of changing harmonies.

Harmony. (1) Any simultaneous combination of sounds; a chord; (2) the chordal or "vertical" aspect of a musical composition as contrasted with melodic, contrapuntal, rhythmic, coloristic, or other aspects; (3) the style of a composition considered with respect to the chords employed and the principles governing their succession (see also *harmonic*).

Hemiola (literally, "one and one-half"). A mensural device in the notation of the fifteenth and sixteenth centuries which in effect alters the movement from | ♩.♩. | to | ♩ ♩ ♩ |. Hence, in Baroque music, a common cadential formula in triple meter, by which two measures of 3/4 time are made to sound like one measure of 3/2 time: | ♩ ♩ | ♩ ♩ |.

Heterophony. The sounding of a melody simultaneously in a simple and an ornamented form.

Homophony. A texture in which all the voice parts move in the same or nearly the same rhythm.

Imitation. The closely following restatement of a melody or phrase by another voice or voices in a contrapuntal texture. If the restatement is exact, it is called *strict* imitation; if similar, but not exact, *free* imitation.

Indeterminacy. Method of composition in which certain factors (e.g., pitches, duration, rhythms, textures, order of succession) are not, or not wholly, specified by the composer. Also called *aleatory*.

Interval. The distance in pitch between two tones, simultaneous or successive. Intervals are measured (usually upward) by scale degrees or steps, counting both the first and last tones; thus, C–E is a third, D–G is a fourth, and so on.

Inversion. Substitution of a higher for a lower note. An interval is inverted when its higher note is placed below its originally lower note: a chord is inverted (or *in inversion*) when any of its notes other than the root is in the bass; a melody is inverted when an equal descending interval is substituted for every ascending interval and *vice versa;* two or more melodic lines in counterpoint are inverted when one of them, originally higher, is placed below the other.

Key, keynote. A tone (including its duplication in any octave) to which the other tones of the octave stand in subordinate relation.

Key signature. Sharp(s) ♯ or flat(s) ♭ placed on line(s) or spaces(s) at the beginning of each staff; all notes on the lines or spaces so indicated are to be raised or lowered respectively one semitone (unless the effect of the sharp or flat is cancelled by a natural ♮). A particular combination of sharps or flats may indicate the key of a composition.

Keyboard music. Music for a keyboard instrument (organ, harpsichord, clavichord, piano).

Line. A melody or part of a melody, considered either by itself or as a constituent in a polyphonic (especially a contrapuntal) texture.

Measure. (1) A unit of time, usually comprising two to six smaller units (*beats*); (2) the space between two bar lines.

Melody. A succession of tones perceived as an entity.

Metrical rhythm. Rhythm in which the duration of every note and rest is a fixed multiple or fraction of a common unit of duration.

Microtone. Any interval smaller than a semitone.

Mixture. An organ stop by which certain higher tones ("harmonics") are artificially made to sound along with the fundamental tone.

Modality. The quality of music written more or less definitely in accordance with the system of the modes of medieval music instead of the major or minor scales.

Modulation. Harmonic movement from one key to a different key in the course of a composition.

Monophony (monophonic). A musical texture consisting of a single line of melody without accompaniment; opposite of *polyphony*.

Motive, motif. The smallest unit of a musical idea (see also *phrase, theme*).

Musette. (1) A form of bagpipe; (2) a piece in pastoral style and light dance-like rhythm, with a drone bass.

Nonharmonic tone. A tone foreign to, and therefore dissonant with, the basic harmony or chord with which it is sounding.

Note. (1) A graphic sign directing a performer to produce a tone of a certain pitch and duration; (2) the tone represented by such a sign.

Note designation. In this book, a note referred to without regard to its octave register is designated by a capital letter (A). A note in a particular octave is designated by a letter according to the following scheme:

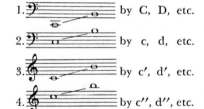

732

Oblique motion. Movement of two voices in which one remains at the same pitch while the other moves to a different pitch.

Ornament, ornamentation. Decorative notes added to a melodic line.

Ostinato. (1) A short melodic figure persistently repeated, usually in the same voice and at the same pitch, throughout a composition or section of a composition; (2) a persistently repeated pattern of rhythm, not necessarily coinciding with any repeated melodic or harmonic pattern.

Parallel motion. Two or more voices moving constantly at the same interval from one another.

Part. (1) A section of a composition; (2) a voice in contrapuntal texture.

Partial signature. A signature applied to fewer than all the voices of a polyphonic composition.

Phrase. A musical unit made up of one or more motives, and corresponding to a sentence in speech.

Pivot chord. In modulation, the chord which is heard as common to both the initial key and the new key.

Polyphony (polyphonic). "Many-voiced"; a musical texture consisting of two or more lines of melody (see *counterpoint*), or melody and accompaniment, or chords. In this book *polyphonic* is used in contrast to *monophonic*, as a general term including both contrapuntal and harmonic textures (see also *monophonic, counterpoint, harmony*).

Prepared piano. Made by affixing to or near to the wires of a piano, various objects of metal, rubber, etc., producing on the notes so prepared tinkling, damped, pizzicato, buzzing, etc. sounds. Used by John Cage for his *Sonatas and Interludes* (1948).

Principal. An organ stop controlling the pipes which produce the basic, characteristic tone color of the instrument.

Recitative. A style of vocal writing based on imitating the rhythms and inflections of speech, with a minimum of musical structure.

Resolution. The movement of a dissonant interval or chord to a more consonant one, producing an effect of completion or of comparative repose.

Root. The lowest note of a chord considered as a combination of tones built up by successive thirds (see also *root position, triad, inversion*).

Root position. A chord is in root position when its root is the lowest sounding note (compare *inversion*).

Round. A canon, usually vocal, in which each voice continues to repeat its part as many times as desired (see *canon*).

Rubato. A slight modification of the regularity of the beat, introduced by the performer for the purpose of musical expression.

Serial, serialism. Technique of composition in which the principle of ordered pitches of twelve-tone music is extended to other parameters such as duration, intensity, timbre, etc.

Shawms. Double-reed instruments of the oboe family, of various sizes, in use from the thirteenth to the seventeenth centuries.

Signature, see *key signature, time signature.*

Stop. A mechanism of the organ enabling the player to bring on or shut off different ranks of pipes at will.

Stretto. (1) A portion of a fugal composition in which imitations of the subject occur at closer time intervals than in the original presentation of the subject; (2) a closing portion, in quicker time, of a movement in fast tempo.

Subject. The theme of a fugue.

Suspension. A nonharmonic tone held over (*suspended*) on a strong beat from a previous harmony in which it was a harmonic tone, and then resolved (regularly by step downward) to a harmonic tone on a weaker beat (compare *appoggiatura*).

Syncopation. Displacement of the normal accent by transferring it from a strong to a weak beat, or from a strong to a weak part of a beat.

Tempered, see *equal temperament.*

Texture. The character of a musical composition in terms of its density, tone colors, and relative levels of activity in the different voice parts. With regard to the last criterion, textures range from those in which the level of activity is the same in all voices (*homophony*) to those in which the levels of activity are markedly distinct while the voices retain equal melodic importance (*counterpoint*).

Theme. A characteristic musical idea which serves as the basis for development of a composition or section of a composition.

Thirds, see *interval.*

Timbre. The characteristic color or quality of a musical sound as produced by various instruments—as the timbre of the clarinet, oboe, and so on (see also *color*).

Time signature. A sign placed at the beginning of a composition to indicate either (a) the proportion according to which longer time values are to be divided into shorter ones; or (b) the number of beats in each measure and the kind of note that represents a single beat: a time signature of 3/4 means three beats in a measure, a quarter note representing one beat.

Tonality (tonal). (1) The quality by virtue of which a musical composition, or a part of a composition, is organized harmonically around a constant central tone (compare *atonality, modality*); (2) the central tone or key of a composition.

Tone. A musical sound of definite pitch.

Tonic. The first note of the scale; the key note.

Triad. A chord consisting of three notes: one, the root, and two others respectively a third and a fifth above the root (see also *root position, inversion*).

Trio. (1) A composition, or section of a composition, in three voices; (2) a composition for three performers; (3) in Classical sonatas and symphonies, a second two-part section following a minuet or scherzo, and followed by a repetition of the minuet or scherzo.

Tritone. The interval of the augmented fourth, which contains three whole tones, as F–B♮, C–F♯, B♭–E. In strict contrapuntal writing this interval may not occur harmonically between the bass and an upper voice, or melodically as two successive notes in any voice.

Twelve-tone music. Music in which a certain order of the twelve tones of the chromatic scale, and derivations of that order, are systematically adhered to throughout a composition.

Vibrato. A slight fluctuation of pitch, used especially by singers and by players of bowed string instruments to make the tone more expressive.

Voice. A melodic line, especially in contrapuntal texture.

Abbreviations

AIM   *American Institute of Musicology;* publications include CEKM, CMM, CSM, MD, MSD. For lists, see MD 25 (1971), 229–51.

CDMI   *I Classici della Musica Italiana,* Milan, 1918–20 (36 vols.).

CEKM   *Corpus of Early Keyboard Music,* AIM, 1963– .

CM   *Collegium Musicum,* New Haven, 1955– ; second series, New Haven and Madison, 1969– .

CMI   *I Classici Musicali Italiani,* Milan, 1941–43, 1956 (15 vols.).

CMM   *Corpus mensurabilis musicae,* AIM, 1948– .

CSM   *Corpus scriptorum de musica,* AIM, 1950– .

DdT   *Denkmäler deutscher Tonkunst,* Leipzig, 1892–1931 (65 vols.); reprinted, Wiesbaden, 1957–61.

DTB   *Denkmäler deutscher Tonkunst, 2. Folge: Denkmäler der Tonkunst in Bayern,* Braunschweig, 1900–38 (38 vols., many of which are subdivided).

DTOe   *Denkmäler der Tonkunst in Oesterreich,* Vienna, 1894–19–. Numbers by volumes and also, up to Vol. 83, by years (*Jahrgänge*); many of the yearly volumes are subdivided: for example, Vol. 39 is Jahrgang 19/2; reprinted, Graz, 1959– .

EE   Alfred Einstein, Appendix to *A Short History of Music,* New York, 1947. Contains notes, some translations, and many musical examples.

EP   R. Eitner, ed., *Publikationen älterer praktischer und theoretischer Musikwerke, vorzugsweise des XV. und XVI. Jahrhunderts,* Berlin, 1873–1905 (29 vols, in 33 *Jahrgänge*).

GMB   Arnold Schering, ed., *Geschichte der Musik in Beispielen* [*History of Music in Examples*], Leipzig, 1931. Notes and translations in German; indications for performance frequently arbitrary.

HAM   Archibald T. Davison and Willi Apel, eds., *Historical Anthology of Music,* Cambridge, 1950. Vol. I: Oriental, Medieval, and Renaissance Music; Vol. II: Baroque, Rococo, and Pre-Classical Music. Notes and translations.

JAMS   *Journal of the American Musicological Society,* 1948– .

JMT   *Journal of Music Theory,* 1957– .

LSS   Edward R. Lerner, ed., *Study Scores of Musical Styles,* New York, 1968.

MB   *Musica Britannica,* London, 1951– .

MD   *Musica Disciplina,* 1946– .

MM   Carl Parrish and John F. Ohl, eds., *Masterpieces of Music Before 1750,* New York, 1951. Translations, good editorial notes.

MMA   Gustave Reese, *Music in the Middle Ages,* New York, 1940.

MQ   *The Musical Quarterly,* 1915– .

MR   Gustave Reese, *Music in the Renaissance,* 2nd ed., New York, 1959.

MRM   Edward Lowinsky, ed., *Monuments of Renaissance Music,* Chicago, 1964– .

MSD   *Musicological Studies and Documents,* AIM, 1951– .

NOHM   *New Oxford History of Music,* London and New York, 1954– . Vol. I, *Ancient and Oriental Music,* 1957; Vol. II, *Early Medieval Music up to 1300,* 1954; Vol. III, *Ars Nova and the Renaissance, 1300–1540,* 1960; Vol. IV, *The Age of Humanism, 1540–1630,* 1968.

PAM   *Publikationen älterer Musik . . . bei der deutschen Musikgesellschaft,* Leipzig, 1926–40.

PMMM   *Publications of Medieval Music Manuscripts,* Brooklyn, Institute of Medieval Music, 1957– .

RMAW   Curt Sachs, *The Rise of Music in the Ancient World,* New York, 1943.

SR   Oliver Strunk, *Source Readings in Music History,* New York, 1950. Also published as separate paperbacks, which are indicated as follows:

SRA   —— *Source Readings in Music History: Antiquity and the Middle Ages.*

SRRe   —— *Source Readings in Music History: The Renaissance.*

SRB   —— *Source Readings in Music History: The Baroque Era.*

SRC   —— *Source Readings in Music History: The Classic Era.*

SRRo   —— *Source Readings in Music History: The Romantic Era.*

TEM   Carl Parrish, ed., *A Treasury of Early Music,* New York, 1958.

WM   Johannes Wolf, *Music of Earlier Times;* the American edition of Wolf's *Sing- und Spielmusik aus älterer Zeit,* 1926. No notes or translations.

For a critical survey of anthologies of music examples, see Edward R. Lerner, "Historical Anthologies of Music—a Review and Critique," *College Music Symposium* 10 (Fall, 1970), 123–33.

Bibliography

General Bibliography

Music Anthologies

In addition to the anthologies of music examples listed below by chapters, the following series will be found useful: *Das Musikwerk; eine Beispielsammlung zur Musikgeschichte,* K. G. Fellerer, ed., Cologne, 1951– ; each volume is devoted to examples of music in a particular form or from a particular period, edited by a specialist, with introduction and notes in English.

Composers and compositions can be located with the help of *Historical Sets, Collected Editions, and Monuments of Music,* compiled by Anna Harriet Heyer, 2nd ed., Chicago, 1969. Many older editions of music are available in reprints: see current catalogues of Broude Bros., Dover Publications, Da Capo Press (all in New York), Gregg Press (Farnborough, England), and others.

There are recordings to accompany MM and TEM, and two sets are in progress to go with HAM (Phonodisc, Pleiades Records, P250– , and Musical Heritage Society, various numbers). Other historical anthologies are: RCA Victor's *History of Music in Sound; Archiv Production,* issued by the History of Music Division of the Deutsche Grammophon Gesellschaft; *L'Anthologie Sonore,* Haydn Society, 1954– , originally recorded at Paris in seventeen albums of 78 r.p.m. records; *Music of the Bach Family,* Boston Records, 1957, a recording of the music in the anthology of the same title edited by K. Geiringer, Cambridge, 1955; *Historical Anthology of Music* (not related to HAM), Bach Guild, 1972– . For others, see current Schwann catalogues.

Reference Works

The leading encyclopedias are: *Die Musik in Geschichte und Gegenwart* (MGG), Friedrich Blume, ed., Kassel, 1949–68, 14 vols., with Supplements, 1968– ; *Grove's Dictionary of Music and Musicians,* Eric Blom, ed., 5th ed., London, 1954, 9 vols. and Supplement, Denis Stevens, ed. (a sixth edition is in preparation); W. W. Cobbett, *Cyclopedic Survey of Chamber Music,* 2nd ed., 1963, 3 vols. (third vol., Colin Mason, ed.). Most convenient, indeed indispensable, are: Willi Apel, *Harvard Dictionary of Music* (HDM), 2nd ed., Cambridge, 1969; and *Baker's Biographical Dictionary of Musicians*, Nicolas Slonimsky, ed., 5th ed., with *Supplement*, 1971.

Other reference works: Keith Mixter, *An Introduction to Library Resources for Music Research*, Columbus, 1963; James Coover, "Music Theory in Translation: a Bibliography," JMT 3 (1959), 70–96; *id., Gesamtausgaben, a Checklist*, Buffalo, 1970; David R. Williams, *A Bibliography of the History of Music Theory*, 2nd ed., Fairport, 1971; Barry S. Brook, *Thematic Catalogues in Music; an Annotated Bibliography*, Hillsdale, 1972; Vinquist, Mary and Neal Zaslaw, *Performance Practice: A Bibliography*, New York, 1971; George Kinsky, *A History of Music in Pictures*, New York, 1951; Emanuel Winternitz, *Musical Autographs from Monteverdi to Hindemith*, New York, 1965, 2 vols.; *Composers' Autographs*, Madison, 1968, 2 vols. (based on three earlier German works), M. Hürlimann, ed., tr. and with a new preface by Ernest Roth; Curt Sachs, *The History of Musical Instruments*, New York, 1940.

Note: Throughout the bibliographies, "Cambridge" as place of publication means Cambridge, Massachusetts, unless otherwise specified. Not all modern reprints are mentioned; see current catalogues.

Chapter I (Pp. 1–34)

Transcriptions of the extant Greek melodies and fragments are given in   *Music*
Théodore Reinach, *La Musique grècque*, Paris, 1926. Examples also in HAM, Nos. 7, 8; GMB, No. 1; EE, No. 2.

The results of labor in the fields of Hebrew and Byzantine music are published in two monumental collections: A. Z. Idelsohn, ed., *Hebräisch-Orientalischer Melodienschatz*, Vol. 1, Leipzig, 1914; Vols. 2–10, Jerusalem, 1922–29; and *Monumenta musicae Byzantinae*, C. Høeg, H. J. W. Tillyard, E. Wellesz, eds., Copenhagen, 1935– ; subdivided into *Monumenta* (facsimiles), *Transcripta* (transcriptions), and other series.

Examples of Hebrew and Byzantine music are given in HAM, Nos. 6 and 8.

For the music of Gregorian Chant, see Bibliography for Chapter II. Examples of chants from other Western liturgies are given in TEM, Nos. 1–3; HAM, Nos. 9 and 10.

Following is a list of some early Christian hymns that are still used in both Catholic and Protestant services:

Title	Author or period	English Version	Number in Episcopal Hymnal (1940)
Phōs hilarion	3rd cent.	Hail, gladdening light	176
Aeterne rerum conditor	St. Ambrose (d. 397)	Framer of the earth and sky	
Splendor paternae gloriae	St. Ambrose	O splendor of Gods glory bright	158
O lux beata Trinitas	St. Ambrose (?)	O Trinity of blessed light	171
Aeterna Christi munera	St. Ambrose	The eternal gifts of Christ	132
Jam lucis orto sidere	5th–6th cent.	Now that the daylight fills the sky	159
Lucis creator	5th–6th cent.	O blest Creator of the light	163
Vexilla regis prodeunt	Venantius Fortunatus (*ca.* 600)	The royal banners forward go	63

Title	Author or period	English Version	Number in Episcopal Hymnal (1940)
Pange lingue . . . certamine	Venantius Fortunatus	Sing, my tongue, the glorious battle	66
Lucis creator optime	6th cent.	O blest Creator of the light	
Conditor alme siderum	6th cent.	Creator of the stars of night	6
Te lucis ante terminem	7th cent.	To Thee before the close of day	164
Urbs beata	7th cent.	Blessed city, heavenly Salem	383
Veni creator spiritus	9th cent.	O come, Creator Spirit	108, 217
Ut queant laxis	Paul the Deacon (*ca.* 780)	O that, once more, to sinful man descending	
Jesu dulcis memoria	Late 12th cent.	Jesu, the very thought of Thee	56
Pange lingue . . . corporis	St. Thomas (*ca.* 1263)	Now, my tongue, the mystery telling	199
Adoro te	St. Thomas (*ca.* 1260)	Humbly I adore Thee	204
O salutaris hostia	St. Thomas (*ca.* 1263)	O Saving Victim	209

*For
Further
Reading*

Books and articles listed under this heading are not offered as bibliography, but are simply suggested readings (mostly in English) which will be profitable to a student beginning the study of music history. Under no circumstances should this reading be regarded as a substitute for the listening or playing experience, or for the study of the music itself.

A basic book is SR (also SRA). For Chapter I, read the selections in the first chapter, "The Greek View of Music," and in the second chapter, "The Early Christian View of Music."

Also see RMAW; and MMA, Chapters 1 through 4.

On Greek music: Plato, *Timaeus; Republic,* Book III, 395–403; Aristotle, *Politics,* Book VIII. A circumstantial technical description of the Dorian, Phrygian, and other modes is given by Aristeides Quintilianus, who claims that the modes he describes are those of which Plato wrote in the *Republic.* Unfortunately, the treatise of Aristeides was written at least five centuries later than Plato, and most modern scholars are not inclined to attach much credit to his testimony. For an account of the modes he describes, and a defense of his authority, see J. F. Mountford, "The Musical Scales of Plato's *Republic," The Classical Quarterly,* 17 (1923), 125–36.

J. F. Mountford, "Greek Music in the Papyri and Inscriptions," in *New Chapters in the History of Greek Literature, Second Series,* J. U. Powell and E. A. Barber, eds., Oxford, 1929, 146–83, surveys the musical sources, with evaluations; also, see R. P. Winnington-Ingram, *Mode in Ancient Greek Music,* Cambridge, England, 1936.

More recent comprehensive studies are Isobel Henderson's chapter "Ancient Greek Music," NOHM, Vol. I; and Edward Lippmann, *Musical Thought in Ancient Greece,* New York, 1964. In Gilbert Highet's *The Classical Tradition,* New York, 1950, 222–24, there is an ingenious explanation of the structure of Pindar's *Odes* based on references to the music and the dance figures with which they were associated. Both MMA and O. Gombosi, "Key, Mode, Species," *JAMS* 4 (1951), 20–26 include comprehensive bibliographies.

In reading about Greek music remember that the terms "up, down" and "high, low" had for the ancient Greeks a meaning opposite to ours; some modern writers use the words in the ancient Greek sense, some in the modern sense, and some shift from one to the other. Furthermore, the actual pitch of the Greek note which we conventionally equate with our e was probably closer to c♯; in other words, the sounds of all the Greek notes which we designate by letters were actually about a minor third lower than the sounds of the notes designated by the same letters in our music.

On Hebrew music: A. Z. Idelsohn, *Jewish Music in Its Historical Development,* New York, 1967. On the many connections between ancient Jewish liturgy and the liturgy and music of the early Church, see Eric Werner, *The Sacred Bridge,* New York, 1959; *id.* "Musical Tradition and its Transmitters between Synagogue and Church," *Yuval: Studies of the Jewish Music Research Center,* Vol. II, Jerusalem, 1971, 163–82 (to be continued in following volumes).

On Byzantine music: see Egon Wellesz, *A History of Byzantine Music and Hymnody,* 2nd ed., Oxford, 1961; *id., Eastern Elements in Western Chant,* Oxford, 1947. Even after the fourth century in many places Greek continued to be used along with Latin for certain parts of the Liturgy. Traces of the Greek language survive in the *Kyrie eleison* of the Mass and in the *Trisagion* of the Good Friday service, where each of the three acclamations is sung first in Greek and immediately repeated in Latin. Wellesz discusses the survival and significance of bilingual singing.

Some details about music at Jerusalem are found in an interesting narrative of a pilgrimmage made to the holy city in 415–17 A.D. by a Spanish nun named Aetheria. It was formerly believed that the author of this narrative was St. Silvia of Acquitania. *The Pilgrimage of S. Silvia of Acquitania to the Holy Places,* ed. John H. Barnes, London, 1891, gives both the original Latin text and an English translation.

The views of the early Church and the Middle Ages generally are given in Théodore Gérold, *Les Pères de l'église et la musique,* Strasbourg, 1931; and Hermann Abert, *Die Musikanschauung des Mittelalters und ihre Grundlagen,* Halle, 1905. See also RMAW; MMA, chs. 1–4; SR (SRA), chs. 1–2.

For better acquaintance with Boethius—and he is well worth knowing—one should read his famous *Consolation of Philosophy,* which is available in many editions and translations. The best short introduction to Boethius is ch. V of E. K. Rand's *Founders of the Middle Ages,* Cambridge, 1929. See also L. Schrade, "Music in the Philosophy of Boethius," MQ 23 (1947), 188–200.

For history of the liturgy, see Adrian Fortescue, *The Mass; a Study of the Roman Liturgy,* London, 1912; and J. A. Jungmann, *The Mass of the Roman Rite,* New York, 1951.

A fascinating book dealing with the influence of ancient and early medieval writings on art and literature is Kathi Meyer-Baer, *Music of the Spheres and the Dance of Death,* Princeton, 1970. Also useful is Edgar de Bruyne, *The Esthetics of the Middle Ages,* New York, 1969.

Chapter II (Pp. 35–74)

Facsimiles and studies of many of the earliest manuscripts of Gregorian Chant are published in *Paléographie musicale; les principaux manuscrits de chant Grégorien, Ambrosien, Mozarabe, Gallican,* Solesmes and Tournai, 1889– ; two series.

Antiphonale Sacrosanctae Romanae Ecclesiae pro diurnis horis, Paris, 1949.

Music Collections (facsimiles and modern editions)

Graduale Sacrosanctae Romanae Ecclesiae, Paris, 1948.
The Liber Usualis with Introduction and Rubrics in English, New York, 1956.

*Chansonniers in facsimile editions (those marked * include transcriptions)*

*Pierre Aubry, Le Chansonnier de l'Arsenal, Paris, 1909.
*Jean Beck, Le Chansonnier Cangé, Philadelphia, 1927. 2 vols.
Jean Beck, Le Manuscrit du Roi, London, 1938. 2 vols.
Alfred Jeanroy, Le Chansonnier d'Arras, Paris, 1925.
Troubadour songs are in Friedrich Gennrich, Lo gai saber, Darmstadt, 1959 and other publications by Gennrich.
See also G. Tintori and R. Monterosso, eds., Orléans, Bibliothèque Municipale Ms. 201 (ten Sacre Rappresentazione; texts, facsimiles, transcriptions); F. Liuzzi, ed., La lauda e i primordi della melodia italiana, Rome, 1935, 2 vols.; B. Bischoff, ed., Carmina burana (PMMM 9; facsimiles).
Edmond de Coussemaker, Drames liturgiques du moyen âge, Rennes, Paris, 1861. This standard collection of liturgical dramas includes music in transcription. Other liturgical dramas: Noah Greenberg, ed., The Play of Daniel, New York, 1959; The Play of Herod, New York, 1965; William Smoldon, ed., Planctus Mariae, London, 1965; Peregrinus, London, 1965; Officium Pastorum, London, 1967.
Johannes Wolf, "Die Tänze des Mittelalters," Archiv für Musikwissenschaft I (1918), 10ff. Transcriptions of medieval dances.

Examples in the Anthologies

Syllabic Chant: MM, No. 3; LSS, Nos. 4, 5, 9; melismatic chant: MM, No. 2; HAM, Nos. 12, 13.

Psalm Tones, with antiphons: MM, No. 1; HAM, No. 11.

Tracts: Graduale, 208, 232.

Graduals: HAM, No. 12; Graduale, 75**; LSS, No. 6.

Alleluias: MM, No. 2; HAM, No. 13; EE, No. 2; LSS, No. 7.

Kyrie: HAM, No. 15a; LSS, No. 2.

Gloria and Sanctus: GMB, No. 2.

Other chants of the Ordinary of the Mass: Liber Usualis, 16–94; LSS, No. 3.

Sequences and proses: HAM, No. 16; MM, No. 3; GMB, Nos. 4–6; EE, No. 5; LSS, No. 9.

Hymn: LSS, No. 8.

Liturgical dramas: TEM, No. 5; GMB, No. 8; LSS, Nos. 10, 11.

Monophonic conductus: HAM, No. 17.

Troubadour songs: TEM, No. 6; HAM, No. 18; GMB, Nos. 11, 13; EE, No. 7; LSS, No. 12.

Trouvère songs: MM, No. 4; HAM, No. 19; GMB, No. 14; LSS, Nos. 13–15.

Minnesongs: MM, No. 5; HAM, No. 20; GMB, Nos. 12, 21; LSS, No. 16.

Meistersongs: TEM, No. 22; HAM, No. 24; GMB, Nos. 78, 79; EE, No. 8.

Other monophonic songs: TEM, Nos. 7, 8; HAM, Nos. 21–23; GMB, No. 25; LSS, Nos. 17–21.

Instrumental pieces: MM, No. 12; HAM, Nos. 40, 41, 58, 59; GMB, No. 28.

For Further Reading

For a comprehensive account of the chant (not primarily historical) see Willi Apel, Gregorian Chant, Bloomington, 1958.

Rev. Dom Dominic Johner, *A New School of Gregorian Chant*, New York, 1925. A practical introduction to the subject of Gregorian Chant, with much historical and liturgical information.

Section 7 of RMAW discusses the connection between melodic thirds and the rise of modern major-minor tonality.

Dom André Mocquereau, *Le Nombre musical Grégorien ou rhythmique Grégorienne*. Rome, 1908, 1927, 2 vols. The definitive exposition of the rhythmic principles governing the editions of Gregorian Chant in present-day liturgical books.

J. R. Bryden and D. Hughes, *An Index of Gregorian Chant*, Cambridge, 1969, 2 vols.

See also H. J. Waddell, *The Wandering Scholars*, New York, 1961; F. Gennrich, ed., *Troubadours, Trouvères, Minne- and Meistersingers*, Cologne, 1960; R. J. Taylor, *The Art of the Minnesinger*, Cardiff. 1968, 2 vols. Hendrik Van der Werf, *The Chansons of the Troubadours and Trouvères*, Utrecht, 1972. On other non-liturgical and secular monophony, see the chapters "Liturgical Drama" by W. L. Smoldon and "Medieval Song" by J. A. Westrup in NOHM II, London, 1954. On medieval instruments: Edward A. Bowles, "Haut and Bas," MD 8 (1954), 115–41; *id.* "The Role of Musical Instruments in Medieval Sacred Drama," MQ 45 (1959), 67–84. Special topics: Paul Evans, *The Early Trope Repertoire of St. Martial*, Princeton, 1970; Don Randel, *The Responsorial Psalm Tones for the Mozarabic Office*, Princeton, 1969.

Chapter III (Pp. 75–115)

J. H. Baxter, ed., *An Old St. Andrews Music Book*, London, 1931. A facsimile of the manuscript Wolfenbüttel 677, containing organa, conducti, and other compositions of the Notre Dame school.

William G. Waite, *The Rhythm of Twelfth-Century Polyphony*, New Haven, 1954. The musical supplement is a transcription of Leonin's organa in the *Magnus liber organi*.

Luther Dittmer, ed., *Facsimile Reproduction of the Manuscript, Madrid 20486, with an Introduction*, New York, 1957. One of the important sources (with Wolfenbüttel 677) of the music of the Notre Dame school; the contents are mostly conducti and motets.

Perotin's organum quadruplum *Sederunt principes* is published in H. Husmann, ed., *Die drei- und vierstimmige Notre-Dame-Organa*, PAM 11.

Examples of conducti, and lists of other transcribed examples, may be found in Leonard Ellinwood, "The Conductus," *MQ*, 27 (1941), 165–204; see also Janet Knapp, ed., *Thirty-five Conductus*, CM 6.

Motet collections:

1. The Montpellier Codex: Yvonne Rokseth, *Polyphonies du XIIIe siècle; le manuscrit H 196 de la Faculté de Médecine de Montpellier*, Paris, 1935–39, 4 volumes: I, Facsimiles; II, III, Transcriptions; IV, Commentary.

2. The Bamberg Codex: Pierre·Aubry, *Cent Motets du XIIIe siècle publiés d'après le manuscrit Ed. IV. 6 de Bamberg*, Paris, 1908, 3 volumes: I, Facsimiles; II, Transcriptions; III, Commentary.

3. The Las Huelgas Codex: Higini Anglès, *El còdex musical de Las Huelgas (múcisa a veus dels segles XIII–XIV)*, Barcelona, 1931, 3 volumes: I, Commentary; II, Facsimiles; III, Transcriptions.

Other twelfth- and thirteenth-century manuscripts in modern editions are:

Music Collections (facsimiles and modern editions)

Winchester Troper: W. H. Frere, ed., London, 1894, Introduction and facsimiles; see also A. Holschneider, *Die Organa von Winchester,* Hildesheim, 1968.

Compostela: P. Wagner, *Die Gesänge der Jakobsliturgie zu Santiago de Compostela,* Freiburg, 1931. See also W. M. Whitehill and G. Prado, *Liber Sancti Jacobi, Codex Calixtinus,* Santiago de Compostela, 1944, 3 vols. (facsimiles, transcription, commentary).

Florence, Biblioteca Medicea, Pluteus 29, 1: facsimile, PMMM 1.

Wolfenbüttel 677 (628), called W₁: facsimile, Baxter, *An Old St. Andrews Music Book,* London, 1931.

Wolfenbüttel 1099 (1206), called W₂: facsimile, PMMM 2.

Selection of thirteenth-century motets in F. Gennrich, *Florilegium motettorum,* Frankfurt, 1966.

Adam de la Halle: E. de Coussemaker, ed., *Oeuvres complètes du trouvère Adam de la Halle,* Paris, 1872. Includes both poetic and musical works. *Le jeu de Robin et Marion,* F. Gennrich, ed., Frankfurt, 1962. See also CMM 44.

Examples in the Anthologies

Early organum: MM, No. 6; HAM, No. 25.

Eleventh-century counterpoint: MM, No. 7; HAM, No. 26; GMB, No. 9.

St. Martial organum: MM, No. 8; HAM, No. 27.

Notre Dame organum (period of Leonin): TEM, No. 9; HAM, Nos. 28 c-e, 29; LSS, No. 22.

Clausulae: HAM, No. 30.

Notre Dame organum (period of Perotin): MM, No. 9; HAM, No. 31; LSS, No. 23.

Conductus: MM, No. 11; HAM, Nos. 38, 39; GMB, No. 16; EE, No. 6; LSS, No. 24.

Conductus style: HAM, No. 32c.

Interchanged voices (*Stimmtausch*): MM, No. 10; HAM, Nos. 32c, 33a.

Motet: TEM, Nos. 10, 12; MM, No. 10; HAM, Nos. 28f-i, 32–35; GMB, Nos. 18–20; EE, No. 9; WM, No. 3.

Miscellaneous cantilena types: HAM, No. 36.

Hocket: TEM, No. 11; LSS, No. 25.

Rota (*Sumer* canon): HAM, No. 42; GMB, No. 17.

Dance: LSS, No. 26.

For Further Reading

For a list of the principal theorists, with indication of modern editions, see HDM, art. "Theory," Part I.

The principal modern collections of medieval music treatises are:

Martin Gerbert, ed., *Scriptores ecclesiastici de musica,* Milan, 1931. 3 vols. A facsimile reprint of the original edition of 1784. (*Musica enchiriadis* is in Vol. I, pp. 152–73)

E. de Coussemaker, ed., *Scriptorum de musica medii ævi novam seriem,* Milan, 1931. 4 vols. A facsimile reprint of the original Paris edition of 1864.

Several important treatises are translated in ..e or in part in SR (also, SRA); see especially selections from the *Schol.. enchiriadis,* 126–38, and Franco of Cologne's *Ars cantus mensurabilis,* 139–59. A typical medieval explanation of the perfection of the number 3 is given in the paragraphs from Jean de Muris's *Ars novae musicae* (1319), 173.

For details of the notation of twelfth- and thirteenth-century polyphonic music, see Willi Apel, *The Notation of Polyphonic Music,* Cambridge, 1961, 5th ed.; Waite, *The Rhythm of Twelfth-Century Polyphony.*

Chapter IV (Pp. 116–45)

Polyphonic Music of the Fourteenth Century, Monaco, 1956– , Leo
Schrade (Vols. 1–4) and Frank Ll. Harrison, eds. (Machaut, Vols. 2–3;
Landini, Vol. 4.)

Machaut, *Musikalische Werke,* Fr. Ludwig, ed., Leipzig, 1954; 4 vols.

The following numbers of CMM: 2 (Machaut), 8 (Music of Fourteenth-
Century Italy), 11 (Early Fifteenth-Century Music), 13 (Mass of Tournai),
29 (Fourteenth-Century Mass Music in France), 36–37 (Codex Reina), 39
(Codex Chantilly), 53 (French secular compositions).

Squarcialupi Codex, J. Wolf, ed., Lippstadt, 1955.

CEKM, No. 1 (Keyboard Music of the Fourteenth and Fifteenth Centuries); see also Codex Faenza (facsimile) in MD 13 (1959) 79–107, and
article by D. Plamenac in JAMS 4 (1951).

Additional examples of late fourteenth- and early fifteenth-century
church music may be found in Amédée Gastoué, ed., *Le Manuscrit de
musique polyphonique du Trésor d'Apt,* Paris, 1936; this is a transcription
of a French manuscript containing 51 sections of the Ordinary, hymns, and
motets from the period *ca.* 1380–1420. See also Vol. 76 (Year 40) of the
DTOe, which contains 36 motets of the fourteenth and early fifteenth centuries. The transcriptions in this last volume are an unfortunate compromise between a facsimile and a modern edition.

Willi Apel, ed., *French Secular Music of the Late Fourteenth Century,*
Cambridge, 1950, contains 81 compositions of both southern and northern
French origin, with commentary and eight facsimiles.

Reproductions of the portrait miniatures of the Squarcialupi Codex
appear in Riccardo Gandolfi, *Illustrazioni di alucuni cimelli concernenti
l'arte musicale in Firenze,* Florence, 1892.

W. Thomas Marrocco, ed., *Fourteenth-Century Italian Cacce,* 2nd ed.,
Cambridge, 1961; id., *The Music of Jacopo da Bologna,* Berkeley, 1954.

Nigel Wilkins, ed., *One Hundred Ballades, Rondeaux and Virelais from
the Late Middle Ages,* Cambridge, England, 1969.

Leonard Ellinwood, ed., *The Works of Francesco Landini,* Cambridge,
1945, has transcriptions of Landini's complete works, with introduction,
bibliography, and facsimiles.

Music Collections (facsimiles and modern editions)

Motets from the *Roman de Fauvel:* HAM, No. 43.
Works of Guillaume de Machaut:
  Chansons balladées: HAM, No. 46; GMB, No. 26b.
  Motets: HAM, No. 44; GMB, No. 27; WM, No. 5; LSS, No. 27.
  Ballades: HAM, No. 45; GMB, No. 26a; EE, No. 11.
  Mass: MM, No. 13 (Agnus Dei).
Church music of the fourteenth and early fifteenth centuries: TEM, Nos.
  13, 14; HAM, Nos. 55, 56; GMB, No. 29.
Late fourteenth-century secular French music: TEM, No. 17; HAM, Nos.
  47, 48; GMB, No. 24; LSS, No. 30.
Italian music of the fourteenth century:
  Madrigals: HAM, Nos. 49, 50; GMB, No. 22; LSS, No. 28.
  Cacce: TEM, No. 16; HAM, No. 52; WM, No. 7; LSS, No. 29.
  Ballata: HAM, No. 51 (also in EE, No. 10)
Works of Francesco Landini:
  Madrigal: HAM, No. 54.
  Ballate: MM, No. 14; HAM, No. 53; GMB, No. 23; WM, No. 6.
Instrumental music: TEM, No. 15; HAM, Nos. 58, 59.

Examples in the Anthologies

Bibliography to Chapter V

For
Further
Reading

Selections from fourteenth-century treatises in SR (also, SRA): Marchetto da Padua, 160–71; Jean de Muris, 172–79; and Jacob of Liège, 180–90; translation of Philippe de Vitry's *Ars nova* by Leon Plantinga in JMT 5 (1961), 204–23; see also CSM 8.

On Guillaume de Machaut: George Perle, "Integrative Devices in the Music of Machaut," *MQ* 24 (1948), 169–76; Otto Gombosi, "Machaut's *Messe Notre-Dame*," *MQ* 36 (1950), 204–24; Gilbert Reaney, "Voices and Instruments in the Music of Guillaume de Machault," *Revue Belge de Musicologie* 10 (1956), 3–17, 93–104.

On Marchetto da Padua: Nino Pirrotta, in MD 9 (1955), 57–73.

The original Latin text of Pope John XXII's decree of 1324 concerning church music is in Vol. I of the old *Oxford History of Music,* London, 1929, 294–95. For some other pronouncements on this subject see MMA, 321, 390; and P. H. Lang, *Music in Western Civilization,* New York, 1941, 140, 163.

On partial signatures: Edward Lowinsky, "The Function of Conflicting Signatures," MQ 31 (1945), 227 (summarized in MR 45–48); see also Richard H. Hoppin, "Partial Signatures and Musica Ficta in Some Early 15th-Century Sources," *JAMS* 6 (1953), 197–215; Edward Lowinsky, "Conflicting Views on Conflicting Signatures," *JAMS* 7 (1954), 181–204; Hoppin, "Conflicting Signatures Reviewed," *JAMS* 9 (1956), 97–115.

On instruments in the music of this period, see essays by E. A. Bowles, F. Ll. Harrison, and G. Reaney in Jan LaRue, ed., *Aspects of Medieval and Renaissance Music,* New York, 1966.

E. H. Sanders, "Cantilena and Discant in 14th-century England," MD 19 (1965), 7–52.

Chapter V (Pp. 146–71)

Music
Collections
(facsimiles
and modern
editions)

H. E. Wooldridge, ed., *Early English Harmony from the 10th to the 15th Century,* London, 1897–1913, 2 volumes: Vol. I, Facsimiles; Vol. II, Transcriptions and notes.

Dom Anselm Hughes, ed., *Worcester Mediæval Harmony of the Thirteenth and Fourteenth Centuries,* Nashdom Abbey, 1928.

Luther A. Dittmer, ed., *The Worcester Fragments; a Catalogue Raisonné and Transcription,* Rome, 1957. For all practical purposes this edition supersedes Hughes' *Worcester Mediæval Harmony.* See also PMMM 5, 6.

The Old Hall Manuscript, A. Hughes and M. Bent, eds., 4 vols. (CMM 46) (to replace the ed. by A. Ramsbotham, 1933–38).

John Dunstable, *Complete Works,* Manfred F. Bukofzer, ed., London, 1970 (MB 8).

John Stevens, ed., *Mediaeval Carols,* London, 1952 (MB 4). The extant polyphonic carols of the fifteenth century.

Guillaume Dufay, *Opera omnia,* H. Besseler, ed., Rome, 1951–66, six vols. (CMM 1); Dufay's Hymns for three and four voices also in an edition by R. Gerber, 1937-*Das Chorwerk,* Jg. 9 and 49.

Miscellaneous collections of fifteenth-century music, chiefly of English, French and Burgundian composers:

Sir John Stainer, ed., *Dufay and His Contemporaries,* London, 1898; reprinted, Hilversum, 1966: fifty secular compositions from the Bodleian Ms. Canonici misc. 213. Transcriptions in modern clefs; introduction and notes in English. Inventory of the manuscript by Gilbert Reaney in MD 9 (1955), 73–104.

Polyphonia sacra contains Latin compositions of the Canonici Ms., first ed. C. van den Borren, 1932; rev. ed., University Park, Pa., 1963.

The Trent Codices are transcribed (not entire) in the following volumes of the DTOe: Vol. 14/15 (Year 7); Vol. 22 (Year 11, Pt. 1); Vol. 38 (Year 19, Pt. 1); Vol. 53 (Year 27, Pt. 1); Vol. 61 (Year 31); and Vol. 76 (Year 40).

Jeanne Marix, ed., *Les Musiciens de la Cour de Bourgogne au XVe siècle (1420–1467)*, Paris, 1937. 81 chansons, 4 *Magnificats*, 10 sections of Masses, and 19 motets, from manuscripts other than the Oxford and Trent codices.

Eugénie Droz and G. Thibault, eds., *Poètes et musiciens du XVe siècle*, Paris, 1924. See also E. Droz, ed., *Trois Chansonniers français du XVe siècle*, Paris, 1927.

Knud Jeppesen, ed., *Der Kopenhagener Chansonnier*, Leipzig, 1927.

Charles van den Borren, ed., *Pièces polyphoniques de provenance Liégeoise*, Brussels, 1950–   ; chansons by Netherlands composers, from various manuscripts.

English medieval carols are in MB 4. The Eton Choirbook, transcribed by F. Ll. Harrison, is in MB 10–12; description and catalogue in *Annales musicologiques* 1 (1953), 151–75.

The Worcester fragments: MSD 2.

See also CMM 9, 19, 21, 50; *Early English Church Music*, F. Ll. Harrison, ed. (London, 1963–   ), Vol. 8.

The following collections are exclusively sacred music:

Laurence Feininger, ed., *Documenta polyphoniæ liturgicæ*, Rome, 1947–   ; performing editions, chiefly Masses and parts of Masses from the Trent Codices.

Laurence Feininger, ed., *Monumenta polyphoniæ liturgicæ*, Rome, 1947–   ; Series I, Ordinary of the Mass; Vol. I of this series contains ten early Masses on *L'homme armé*; Series II, Proper of the Mass. Scholarly editions preserving all features of the original manuscripts.

English music of the fourteenth and early fifteenth centuries, other than Dunstable: HAM, Nos. 57, 63, 64 (compare also HAM, Nos. 25c, 33a, 37, 42 and EE, No. 6). *Examples in the Anthologies*

Dunstable: TEM, No. 18; HAM, Nos. 61, 62; GMB, No. 35; WM, No. 11; LSS, No. 31. (The transcriptions of GMB, Nos. 32 and 34 are not reliable.)

The Burgundian School: *Chansons:* MM, No. 16; HAM, Nos. 67, 68, 69, 70, 71, 72; GMB, Nos. 40, 41, 42; LSS, No. 35. *Motets:* HAM, No. 65; GMB, Nos. 38, 43; WM, No. 12; LSS, No. 33. *Masses:* MM, No. 15; HAM, No. 66 (and compare Nos. 73, 92); GMB, No. 39; EE, No. 12; LSS, No. 34.

Frank Ll. Harrison, *Music in Medieval Britain*, London, 1958. An excellent study of the period from the eleventh century to the Reformation; it deals not only with musical style but also with the institutions under whose patronage the music was composed and performed. *For Further Reading*

Sylvia W. Kenney, *Walter Frye and the contenance angloise*, New Haven, 1964.

Edgar H. Sparks, *Cantus Firmus in Mass and Motet, 1420–1520*, Berkeley, 1963.

Philip Gossett, "Techniques of Unification in Early Cyclic Masses and Mass Pairs," JAMS 19 (1966), 205–31.

Manfred F. Bukofzer, *Studies in Medieval and Renaissance Music*, New York, 1950. The first four essays in this volume are concerned with English music of the fourteenth and early fifteenth centuries. The seventh essay ("*Caput:* a Liturgico-Musical Study") deals with the origins of the cyclic

Mass and contains an analysis of three Masses based on the *"Caput" cantus firmus.*

Manfred F. Bukofzer, "John Dunstable: A Quincentenary Report," *MQ* 40 (1954), 29–49. Biography, musical sources, style, and significance, in brief and attractive form.

Charles Hamm, *A Chronology of the Works of Guillaume Dufay,* Princeton, 1964.

Richard Leighton Greene, *The Early English Carols,* Oxford, 1935. The fundamental work on the form of the carol; includes a collection of all extant carol texts to 1550.

Jeanne Marix, *Histoire de la musique et des musiciens de la Cour de Bourgogne sous le règne de Philippe le Bon (1420–1467),* Strasbourg, 1939.

Howard M. Brown, *Music in the French Secular Theatre, 1400–1550* and the companion volume *Theatrical Chansons of the Fifteenth and Early Sixteenth Centuries,* Cambridge, 1963.

Nino Pirrotta, "Music and Cultural Tendencies in 15th Century Italy," JAMS 19 (1966), 127–61.

Chapter VI (Pp. 172–206)

*Music
Collections
(facsimiles
and modern
editions)*

Modern editions of music by the composers mentioned in this chapter include:

Ockeghem: *Collected Works,* D. Plamenac, ed., 2nd ed., New York, 1959, 3 vols.

Obrecht: *Werken,* J. Wolf, ed., Amsterdam, 1908–21, 8 vols. (reprinted 1968, Gregg Press). *Opera omnia,* A. Smijers, ed., Amsterdam, 1953– .

Josquin des Prez: complete works, A. Smijers, ed., Amsterdam, 1925– ; *Opera omnia,* Amsterdam, 1957– ; see also *Das Chorwerk,* Vols. 1, 3, 18, 20, 23, 30, 33, 42.

Isaac: *Choralis Constantinus,* Books I and II, DTOe, Vols. 10, 33; Book III, L. Cuyler, ed., Ann Arbor, 1950; *Five Polyphonic Masses,* L. Cuyler, ed., Ann Arbor, 1956; miscellaneous secular vocal and instrumental works, DTOe, Vol. 28.

Mouton: CMM 43

Verdelot: CMM 28

Petrucci's *Odhecaton:* facsimile, Milan, 1931; *Canti A,* H. Hewitt, ed., Cambridge, 1942; *Canti B,* H. Hewitt, ed., MRM 2.

La Rue's Mass *Ave Sanctissima* is published in a performing edition by L. Feininger in *Documenta polyphoniæ liturgicæ,* Series IB, No. 1, Rome, 1950; see also A. Tirabassi, ed., *Liber missarum P. de la Rue,* Malines, 1941, 135–65. The motet on which this Mass is parodied is given in GMB, No. 97.

See also *Music of the Polish Renaissance,* J. Chominski and Z. Lissa, eds., Cracow, 1955; MRM 3–5; CM, series I, No. 5 (three *Caput* Masses); CMM 5, 7, 10, 15, 18, 22, 23, 29, 34, 49.

*Examples
in the
Anthologies*

(The following is only a partial list; for additional examples consult the anthologies.)

Ockeghem: MM, No. 17; HAM, Nos. 73 (the very strict treatment of the *cantus firmus* in this example is exceptional in Ockeghem), 74, 75; LSS, No. 36.

Canonic devices in Netherlands music: MM, No. 17, with introductory commentary; HAM, Nos. 66c, 89, 91, 92, with commentary on pages 223, 225–26.

Obrecht: MM, No. 18; HAM, Nos. 77, 78.

The Netherlands chanson in the early sixteenth century: HAM, Nos. 68, 69, 70, 72, 74, 75, 79 (an exceptional type, the motet chanson), 91; GMB, No. 53. For instrumental pieces in vocal collections dated around 1500, see HAM, Nos. 78, 83; GMB, Nos. 56, 62b, 67, 68.

Josquin des Prez: MM, No. 19; HAM, Nos. 90, 91; LSS, No. 37. The motet *Absalon fili mi* is in the *Oxford History of Music,* Vol. II, 77–83. The Mass *Pange lingua* is Vol. I of Blume, *Das Chorwerk.*

Contemporaries of Obrecht and Josquin: HAM, Nos. 88, 92

For Further Reading

The indispensable starting point for any detailed study of this period is Gustave Reese, *Music in the Renaissance,* New York, 1959, a comprehensive, concrete, and accurate account of every phase of musical activity from 1400–1600. Very full bibliographical references are included.

An excellent survey of this and the following era is Friedrich Blume, *Renaissance and Baroque Music,* New York, 1967. See also Edward Lowinsky, *Tonality and Atonality in Sixteenth-Century Music,* Berkeley, 1961.

Helmuth Osthoff, *Josquin Desprez* (Tutzing, 1962–65, 2 vols.) is the standard work on this composer. On Spanish music, see Robert Stevenson, *Spanish Music in the Age of Columbus,* The Hague, 1960.

Chapters V, VI, and VII of Manfred Bukofzer's *Studies in Medieval and Renaissance Music* deal chiefly with the period 1450–1550.

For a complete list, with descriptions, of the publications of Petrucci, see Claudio Sartori, *Bibliografia delle opere musicali stampate da Ottaviano Petrucci,* Florence, 1948.

A good succinct account, with illustrations, is A. Hyatt King's *Four Hundred Years of Music Printing,* 2nd ed., London, 1968. See also the same author's "The Significance of John Rastell in Early Music Printing," *The Library,* Vol. XXVI, No. 3 (September 1971), 197–214.

Howard M. Brown, *Instrumental Music Printed before 1600,* Cambridge, 1965.

Accounts of the earliest music printers in France, with intelligent discussions of the technical, commercial, and general social conditions under which they carried on their business, may be found in Daniel Heartz, *Pierre Attaingnant, Royal Printer of Music,* Berkeley, 1968; and Samuel F. Pogue, *Jacques Moderne, Lyons Music Printer of the Sixteenth Century,* Geneva, 1969.

On the Parody Mass, see two articles by Lewis Lockwood: "On 'Parody' as a Term and Concept" in Jan LaRue, ed., *Aspects of Medieval and Renaissance Music,* New York, 1966, 560–75; and "A View of the Early Sixteenth-Century Parody Mass" in Albert Mell, ed., *Twenty-Fifth Anniversary Festschrift* [of the Music Department of Queen's College], New York, 1964, 53–77.

Evidence for the use of scores by sixteenth-century composers is presented in Edward Lowinsky, "Early Scores in Manuscript," JAMS 13 (1960), 126–73.

Concerning the texture of parallel tenths in music of the late fifteenth century, see Charles Warren Fox, "Non-Quartal Harmony in Renaissance Music" *MQ* 31 (1945), 33–53. In the Agnus Dei of a Mass by Isaac (Sistine Chapel Ms. 35, fol. 36ᵛ), the superius and bassus move entirely in parallel tenths; the bass is not written out, but is derived from a playful canonic inscription over the superius, the scriptural verse "I give tithes [*tenths*] of all that I possess."

On *musica reservata,* see Edward Lowinsky, *Secret Chromatic Art in the Netherlands Motet,* New York, 1946, Ch. VII; M. van Crevel, *Adrianus Petit Coclico,* Den Haag, 1940, 293–326 *et passim;* Claude Palisca, "A Clarification of 'Musica Reservata,' " in *Acta Musicologica* 31 (1959), 133–61. Concerning Josquin's motet *Absalon fili mi*, see Lowinsky, *op. cit.,* 24ff and his Example 23.

Chapter VII (Pp. 207–51)

Music Collections (Modern editions and facsimiles)

Modern collected editions of the works of composers mentioned in this chapter:

Gombert: CMM 6, J. Schmidt-Görg, ed.

Clemens: CMM 4, K. Ph. Bernet Kempers, ed.

Senfl: *Sämtliche Werke,* Basel, 1937– (Vol. 9, 1971).

Willaert: CMM 3, H. Zenck and W. Gerstenberg, eds.

Sermisy: CMM 52, G. Allaire and I. Cazeaux, eds.

Jannequin: Chansons, A. T. Merritt and F. Lesure, eds., Monaco, 1965– .

Hofhaimer: Supplement to H. J. Moser, *Paul Hofhaimer,* Stuttgart, 1929.

Morales: *Monumentos de la Música Española,* H. Anglès, ed., Vols. 11, 13, 15, 17, 20, 21, 24.

Fayrfax: CMM 17, E. B. Warren, ed.

Ludford: CMM 27, J. Bergsagel, ed.

John of Lublin: CEKM 6, J. R. White, ed.

Festa: CMM 25, A. Main, ed.

Arcadelt: CMM 31, A. Seay, ed.

Rore: CMM 14, B. Meier, ed.

Lasso: Haberl and Sandberger, eds., Leipzig, 1894–1927, 21 vols.; reprinted, Wiesbaden, 196?; W. Boetticher, ed., Kassel, 1956– .

Monte: Van den Borren and Nuffel, eds., Düsseldorf, 1927–39, 31 vols.; reprinted, New York, 1965.

Wert: CMM 24, C. MacClintock and M. Bernstein, eds.

Monteverdi: G. F. Malipiero, ed., Asola, 1926–66, 17 vols.; reprinted, Vienna, 1967.

Sweelinck: *Werken,* M. Seiffert, ed., Leipzig, 1894–1901, 10 vols. and 1 vol. supplement. (Vols. 1 and 6 have been reissued). Reprinted Amsterdam, 1943– ; Gregg Press, 1968. *Opera omnia,* Amsterdam, 1965– .

Campion: W. R. Davis, ed.; New York, 1967.

Miscellaneous Collections (short list; for more information see the article "Editions, historical" in HDM):

Motets by French and Franco-Flemish composers of the first half of the sixteenth century are published in A. Smijers, ed., *Treize Livres de motets parus chez Pierre Attaingnant en 1534 et 1535,* Paris 1934–36; 3 vols.; see also H. Expert, ed., *Monuments de la musique française au temps de la Renaissance,* Vol. 2, Paris, 1925; CMM 48 (works of Lhéritier, L. Perkins, ed., with extensive introduction and commentary).

Examples of the frottola and kindred forms are in Alfred Einstein's *The Italian Madrigal,* Princeton, 1949, Vol. III, Nos. 1–14. See also R. Schwarz's edition of Petrucci's first and fourth books of *frottole* in PAM 8; and R. Monterosso, ed., *Frottole nell'edizione principe di O. Petrucci,* Cremona, 1954. O. Gombosi, ed., *Composizione di Meser Vincenzo Capirola,* Paris, 1955, contains lute transcriptions of *frottole.*

Knud Jeppesen's *Die mehrstimmige italienische Laude um 1500,* Leipzig, 1935, contains 98 *laude* in transcription, as well as detailed analysis of the poetry and music.

Other collections of early sixteenth-century Italian music: F. D'Accone, ed., *Music of the Florentine Renaissance,* 4 vols. (CMM 32); C. Gallico, ed. *Un canzoniero musicale italiano del cinquecento,* Florence, 1961.

For examples of the French chanson from the first half of the sixteenth century see F. Lesure, ed., *Anthologie de la chanson parisienne au XVIe siècle,* Monaco, 1953; H. Expert, ed., *Les Maîtres musiciens de la Renaissance française* (Paris, 1894ff), Vols. 5 and 7; and H. Expert, ed., *Florilège du concert vocal de la Renaissance,* Paris, 1928–29, Nos. 1, 3. EP, Year 27, Vol. 23, contains chansons by French and Netherlandish composers. More recent modern editions are: CM I, No. 2, A. Seay, ed.; by the same editor, CMM 47, CMM 20; M. Picker, ed., *Chanson Albums of Marguerite of Austria,* Berkeley, 1965; see also D. Heartz, ed., *Preludes, Chansons and Dances for Lute . . . Attaignant 1529–30,* Neuilly-sur-Seine, 1964.

Many French chansons of the latter part of the sixteenth century are to be found in the following publications, all edited by Henry Expert: *Les Maîtres Musiciens de la Renaissance française,* Paris, 1894–1908 (23 vols.), Vols. 1, 3, 10, 12–19; *Monuments de la musique française au temps de la Renaissance,* Paris, 1924–29 (10 vols.), Vols. 1, 3, 4–7; and *Florilège du concert vocal de la Renaissance,* Paris, 1928–29, Nos. 2, 4–6, 8. The chansons of Sweelinck are published in his *Werken,* The Hague, 1894–1901 (12 vols.), Vols. 9 and 10. See also L. de La Laurencie, ed., *Chansons au luth et Airs de cour français du XVIe siècle,* Paris, 1934.

See also F. Lesure and G. Thibault, *Bibliographie des éditions d'Adrien Le Roy et Robert Ballard,* Paris, 1955; Heartz, *Pierre Attaingnant;* Pogue, *Jacques Moderne.*

Polyphonic songs on Dutch texts are included in R. Lenaerts, *Het nederlands polifonies lied,* Mechelen-Amsterdam, 1933.

The Lochamer *Liederbuch* was published in a facsimile edition by K. Ameln, Berlin, 1925 and in modern transcription by K. Escher and W. Lott, Berlin, 1926 (reprinted, Wiesbaden, 1969); the polyphonic compositions from this book were published in transcription by K. Ameln, Augsburg, 1926. A modern edition of the Glogauer *Liederbuch* is in *Das Erbe deutscher Musik, Series I,* Vols. 4 and 8, Leipzig, 1936–37.

German *Lieder* of the first half of the sixteenth century are in EP, Years 1–4, 7–8, 33; compositions by H. L. Hassler are published in DdT 2, 7, 24–25; DTB IV, 2; V, 2; XI, 1; EP, Year 15; Collected Works, C. R. Crosby, ed., Wiesbaden 1961– . Other late sixteenth-century *Lieder* are in EP, Years 23 (Regnart) and 25 (Eccard).

For modern editions of Spanish music of the sixteenth century see the various volumes of the series *Monumentos de la música española,* H. Anglès, general editor, 1941– ; also the series *Hispaniæ scholæ musica sacra,* F. Pedrell, ed., 1894–98; also the edition by Jesus Bal y Gay of the *Cancionero de Upsala,* Mexico, 1944, with historical essay on the polyphonic villancico by Isabel Pope. See also the series *Portugaliæ musica,* M. S. Kastner and others, eds., 1959– .

English sacred music of the early sixteenth century is published in *Tudor Church Music,* 10 vols., London 1923–29. The anonymous Mass *O quam suavis* (ca. 1500) has been edited by H. B. Collins and published by the Plainsong and Mediæval Music Society, 1927. See also the series *Early English Church Music* (London, 1963–), F. Ll. Harrison, ed., Vols. 1, 2, 4, 6, 7, 10, 12, 13; MB 15 (*Music of Scotland,* 1500–1700).

One of the English manuscripts containing secular music from the time of Henry VIII is edited by John Stevens in MB 18 (see also Stevens's book *Music and Poetry in the Early Tudor Court,* London, 1961); also from this period is the announced Vol. 35 of MB (*Early Tudor Songs and Carols*).

Organ pieces based on *cantus firmi* are contained in Y. Rokseth, ed., *Deux Livres d'orgue parus chez Pierre Attaingnant*, Paris, 1925; and D. Stevens, ed., *The Mulliner Book*, Vol. I of MB. Transcriptions of vocal pieces for organ are found in K. Jeppesen, ed., *Die italienische Orgelmusik am Anfang des Cinquecento*, Copenhagen, 1943; 2nd ed, 1960.

Luis Milan's *Libro de musica de vihuela de mano intitulado El Maestro*, Leo Schrade, ed., is in PAM, Year 2, Part 1 (reprinted, Hildesheim, 1967). For other examples of early Spanish lute music see G. Morphy, ed., *Les Luthistes espagnols du XVIe siècle*, Leipzig, 1902, 2 vols.; *Monumentos de la Música Española*, Vols. II, III, VII. Examples of Italian lute music are found in A. Ness, ed., *The Lute Music of Francesco Canova da Milano*, 2 vols., Cambridge, 1970 (Harvard Publications in Music 3, 4).

Improvisation in musical performance in the Renaissance and other periods is illustrated in an interesting collection of examples edited by Ernest T. Ferand, *Die Improvisation in Beispielen aus neun Jahrhunderten abendländischer Musik*, Cologne, 1956; see also examples in Imogene Horsley, "Improvised Embellishment in the Performance of Renaissance Polyphonic Music," *JAMS* 4 (1951), 3–19.

Examples of Italian madrigals and related forms of Italian secular vocal music are given in Vol. III of Einstein's *The Italian Madrigal*. Some of Monte's madrigals are in Vols. 6 and 19 of his collected works. A collected edition of Marenzio's works under the editorship of Alfred Einstein was begun in PAM, Years IV, Part 1, and VI. Books I–IV of Monteverdi's madrigals are the first four volumes in his collected works.

The original printed editions of Italian secular vocal works of the sixteenth and seventeenth centuries are listed, with their contents, in Emil Vogel's *Bibliothek der gedruckten weltlichen Vokalmusik Italiens aus den Jahren 1500–1700*, Berlin, 1892; a new edition of Vogel (Hildesheim, 1962; 2 vols.) incorporates the revisions and additions by Alfred Einstein originally published in *Notes of the Music Library Association* II, 3 (June 1945); IV, 3 (June 1947); V, 1 (December 1947); and V, 4 (September 1948).

English madrigals are published in E. H. Fellowes, ed., *The English Madrigal School*, London, 1913–24 (36 vols.); and ayres in Fellowes, *The English School of Lutenist Song Writers*, London, 1920–32 (16 vols.); second series, London, 1925–27 (16 vols.).

Other English music of this period is in MB 6, 22, 29; music by Anthony Holborne (d. 1602) in a collected edition, M. Kanasawa, ed., Cambridge, 1967– .

Examples in the Anthologies

(The following is a partial list; for additional examples, consult the anthologies.)

Netherlands composers 1520–*ca.* 1550: HAM, Nos. 106, 109, 113, 114, 125; EE, No. 15; WM, No. 27; GMB, No. 118.

National schools of the early sixteenth century: *Italy:* TEM, Nos. 20, 21; HAM, Nos. 94 (the use of an antiphon melody [see MM, p. 63] in this lauda is exceptional, as are likewise the antiphonal two-voice phrases and, to a lesser degree, the imitations in measures 29 to 37), 95; WM, Nos. 20–23; GMB, Nos. 69–72. *France:* HAM, No. 107; EE, No. 16. *Germany:* TEM, No. 32; HAM, Nos. 81, 82, 87, 93, 110; GMB, No. 87; Quodlibets: TEM, No. 31; HAM, No. 82; GMB, No. 111; Ode, GMB, No. 73. *Spain:* HAM, Nos 97, 98, 128; TEM, Nos. 19, 23; GMB, No. 96. *England:* HAM, Nos. 86, 112, 127.

Instrumental music:

Organ pieces on a *cantus firmus:* HAM, Nos. 100, 101, 120, 133.

Vocal compositions transcribed: GMB, Nos. 62b, 63a; from a later date, but illustrative of the technique of transcription, are the compositions in MM, Nos. 20, 21; HAM, No. 145.

Ricercare (imitative): HAM, Nos. 115, 116; GMB, Nos. 105, 113; EE, No. 22.

Ricercare (non-imitative): GMB, Nos. 94, 115.

Canzona: HAM, No. 118 (also compare No. 91).

Dances: HAM, No. 137; MM, No. 22; GMB, Nos. 90, 91; LSS, Nos. 46, 48.

Improvisatory pieces: HAM, Nos. 84, 99, 121; GMB, Nos. 63b, 93.

Variations: HAM, Nos. 122, 124, 134; compare No. 103 (ostinato pattern).

Secular vocal music of the late sixteenth century:

Italy: TEM, No. 33; MM, No. 27; HAM, Nos. 129–131, 155, 158, 161, 188; GMB, Nos. 98, 100, 101, 106, 140, 165 (the lower voices arbitrarily edited for instruments), 167; EE, Nos. 18, 20; WM, Nos. 38, 46, 47; LSS, Nos. 38, 39, 47, 60.

Spain: LSS, No. 40.

Germany and France: HAM, Nos. 138, 142, 145a, 146a, 147, 165, 168; GMB, Nos. 124, 125, 139, 141, 144, 152; LSS, Nos. 41–42, 45, 49.

England: TEM, No. 34; MM, No. 28; HAM, Nos. 159, 162, 163, 170; GMB, Nos. 145, 146; LSS, Nos. 56, 57.

Edward Lowinsky, *Secret Chromatic Art in the Netherlands Motet* brilliantly presents a theory which, although controversial in some details, is well established in essentials. A related article is Lowinsky's "The Goddess Fortuna in Music," *MQ* 29 (1943), 45–77.

For Further Reading

Alfred Einstein, *The Italian Madrigal,* Princeton, 1949 (3 vols.), is the definitive work on this subject, a rare combination of scholarly accuracy, wide knowledge, and attractive presentation. Chapter I deals with the frottola and other forerunners of the madrigal in Italy. On the interrelationship of various forms of secular vocal music in this period see James Haar, ed., *Chanson and Madrigal 1480–1530,* Cambridge, 1964.

Sebastian Virdung's *Musica getutscht* is published in facsimile in EP, Year 10 (Vol. 11), and also in a facsimile edition, Kassel, 1931.

The second volume of Praetorius's *Syntagma,* entitled *De organographia* (*Description of instruments*), has a supplement of woodcut illustrations which was published in 1620. There are two modern editions of this work: EP, Year 12 (Vol. 13); and an edition by W. Gurlitt, Kassel, 1929.

On improvisation in Renaissance music, see E. Ferand, " 'Sodaine and Unexpected' Music in the Renaissance," *MQ* 37 (1951), 10–27.

A detailed analysis of Cabezon's variations on the *Song of the Cavalier* is given in Robert U. Nelson's *The Technique of Variation,* Berkeley, 1948, 131–34.

For examples of Italian madrigal poetry in accurate but inelegant translation, see HAM, Vol. I, 251ff and MM, No. 27. On madrigal poetry in general, see Walter Rubsamen, *Literary Sources of Secular Music in Italy* (*ca. 1500*), Berkeley, 1943; Einstein, *The Italian Madrigal,* Vol. I, 166–212; and E. H. Fellowes, *English Madrigal Verse,* Oxford, 1929.

On the life and music of Gesualdo, see Cecil Gray and Philip Heseltine, *Carlo Gesualdo, Prince of Venosa, Musician and Murderer,* London, 1926; on Monteverdi: Leo Schrade, *Monteverdi, Creator of Modern Music,* New York, 1950.

For information about English music of the early sixteenth century: John Stevens, *Music & Poetry in the Early Tudor Court,* Lincoln, Neb., 1961; and Paul Doe, *Tallis,* London and New York, 1968; of the Elizabethan age: E. H. Fellowes, *The English Madrigal Composers,* Oxford, 1921; Peter Warlock (pseudonym for Philip Heseltine), *The English Ayre,* London,

1926; Ernest Walker, *A History of Music in England*, Oxford, 1952, Ch. IV; Walter L. Woodfill, *Musicians in English Society*, New York, 1969; Charles Kennedy Scott, *Madrigal Singing*, London, 1931; Joseph Kerman, *The Elizabethan Madrigal*, New York, 1962; David Brown, *Thomas Weelkes*, London, 1969; Philip Brett, "The English Consort Song" in *Proceedings of the Royal Musical Association* 88 (1961–62), 73–88; Denis Stevens, *Tudor Church Music*, London, 1966.

has been published in a modern edition, with the spelling brought up to date and the musical examples transcribed in modern notation, by R. Alec Harman, New York, 1952. See also SR Nos. 29 and 37 (SRRe Nos. 8 and 16) by Morley and Henry Peacham, respectively.

Chapter VIII (Pp. 252–92)

Music Collections (Modern editions and facsimiles)

Luther's *Deudsche Messe* (1526) is published in facsimíle by Bärenreiter, Kassel, 1934.

Johann Walther's *Geystliche gesangk Buchleyn* of 1524 is published in EP, Vol. 7 (Year 6); also as Vol. 1 of his *Sämtliche Werke*, Kassel/St. Louis, 1953– . Rhaw's collection of 1544, *Newe deudsche geistliche Gesenge CXXIII* is Vol. 34 of the DdT.

Michael Praetorius, *Gesamtausgabe der musikalischen Werke*, F. Blume, A. Mendelssohn, W. Gurlitt, eds., Wolfenbüttel, 1928–40 (20 vols.).

For church music of the Reformation in France and the Netherlands see: Pierre Pidoux, *Le Psautier Huguenot du XVIe siècle*, Basle, 1962 (2 vols.); Waldo Selden Pratt, *The Music of the French Psalter of 1562*, New York, 1939; H. Expert, ed., *Maîtres musiciens de la Renaissance française*, Vols. 2, 4, 6 (Goudimel), and 11, 21, 22, 23 (le Jeune); Sweelinck, *Werken*, Vols. 2–5.

A facsimile reprint of the *Bay Psalm Book* has been published by the Chicago University Press, 1956.

For church music by Orlando Gibbons see *Tudor Church Music*, Vol. 4; by Byrd, *The Collected Vocal Works of William Byrd*, E. H. Fellowes, ed., London, 1937–50. Church music by Byrd is published also in *Tudor Church Music*, Vols. 2, 7, and 9; by Weelkes in MB 23.

De Kerle's *Preces speciales* are in DTB, Year 26.

There are two collected editions of Palestrina's works: one, Theodor de Witt, F. X. Haberl, *et al.*, eds., Leipzig 1862–1907 (33 vols.); reprinted, Gregg Press, 1968. The other edition uses modern clefs and a different system of barring: R. Casimiri and L. Virgili, eds., Rome, 1939– . Palestrina's motet on which his Mass *Veni sponsa Christi* (MM, No. 24) is parodied is in Vol. 5 of the Haberl edition.

Victoria's complete works, F. Pedrell, ed., Leipzig 1902–13, 8 vols., reprinted 1965–66 by Gregg Press; *Opera omnia*, corrected and augmented, H. Anglès, ed., *Monumentos de la Música Española*, Vols. 25, 26, 30, 31. Works of Guerrero, M. Querol Gavaldá, ed., in the same series, Vols. 16, 19. Collected works of Pujol, Anglès, ed., Biblioteca de Cataluña, Dep. de Música, Vols. 3, 7.

Handl's *Moralia* (1596), A. B. Skei, ed., Madison, Wis., 1970, 2 vols; Collected Edition, D. Cvetko, ed., Ljubljana, 1966– ; DTOe, Vols. 12, 24, 30, 40, 48, 51, 52, 78.

For examples of Italian keyboard music from the sixteenth to the early eighteenth centuries see L. Torchi, ed., *L'arte musicale in Italia*, Milan, 1897–1908 (7 vols.), Vol. 3. Italian and other keyboard music of the sixteenth century in CEKM 2, 6 (John of Lublin), 9, 12, 14, 33, 34.

English keyboard music in MB: 1, The Mulliner Book (*ca.* 1560); 5, Tomkins; 14, 19, Bull; 20, O. Gibbons; 24, Farnaby; 27, 28, Byrd. Other editions: John Ward, ed., *The Dublin Virginal Manuscript* [*ca.* 1570], Wellesley, 1954; a facsimile ed. by O. Deutsch of *Parthenia* (the first printed collection [1611] of virginal music), Cambridge, 1942; *The Fitzwilliam Virginal Book,* Fuller-Maitland and B. Squire, eds., New York, Broude, 1949 (2 vols.); Byrd's *My Ladye Nevells Booke,* H. Andrews, ed., London, 1926; Byrd, *Forty-five Pieces for Keyboard Instruments,* S. D. Tuttle, ed., Paris, 1939; Gibbons, *Complete Keyboard Works,* M. Glyn, ed., London, 1922–25 (5 vols.).

Compositions by Andrea and Giovanni Gabrieli are published in the first two volumes of *Istituzioni e monumenti dell'arte musicale italiana,* Milan, 1931–41 (7 vols.). Collected edition of G. Gabrieli, CMM 12; of Merulo, CMM 51.

Music by H. Praetorius: DdT, Vol. 23. For Hassler, see Bibliography for Chapter VII.

Examples in the Anthologies

Protestant church music: *Lutheran:* TEM, No. 24; HAM, Nos. 108, 111, 167a; GMB, Nos. 77, 80, 84, 108–110, 123, 143, 159–162; WM, No. 35; LSS, Nos. 43–44. *Calvinist:* TEM, Nos. 25, 26; HAM, Nos. 126, 132; GMB, No. 142. *Anglican:* TEM, No. 27; HAM, Nos. 151, 169, 171, 172; LSS, No. 58.

Catholic church music of the late Renaissance: MM, Nos., 23–25; HAM, Nos. 139–141, 143, 144, 146b, 148–150, 152, 156, 164, 166; GMB, Nos. 120–122, 126–129, 131, 179; WM, No. 41; LSS, Nos. 50, 51–52.

Instrumental music of the late Renaissance: TEM, Nos. 29, 30, 35, 36; MM, No. 29; HAM, Nos. 135–137, 145b, 153, 154, 160b, 167b, 173–180; GMB, Nos. 134–138, 147–151, 153, 155–157, 174; EE, Nos. 22, 25, 26; WM, Nos. 39, 40, 43, 56, 57; LSS, No. 55.

The Venetian School: TEM, No. 28; HAM, Nos. 157, 173; GMB, Nos. 130, 148; EE, No. 19; LSS, Nos. 53, 54.

For Further Reading

SR, Nos. 28, 29, 34–36, 38, 40, 43–45. (SRRe 7, 8, 13–15, 17, 19, 22–24.)

The basic work on Lutheran church music is Friedrich Blume, *Geschichte der evangelischen Kirchenmusik,* Kassel, 1965; scheduled for publication in English translation.

On Spanish music of the period covered in this chapter see Robert Stevenson, *Spanish Cathedral Music in the Golden Age,* Berkeley, 1961.

Waldo S. Pratt, *The Music of the Pilgrims,* Boston, 1921, contains a description of the Ainsworth Psalter; see also Irving Lowens, "The Bay Psalm Book in 17th-Century New England," *JAMS* 8 (1955), 22–29.

Palestrina's music is subjected to detailed analysis in Knud Jeppesen's *The Style of Palestrina and the Dissonance,* London, 1927. Some counterpoint textbooks based on the Palestrina style are: R. O. Morris, *Contrapuntal Technique in the Sixteenth Century,* Oxford, 1922; K. Jeppesen, *Counterpoint,* tr. G. Haydon, New York, 1929; A. T. Merritt, *Sixteenth Century Polyphony,* Cambridge, 1939.

On the subject of choral sonority, see Archibald T. Davison, *The Technique of Choral Composition,* Cambridge, 1945, 20–31 *et passim.*

English translation of Thoinot-Arbeau's *Orchésographie* (1588): Jehan Tabourot, *Orchesography by Thoinot-Arbeau,* tr. M. S. Evans, New York, 1948, reprinted 1967.

On English music of the late sixteenth and early seventeenth centuries: M. C. Boyd, *Elizabethan Music and Musical Criticism,* 2nd ed., Philadelphia, 1962; Gretchen L. Finney, *Musical Backgrounds for English Literature 1580–1650,* New Brunswick, 1962; *id.,* "Music; a Book of Knowledge in Renaissance England," *Studies in the Renaissance* 6 (1959), 36–63 (a study of the interrelations of music with the sciences and with nature, as conceived by Renaissance writers, with many quotations); Joseph Kerman, "On William Byrd's *Emendemus in melius*," MQ 49 (1963), 431–49 (a model of musical analysis); E. H. Fellowes, *William Byrd*, London, 1948; *id., English Cathedral Music,* new ed., rev. J. A. Westrup, New York, 1969; D. Stevens, *Thomas Tomkins*, New York, 1967; see also W. Mellers, "John Bull and English Keyboard Music," MQ 40 (1954), 364–83, 548–71.

Egon Kenton, *Giovanni Gabrieli, Life and Works,* MSD 16.

Chapter IX (Pp. 293–340)

*Music
Collections
and modern
editions*

Music by Vincenzo Galilei is in Vol. 4 of the *Instituzioni e monumenti dell'arte musicale italiana,* and Vol. 8 of the *Smith College Music Archives.*

A facsimile edition of Peri's *Euridice* was published at Rome, 1934; a modern edition appears in Torchi, *L'arte musicale in Italia,* Vol. 6; Caccini's setting (incomplete) is in EP, Vol. 10 (Year 9).

Monteverdi, *Tutte le opere,* G. F. Malipiero, ed., Asolo, 1926–42 (16 vols.). The eight books of madrigals are Vols. 1–8 of this edition; other vocal chamber music, Vols. 9 and 10; *Orfeo* and the Lament from *Arianna,* Vol. 11; *Ulisse,* Vol. 12, *Poppea,* Vol. 13; sacred music, Vols. 14–16. Modern edition of *Orfeo,* Denis Stevens, ed., London, 1967. Facsimiles: *Orfeo,* Augsburg, 1927; *Poppea,* Milan, 1938.
1938.

Cavalli's *Giasone* (prologue and Act I only) EP, Vol. 12.

Cesti's *Orontea,* W. C. Holmes, ed., Wellesley, 1973.

Knud Jeppesen, ed., *La Flora,* Copenhagen, 1949 (3 vols.) is a good collection of Italian songs and cantatas from the seventeenth and eighteenth centuries.

H. Schütz, *Sämtliche Werke,* Spitta and Schering, eds., Leipzig, 1885–1927 (18 vols.); *Neue Ausgabe sämtlicher Werke* (performing editions), Kassel, 1955– ; *Stuttgarter Schützausgabe,* G. Graulich and P. Horn, eds., Stuttgart-Hohenheim, 1967– (projected 36 vols.).

Music by John Jenkins is in the Wellesley Edition, Vols. 1 and 10, and MB 26. Other English consort music of this period: MB 9, 21, 31, 32; vocal music, MB 2, 25, 33.

Benevoli's Salzburg Festival Mass is in the DTOe, Vol. 20 (Year 11, Part 1); other works of Benevoli, L. Feininger, ed., Societas universalis Sanctæ Ceciliæ, Rome, 1950– ; *Opera Omnia,* Rome, 1966– .

The works of Cererols are in Vols. 1–3 of the series *Mestres de l'Escalonia de Montserrat,* Montserrat, 1930–32.

Cavalieri's *Rappresentazione di animo e di corpo,* facsimile edition, Rome, 1912; selections in CDMI, Vol. 10.

Carissimi's oratorios are published by the Istituto Italiano per la Storia della Musica, L. Bianchi, ed., Rome, 1951– .

A collected edition of Frescobaldi's music, F. Germani, ed., Rome, 196– . The keyboard works have been edited by P. Pidoux, Kassel, 1950– (5 vols.); the ricercari, etc., by F. Boghen, Milan, 1918, 1922 (4 vols.).

Keyboard pieces by Froberger, G. Adler, ed., are in the DTOe, Vols. 8, 13, 21 (Years 4, Part 1; 6, Part 2; 10, Part 2).

Scheidt's collected works have been edited by G. Harms and C. Mahrenholz, Klecken, 1923– (13 vols.); the *Tabulatura nova* is in DdT, Vol. 1.

J. H. Schein's collected works have been edited by A. Prüfer, Leipzig,

1901–23 (7 vols.); reprinted 1970 by Gregg Press. New ed. by A. Adrio, Kassel, 1963– .

Gaultier's *Rhétorique des dieux* (facsimile and transcription) is in Vols. 6 and 7 of the *Publications de la Société française de musicologie,* Paris, 1932–33; also transcribed (complete) by O. Fleischer in his monograph on Gaultier in the *Vierteljahrsschrift für Musikwissenschaft* 2 (1886). See also A. Verchaly, ed., *Airs de Cour pour voix et luth (1603–43),* Paris, 1961; and D. Launay, ed., *Anthologie du motet latin . . . 1609–61,* Paris, 1963.

For Polish music of the seventeenth and eighteenth centuries, see the *Denkmäler altpolnischer Musik (Wydawnictwo Dawnej Muzyki Polskiej),* A. Chybiński, ed., Warsaw, 193?– (52 vols.).

Chambonnières, *Oeuvres complètes,* P. Brunold and A. Tessier, eds., Paris, 1925.

J. H. d'Anglebert, *Pièces de clavecin,* M. Roesgen-Champion, ed., Paris, 1934.

Louis Couperin, *Oeuvres complètes,* P. Brunold, ed., Paris, 1936; *Pièces de clavecin,* P. Brunold and T. Dart, eds., Monaco, 1959.

See also the relevant volumes in CEKM.

Examples in the Anthologies

The opera and its forerunners: MM, No. 31; HAM, Nos. 182, 186, 187, 206, 208, 209, 221, 230; GMB, Nos. 164, 166, 171, 175–178, 199–204; EE, No. 24; WM, No. 48; LSS, Nos. 59, 62, 63.

Vocal chamber music: MM, No. 30; HAM, Nos. 184, 189, 203–205; GMB, Nos. 170, 172, 173, 187, 193, 194, 197; WM, Nos. 49, 53, 65, 66.

Catholic church music and oratorio: TEM, No. 37; MM, No. 32; HAM, Nos. 183, 185, 207; GMB, Nos. 168, 169, 180, 198; WM, No. 52; LSS, Nos. 61, 68.

Lutheran church music in Germany: TEM, No. 38; MM, No. 33; HAM, Nos. 201, 202, 213; GMB, Nos. 188–192; EE, No. 27; LSS, No. 64.

Instrumental music: TEM, No. 39; MM, Nos. 26, 34, 35; HAM, Nos. 190a, 191–199, 210–212, 215–217, 229, 230, 256; GMB, Nos. 153, 155–158, 182–185, 196, 205, 207 (compare 206), 215, 216, 218; EE, No. 26; WM, Nos. 54–56, 63, 64; LSS, Nos. 65, 66, 67.

For Further Reading

SR, Nos. 46–56 (SRB 1–11).

Manfred F. Bukofzer, *Music in the Baroque Era,* New York, 1947. A comprehensive survey of the entire Baroque, with music examples and bibliographies.

On the interrelation of music and the other arts in general, see Curt Sachs, *The Commonwealth of Art,* New York, 1946; in the Baroque particularly, Suzanne Clercx, *Le Baroque et la musique,* Bruxelles, 1948.

Frank Arnold's *The Art of Accompaniment from a Thorough-Bass as Practiced in the XVIIth and XVIIIth Centuries,* New York, 1965, is the basic work on this subject, with copious quotations and examples from the sources. A very useful introduction, both scholarly and practical, is Peter F. Williams, *Figured Bass Accompaniment,* Edinburgh and Chicago, 1970, 2 vols. See also G. J. Buelow, *Thorough-Bass Accompaniment according to Johann David Heinichen,* Berkeley, 1966; and Francesco Gasparini [1668–1727], *L'armonico pratico al cimbalo* [1708], tr. and ed. by F. S. Stillings and D. Burrows as *The Practical Harmonist at the Harpsichord,* New Haven, 1963.

On the opera, in the Baroque and later periods, see D. J. Grout, *A Short History of Opera,* New York, 1965, 2nd edition; Joseph Kerman, *Opera as Drama,* New York, 1956. Egon Wellesz, *Essays on Opera,* London, 1950, deals for the most part with seventeenth-century works.

On the Florentine Camerata and Italian vocal chamber music, see Claude Palisca, "Girolamo Mei," *MQ* 40 (1954), 1–20; *idem, Girolamo Mei, Letters on Ancient and Modern Music,* American Institute of Musicology, 1960; Nino Pirrotta, "Temperaments and Tendencies in the Florentine Camerata," *MQ* 40 (1954), 169–89; Nigel Fortune, "Italian Secular Monody from 1600 to 1635; an Introductory Survey," *MQ* 39 (1953), 171–95. Putnam Aldrich, *Rhythm in Seventeenth-Century Monody,* New York, 1966.

Other aspects of Baroque music are treated in Curt Sachs, *A World History of the Dance,* New York, 1937; Leo Schrade, *Monteverdi,* New York, 1950; D. Arnold and N. Fortune, eds., *The Monteverdi Companion,* New York, 1968; Alan Curtis, *Sweelinck's Keyboard Music.* Leiden, 1969; R. Jackson, "On Frescobaldi's Chromaticism," MQ 57 (1971), 255–69; H. J. Moser, *Heinrich Schütz,* C. F. Pfatteicher, tr., St. Louis, 1959; D. Boyden, *The History of Violin Playing from Its Origins to 1761,* London, 1965; Gotthold Frotscher, *Geschichte des Orgel-Spiels und der Orgel-Komposition,* Berlin, 1935–36 (2 vols.); William S. Newman, *The Sonata in the Baroque Era,* Chapel Hill, 1959. On the curious and complicated history of the chaconne, passacaglia, and related patterns, see articles by Thomas Walker in JAMS 21 (1968), 300–20 and by Richard Hudson in JAMS 23 (1970), 302–14, MD 25 (1971), 199–222, and JAMS 24 (1971), 364–94.

Chapter X (Pp. 341–73)

Music Collections and modern editions

One opera of Steffani (*Alarico,* 1687) is published in the DTB, Vol. 11, Part 2; excerpts from others, DTB, Vol. 12, Part 1; *Enrico Leone,* Th. Werner, ed., is in *Musikalische Denkwürdigkeiten,* Hanover, 1926, Vol. I; *Tassilone,* G. Croll, ed., is in *Denkmäler rheinischer Musik,* Düsseldorf, 1958, Vol. 8.

A. Scarlatti's oratorios are in course of publication, L. Bianchi, ed., Rome, 1965– ; the operas, D. J. Grout and others, eds., Cambridge, 1972– .

There is a collected edition (incomplete) of the works of Lully, H. Prunières, ed., Paris, 1930–39 (10 vols.); reprinted, New York, 1966. Operas of Lully and other composers, mostly French, of the seventeenth and eighteenth centuries are published in the series *Les Chefs d'Oeuvre classiques de l'opéra français,* Leipzig, *ca.* 1880 (40 vols.); reprinted, New York, 196– .

Examples of French opera overtures may be found in MM, No. 36 and HAM, Nos. 223 and 224; examples of the same form in other contexts are EE, No. 30 and GMB, Nos. 278 and 292. Some other examples are: J. S. Bach, the four Suites (*Ouvertures*) for orchestra, and the opening movements of the cantatas Nos. 61, 97, 119; Handel, Overture to *Messiah* and first movements of the *Concerti Grossi* Nos. 10 and 12.

The works of Purcell are published in a complete edition of 32 volumes, London 1878– . Vols. 1–26, revised ed., London, 1961– . *Dido and Aeneas* is Vol. 3; *Ode for St. Cecilia's Day,* Vol. 8. For study of Purcell's theatre music the complete scores of *Dioclesian* (Vol. 9; particularly the masque in the fifth act), *King Arthur* (Vol. 26), and *The Fairy Queen* (Vol. 12) are recommended.

The following examples of the passacaglia form in Baroque music may be compared with Purcell's aria "When I am laid in earth" from *Dido and Aeneas:* HAM, Nos. 222, 238; GMB, Nos. 230, 231, 233; and the "Crucifixus" from Bach's *Mass in B Minor.*

Modern editions of Keiser's operas are printed in Vol. 6 of the supplement to the Händelgesellschaft edition of Handel's works, F. Chrysander, ed., Leipzig, 1858–94 (*Octavia,* 1705); also in DdT, Vol. 37/38 (*Croesus,* 1710 and 1732; *L'inganno fedele,* 1714, incomplete); and EP, Vol. 18, Year 21/22 (*Der lächerliche Prinz Jodelet,* 1726).

G. C. Schürmann's opera *Ludovicus Pius* (1726) is published (incomplete) in EP, Vol. 17 (Year 19/20).

J. J. Fux, *Sämtliche Werke,* H. Federhofer, ed., Kassel, 1959– .

Some examples of vocal chamber duets in the manner of Steffani are the "Christe eleison" from Bach's *Mass in B Minor;* and the duets in Vol. 32 of the Händelgesellschaft edition of the works of Handel.

Some modern editions of Italian vocal chamber music of the seventeenth and eighteenth centuries are: CDMI, Vols. 2 (G. B. Bassani), 17 (Marcello), 30 (A. Scarlatti); CMI, Vol. 2 (Marcello); K. Jeppeson, ed., *La Flora;* H. Riemann, ed., *Kantaten Frühling, 1633–1682,* Leipzig, no date (2 vols.); H. Riemann, ed., *Ausgewählte Kammer-Kantaten der Zeit um 1700,* Leipzig, no date, 6 numbers. For others, see Bukofzer, *Music in the Baroque Era,* 462–63.

Krieger's *Neue Arien* are in DdT, Vol. 19.

Selections from the musical works of the Emperors Ferdinand III (*reg.* 1637–57), Leopold I (1658–1705), and Joseph I (1705–11) are published in an edition by G. Adler, Vienna, 1892–93 (2 vols.); see also *Vierteljahrsschrift für Musikwissenschaft* 8 (1892), 252–74.

Modern editions of south German Catholic church music are printed in the DTOe, Vols. 1, 3, 26, 46, 49, 59, 80 (Years 1,1; 2,1; 13,1; 23,1; 25,1; 30,1; 43,1) and in DdT, Vols. 20, 49/50, 60.

Marcello's oratorio *Gioaz* is Vol. 8 of CMI.

François Couperin, *Oeuvres complètes,* Paris, 1932–33 (12 vols); M. A. Charpentier, *Oeuvres,* G. Lambert, ed., Paris, 1948–53, (15 vols.).

John Blow's Coronation Anthems are in MB 7; Pelham Humfrey's church music in MB 34.

The seven volumes of *Dietrich Buxtehudes Werke,* Klecken, 1925–37, contain only vocal works. The cantata *Wachet auf* to which reference is made in the text is in Vol. 6 of this edition. (There is a different setting by Buxtehude of these words in DdT, Vol. 14, 139.)

Zachow's cantatas are printed in Vol. 21/22 of the DdT. For other examples of Lutheran Church music in the seventeenth and eighteenth centuries see *Das Erbe deutscher Musik, Series I* (Reichsdenkmale), Vols. 1, 2, 45/46, 48; and Series II (Landschaftsdenkmale), Schleswig-Holstein, Vol. 4. Also, DdT, Vols. 3, 6, 14, 17 (*Passions* of Theile and Sebastiani), 28, 40, 45, 48, 56, 58, 59; and DTB, Year 6,1.

Examples in the Anthologies

Opera: TEM, Nos. 44, 46; MM, No. 36; HAM, Nos. 222–225, 241, 243, 244, 255, 267, 281; GMB, Nos. 195, 222–224, 226, 227, 231, 232, 233, 234, 236, 247, 250, 258, 259, 261, 266, 268–270, 272, 274, 293; EE, No. 30; LSS, Nos. 69, 71, 72, 78–79.

Cantata and song: TEM, No. 49; HAM, Nos. 228, 251, 258, 273 (by Francesco Durante, 1684–1755; a *tour de force* of chromatic harmonies and remote modulations; compare also GMB, No. 197 and TEM, No. 49); GMB, Nos. 209, 210, 217, 235, 242, 248, 254, 256, 260, 262, 287; EE, No. 28; LSS, No. 73.

Roman Catholic and Anglican church music: TEM, Nos. 42, 43; HAM, Nos. 218, 226, 242, 257, 266, 268; GMB, Nos. 225, 230, 246, 271, 273, 275, 310; LSS, Nos. 70, 74.

Lutheran church music: HAM, Nos. 213, 214, 235, 272; GMB, Nos. 208, 211, 212, 267, 290.

For
Further
Reading

SR, Nos. 57–64 (SRB, Nos. 12–19).

Beekman C. Cannon, *Johann Mattheson, Spectator in Music,* New Haven, 1947, an account of the famous theorist of the early eighteenth century, a contemporary of Bach and Handel. Mattheson's *Der vollkommene Capellmeister* [*The Perfect Music Director*] of 1739 has been published in a facsimile edition, Kassel, 1954.

The *Musikalisches Lexikon* [*Encyclopedia of Music;* 1732] by Johann Gottfried Walther (1684–1748) is also published in facsimile, Kassel, 1953.

H. Wiley Hitchcock, "The Latin Oratorios of Marc-Antoine Charpentier," *MQ* 41 (1955), 41–65, surveys the historical background and style of Charpentier's work and gives a catalogue of his oratorios, as well as his table of the "key-feelings" of eighteen major and minor keys.

Wilfred Mellers, *François Couperin and the French Classical Tradition,* New York, 1968.

On English opera of this period the basic work is E. J. Dent, *Foundations of English Opera,* New York, 1965. On Venetian opera in the second half of the seventeenth century, see Simon Towneley Worsthorne, *Venetian Opera in the Seventeenth Century,* Oxford, 1954.

On Scarlatti: E. J. Dent, *Alessandro Scarlatti,* second impression, London, 1960.

On Purcell: J. A. Westrup, *Purcell,* New York, 1962; F. B. Zimmerman, *Henry Purcell, His Life and Times,* London, 1967; *id., Henry Purcell, an Analytical Catalogue of His Music,* New York, 1963; Robert E. Moore, *Henry Purcell and the Restoration Theatre,* Cambridge, 1961.

The books listed in the Appendix to Chapter IX should also be consulted for supplementary reading for the material in Chapter X.

Chapter XI (Pp. 374–401)

Music
Collections
and modern
editions

Collected editions (see also those listed under Chapter X):

Georg Böhm, *Sämtliche Werke,* J. Wolgast, ed., Leipzig, 1927, 1932, 2 vols.; G. Wolgast, ed., Wiesbaden, n.d., 4 vols.

Dietrich Buxtehude, *Werke,* W. Gurlitt and others, eds., Klecken, 1925–37; 7 vols., vocal works only. *Sämtliche Orgelwerke,* J. Hedar, ed., Copenhagen, 1952, 4 vols.

Juan Cabanilles, *Opera omnia,* H. Anglès, ed., Barcelona, 1927–36, 3 vols.

Arcangelo Corelli, *Oeuvres,* J. Joachim and F. Chrysander, eds., London, 1888–91, 5 vols.; reprinted 1952.

Georg Philip Telemann, *Musikalische Werke,* Kassel and Basel, 1950– .

J. C. F. Fischer, collected keyboard works, Leipzig, 1901; reprinted, New York, 1965.

Music in other modern collections:

A selection of chorale preludes by contemporaries of J. S. Bach is given in Vol. 9 of *Das Erbe deutscher Musik,* Series I (Reichsdenkmale). See also: DdT, Vols. 26, 27; DTB, Year 2,2; DTOe, Vols. 17, 58 (Years 8,2 and 29,2); Karl Straube, ed., *Choralvorspiele alter Meister,* Edition Peters No. 3048, and *Alte Meister des Orgelspiels,* Edition Peters No. 4301a-b (2 vols.); for other collections, see list in Bukofzer, *Music in the Baroque Era,* 463–64.

French composers of organ music are represented in Alexandre Guilmant, ed., *Archives des maîtres de l'orgue,* Paris, 1898–1910 (10 vols.).

Keyboard works by Belgian composers are in the *Monumenta musicæ belgicæ,* Antwerp, 1932– . See also the relevant volumes of CEKM.

Compositions for lute by E. Reusner and S. L. Weiss are published in *Das Erbe deutscher Musik,* Series I (Reichsdenkmale), Vol. 12; see also DTOe, Vols. 50 (Year 25,2) and 84.

Instrumental ensemble works by G. B. Vitali, G. B. Bassani, and other Italian composers are in Vol. 7 of Torchi's *L'arte musicale in Italia*. Sonatas by T. A. Vitali are given in *Smith College Music Archives*, Vol. 12, Northampton, 1954.

J. J. Walther's *Scherzi* are published in Vol. 17 of *Das Erbe deutscher Musik*, Series I.

Some of Biber's works are published in the DTOe: Vol. 11 (Year 5,2), the violin sonatas of 1681; Vol. 25 (Year 12,2), the "Biblical" violin sonatas (the first printing was faulty because the composer's *scordatura* was misread; separate sheets were issued later to correct the mistakes, but not all libraries have these); Vol. 49 (Year 25,1), Masses; and Vol. 59 (Year 30,1), Requiem.

The twelve sonatas of Geminiani's Op. 1 (1716), R. L. Finney, ed., are in Vol. 1 of the *Smith College Music Archives*, Northampton, 1935.

Violin sonatas by J. M. Leclair are in EP, Vol. 27 (Year 31); six sonatas were published by Oiseau-Lyre, 1952.

Rosenmüller's *Sonate da camera* are in DdT, Vol. 18.

Muffat's *Florilegium* is published in the DTOe, Vols. 2 and 4 (Years 1,2 and 2,2); Fischer's *Journal de Printemps* is in the DdT, Vol. 10, together with another collection of orchestral suites, the *Zodiacus musicus Part I* (1698) of J. A. Schmicorer. Suites by Fux (called *Ouverture, Sinfonia,* or *Serenada*) are found in his *Concentus musico-instrumentalis* (1701) printed in DTOe, Vol. 47 (Year 23,2); suites by Telemann (*Musique de Table,* 1733) in DdT, Vol. 61/62.

Concertos and other instrumental ensemble pieces by Georg Muffat are in the DTOe, Vols. 23 (Year 11,2) and 89. See also DdT, Vol. 29/30.

Selections from dall'Abaco's sonatas and concertos are published in the DTB, Years 1 and 9,1.

Music for organ: TEM, No. 41; MM, No. 37; HAM, Nos. 190b,c,d, 215, 231, 234, 237, 239, 247, 249a,b, 251; GMB, Nos. 243, 249, 263, 265, 291; EE, No. 35. *Examples in the Anthologies*

Music for lute, harpsichord, and clavichord: TEM, No. 40; MM, Nos. 38, 40; HAM, Nos. 212, 232, 233, 236, 240, 248, 250, 261, 265a, 265b, 280; GMB, Nos. 215, 216, 218, 244, 253, 264; LSS, Nos. 82, 83. The keyboard suite by J. K. F. Fischer in HAM, No. 248 has for its second movement a "passacaille"; in this passacaglia the theme, instead of being continuously repeated, recurs like a refrain, with contrasting interludes. The movement thus assumes the form of a rondeau (compare HAM, No. 265b). The French clavecinists used the terms *chaconne* or *passacaglia* for pieces of this kind (compare HAM, No. 212; HAM, No. 240 combines the regular passacaglia with the rondeau form).

Solo sonatas with basso continuo: HAM, Nos. 219, 238, 252, 253, 275, 278; GMB, Nos. 238, 245, 294, 295; EE, No. 32; LSS, No. 75.

Trio sonatas: MM, No. 39; HAM, Nos. 245, 263, 269; GMB, Nos. 240, 241; EE, No. 29; LSS, No. 76.

Works for larger ensembles: TEM, No. 45 (chaconne); HAM, Nos. 220, 223; GMB, Nos. 214, 220, 221, 224, 233, 252.

Orchestral suites and concertos: HAM, Nos. 246, 260; GMB, Nos. 251, 257, 277.

Claudio Sartori, *Bibliografia della musica strumentale italiana stampata in Italia fino al 1700*, Florence, 1952–68, 2 vols. *For Further Reading*

J. J. Fux, *Gradus ad Parnassum* (facsimile), New York, 1966 (Monuments of Music and Music Literature in Facsimile, Ser. 2, No. 24); *The Study of Counterpoint from Johann Joseph Fux's Gradus ad Parnassum*, rev. ed., tr. and ed. A. Mann and J. Edmunds, New York, 1965.

Francesco Geminiani, *Art of Playing on the Violin* (facsimile), D. Boyden, ed., London, 1952; *id., A Treatise of Good Taste in the Art of Musick* (facsimile), with introd. by R. Donington, New York, 1969.

Henry Mishkin, "The Solo Violin Sonata of the Bologna School," *MQ* 29 (1943), 92–112.

Ernst H. Meyer, *English Chamber Music,* 2nd ed., London, 1951.

Marc Pincherle, *Corelli et son temps,* Paris, 1954; H. E. M. Russell, tr., *Corelli, His Life, His Music,* New York, 1968.

William Klenz, *Giovanni Maria Bononcini, a Chapter in Baroque Instrumental Music,* Durham, 1962.

Arthur Hutchings, *The Baroque Concerto,* 2nd ed., London, 1963.

On the history of the Sarabande, see articles by Robert Stevenson in *Inter-American Music Bulletin* Nos. 30 (July, 1962) and 33 (January, 1963); also articles by T. Walker and R. Hudson referred to under Ch. IX.

Chapter XII (Pp. 402–46)

Music Collected editions

Very little of Vivaldi's vocal music, and only about half of his instrumental music, is available in modern editions. A collected edition, A. Fanna, ed., Rome, 1947– ; thematic catalogue of the instrumental works by A. Fanna, Milan, 1968. There are several other thematic catalogues, including one which constitutes the second volume of M. Pincherle, *Vivaldi,* Paris, 1948.

Rameau, *Oeuvres complètes,* C. Saint-Saens, ed., Paris, 1896–1924; 18 vols. in 21; reprinted, New York, 1968. A luxurious edition, but despite the title not complete; a new edition is projected.

Johann Sebastian Bach, *Werke,* Leipzig, 1851–99 and supplementary volume, 1926; 61 vols. in 47 Jahrgänge. Reprinted (except Jg. 47) Ann Arbor, 1947; reprinted by Gregg Press, 1968; by Kalmus (in miniature format), 1969. *Neue Ausgabe sämtlicher Werke,* Kassel and Basel, 1954– . *Faksimile-Reihe Bachser Werke und Schriftstücke,* Leipzig, 1955– . *Mass in B minor,* A. Dürr, ed., Kassel and New York, 1965 (facsimile and commentary). *Cantata No. 4, Christ lag in Todesbanden,* G. Herz, ed., New York, 1967. *Cantata No. 140, Wachet auf,* G. Herz, ed., New York, 1972; contains table showing the new chronology of Bach's vocal music.

Wolfgang Schmieder, ed., *Thematisch-systematisches Verzeichnis der musikalischen Werke von Johann Sebastian Bach (BWV),* Leipzig, 1950. A complete systematic-thematic index of Bach's works, with references to the Bach Society edition and also to other standard modern editions.

Georg Friedrich Händel, *Werke,* F. Chrysander, ed., Leipzig, 1858–1903. (Vols. 1–48 & 50–94 and six vols. of supplements; vols. 49 and 95–96 never appeared); reprinted in 1966 by Gregg Press. *Hallische Händel-Ausgabe,* M. Schneider and R. Steglich, eds., Kassel, 1955– .

Examples in the Anthologies

Vivaldi: TEM, No. 47; HAM, No. 270; GMB, No. 276; LSS, No. 77.
Rameau: MM, No. 41; HAM, Nos. 276, 277; GMB, Nos. 296, 297.
Bach: MM, Nos. 46–50; HAM, No. 190d; GMB, Nos. 283–285, 286[?]; EE, No. 33; LSS, Nos. 84, 85, 86.
Handel: MM, Nos. 43–45; GMB, Nos. 278–280; LSS, Nos. 80, 81.

For Further Reading

Vivaldi: Marc Pincherle, *Antonio Vivaldi et la musique instrumentale,* Paris, 1948; reprinted, New York, 1968; some of the material appears in Pincherle's article, "Vivaldi and the *Ospitali* of Venice," *MQ* 24 (1938), 300–12. The best comprehensive study is Walter Kolneder, *Vivaldi,* B.

Hopkins, tr., Berkeley, 1971. The general structure of the Vivaldi concerto is so clearly reflected in J. J. Quantz's *Essay on How to Play the Flute* of 1752 (see SR, 583–88 or SRC, 9–14) that we may suppose the author to have had Vivaldi's works in mind as a model.

Rameau: Complete Theoretical Writings, E. Jacobi, ed., 6 vols. (AIM, Series Misc. 3); *Treatise on Harmony*, tr. with introduction and notes by P. Gossett, New York, 1971. The best comprehensive study in English is Cuthbert Girdlestone, *Jean-Philippe Rameau, His Life and Work*, New York, 1969. For background on Rameau, read Georges Cucuel, *La Pouplinière et la musique de chambre au XVIIIe siècle*, Paris, 1913; a detailed stylistic study of Rameau's operas is Paul-Marie Masson, *L'Opéra de Rameau*, Paris, 1930.

Bach: The standard work is Philipp Spitta, *Johann Sebastian Bach*, 4th ed., Leipzig, 1930 (2 vols.). An English translation in three volumes, published at London in 1889, has been reissued: *Johann Sebastian Bach, His Work and Influence on the Music of Germany*, New York, 1951. A good general study is Karl Geiringer, *Johann Sebastian Bach; the Culmination of an Epoch*, New York, 1966.

An invaluable book is Hans David and Arthur Mendel, *The Bach Reader*, New York, 1966; it contains (in English translation) "all the surviving sources of any importance from which our knowledge of Bach's life and reputation has been drawn," as well as essays on Bach's life and music and on the history of his fame.

A detailed account of Bach's life is given in Charles Sanford Terry, *Bach, a Biography*, London, 1928; the same author's *Bach, the Historical Approach* is semipopular in style but sound in substance. Albert Schweitzer, *J. S. Bach*, first published in 1908 (English translation, New York, 1966) has been an influential book, but its historical conclusions and treatment of Bach's musical symbolism can no longer be accepted uncritically.

Handel: The essential books are: P. H. Lang, *George Frideric Handel*, New York, 1966; and O. E. Deutsch, *Handel, a Documentary Biography*, New York, 1954, a "collection of all known and many hitherto unknown or overlooked documents referring to Handel's life"; it contains also a large bibliography.

The long chapter entitled "Origin of the Italian Opera in England and its Progress There during the Present Century" in Burney's *General History of Music* (Book IV, Ch. 6) includes a detailed account of Handel's operas in London and many observations on the music. This chapter is found in the second edition of Burney's work, F. Mercer, ed., New York, 1935 (2 vols.), II, 651–904.

On *Messiah*, see Robert Manson Myers, *Handel's Messiah, a Touchstone of Taste*, New York, 1948; and Jens Peter Larsen, *Handel's Messiah; Origins, Composition, Sources*, New York, 1972. See also Winton Dean, *Handel's Dramatic Oratorios and Masques*, London, 1959; id., *Handel and the Opera Seria*, Berkeley, 1969.

Chapter XIII (Pp. 447–75)

A collected edition of Domenico Scarlatti's sonatas was made by A. Longo, New York, 1947–51 (10 vols. and supplementary vol.). A representative selection in a superior edition by Ralph Kirkpatrick is published by G. Schirmer, New York (2 vols.); *Complete Keyboard Works*, ed. in facsimile by Ralph Kirkpatrick, 18 vols., New York, 1971– .

Music Collections and modern editions

For Italian keyboard music, see CDMI, Vols. 8, 18, 22, 25, 27, 28, 29; and CMI, Vols. 3, 4, 12, 13.

A valuable selection of eighteenth- and early nineteenth-century compositions is *Thirteen Keyboard Sonatas*, ed. with critical commentaries by William S. Newman, Chapel Hill, 1947.

Pergolesi's collected works: *Opera omnia*, F. Caffarelli, ed., Rome, 1939–42, 26 vols. in 5. Vocal works have the accompaniments in piano score with instrumental cues. This edition contains some works that have since been rejected as spurious; sources are not named, and the editing is sometimes questionable. For study of a complete *opera seria*, Pergolesi's *Olimpiade* (1735; libretto by Metastasio) is suggested (Vol. 24 of this edition).

A selection of compositions by ancestors and descendants of J. S. Bach is found in Karl Geiringer, ed., *Music of the Bach Family,* Cambridge, 1955.

Selections from the works of Schobert are published in the DdT, Vol. 39.

Symphonies by Mannheim composers are found in DTB, Vols. 3,1; 7,2; and 8,2; a reprint of the music in two volumes entitled *Mannheim Symphonists* is published by Broude Bros., New York, 1956. Mannheim chamber music is in DTB, Vols. 15 and 16. Symphonies by Viennese composers are in DTOe, Vols. 31 and 39 (Years 15,2 and 19,2); North German symphonies, DdT, Vols. 51, 52; symphonies by C. P. E. Bach, *Das Erbe deutscher Musik,* Series I, Vol. 18; chamber and symphonic music by Johann Christian Bach, *id.,* Vols. 3, 30. Instrumental works of Michael Haydn, DTOe, Vol. 29 (Year 14,2); of Dittersdorf, DTOe, Vol. 81 (Year 43,2). *The Symphonies of G. B. Sammartini,* B. Churgin, ed., Cambridge, 1968–   .

Graun's *Montezuma* is published in DdT, Vol. 15; Jommelli's *Fetonte* in DdT, Vols. 32/33; selections from Traetta's operas in DTB, Vols. 14,1 and 17; Hasse's *Arminio* is in *Das Erbe deutscher Musik*, Series I, Vols. 27/28.

Gluck's principal operas, beginning with *Orfeo,* were published in a sumptuous edition by J. Pelletan and others, Leipzig, 1873–96 (7 vols.); a new edition of the complete works, R. Gerber, ed., Kassel and Basel, 1951–   . See also DTB, Vol. 14,2; and DTOe, Vols. 44a, 60, 82 (Years 21,2, 30,2, 44).

Italian comic operas are published in CDMI, Vols. 13 (Galuppi) and 20 (Paisiello); and in CMI, Vol. 7 (Piccinni).

A collected edition of the works of Grétry was published by the Belgian government, Leipzig, 1884–1936 (49 vols.); reprint, New York, 197-.

German singspiels are available in modern editions as follows: Viennese: *Die Bergknappen (The Miners),* by Ignaz Umlauf (1746–96), DTOe, Vol. 36 (Year 18,1); *Der Dorfbarbier (The Village Barber),* by Johann Schenk (1753–1836), DTOe, Vol. 48 (Year 24). See also the songs in DTOe, Vol. 64 (Year 33,1). North German: *Der Jahrmarkt (The Fair),* by Georg Benda (1722–95), DdT, Vol. 64.

The second part of Vol. 1 of Max Friedländer's *Das deutsche Lied im 18. Jahrhundert,* Stuttgart 1902, contains 236 songs, mostly from eighteenth-century collections. See also DTOe, Vols. 54 and 79 (Years 37,2 and 42,2); and DdT, Vols. 35/36 (Sperontes) and 57.

Viennese church music of the late eighteenth century is published in DTOe, Vols. 62 and 83 (Years 33,1 and 45). Hasse's oratorio, *The Conversion of St. Augustine,* is in DdT, Vol. 20; Jommelli's *Passione di Gesù Cristo* is in CDMI, Vol. 15.

*Examples
in the
Anthologies*

For one aspect of the contrast between Baroque and Classic, compare the complex phrase structure of Vivaldi's Concerto Grosso in A minor (HAM, No. 270) with the regular two- and four-measure phrases of Stamitz's Symphony in D (HAM, No. 294).

Examples of Classical melodic styles: *Chord outlining,* GMB, No. 304, Pt. 2; HAM, Nos. 294, 304. *Parlando,* HAM, No. 284 (compare No. 287). *Singing allegro,* HAM, No. 303. *Momentary shifts to minor,* GMB, Nos. 282 (Pt. 2) and 303. For the *Alberti bass,* see HAM, No. 304.

Sonatas by Domenico Scarlatti are in MM, No. 42; HAM, No. 274; GMB, No. 282. The sonata movement in F-sharp minor by Manuel Blasco de Nebra, HAM, No. 308, has some of the qualities of rhythmic alertness, coloristic dissonances, and use of repeated phrases characteristic of Scarlatti.

HAM, No. 284, is the last movement of a sonata by Giovanni Platti (1690–1763), composed probably about 1740. On the basis of its resemblance to the concerto form, this movement may be analyzed as follows (the sign ≅ means "equivalent to"):

Ritornello I (C): measures 1–12
Solo I (C-G): 12–43
    Sequential extension leading to V of G: 14–19
    V of G: 21–28
    Cadential closing section, reiterated I-V-I G*: 29–43.
Ritornello II (G): 44–45 (≅ 1–12)
Solo II (G-a); 55–82
    Sequential extension in a: 60–66 (motive from m. 25) 66–74 ≅ 35–43
      with interrupted cadence in a
    Close in a: 74–82 (motives in 75–80 from 25–28)
Ritornello III (C) = Ritornello I (1–12): 83–94
Solo III (C): 94–124 (≅ 12–43)
    Sequential extension leading to V of C: 95–101 (≅ 14–19)
    V of C: 102–9 (≅ 21–28)
    Cadential closing section I-V-I in C: 110–124 (≅ 29–43)
Ritornello IV (C), shortened (first motive of Ritornello I, with cadential
    phrase): 124–130
* Grouping of measures 29–43: 29–31 32–34 35–36 37–38 39 40 41–43

If we prefer to think of this piece in terms of Classical sonata-form we may subdivide it in this way:

Exposition: 1–43
    First theme group in C (two themes): 1–12
    Transition to dominant (three [or two] themes): 12–29
    Second theme group in G (two themes): 29–43
First theme group in G: 44–55
"Development" section: 55–82
Recapitulation: 83–124, and cadential close: 124–130

The sonata movement by G. M. P. Rutini (1723–97) printed in HAM, No. 302, which was written about 1760, sounds rather like the gigue finale of a Baroque suite, although the consistent two-voice homophonic texture, the many repeated phrases, and the Alberti bass are Rococo features. There is a very slight thematic contrast between the opening material and what might be called the second theme (measures 9 ff.). The section after the double bar begins with the opening material in the dominant key. There is no recapitulation of this material in the tonic, but the closing eight measures of both sections are identical except in key.

The two movements of a sonata by Tartini in GMB, No. 295, are from an early, not really representative work. The *Presto assai* in HAM, No. 275, from a set of twelve sonatas published at Rome in 1745, though typical in form and texture for its period, is of little interest as far as its musical content is concerned. A more adequate idea of Tartini's work can be obtained from the two concertos published in the *Smith College Music Archives,* Vol. 9, Northampton, 1948.

Additional examples:

The *empfindsamer Stil;* C. P. E. Bach: HAM, Nos. 288, 289, 296, 297; GMB, Nos. 303, 304 (Pt. 1).

Symphony and chamber music: HAM, Nos. 271, 283, 294, 295, 304, 307; GMB, Nos. 305–307; EE, No. 31. (*Note:* the edition from which HAM No. 283 is taken has added a second violin part to Sammartini's original score and rewritten the recapitulation so as to make it conform to the exposition.)

Italian *opera seria:* HAM, Nos. 262, 282; GMB, No. 298.

Gluck: HAM, Nos. 292, 293; GMB, No. 313; EE, No. 39.

Comic opera: TEM, No. 50; HAM, Nos. 264, 285–287, 291, 300, 301, 305, 306; GMB, Nos. 281, 309; EE, No. 36.

The Lied: GMB, Nos. 287, 289, 299–301.

Church music and oratorio: HAM, Nos. 272, 279, 281, 298, 299; GMB, Nos. 308, 310.

For Further Reading

SR, Nos. 65–77 (SRC)

C. P. E. Bach's *Versuch über die wahre Art, das Clavier zu spielen* was first published in 1753 (Part One) and 1762 (Part Two); a facsimile of the first edition, ed. L. Hoffmann-Erbrecht, was published at Leipzig in 1957. An English translation by William J. Mitchell, *Essay on the True Art of Playing Keyboard Instruments,* New York, 1949, combines the original and revised editions of the eighteenth century. Excerpt in SR, No. 67 (SRC, No. 3). Bach's autobiography (1773) is available in a facsimile edition with critical annotations by William S. Newman, Hilversum, 1967.

The *Versuch einer Anweisung, die Flöte traversiere zu spielen* [*Essay on the Method of Playing the Transverse Flute*] by Johann Joachim Quantz (1697–1773), another important treatise of this period, was first published in 1752. There is a facsimile of the third edition of 1789, Kassel, 1953; English translation by E. R. Reilly, New York, 1966. Excerpts in SR, No. 65 (SRC, No. 1).

On the sonata, see William S. Newman, *The Sonata in the Classic Era,* Chapel Hill, 1963.

The best book about D. Scarlatti is Ralph Kirkpatrick, *Domenico Scarlatti,* New York, 1968, a model of scholarly authority and musical insight.

For an account of the life and music of J. S. Bach's sons, see Karl Geiringer, *The Bach Family,* New York, 1954; P. M. Young, *The Bachs, 1500–1850,* New York, 1970. The standard biography of Johann Christian Bach is by Charles Sanford Terry, London and New York, 1967.

Marcello's *Teatro alla moda,* in an annotated English translation by R. G. Pauly, is in *MQ* 34 (1948), 371–403; and 35 (1949), 85–105.

Important sources of information about eighteenth-century musical life are Dr. Charles Burney's *General History of Music* and his two travel books: *The present State of Music in France and Italy,* London, 1771, and *The Present State of Music in Germany, The Netherlands, and the United Provinces,* London, 1775 (2 vols.), as well as his *Memoirs of the Life and Writings of the Abate Metastasio, in Which Are Incorporated Translations of His Principal Letters,* London, 1796 (3 vols.). Excerpts from *The Present State of Music In France and Italy* are in SR, No. 74 (SRC, No. 10); a new edition, under the title *Music, Men and Manners in France and Italy, 1770,* H. E. Poole, ed., London, 1969. Brief excerpts from the travel books and Burney's journals, with connecting summaries by the editor, are found in Cedric Howard Glover, *Dr. Charles Burney's Continental Travels 1700–1772,* London, 1927. See also Percy A. Scholes, *The Great Dr. Burney; His Life, His Travels, His Works, His Family and His Friends,* London, 1948 (2 vols.). Scholes also edited Burney's two travel books under the titles *An*

Eighteenth-Century Musical Tour in France and Italy and *An Eighteenth-Century Musical Tour in Central Europe and the Netherlands,* both London and New York, 1959.

On the sixty-odd distinct meanings attached to the catchwords "nature" and "natural" by various writers, see entries in the index to Arthur Lovejoy, *Essays in the History of Ideas,* New York, 1955, and Ch. ii of C. S. Lewis, *Studies in Words,* Cambridge (England), 1960.

On the *symphonie concertante,* see Barry S. Brook, *La Symphonie française dans la seconde moitié du XVIIIe siècle,* Paris, 1962 (3 vols., including one volume of music).

Martin Cooper, *Gluck,* New York, 1935, and Alfred Einstein, *Gluck,* London and New York, 1954, are comprehensive studies of the life, works, and musical environment of this composer.; *Collected Correspondence,* H. and E. H. Mueller von Asow, eds., S. Thomson, tr., London 1962; Ernest Newman, *Gluck and the Opera,* London, 1967; A. Wotquenne, *Catalogue thématique des oeuvres,* Leipzig, 1904, reprinted Hildesheim, 1967. Bibliography of Gluck's printed works by C. Hopkinson, 2nd. ed., New York, 1967.

Chapter XIV (Pp. 476–511)

Friedrich Blume, *Classic and Romantic Music,* New York, 1970, is a comprehensive survey of all aspects of music in the period *ca.* 1770–1910. Charles Rosen, *The Classical Style: Haydn, Mozart, Beethoven,* New York, 1971, is strongly recommended; likewise, for those who can read German, Ludwig Finscher, "Zum Begriff der Klassik in der Musik," *Deutsches Jahrbuch der Musikwissenschaft* XI (1966), 9–34. See also H. C. Robbins Landon, *Essays on the Viennese Classical Style: Gluck, Haydn, Mozart, Beethoven,* New York, 1970.

General Reading

The definitive edition of his works is in course of publication by the Haydn Institute of Cologne under the direction of J. P. Larsen, Munich-Duisberg, 1958–   ; thematic catalogue by A. van Hoboken, Mainz, 1957–71, 2 vols.

Haydn

The basis for Haydn research was laid by J. P. Larsen in *Die Haydn-Überlieferungen,* 2 vols., Copenhagen, 1939. Source material is in H. C. Robbins Landon, ed. *The Collected Correspondence and London Notebooks of Joseph Haydn,* London and New York, 1959. The best general biographies in English are: Karl Geiringer, *Haydn, a Creative Life in Music,* Berkeley, 1968; and Rosemary Hughes, *Haydn,* London, 1946. On the symphonies: H. C. Robbins Landon, *The Symphonies of Joseph Haydn,* London 1955 with *Supplement,* New York, 1961; D. F. Tovey, *Essays in Musical Analysis,* Vol. I, London, 1935, is a mine of entertainment, information, and enlightenment about the late Haydn symphonies as well as the symphonies of Mozart, Beethoven, Schubert, and Brahms. On the quartets, see Tovey's article "Haydn" in *Cobbett's Cyclopedic Survey of Chamber Music,* London, 1963.

The standard collected edition is *W. A. Mozart's Sämtliche Werke,* Leipzig, 1876–1907; 14 series including supplementary volumes; reprinted, Ann Arbor, 1951–56, and New York, 1968 in miniature format. Eventually this edition will be superseded by the *Neue Ausgabe sämtlicher Werke* (Salzburg, International Mozart Foundation, 1956–   ), now at about Vol. 65 of the planned 110 volumes.

Mozart

Ludwig Köchel, *Chronologisch-thematisches Verzeichnis,* 6th ed., Wiesbaden, 1964.

O. E. Deutsch, *Mozart, a Documentary Biography,* 2nd ed., London, 1966.

The standard book about Mozart's life and music is Hermann Abert, *W. A. Mozart,* Leipzig, 1956 (2 vols.). This is a revision of Otto Jahn's *Mozart,* which was first published in four volumes in 1856–59; an English translation in three volumes appeared at London in 1882; reprinted, New York, 1969.

T. de Wyzewa and G. de Saint-Foix, *W.-A. Mozart, sa vie musicale et son oeuvre de l'enfance à la pleine maturité,* Paris, 1912–46 (5 vols.) is an important work, although marred by inaccuracies. Jean and Brigitte Massin, *Wolfgang Amadeus Mozart,* Paris, 1970, is a vivid and imaginative work —too imaginative in some respects, though accurate as to facts, and lively reading. A. Hyatt King's *Mozart,* Hamden, Conn., 1970, is a convenient short biography; it includes useful annotated lists of books about Mozart in English and a bibliography of Mozart editions.

Useful books about Mozart in English are: Alfred Einstein, *Mozart: His Character, His Work,* tr. A. Mendel and N. Broder, New York, 1962; A. Hyatt King, *Mozart in Retrospect,* 3rd ed., London, 1970; H. C. Robbins Landon and D. Mitchell, eds., *The Mozart Companion,* New York, 1969.

Important and interesting source material is found in *The Letters of Mozart and His Family,* Emily Anderson, ed., London and New York, 1966 (2 vols.).

Special topics: C. M. Girdlestone, *Mozart and His Piano Concertos,* New York, 1964 and Gloucester, Mass., 1966; E. J. Dent, *Mozart's Operas,* 2nd ed., London, 1960. Leopold Mozart's *Gründliche Violinschule* (1756) is published in facsimile, Leipzig, 1956, and in an English tr. by E. Knocker as *A Treatise on the Fundamental Principles of Violin Playing,* London, 1951.

Chapter XV (Pp. 512–36)

Beethoven

Collected edition: *Ludwig van Beethovens Werke,* Leipzig, 1864–90 (24 series and supplementary volume; reprinted, Ann Arbor, 1949 and New York, 1967 (also in miniature format). *Supplemente zur Gesamtausgabe,* W. Hess, ed., Wiesbaden, 1959– . *Sämtliche Werke,* Schmidt-Görg, ed., Munich, 1960– .

Thematic index: Georg Kinsky and Hans Halm, *Das Werk Beethovens; Verzeichnis seiner sämtlich vollendeten Kompositionen,* Munich, 1955.

The Letters of Beethoven, tr. and ed. Emily Anderson, New York, 1961 (3 vols.).

The standard biography is *Thayer's Life of Beethoven,* rev. and ed. Elliot Forbes, Princeton, 1969, 2 vols. Special insights into Beethoven's life and personality may be gained from Anton Schindler's *Beethoven as I Knew Him* (1840), D. W. MacArdle, ed., C. S. Jolly, tr., Chapel Hill, 1966; and O. G. Sonneck, ed., *Beethoven: Impressions by His Contemporaries,* New York, 1967. General works in English include: H. C. Robbins Landon, comp., *Beethoven; a Documentary Study,* New York, 1970; D. Arnold and N. Fortune, eds., *The Beethoven Reader,* New York, 1971; P. H. Lang, ed., *The Creative World of Beethoven,* New York, 1971 (see particularly D. Bartha's illuminating essay "On Beethoven's Thematic Structure"); Martin Cooper, *Beethoven, the Last Decade, 1817–1827* (a very careful study; the Appendix, "Beethoven's Medical History," by Edward

Larkin, debunks a number of pseudo-Freudian notions of the sort that are always creeping into the biographies of dead-and-gone composers).

Of the innumerable books about Beethoven's music we cite only: D. F. Tovey, *Beethoven* (London, 1945), the unfinished last work of one of the most perceptive musicians of the present century; J. Kerman, *The Beethoven Quartets,* New York, 1967; and the classic *Beethoven and His Nine Symphonies* by Sir George Grove, first published in 1896 and republished (from the third edition) New York, 1962.

On Beethoven's sketches and sketchbooks—currently a live topic of research—see Hans Schmidt, "Verzeichnis der Skizzen Beethovens," *Beethoven-Jahrbuch,* 2. Reihe VI (1965–68), 7–128 (a summary list of the known sketches, with locations); A. Tyson, "Sketches and Autographs" in *The Beethoven Reader,* pp. 443–58 (see also the numerous references under this heading in the Index of the same work); Gustav Nottebohm's *Beethoveniana* (1872) and *Zweite Beethoveniana* (1887) have been reprinted, New York, 1970; also his *Zwei Skizzenbücher . . . 1801 bis 1803,* Paul Mies, ed., Wiesbaden, 1970. Beethoven's *Studien in Generalbass . . . gesammelt von Seyfried* (1832) exists in a revised and augmented edition by H. H. Pierson, Hildesheim, 1967. See also Paul Mies, *Beethoven's Sketches, an Analysis of His Style Based on a Study of His Sketch-Books,* D. L. Mackinnon, tr., New York, 1969; and J. Kerman, ed., *Ludwig van Beethoven, Autograph Miscellany from circa 1786 to 1799,* London, 1970, 2 vols.

Chapters XVI and XVII (Pp. 537–94)

Berlioz: *Werke,* Leipzig, 1900–1907; nine series in twenty vols.; lacks the operas *Benvenuto Cellini* and *Les Troyens;* reprinted New York, 1969 (and in miniature format), including the missing operas. *Neue Berlioz-Ausgabe,* Kassel, 1967– .

Brahms: *Sämtliche Werke,* Leipzig, 1926–27, 26 vols. Reprinted, Ann Arbor, 1949 and Wiesbaden, 1965; in miniature format, New York, 1970.

Bruckner: *Sämtliche Werke,* R. Haas et al., eds., Augsburg, 1930–44, 11 vols. *Sämtliche Werke, kritische Gesamtausgabe,* L. Nowak, ed., Vienna, 1953– .

Chopin: *Werke,* Leipzig, 1878–80, 14 vols.; Supplements and Revisionsbericht, 1878–1902. *Complete Works,* I. Paderewski and others, eds., Warsaw, 1949–62.

Dvořák: *Collected edition,* Prague, 1955– .

Liszt: *Musikalische Werke,* Leipzig, 1907–36; 34 vols, incomplete. Reprint, Gregg Press, 1967. *Liszt Society Publications,* London, 1950– . A new edition is in preparation by the Hungarian State Publishing House.

Mendelssohn: *Kritisch durchgesehene Ausgabe,* Leipzig, 1874–77, 19 series in 35 vols. Reprint, Gregg Press, 1967; Wiesbaden, 1968; and in miniature format, New York, 1970. *Leipziger Ausgabe der Werke,* Leipzig, 1960– .

Schubert: *Kritisch durchgesehene Ausgabe,* Leipzig, 1888–97; 21 series in 41 vols., 10 separate Revisionsberichte; reprinted New York, 196?, and in miniature format, New York, 1970. *Neue Ausgabe sämtlicher Werke,* Kassel, 1964– . (The *Lieder* are published in a complete edition by Peters, 7 vols.)

Schumann: *Werke,* Leipzig, 1881–93, 14 series in 31 vols; reprinted in miniature format, New York, 1970.

Tchaikovsky: Collected Edition, Moscow, 194?– .

*Music
Collected
editions*

For
Further
Reading
General

    Logan Pearsall Smith, in his fascinating short essay *Four Words: Romantic, Originality, Creative, Genius,* London, 1924, traces the history of the ideas that have been denoted by these words at various periods. On "romantic" see also the valuable chapters viii–xii in Arthur Lovejoy, *Essays in the History of Ideas,* New York, 1955, and the same author's "The Meaning of Romanticism for the History of Ideas," *Journal of the History of Ideas* (June 1941), 257–78; for an interesting personal interpretation, see Preface to the third edition of C. S. Lewis, *The Pilgrim's Regress,* London, 1943. A general survey is H. G. Schenk, *The Mind of the European Romantics,* New York, 1969.

    On nineteenth-century music in general: SR, Nos. 78–82, 85, 86 (SRRo, Nos. 1–5, 8, 9); Alfred Einstein, *Music in the Romantic Era,* New York, 1947; Gerald Abraham, *A Hundred Years of Music,* 3rd ed., Chicago, 1964; W. S. Newman, *The Sonata Since Beethoven,* Chapel Hill, 1969.

    On the social history of the piano, see Arthur Loesser, *Men, Women, and Pianos,* New York, 1954; on its mechanical history, R. E. M. Harding, *The Piano-Forte; Its History to the Great Exhibition of 1851,* Cambridge, England, 1933.

Composers

    Berlioz: His *Treatise on Instrumentation* (1843), rev. and enl. by Richard Strauss (1905), is published in English translation, New York, 1948; his *Memoirs,* tr. and ed. D. Cairns, New York, 1969. See also Cecil Hopkinson, *A Bibliography of the Works of Hector Berlioz,* Edinburgh, 1951; Jacques Barzun, *Berlioz and the Romantic Century,* 3rd ed., New York, 1969, 2 vols.; Aaron Copland, "Berlioz Today," in *Copland on Music,* New York, 1960, and reprinted in the Norton Critical Scores edition of the *Fantastic Symphony,* E. T. Cone, ed., New York, 1971.

    Brahms: Biography by Walter Niemann, C. A. Phillips, tr., New York, 1969; A. Schoenberg, "Brahms the Progressive," in his *Style and Idea,* New York, 1950; Edwin Evans, *Handbook to the Chamber and Orchestral Music,* London, 1933–35, 2 vols.

    Bruckner: A helpful introduction is Robert Simpson, *The Essence of Bruckner,* London, 1967; see also Erwin Doernberg, *The Life and Symphonies of Anton Bruckner,* London, 1960.

    Chopin: Maurice J. E. Brown, *Chopin: an Index of His Works in Chronological Order,* London, 1960; the standard study is G. Abraham, *Chopin's Musical Style,* London, 1960; see also André Gide, *Notes sur Chopin,* Paris, 1948 and in English tr. New York, 1949; G. S. Golos, "Some Slavic Predecessors of Chopin," MQ 41 (1960), 437–47.

    Dvořák: J. Burghauser, *Thematic Catalogue,* Prague, 1960 (in Czech, German, and English); *Letters and Reminiscences,* O. Sourek, ed., Prague, 1954; the best book in English is John Clapham, *Antonín Dvořák,* London, 1966.

    Franck: Vincent d'Indy, *César Franck,* New York, 1910; N. Demuth, *César Franck,* New York, 1949.

    Liszt: Alan Walker, comp., *Franz Liszt; the Man and His Music,* New York, 1970; Sacheverell Sitwell, *Liszt,* New York, 1967; H. Searle, *The Music of Liszt,* 2nd ed., New York, 1966; B. Johnsson, "Modernities in Liszt's Works," *Svensk Tidskrift för Musikforskning* 46 (1964), 83–118.

    Mendelssohn: Thematic Catalogue, 3rd augm. ed., London, 1966 (first publ. 1882); Philip Radcliffe, *Mendelssohn,* London, 1954. Mendelssohn's letters are available in various English editions.

    Paganini: G. I. C. de Courcy, *Paganini the Genoese,* Norman, Oklahoma, 1957, 2 vols.

    Schubert: Thematic Catalogue by O. E. Deutsch, New York, 1951;

Deutsch, ed., *The Schubert Reader,* New York, 1947; *id., Schubert: Memoirs by His Friends,* New York, 1958; Maurice J. E. Brown, *Schubert: a Critical Biography,* New York, 1958; *id., Essays on Schubert,* London and New York, 1966; G. Abraham, ed., *The Music of Schubert,* New York, 1947; R. Capell, *Schubert's Songs,* New York, 1957.

Schumann: Thematic Catalogue, 4th augm. ed., London, 1966 (first publ. 1860); *Gesammelte Schriften über Musik und Musiker,* Leipzig, 1891, 2 vols.; Marcel Brion, *Schumann and the Romantic Age,* G. Sainsbury, tr., London, 1956; G. Abraham, ed., *Schumann, a Symposium,* New York, 1952.

Tchaikovsky: Thematic Catalogue, London, 1966 (first publ. 1897); G. Abraham, ed., *The Music of Tchaikovsky,* New York, 1946.

Chapter XVIII (Pp. 595–617)

For collected editions, see below; see also under names under Ch. XVI–XVII.

Music Collected editions

Wagner's *Musikalische Werke* were published at Leipzig, 1912–22, M. Balling, ed.; this incomplete edition has been reprinted, New York, 1969. A new edition, presumably to be complete and authoritative, was begun at Mainz, C. Dahlhaus, ed., 1970– .

Non-operatic works of Rossini appear in the *Quaderni Rossiniani,* Pesaro, 1954– .

Most of the operas mentioned in this chapter are available in piano-vocal scores, a few in full or miniature orchestral scores.

SR, Nos. 83, 84, 87 (SRRo, Nos. 6, 7, 10)

For Further Reading

Bizet: Mina Curtiss, *Bizet and His World,* New York, 1958; Winton Dean, *Georges Bizet, His Life and Work,* London, 1965.

Rossini: biography by Herbert Weinstock, New York, 1968. Stendhal's *Life of Rossini* (1824), New York, 1957, gives delightful insights into the way the composer was regarded by a hero-worshipping contemporary who evidently regarded factual accuracy as a negligible requirement.

Donizetti: see works on this composer by H. Weinstock, New York, 1963, and W. Ashbrook, London, 1965.

Bellini: An extraordinarily sensitive and penetrating study of the style of this composer is Ildebrando Pizzetti, *La musica di Vincenzo Bellini,* Florence, 1915, and in *La Musica italiana dell'ottocento,* Turin, 1947, pp. 149–228. See also the recent biography by Herbert Weinstock, New York, 1971.

Verdi: Francis Toye, *Giuseppe Verdi, His Life and Works,* New York, 1946, is an excellent introduction. The best biography is Frank Walker, *The Man Verdi,* New York, 1962.

Weber: J. H. Warrack, *Carl Maria von Weber,* London and New York, 1968, is the best book about this composer, his works, and his position in the history of nineteenth-century music. Weber's biography by his son, Max von Weber, was published in an English adaptation at London in 1865 (2 vols.) and has been reprinted, New York, 1969.

Wagner: The standard biography is Ernest Newman's *Life of Richard Wagner,* 4 vols., New York, 1933–46. See also Wagner's *Prose Works,* W. A. Ellis, tr., London, 1892–99 (8 vols.), especially Vol. I ("Art and Revolution" and "The Art-Work of the Future") and Vol. II ("Opera and Drama"). The complex of forms in Wagner's music dramas has been analyzed in detail, with addition of irrelevant metaphysical fancies, by Alfred Lorenz in four volumes collectively entitled *Das Geheimnis der Form bei Richard Wagner,* Berlin, 1924–33. An example of Lorenz's methods of analysis, as well as a good summary of the contents of Wagner's *Opera and Drama,* is given in Gerald Abraham, *A Hundred Years of Music,* Chicago, 1964, Part II. An interesting recent book is R. Donington, *Wagner's Ring and Its Symbols,* New York, 1969.

Chapter XIX (Pp. 618–61)

For
Further
Reading

An excellent survey of the period covered in this chapter will be found in Gerald Abraham, *A Hundred Years of Music;* Neville Cardus, *A Composers Eleven,* London, 1958, contains good nontechnical essays on Schubert, Wagner, Brahms, Bruckner, Mahler, Richard Strauss, César Franck, Debussy, Elgar, Delius, and Sibelius.

Late Romanticism: On Wolf, see Frank Walker, *Hugo Wolf, a Biography,* 2nd ed., New York, 1968; Eric Sams, *The Songs of Hugo Wolf,* London, 1961. Wolf's songs are published in an edition by Peters in 23 volumes, and a new critical edition is in progress.

Mahler: H. F. Redlich, *Bruckner and Mahler,* London, 1955; N. Cardus, *Gustav Mahler, His Mind and His Music,* London, 1965; Alma Mahler Werfel, *Mahler: Memories and Letters,* D. Mitchell, ed., B. Creighton, tr., New York, 1969; Arnold Schoenberg, "Gustav Mahler," in *Style and Idea,* New York, 1950. A critical edition of Mahler's works is in progress, Vienna, 1960– .

Strauss: The composer's own *Recollections and Reflections,* London, 1953. Of the published correspondence, the following volumes are available in translation: with von Hoffmansthal, under the title *A Working Friendship,* New York, 1961; with von Bülow, London, 1953; with Romain Rolland, Berkeley, 1968. For biography, see Norman Del Mar, *Richard Strauss; a Critical Commentary on His Life and Work,* 3 vols., New York and Philadelphia, 1962, 1969, 1972. Ernst Krause, *Richard Strauss, Gestalt und Werk,* Leipzig, 1955, is an excellent study, unfortunately not yet available in translation.

Max Reger's works are issued in a collected edition by the Max Reger Institute, Wiesbaden, 1954–70. Fritz Stein, *Thematisches Verzeichnis der im Druck erschienenen Werke von Max Reger,* Leipzig, 1953, includes an extensive bibliography. See also Mitchell, "Max Reger," *The Music Review* 12 (1951), 279–88.

Example of Dutch music 1890–1960 are given in E. Reeser, comp., *Stijlproeven van Nederlandse Muziek,* published by Donemus, Amsterdam (2 vols. and a third to follow).

Nationalism Old and New: On Russian music in general, see Gerald Abraham, *Studies in Russian Music,* New York, 1968; id. *On Russian Music,* London, 1939; id., *Slavonic and Romantic Music,* New York, 1968; M. D. Calvocoressi and G. Abraham, *Masters of Russian Music,* New York, 1971.

Collected editions of the music of Russian composers include the works of Glinka (Moscow, 1955–57), Borodin (Moscow, 1938–), Mussorgsky (Moscow and Vienna, 1928–34, reprinted New York 1969; Russian State Edition, 1939–); and Rimsky-Korsakov (Moscow, 1948–).

Glinka's *Memoirs,* R. B. Mudge, tr., Norman, Oklahoma, 1963; Edward Garden, *Balakirev, a Critical Study,* New York, 1967.

On Mussorgsky: J. Leyda and S. Bertensson, eds., *The Mussorgsky Reader,* New York, 1947; M. D. Calvocoressi, *Mussorgsky,* New York, 1962.

The subject of modality in Western music is well covered in John Vincent, *The Diatonic Modes in Modern Music,* Berkeley, 1951; on Russian music, see especially Ch. 28.

Rimsky-Korsakov's *Memoirs* were published in 1908; first unabridged Russian edition, 1928; in English translation, 1942. His *Principles of Orchestration,* with musical examples from his own works, in English translation, New York, 1933.

The analyses of Scriabin's harmony in A. Eaglefield Hull, *A Great Musical Tone Poet: Scriabin,* London, 1918, are suggestive but not detailed nor altogether satisfactory.

On Janáček, see biography by J. Vogel, G. Thomsen-Muchová, tr., London, 1963.

On Grieg, see *Grieg: a Symposium,* Gerald Abraham, ed., Norman, Oklahoma, 1950; biography by David M. Johansen (in English translation), Princeton and New York, 1938. On Nielsen: Robert W. Simpson, *Carl Nielsen, Symphonist,* London, 1964; Nielsen, *Living Music* and *My Childhood,* both London, 1953.

For general survey of music of the United States of America, see Gilbert Chase, *America's Music,* New York, 1955; H. Wiley Hitchcock, *Music in the United States: a Historical Introduction,* Englewood Cliffs, 1969; Eileen Southern, *The Music of Black Americans,* New York, 1971; id., *Readings in Black American Music,* New York, 1971. For more specialized studies: Robert Stevenson, *Protestant Church Music in America,* New York, 1966; Irving Lowens, *Music and Musicians in Early America,* New York, 1964; Thomas Marrocco and Harold Gleason, eds., *Music in America: an Anthology . . . 1620–1865,* New York, 1964; William Billings, *The Continental Harmony,* H. Nathan, ed., Cambridge, 1961; R. Offergeld, "The Centennial Catalogue of the Published and Unpublished Compositions of Louis Moreau Gottschalk," *Stereo Review,* New York, 1970; Edward MacDowell, *Critical and Historical Essays,* W. J. Baltzell, ed., New York, 1969.

Ives: His *Essays Before a Sonata and Other Writings,* H. Boatwright, ed., New York, 1962; his *Memos,* J. Kirkpatrick, ed., New York, 1972; H. and S. Cowell, *Charles Ives and His Music,* New York, 1955. Ives's numerous manuscripts and sketches in the Yale University Library have been catalogued by John Kirkpatrick, the pianist who has done much to bring this composer's work to public attention.

Sibelius: Gerald Abraham, ed., *The Music of Sibelius,* New York, 1947; Cecil Gray, *Sibelius,* London, 1934; id., *Sibelius: the Symphonies,* London, 1935; H. E. Johnson, *Jan Sibelius,* New York, 1959; Simon Parmet, *The Symphonies of Sibelius,* London, 1959.

For English musical nationalism in the early twentieth century, see Ch. 13 of Ernest Walker, *History of Music in England,* Oxford, 1952.

Elgar: Diana McVeagh, *Edward Elgar: His Life and Music,* London, 1955; Percy Young, ed., *Letters of Elgar and Other Writings,* London, 1956; Michael Kennedy, *Portrait of Elgar,* London and New York, 1968; see also Robert A. Hall, Jr., "Elgar and the Intonation of British English," *The Gramophone,* June, 1953.

Falla: Jaime Pahissa, *Manuel de Falla: His Life and Works,* London, 1954.

New Currents in France: Martin Cooper, *French Music from the Death of Berlioz to the Death of Fauré,* London, 1961; Paul Collaer, *A History of Modern Music,* New York, 1961, chs. 4–7.

d'Indy: Norman Demuth, *Vincent d'Indy,* London, 1951. Preferably, however, d'Indy's own writings, especially his *Cours de composition musicale,* Paris, 1903–50, 4 vols.

Fauré: Norman Suckling, *Fauré,* London, 1946.

Debussy: Debussy's essays were published at Paris in 1923 under the title *Monsieur Croche, anti-dilettante;* in translation, *Monsieur Croche, the Dilettante Hater,* New York, 1928, and in *Three Classics in the Aesthetic of Music,* New York, 1962. The best biography is Edward Lockspeiser, *Debussy: His Life and Mind,* London, 1965–66, 2 vols.

Books about other French composers: Basil Deane, *Albert Roussel,* London, 1961; Norman Demuth, *Ravel,* New York, 1962, Rollo Myers, *Eric Satie,* New York, 1968; see also the two chapters on Satie in Roger Shattuck, *The Banquet Years,* New York, 1958.

Chapter XX (Pp. 662–728)

For Further Reading

1900–1970 in general: William W. Austin, *Music in the Twentieth Century from Debussy through Stravinsky,* New York, 1966 (includes copious annotated bibliographies); Eric Salzman, *Twentieth-Century Music; an Introduction,* Englewood Cliffs, 1967 (complements Austin, with more information on American music and the period since 1950); Nicolas Slonimsky, *Music since 1900,* 4th ed., New York, 1971; Elliott Schwarz and Barney Childs, eds., *Contemporary Composers on Contemporary Music,* New York, 1967; Paul Collaer, *A History of Modern Music,* New York, 1961; P. H. Lang and N. Broder, eds., *Contemporary Music in Europe,* New York, 1965; Leonard B. Meyer, *Music, the Arts, and Ideas; Patterns and Predictions in Twentieth-Century Culture,* Chicago, 1967; Allen Forte, *Contemporary Tone Structures,* New York, 1955; André Hodeir, *Since Debussy; a View of Contemporary Music,* N. Burch, tr., New York, 1961 (a stimulating book, strongly French-oriented and very sure of the future); Josef Häusler, *Musik im 20, Jahrhundert von Schönberg zu Penderecki,* Bremen, 1969 (introduction, pp. 9–88, followed by "Porträtskizzen" of 56 composers including the Americans Cage, Cowell, Ives, and Varèse.)

Bartók: Halsey Stevens, *The Life and Music of Béla Bartók,* London, 1964.

Soviet Composers: Gerald Abraham, *Eight Soviet Composers,* New York, 1943; I. V. Nestyev, *Prokofiev,* F. Jonas, tr., Stanford, 1960 (3rd ed. in preparation); D. Shostakovich, *The Power of Music,* New York, 1968; B. Schwarz, *Music and Musical Life in Soviet Russia, 1917–1970,* New York, 1972.

Vaughan Williams: A. E. F. Dickinson, *Vaughan Williams,* London, 1963; Ursula Vaughan Williams, *R. V. W., a Biography,* London, 1964; Michael Kennedy, *The Works of Ralph Vaughan Williams,* London, 1964; and the composer's own writings, including *National Music,* London 1934.

Holst: Imogen Holst, *The Music of Gustav Holst,* 2nd ed., London and New York, 1968; id., *Gustav Holst, a Biography,* 2nd ed., New York, 1969.

Britten: Eric W. White, *Benjamin Britten, His Life and Operas,* Berkeley, 1970.

Copland: his own writings, including *Music and Imagination,* New York, 1959; *The New Music 1900–1960,* rev. ed., New York, 1968; *Copland on Music,* New York, 1963.

Thomson: Kathleen Hoover and John Cage, *Virgil Thomson, His Life and Music,* New York, 1970; the composer's own writings, including *Virgil Thomson,* London, 1967; *American Music Since 1910,* New York, 1971; *The Art of Judging Music,* New York, 1948.

Sessions: Oliver Daniel and others, *Roger Sessions,* New York, 1965; Sessions, *The Musical Experience of Composer, Performer, Listener,* New York, 1962, and *Questions about Music,* New York, 1970.

Carter: Allen Edwards, ed., *Flawed Words and Stubborn Sounds; a Conversation with Elliott Carter,* New York, 1971.

Milhaud: his autobiography, *Notes Without Music,* D. Evans, tr., New York, 1970.

Messiaen: his *The Technique of My Musical Language,* Paris, 1956; articles by David Drew in *The Score* (London), December, 1954 and September and December, 1955; Antoine Goléa, *Recontres avec Olivier Messiaen,* Paris, 1961; Claude Samuel, *Entretiens avec Olivier Messiaen,* Paris, 1967.

Hindemith: his *The Craft of Musical Composition,* New York, 1945, and *A Composer's World; Horizons and Limitations,* New York, 1961; Helmut Rosner, *Paul Hindemith: Katalog seiner Werke, Diskographie, Bibliographie, Einführung in das Schaffen,* Frankfurt a.M., 1970.

Stravinsky: his *Autobiography,* New York, 1962, and *Poetics of Music,* New York, 1956. Stravinsky's numerous books in collaboration with Robert Craft, 1959–69, contain many wise and penetrating observations on music and musicians in the twentieth century; see also Eric W. White, *Stravinsky: the Composer and His Works,* Berkeley, 1966; Roman Vlad, *Stravinsky,* F. and A. Fuller, trs., 2nd ed., New York, 1967.

Schoenberg: Sämtliche Werke, Josef Rufer, ed., Mainz, 1966– ; Rufer, *The Works of Arnold Schoenberg: a Catalogue of His Compositions, Writings, and Paintings,* D. Newlin, tr., New York, 1963; the composer's *Letters,* E. Stein, ed., New York, 1965 and essays *Style and Idea,* D. Newlin, tr., New York, 1950; Willi Reich, *Schoenberg, a Critical Biography,* New York, 1972; George Perle, *Serial Composition and Atonality,* 3rd ed., 1971; Alban Berg, "Why Is Schoenberg's Music So Hard to Understand?", *The Music Review* 13 (1952), 187–96.

Berg: Willi Reich, *The Life and Works of Alban Berg,* C. Cardew, tr., London, 1965.

Webern: his *Letters,* J. Polnauer, ed., C. Cardew, tr., Bryn Mawr, 1967; and *The Path to New Music,* L. Black, tr., Bryn Mawr, 1963; Walter Kolneder, *Anton Webern; an Introduction to His Works,* H. Searle, tr., Berkeley, 1968; H. Moldenhauer, comp., and D. Irvine, ed., *Anton Webern: Perspectives,* Seattle, 1966.

Boulez: his *Notes of an Apprenticeship,* H. Weinstock, tr., New York, 1968; *Boulez on Music Today,* S. Bradshaw and R. R. Bennett, trs., Cambridge, 1971.

Stockhausen: his *Texte,* 2 vols., Cologne, 1963; Alan Rich, "Stockhausen" in *International Cyclopedia of Music and Musicians,* 9th ed. (New York, 1964), pp. 2113–17; Karl H. Wörner, *Karlheinz Stockhausen, Werk und Wollen, 1950–1962,* Rodenkirchen, 1963.

Cage: His own writings, particularly *Silence,* London, 1968, which gives the best idea of his work and theories; *A Year from Monday,* Middletown, 1967, also occasionally mentions music.

Varèse: Louise Varèse, *Varèse: A Looking-Glass Diary,* Vol. I (1883–1928), New York, 1972.

Chronology

This chronology is intended to provide a background for the history of music, and to enable the reader to see the individual works and composers in relation to their times.

Entries fall into three categories, each listed in a separate paragraph under the given date:

(M) Significant musical events.
(H) Concurrent events in political, social, and intellectual history.
(A) Representative works and events in the other arts.

The first time a writer's or artist's name appears it is given in full, together with dates of birth and death. Thereafter, unless there is a chance of confusion, it appears in the surname form alone.

800–461 B.C.
(H) Rise of city states in Greece.

753 B.C.
(H) Traditional date of founding of Rome.

586 B.C.
(M) Sakadas of Argos wins Pythian Games with *Nomos Pythicos*.

500 B.C.
(M) Pythagoras (d. *ca.* 497).
(A) Pindar (522–443), *Odes*.
(H) Establishment of early Roman Republic.

461–429 B.C.
(H) Age of Pericles.

458 B.C.
(A) Aeschylus (525–456), *Agamemnon*.

432 B.C.
(A) Parthenon completed.

431–404 B.C.
(H) Peloponnesian War.

429 B.C.
(H) Death of Pericles.
(A) Sophocles (446–406), *Oedipus Rex*.

414 B.C.
(A) Euripides (480–406), *Iphigenia in Tauris*.

401 B.C.
(A) Xenophon (434–255), *Anabasis*.

400 B.C.
(H) Athens defeated by Sparta; decline of democracy in Greece.

399 B.C.
(H) Death of Socrates.

380 B.C.
(A) Plato (427?–347), *Republic*.

350 B.C.

(A) Aristotle (384–322), *Politics*, Praxiteles. (4th c. B.C.), *Hermes with Infant Dionysos*.

338–337 B.C.

(H) Macedonian conquest of Greece.

336–323 B.C.

(H) Conquests of Alexander the Great and subsequent division of his Empire.

330 B.C.

(M) Aristoxenus (b. *ca.* 354), *Harmonic Elements*.

323 B.C.

(H) Hellenistic Age.

306 B.C.

(A) Nike of Samothrace.

286 B.C.

(H) Library at Alexandria founded.

175 B.C.

(A) Frieze from Altar of Zeus at Pergamon.

150 B.C.

(M) Delphic *Hymn to Apollo*.

146 B.C.

(H) Greece under Roman rule.

60 B.C.

(A) Lucretius (*ca.* 96–55), *De Rerum Natura*.

58–51 B.C.

(H) Julius Caesar (100–44) invades Gaul and Britain.

46 B.C.

(H) Julius Caesar becomes dictator.

27 B.C.

(H) Augustus Caesar (63 B.C.–14 A.D.) first Emperor of Rome; Principate or Early Empire (27 B.C.–284 A.D.).
(A) Vergil (70–19), *Aeneid;* Horace (65–3), *Ars Poetica;* Ovid (43 B.C.–17 A.D.), *Metamorphoses*.

4 B.C.

(H) Birth of Jesus.

Ca. **33 A.D.**

(H) The Crucifixion.

50

(H) Rise of the Papacy (to *ca.* 300).

54

(H) Nero (37–68) Emperor of Rome.

65

(H) First persecution of Christians in Rome.

70

(H) Temple at Jerusalem destroyed.
(A) Colosseum begun at Rome.

81

(A) Arch of Titus completed.

100

(M) Plutarch (50–120), *On Music*.
(H) Germanic migrations and invasions begin (to *ca.* 600).

112

(M) Pliny the Younger (62–113) reports hymn singing by Christians.

118

(A) Pantheon begun (till 126).

150

(M) Ptolemy, *Harmonics*.

211

(A) Baths of Caracalla started (till 217).

284

(H) Diocletian becomes Emperor; beginning of Late Roman Empire (284–476).

285

(M) Oxyrhynchos hymn fragment.

313

(H) Constantine I (306–337) issues Edict of Milan.

325

(H) Council of Nicea.

330

(H) Constantinople established as new capital of Roman Empire.

374

(H) St. Ambrose (340–397) consecrated as Bishop of Milan.

395

(H) Separation of Eastern and Western Roman Empires.

410

(H) Sack of Rome by Alaric the Visigoth; invasion of Britain by Angles and Saxons.

413

(A) St. Augustine (354–430), *City of God*.

Ca. **450**

(A) Establishment of seven liberal arts as course of study.

452

(H) Invasion of Italy by Attila the Hun; Venice founded.

455

(H) Rome sacked by Vandals.

476

(H) Romulus Augustulus deposed; traditional date of end of Roman Empire.

481

(H) Merovingian dynasty in France established (till 751).

493

(H) Ostrogothic rule in Italy established (till 552).

500

(M) Boethius (480–524), *De institutione musica*.

527

(H) Justinian becomes Emperor of Eastern Roman Empire.
(A) Construction started on Hagia Sophia, Constantinople (finished 565).

529

(H) Benedictine order founded.

568

(H) Lombard invasion of northern Italy.

590

(H) Election of Pope Gregory the Great (*ca.* 540–604).

622

(M) Isidore of Seville (*ca.* 560–636), treatise on the arts.
(H) Hegira of Mohammed (*ca.* 570–632).

630

(H) Capture of Mecca.

633

(H) Council of Toledo.

650

(H) Rise of monasteries (to *ca.* 700); Arab conquests in Asia and North Africa.

700

(H) Irish and Anglo-Saxon missionaries on Continent; monastic schools flourish.

735

(H) Death of the Venerable Bede (673–735).

750

(H) Arabic science brought to Europe.

768

(H) Charlemagne (742–814) King of the Franks.

800

(M) Cultivation of music in the monasteries.
(H) Charlemagne crowned Emperor by Pope at Rome; Arabic culture appears in Europe; Viking raids and conquests begin.

805

(A) Minster of Aix-la-Chapelle dedicated.

830

(A) The Utrecht Psalter.

850

(H) University of Constantinople opened.

871

(H) Alfred the Great (849–899) King of England.

900

(M) Arabic musical instruments introduced into Europe; tropes and sequences; *Musica enchiriadis*.

962

(H) Otto the Great (912–973) crowned first Emperor of the Holy Roman Empire.

987

(H) Hugh Capet (*ca.* 940–996) elected King of France.

1025

(M) Guido of Arezzo's (*ca.* 955–1050) first writings on music.

1050

(A) *Chanson de Roland*.

1054

(H) Final separation of Eastern and Western Churches.

1066

(H) Norman invasion of England; Battle of Hastings.

1073

(M) Winchester Tropes.

1080

(A) The Bayeux Tapestry.

1086

(H) Domesday Book compiled.

1094

(A) St. Mark's Cathedral, Venice, begun.

1096

(H) First Crusade (till 1099).

1100

(M) Beginnings of St.-Martial organum.

1145

(A) Chartres Cathedral begun.

1150

(M) Troubadours flourish in Provence; Notre Dame School assumes musical leadership; liturgical dramas appear.
(A) Cathedrals at Sens, Senlis, and Noyen begun.
(H) Rise of universities throughout Europe; high point of Scholasticism.

1160

(A) Laon Cathedral begun (till 1205).

1163

(A) Cornerstone of Notre Dame at Paris laid.

1167
(H) Beginning of Oxford University.

1170
(H) Beginning of the University of Paris. Murder of Thomas Becket at Canterbury.

1175
(M) Leonin, master of Notre Dame School (fl. after 1150), *Magnus liber organi*.
(A) Canterbury Cathedral begun.

1183
(M) Perotin active at Notre Dame.

1189
(H) Richard Coeur de Lion (1157–99) King of England.

1200
(M) Trouvères flourish in France, Minnesingers in Germany.
(A) Reims Cathedral begun.

1209
(H) St. Francis of Assisi (1182–1226) founds the Franciscan Order; Cambridge University founded.

1213
(A) The Alhambra begun (completed 1388).

1215
(H) Magna Charta signed by King John.

1240
(M) Motet becomes important type of polyphonic composition. *Sumer* canon.
(A) Chartres Cathedral rebuilt.

1248
(M) Sequence *Dies irae*, attributed to Thomas of Celano.
(A) Cologne Cathedral begun; Sainte-Chapelle, Paris, built.

1250
(M) Period of *ars antiqua*.

1260
(M) Franco of Cologne (active 1250–80), *Ars cantus mensurabilis*.
(A) Nicola Pisano (*ca.* 1225–*ca.* 1278), pulpit of baptistry, Pisa.

1270
(M) English musicians in Paris; Cantigas de Santa Maria; Petrus de Cruce active; Motets of Bamberg Codex.
(A) Roger Bacon (*ca.* 1214–94), *Opus maius;* St. Thomas Aquinas (1225–74), *Summa theologica*.
(H) Start of Louis' Second Crusade; Sicilian Vespers.

1284
(M) Adam de la Hale (*ca.* 1230–88), *Robin et Marion*.

1297
(A) Marco Polo (*ca.* 1254–*ca.* 1324), *Book of Various Experiences*.

1300
(M) Beginning of French *Ars nova* (to *ca.* 1370); Treatises of Walter Odington and Johannes de Grocheo.
(H) Papal jubilee in Rome; feudalism declines.

1305
(A) Arena chapel frescoes by Giotto (1266–1337).
(H) The papacy in exile at Avignon.

1307
(A) Dante (1265–1321), *The Divine Comedy*.

1308
(A) Duccio (1268–1319) begins painting Siena panels.

1316
(M) Illuminated manuscript of *Roman de Fauvel;* Philippe de Vitry (1291–1361), *Ars nova*.
(H) Pope John XXII elected (till 1334).

1318
(M) Marchetto da Padua, *Pomerium artis musicae mensurabilis*.

1319
(M) Jean de Muris (*ca.* 1290–*ca.* 1351), *Ars novae musicae*.

1325
(M) Robertsbridge Codex.

1327
(A) Petrarch (1304–74) meets Laura.

1330
(M) Italian *Ars nova* (till 1410); Jacob of Liège (fl. 14th c.), *Speculum musicae*.

1337
(H) Outbreak of the Hundred Years' War.

1348
(H) The Black Death.

1353
(A) Boccaccio (1313–75), *Decameron*.

1360
(M) Guillaume de Machaut (*ca.* 1300–77), *Messe de Notre Dame*.

1362
(A) William Langland, *The Vision of Piers Plowman*.

1376
(A) Wycliffe's (*ca.* 1320–84) translation of the Bible.

1378
(H) Start of Papal schism.

1385

(H) Heidelberg University chartered.

1386

(A) Chaucer (*ca.* 1340–1400), *The Canterbury Tales.*

1405

(H) Duchy of Burgundy (till 1477).

1415

(H) Battle of Agincourt; Council of Constance.

1416

(A) *Très riches heures* of the Duc de Berry.

1417

(H) End of Papal schism.

1420

(M) Squarcialupi Codex; Old Hall Manuscript; Trent Codices (to 1480).
(A) Thomas à Kempis, *Imitatio Christi.*

1425

(M) White notation introduced in England.
(A) Giovanni da Prato, *Paradiso degli Alberti.* Ghiberti (1378–1455) begins *Gates of Paradise* for Baptistry at Florence.

1426

(A) Jan (ca. 1390–1440) and Hubert (*ca.* 1370–*ca.* 1440) Van Eyck begin the Ghent Altarpiece.

1431

(A) Lucca della Robbia (*ca.* 1400–82) starts work on *Cantoria.*
(H) Jeanne d'Arc executed.

1434

(H) Medici powerful at Florence (till 1494).

1435

(A) Donatello (*ca.* 1386–1466), *David.*

1436

(M) Guillaume Dufay (*ca.* 1400–74), *Nuper rosarum flores.*

1439

(H) Great Church Council of Florence.

1440

(M) Meistersinger in Germany; Canonici Manuscript.

1447

(H) Pope Nicholas V elected (till 1455); Vatican Library founded.
(A) Humanism rises in Italy.

1452

(H) Emperor Frederic III (till 1493), last Holy Roman Emperor to be crowned at Rome.

(A) Fouquet (*ca.* 1420–81), *Book of Hours of Etienne Chevalier.*

1453

(H) End of Hundred Years' War; Constantinople conquered.

1454

(H) Gutenberg (1398–1468) invents printing from movable metal type.
(A) Andrea Mantegna (1431–1506), *St. James Led to Martyrdom.*

1455

(M) Lochamer *Liederbuch.*
(H) Beginning of War of the Roses (till 1485).

1456

(H) Gutenberg prints the Mazarin Bible.

1460

(M) Dufay, Mass *Se la face ay pale;* first Doctor of Music degree awarded at Oxford.

1471

(A) Poliziano, *Orfeo.*

1478

(H) Lorenzo de' Medici (1449–92; the "Magnificent") ruler in Florence.
(A) Sandro Botticelli (*ca.* 1444–1510), *La Primavera.*

1480

(M) Jacob Obrecht (*ca.* 1452–1505), first Masses.

1481

(A) Andrea del Verrocchio (1435–1488), *Colleoni.*

1484

(A) Sir Thomas Malory, *Morte d'Arthur,* printed by Caxton.

1485

(H) Tudor dynasty in England (till 1603).

1486

(M) Josquin des Prez (*ca.* 1440–1521) at Rome, Papal Chapel.

1487

(A) Giovanni Bellini (*ca.* 1430–1516), San Giobbe Altarpiece.

1492

(M) Obrecht at Antwerp (till 1504).
(H) Unification of Spain; first voyage of Columbus; Alexander VI (Borgia) elected Pope.

1495

(A) Hieronymus Bosch (*ca.* 1450–1516), *Temptation of St. Anthony;* Leonardo da Vinci (1452–1519), *Last Supper.*

1496

(M) Franchino Gafori (1451–1522), *Practica musicae.*

1497
(H) Voyage of John Cabot (1450–98) to Canada; Vasco da Gama (*ca.* 1469–1524), voyage to India; first voyage of Amerigo Vespucci.

1498
(M) License to print music granted to Ottaviano dei Petrucci, Venetian music publisher; first to print complete song collections from movable type.
(H) Execution of Savonarola (1452–98) at Florence.

1501
(M) Petrucci publishes *Odhecaton*, first book of Josquin's Masses, first book of frottole.

1502
(A) Donato Bramante (1444–1514) *Tempietto*, Rome.

1503
(M) Obrecht Masses printed by Petrucci.
(A) Henry VII's chapel, Westminster; Leonardo da Vinci (1452–1519), *Mona Lisa.*

1504
(M) Josquin leaves Italy for France.
(A) Michelangelo Buonarotti (1475–1564), *David.*

1505
(A) Giorgione (*ca.* 1475-1510), *Fête Champêtre.*

1506
(A) St. Peter's begun at Rome, under Bramante's direction.

1507
(A) Albrecht Dürer (1471–1528), *Adam and Eve.*
(M) Petrucci issues first printed lute tablature.

1508
(A) Michelangelo begins Sistine Chapel ceiling.

1509
(A) Raphael (1483–1520), *School of Athens.*
(H) Henry VIII King of England (till 1547).

1511
(M) Sebastian Virdung, *Musica getutscht.*
(A) Desiderius Erasmus (1466–1536), *The Praise of Folly.*

1512
(M) Oeglin's *Liederbuch.*

1513
(H) Balboa (1475–1517) discovers the Pacific Ocean; election of Pope Leo X (Giovanni de' Medici).
(A) Matthias Grünewald (1485–1530), Isenheim Altarpiece.

1514
(A) Dürer, *St. Jerome in His Study;* Niccolò Machiavelli (1469–1527), *The Prince.*

1516
(A) Raphael, *Sistine Madonna;* Sir Thomas More (1478–1535), *Utopia;* Lodovico Ariosto (1474–1533), *Orlando Furioso.*

1517
(H) Martin Luther (1483–1546), ninety-five theses.

1518
(H) Conquest of Mexico by Cortes.
(A) Pontormo (1494–1557), *Joseph in Egypt.*

1519
(H) Ferdinand Magellan (*ca.* 1480–1521) circumnavigates the globe; Charles V (1500–58), Holy Roman Emperor (till 1556).

1520
(A) Michelangelo, sculpture for Medici tombs.
(H) Field of the Cloth of Gold.

1524
(M) Johann Walter (1496–1570), *Geystliche Gesangk Buchleyn.*

1525
(A) Titian, *Deposition.*

1526
(A) Luther, *Deudsche Messe.*

1527
(M) Pierre Attaingnant's (d. 1552) first publication, *Brevarium noviomense.*
(H) Sack of Rome.

1528
(A) Conte Baldassare Castighone (1478–1529), *The Courtier.*

1530
(A) Nicolaus Copernicus (1473–1543), *De Revolutionibus Orbium Coelesticum.*

1532
(A) François Rabelais (1494?–1553), *Gargantua.*

1533
(M) First Italian madrigals.
(A) Hans Holbein the Younger (1497–1543), *The Ambassadors.*

1534
(H) Act of Supremacy separates Church of England from the Papacy.

1535
(A) Angelo Bronzino (1503–72), *Portrait of a Young Man.* Il Parmigianino (1503–1540), *Madonna del Collo Lungo.*

1536
(M) First music publications of Gardano (Venice) and Petreius (Nuremberg).
(A) Library at Venice founded.

1538
(A) Titian, *Venus of Urbino*.

1539
(M) Jacob Arcadelt (*ca.* 1505–*ca.* 1560), first book of five-part madrigals.
(H) Statute of the Six Articles.

1540
(H) Society of Jesus founded.

1541
(H) Hernando de Soto (1500–42) discovers Mississippi River.
(A) Michelangelo, *Last Judgment* in Sistine Chapel.

1542
(M) Cipriano de Rore (1516–65), first book of madrigals.
(H) Ireland made a kingdom.

1545
(H) Council of Trent (till 1563).

1547
(M) Glareanus (1488–1563), *Dodecachordon*.
(A) Benevenuto Cellini (1500–71), *Perseus*.
(H) Edward VI King of England (till 1553).

1549
(M) Adrian Willaert (*ca.* 1490–1562), *ricercari*.
(H) Book of Common Prayer authorized by Edward VI.

1551
(M) Claude Goudimel (1505–72), *First Book of Psalms*.

1553
(H) Catholicism restored in England under Queen Mary (till 1558).

1554
(M) Giovanni Palestrina (*ca.* 1526–94), first book of Masses; Philippe de Monte (1521–1603), first book of madrigals.

1555
(M) Orlando di Lasso (*ca.* 1532–94), first book of madrigals.
(H) Peace of Augsburg.

1557
(M) Claudio Merulo (1533–1604) at San Marco.

1558
(M) Gioseffo Zarlino (1517–1590), *Istitutioni harmoniche;* Willaert, *Musica nova*.
(H) Elizabeth I, Queen of England (till 1603).

1561
(M) Palestrina, *Improperia*.

1562
(H) Religious wars of the French Huguenots.

1563
(H) Establishment of the Church of England.

1565
(M) Lasso, *Penitential Psalms*.

1566
(A) Pieter Brueghel the Elder (*ca.* 1525–69), *The Wedding Dance*.

1568
(H) Revolt of the Netherlands.

1569
(M) Palestrina, first book of motets.

1571
(H) Naval battle of Lepanto.

1572
(H) Massacre of Protestants in Paris.
(A) Giovanni da Bologna (*ca.* 1529–1608), *Mercury*.

1575
(M) William Byrd (1543–1623) and Thomas Tallis (*ca.* 1505–85), *Cantiones sacrae*.

1576
(A) Tintoretto (1518–94), *Ascension of Christ*.

1577
(M) Monte at Prague.
(H) Sir Francis Drake (1540–96) starts voyage around the world.

1580
(A) Michel Eyquem de Montaigne (1533–92), *Essays*.

1581
(M) Vincenzo Galileo (*ca.* 1520–91), *Dialogo della musica antica e della moderna*.

1582
(H) Calendar reform by Pope Gregory XIII.

1586
(M) Jakob Handl (Gallus; 1550–91), *Opus musicum*.

1587
(M) Claudio Monteverdi (*ca.* 1567–1643), first book of madrigals.

1588
(M) Nicholas Yonge (d. 1619) issues *Musica transalpina*.
(H) War between Spain and England; defeat of the Spanish Armada.

(A) Christopher Marlowe (1564–93), *Doctor Faustus*.

1589

(M) Byrd, *Cantiones sacrae, Songs of Sundrie Natures*.

1590

(A) Edmund Spenser (1552–99), *The Faerie Queene*.

1592

(A) Tintoretto, *The Last Supper*.

1594

(M) Thomas Morley (1557–1602) *The First Book of Ballets for Five Voices;* Orazio Vecchi (1540–1603), *Amfiparnaso;* Carlo Gesualdo (*ca.* 1560–1613), first book of madrigals.
(A) William Shakespeare (1564–1616), *Romeo and Juliet*.

1597

(M) Morley, *A Plaine and Easie Introduction to Practicall Musicke;* Jacopo Peri (1561–1633), *Dafne;* John Dowland (1562–1626), *First Book of Songs or Ayres;* Giovanni Gabrieli (*ca.* 1554–1612), *Symphoniae sacrae*.

1600

(M) Peri, *Euridice;* Giulio Caccini (1546–1618), *Euridice;* Emilio de' Cavalieri (1550–1602), *La Rappresentazione di anima e di corpo*.
(H) Henry IV marries Marie de' Medici; Giordano Bruno (1548–1600) burned at stake.
(A) Annibale Carracci (1560–1609), *Polyphemus Hurling Rocks at Acis*.

1601

(M) Caccini, *Le Nuove Musiche*.
(A) Shakespeare, *Hamlet*.

1602

(M) Lodovico Viadana (1564–1645), *Cento concerti ecclesiastici.*
(H) Galileo Galilei (1564–1642) discovers law of falling bodies; Dutch East India Company founded.

1603

(H) James I of England (James VI of Scotland) crowned (till 1625).

1604

(A) Shakespeare, *Othello*.

1605

(M) Monteverdi, *Fifth Book of Madrigals;* Michael Praetorius (1571–1621), *Musae Sioniae;* Thomas Luis de Victoria (*ca.* 1549–1611), *Requiem;* John Dowland (1562–1626), *Lachrymae*.
(H) Gunpowder plot; Pope Paul V crowned (till 1621).
(A) Miguel de Cervantes (1547–1616), Part I of *Don Quixote;* Francis Bacon (1561–1626), *On the Advancement of Learning;* Ben Jonson (*ca.* 1573–1637), *Volpone.*

1606

(A) Shakespeare, *Macbeth*.

1607

(M) Monteverdi, *Orfeo;* Marco da Gagliano (*ca.* 1575–1642), *Dafne;* Agostino Agazzari (1578–1640), *Del sonare sopra il basso*.
(H) Founding of Jamestown Colony.

1608

(M) Monteverdi, *Arianna;* Girolamo Frescobaldi (1583–1643), organist at St. Peter's.
(H) Quebec founded by Champlain.

1609

(M) Heinrich Schütz (1585–1672) and G. Gabrieli at Venice; Peri, *Le varie musiche*.
(H) Henry Hudson (d. 1611) explores Hudson River; Johannes Kepler (1571–1630), *Astronomia nova*.

1610

(H) Louis XIII crowned (till 1643).
(A) Honoré d' Urfé (1568–1625), *L'Astrée*.

1611

(M) *Parthenia* published.
(A) King James version of Bible.

1612

(A) Bacon, *Novum organum.*
(H) Louvre begun (till 1690).

1613

(M) Domenico Cerone (*ca.* 1560–1626), *The Art of Music and Instructor;* Monteverdi at San Marco.

1614

(M) *Medicean Gradual* published at Rome.
(A) Peter Paul Rubens (1577–1646), *The Descent from the Cross*.

1615

(M) G. Gabrieli, *Canzoni e sonate, Symphoniae sacrae II*.

1617

(M) Biagio Marini (1595–1665), *Affetti musicali;* J. H. Schein (1586–1630), *Banchetto musicale;* Schütz at Dresden.

1618

(M) Schein, *Opella nova*.
(H) Start of Thirty Years' War.

1619

(M) Praetorius, *Syntagma musicum*.
(H) Ferdinand II Holy Roman Emperor (till 1637).

1620

(H) Pilgrims arrive at Cape Cod; Mayflower Compact.

1621

(M) Schein, *Musica Boscareccia*.
(H) Gregory XV Pope (till 1623); Philip IV King of Spain (till 1665).

783

1623

(M) Schütz, *Historia der fröhlichen und siegreichen Auferstehung.*
(A) Shakespeare first folio; Marino, *Adone.*

1624

(M) Monteverdi, *Il Combattimento di Tancredi e Clorinda;* Samuel Scheidt (1587–1654), *Tabulatura nova.*
(H) Cardinal Richelieu in power in France (till 1642).
(A) Franz Hals (*ca.* 1580–1666), *The Laughing Cavalier;* Jakob Böhme (1572–1624), *Der Weg zu Christo.*

1625

(M) Schütz, *Cantiones sacrae.*
(H) Charles I crowned King of England (till 1649).

1626

(M) Domenico Mazzocchi (1592–1655), *La Catena d' Adone.*
(H) Manhattan Island bought by Peter Minuit.

1627

(M) Schein, *Leipziger Kantional;* Schütz, *Dafne.*

1628

(M) Orazio Benevoli (1605–72), *Salzburg Festival* Mass. Gagliano and Peri, *La Flora;* Schütz, *Psalms of David;* Carissimi (1605–74) at San Apollinare in Rome.
(A) William Harvey (1578–1657), *Essay on the Motion of the Heart and the Blood.*
(H) La Rochelle captured; end of Huguenot power in France.

1629

(M) Schütz, *Symphoniae Sacrae I.*

1630

(H) Puritans establish Boston.

1631

(H) Battle of Lützen; Galilei, *Dialogo dei due massimi sistemi del mondo.*
(A) Rembrandt van Rijn (1606–1669), *The Anatomy Lesson.*

1633

(M) Schütz at Copenhagen; Dresden Chapel closed.

1634

(M) Stefano Landi (*ca.* 1590–1655), *Il Sant' Alessio;* Henry Lawes (1596–1662), *Comus.*
(A) Taj Mahal begun (till 1653).

1635

(H) Académie Française founded.
(A) Diego Velasquez (1599–1660), *Surrender of Breda.*

1636

(M) Marin Mersenne (1588–1648), *Harmonie Universelle.*

(H) Founding of Harvard College; Roger Williams' first settlement in Rhode Island.
(A) Pierre Corneille (1606–1684), *Le Cid.*

1637

(M) Johann Froberger (1616–67), organist at court chapel, Vienna; Giovanni Doni (1594–1647), *Della musica scenica;* first public opera theatre (Venice).
(A) René Descartes (1596–1650), *Discourse on Method;* Anthony van' Dycke (1599–1641), *The Children of Charles I.*
(H) Ferdinand III Holy Roman Emperor (till 1657).

1638

(M) Heinrich Albert (1604–51), first arias; Mazzocchi, *Madrigali a 5 voci in partitura;* Monteverdi, *Madrigali guerrieri et amorosi;* Pier Francesco Cavalli (1602–76), second organist at San Marco.

1639

(M) Virgilio Mazzocchi (1597–1646) and Marco Marazzoli (1600–62) compose first comic opera, *Chi soffre, speri;* Loreto Vittori (1604–70), *La Galatea.*
(A) Nicolas Poussin (1594–1665), *Shepherds in Arcadia.*

1640

(H) Frederick William becomes Elector of Brandenburg. *The Bay Psalm Book,* first book printed in English colonies.

1642

(M) Monteverdi, *L'incoronazione di Poppea.*
(A) Rembrandt, *The Night Watch.*

1643

(H) Louis XIV King of France at age of five (till 1715).

1644

(A) Giovanni Lorenzo Bernini (1598–1680), *The Ecstasy of St. Teresa.*

1645

(M) Andreas Hammerschmidt (1612–75), *Dialogues;* Schütz, *Seven Last Words.*

1647

(M) Luigi Rossi's (1597–1653) *Orfeo* staged in Paris; Johann Crüger (1598–1662), *Praxis pietatis melica.*

1648

(M) Schütz, *Geistliche Chormusik.*
(H) Treaty of Westphalia; end of Thirty Years' War.

1649

(M) Cavalli, *Giasone;* Marc' Antonio Cesti (1623–69), *Orontea.*
(H) King Charles I beheaded; Commonwealth established (till 1660).

1650

(M) Carissimi, *Jephtha;* Samuel Scheidt (1587–1654), chorales for organ; Schütz,

Symphoniae sacrae, Part III; Athanasius Kircher (1602–80), *Musurgia universalis.*
(A) Descartes, *Musicae compendium.*

1651

(A) Thomas Hobbes (1588–1679), *Leviathan.*

1653

(M) Jean-Baptiste Lully (1632–87) court composer at Paris.
(H) Oliver Cromwell (1599–1658) dissolves Parliament.

1656

(A) Velasquez, *The Maids of Honor.*

1660

(M) Cavalli, *Serse.*
(H) Restoration of Charles II in England (till 1685).
(A) Samuel Pepys (1633–1703), *Diary.*

1661

(M) Marc' Antonio Cesti, *Dori.*
(H) Absolute reign of Louis XIV (till 1715).

1662

(M) Cavalli, *Ercole amante.*
(A) Molière (1622–73), *Ecole des Femmes.*

1664

(M) Schütz, *Christmas Oratorio.*
(H) New Amsterdam becomes New York.

1665

(M) Schütz, *St. John Passion.*
(H) Charles II of Spain crowned (till 1700); plague in London.
(A) Baruch Spinoza (1632–77), *Ethics.*

1666

(M) Schütz, *St. Matthew Passion.*
(H) Great fire of London.

1667

(M) Johann Rosenmüller (*ca.* 1620–84), *12 Sonate da camera a 5 stromenti;* M. A. Cesti (1623–69), *Il pomo d'Oro.*
(A) John Milton (1608–74), *Paradise Lost;* Bernini, colonnade of St. Peter's.

1668

(A) La Fontaine (1621–95), *Fables.*

1669

(M) Paris Academy of Music founded.
(A) Claude Gellée Lorrain (1600–82), *Egeria.*

1670

(M) Jacques Chambonnières (*ca.* 1602–72), clavecin pieces.
(A) Blaise Pascal (1623–62), *Pensées;* Molière, *Le Bourgeois Gentilhomme.*

1674

(A) Nicolas Boileau-Despréaux (1636–1711), *L'Art Poétique.*

1675

(M) Lully, *Thésée.*
(A) Sir Christopher Wren (1632–1723) begins St. Paul's Cathedral.

1677

(A) Jean Baptiste Racine (1639–99), *Phèdre.*

1678

(A) Bartolomé Murillo (1617–82), *Mystery of the Immaculate Conception;* John Bunyan (1628–88), *Pilgrim's Progress.*

1681

(M) Arcangelo Corelli (1653–1713), first trio sonatas.

1682

(H) Reign of Peter the Great (till 1725); La Salle explores the Mississippi; Philadelphia founded by William Penn.

1685

(M) Giovanni Legrenzi (1626–90) at San Marco; John Playford (1623–86), *The Division Violist.*
(H) James II of England crowned (till 1688); revocation of the Edict of Nantes.

1686

(M) Lully, *Armide.*

1687

(A) Isaac Newton (1642–1727), *Principia mathematica.*

1689

(M) Agostino Steffani (1654–1728), *Enrico detto il Leone;* Henry Purcell (*ca.* 1659–95), *Dido and Aeneas;* Johann Kuhnau (1660–1722), Clavier Sonatas.
(H) William III and Mary (d. 1694) rulers of England (till 1702).
(A) Thomas Burnet, *The Sacred Theory of the Earth.*

1690

(M) Georg Muffat (1653–1704), *Apparatus musico-organisticus.*
(A) John Locke (1632–1704), *An Essay Concerning Human Understanding.*

1692

(H) Salem witchcraft trials; College of William and Mary chartered.

1695

(M) Muffat, *Florilegium I;* Reinhard Keiser (1674–1739) director of Hamburg opera.

1696

(M) Kuhnau, *Frische Klavier Früchte.*

1697

(M) André Campra (1660–1744), *L'Europe galante.*
(A) John Dryden (1631–1700), *Alexander's Feast.*

1698

(M) Giuseppe Torelli (1658–1709), Violin Concertos Op. 6; *Bay Psalm Book,* first edition with music.

1700

(M) Johann Sebastian Bach (1685–1750) at Lüneburg.
(H) Philip V of Spain crowned (till 1746).

1701

(M) Muffat, *12 Concerti Grossi.*
(H) Frederick I of Prussia crowned; war of the Spanish Succession (till 1714); Detroit founded; Yale College founded.

1702

(H) Queen Anne of England crowned.

1703

(M) George Frideric Handel (1685–1759) at Hamburg.
(H) St. Petersburg founded.

1704

(M) Handel, *St. John Passion.* Georg Telemann (1681–1761) founds Collegium musicum at Leipzig.

1706

(M) Jean-Philippe Rameau (1683–1764), first book of clavecin pieces; Handel in Italy.

1707

(M) Alessandro Scarlatti (1660–1725), *Mitridate eupatore;* first Bach cantatas.

1708

(M) Bach at Weimar.

1709

(M) First pianoforte built; *opera buffa* in Italy.
(A) *The Tatler* and *the Spectator* founded.

1710

(M) Campra, *Fêtes Vénitiennes;* Handel in England; Academy of Ancient Music founded at London.
(A) George Berkeley (1685–1753), *A Treatise Concerning the Principles of Human Knowledge.*

1711

(M) Keiser, *Croesus;* Handel, *Rinaldo.*
(H) Charles VI crowned Holy Roman Emperor (till 1740).
(A) Alexander Pope (1688–1744), *Essay on Criticism.*

1712

(M) Antonio Vivaldi (1678–1741), Concertos, Op. 3. Handel settles in London.
(H) Toleration Act, London.
(A) Pope, *Rape of the Lock.*

1713

(M) François Couperin (1668–1733), *Pièces de Clavecin,* I; Bach, *Ich hatte viel Bekümmernis.*
(H) Peace of Utrecht.

1714

(M) Silbermann's organ at Freiburg.
(H) George I of England (Handel's patron).
(A) Gottfried Leibnitz (1646–1716), *Monadologie.*

1715

(M) First *opéra comique* founded; A. Scarlatti, *Tigrane.*
(H) Louis XV of France crowned (till 1774).
(A) Alain Lesage (1668–1747), *L'Histoire de Gil Blas de Santillane.*

1716

(M) Handel, *Passion;* Couperin, *L'Art de Toucher le Clavecin* and *Pièces de Clavecin, II.*

1717

(M) Bach at Cöthen—*Orgelbüchlein.*
(H) Triple Alliance.
(A) Jean Watteau (1684–1721), *Embarkation for Cythera.*

1719

(H) Herculaneum and Pompeii rediscovered.
(A) Daniel Defoe (*ca.* 1659–*ca.* 1731), *Robinson Crusoe.*

1720

(M) Benedetto Marcello (1686–1739), *Il teatro alla moda.*
(H) South Sea and Mississippi bubbles.

1721

(M) Bach: *Brandenburg Concertos; French* and *English Suites.*
(A) Baron de Montesquieu (1689–1755), *Lettres Persanes.*

1722

(M) Bach, *The Well-Tempered Clavier, I;* Rameau, *Traité de l'Harmonie.*

1723

(A) François Voltaire (1694–1778), *Henriade.*

1724

(M) Handel, *Giulio Cesare;* Bach, *St. John Passion;* cantata, *Ein' feste Burg.*

1725

(M) *Concerts spirituels* at Paris; Johann Fux (1660–1741), *Gradus ad Parnassum.*

1726

(M) Vivaldi, *The Seasons;* Rameau, *Nouveau système de musique théorique.*
(A) Jonathan Swift (1667–1745), *Gulliver's Travels.*

1727

(M) Handel, *Coronation Anthem.*
(H) George II of England crowned.

1728

(M) John Gay (1685–1732), *Beggar's Opera.*

1729
(M) Bach, *St. Matthew Passion.*

1730
(M) Johann Hasse (1699–1783), *Artaserse.*

1731
(M) Bach, *Klavierübung, I.*
(H) Treaty of Vienna.
(A) Abbé Prévost (1697–1763), *Manon Lescaut.*

1732
(A) Voltaire, *Zaïre;* William Hogarth (1697–1764), *A Harlot's Progress.*

1733
(M) Giovanni Pergolesi (1710–36), *La Serva padrona.*
(H) Founding of Georgia; War of Polish Succession.

1734
(M) Bach, *Christmas Oratorio;* Giuseppe Tartini (1692–1770), Sonatas, Op. 1.
(A) François Boucher (1703–70), *Rinaldo and Armida.*

1735
(M) Rameau, *Les Indes Galantes.*
(H) Carolus Linnaeus (1707–78), *Systema naturae.*
(A) Hogarth, *A Rake's Progress.*

1736
(M) Handel, *Alexander's Feast.*

1737
(M) Rameau, *Castor et Pollux;* Domenico Scarlatti (1685–1757), first published sonatas; San Carlo Opera opens, Naples.
(H) First lodge of Freemasons in Germany.

1738
(M) D. Scarlatti, *Essercizi;* Bach *Mass in B minor;* Handel, *Saul, Israel in Egypt, Serse.*
(H) Methodist church founded by Wesley and Whitefield.

1739
(M) Handel, *Concerti grossi;* Johann Mattheson (1681–1764), *Der vollkommene Capellmeister.*
(A) David Hume (1711–76), *A Treatise of Human Nature.*

1740
(H) Age of enlightened despots (till 1796); Frederick the Great of Prussia (till 1786).
(A) Giovanni Tiepolo (1696–1770), *Triumph of Amphitrite;* Samuel Richardson (1689–1761), *Pamela.*

1741
(M) Christoph Gluck (1714–87), *Artaserse.*

1742
(M) Bach, *Goldberg Variations;* Handel, *Messiah* performed at Dublin; C. P. E. Bach (1714–88), *Prussian Sonatas.*

(H) Charles VII Holy Roman Emperor (till 1745).

1743
(M) Handel, *Samson.*
(H) Treaty of Fontainebleau.
(A) Voltaire, *Mérope.*

1744
(M) C. P. E. Bach, *Württemberg Sonatas.*

1745
(M) Gluck in England; Johann Stamitz (1717–57) at Mannheim.

1746
(M) Handel, *Judas Maccabaeus.*
(H) Ferdinand I of Spain crowned (till 1759).
(A) Boucher, *Toilet of Venus.*

1747
(M) Handel, *Joshua.* J. S. Bach, *Musical Offering.*
(A) Sans Souci castle at Potsdam.

1748
(H) End of war of Austrian Succession.
(A) Montesquieu, *Esprit des lois;* Voltaire, *Zadig;* Gottlieb Klopstock (1724–1803), *Der Messias.*

1749
(M) Rameau, *Zoroastre;* J. S. Bach, *Die Kunst der Fuge.*
(A) Henry Fielding (1707–54), *Tom Jones.*

1750
(M) Johann Quantz (1697–1773), Flute Concertos.
(A) George Buffon (1707–88), *Histoire Naturelle.*

1751
(M) Handel, *Jephtha.*
(H) First volumes of *Encyclopédie;* Benjamin Franklin (1706–90), *Experiments and Observation on Electricity.*
(A) Thomas Gray (1716–71), *Elegy Written in a Country Churchyard;* Voltaire, *Le Siècle de Louis XIV.*

1752
(M) Quantz, *Versuch einer Anweisung die Flöte traversiere zu spielen;* War of the Buffons in Paris; first German *Singspiele.*

1753
(M) C. P. E. Bach, *Versuch über die Wahre Art.* Jean-Jacques Rousseau (1712–78), *Lettre sur la musique française.*

1754
(M) Rameau, *Observations sur notre instinct pour la musique.*
(A) Samuel Johnson (1709–84), *Dictionary;* Thomas Chippendale manufacturing furniture.

1755
(M) Franz Joseph Haydn (1732–1809),

first quartets. Karl Graun (1701–59), *Der Tod Jesu.*
(H) Lisbon earthquake; Moscow University founded.
(A) Gotthold Lessing (1729–81), *Miss Sara Sampson.*

1756
(H) French and Indian Wars.
(A) Voltaire, *Essai sur les moeurs;* Piranesi's engravings of ancient Roman ruins.

1759
(H) Wolfe captures Quebec.
(A) Voltaire, *Candide;* Laurence Sterne (1713–1768), *Tristram Shandy.*

1760
(H) George III of England crowned (till 1820).
(A) Jean Fragonard (1732–1806), Park of the Villa D'Este in Tivoli, James Macpherson (1736–96), *Ossian.*

1761
(M) Haydn at Eisenstadt; Gluck, *Le Cadi dupé; Don Juan.*

1762
(M) Gluck, *Orfeo ed Euridice.*
(A) Rousseau, *Le Contrat Social, Emile, Pygmalion.*

1763
(H) Beginnings of excavations at Pompeii and Herculaneum; Treaty of Paris; Canada ceded to England.

1764
(M) Gluck, *La Rencontre imprévue;* Mozart (1756–91) in London.
(A) Voltaire, *Dictionnaire philosophique;* Johann Winckelmann (1717–68), *Geschichte der Kunst des Altertums.*

1766
(M) Haydn, Quartets, Op. 9.
(A) Petit Trianon built. Lessing, *Laokoon;* Oliver Goldsmith (1728–74), *The Vicar of Wakefield.*

1767
(M) Haydn, Symphonies 35–38; Gluck, *Alceste;* Rousseau, *Dictionnaire de musique.*

1768
(M) Mozart, *Bastien und Bastienne.*
(A) Leonhard Euler (1707–83), *Lettres à une princesse d'Allemagne;* Sterne, *Sentimental Journey.*

1769
(M) Mozart in Italy.
(H) Watt's steam engine patented.

1770
(M) Mozart, first quartets; William Billings (1746–1800) *The New England Psalm Singer.*

(H) Beginning of the factory system; James Hargreaves (d. 1778), spinning jenny patented.
(A) Thomas Gainsborough (1727–88), *The Blue Boy.*

1771
(H) First edition of *Encyclopedia Britannica.*

1772
(M) Haydn, *Sun* Quartets, Op. 20.
(H) First partition of Poland.

1773
(M) Mozart, Symphonies K. 183, 201.
(H) Dissolution of Jesuit order by Clement XIV.

1774
(M) Gluck, *Iphigénie en Aulide, Orphée et Euridice.*
(H) First Continental Congress assembled at Philadelphia; Louis XVI King of France (till 1792); Joseph Priestley discovers oxygen.

1775
(H) Volta's electric battery invented; American Revolution (till 1783).
(A) Pierre Beaumarchais (1732–99), *Le Barbière de Séville.*

1776
(M) Sir John Hawkins (1719–89) and Charles Burney (1726–1814), general histories of music; Gluck, *Alceste.*
(H) Declaration of Independence; discovery of hydrogen.
(A) Thomas Paine, *Common Sense;* Adam Smith (1732–90), *The Wealth of Nations.*

1777
(M) Gluck, *Armide.*
(H) Articles of Confederation.
(A) Richard Sheridan (1751–1816), *The School for Scandal.*

1778
(M) Mozart, Piano Sonatas K. 310, 330–333, Violin Sonatas K. 296, 301–306; La Scala Opera opens in Milan.

1779
(M) Gluck, *Iphigénie en Tauride.*
(A) Lessing, *Nathan der Weise;* Sheridan, *The Critic.*

1780
(M) Haydn, Quartets, Op. 33.
(H) Cornwallis surrenders at Yorktown.

1781
(M) Haydn, *Jungfrau* Quartets; Mozart, *Idomeneo.*
(A) Immanuel Kant (1724–1804), *Critique of Pure Reason;* Jean Houdon (1741–1828), *Voltaire.*

1782

(M) Mozart, *Die Entführung.*
(A) Johann Schiller (1759–1805) *Die Räuber;* Rousseau, *Confessions.*

1784

(M) Andre Grétry (1741–1813), *Richard Coeur de Lion;* Martin Gerbert (1720–93), *Scriptores ecclesiastici.*
(A) Beaumarchais, *Le Mariage de Figaro.*

1785

(M) Haydn, *Seven Last Words;* Mozart, *Haydn* Quartets.
(A) Thomas Jefferson (1743–1826), design for Virginia State Capitol.

1786

(M) Mozart, *Le nozze di Figaro;* Haydn, *Paris* Symphonies.
(H) Frederick Wilhelm II of Prussia (till 1797).
(A) Robert Burns (1759–96), first edition of poetry; Joshua Reynolds (1723–92), *The Duchess of Devonshire.*

1787

(M) Mozart, *Don Giovanni,* Quintets K. 515, 516.
(H) American Constitutional Convention.
(A) Schiller, *Don Carlo;* Johann Goethe (1749–1832), *Iphigenia.*

1788

(M) Mozart, last three symphonies.
(H) John Fitch's steamboat invented; American constitution ratified.
(A) Edward Gibbon (1737–94), *The History of the Decline and Fall of the Roman Empire;* Goethe, *Egmont;* Jacques David (1718–1825), *Paris and Helen.*

1789

(M) Haydn, Quartets, Opp. 54, 55.
(H) French Revolution (till 1794); George Washington first president of United States.
(A) Goethe, *Torquato Tasso.*

1790

(M) Mozart, *Così fan tutte;* Haydn in London.
(A) Kant, *Critique of Judgment.*

1791

(M) Mozart, *The Magic Flute, Requiem;* Haydn, first *London* Symphonies.
(H) Bill of Rights.
(A) James Boswell (1740–95), *Life of Samuel Johnson.*

1792

(M) Domenico Cimarosa (1749–1801), *Il Matrimonio segreto;* Ludwig van Beethoven (1770–1827) at Vienna.
(H) France declared a republic.

1793

(H) Reign of Terror; Eli Whitney invents cotton gin.

(A) David, *Death of Marat;* William Blake (1757–1827), *Marriage of Heaven and Hell.*

1794

(M) Haydn, second trip to London.
(A) J. G. Fichte (1762–1814), *Uber den Begriff der Wissenschaftslehre.*

1795

(M) Beethoven, Trios Op. 1; Paris Conservatory founded.

1796

(M) Haydn, *Missa in tempore belli.*
(H) Jenner's first vaccination; Paul I of Russia (till 1801); Napoleon in Italy; Battle of Lodi.

1797

(M) Luigi Cherubini (1760–1842), *Médée.*
(A) Wilhelm Wackenroder (1773–98), *Herzensergiessungen.* François Gérard (1770–1837), *Cupid and Psyche.*

1798

(M) Haydn, *The Creation, Imperial Mass.*
(H) Napoleon in Egypt.
(A) Samuel Coleridge (1772–1834) and William Wordsworth (1770–1850), *Lyrical Ballads;* Thomas Malthus (1766–1834), *Essay on the Principle of Population;* Charles Bulfinch (1763–1844) designs the Massachusetts State House.

1799

(M) Beethoven, First Symphony, *Sonata Pathétique.*
(H) Napoleon becomes First Consul.
(A) Schiller, *Wallenstein;* Friedrich Hölderlin (1770–1843), *Hyperion*

1800

(M) Haydn, *The Seasons.*
(H) Discovery of ultraviolet rays; Volta invents voltaic pile.
(A) David, *Madame Recamier;* Schiller, *Die Jungfrau von Orleans.*

1802

(M) Beethoven, Second Symphony.
(H) Napoleon made Consul for life.
(A) Chateaubriand, *Génie du Christianisme.*

1803

(M) Haydn, Quartets, Op. 103; Beethoven, *Eroica Symphony, Kreutzer Sonata.*
(H) Louisiana Purchase.

1804

(M) Beethoven, Sonata, Op. 53.
(H) Napoleon crowned Emperor; Lewis and Clark expedition.
(A) Schiller, *Wilhelm Tell;* Jean Paul Richter (1763–1825), *Die Flegeljahre;* Jean Ingres (1780–1867), *Mme. Rivière.*

1805

(M) Beethoven, *Fidelio,* Sonata, Op. 54.
(H) Battle of Trafalgar.

(A) Ludwig Arnim (1781–1831) and Clemens Brentano (1778–1842), *Des Knaben Wunderhorn.*

1806

(M) Beethoven, Fourth Symphony, Violin Concerto, Sonata, Op. 57.
(H) Formal dissolution of the Holy Roman Empire; Lewis and Clark reach Pacific.

1807

(M) Beethoven, Fifth Symphony, *Coriolanus Overture.*
(H) Fulton builds the first commercial steamboat; London streets lighted by gas; Hegel, *Phenomenology of the Spirit.*
(A) Wordsworth, *Intimations of Immortality.*

1808

(A) Goethe, *Faust, Part I.*

1810

(M) John Wyeth (1770–1858), *Repository of Sacred Music.*
(A) Sir Walter Scott (1771–1832), *The Lady of the Lake.*

1811

(M) Franz Schubert (1797–1828), first *Lieder.*
(A) Goethe, *Dichtung und Wahrheit.*

1812

(M) Beethoven, Seventh and Eighth Symphonies, Violin Sonata, Op. 96.
(H) Napoleon retreats from Moscow.
(A) George Byron (1788–1824), *Childe Harold's Pilgrimage;* Jacob (1785–1863) and Wilhelm (1786–1859) Grimm, *Kinder- und Hausmärchen.*

1813

(M) London Philharmonic Society founded.
(H) Napoleon abdicates.
(A) Jane Austen (1775–1817), *Pride and Prejudice.*

1814

(M) Schubert, *Gretchen am Spinnrad.*
(H) Napoleon to Elba; Congress of Vienna.
(A) Scott, *Waverly;* Francisco Goya (1746–1828), *King Ferdinand VII.*

1815

(M) Invention of the metronome; Schubert, *Der Erlkönig,* Third Symphony.
(H) Battle of Waterloo; the Holy Alliance.
(A) Goya, *Witch's Sabbath.*

1816

(M) Schubert, Fourth and Fifth Symphonies, Third Piano Sonata, Mass in C; Gioacchino Rossini (1792–1868), *The Barber of Seville, Otello.*
(A) Percy Bysshe Shelley (1792–1822), *Alastor, or the Spirit of Solitude.*

1817

(M) Muzio Clementi (1752–1832), *Gradus ad Parnassum.*

(A) David Ricardo (1772–1823), *Principles of Political Economy and Taxation;* John Keats (1795–1821), *Endymion;* Byron, *Manfred.*

1818

(M) Beethoven, Sonata, Op. 106; Schubert, Sixth Symphony, Quartet in E.

1819

(M) Schubert, *Forellen* Quintet, Piano Sonata No. 13.
(H) First steamship crosses Atlantic; Florida purchased from Spain.
(A) Scott, *Ivanhoe.*

1820

(M) Anthony Philip Heinrich (1781–1861), *Dawning of Music in Kentucky.*
(A) Shelley, *Prometheus Unbound;* Blake, *Jerusalem.* Alphonse Lamartine (1790–1869), *Méditations Poétiques.*

1821

(M) Carl Maria von Weber (1786–1826), *Der Freischütz;* Beethoven, Sonatas, Opp. 110, 111.
(H) Faraday's electric motor and generator.
(A) John Constable (1776–1837), *The Hay Wain.*

1822

(M) Beethoven, *Missa solemnis;* Schubert, *Unfinished Symphony.*

1823

(M) Weber, *Euryanthe;* Beethoven, Ninth Symphony, *Diabelli Variations;* Schubert, *Die schöne Müllerin.*
(H) Monroe Doctrine.

1824

(H) Charles X of France crowned.

1825

(M) Beethoven, Quartets, Opp. 127, 132; Felix Mendelssohn (1809–1847), String Octet.
(H) Erie Canal opened; Ludwig I of Bavaria crowned.
(A) Alessandro Manzoni (1785–1873), *I Promessi Sposi;* Alexander Pushkin (1799–1837), *Boris Godunov.*

1826

(M) Beethoven, Quartets, Opp. 130, 135; Schubert, *Die Winterreise;* Mendelssohn, *Midsummer Night's Dream Overture.*
(A) James Fenimore Cooper (1789–1851), *The Last of the Mohicans.*

1827

(M) Beethoven, Quartet, Op. 131.
(H) Mormon church founded.
(A) Heinrich Heine (1797–1856), *Buch der Lieder.*

1828

(M) Rossini, *Le Comte Ory;* Schubert,

Symphony in C, last three piano sonatas, string quintet; Paganini concerts.
(A) First performance of Goethe's *Faust*.

1829

(M) Hector Berlioz (1803–69), *Symphonie Fantastique;* Rossini, *Guillaume Tell.*
(H) Independence of Greece.
(A) Honoré de Balzac (1799–1850), *La Comédie Humaine.* Victor Hugo (1802–85), *Les Orientales;* James Mill (1773–1836), *Analysis of the Mind.*

1830

(M) Daniel Auber (1782–1871), *Fra Diavolo;* Robert Schumann (1810–56), *Abegg Variations,* Op. 1; Mendelssohn's first *Songs Without Words.*
(H) First railroad, Liverpool to Manchester; July Revolution in France.
(A) Lamartine, *Harmonies poétiques et religieuses;* Hugo, *Hernani;* Stendhal (1783–1842), *Le Rouge et le Noir.*

1831

(M) Vincenzo Bellini (1801–35), *Norma;* Schumann, *Papillons.*
(H) William Lloyd Garrison founds the *Liberator;* beginning of anti-slavery movement.
(A) Hugo, *Notre Dame de Paris.*

1832

(M) Frédéric Chopin (1810–49), *Etudes,* Op. 10, *Mazurkas,* Op. 6; Mendelssohn, *Hebrides Overture;* Rossini, *Stabat Mater;* G. Donizetti (1797–1848), *L'Elisir d'Amore;* *Concerts historiques* founded at Paris.

1833

(M) Wagner, *Die Feen.*
(H) Slavery outlawed in British Empire.
(A) Thomas Carlyle (1795–1881), *Sartor Resartus.*

1834

(M) Berlioz, *Harold in Italy; Neue Zeitschrift für Musik* founded by Schumann.
(H) McCormick patents mechanical reaper.
(A) Edward Lytton (1803–73), *The Last Days of Pompeii.*

1835

(M) Donizetti, *Lucia di Lammermoor;* Schumann, Symphonic Etudes, Op. 13, *Carnaval,* Op. 9; Bellini, *I Puritani.*

1836

(M) Giacomo Meyerbeer (1791–1864), *Les Huguenots;* Michael Glinka (1803–57), *A Life for the Tsar.* Chopin, Ballades, Op. 23.
(A) Charles Dickens (1812–70), *The Pickwick Papers;* Sir Charles Barry designs Houses of Parliament, London.
(H) Independence of Texas.

1837

(M) Berlioz, *Requiem;* Franz Liszt (1811–86), *Années de Pèlerinage.*
(H) Morse's telegraph; Queen Victoria crowned; Mount Holyoke College founded.
(A) Carlyle, *The French Revolution.*

1838

(M) Schumann, *Kinderszenen, Kreisleriana;* Berlioz, *Benvenuto Cellini;* first public school instruction in music (Boston).
(H) Daguerre (1789–1851) takes first photographs.
(A) Ferdinand Delacroix (1798–1863), *The Capture of Constantinople.*

1839

(M) Chopin, Préludes, Op. 28; New York Philharmonic Society founded; Vienna Philharmonic founded; Berlioz, *Romeo and Juliet;* Schumann, *Nachtstücke.*
(A) Joseph Turner (1775–1851), *The Fighting Temeraire;* Edgar Allan Poe (1809–49), *Tales of the Grotesque and Arabesque;* Stendhal, *The Charterhouse of Parma.*

1840

(M) Schumann, *Lieder;* Donizetti, *The Daughter of the Regiment.*
(H) First incandescent electric bulb.

1841

(M) Schumann, First and Fourth Symphonies.
(H) Invention of the saxophone.
(A) *Punch* founded.

1842

(M) Wagner, *Rienzi;* Glinka, *Russlan and Ludmilla;* Giuseppe Verdi (1813–1901), *Nabucco;* Third New York Philharmonic Society founded.

1843

(M) Wagner, *Der fliegende Holländer;* Donizetti, *Don Pasquale.*
(A) Sören Kierkegaard (1813–55), *Fear and Trembling.*

1844

(M) Verdi, *Ernani;* Mendelssohn, Violin Concerto; B. F. White (1800–79), *The Sacred Harp.*
(H) First telegraph message transmitted.
(A) Alexandre Dumas (1824–95), *The Three Musketeers.*

1845

(M) Liszt, *Les Préludes;* Wagner, *Tannhäuser;* Louis Moreau Gottschalk (1829–69), *La Bamboula.*
(A) Dumas, *The Count of Monte Cristo.*

1846

(M) Berlioz, *The Damnation of Faust;* Mendelssohn, *Elijah.*
(H) First use of ether as an anesthetic; Howe's sewing machine patented; Smithsonian Institution founded.

1847

(M) Verdi, *Macbeth;* Friedrich von Flotow (1812–83), *Martha.*

791

1848

(H) Potato famine in Ireland; gold rush in California; first Women's Rights Convention; revolutionary uprisings in Europe.
(A) Thomas Macaulay (1800–59), *History of England;* William Thackeray (1811–63), *Vanity Fair;* Alexandre Dumas *fils, La Dame aux Camélias;* Karl Marx (1818–83) and Friedrich Engels (1820–95), *Communist Manifesto.*

1849

(M) Wagner, *Die Kunst und die Revolution;* Meyerbeer, *Le Prophète;* Anton Bruckner (1824–96), *Requiem.*
(A) Gustave Courbet (1819–77), *The Stone Breaker;* Dickens, *David Copperfield.*

1850

(M) Bachgesellschaft founded; Wagner, *Lohengrin.*
(A) Nathaniel Hawthorne (1804–64), *The Scarlet Letter;* Dante Rossetti (1828–82), *The Annunciation;* Theodor Storm (1817–88), *Immensee;* Henry Wadsworth Longfellow (1807–82), *Evangeline.*

1851

(M) Wagner, *Oper und Drama;* Schumann, Third Symphony; Verdi, *Rigoletto;* Stephen Foster (1826–64), *Old Folks at Home.*
(H) First submarine telegraph cable.
(A) Herman Melville (1819–91), *Moby Dick;* Jean Millet (1814–75), *The Gleaners.*

1852

(H) Second Empire under Napoleon III.
(A) Harriet Beecher Stowe (1811–96), *Uncle Tom's Cabin.*

1853

(M) Verdi, *Il Trovatore, La Traviata.*
(H) Crimean War; Commodore Perry opens Japan to the West; first rail connection New York-Chicago.

1854

(M) Liszt, Sonata in B minor.
(A) Henry David Thoreau (1817–62), *Walden.*

1855

(M) Liszt, *Faust* Symphony; Verdi, *Vespri siciliani.*
(H) Charge of the Light Brigade.
(A) Walt Whitman (1819–92), *Leaves of Grass.*

1856

(M) Liszt, *Hungarian Rhapsodies.*

1857

(H) Dred Scott decision.
(A) Gustave Flaubert (1821–80), *Madame Bovary;* Currier and Ives publish prints; Pierre Baudelaire (1821–67), *Les Fleurs du Mal.*

1858

(M) Berlioz, *Les Troyens;* Verdi, *Un Ballo in Maschera;* Jacques Offenbach (1819–80), *Orphée aux enfers.*
(H) Covent Garden opera house opens.

1859

(M) Charles Gounod (1818–93), *Faust;* Wagner, *Tristan und Isolde.*
(H) Charles Darwin (1809–82), *Origin of Species;* John Brown raids Harper's Ferry.
(A) Millet, *The Angelus;* Alfred Lord Tennyson (1809–92), *Idylls of the King.*

1861

(M) *Tannhäuser* performed at Paris.
(H) Serfs emancipated in Russia; unification of Italy; Civil War in America (till 1865).
(A) George Eliot (1819–80), *Silas Marner.*

1862

(M) Verdi, *La Forza del Destino;* Köchel's Mozart catalogue begun.
(H) Bismarck chancellor of Prussia.
(A) Ivan Turgenev (1818–83), *Fathers and Sons;* Honoré Daumier (1808–79), *Third Class Carriage.*

1863

(M) Berlioz, *Les Troyens* (first performance).
(H) Gettysburg Address; Emancipation Proclamation.
(A) Edouard Manet (1832–83), *Olympia.*

1864

(M) Johannes Brahms (1833–97), Piano Quintet in F minor, *Lieder,* Op. 33; Bruckner, First Symphony; Offenbach, *La Belle Hélène.*
(H) First International founded by Karl Marx; first ascent of the Matterhorn; first successful transatlantic cable.
(A) Lewis Carroll (1832–98), *Alice in Wonderland;* Leo Tolstoy (1828–1910), *War and Peace.*

1865

(H) Lincoln assassinated; Thirteenth Amendment ratified, outlawing slavery.

1866

(M) Ambroise Thomas (1811–96), *Mignon;* Bedřich Smetana (1824–84), *The Bartered Bride.*
(H) Christian Science founded by Mary Baker Eddy.
(A) Feodor Dostoyevsky (1821–81), *Crime and Punishment.*

1867

(M) Verdi, *Don Carlo;* Johann Strauss (1825–99), *On the Beautiful Blue Danube;* first collection of Negro spirituals.
(H) Purchase of Alaska; Franz Joseph I of Austria-Hungary (till 1916).
(A) Henrik Ibsen (1828–1906), *Peer Gynt;* Marx, *Das Kapital.*

1868

(M) Brahms, *A German Requiem;* Mage-

lone songs, Op. 33; Gesellschaft für Musik-forschung founded at Berlin.
(A) Robert Browning (1812–89), *The Ring and the Book;* Dostoyevsky, *The Idiot.*

1869

(H) Suez Canal opened; first American transcontinental railroad.
(A) Jules Verne (1828–1905), *Twenty Thousand Leagues Under the Sea.*

1870

(M) Wagner, *Die Walküre* performed.
(H) Heinrich Schliemann (1822–90) excavates the site of Troy; Rome becomes the capital of Italy; Franco-Prussian War; Vatican Council proclaims papal infallibility.

1871

(M) Verdi, *Aïda;* Brahms, *Schicksalslied;* Edvard Grieg (1843–1907), first lyric pieces for piano.
(H) Bismarck chancellor of Germany; Paris Commune, Third Republic.
(A) Ralph Waldo Emerson (1860–1927), *Essays;* Darwin, *The Descent of Man.*

1872

(M) Georges Bizet (1838–75), *L'Arlésienne;* Bruckner, Mass in F minor.
(A) Eliot, *Middlemarch;* James Whistler (1834–1903), *Portrait of Miss Alexander;* Alphonse Daudet (1840–97), *Tartarin de Tarascon;* Friedrich Nietzsche (1844–1900), *The Birth of Tragedy.*

1873

(M) Bruckner, Third Symphony; Brahms, Quartet, Op. 51.
(A) Edgar Degas (1834–1917), *Place de la Concorde.*

1874

(M) Modest Mussorgsky (1839–81), *Boris Godunov, Pictures at an Exhibition;* Verdi, *Requiem;* J. Strauss, *Die Fledermaus.*

1875

(M) New Paris opera house opened; Bizet, *Carmen;* Smetana, *My Fatherland.*
(A) Mary Baker Eddy (1821–1910), *Science and Health;* Tolstoy, *Anna Karenina.*

1876

(M) First Wagner festival at Bayreuth.
(H) Telephone invented by Bell.
(A) Stéphane Mallarmé (1842–98), *L'-Après-midi d'un Faune;* Mark Twain (1835–1910), *Tom Sawyer;* Pierre Renoir (1841–1919), *Le Bal du Moulin de la Galette.*

1877

(M) Wagner, *Parsifal;* Brahms, First and Second Symphonies; Camille Saint-Saëns (1835–1921), *Samson and Delilah.*
(H) Edison invents the phonograph.
(A) Claude Monet (1840–1926), *Gare Saint-Lazare.*

1878

(M) Brahms, Violin Concerto; James Bland's (1854–1911) song "Carry Me Back to Old Virginny" published.

1879

(M) Tchaikovsky, *Eugen Onegin;* Sir George Grove (1820–1900), *Dictionary of Music and Musicians.*
(H) Edison invents an improved incandescent electric light.
(A) Henry George (1839–97), *Progress and Poverty;* Ibsen, *The Doll's House;* Dostoyevsky, *The Brothers Karamazov.*

1880

(H) Irish insurrection; Pavlov's experiments on conditioned reflexes.
(A) Emile Zola (1840–1902), *Nana.*

1881

(M) Offenbach, *Tales of Hoffmann;* Boston Symphony founded; John Knowles Paine (1839–1906), music for *Oedipus Tyrannus.*
(H) Tsar Alexander II assassinated; President Garfield shot; Panama Canal built.
(A) Renoir, *Luncheon of the Boating Party;* Henry James (1843–1916), *Portrait of a Lady.*

1882

(M) Berlin Philharmonia founded.
(H) Koch discovers tuberculosis germs; Triple Alliance.
(A) Manet, *The Bar at the Folies Bergères.*

1883

(M) Brahms, Third Symphony; Metropolitan Opera opened; Amsterdam Concertgebouw founded.
(H) Gottlieb Daimler (1834–1900) patents automobile motor.
(A) Nietzsche, *Also sprach Zarathustra;* Robert Louis Stevenson (1850–94), *Treasure Island.*

1884

(M) Jules Massenet (1842–1912), *Manon.*
(H) Pasteur innoculates against rabies; mean solar day adopted as unit of universal time.
(A) Auguste Rodin (1840–1917), *The Burghers of Calais;* Georges Seurat (1859–91), *Sunday Afternoon on Grande Jatte;* Twain, *Huckleberry Finn.*

1885

(M) Bruckner, *Te Deum;* J. Strauss, *Der Zigeunerbaron;* Brahms, Fourth Symphony; Sir William Gilbert (1836–1911) and Sir Arthur Sullivan (1842–1900), *The Mikado.*
(H) First American electric street railway; Brooklyn Bridge built.
(A) Henry Richardson (1838–86) designs Marshall Field warehouse; Guy de Maupassant (1850–93), *Contes et Nouvelles;*

793

Paul Cézanne (1839–1906), *Mont St. Victoire;* William Dean Howells (1839–1920), *The Rise of Silas Lapham.*

1886

(M) César Franck (1822–90), *Violin Sonata.*

(H) American Federation of Labor organized, Statue of Liberty unveiled in New York Harbor.

(A) Nietzsche, *Jenseits von Gut und Böse;* Pierre Loti (1850–1923), *Pêcheur d'Islande;* Henri Rousseau (1844–1910), *Un Soir de carnaval.*

1887

(M) Verdi, *Otello.*

(A) A. Strindberg (1849–1912), *Der Vater.*

1888

(M) Franck, *Symphony in D minor;* Nikolas Rimsky-Korsakov (1844–1908), *Scheherazade;* Erik Satie (1866–1925), *Gymnopédies;* Hugo Wolf (1860–1903), *Mörike Lieder;* Tchaikovsky, Fifth Symphony.

(H) Kaiser Wilhelm II crowned (till 1918).

(A) Vincent van Gogh (1853–1900), *The Sunflowers.*

1889

(M) Richard Strauss (1864–1949), *Don Juan;* Wolf, *Spanisches Liederbuch;* Mahler, First Symphony.

(H) Paris World's Fair opened; Brazil expels emperor, becomes republic.

(A) Eiffel Tower completed; Henry Adams (1838–1918), *History of the United States* (1889–91); Auguste Rodin (1840–1917), *The Thinker.*

1890

(M) Pietro Mascagni (1863–1945), *Cavalleria Rusticana;* R. Strauss, *Death and Transfiguration;* Tchaikovsky, *Pique Dame.* Alexander Borodin (1833–87), *Prince Igor* (first performance).

(A) Ibsen, *Hedda Gabler.*

1891

(M) Wolf, *Italienisches Liederbuch.*

(A) Sir Arthur Conan Doyle (1859–1930), *Adventures of Sherlock Holmes;* Augustus Saint-Gaudens (1848–1907), Adams Memorial.

1892

(M) Gabriel Fauré (1845–1924), *La Bonne Chanson;* Bruckner, Eighth Symphony; Ruggiero Leoncavallo (1858–1919), *I Pagliacci.*

(A) Cézanne, *The Card Players;* Maurice Maeterlinck (1862–1949), *Pelléas et Mélisande;* Henri de Toulouse-Lautrec (1864–1901), *At the Moulin Rouge.*

1893

(M) Engelbert Humperdinck (1854–1921), *Hansel und Gretel;* Giacomo Puccini (1858–1924), *Manon Lescaut;* Verdi, *Falstaff;*

Tchaikovsky, Sixth Symphony; Horatio Parker (1863–1919), *Hora Novissima.*

(A) Stephen Crane (1871–1900), *The Red Badge of Courage;* Oscar Wilde (1856–1900), *Salome;* Louis Sullivan (1856–1924), Transportation Building at World's Columbian Exposition.

1894

(M) Anton Dvořák (1841–1904,) *New World Symphony;* Debussy, *Prélude à l'après-midi d'un faune.*

(H) Nicholas II crowned; last Czar of Russia; Dreyfus Affair (till 1905).

(A) Rudyard Kipling (1865–1936), *Jungle Book;* George Bernard Shaw (1856–1950), *Candida.*

1895

(M) Strauss, *Till Eulenspiegel.*

(H) Wilhelm Roentgen (1845–1923) discovers X-rays.

(A) Winslow Homer (1836–1910), *Northeaster.*

1896

(M) Brahms, *Vier ernste Gesänge;* Vincent d'Indy (1851–1931), *Istar;* Edward MacDowell (1861–1908), *Indian Suite;* Puccini, *La Bohème;* Wolf, *Der Corregidor.*

(A) Paul Gauguin (1843–1903), *Maternity;* A. E. Housman (1859–1936), *A Shropshire Lad.*

1897

(M) d'Indy, *Fervaal;* Strauss, *Don Quixote;* John Philip Sousa (1845–1932), *The Stars and Stripes Forever.*

1898

(M) Rimsky-Korsakov, *Sadko;* MacDowell, *Sea Pieces;* R. Strauss, *Ein Heldenleben.*

(H) Spanish-American War.

(A) Edmond Rostand (1868–1918), *Cyrano de Bergerac.*

1899

(M) Maurice Ravel (1875–1937), *Pavane pour une infante défunte;* Arnold Schoenberg (1874–1950), *Verklärte Nacht;* Jean Sibelius (1865–1957), *Finlandia;* Scott Joplin (1868–1917), *Maple Leaf Rag.* Internationale Musikgesellschaft founded at Leipzig.

(H) Boer War.

1900

(M) Edward Elgar (1857–1934), *The Dream of Gerontius;* Puccini, *Tosca;* Debussy, *Nocturnes;* Gustave Charpentier (1860–1956), *Louise.* Philadelphia Orchestra founded.

(H) Boxer Rebellion; Count Ferdinand Zeppelin constructs first dirigible; Sigmund Freud (1856–1939) *The Interpretation of Dreams;* Hopkins, first studies of vitamins.

(A) Joseph Conrad (1857–1924), *Lord Jim;* John Singer Sargent (1856–1925), *The Wyndham Sisters;* Tolstoy, *Resurrection.*

1901

(M) Gustav Mahler (1860–1911), Fourth Symphony; Schoenberg, *Gurrelieder;* Sergei Rachmaninov (1873–1943), Second Piano Concerto; Charles Martin Loeffler (1861–1935), *A Pagan Poem.*
(H) Edward VII King of England (till 1910); Guglielmo Marconi transmits wireless telegraph signals across the Atlantic; Max Planck develops quantum theory.
(A) Shaw, *Caesar and Cleopatra;* Aristide Maillol (1861–1944), *Mediterranean;* Thomas Mann (1875–1955), *Buddenbrooks.*

1902

(M) Sibelius, Second Symphony; Debussy, *Pelléas et Mélisande.*
(H) Discovery of radium by Pierre (1859–1906) and Marie (1867–1934) Curie.
(A) Maxim Gorky (1868–1936), *Tales;* Claude Monet (1840–1926), *Waterloo Bridge.*

1903

(M) Leos Janácek (1854–1928), *Její Pastorkyňa (Jenufa)* composed; Strauss, *Sinfonia domestica.*
(H) Wilbur (1867–1912) and Orville (1871–1948) Wright, first successful airplane flight; Encyclical *Motu proprio* of Pope Pius X; Twsett, studies in adsorption chromatography.
(A) Shaw, *Man and Superman.*

1904

(M) Puccini, *Madama Butterfly;* Ravel, *Quartet in F.* London Symphony founded.
(H) Russo-Japanese War.
(A) Anton Chekhov (1860–1904), *The Cherry Orchard;* James Barrie (1860–1937), *Peter Pan;* Romain Rolland (1866–1943), *Jean Christophe.*

1905

(M) Debussy, *La Mer;* Strauss, *Salome;* Franz Lehár (1870–1948), *The Merry Widow.*
(H) Norway separates from Sweden; First Russian Revolution. Albert Einstein (1879–1955), special relativity theory; Wilstätter, first chemical investigations in photosynthesis.

1906

(M) First Mozart festival at Salzburg. Schoenberg, *Kammersymphonie,* First Quartet.
(H) San Francisco earthquake and fire.
(A) André Derain (1880–1954), *London Bridge.*

1907

(M) Alexander Scriabin (1872–1915), *Poem of Ecstasy;* Rimsky-Korsakov, *The Golden Cockerel.* First music broadcast.
(H) Second Hague Conference; Triple Entente.
(A) J. M. Synge (1871–1909), *The Playboy of the Western World;* William James

(1842–1910), *Pragmatism;* Pablo Picasso (1881–1973), *Les Demoiselles d'Avignon.*

1908

(M) Ravel, *Rapsodie Espagnole;* Debussy, *Children's Corner;* Béla Bartók (1881–1945), First Quartet.
(H) Model "T" Ford produced.
(A) Rainer Maria Rilke (1875–1926), *Neue Gedichte.*

1909

(M) Schoenberg, Piano Pieces Op. 11; Ralph Vaughan Williams (1872–1958), *Fantasia on a Theme of Thomas Tallis;* Strauss, *Elektra.*
(H) Robert Peary (1856–1920) reaches North Pole.
(A) Frank Lloyd Wright (1869–1959), Robie House, Chicago; Ferenc Molnár (1878–1952), *Liliom.*

1910

(M) Ravel, *Daphnis et Chloé, Ma Mère l'Oye;* Bartók, *Allegro Barbaro;* Igor Stravinsky (1882–1971), *The Fire Bird;* Vaughan Williams, *Sea Symphony;* Mahler's Eighth Symphony performed; Debussy, *Préludes,* Book I.
(H) Discovery of protons and electrons; George V King of England (till 1936).
(A) Bertrand Russell (1872–1970) and Alfred North Whitehead (1861–1947), *Principia Mathematica;* John Masefield (1878–1959), *The Tragedy of Pompey the Great.*

1911

(M) Mahler, *Das Lied von der Erde;* Strauss, *Der Rosenkavalier;* Sibelius, Fourth Symphony; Bartók, *Duke Bluebeard's Castle;* Stravinsky, *Petrushka;* Ravel, *L'Heure espagnole;* Scott Joplin's opera *Treemonisha* performed at New York.
(H) Roald Amundsen (1872–1928) reaches the South Pole.
(A) Edith Wharton (1862–1937), *Ethan Frome;* Giorgio de Chirico (1888–), *La Nostalgie de l'infini.*

1912

(M) Schoenberg, *Pierrot Lunaire;* Strauss, *Ariadne auf Naxos.*
(H) *Titanic* disaster; Balkan wars.
(A) Marcel Duchamp (1887–1968), *Nude Descending a Staircase;* Wassily Kandinsky (1866–1944), *Improvisation.*

1913

(M) Anton Webern (1883–1945), *Six Orchestral Pieces;* Stravinsky, *Sacre du Printemps;* Manuel de Falla (1876–1946), *La vida breve;* Satie, *Descriptions automatiques.*
(A) D. H. Lawrence (1885–1930), *Sons and Lovers;* Thomas Mann, *Death in Venice;* John Sloane (1871–1955), *Sunday, Women Drying their Hair;* Georges Braque (1881–1963), *Musical Forms;* Marcel Proust (1871–1922), *Remembrance of Things Past.*

1914

(M) Vaughan Williams, *A London Symphony;* W. C. Handy (1873–1958), *St. Louis Blues.*
(H) First World War (till 1918); Panama Canal opened.
(A) Robert Frost (1876–1963), *North of Boston;* Vachel Lindsay (1879–1940), *The Congo and Other Poems;* D. W. Griffith (1875–1948), *The Birth of a Nation.*

1915

(M) Bartók, *Piano Sonatina;* Debussy, *Etudes;* Max Reger (1873–1916), *Mozart Variations for Orchestra;* Charles Ives (1874–1954), *Concord Sonata;* Ferdinand Morton (1885–1942), *Jelly Roll Blues* published.
(H) Bragg, *X-Rays and Crystal Structure;* T. H. Morgan, *Mechanism of Mendelian Heredity* (theory of the gene).
(A) W. Somerset Maugham (1874–1965), *Of Human Bondage.*

1916

(M) Ernest Bloch (1880–1959), *Schelomo;* Enrique Granados (1894–1928), *Goyescas;* Ives, Fourth Symphony composed.
(H) Einstein, general relativity theory; Bolshevik revolution in Russia; Battle of Verdun.
(A) Wright, Imperial Hotel in Tokio.

1917

(M) Ottorino Respighi (1879–1936), *Fountains of Rome;* Schoenberg, *Four Songs for Voice and Orchestra,* Op. 22; Hans Pfitzner (1869–1949), *Palestrina.*
(H) U.S. enters World War I.
(A) Georges Rouault (1871–1958), *Three Clowns;* W. B. Yeats (1865–1939), *Wild Swans at Coole.*

1918

(M) Puccini, *Il Tabarro, Gianni Schicchi;* Stravinsky, *L'Histoire du Soldat;* Sergei Prokofiev (1891–1952), *Classical Symphony.*
(A) Willa Cather (1873–1916), *My Antonia;* Oswald Spengler (1880–1936), *Decline of the West.*

1919

(M) Falla, *The Three-Cornered Hat;* Strauss, *Die Frau ohne Schatten.*
(H) Treaty of Versailles; League of Nations; first Atlantic airplane crossing.
(A) André Gide (1869–1951), *La Symphonie Pastorale;* Fernand Léger (1881–1955), *The City;* Paul Claudel (1868–1955), *Le Père Humilié.*

1920

(M) Gustav Holst (1874–1934), *The Planets;* Ravel, *Le Tombeau de Couperin, La Valse;* Satie, *Socrate.*
(H) First commercial radio broadcast.
(A) Sinclair Lewis (1885–1951), *Main Street.*

1921

(M) Arthur Honegger (1892–1955), *King David;* Prokofiev, *The Love for Three Oranges;* Vaughan Williams, *Pastoral Symphony;* Stravinsky, *Symphony for Wind Instruments;* Janácek, *Katya Kabanova;* Darius Milhaud (1892–), *Saudades do Brasil.*
(A) Picasso, *Three Musicians;* Piet Mondriaan (1872–1944), *Painting No. 1;* Charlie Chaplin, *The Kid.*

1922

(M) Schoenberg, method of composing with twelve tones; Carl Nielsen (1865–1931), Fifth Symphony.
(H) Fascist revolution in Italy; discovery of insulin.
(A) John Galsworthy (1867–1933), *The Forsyte Saga;* T. S. Eliot (1888–1965), *The Waste Land;* James Joyce (1882–1941), *Ulysses;* Rilke, *Duino Elegies, Sonnets to Orpheus.*

1923

(M) Stravinsky, *Les Noces, Octet;* Sibelius, Sixth Symphony; Paul Hindemith (1895–1963), *Das Marienleben;* Honegger, *Pacific 231.*
(H) Hitler-Ludendorff Putsch in Munich.
(A) Paul Klee (1879–1940), *At the Mountain of the Bull.*

1924

(M) George Gershwin (1898–1937), *Rhapsody in Blue;* Schoenberg, *Serenade, Woodwind Quintet;* Puccini, *Turandot.*
(H) Stalin becomes dictator in Russia.
(A) Shaw, *Saint Joan;* Mann, *The Magic Mountain;* Franz Kafka (1883–1924), *The Trial.*

1925

(M) Alban Berg (1885–1935), *Wozzeck;* Bloch, *Concerto Grosso.*
(H) Keilin, discovery of cytochromes and beginning of molecular biology.
(A) Theodore Dreiser (1871–1945), *An American Tragedy;* F. Scott Fitzgerald (1896–1940), *The Great Gatsby.*

1926

(M) Zoltán Kodály (1882–1967), *Háry János;* Dimitri Shostakovich (1906–), First Symphony.
(A) Ernest Hemingway (1899–1961), *The Sun Also Rises.* First all-sound films.

1927

(M) Stravinsky, *Oedipus. Rex.* International Musicological Society founded at Basle.
(H) Charles Lindbergh, solo flight across the Atlantic; first television transmission; W. Heisenberg and others propound "uncertainty principle" in quantum physics.
(A) Sir Jacob Epstein (1880–1959), *Madonna and Child;* Ole Rölvaag (1876–1931),

Giants in the Earth; Virginia Woolf (1882–1945), *To the Lighthouse;* Eugene O'Neill (1888–1953), *Strange Interlude.*

1928

(M) Kurt Weill (1900–1950), *Three-penny Opera;* Ravel, *Bolero;* Webern, Symphony, Op. 21.
(H) Dirigible Graf Zeppelin crosses Atlantic; first radio broadcast of New York Philharmonic.
(A) Lawrence, *Lady Chatterly's Lover;* Aldous Huxley (1894–1963), *Point Counter Point;* Stephen Vincent Benét (1898–1943), *John Brown's Body.*

1929

(M) Hindemith, *Neues vom Tage.*
(H) New York stock market crash; beginning of world-wide depression.
(A) Mies Van der Rohe (1886–1969), German pavilion; Jean Giraudoux (1882–1944), *Amphitryon 38;* Thomas Wolfe (1900–1938), *Look Homeward, Angel;* William Faulkner (1897–1962), *The Sound and the Fury.*

1930

(M) Milhaud, *Christophe Colomb;* Stravinsky, *Symphony of Psalms;* Prokofiev, Fourth Symphony.
(A) Mondriaan, *Fox Trot;* Edward Hopper (1882–1967), *Early Sunday Morning;* Grant Wood (1892–1942), *American Gothic;* José Ortega y Gasset (1883–1954), *The Revolt of the Masses;* Hart Crane (1899–1932), *The Bridge.*

1931

(M) William Walton (1902–), *Belshazzar's Feast;* Gershwin, *Of Thee I Sing;* Edgard Varèse (1885–1965), *Ionisation.*
(H) Japan invades Manchuria.
(A) O'Neill, *Mourning Becomes Electra.*

1932

(M) Prokofiev, Fifth Piano Concerto; Ravel, two piano concertos.
(H) Discovery of the neutron.
(A) Gertrude Stein (1874–1946), *Matisse, Picasso and Gertrude Stein.*

1933

(M) Hindemith, *Mathis der Maler;* Strauss, *Arabella;* Stravinsky, *Perséphone;* Shostakovich, First Piano Concerto.
(H) Franklin D. Roosevelt (1882–1945) President of the United States; Adolf Hitler (1889–1945) Chancellor of Germany.
(A) Joan Miró (1893–), *Composition;* Arnold Toynbee (1889–), *A Study of History.*

1934

(M) Virgil Thomson (1898–). *Four Saints in Three Acts.* American Musicological Society founded at New York.
(H) Adrian, studies in the electric nature of nerve impulses; Joliot, discovery of induced radioactivity.
(A) Mann, *Joseph and His Brothers.*

1935

(M) Berg, *Violin Concerto;* Gershwin, *Porgy and Bess;* Honegger, *Joan of Arc at the Stake.*
(H) Italy invades Ethiopia.
(A) Eliot, *Murder in the Cathedral;* José Orozco (1883–1949), *Man in Four Aspects.*

1936

(M) Prokofiev, *Peter and the Wolf.* 440 adopted as standard pitch.
(H) Spanish Civil War.
(A) John Dos Passos (1896–), *U. S. A.*

1937

(M) Carl Orff (1895–), *Carmina Burana;* Berg, *Lulu;* Shostakovich, Fifth Symphony.
(H) Japan invades China. Andersson, discovery of positive electrons and mesons; Krebs, metabolic pathways; Hill, demonstration of chloroplast reaction in plants.
(A) Picasso, *Guernica;* John Marquand (1893–1960), *The Late George Apley.*

1938

(M) Walter Piston (1894–), *The Incredible Flutist;* Bartók, *Violin Concerto.*
(H) Hans Bethe, *Energy Production in Stars;* discovery of nuclear fission; development of penicillin.
(A) Raoul Dufy (1879–1953), *Regatta.*

1939

(M) Bartók, Sixth Quartet; Prokofiev, *Alexander Nevsky;* Roy Harris (1898–), Third Symphony.
(H) World War II (till 1945).
(A) Joyce, *Finnegans Wake;* C. S. Forester (1899–1966), *Captain Horatio Hornblower;* John Steinbeck (1902–1968), *The Grapes of Wrath.*

1940

(M) Stravinsky, *Symphony in C Major.*
(H) First radio broadcast of the Metropolitan Opera; Roosevelt elected to third term; first commercial electron microscope; microwave radar.
(A) Hemingway, *For Whom the Bell Tolls.*

1941

(M) Aaron Copland (1900–), *Piano Sonata.*
(H) United States enters war; Atlantic Charter.

1942

(M) Shostakovich, Seventh Symphony; Heitor Villa-Lobos (1887–1959), *Choros No. 11.*
(H) United Nations Alliance.

1943

(M) Vaughan Williams, Fifth Symphony.
(A) Marc Chagall (1887–), *Crucifixion.*

1944

(M) Copland, *Appalachian Spring;* Bartók, *Concerto for Orchestra;* Hindemith, *Ludus Tonalis.*

(H) Roosevelt elected to fourth term; Allied armies invade Germany.

1945

(M) Benjamin Britten (1913–), *Peter Grimes;* Bartók, Third Piano Concerto; Strauss, *Metamorphosen.*
(H) Surrender of Germany; atomic bomb used against Japan; New York chosen as seat of United Nations. Radio astronomy; jet planes and rockets.

1946

(M) Shostakovich, Ninth Symphony; Britten, *The Rape of Lucretia;* Copland, Third Symphony.
(H) First Assembly of United Nations; Nuremberg trials.
(A) Le Corbusier (1887–1965), Unité d'Habitation, Marseilles; Dylan Thomas (1914–1953), *Deaths and Entrances.*

1947

(M) Prokofiev, *War and Peace;* Piston, Third Quartet.
(H) Marshall Plan; independence of India. Perutz, X-ray studies on crystalline proteins.
(A) Tennessee Williams (1914–), *A Streetcar Named Desire.*

1948

(M) Piston, Third Symphony; Stravinsky, *Mass;* Vaughan Williams, Sixth Symphony; John Cage, *Sonatas and Interludes* for prepared piano.

1949

(M) Orff, *Antigonae;* Samuel Barber (1910–), *Knoxville: Summer of 1915;* Olivier Messaien (1908–), *Turangalila Symphony.*
(H) North Atlantic Defense Pact; Communist government in China.
(A) George Orwell (1903–1950), *1984;* Arthur Miller (1916–), *Death of a Salesman.*

1950

(M) Honegger, Fifth Symphony; Gian Carlo Menotti (1911–), *The Consul.*
(H) Korean War; hydrogen bomb.
(A) Eliot, *The Cocktail Party.*

1951

(M) Menotti, *Amahl and the Night Visitors;* Stravinsky, *The Rake's Progress;* Pierre Boulez (1925–), *Polyphonie X.*
(H) NATO formed from North Atlantic Pact.
(A) Jacques Lipchitz (1891–), *Birth of Venus.*

1952

(M) Columbia University Electronic Studio founded.
(A) Alexander Calder (1898–), *Giraffe;* Albert Camus (1913–1960), *L'Homme revolté;* Eliot, *Complete Plays and Poems;* André Maurois (1885–1967), *Lélia, ou la vie de George Sand.*

1953

(M) Karlheinz Stockhausen (1928–), *Kontra-Punkte.*
(H) Malenkov succeeds Stalin in Russia. Watson-Crick model of DNA molecule.
(A) Reg Butler (1917–), *The Unknown Political Prisoner;* Churchill, *History of the Second World War;* Samuel Beckett (1906–), *En attendant Godot.*

1954

(H) Gordon, Zeiger, and Townes, molecular amplification by stimulated emission of radiation (Maser); U. S. Supreme Court decision outlawing school segregation.
(A) e. e. cummings (1894–1962), *Poems 1923–1954;* Thomas, *Under Milk Wood.*

1955

(M) Luigi Nono (1924–), *Incontri;* Boulez, *Le Marteau sans maître.*
(H) E. R. Andrew, *Nuclear Magnetic Resonance.*
(A) W. H. Auden (1907–), *The Shield of Achilles.*

1956

(M) Stravinsky, *Canticum sacrum;* Ernst Pepping (1901–), *Te Deum;* Stockhausen, *Gesang der Jünglinge.*
(H) Revolt in Hungary.

1957

(M) Stravinsky, *Agon;* Wolfgang Fortner (1907–), *Bluthochzeit;* Francis Poulenc (1899–1963), *Dialogues des Carmélites;* Hindemith, *Die Harmonie der Welt;* Leonard Bernstein (1918–), *West Side Story.*
(H) First Sputnik launched; International Geophysical Year begins; T. D. Lee and C. N. Yang awarded Nobel Prize for discovery of principle of non-conservation of parity.

1958

(M) Stravinsky, *Threni;* Witold Lutoslawski (1913–), *Funeral Music;* Messiaen, *Catalogue des oiseaux.*
(H) Explorer I (U.S. satellite); voyage of the *Nautilus;* Khrushchev becomes Premier of U.S.S.R.

1959

(M) Orff, *Oedipus der Tyrann.*
(H) First moon rockets; studies in the structure of viruses.

1960

(M) Copland, *Nonet for Strings;* Messiaen, *Chronochromie;* Boulez, *Pli selon pli;* Frank Martin (1890–), *Mystère de la Nativité;* Niccolo Castiglione (1932–), *Aprèsludes.*
(H) 25 artificial satellites now in orbit; first working laser.
(A) Jean Tinguely (1925–), *Homage to New York.*

1961

(M) Elliott Carter (1908–), *Double Concerto;* Nono, *Intolleranza 1960;*

Krzysztof Penderecki (1933–), *Lament for the Victims of Hiroshima.*
(H) Peace Corps established; Berlin Wall erected; first manned space flights.
(A) Claes Oldenburg's (1929–) "Store" opens in New York; "Art of Assemblage" show at Museum of Modern Art; David Smith (1906–1965), "Cubi" sculptures.

1962

(M) Britten, *War Requiem;* Stravinsky, *A Sermon, a Narrative, and a Prayer.*
(H) Vatican Council II convenes; Cuban missile crisis.
(A) Edward Albee (1928–), *Who's Afraid of Virginia Woolf?*

1963

(H) President J. F. Kennedy assassinated; increasing U. S. involvement in Vietnam.
(A) Rachel Carson (1917–1964), *Silent Spring.*

1964

(M) Roger Sessions (1896–), *Montezuma;* Yannis Xenakis (1922–), *Strategy;* György Ligeti (1923–), *Requiem;* Britten, *Curlew River.*
(H) Kosygin becomes Premier of U.S.S.R.

1965

(M) First performance of Ives's Fourth Symphony.
(H) Gemini space vehicles; Civil Rights march in Alabama.
(A) *The Autobiography of Malcolm X;* Peter Weiss (1916–), *The Persecution and Assassination of Jean-Paul Marat* (Marat-Sade).

1966

(M) Penderecki, *St. Luke Passion;* Gunther Schuller (1925–), *The Visitation;* Britten, *The Burning Fiery Furnace.*
(A) Harold Pinter (1930–), *The Homecoming.*

1967

(M) Alberto Ginastera (1916–), *Bomarzo* (opera); Copland, *Inscape;* Stockhausen *Hymnen;* the Beatles, *Sergeant Pepper's Lonely Hearts Club Band.*
(H) Israeli-Arab Six-Day War. Development of astrophysics; G. and M. Burbidge, *Quasi-Stellar Objects* ("quasars"); J. C. Lilly, *The Mind of the Dolphin.* Length of one second of time now determinable within limit of error of 1-2 parts in 10^{10}.

1968

(M) Luciano Berio (1925–), *Sinfonia;* Orff, *Prometheus;* Britten, *The Prodigal Son.*
(H) Soviet invasion of Czechoslovakia; student uprisings in France; massive anti-war protests in U.S.A.; assassinations of Martin Luther King and Robert F. Kennedy.

1969

(H) First men on the moon.

1970

(A) Alvin Toffler (1928–), *Future Shock;* Charles Reich (1928–), *The Greening of America.*

1971

(H) Indo-Pakistan war; independence of Bangladesh.

1972

(M) Complete Works of Scott Joplin published at New York.

Index

Index

Index

Index

Index

Index

Index

Index

Index

Index

Index

Index